NO WIDER WAR

OSPREY
PUBLISHING

DEDICATION

To my nieces
Teresa, Sophia, and Isabel

NO WIDER WAR

A History of the Vietnam War
Volume 2: 1965–75

SERGIO MILLER

OSPREY PUBLISHING
Bloomsbury Publishing Plc
Kemp House, Chawley Park, Cumnor Hill, Oxford OX2 9PH, UK
29 Earlsfort Terrace, Dublin 2, Ireland
1385 Broadway New York NY 10018 USA
E-mail: info@ospreypublishing.com
www.ospreypublishing.com

OSPREY is a trademark of Osprey Publishing Ltd

First published in Great Britain in 2021

A catalog record for this book is available from the British Library.

ISBN: HB 978 1 4728 3851 3; PB 978 1 4728 3852 0; eBook 978 1 4728 3850 6; ePDF 978 1 4728 3848 3; XML 978 1 4728 3849 0

21 22 23 24 25   10 9 8 7 6 5 4 3 2 1

Maps by Bounford.com
Index by Angela Hall

Typeset by Deanta Global Publishing Services, Chennai, India
Printed and bound in Great Britain by CPI (Group) UK Ltd, Croydon CR0 4YY

Osprey Publishing supports the Woodland Trust, the UK's leading woodland conservation charity.

To find out more about our authors and books visit www.ospreypublishing.com. Here you will find extracts, author interviews, details of forthcoming events and the option to sign up for our newsletter.

CONTENTS

LIST OF MAPS

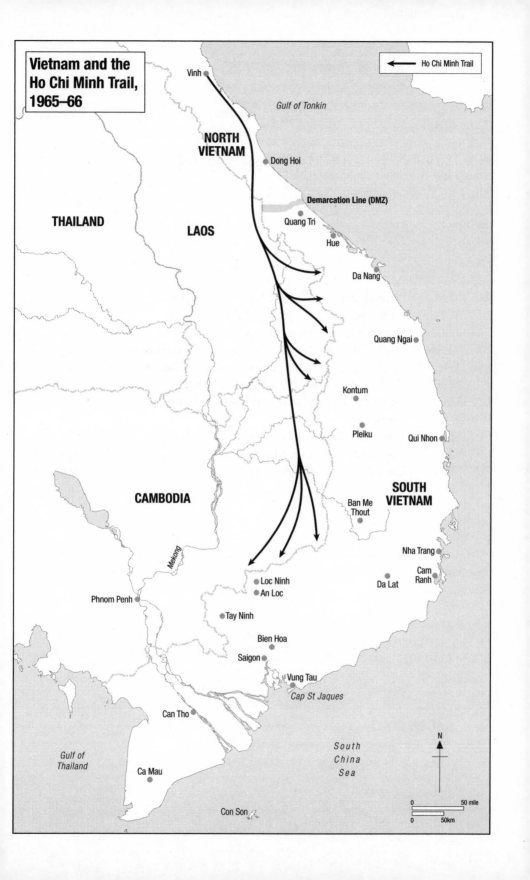

Vietnam and the Ho Chi Minh Trail, 1965–66

Ho Chi Minh Trail

Gulf of Tonkin

NORTH VIETNAM

Vinh

Dong Hoi

THAILAND

LAOS

Demarcation Line (DMZ)

Quang Tri

Hue

Da Nang

Quang Ngai

Kontum

Pleiku

Qui Nhon

CAMBODIA

SOUTH VIETNAM

Ban Me Thout

Mekong

Loc Ninh

An Loc

Nha Trang

Cam Ranh

Da Lat

Phnom Penh

Tay Ninh

Bien Hoa

Saigon

Vung Tau

Cap St Jaques

Can Tho

Gulf of Thailand

South China Sea

N

Ca Mau

Con Son

0   50 mile

0   50km

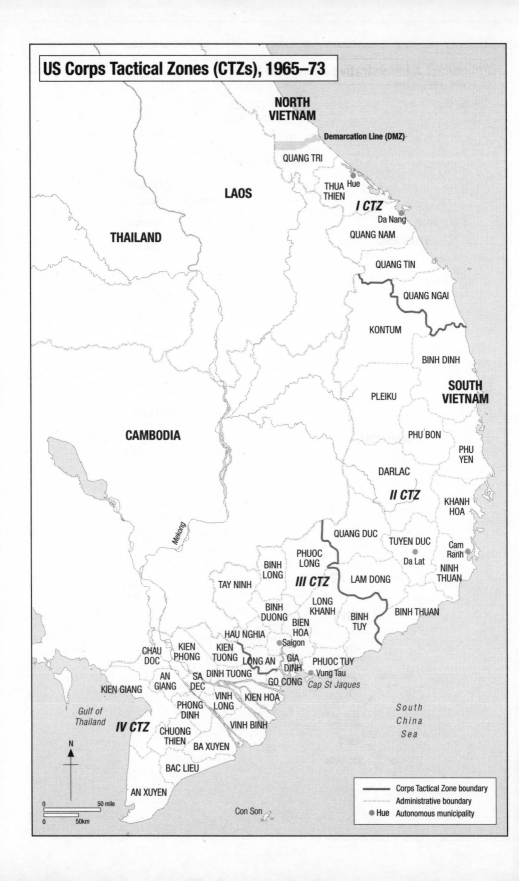

US Corps Tactical Zones (CTZs), 1965–73

NORTH VIETNAM

Demarcation Line (DMZ)

QUANG TRI

THUA THIEN   Hue

I CTZ

Da Nang

QUANG NAM

LAOS

THAILAND

QUANG TIN

QUANG NGAI

KONTUM

BINH DINH

SOUTH VIETNAM

PLEIKU

PHU BON

PHU YEN

CAMBODIA

DARLAC

KHANH HOA

II CTZ

QUANG DUC

TUYEN DUC

Da Lat

Cam Ranh

NINH THUAN

PHUOC LONG

LAM DONG

Mekong

BINH LONG

III CTZ

TAY NINH

LONG KHANH

BINH THUAN

BINH DUONG

BIEN HOA

BINH TUY

HAU NGHIA

Saigon

CHAU DOC

KIEN PHONG

KIEN TUONG

LONG AN

GIA DINH

PHUOC TUY

AN GIANG

SA DEC

DINH TUONG

GO CONG

Vung Tau

Cap St Jaques

KIEN GIANG

VINH LONG

KIEN HOA

Gulf of Thailand

PHONG DINH

IV CTZ

VINH BINH

South China Sea

CHUONG THIEN

BA XUYEN

N

BAC LIEU

AN XUYEN

| 0 | 50 mile |
| 0 | 50km |

Con Son

———	Corps Tactical Zone boundary
- - -	Administrative boundary
● Hue	Autonomous municipality

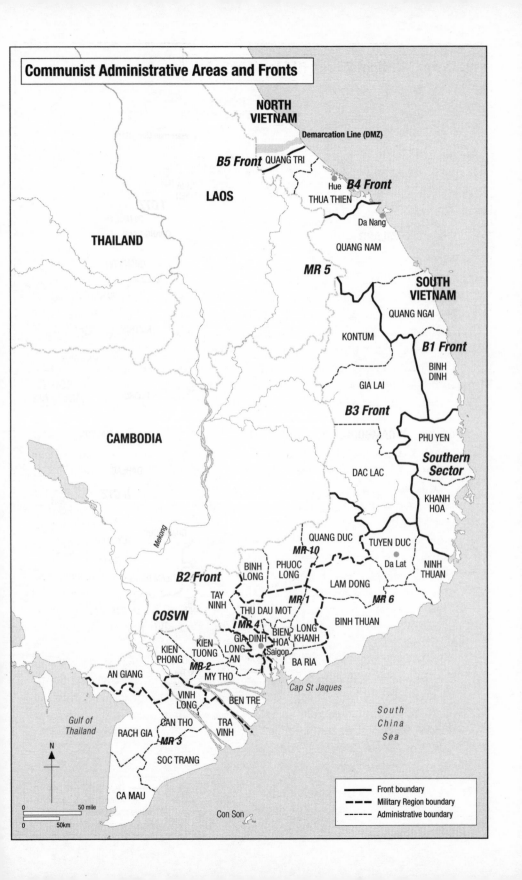

Communist Administrative Areas and Fronts

NORTH
VIETNAM

Demarcation Line (DMZ)

B5 Front QUANG TRI

LAOS

Hue *B4 Front*

THUA THIEN

Da Nang

THAILAND

QUANG NAM

MR 5

SOUTH
VIETNAM

QUANG NGAI

KONTUM

B1 Front

BINH
DINH

GIA LAI

B3 Front

PHU YEN

CAMBODIA

*Southern
Sector*

DAC LAC

KHANH
HOA

QUANG DUC

TUYEN DUC

MR 10

PHUOC
LONG

Da Lat

NINH
THUAN

B2 Front

BINH
LONG

LAM DONG

TAY
NINH

MR 1

MR 6

COSVN

THU DAU MOT

BINH THUAN

MR 4

BIEN
HOA

LONG
KHANH

KIEN
PHONG

KIEN
TUONG

GIA DINH

LONG
AN

Saigon

MR 2

MY THO

BA RIA

AN GIANG

Mekong

VINH
LONG

BEN TRE

Cap St Jaques

South
China
Sea

CAN THO

TRA
VINH

Gulf of
Thailand

RACH GIA

MR 3

N

SOC TRANG

CA MAU

0   50 mile

0   50km

Con Son

	Front boundary
	Military Region boundary
	Administrative boundary

PREFACE

A matter of days following the Japanese surrender in August 1945, a barely known Vietnamese nationalist calling himself Ho Chi Minh declared the independence of Vietnam from colonial French Indochina. The "shouts from the heart" that accompanied the proclamation were premature. Aided by the British, French troops returned to recover lost possessions and became embroiled in a forlorn-hope guerrilla war against the communist Viet Minh. American policy was divided. A traditional anti-colonialist stance vied with the need to support a weakened ally in the face of the Stalinist menace in Europe. But whatever doubts existed in the White House evaporated when North Korea launched its surprise attack on the South in 1950. France's war in Indochina became an American cause against global communism.

This was the story told in volume 1 of this two-part history of the Vietnam War, *In Good Faith*. Four American presidents found themselves drawn deeper into a conflict underwritten by a political theory based on a barroom game: if one domino fell, all the dominoes in Southeast Asia would fall. Successive commanders posted to a newly raised Military Assistance Command Vietnam (MACV) dangled the promise of success with more American trainers and military hardware. Kennedy fretted that America had become godparents of "little Vietnam" and far-seeing officials warned of a quagmire, but the promise of Camelot ended with an assassin's bullet in Dallas, Texas, and by then the South had become a cockpit of squabbling, venal generals.

Volume 2, *No Wider War*, picks up the story from the deployment of the two marine battalion landing teams to Da Nang in March 1965. South Vietnam already hosted over 16,000 American servicemen, but the arrival of the marines marked the symbolic threshold after which the South's war became Washington's conflict. For Johnson, the agony of deciding whether to "get in or get out" was over, but another agony was about to unfold.

The splendid little war barely lasted the summer. *No Wider War* unpicks the tortuous path of "escalation" as one troop request inevitably led to further requests for more soldiers. The vanguard arrived with the optimism of all new boys to a war, mounting ambitious, sweeping operations. At Ia Drang American cavalrymen clashed for a first time with Hanoi's soldiers, leaving several hundred dead and wounded – and many unanswered questions.

The numerous operations mounted from 1966 to the Tet Offensive in February 1968 can be brushed over in histories of the war, but *No Wider War* guides the reader through this multifaceted period of campaigning when Commander MACV General William Westmoreland sincerely believed in the possibility of "winning it" even though the numbers were beginning to tell a very different story. Tet, of course, changed everything, including a president, and ushered in the great double act of the war: Nixon and Kissinger.

Nixon's war was memorably described as "backing out of the saloon with both guns firing." By the beginning of the 1970s America had to get out of a conflict that was rending the country apart. But nobody had a monopoly on the anguish, as Kissinger eloquently put it, and Nixon was not a president willing to lose a war. Volume 2 describes how a withdrawing MACV mounted controversial incursions into Laos; backed the South's incursion into Cambodia; and stepped up the bombing. Even as the war wound down for Americans there were still horrors to face. *No Wider War* candidly examines My Lai and the wider decline of a 1960s soldiery questioning the point of the war.

There was, as Kissinger wrote in the margins of a policy paper, a decent interval. But it only lasted two years. Saigon's finale is vividly told in *No Wider War*. Washington could not undo the mistakes of three decades but the manner in which Americans made one last supreme effort to rescue South Vietnamese fleeing the communist onslaught speaks of "an honorable people who lived up to their pledge to defend democracy, and did the best they could."

Chapter 1

BATTLE OF THE BEACHHEADS, MARCH–DECEMBER 1965

Washington's war began in the skies, but it was in the ground war where America had to succeed, or accept the entire venture was doomed. This undertaking began where the first Portuguese explorer António de Faria alighted in Indochina in 1535, and where French imperialism, fueled by the portly Admiral Charles Rigault de Genouilly, seized its first settlement in 1858 – Da Nang. Between these two historical markers, various French, Spanish, American, and British trade missions arrived and departed. None succeeded in establishing a foothold in this harbor town, inhabited by suspicious Dai Viet ("Great Viet") who spoke a dialect which has remained distinct to official Hanoi Vietnamese to this day.

The stunning bay at Da Nang, it seems, had always invited human occupation, framed by the Hai Van peninsula to the north and the scenic Monkey Mountain to the south. The earliest occupation dated to the second century AD when the region fell under the sway of the Hindu Champa (founding the original coastal settlement, Da Nak). The Champa were defeated by the Dai Viet Emperor Tran Thanh Tong at the end of the fifteenth century. It would take a further 350 years before this mysterious, and today persecuted minority culture, was finally quashed. In the early 1800s, a visiting British watercolorist depicted a small, idyllic fishing town on the later-named China Beach, one of scores of such settlements along this stretch of the coastline. The French, with imperial insensitivity, renamed the town Tourane. They eventually expanded the settlement away from the beach to the protected lee of Monkey Mountain.

The French had found a town ringed by forts, moats, and earthworks. Vietnamese resistance proved stubborn. Intermittent fighting as well as disease drained manpower. Pacification was never fully achieved beyond the immediate hinterlands. Over the succeeding decades, the better impulses of a French *mission civilisatrice* added the impediments of Western culture: a commissariat de la République, a *chambre de commerce et d'agriculture*, a Blaise Pascal school, a hospital, a *jardin de la ville*, a neo-classical Musée Chams, and many modern conveniences. A European quarter grew with place names recalling the mother country: Rue Verdun, Quai Courbet, and the pleasant Avenue Rivière.

By the time the French quit Indochina, Da Nang had grown considerably as a road and rail hub. To the west of the urban sprawl, American engineers expanded the existing French air base to include a 10,000-foot runway. This became the busiest single runway in the world, recording an average of 1,500 landings and takeoffs every day, and as many as 67,000 per month at the peak of operations.[1] A marine, Paul O'Connell, who later served at Da Nang, related, "The air field is right beside my hut and those Phantoms and Skyhawks fly out of here 24 hours a day. About 80 go out an hour."[2] They would continue to do so almost to the end.

Fortunately for its citizens, the town was ultimately spared destruction. Modern-day Da Nang has sprawled further into a busy, commercial port and popular tourist destination. There are over 100 hotels. Five-star resorts jostle with gift shops and boutique cafes. The spot where the first American marines landed is now beached by middle-aged, overweight Australians. The giant air base has survived, along with the French-built railway station, neo-Gothic cathedral, and several churches, relics of a bygone era. In walking distance of both, as a reminder that the spoils go to the victor, is a Ho Chi Minh Museum.

The deployment of the first combat ground troops to South Vietnam – Military Assistance Command Vietnam (MACV) was already 23,000 strong by the spring of 1965 – had roots in the Gulf of Tonkin incident the previous August. The subsequent reprisal air strikes were one element of a raft of contingencies prepared by the Pentagon which included the emergency deployment of elements of III Marine Expeditionary Force (MEF).[3] There was nothing unusual about this; Marine units had been stood up previously for rapid deployment during the 1961 Laos crisis under Kennedy, and a small contingent had deployed to the Thailand border. America was already fighting a ground war in Indochina, albeit a small-scale and covert counter-guerrilla war waged by 5th Special Forces Group, with few casualties and well away from the attentions of the media.

At the beginning of the New Year, III MEF was placed on heightened alert but with no fixed plans for commitment to Vietnam. However, Viet

Cong attacks on American servicemen at Pleiku (February 7) and Qui Nhon (February 10) changed this. In the beginning, the rationale for the deployment of the marines was modest and precautionary. A review of the US military footprint in Vietnam had recorded that servicemen were now based in 16 airfields, nine communications sites, and as many as 289 other installations, all vulnerable to guerrilla attacks.[4] The previous November, the air force had been embarrassed by the destruction and damage of 31 aircraft at Bien Hoa Air Base following a surprise Viet Cong attack. The lesson had not been forgotten.[5] There were some 220 USAF aircraft in South Vietnam, virtually all concentrated in just three bases: Tan Son Nhut, Bien Hoa, and Da Nang.[6] Relying on South Vietnamese guards risked further embarrassments and setbacks, although no amount of security would in the end prove sufficient. US air bases in Vietnam and Thailand would be attacked 478 times from 1964 to 1973. These would result in the loss of 375 allied aircraft with damage to a further 1,203.[7]

MACV at the time estimated there were around 12 Viet Cong battalions in the area of Da Nang, numbering perhaps 6,000 strong. The small town of Mieu King, just three miles south of the base, had already been attacked by guerrillas. By February 1965, Da Nang had become the home of 613th Tactical Fighter Squadron, flying the F-100 Super Sabres undertaking raids on North Vietnam just 85 miles to the north. F-102 Delta Daggers from 509th Fighter Interceptor Squadron – "the Deuces" – had been based there since August 1964. The base would eventually become home to 366th Tactical Fighter Wing – a formation with a heritage dating back to the Normandy landings – with three fighter squadrons, the 389th, 390th, and 480th. One line company from 1/3 Marines had joined the airmen along with support troops (in fact, there were already 1,300 marines deployed in Da Nang in one capacity or other).[8] A marine Hawk antiaircraft battery had been despatched to Da Nang on February 7. The air base, then, was already well established, surrounded by guerrillas, and likely to become more important with the expansion of the air war. There was a real fear, expressed by Commander-in-Chief Pacific Command (CINCPAC) Admiral Ulysses Simpson Grant Sharp and others, that the situation might unravel, leaving the United States in the difficult position of extracting its force from Da Nang under fire. These fears were not unreasonable. On July 1, the air base would record its first direct attack; a 14-strong "suicide squad" penetrated the base and destroyed three aircraft.

It was against this background that General William Westmoreland – laboring under the wordy title Commander United States Military Assistance Command Vietnam (COMUSMACV) – submitted a request for the deployment of two marine battalions as an air base protection force on February 22. The Joint Chiefs of Staff (JCS) had already recommended the deployment of a USMC Marine Expeditionary Brigade (MEB) to Da Nang and an army brigade to Thailand as deterrence two weeks previously.[9] A suggestion to deploy a multinational force was also circulating at the time (2,000 South Korean marines had already arrived in January). Ambassador Maxwell Taylor felt obliged to comment on the request (which he supported in principle), warning that such a deployment might cross a line and invite wider US involvement in the ground war. This was a task which he felt the "white-faced" soldier was ill-equipped to undertake. Would American soldiers adapt to jungle warfare? How would an American boy distinguish a guerrilla from an innocent civilian? – a question that would hang with tragic weight over the entire war.

Concerns over the interaction between foreign soldiers and the locals were such that when the marines were finally allocated a patch of Da Nang to defend, care was taken to ensure that it included the fewest possible number of civilians (just 1,930).[10] Even this small step had provoked heated discussions in Saigon.[11] It would have been surprising if it had not, given that the numbers and operational parameters of possible US ground troop involvement had been the subject of continuous examination and revision for the last four years.

But the practicality and necessity of this measure seemed clear to all, with or without Taylor's "grave reservations," and it took just four days to secure Defense Secretary Robert McNamara's approval. Decision-makers in Washington did not share Taylor's cavilling, and nor did they view the proposed Da Nang deployment as momentous or worthy of lengthy deliberations. Nobody viewed reinforcing a coastal air base as the prelude to a major US ground intervention – not even Westmoreland. With hindsight, one of the arresting aspects of the American entry into the Vietnam ground war was that it happened thus, without great consideration. In the reflection of an anonymous author of the later-leaked Pentagon Papers:

> Whereas the decision to begin bombing North Vietnam was the product of a year's discussion, debate, and a lot of paper, and whereas the consideration of the pacification policies reached Talmudic proportions over the years, this decision [the deployment of two marine battalions to Da Nang] created less than a ripple.[12]

Up to this moment, the only serious discussion over the commitment of ground troops had been in the context of a North Vietnamese invasion across the Demilitarized Zone (DMZ). The model and memory was Korea. The first reference of the deployment of marines was in August 1964, a proposal by Taylor to bolster the defense of precisely Da Nang.[13] This was repeated in late November by the JCS.[14] The response was intended as part of a contingency formulated in OPLAN (Operations Plan) 32-64 which had been sitting on the shelves in the Pentagon since 1959. OPLAN 32-64 in its broadest implementation envisaged a full-scale war across Southeast Asia, from Vietnam to Malaysia, a somewhat pessimistic and fantastic proposition.

Phase I of this plan had been activated on January 1, placing III MEF on a higher state of alert. The matter seemed to be settled by General John Throckmorton, Westmoreland's deputy, who visited Da Nang and was so alarmed by what he found that he recommended the prompt despatch of ground troop reinforcements to protect the vulnerable air base. Thus, on March 8, just six days after the first Operation *Rolling Thunder* bombing mission against North Vietnam, Lieutenant Colonel Charles McPartlin's 3/9 Battalion Landing Team (BLT), which had spent a month at sea on standby, duly landed at Da Nang in high waves and a fanfare of publicity. H-Hour was delayed by one hour because "swells, estimated to be 8–19 feet, played havoc with personnel and equipment during debarkation process."[15] McPartlin's orders read that 3/9 BLT was to "land in Republic of Vietnam to conduct security missions, reconnaissance operations, and offensive/defensive operations as directed,"[16] tasks that may have raised a few eyebrows in Washington where the understanding was that the deployment was just about air base security.

The overall 3,500-strong force was led by Brigadier General Frederick Karch, in his role as Commander 9th Marine Expeditionary Brigade. This Second World War veteran with Hollywood film star pencil mustache and sharply pressed uniform would only play a cameo role. By December he was posted home and would retire from the service shortly afterwards. Yet who could forget the scenes? Karch became one of the early faces of the Vietnam War: a dilettantish figure with shouldered pistol, adorned with a welcoming garland of red, white, and yellow flowers on Nam O Beach, redesignated Red Beach 2 for the purposes of the staged landing. The second battalion – 1/3 Marines – sensibly arrived in C-130 transport aircraft, escaping the media attention and embarrassment endured by their comrades in arms.

The operation was less a typical marine amphibious landing and more a circus. The South Vietnamese government was only informed at the very last minute, provoking a flurry of panicked reception arrangements. The ringmaster was the local corps commander, a beaming General Nguyen Chanh Thi in trademark red beret, suspected by the Saigon generals of being in cahoots with Hanoi. He chose as his ring assistants a bevy of giggling girls, dressed in traditional *ao dai* dresses but with jerseys to protect against the unseasonal cold weather (duly captured for posterity by photographer Larry Burrows). The mademoiselles presented the bemused servicemen with garlands of flowers, somewhat deflating the expectations of the marines digging foxholes on the beach. George McArthur, the Bureau Chief with AP, memorably recalled them as "little Vietnamese ladies" with "owl's eyes."[17] A posse of cameramen and photographers mingled with the marines. A banner was erected: "Thanks to the U.S. Government and People for their determination in protecting the freedom of the people of V.N." Ironically, when the Da Nang deployment was first broached to the Saigon generals it caused such alarm the embassy was advised that they should be "brought ashore in the most inconspicuous way feasible."[18]

Karch was clear that his mission was to defend the air base, the official intent expressed in a Pentagon press release.[19] But in Karch's own words, this would be an "aggressive defense" – the best way to defend a base. The apparent paradox was obvious to anyone familiar with the topography of Da Nang. If you stood on the runway and looked west, you saw a line of jungle-shrouded hills overlooking the base. From north to south, there were four such spot heights; Hills 282, 364, 268, and 327. To secure the base, Karch would have to secure these knolls (in fact, the base perimeter was so great that even with two battalions Karch was only able to fully occupy one hill). But what if the VC (Viet Cong) starting shooting from the ridgeline beyond, a reporter asked? We will occupy that one as well, Karch bullishly replied. The marines couldn't do that either with their limited numbers, and where would it end anyway? These questions remained hanging and unanswered. Commentators in Saigon and in Washington fully expected the marines to take the war to the enemy and generally welcomed the shift in policy. Despite Pentagon denials – genuine at this point – virtually all the press pack assumed that the arrival of the marines would be the prelude to further ground operations.

It was fortunate that amongst the first arrivals in Da Nang was a second lieutenant, Philip Caputo, serving with 1/3 Marines. He would become one of the great chroniclers of the war in *A Rumor of War*. Caputo's sensitive eye missed nothing. He accurately captured this period of a phony war, the "splendid little war," when Vietnam still had a ring of adventure about it without the body counts. His first impressions were dominated by the heat, mosquitoes, boredom, and mud – all the staples of fighting in a tropical climate. The command history recorded with some understatement, "the effects from terrain and weather have been somewhat of a problem."[20] However, "the largest problem" one unit diary recorded, "has been the explosion of mines in Company 'C' area by dogs crossing minefields."[21] The young marines stared at elephant tracks and were impressed by the ubiquitous water buffalo. The battalion did not see "action" for a month and most casualties seem to be self-inflicted from accidents. On March 16, just one week into the deployment, a jumpy member of I Company accidentally killed two fellow marines.

When Caputo's battalion started offensive operations, the mood changed and the casualties began to mount. By May, around 200 marines had been injured and 18 killed.[22] One of the fallen would have a frigate named after him (the USS *Reasoner*, a ship that would feature in the popular song "In the Navy" performed by The Village People).[23] By June, the deadpan reporting of military deaths was beginning to take on a routine aspect. "On the morning of 5 June, one (1) marine stepped on a mine and was critically wounded," a unit entry read. This was Private First Class McNees R.H. 2072657. The record continued, "He was DOA [Dead on Arrival] upon evacuation to CandC Company."[24] McNees had stepped on a mine in a corner of a cleared field. It went off "when he was one or two steps past it," an experience hundreds of American foot soldiers would suffer in the succeeding years.

Ominously, the marines noted, "Methods of identification of Vietnamese are not effective." This had terrible consequences from the very beginnings. From the perspective of the suspicious soldiers, a young Vietnamese male found in a field was presumed a potential "guerrilla." As the frustration mounted, "guerrilla" became "target."

The tough lessons of jungle warfare were quickly learned: the near-invisibility of the enemy; the hours spent trekking fruitlessly in the bush; and the sudden violence of a "contact." One company commander reported:

> Because of the heavy vegetation causing efficient movement to be restricted to the roads, trails and stream beds, and inaccuracies in the standard tactical map, IT IS ESSENTIAL that any company working in this area have a set of aeriel [sic] photographs, (verticals) for use as map supplements.[25]

Mostly, however, the company diaries recorded "negative results." Callousness over the taking of human life set in quickly, verging on unfeigned pleasure in some hardened cases. By the time Caputo was posted out of the battalion in the summer, to assume a staff job as "officer in charge of the dead," the boy from Illinois had been quite changed, as had the survivors of his original platoon.

Could Caputo have imagined that 9th Marines' landing would be the first of 62 amphibious assault operations along the South Vietnamese coastline over the next four years, commonly against the same areas, no sooner "cleared" than re-infiltrated by the Viet Cong? The last would be mounted on September 7, 1969 at Barrier Island (Operation *Defiant Stand*), just 34 miles south of where Caputo first pitched his bivouac.[26] Would he have believed that in all that time the contested areas had not greatly changed?

The deployment of the marine battalions to Da Nang, important though it was, was overtaken by poor domestic news. In the same week that Caputo landed in Da Nang, a Civil Rights march in Selma, Alabama was met by bull whips, billy clubs, and cheers from loutish white onlookers. Dr Martin Luther King, a prominent Civil Rights leader with a growing reputation, declared that he would prefer to die than butcher his conscience. A second march then led to tragedy. Johnson was in Camp David with McNamara and Secretary of State Dean Rusk, discussing Vietnam, when the news filtered through that a Reverend James Reeb, a white Unitarian Universalist preacher, had been murdered by Southern bigots. These clashes were amplified by student unrest, ushering another great theme of the Johnson presidency.

The next spin of the wheel was given by Army Chief of Staff General Harold Johnson whose visit to Vietnam from March 5 to 12 resulted in a lengthy 21-point plan. Johnson had been a double survivor, first of the Bataan death march, and later the sinking of the *Oryoku Maru* in which 300 allied POWs drowned. He arrived in Saigon, reportedly telling the MACV leadership that he came with a "blank check" from the President.[27] If true, this was not how the President subsequently responded to his plan. By the first winter Harold Johnson would become a critic of the war, later regretting not resigning in protest: "I am going to my grave with that lapse in moral courage on my back."[28]

These cavils were for later. At the time, Westmoreland concurred with the plan which "reflected much of my thinking."[29] This was expected as Johnson had lifted passages from an estimate of the situation generated by HQ MACV. A week before the arrival of the Chief of Staff, COMUSMACV had in fact published a study that drew a deeply pessimistic conclusion:

> With the continuance of present trends, and provided that no new power elements are brought into play, six months from now the configuration of the RVNAF [Republic of Vietnam Armed Forces] will essentially be a series of islands of strength clustered around district and province capitals clogged with large numbers of refugees in a generally subverted countryside; and the GVN [Government] itself will be beset by "end the war" groups openly advocating a negotiated settlement. We are headed toward a VC takeover of the country, sooner or later, if we continue down the present road at the present level of effort.[30]

Despite this dire prognosis, Westmoreland did not make a pitch for a massive US reinforcement. It was Johnson who broadened the scope of discussions and floated ideas over the deployment of US ground troops, supported by SEATO (Southeast Asia Treaty Organization) or South Korean troops. Sensitive to political considerations, he suggested these would release South Vietnamese troops for combat operations, but who would not take part in combat operations themselves. In Johnson's reckoning, at least a division would be required at Bien Hoa and Tan Son Nhut air bases, as well as in enclaves at Pleiku, Kontum, and Darlac in the Central Highlands. The Marine Corps supported this proposal, recommending the establishment of another six coastal enclaves.[31] In Johnson's most ambitious third option, as many as four divisions might eventually be required from the DMZ (Demilitarized Zone) on the 17th parallel to the Laotian panhandle in the south.

On March 15, the White House broadly endorsed Johnson's 21 points (relating to improving the bombing campaign, not ground reinforcements), without making any commitments. Typically, it was McNamara who seized on the unconvincing arithmetic. Even if the US deployed one of Johnson's "tailored divisions" of 23,000 soldiers, this would probably only result in the release of 5,000 ARVN (Army of Vietnam) to pursue offensive operations. What was the point of that?

Subtly, and in ways that the personae living through the drama tacitly accepted, an atmosphere was being created where discussion over the deployment of a US division to South Vietnam was no longer controversial, but a refrain. The day after Johnson boarded the plane to return to Washington, Westmoreland instructed his staffs to prepare contingency plans for further deployments of US ground troops – a proposal he would have discounted just one month previously, and that Ambassador Taylor would certainly have challenged. Far from being the hidden hand behind Washington's precipitous leap into Vietnam, it appears that it was Harold Johnson who prodded a rather cautious Westmoreland into action.

In anticipation of possible future reorganizations, on the same day, Field Force Vietnam became I Field Force with its own bayonet logo, and II Field Force was created, assigned to the III Corps area (Saigon and environs).[32] Two days later, Westmoreland requested the deployment of a further marine battalion to Phu Bai 30 miles north of Da Nang, partly to relieve the congestion at Da Nang.[33] This was endorsed by CINCPAC, Admiral Ulysses Simpson Grant Sharp, who recommended the deployment of the entire Marine Expeditionary Brigade within the month. The JCS went further and submitted a proposal for three divisions (two US and one South Korean) on March 20.[34] This proposal went far beyond airbase protection or defensive enclaves and endorsed the employment of US ground troops in offensive operations against the Viet Cong. General Johnson's political finessing over the role of US troops had been dropped within the week. Now the talk was of marching to the enemy, not manning perimeter wires at air bases and waiting for the enemy to march to you.

The theme was picked up on March 27 by Westmoreland who circulated a fat volume entitled "Commander's Estimate of the Military Situation in South Vietnam."[35] Encouraged by the Johnson visit and by all the discussions in Washington, it was now Westmoreland's turn to ratchet up the stakes. The Commander's Estimate was half an inch thick, a classic Leavenworth-style analysis, and dull in a way that only military estimates can be. It was grounded on an assumption that the bombing campaign would eventually end Hanoi's support for the insurgency, a belief universally shared in Defense and State. In the meanwhile, a ground campaign was necessary "to contain and then defeat the VC." Based on a belief that only American troops could shore up the South and buy time for *Rolling Thunder* to succeed, the study proposed offensive ground operations. Concretely, Westmoreland advised that an airmobile division be deployed and start operating between Qui Nhon on the coast and Pleiku in the Central Highlands. Alternatively, a division might be deployed to seize coastal enclaves in Tuy Hoa, Nha Trang, and Qui Nhon. Another brigade would provide security at Bien Hoa and Vung Tau, and conduct offensive operations north of Saigon. With additional marine reinforcements in Da Nang and Phu Bai, this would amount to another 17 battalions and supporting elements. In just 19 days, the matter had been elevated from an emergency deployment of two marine battalions to protect an air base to a full-scale commitment of US troops.

Without waiting to see how the political or military situation might develop over the summer, Westmoreland had forwarded a concept of operations to Washington that effectively became the blueprint for the next three years of the war. In the short term, the Commander's Estimate provided the Joint Chiefs with a solid foundation on which to build their case for massive reinforcement of South Vietnam – indeed, it acted as another spur to the necessary planning, despite the fact that at this stage no political authorization whatsoever had been secured to ramp up the mission.

What Westmoreland offered was an enclave strategy migrating inland, or effectively an invasion of South Vietnam with the forced compliance of the hosts. There would be three stages: in the first, the coastal enclaves would be secured; in the second, US forces would embark on deep patrolling and offensive operations; and in the final phase there would be big-unit search and destroy operations. By 1967, Westmoreland optimistically posited, the war might be won. In fact, by this date there would be 107 US combat battalions in South Vietnam, within a total force of 525,000 men, and the war would only just be starting.

In truth, Westmoreland's March estimate was not as original as it seemed. A plan to deploy US troops to the Central Highlands (and Laos) was a reprise of long-standing proposals first aired by the Joint Chiefs on October 9, 1961 in JCSM (Joint Chiefs of Staff Memorandum) 717-61. This had argued for the deployment of a 20,000-strong force in Indochina (quickly bumped up to 40,000 troops by the time the Chiefs met with Kennedy two days later at a National Security Council (NSC) meeting). The proposal followed logically from the May 10 JCSM 320-61 which had recommended, somewhat more vaguely, the deployment of a deterrent force but left open the questions of what force and to where. Taken together, these two memoranda from the Joint Chiefs illustrated a danger unnoticed by contemporaries. Rejected plans did not end up in a historical graveyard of what might have been. They sat in files waiting to be re-warmed by the next incumbent general. If this president won't buy it, perhaps the next one will.

In the usual way, Westmoreland's scheme only served to highlight divisions. Taylor and most of the JCS supported remaining in the coastal enclaves and constraining the commitment. General Earle Wheeler, Admiral Sharp, and General Johnson backed Westmoreland. In the State Department there were mutterings about jungle wars without prospects for a clear victory. At the back of everyone's minds was the novel development of the detonation of China's second atomic bomb.

The Hanoi Politburo was not complacent over these developments. Concurrently with Westmoreland's publication of his Commander's Estimate, an 11th Plenum (Special Session) of the Party Central Committee was held on March 25–27. The title of the Plenum was "On the Immediate Situation and Urgent Responsibilities." The principal resolutions related to intensifying "our diplomatic struggle operations" against Washington. Counter-matching the domino theory, Hanoi asserted its own exaggerated theory of American neo-colonialism:

> the American imperialists are using South Vietnam as a testing ground for their "special warfare" strategy, which is aimed at extinguishing the struggle for liberation by the peoples of all nations, and especially by the peoples of the nations of Asia, Africa, and Latin America, at carrying out a policy of neo-colonialism, and at preparing for a new world war.[36]

With both sides girded with bankrupt abstract theories portraying the other as existential enemy, collision was inevitable.

An uncontrolled momentum, rather than conspiracy, was the motor to the subsequent rapid developments. This gave the events the quality of an unlucky accident. All the actors responded rationally to a situation that was perceived to be worsening with potentially fatal consequences to MACV, and to wider US policy in Indochina. The collapsing South Vietnamese hooch needed a plank or two to shore it up and, in March 1965, this support was provided. The most that can be said is that the marines deployed within the context of an established contingency plan that envisaged divisional deployments in a full-blown war. This predisposed but did not oblige the Johnson administration to jump from battalions to divisions.

What was happening in Washington was more elusive and largely overlooked. To query was to raise questions over your loyalty and imperil your career. Over time, all the dissenting and skeptical voices had already fallen, or were falling, by the wayside. Some, more dishonestly, were concealing their feelings. By the spring of 1965, the roll call of the fallen and silent had lengthened, and with it, resistance to an American intervention in Vietnam.[37] The first major figure to depart was Bill Trueheart, the Deputy Chief of Mission in Saigon, in December 1963. Trueheart had challenged the former MACV commander General Harkins' optimistic reporting and the general direction of US policy in Indochina. He was recalled to Washington and re-assigned as a desk officer on a Southeast Asia desk that did not include Vietnam. In early 1964, State official Paul Kattenburg, an Indochina veteran from the 1950s who prognosticated a lost war, was moved out of the Interdepartmental Working Group on Vietnam and posted to the toothless Policy Planning Council, where he could cause no ructions. In February 1965, Roger Hilsman in the Bureau of Far Eastern Affairs resigned or was sacked, and was replaced by the more amenable William Bundy. In March, Michael Forrestal quit in a depression. He had already been moved from supporting National Security Advisor McGeorge Bundy to a less-influential Vietnam desk in State. In April, CIA Director McCone resigned.

Others like Deputy Secretary of Defense John McNaughton – in public "one of the team" but privately perceived to be a mid-Western isolationist – continued to play an intellectually dubious double game. In Saigon, Taylor abandoned his better instincts and switched from warning of deeper American involvement to supporting his former military colleagues in the hawkish JCS. Within the subterranean world of Defense, a brilliant RAND Corporation analyst, Daniel Ellsberg, was quietly digging up secrets which he would later reveal to the world in the biggest security leak in American history. Over the same period, McNamara protégé Alain Enthoven was moved from the post of Deputy Assistant Secretary to the Defense Office for Systems Analysis. This sideways promotion in fact only served to place him in a better position to unscramble the awful arithmetic of the war and offer it like so many poisoned chalices. Veteran Averell Harriman, now one of the unwanted old guard, was shoved off to the Congo. In State, George Ball's long-standing dissent had become the isolated voice. "No one can assure you," he warned Johnson, "that we can beat the Viet Cong or even force them to the conference table on our terms, no matter how many hundred thousand *white, foreign* (U.S.) troops we deploy."[38] It was a measure of Johnson's private turmoil that rather than shoot the messenger, he welcomed "the negative advice that I was giving him."[39]

The remainder of his entourage was not so complaisant. As David Halberstam later observed,

> Thus, without attracting much attention, without anyone commenting on it, the men who had been the greatest doubters on Vietnam, who were more politically oriented in their view of the war than militarily, were moved out … in the struggle almost all the doubters had become marked men; they would not be players again on Vietnam, because they had antagonized Lyndon Johnson with their opposition.[40]

The deployment of the two marine battalions prompted a necessary re-formulation of US policy in South Vietnam by the National Security Council. This came in the form of the 6 April NSAM (National Security Action Memorandum) 328. This did not overturn the basic posture of no combat troop involvement, but it did open the door a little wider. Haunting the discussions round the cabinet table was McNaughton's "trilemma." McNaughton had returned from a fact-finding mission to Saigon in a mood so gloomy it prompted him to write: "Place in unholy mess. We control next to no territory. Fear economic collapse. Militarily will be in the same place a year from now. Pacification won't get off ground for a year."[41] His official assessment was equally pessimistic:

> The situation is bad and deteriorating. The VC have the initiative. Defeatism is gaining among the rural population, somewhat in the cities, and even among the soldiers … [the] area around Saigon is making little progress; the Delta stays bad; the country is severed in the north. GVN control is shrinking to enclaves, some burdened by refugees.

"Can the situation inside SVN be bottomed out," he asked, "(a) without extreme measures against the DRV [Hanoi] and/or (b) without the large deployment of US … combat troops inside SVN?" Answering his own question, he suggested "probably not."[42]

The three options of all-out bombing, massive ground reinforcement, and withdrawal had all been tasted and spat out as too sour in previous NSC meetings. What choice remained given that if one or both of the first two options were not selected, everyone agreed that South Vietnam was unlikely to survive much longer?

However, Johnson's anti-war instincts had not deserted him at this stage. After all the froth of the last month, and however gloomy the picture, the prospect of Americans locked in an Asian land war was temporarily killed off. The focus of this memorandum was thus primarily on non-military actions. In total, there were 41 recommended actions, all of which were accepted. General Johnson's 21 points aimed at improving the effectiveness of the bombing campaign were also all formally accepted. A modest 12 covert actions under OPLAN 34-A were sanctioned. Additional ground forces were very much a last consideration and, in this context, SEATO involvement was urged. Westmoreland's Commander's Estimate had failed to sway opinions. As part of these final provisions it was agreed that just two more marine battalions would be deployed – still within contingency OPLAN 32-64. The first would deploy to Phu Bai, as requested by Westmoreland, and the second to Chu Lai, nearly 60 miles south.

Concerns over the fragility of the Central Highlands influenced this decision-making. Da Nang was the I Corps military anchor to Binh Dinh Province. This province mattered to the entire security of the northern half of the country, as it had done during the First Indochina War. Two major routes bisected in Binh Dinh: Highway 1, the coastal road running south to north; and Highway 19, running from the coastal town of Qui Nhon, west to An Khe and on to Pleiku, where US special forces detachments operated. If the Viet Cong seized or even successfully interdicted these arterial routes, there was a real prospect that South Vietnam would be cut in half. Securing Phu Bai and Chu Lai added more points of support to the anchor at Da Nang.

NSAM 328 also authorized up to 20,000 further troops to MACV, but "to fill out existing units and supply needed logistic personnel." These additional troops caused some confusion: the Joint Chiefs seemed to assume, or perhaps anticipated hopefully, that these would be the logistic advance guard for their cherished divisional deployments. McNamara quickly scotched this suggestion and insisted they were merely necessary support for troops already deployed in South Vietnam.

However, it was evident by the beginning of April, that the Joint Chiefs were already acting as if they would win the argument, regardless of clear direction from the White House away from an expanded military involvement. In an insubordinate April 2 memo, the Chiefs almost seemed to instruct McNamara to get out of the way and let them run the war. The decks should be cleared, they peremptorily told the defense secretary, of "all administrative and procedural impediments that hamper us in the prosecution of this war."[43] McNamara privately fumed at this challenge and indeed did not formally respond until May 14, a sign of his displeasure. But it is also the case, recorded in the Pentagon Papers, that the defense secretary was personally and carefully ensuring that his department was ready to provide efficient and sufficient support to the fighting elements in Vietnam. What mattered to McNamara more than any point of contention was good management, not any particular strategy.

As a sop, the rules of engagement were relaxed to permit "a more active role," but this relaxation was not made in the context of entering a ground war but rather to offer the marines more flexibility to defend themselves more effectively. An aggressive interpretation of this phrase was made by Taylor who hitherto had counseled caution. Unless otherwise advised, the marines would be permitted to engage in "mobile counterinsurgency" operations up to 50 miles from their coastal bases, a number seemingly chosen at random.[44] What had begun as a security strategy – that is, the security of US air bases – had swiftly mutated into a strategy for using these secure enclaves as bases from which to launch aggressive operations against the Viet Cong, notwithstanding the President's lukewarm stance over ground operations.

The next decisive turn came in the Honolulu Planning Conference held on April 10. This was convened primarily to smooth out divisions over the bombing campaign, but it also addressed the question of combat troop deployments. The planning conference was only attended by JCS and PACOM (Pacific Command) representatives, to lay the foundations for the full conference the following week. Without a civilian input, the attendees almost inevitably considered military options outside political considerations. Wheeler's three-division plan came to the fore again. Army planners offered two concrete recommendations for immediate troop deployments: send 173rd Airborne Brigade to Bien Hoa-Vung Tau, north of Saigon, and a second army brigade to Qui Nhon-Nha Trang as an advance force for a possible, future divisional deployment in the Central Highlands (the latter triggered a warning order to 1st Infantry Division, "the Big Red One," even though this remained just a recommendation and it had not been endorsed or even, it appears, the subject of consultation with the White House). Although Westmoreland did not personally attend this conference, he could not resist signaling CINCPAC to repeat the argument for the deployment of an army division to the Central Highlands.[45] Westmoreland notably conceded that this request was unlikely to be accepted. By the second week of April, the military staffs were thus planning various expansive options – as they were bound to do, they would have argued – while ruefully recognizing a cautious political leadership.

A certain institutional anarchy then seemed to set in. On April 14, the JCS approved the deployment of the airborne brigade. On the same day, Major General Jonathan O. Seaman, a wartime artilleryman, was instructed to stand up 2nd Brigade 1st Infantry Division for operations. This brigade was unrealistically given just one month to ready itself, provoking logistic bedlam.[46] In a decision he later came to regret, Seaman "really tore that division apart," posting all the best officers and NCOs into 2nd Brigade and cannibalizing the remainder of the division for equipment. The secrecy was such that the troops were not actually told where they were deploying (although most guessed) until they were on board the navy troopships. The spirit of NSAM 328 agreed just two weeks previously – which had explicitly rejected increasing a ground combat commitment – was being roundly ignored.

The decision to deploy the paratroopers arrived as a bolt out of the blue and seemed to catch some of the protagonists by surprise. An exasperated Taylor immediately reacted by requesting the decision be put on hold.[47] Although he had been one of the originators of an enclave strategy, his misgivings over precipitate action were deep. Since the beginning of the year, Taylor had become increasingly frustrated with "firemen" arriving from Washington, making necessarily hurried evaluations, proposing short-term solutions, all of which was resulting in Saigon being "helped to death." The authorization to deploy the paratroopers was the final straw and it provoked a flurry of signals and counter-signals between Taylor, the JCS, and McNaughton. The latter leaped in intemperately and proposed his own 7-point plan, prompting Taylor to famously respond that Saigon was being asked to implement a 21-point military program, a 41-point non-military program, a 16-point USIS program, and a 12-point CIA program, "as if we can win here somehow on a point score."[48] Whether McNamara was aware that his deputy was strategizing in this manner remains unclear. McNamara only finally approved of the airborne brigade deployment two weeks later (on April 30) suggesting that the Joint Chiefs had committed the faux pas of anticipating a decision from the defense secretary which in the normal course of events would have required presidential sanction. Indeed, who did ask Johnson? What was clear was that all the actors were heading for a showdown and it came at the second Honolulu Conference on April 20.

Honolulu was the first opportunity for all parties to speak face-to-face, with the benefit of some experience of the effects of the bombing campaign, and with the deployment of ground troops to Da Nang now a reality. But the point of this experience was that it was very limited. *Rolling Thunder* had only been running for seven weeks and there had only been four missions (*Rolling Thunder V* to *IX*). The marines had barely settled down to eat their C-Rations. Anyone seeking to draw conclusions from these expedient measures was on shaky ground, but an overwhelming compulsion to do something, forceful and decisive, seemed to overtake the deliberations. The responsibility (or culpability) was evenly distributed between McNamara and McNaughton from Defense, William Bundy and Taylor from State, and the three principal senior officers, Wheeler, Sharp, and Westmoreland. All contributed to the momentous decisions taken in the nondescript three-story HQ building on Makalapa Drive.

At Honolulu – from discussions that lasted just one day – the emphasis switched from air war to ground war, and from influencing Hanoi to denying victory to the Viet Cong in the South. This was the important shift that would lead irreversibly to an American war in South Vietnam. At the conclusion of the conference it was proposed that four "enclaves" would be established: at Bien Hoa-Vung Tau in the south; at Chu Lai and Qui Nhon; at the airbase in Da Nang; and at the coastal town of Quang Ngai. Each would require a brigade-sized force. A quick bit of arithmetic yielded 17 battalions (Westmoreland's March estimate). NSAM 328 had already authorized the deployment of four marine battalions, which implied that 13 additional battalions would be required, raising US troop levels to 82,000. These would hopefully be augmented with contributions from what were being dubbed the Free World Military Assistance Forces (FWMAF). With 8,000-odd South Koreans (ROK) already deployed in South Vietnam since the beginning of the year perhaps this number could be reached without too much difficulty. In June, they would be joined by the 1st Battalion Royal Australian Regiment (1 RAR). With presidential approval, which was far from certain at this stage, the plan implied confirmation of Wheeler's three-division proposal made up from the balance of III MEF, a US Army division spearheaded by 173rd Airborne Brigade, and a ROK division.

Missing from the crucial April 20 Honolulu Conference was any South Vietnamese participation. It was as if the doctors had huddled in a corner and quite ignored the demands of the patient. This raises the question: what did the patient make of this prescribed medicine? After the war, General Nguyen Khanh was posed the question he was not given a chance to answer in the spring of 1965 when he was serving as interim president. "How did you feel about the idea of bringing American combat troops into Vietnam?"[49] For Khanh, without reservations, this was "the main error we made." Diem would never have sanctioned the deployment of US combat troops in his country. The Saigon generals in the Armed Forces Council did not want to go down this path either. Suspicion of foreign troops was deeply rooted in Vietnamese culture; the experiences had all been bad. The Joint Chiefs drove a coach and horses through the wishes of the South Vietnamese military and civilian leadership, which they did not even consult. The unhappy passenger on this bumpy ride was a reluctant Johnson administration. Ironically, this was made possible because a US-backed coup (or more finely, a coup tacitly encouraged by Henry Cabot Lodge) had left behind the wreck of a divided and weak government.

Khanh was against the deployment of US combat troops "for the simple reason that we do not need that [sic]."[50] Whether or not Khanh was right remains speculative. Few would contend that a separate South Vietnam could have survived much longer without American support, but equally, few would dispute that the path to unification would have been quite so bloody. A US government took a crucial decision to flood a foreign country with troops, against the instincts and wishes of the national leadership. Whereas alarmist American reporting was predicting the collapse of South Vietnam by the end of the year, followed by the spreading infection of communism across Southeast Asia, Vietnamese were more passively resigned to the eddies and currents, or just long-suffering. Was this really any worse than the French occupation, the Japanese occupation, the turbulent postwar years, the years of famine and starvation, or the militia wars of the mid-1950s? Accommodation with Hanoi had been flirted with; the possibility of a "neutralist" solution had been raised. This was an internal Vietnamese nationalist struggle, not a global war against international communism. In the spring of 1965 Ho Chi Minh would have won a freely held election across the partitioned Vietnam.

Sensitive to Johnson's reservations over combat troops, the official mission remained unchanged: it was about averting a "catastrophe" at one of the large US air bases – the hoodoo that first raised its head in January – and releasing South Vietnamese forces to engage in the fighting. The fact was that neither Johnson nor McNamara immediately authorized the principal Honolulu recommendation to establish four brigade enclaves. In Saigon, the newly installed Quat government was not even prepared to discuss further deployments of US troops with Taylor, a point totally ignored by the Honolulu conferees.[51] Only modest augmentations were authorized, although even these raised the MACV troop levels to a total of 69,143.[52] The deployment of 173rd Airborne Brigade and the additional marine battalions was accepted as a fait accompli, but at this stage no more reinforcements were agreed – at all. When the privately exasperated McNamara finally replied to the Joint Chiefs in mid-May, he firmly reminded them that "he considered as approved only so much of the remainder of the Honolulu recommendations as applied to the Australian Battalion, the ROK [Korean] Regimental Combat Team and some MACV augmentations."[53] That was it.

If Johnson had stuck to this posture, by June, there would only have been nine US battalions in-country, all committed to providing security and not engaged in combat. The sense that they were also there to establish small enclaves was present, but not in any formal arrangement and rather as an experiment. However, this ambiguous stance suited the Joint Chiefs who exploited it to press for more battalions under the guise of security. By the end of the year, 21 of the 44 battalions authorized to MACV would be committed under this rationale, although, by this time, the notion that US troops were being sent to South Vietnam to bolster air base security was a "dead letter."[54]

The problem with the enclave strategy was evident from the beginning and it was voiced by Westmoreland – denying victory to your enemy was no strategy at all. Westmoreland would be blamed for championing "search and destroy" – the basic tactic that dominated the American ground war – but he was chiefly reacting to what he perceived to be a timid and unsatisfactory strategy offered by his civilian and some military superiors (indeed, it appears that his aggressive deputy William DePuy was the real engine behind sallying out, searching for "the bastards," and destroying them, as he put it).[55] Westmoreland, not improperly, believed the war should be won, not just drawn. From a military viewpoint, it made no sense to enter a war except with an intention to win. In this respect, he was a conjoined twin with his frustrated Air Force Chief General John McConnell. If you go to war, you must unleash the dogs of war.

Regardless of the discussions taking place in the air-conditioned sanctum of CINCPAC's headquarters, the dogs had already been unleashed. A sense that all was not well was brought home in photographer Larry Burrow's essay on Yankee Papa 13, the crew of a UH-34D Seahorse, published just days before the Honolulu Conference for *Life* magazine.[56] Burrow's story was not shocking because it revealed a war hitherto hidden from Americans. *Life* had run several features on Vietnam in the preceding years, many in color and sparing readers no gore. But the bloodied bodies were Vietnamese. What was especially shocking about the April 16 story was that this was about Americans dying, when they were not supposed to be dying. This was innocence lost to the unseen rapist. The only missing actor in Burrow's *mise en scène* was the Viet Cong gunner who killed the crewmen. All the other actors played their parts in the full glare of the camera lights.

Burrows had been despatched to cover a routine story on "our boys in Da Nang" and this was the story he in fact set about recording, hosted by 163rd Marine Helicopter Squadron. The aircraft the squadron flew were brand new, literally off the production lines, but only around 150 would ever be built and virtually all lost. The UH-34D Seahorse and Army variant were rugged and simple, but also vulnerable because of their size and slow speed, chugging along at much less than 100 knots. The marines were the first to arm them and named their hybrid gunships "Stingers."

They were a swaggering lot, these marines – in their tiger camouflage suits, festooned with side arms, knives, and bandoliers of ammunition. They were also very young (the two main protagonists just 20 and 21), and like all young men quick with their smiles and joking. The day before the fateful mission, crew chief Lance Corporal James Farley and his gunner Private First Class Wayne Hoilien headed into Da Nang, to do some shopping. They looked like a couple of excited tourists; Farley trying on hats and looking out for jade jewelry which a friend back in Tucson had advised him was a bargain in South Vietnam.

The mission involved landing a battalion of South Vietnamese soldiers just 20 miles from Da Nang, such was the proximity of the front line, on a suspected Viet Cong position. Seventeen Seahorses took part, landing in a wide expanse of elephant grass that had been designated as the Landing Site (LS). Unfortunately for the crews, the tree lines defining the edges of the LS concealed guerrillas who opened fire and soon the helicopters were being hit. Yankee Papa 13, piloted by Captain Peter Vogel, evaded the raking fire and returned to the rendezvous point to pick up more South Vietnamese soldiers. On his second run Vogel noticed the stricken Yankee Papa 3. Two wounded crewmen came stumbling towards Yankee Papa 13. At this point, Farley, followed by Burrows, raced to the casualty helicopter and tried to recover the pilot's apparently lifeless body. A machine gun position less than 100 yards away peppered the helicopter and Farley was forced to abandon the dead pilot (in fact the pilot, shot in the neck, was alive and would later be evacuated by another crew). By the time they returned to Yankee Papa 13, the helicopter was in a desperate situation. The plexiglass had been blown out of the cockpit, the instruments had been damaged, and Private Hoilien was fighting for his life. Vogel lifted off. Farley, now back on his M60 machine gun, poured fire into the tree lines.

Burrows then captured the last moments of Lieutenant James Magel's life, draining on the floor of the helicopter. Wounded gunner Billie Owens looked on in a daze. Magel had been hit below the armpit and was dying of internal bleeding. Owens had been hit in the shoulder and fell silent behind his sunglasses. When they got back to base, the 21-year-old Farley broke down. Four of the 17 helicopters had been destroyed, two marines had been killed, and 14 had been wounded. One month after their arrival in Da Nang, 163rd Helicopter Squadron had been blooded.

At the time, there were over 400 American helicopters in South Vietnam. It was just a matter of time before the vignette captured by Burrows would be repeated in fields across the length and breadth of the country. Hallowed by death, Vietnam was becoming a country of sacrificial fascination. In the summer of 1965, *Life* correspondent Loudon Wainwright wrote:

> It is a one-subject, single-preoccupation country, and no American I talked to was much interested in anything else but the struggle that is going on here. They bitch about the heat and the food, gab about home and sex, but mainly they are fascinated even obsessed, with the problems at hand ... it is almost contagious for the passer-by.[57]

This fascination began to manifest itself in numbers, relatively modest but later prodigious. Ten days after Honolulu, the JCS finalized plans for the deployment of up to 48,000 US troops and 5,250 FWMAF. These would make up four, roughly brigade-sized forces that would establish the foundations for the deployment of an airmobile division (Westmoreland's request) to the Central Highlands.[58]

On May 5, the first elements of 173rd Airborne Brigade arrived at Bien Hoa-Vung Tau to secure the air base, thus becoming the first regular Army formation deployed to South Vietnam. The airlift was stupendous: in just a matter of two days, the bulk of the soldiers were shifted from Okinawa in 150 C-130 flights and 11 C-124 Globemaster lifts. Almost concurrently a fourth marine battalion landed at Chu Lai.

The airborne brigade was commanded by Brigadier General Ellis W. Williamson, a world war veteran who started his career as an infantry private. 1/503rd deployed to Vung Tau and 2/503rd to Bien Hoa. In June they would be joined by the Australian battalion.[59] The speed of the deployment meant that little consideration was given to how the soldiers would be sustained. This meant that for the next few weeks every item of resupply had to be flown in by C-130 from Okinawa. Despite subsisting on this airborne umbilical cord, the brigade was soon caught up in scrapes west of Saigon and northern Binh Dinh Province where an advance element was deployed. The action by the paratroopers in the so-called War Zone D north of Saigon on June 27–30 – involving a staggering 140 UH-1s, each flying multiple sorties – was the first major operation by the US Army in South Vietnam.[60] In none of the early operations did Williamson consider consulting, still less coordinating with, ARVN units in the area. His attitude, soon shaken, seemed to be that this was now an American war and that the South Vietnamese should step aside and let him win it.

The enemy was hardly going to be idle while all these deliberations were taking place. There were in the order of 93,000–113,000 Viet Cong in South Vietnam.[61] Intelligence estimates had been warning that the spring lull would be followed by a summer monsoon offensive and this is what transpired. On May 11, the Viet Cong mounted a regiment-sized attack on Song Be, the capital of Phuoc Long Province. This was followed with the decimation of ARVN battalions in Quang Ngai and Dong Xoai in the I Corps area, just south of the DMZ. A second, multiple-battalion attack was launched at Duc Hao. In Saigon, widely reported terrorist attacks at Tan Son Nhut airport and at the fashionable My Canh restaurant left over 100 civilians dead or wounded. To some American observers, the nightmare of collapsing South Vietnamese forces augured in the New Year was witnessing its fulfillment. It was just a matter of time before the Central Highlands fell, so the pessimists argued.

These were unduly exaggerated assessments. At Song Be, the guerrillas were ejected after one day, leaving behind many dead. At Quang Ngai, the ineptitude of an ARVN commander had been the determining factor, not guerrilla competence. Terrorist attacks were nothing new but rather a weekly occurrence that South Vietnamese had long learned to live with. In themselves, none of these events presaged collapse although the situation was undeniably dire in the countryside, as it had been for over a year.

What Westmoreland seized on was not these attacks but rather the presence of a North Vietnamese Army regiment from 325th PAVN (People's Army of Vietnam) Division in the Central Highlands (in fact, this division was one of five that had been filled with Southern Vietnamese who had migrated north during the *regroupements* following the 1954 Geneva Accords).[62] This was the first unambiguous reporting of North Vietnamese troops on Southern soil and Westmoreland fell for the classic temptation of adding a general's spin to the intelligence. CIA reporting accurately assessed one regiment in the highlands. In his cable to CINCPAC Westmoreland inflated this to one division. "It is quite possible," he wrote, "that the major portion, if not all, of the division is now deployed in the Kontum, Pleiku, Pau Bon area."[63] This was untrue. To add to the alarm, he suggested that 304th PAVN Division, currently in the Laotian panhandle, could soon join them. In a subsequent paragraph he shifted them westward with a sleight of words – "Whether or not the 304th Div is in, or moving towards SVN [South Vietnam]" – thus painting a picture of an invasion of the Central Highlands. Later in the war, Westmoreland would come into conflict with his intelligence chief, Brigadier General Joseph McChristian, over alleged manipulation of enemy strengths to better serve his arguments with Washington. The temptation and habit were apparent from the beginning. Westmoreland's conclusion, reached after several lengthy paragraphs developing the theme of the growing threat and unfavorable force ratios, foreclosed all options except greater US commitment:

> In order to cope with the situation outlined above, I see no course of action open to us except to reinforce our efforts in SVN with additional U.S. or Third Country forces as rapidly as is practical during the critical weeks ahead. Additionally, studies must continue and plans developed to deploy even greater forces, if and when required, to attain our objectives or counter enemy initiatives. Ground forces deployed to selected areas along the coast and inland will be used both offensively and defensively. U.S. ground troops are gaining experience and thus far have performed well. Although they have not yet engaged the enemy in strength, I am convinced that U.S. troops with their energy, mobility and firepower can successfully take the fight to the VC. The basic purpose of the additional deployments recommended below is to give us a substantial and hard-hitting offensive capability on the ground to convince the VC that they cannot win.[64]

At a stroke, Washington had a strategy, or at least an aim, that a raft of NSAMs had failed to deliver: convincing the Viet Cong and Hanoi that they could not win. This was not quite the outright "victory strategy" of Westmoreland's March Estimate but it dovetailed more closely with the fears of the enclavists who were still holding out for a more cautious approach.

Even as McNamara was preparing for another fact-finding mission, Wheeler at the JCS was advising him, "There appears to be no reason we cannot win if such is our will – and if that will is manifested in strategy and tactical options."[65]At McNamara's request a study group was formed to examine this proposition. Assistant Secretary McNaughton's terms of reference to the JCS exactly addressed the question – what does "to win" mean? – and the answer was a mirror of the Saigon view:

> With respect to the word "win," I think this means that we succeed in demonstrating to the VC that they cannot win; this, of course is victory for us only if it is, with a high degree of probability, a way station toward a favorable settlement in South Vietnam.[66]

Over the summer, this highly dubious proposition was refined and ultimately became the "USMACV Concept of Operations" published on August 30.

The problem with the proposed strategy was that it was no strategy at all. Playing for a draw conditional on a degree of probability was not a binding reason to take a country to war. It rested on two baseless assumptions: that the other side would accept a draw, and that an American intervention would force a draw at a tolerable cost and in a realistic time frame. It was a measure of just how obsessed the administration had become with an imagined imminent collapse of South Vietnam that such a strategy was acceptable at all.

Thus, on June 7, just six weeks after the Honolulu agreement for a reinforcement of only 17 battalions, including FWMAF contingents, Westmoreland dropped his famous "44 battalion request" on McNamara's desk.[67] The defense secretary later described this as the most shocking memo he received during his eight-year tenure at the Pentagon. The following night, a tormented Johnson, unable to sleep, telephoned one of his oldest confidantes, Senator Mike Mansfield. He was desperate to find some way out of sending more troops to South Vietnam. In a startling admission, he confessed to Mansfield, "Rusk doesn't know that I'm thinking this. McNamara doesn't know I'm thinking this. Bundy doesn't. I haven't talked to a human."[68] Isolated in his thoughts from his own secretaries and aides, the pressure on Johnson was unbearable. "If they get 150 [reinforcements]," he whinged, "they will have to have another 150. And then they'll have to have another 150. So, the big question then is, what does the Congress want to do about it, under these circumstances? Would the country support such a move now or in six months' time?"

Johnson was right, of course. Once committed, there would be no turning back, and the requests for reinforcements would multiply. His relationship with Congress and with that great abstract, "the American people," would be transformed irrevocably. Despatching the divisions made sense, if there was a prospect of winning, but nobody was promising the President this prize. All his counselors were prophesying collapse. "*We* think they are winning," Johnson confided to Mansfield. "Now if we think they are winning, you can imagine what they are thinking." "Yes," Mansfield replied bluntly, "they know they are winning." Cornered by the old dilemma – "you either get out or you get in" – Johnson asked Mansfield, "Where do you go?" – perhaps hoping for a signal from the senior congressman that America's first president to quit a war would not be pilloried, or that Congress would back him if he "got in." If this is what he hoped, he was disappointed. Mansfield was as muddled as his President. Having first offered that America already had too many troops in South Vietnam, and that if a "white man's war" were sparked, "you might as well say goodbye to all of Asia and to most of the world," Mansfield then backtracked, urging Johnson to consolidate, "and that may take more troops." Fed a diet of such contradictory advice, it was little wonder that Johnson felt a helpless victim on the wheel of fate.

Johnson had always and sincerely contended "we seek no wider war," but this is what happened.[69] Westmoreland got his way and what followed was the battle of the beachheads – a summer of violence that completely altered the facts on the ground and which removed any further obstacles to restraint. This was when and where the war started: in Phu Bai, Da Nang, and Chu Lai; in Qui Nhon, Nha Trang, and Cam Ranh Bay; and in Vung Tau and Bien Hao in the south. Indeed, the only restraint was logistics. South Vietnam could not possibly absorb all the troops and their equipment at a quick-enough rate, a fact readily appreciated by the military planners which led to the development of Cam Ranh Bay into the biggest military hub in Southeast Asia.[70] When the Seabees (navy engineers) deployed to start the construction of the base, they did so over the remains of a Japanese base destroyed in 1944, and an even earlier French base. The magnificent deep-water harbor had witnessed many armies come and go.

On June 10, McNamara attempted a belated rearguard action, warning Johnson that the military build-up should be slowed down, or halted, "unless we really are willing to go to a full potential land war."[71] "This is a hard one to argue out with the Chiefs, you see," McNamara hinted, "because at the back of my mind, I have a very definite limitation on commitment in mind, and

I don't think the Chiefs do. In fact, I know they don't."[72] Johnson pleading faux ignorance could not have reassured his defense secretary: "Well, now, on companies and platoons and battalions and brigade," he replied evasively, "none of them mean anything to me because there are so many different numbers and different ones."

Then, as if impelled by a mysterious force, the wheel spun uncontrollably. On June 11, the Joint Chiefs recommended a commitment of 116,793 US troops and 19,750 FWMAF.[73] On June 16, McNamara announced that up to 75,000 US troops would be deployed to Vietnam and gave his approval for planning the deployment of an airmobile division. On June 18, the JCS revised its figures again and called for 120,839 US troops.[74] The next day McNamara authorized the permanent deployment of 1st Cavalry Division to South Vietnam and the formation began its preparations for deployment the following week. On June 26, MACV was authorized to commit ground troops anywhere in South Vietnam in offensive operations (oddly by diplomatic telegram from the State Department).[75] Without delay, 173rd Airborne Brigade was despatched on its first search and destroy operation into the Viet Cong base area of War Zone D, northwest of Saigon.

At State, George Ball made one last attempt to arrest the slide to war in a July 1 memo to Johnson entitled "A Compromise Solution for South Vietnam." But by his own admission, "I had a feeling that in trying to stop it I was in effect swimming up Niagara Falls."[76] He wrote:

> So long as our forces are restricted to advising and assisting the South Vietnamese, the struggle will remain a civil war between Asian peoples. Once we deploy substantial numbers of troops in combat it will become a war between the U.S. and a large part of the population of South Vietnam, organized and directed from North Vietnam and backed by the resources of both Moscow and Peiping.
>
> The decision you face now, therefore, is crucial. Once large numbers of U.S. troops are committed to direct combat, they will begin to take heavy casualties in a war they are ill-equipped to fight in a non-cooperative if not downright hostile countryside.
>
> Once we suffer large casualties, we will have started a well-nigh irreversible process. Our involvement will be so great that we cannot – without national humiliation – stop short of achieving our complete objectives. Of the two possibilities I think humiliation would be more likely than the achievement of our objectives – even after we have paid terrible costs.[77]

This Solomonic prescience was swiftly despatched by the saber-rattling JCS. By July 2, the number of desirable US troops in Vietnam had jumped to

175,000.[78] Johnson, "like a hitchhiker caught in a hailstorm on a Texas highway," acknowledged this number but held back on authorization.[79] Even if he threw the full weight of America's military strength against Hanoi, he probed McNamara, "can we really have any assurance that we can win … can the Vietcong [still] come in and tear us up and continue this thing indefinitely and never really bring it to an end?"[80] His defense secretary could offer no positive answer.

Remarkably, given the momentousness of the decision-making, there was no consultation with Prime Minister Ky in Saigon.[81] On July 9, McNamara gave the JCS the nod to plan for 44 battalions and the possibility of an additional division and six independent brigades. To make up the numbers, perhaps 100,000 national guardsmen and reserves might need to be called up. On July 12, the first elements of 2nd Brigade, 1st Infantry Division finally deployed arriving at the coastal towns of Qui Nhon and Nha Trang. Seaman, the divisional commander, deployed with the force although the brigade was commanded by his subordinate, Colonel James E. Simmons. Once in-country, he deployed 2/16th Infantry and 2/18th Infantry to Bien Hoa, and 1/18th Infantry to Cam Ranh Bay.[82]

On July 20, there was a request for a further 24 battalions. In case anyone was forgetting there was an air war in progress, the first US aircraft lost to newly delivered Russian SAMs was downed on July 24. In the same month the number of fighter-attack squadrons was raised to 18 and the number of B-52 sorties to 800 per month. On the ground, the sense of crisis was not manufactured. The previous month, ARVN fatalities were twice that recorded in any other week of the war. Five regiments and nine battalions were effectively written off. This included the decimation of two ARVN battalions at Ba Gia in the north, followed by a disastrous performance of South Vietnamese Rangers in a battle at Dong Xoai (some 416 killed, 174 wounded, and 233 missing). These were deeply shocking numbers to Washington and to MACV that had expended so much effort and treasure building up and training the ARVN. The fall of the Quat government on June 12 only deepened a widespread view that South Vietnam was about to fall apart.

The institutional organism of decision-making – as Dean Rusk may have described it – could not go on indefinitely. On July 21–26, Johnson pressed the pause button and held a series of meetings with McNamara, Wheeler, the Joint Chiefs, State, and the Treasury. Special advisor Jack Valenti retrospectively judged them "the most crucial meetings that he held in all of the Vietnam adventure."[83] This was true, but Johnson had already jumped off the diving board, to borrow an analogy he used with his staffs.[84] On July 17, while McNamara was in Saigon, he gave approval – but stopped short of formal authorization – to Westmoreland's "44 battalion request," blind-siding his own defense secretary.

Back in Washington, the atmosphere was anxious and tense. "Every time we have gotten near the culmination of our dreams," Johnson moaned, "the war bells have rung."[85] In a private moment, he despondently bleated to Valenti: "God, we've got to find some way to get out of this war."[86] But none of his advisors were offering a way out. "Why won't Ho Chi Minh match us for every man we send in?" he demanded of Wheeler. Johnson begged,

> You are asking for 200,000 men – in two or three years' time will you ask for 500,000? Can Westerners even win a jungle war? How can we fight a war alongside governments that keep toppling like bowling balls? Now, somebody answer these questions for me.

Nobody did, convincingly. For the protagonists in the room, "the idea that a few pajama-clad guerrillas could defeat the mightiest power on earth was absurd."[87]

Resigned if not defeated, on July 27, Johnson formally authorized the 44-battalion reinforcement but rejected calls for a reserve call-up, fearing a Congressional backlash. This well-founded fear proved to be the main restraint on a quick and massive troop build-up in South Vietnam, and by now the only real point of dispute between the President and his generals. The following day, Johnson went on television to explain his decision to the nation in what became known as the "Why We Are in Vietnam" speech. He stood in front of a plain curtain in the White House, reading the script without his glasses to an expectant press. He spoke of the agony of the decision, but at least one agony was over: the dilemma, get in or get out, was finally and irreversibly settled. Johnson could not now turn back.

In McGeorge Bundy's judgment, Johnson had already made up his mind at the beginning of July.[88] By this stage, McNamara had approved a divisional-level deployment (1st Cavalry) and the pressure to raise the stakes was becoming unstoppable. McNamara's final fact-finding mission in July was a cosmetic exercise, "confirming judgements already made up in his [Johnson's] own mind."[89] The primary concern had shifted from how many, to how to sell the ramped-up effort with "as low-key announcement as he could make and with as little energetic public debate." Johnson did not "want to seem to be going like Custer to Little Big Horn – bugles blowing, banners waving, confident of an all-out and successful confrontation." Domestic backlash was a concern – Johnson fretted with reason over the consequences a full-blown military commitment with reservist call-out would have on Congressional support for his Great Society programs – but as importantly, the administration wanted to keep the door open for negotiations.[90]

In dampening domestic debate, Johnson mostly succeeded. In five months, America had swung from a retaliatory air raid to the deployment of three divisions, without Congressional debate, or great media debate. Johnson had been warned that joining a war implied going to war. In July 1965 he slipped the country into war, unguarded and unchecked. The day after his television announcement a third Army brigade deployed: 1st Brigade, 101st Airborne Division "Screaming Eagles" arrived at Cam Ranh Bay.[91] This formation was commanded by Colonel James S. Timothy and his paratroopers would soon become known as "Tim's Travelling Trouble."[92]

Lurking beneath the craziness of the numbers was a growing rift between Johnson and his generals – in particular General Harold Johnson. It was a measure of just how dramatically opinion had swung in the JCS that anyone not advocating massive reinforcement and a general mobilization – an option that would have been dismissed as mad just a few months previously – was now on the wrong side of the argument. In a June 24 diary entry, McNaughton, McNamara's most intimate and intelligent advisor, wrote how everyone was now playing departmental games, anxious to be on the right side of the argument, even if the argument was plainly flawed.[93] This is precisely what was happening: counsel was being adjusted according to the tide, in an adversarial game between the White House, Defense, the Joint Chiefs, and State. Johnson's authorization of the 44-battalion reinforcement, far from pleasing the Joint Chiefs, provoked frustration. General Johnson considered resignation and later professed that his decision to stay in post was the most immoral of his career. Wheeler also concealed his true feelings.[94] The only official in the administration truly testing the temperature of the over-heated JCS was McNamara. Rather than cooling heads, he addled them more by encouraging the generals to plan expansively. What to McNamara was necessary contingency planning to the JCS was vindication that they were right all along. Possibility became actuality; you just had to keep lobbying hard enough and you eventually got your troops.

The background friction to all these requests was the awful job Taylor at the Saigon Embassy was having maintaining meaningful relations with the South Vietnamese Government. For several months, there was no government, only revolving doors, coups and counter-coups. In Washington, Johnson's frustration over the unreliable South Vietnamese ally was palpable: "I don't wanna hear any more of this coup shit."[95] In these circumstances, the temptation to take over the war was strong. On January 26, the Armed Forces Council had removed Huong as Prime Minister and installed General Nguyen Khanh as his replacement. President Suu was allowed to keep his position but became a marginalized figure. In a wave of anti-US feeling, a USIS library was burned and Taylor became a popular hate figure in street protests. Khanh barely lasted two months. In March, he was deposed in a coup (the eighth since the assassination of Diem) and Phan Huy Quat, a civilian, took his place. The two coup leaders, General Tran Thiem Khien and Colonel Pham Ngoc Thao, Ho Chi Minh's intelligence chief in a previous life, were in Washington at the time, cleverly distancing themselves from the taint of being directly involved in the coup. Quat also only lasted two months. On June 19, he was forced to resign. Following a two-day conference attended by some 70 senior officers, Air Vice Marshal Nguyen Cao Ky was appointed Prime Minister and Major General Nguyen Van Thieu became Chief of State. Neither man pushed his candidacy – the lack of willing contenders acted as the selection mechanism. In the words of one US official, they were "the bottom of the barrel."[96]

The new political arrangement was dysfunctional at best and it effectively militarized the South Vietnamese government with a National Leadership Committee (more commonly known as "The Directory"). The pipe-puffing Nguyen Van Thieu headed the Directory, supported by nine generals: Ky as Prime Minister; the intense Lieutenant General Nguyen Huu Co as joint Deputy Prime Minister with Lieutenant General Pham Xuan Chieu; and Lieutenant General Cao Van Vien as Chief of Staff. The other five were the corps commanders and the Saigon commander, of which the most unpredictable was the I Corps commander, Lieutenant General Nguyen Chanh Thi.

The youthful and zealous Ky would become one of the most important figures in this cabal of generals, but not before Washington had foreclosed any possibility of independent South Vietnamese decision-making by rushing US troops to fill the political vacuum. Ky was distrustful of his American allies and quite open about it, but his policy of avoiding communication with the US Embassy amounted to feckless protest which he soon abandoned. This 34-year-old pilot with a penchant for flashy uniforms arrived with the slogan "I'm a revolutionary" and in many ways he was more communist than the communists. Chain-smoking, agitated, and posturing, he talked of purges, mass mobilizations, and of a complete re-ordering of Vietnamese society. He was dismissive of fellow senior officers (not one killed in ten years of fighting); of politicians (all corrupt); and of his fellow Vietnamese (all dishonest). More than any other South Vietnamese general, Ky believed the South's salvation lay in an invasion of the North, a proposal scotched by Rusk and Johnson at the 1964 Guam conference.[97] He aspired to be the purgatorial fire that South Vietnamese politics needed, but joined an already raging bonfire.

The point on which there was universal agreement was the deteriorating situation in the countryside, but it was precisely this orthodoxy that began to be questioned as the reality of massive troop deployments began to dawn on several personalities. Was it really that bad? Was catastrophe looming unless

Washington acted now, or was South Vietnam experiencing one of its episodic dips? After all, in the spring, all the talk had been of cautious optimism. Why the sudden swing from optimism to deep pessimism? Deputy Ambassador U. Alexis Johnson thought the matter was being exaggerated, echoing his boss Taylor. Opinion in the State Department was also solidly skeptical, especially of America's capacity to actually win a war in Vietnam. Ball went so far as to send his prophetic July 1 memo to Johnson advising him to quit now from what was a doomed project.[98] "You know, once on the tiger's back, we can't pick the time to dismount. You're going to lose control of this situation and this could be very serious."[99] Taylor continued to express doubts. All these reservations were now being voiced far too late in what had become an unstoppable march to war.

Whether or not South Vietnam was collapsing, it was incontrovertibly the case that the dry season Viet Cong offensive had picked up steam. With the capture of Chinese weapons later in the year, it was clear that this offensive, in part, was inflated by the wind of fraternal communist support from the northern neighbor. A special forces camp and District HQ in Dong Xoai, in War Zone C, were attacked, 55 miles north of Saigon. The resulting battle lasted five days and required the deployment of US paratroopers to restore the situation. Twenty-one US soldiers were killed and the guerrillas were thoroughly drubbed, but the real significance of this encounter was the destruction of another strategic hamlet. By the end of the fighting, Dong Xoai had been reduced to ruins and the civilian population joined the 400,000 refugees that had by now migrated to the Delta and greater Saigon areas. This mattered because the official strategy in Vietnam, notwithstanding the dramatic developments of the last few months, was and remained pacification. Hundreds of millions of dollars were being expended in the name of this strategy. Scores of programs and budgets were linked to pacification. Hundreds of staff worked to this aim, irrespective almost of the developments of the summer. The tap of pacification could not be switched off to accommodate the arriviste enclave or search and destroy strategies. The vignette at Dong Xoai served as a reminder to everyone that pacification had in effect "stalled," in the words of a CIA report.

Tou Morong District HQ in Kontum Province then fell, it was rumored, to North Vietnamese troops. Six more ARVN bases followed, either abandoned or forcibly seized by the Viet Cong. Harassment of lines of communication provoked galloping inflation: in one year the cost of food in urban areas rose by over 40 percent, adding misery to the swelling band of refugees. A revision of enemy strengths suggested as many as 53,000 regular troops and 100,000 guerrillas. Pitted against these were 570,000 ARVN (designated as "RVNAF Regular" in MACV estimates), Regional Forces and Popular Forces. The orthodoxy suggested that a force ratio of 10:1 was needed to stem the Viet Cong, but only a small proportion of South Vietnamese forces were actually usable and competent. It was clear the ratios were miles off the desirable numbers.

———

These provocations were bound to provoke an American reaction. There would soon be 38,000 marines in-country: 23,000 in Da Nang, 13,000 in Chu Lai, and 2,000 in Phu Bai.[100] For III MAF, steeped in a culture of amphibious warfare, the tactical response was a bizarre re-run of world-war-style beach landing operations.[101] US marines began storming the coast of South Vietnam as if engaged in a conventional war. These operations ran through the summer and into the early fall with transient results and at an increasingly heavy cost.

The first was mounted in July against Ky Hoa Island, just three miles north of the marine base at Chu Lai. This tiny island was home to around 1,500 villagers and a small ARVN garrison. When a Viet Cong raiding force sailed down the coast in junks and ejected the South Vietnamese naval garrison (killing two American naval advisors) it was deemed an unacceptable affront. The coastline hosted as many as 50,000 junks, posing an impossibly large maritime policing problem, all the more so because of the custom of night fishing. Earlier in the year, a North Vietnamese ship had been intercepted carrying 100 tons of weapons. In inaccessible coves in Vung Ro Bay, a cache of millions of rounds was found. These represented just a fraction of the war material passing down the "maritime Ho Chi Minh Trail."[102]

Commander III MAF, the Kansan Major General Lewis Walt, big "Silent Lew," ordered an amphibious assault to recapture Ky Hoa Island.[103] This was a general who had the unique distinction of having two ridges named after him following particularly bloody battles in the Pacific War, and who boasted a Silver Star, Purple Heart, and two Navy Crosses. A bump in the Tonkin Gulf was hardly going to stop him.[104] In the course of the subsequent operation, the two hamlets on the island were pummeled with artillery fire killing 50–100 villagers. The Viet Cong skipped back across the mainland to avoid the marines. This small action turned out to be a precursor to the first, major marine operation of the war – Operation *Starlite* (August 18–19).[105]

Once again the target was a large Viet Cong presence insultingly near the marines at Chu Lai. At least a battalion's worth of guerrillas appeared to have ensconced themselves in a village called Ban Tuong on the Batangan Peninsula.[106] Like the precursor operation, *Starlite* did not hold back the punches. The excitement was such, *Life* magazine was invited to cover the beach landing,[107] evoking the glory days of Iwo Jima – literally so, as one of the marine battalions, 2/4 "The Magnificent Bastards" was led by an Iwo

Jima veteran, Joe "Bull" Fisher (the unit appellation was pinched from Lucy Herndon Crockett's 1953 novel by the same title).

There was, in the end, no glory, but there was certainly a great deal of firepower. Four marine battalions took part. A blocking position was established in the north on the Trai Can River. Fifty helicopters were used to drop marines on three landing sites, patriotically named Red, White, and Blue, behind the guerrilla positions, with the intent of entrapping the enemy on the coast. USS *Galveston* and *Cabildo* bombarded the coast, and 3/3 Marines led by Lieutenant Colonel Joseph Muir landed on Green beach meeting little resistance (Muir would be killed three weeks later). Pushing inland, the marines then started running into Viet Cong ambushes. Attack helicopters and artillery fire were called, making way for M-48 Patton tanks that picked their way through the jungle. At one point, an aerial bombardment by F-4 Phantoms caused a landslide on a hill, such was the weight of ordnance expended on the near-invisible enemy (18 tons of bombs and napalm were eventually dropped).

There were many individual acts of bravery. In one incident a 19-year-old "baby-faced" Lance Corporal Joe "JC" Paul laid down suppressive fire to protect a medevac, despite being wounded. He later succumbed to his injuries and was awarded the Medal of Honor. There were also moments of blind panic. When a resupply column was ambushed, Major Comer recalled: "The LVT radio operator kept the microphone button depressed the entire time and pleaded for help. We were unable to quiet him sufficiently to gain essential information as to their location. This continued for an extended period, perhaps an hour."[108] Eventually the beleaguered column was found and rescued. Of the 23 marines in the convoy, five had been killed and several wounded. Only nine had survived unscathed. *Life* magazine had despatched English photographer Tim Page to cover the action. He captured the moment a marine was felled by rifle fire. Instants later he too fell, wounded by shrapnel, the first of four woundings in Vietnam, the last leaving him with a two-inch shard of metal in his head.

By the end of the operation, the marines claimed to have killed over 600 guerrillas but only captured nine, making the figure suspect (III MAF initially claimed it killed 964 VC, a plainly absurd figure that was revised downwards, but not by much). Sixty-odd wounded escapees from the first Chu Lai battle were, it seemed, buried alive in an underground field hospital, but this news was not widely publicized.

Notwithstanding the statistical sleights, the Viet Cong body count was hardly the point. The 24-hour battle for a cluster of hamlets had cost III MAF 45 dead and 203 wounded. Scores of civilians had been killed and one hamlet was largely destroyed. In a land where the enemy could not be distinguished from civilians, every Vietnamese peasant potentially fell into the category of "suspect," and many were rounded up. This was a disaster for innocent peasants. At best a "suspect" merited detention, at worst, torture and summary execution. How many South Vietnamese would eventually perish from this linguistic infelicity can only be guessed. Jim Kehres, then serving with 2/4 Marines, remembered being told there were no civilians in the area, and they were to "just kill everything that was there."[109] General Walt blustered in his after-action report that the battle at Ban Tuong had added "a bright new chapter in the annuls [sic] of our country's historic battles against the enemies of freedom."[110] The Viet Cong also claimed success. But the real significance of Chu Lai was captured by James Reston, a reporter working for the *New York Times*. "Military victories," he wrote, "particularly at lonely military bases along the coast, will not win the country."[111]

As soon as the marines departed, the Viet Cong re-infiltrated the Batangan Peninsula. Victory claims were woefully premature and elevation of this battle in Marine Corps mythology failed to recognize the profound differences between the war in Vietnam and previous conventional wars. In the same month that this single operation was mounted on a pimple on the South Vietnamese coast, there were 52 major VC attacks elsewhere in the country, and 1,597 "terrorist incidents."

More operations then followed: *Piranha, Dagger Thrust, Golden Fleece, Blue Marlin,* and *Harvest Moon*. At the conclusion of each, the Viet Cong returned. Marines found themselves raking over the same paddy fields, and in one operation landing in the vicinity of a beach used in a previous operation. Concurrently, III MAF conducted "thousands of night and day patrols" as well as "hundreds of ambushes and small unit offensive actions." Not everyone was comfortable with the tactics used. Marine Chuck Sawyer took part in ambushes in which the orders were "when they come within range, open fire." But the range and visibility was barely "four, five feet." "This bothered me initially because what if it's a child coming down … You know, what do you do about that? So, I didn't care for that at all."[112] For Marine Calixto Cabrera the mismatch between what he had been taught and the reality he found was stark:

> There was the enemy that I thought that I was going to fight, implacable Communists, madmen that just plunders [sic] villages, tortures and kills anything in the name of their ideology … What I found was a peasant who, for whatever reason, believed that being on the other side was where to be.[113]

The Da Nang perimeter ballooned into a 600 square mile war zone and the casualty lists lengthened.[114] As the area had always been a bastion of resistance since the First Indochina War, it was unlikely that any amount of clearance operations would rid the jungle or villages of guerrillas and sympathizers; indeed, there would be heavy fighting in the area in every subsequent year of the war.

In August 1965, the heaviest fighting took place in the vicinity of a feature called Hill 43. A sense of the futility of *Starlite* can be gained from the fact that in 1970 *Playboy* magazine (what a fall from grace after the rousing, patriotic coverage by *Life*) was reporting on yet another major operation to clear the area.[115] Naval shells and bombs expended from the first operation were found and two miles of tunnels were discovered. In what can only be described as a scorched earth policy, the entire hill was deforested by dozers and the surrounding fields and villages were put to the torch. Contemporary photographs of the area showed a moonscape.[116] All remaining civilians were transported to refugee centers. But the Viet Cong, as before, returned. Today, the surrounding countryside has recovered but the pimple of Hill 43 remains bare. Debris from the fighting is still visible for the curious near a village called Nam Yen.

Even as the marines were fighting their odd battle of the beachheads campaign, the temperature was rising at home. Johnson's decisive switch of strategy in July, from defense of enclaves to offensive operations, had roused "the country" he so feared stirring. How could anyone fail to notice that the President was effectively taking the country to war? An increasingly skeptical public and Senate needed reassurance. The big question overhanging Johnson, which would dog the entire conflict, was: why was America in Vietnam in the first place? His answer was principled. "We just cannot now dishonor our word," he intoned, "or abandon our commitment, or leave those who believed us and who trusted us."[117] It was a matter of honor, or of American "prestige," but it came at a cost. And the price would now be paid by draftees.

Of all the measures announced in the summer of 1965, it was an increase in the draft that proved the most contentious. The draft call would now be doubled to 35,000 per month. There were some 4,000 draft stations across the country implementing the highly controversial, and on several levels iniquitous, Selective Service System. A spate of draft-card burning in the spring had forced the House of Representatives to rush forward a bill setting a maximum five-year prison sentence and $10,000 fine for draft dodgers. Contrary to the popular view, the draft dodgers were not all left-leaning, unpatriotic, "liberal" students. Theoretically, there was a one-in-six chance of being drafted but the selection criteria significantly skewed the odds of avoiding the draft in favor of the wealthy and the smart (the odds, of course, were far worse in North Vietnam; from an overall population of 18 million, around a quarter of all males between 15 and 49 found themselves forcibly drafted into the war; for the communists it was always total war). Worried fathers took huge risks paying bribes to help sons dodge the draft and some ended up in court. College freshmen in the top half of the class were deferred. This resulted in a boom in $1.95 crammers sold on the grounds that the book could save you being sent to Vietnam. No amount of cramming was going to save the children in inadequate public schools, which is why the Vietnam War quickly became "a poor boys' war," with blacks disproportionately represented in the units most likely to suffer the heaviest casualties.

For draftees – even the volunteers – the rude reception in Vietnam could be a shock. When Charles Sabatier questioned why he and his fellow draftees were being picked up at the airport in coaches that "looked like prison buses," he was told that "it was to stop people from running up and throwing grenades into the bus." Are people "gonna try to kill me?" he asked. Dwelling on this troubling thought "was quite a traumatic experience for me."[118]

Ten days later, Sabatier found himself in Cu Chi and wandered into a mess hall looking for comrades from "the 4th and 23rd." Surprised by the deserted hall, he approached a sullen group of soldiers, no more than half a dozen, eating their meal in silence. Where is everybody, he asked. "We are everybody," a soldier replied, one of a handful of survivors from a company recently decimated on operations. A later paralyzed, wiser and angered Sabatier reflected, we were dying for "a stupid slogan" – "we died for the domino theory."

David Adcock, who deployed to An Khe in the Central Highlands, remembered the red dust:

> We hadn't been in-country an hour probably … and there was some guys that had come in from the field … I'll never forget how they looked. They were the most scruffy-looking guys you've ever seen in your life. They needed haircuts and probably needed to be shaved and their clothes, their uniforms, were just red from all that old red mud. Their boots were red. Their skin was red … I didn't realize it but after a while that's the way we'd all be looking.[119]

Others remembered the heat. "It took me a while to get adjusted to the heat," recalled marine officer Charles Allen, "I remember going out and tromping around through the rice paddies just being utterly exhausted and thirsty."[120]

For Dave Crawley the shock of arrival at 3/1 Marines was exacerbated by a macabre (and illegal) initiation rite. He and fellow new arrivals were taken to the edge of a massive crater where "there were hundreds of dead Vietnamese bodies … and they had us all shoot into this hole … I'd never seen that many dead bodies in a big hole like that."[121] The same marine – perhaps in biased recollection from his later anti-war stance – also recalled a bloodthirsty racism in his basic training:

- Throughout all this training, when instructors referred to the Vietnamese, how would they talk about them?
- Oh, they were always gooks.
- Always gooks?
- From boot camp to ITR [Infantry Training Regiment] when you were about to be given a lesson so that they could see the back row, they'd always say, "First two rows down!" and you'd drop to one knee and you'd go, "Kill, kill, kill the gooks!"

Later in his tour he witnessed three fellow marines beating a villager to death, only saved by a "lifer" (career soldier) who intervened.

Marine Anthony Goodrich recalled the same racism used to promote aggression in pugil stick fights during basic training:

I remember Staff Sergeant Soto used to get us out and he would ask us individually, "Why do you want to kill gooks?" I remember that distinctly, and you would have to say, I want to kill gooks because they're Communists … I realized then, even at 18, that they were trying to de-humanize the enemy … I want to kill them because they killed a Marine because they're Communist, because they're godless, all the propaganda we were taught, and I think that was a way for us to de-humanize them for us to be able to kill them.[122]

With the arrival of units from 1st Infantry Division and 101st Airborne Division in July, a reorganization was required. A corps HQ was established at Nha Trang designated I Field Force, embracing the II and III Corps areas in the center of the country. This was commanded by General Stanley Larsen, another wartime infantryman. 1 Corps Tactical Zone (I CTZ) in the north remained a marine command. By November, Task Force Alpha would swell to a two-corps command and be redesignated Field Force Vietnam (FFORCEV). In the meantime, the first elements of 1st Cavalry Division – an elite but untried outfit – began to arrive at An Khe, halfway between Qui Nhon on the coast and Pleiku in the Central Highlands. The former was now invested by the ROK division, 22nd ARVN Division, 2/7 Marines, and 3/7 Marines.

Like their marine counterparts, US Army units were quickly committed to offensive operations. Between June and December 173rd Airborne Brigade conducted five operations in War Zone D, the last appropriately called *Hump*. In August, the formation was used as reserve in the Central Highlands. It was joined by paratrooper brethren from 1/101st Airborne Division tasked to open the notorious Highway 19 that had cost the French so many lives. Like the French, the "Screaming Eagles" soon overextended themselves. When an operation was mounted to trap Viet Cong north of An Khe (Operation *Gibraltar* – September 18), two companies ended up being surrounded and had to be rescued. Over 50 paratroopers were killed or wounded. Twenty-six helicopters were damaged or destroyed and air strikes caused friendly fire fatalities. Westmoreland, however, declared it a "spectacular victory," in the usual way. A more honest David Hackworth, future commander of the controversial Tiger Force, thought it was a disaster. One participant recalled that as night fell, "The cacophony of battle was reduced to the hiss of burnng flames, the moans of the wounded, and the sporadic ratcheting volleys of machine gun fire. The night seemed to last forever."[123]

Civilian casualties also mounted alarmingly, not least because HQ MACV promulgated a directive allowing commanders to use unobserved artillery fire (that is, blind fire against suspected enemy). In populated areas such as hamlets and villages, commanders were given the unrealistic instruction to issue a warning first, unless doing so endangered lives. As few – if any – company commanders were likely to risk the lives of their soldiers attempting to warn villagers speaking an unintelligible language, this directive provided carte blanche to start shelling settlements. This policy was mirrored by the introduction of "free bomb zones," essentially authorizing pilots to drop ordnance without ground control. While all this was unfolding, a tousle-haired pipe fitter and amateur folk singer called Barry McGuire found himself improbably topping the popular music charts with a song called "Eve of Destruction" – what better anthem for the summer of 1965? Patriotic disc jockeys thought otherwise and the "un-American" song was banned from many radio stations. For his five minutes of fame, McGuire received a handsome check, but also sack-loads of hate mail.

Since the summer, American and North Vietnamese units had feinted like two boxers in the ring weighing each other up. This tense situation could not last for ever. The phony war finally ended over four days – from November 14 to 18 – in a valley called Ia Drang ("Ia" meaning "river" in Montagnard, and "Drang" the name of the river).[124]

From the air, Ia Drang gave the appearance of an idyllic, verdant, if impenetrable, bowl of forest ringed on three sides by high features, the most prominent of which was a ten-mile broad granite rock lump, the 2,300-foot Chu Pong massif that straddled both sides of the border. The valleys and ravines falling away from this feature made it the perfect harbor for infiltrating North Vietnamese units. At ground level, the forest revealed wide spaces between the trees and fields of elephant grass. The relatively few natural clearings in the forest offered the only viable Landing Zones (LZs). The valley did not particularly matter and it has been argued the battle should have been named after the Chu Pong massif. But neither side wanted to hold this mountain either, and to focus on the geography was to miss the point. Operation *Silver Bayonet I* – the operation originally launched to relieve a besieged special force camp at Plei Me – was not about seizing and holding ground, and nor was this a war about shoving an enemy off a hill, or clearing a valley.

American soldiers had been despatched to Vietnam to exterminate the enemy – the "body count" as military fetish – and the purity of the idea was compelling. "The basic mission of any military force," Assistant Commander of 1st Cavalry, Brigadier General Richard Knowles, avowed, "is to destroy the enemy."[125] There were no secondary missions in the tactic of "search and destroy." Over the summer and fall, Westmoreland had been denied the opportunity to worship this fetish by the elusiveness of the enemy and the difficulty of the terrain. Now an opportunity presented itself and 234 American soldiers were fated to die in a lowland forest nobody cared for – a higher casualty toll than the weekly average in the Korean War – obeisant to this war of attrition. The People's Army casualties were no less heavy; a low-end estimate was 1,519, and the high figure was 2,262. The true number is unknown and at least one soldier who took part in the battle thought the body count numbers were a joke, with one commanding officer simply quoting the first large number that came to his head.[126] The North Vietnamese would report a far lower number of fatalities; 555 including 346 killed before the two forces clashed, but this also seemed an implausibly low number given the expenditure of ordnance in such a congested battlefield.

The US Army was so unprepared for such a sudden and large loss of life there was no casualty notification system in place. Taxis were used to deliver the notification telegrams to the families at Fort Benning. "The Secretary of the Army has asked me to express his deep regret that your husband ..." became a formula of words that would be repeated many thousands of times over the next few years. But in November 1965 it was still a rarity, like an unfortunate fatal accident. Nobody had thought of providing flags for the coffins that were carried off the back of returning C-130s by civilian workers in jeans and baseball caps.[127]

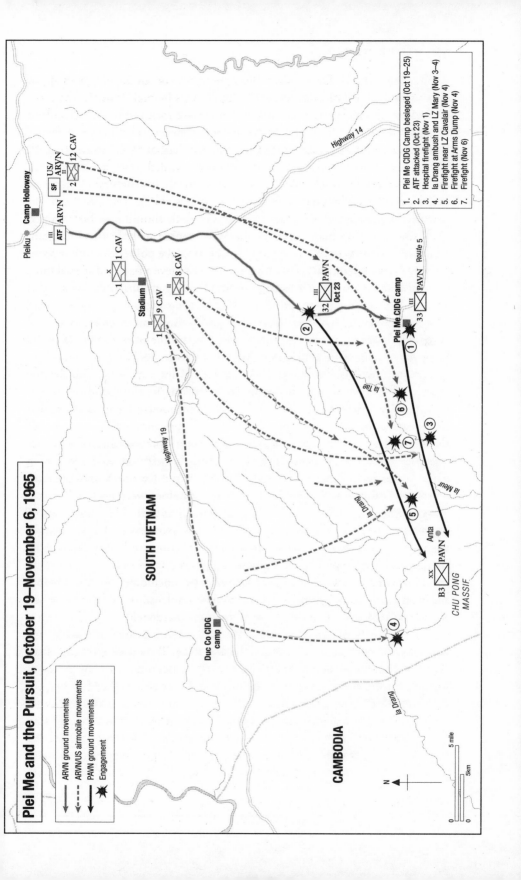

Plei Me and the Pursuit, October 19–November 6, 1965

1. Plei Me CIDG Camp besieged (Oct 19–25)
2. ATF attacked (Oct 23)
3. Hospital firefight (Nov 1)
4. Ia Drang ambush and LZ Mary (Nov 3–4)
5. Firefight near LZ Cavalair (Nov 4)
6. Firefight at Arms Dump (Nov 4)
7. Firefight (Nov 6)

ARVN ground movements
ARVN/US airmobile movements
PAVN ground movements
Engagement

SOUTH VIETNAM

CAMBODIA

CHU PONG MASSIF

Highway 14

Highway 19

Camp Holloway

Pleiku

Stadium

Duc Co CIDG camp

Plei Me CIDG camp

Route 5

Anta

Ia Tae

Ia Meur

Ia Drang

Ia Drang

1 1 CAV

2 8 CAV

1 9 CAV

2 12 CAV

ATF

SF US/ARVN

ARVN

PAVN 32 Oct 23

PAVN 33

PAVN

B3 PAVN

0 5 mile
0 5km

N

The catalyst for the operation was a combined Viet Cong and PAVN attack on Plei Me special force camp in the Central Highlands, just 20 miles east of the Cambodian border. This was home to a handful of Green Berets from Detachment A-217 and 415 Montagnard militia of the CIDG (Civilian Irregular Defense Group). The camp was also shared with around 2,300 Montagnard women and children who scuttled into bunkers when the fighting broke out. For months the PAVN had been building up its forces in the remote and inaccessible valleys and hills just over the Cambodian border. An assault was expected, but in the event failed. Accurate warnings were actually received of the timing of the attack, but these were discounted. When it fell on October 19 it came as a surprise.[128] Elements of 33rd PAVN Regiment led by Lieutenant Colonel Nguyen Huu An surrounded and then attempted to overrun the small, triangular-shaped camp. The assault was beaten off by a massive display of aerial power – as many as ten bombing runs every hour – and the camp suffered only light casualties. An ARVN road relief force, Luat Task Force, based on 3rd Armored Cavalry Regiment, was ambushed by 32nd PAVN Regiment under Lieutenant Colonel To Dinh Khan, but was also seen off.

The most forceful implication that fell out of "the siege of Plei Me," finally relieved after a week, was the growling comment made by a young Major Charlie Beckwith, future founder of Delta Force. Asked by a reporter what he thought of the enemy, he answered: "I would give anything to have 200 of them under my command. They're the finest soldiers I have ever seen." When presented the same question about his South Vietnamese allies, Beckwith could barely bring himself to answer. "I do not want to make any comment on the Vietnamese in the camp," he replied, deflecting the question.[129]

Ia Drang then followed, almost as a trial experiment in finding, fixing, and destroying a concentration of enemy forces using the new and untested tactic of air mobility. This novel doctrine in fact had long roots, dating back to Korea and championed by influential figures like Maxwell Taylor. From the beginnings of the Kennedy presidency, the helicopter had been viewed as the key to unlocking the stalemate in Vietnam. In 1962 McNamara had tasked the Howze Board (after General Hamilton Howze) to study helicopter warfare and develop "a plan for implementing fresh and perhaps unorthodox concepts which will give us a significant increase in mobility."[130] When Kennedy was finally persuaded to increase the troop levels of MACV, it was a small contingent of 33 Shawnee helicopters that was despatched to support the pressed ARVN.

In 1965, "air mobility" was being enthusiastically promoted by Major General Harry Kinnard, Commander of 1st Cavalry, a division sitting on a fleet of over 400 machines. Kinnard importantly had the ear of Westmoreland. A veteran of Normandy, Kinnard followed the scent of an enemy like an excited foxhound in a hunt. Why fight your way through jungle when a bird can drop you on top of the heads of the enemy? II ARVN Corps was also keen to employ the newly deployed resources of its American allies. In the past, the ARVN had always been forced to watch in frustration as North Vietnamese forces withdrew unmolested to Cambodian sanctuaries. The helicopter offered an opportunity to end this game.

Like the tank, it was soon appreciated that mass mattered. A brace of helicopters served little purpose. You needed a flock of the machines, as many as required to land entire battalions or brigades in one swoop (Westmoreland had wanted to split 1st Cavalry on its arrival in South Vietnam, a proposal strongly resisted by Kinnard). As nobody had previously attempted air assault operations on this scale an experimental formation was established – 11th Air Assault Division – later redesignated 1st Cavalry Division. The "Air Cav" sported a patch with a horse head. The officers wore black cavalry hats and maintained perfect creases in their uniforms even on the battlefield. They knew and believed themselves to be elite. They just needed an opportunity to prove it. Or at least this was the myth. Some cavalrymen were dubious of their elite status and lacked confidence in their training. On July 1, the division was still short of 6,000 men. A third of its pilots were untrained in formation flying, and another third lacked aerial gunnery qualification. Thirty-five had not yet passed their general flying course.[131] A battalion like 2/7 Cavalry that would play a prominent and unimpressive role in the forthcoming battle was known to be undertrained, but the drive to build up the troop strength in Vietnam left no time for additional training.

1st Brigade began to arrive at Camp Radcliffe in An Khe in July 1965. By September all three brigades were complete in-country. In total, ten cargo ships, six troopships, and four light aircraft carriers were used to shift the division and its equipment. Qui Nhon had no deep-water piers so every ship had to anchor offshore and be laboriously unloaded in a relay service. It was the last brigade, 3rd Brigade commanded by Colonel Thomas Brown, based at Pleiku just 35 miles from Ia Drang that would be committed to the battle. At the time, only a handful of soldiers in the brigade had actually experienced combat. Some units had barely sorted themselves out following the complicated logistic exercise of shifting 32 battalions and all their equipment to Vietnam, accomplished in two rushed months.

Several commanders faced each other off at the base of the Chu Pong massif. On the American side, the battle was principally commanded and fought by Lieutenant Colonel Harold Moore, Commanding Officer 1/7 Cavalry, a wiry man who roamed the battlefield with his M-16 and bayonet fixed. On the communist side, command was more confused. The People's Army knew this sector as the B3 Front. General Chu Huy Man, a Dien Bien Phu veteran, was overall front commander (or Party Committee Secretary of the Front, in the pompous language of communist military ranks). Lieutenant Colonel Nguyen Huu An was his deputy, also a Dien Bien Phu veteran. It was An – who simultaneously commanded 33rd PAVN Regiment – who effectively assumed overall command of the battle at Chu Pong. After the war, it was An who would strike up a relationship with Moore. But the main fighting was undertaken by 66th PAVN Regiment. This unit was confusingly led by the political officer, La Ngoc Chau, after the military commander absconded.

Both sides would claim victory, but in truth it was a stalemate or pyrrhic victory at best. Westmoreland later reported that this had been the toughest fighting experienced by American troops, and that three North Vietnamese regiments had been destroyed. This was a severe editing of the story, although it is easy to see why from Westmoreland's viewpoint it did seem like a victory. A fairer verdict is that Ia Drang was a confused melee in which both sides blundered into each other, and almost lost control. It is fortunate for historians that the American side – by chance – was accompanied by a combat camera team. Reviewing the footage provokes unavoidable questions: over such ground, wasn't a chaotic fight always likely? Indeed, why did 1/7 Cavalry land at LZ X-Ray in the first place, overlooked by the steep and forested Chu Pong massif?

Following the lifting of the siege at Plei Me, Westmoreland visited the front on October 26–27. Urged to exploit the situation, 1st Cavalry switched from defensive and reactive operations to offensive search and destroy operations. A series of small-unit actions followed that the cavalrymen easily won. But these whitewashes concealed traps. Tactical victories so cheaply won suggested that air mobility was the winning hand. 1st Cavalry only had to keep repeating the trick, "herding" the PAVN and "frog-jumping" all the way to the Cambodian border. More skirmishes followed and the division suffered more fatalities. Still, the high body count being reported up the chain of command (over 1,500 enemy casualties reported by II Corps, a gross exaggeration) and the low level of their own casualties offered the enticement of more cheap wins.[132] Thus inflated with a self-deceiving hubris, Kinnard's men marched ever closer to their Rorke's Drift on the Cambodian border.

On November 14, 1st Cavalry received reports that a second attempt to assault Plei Me was being prepared, inviting a pre-emptive blow against a massing enemy. The intelligence on the whereabouts of the three PAVN regiments was good; an invaluable source was Chinese military advisors who transmitted volubly and in clear, seemingly unaware that their chatter was being intercepted. With some triangulation, it was determined that 66th Regiment was located on the north bank of the Ia Drang and comprised three units, 7th, 8th, and 9th Battalions, mostly intact. The mauled 33rd Regiment had set up camp in Anta, a small village, also with three units, 1st, 2nd, and 3rd Battalions. 32nd Regiment (334th, 645th, and 966th Battalions) was also north of the Ia Drang.[133] This battalion had suffered fewer casualties in the preceding battles.

In later years, An would reveal the positions of the PAVN regiments to American historians of the battle.[134] He drew the unit HQ flags more or less where contemporaneous intelligence reporting had placed them, straddling the Ia Drang, about three miles northwest of the landing zone where Moore's men landed. The nearest unit to 1/7 Cavalry had been 9th Battalion commanded by Nguyen Van Dinh, but even this unit was at least one mile from the LZ and in dead ground to the site, which would explain why the landing was unopposed. If An's recollection was correct it would suggest that his soldiers then made good speed across difficult ground as, within two hours of the landing, 1/7 Cavalry would be locking horns with the enemy. A later captured PAVN map showed that many of the North Vietnamese thrusts had actually advanced from a southwesterly axis, suggesting that the North Vietnamese had been extremely mobile, effectively looping around the southern perimeter of the landing zone and attacking from the rear. In the second half of the battle, almost all the PAVN thrusts were from the east, implying that by this stage the North Vietnamese units had completely encircled the US units to attack from an unexpected direction.

The fitness of the common North Vietnamese soldier had to be respected: 32nd and 33rd Regiments marched 20-odd miles to Plei Me, fought a battle, and then marched back, all before the battles at Ia Drang. These regiments had already trekked the Ho Chi Minh Trail to infiltrate South Vietnam. To get fit, rookie Pham Xuan recalled, recruits undertook long training marches with bamboo baskets loaded with 20 pounds of rocks and soil.[135] On the march south, foot soldiers were issued just ten milk cans of rice which were supposed to last five days' marching, and a single one kilogram can of salted pork, to last three months. They received no other meat, fish, vegetables, or other food; foraging was the order of the day. To avoid detection by American surveillance, recruits were taught to use smokeless Hoang Cam stoves, named after the Viet Minh inventor.[136] Unsurprisingly, dystentry and beriberi decimated their ranks as much as American bombs and bullets.

Dao Van Loi, who made the journey in January 1966, recorded that just 70 percent of a sister unit completed the march, the remainder lost to sickness and desertions.[137] Later that year, now based in Phuoc Long Province, 200 of his comrades perished from malaria, "a very terrible number." Stretcher parties relaying the infirm to rear area clinics were ordered to carry a shovel and hoe. Ailing patients that died before reaching aid were simply buried by the side of the road.

Moore was only given his orders to conduct a search and destroy mission into the Ia Drang – Operation *Silver Bayonet I* – the night before the operation, on November 13:

> 1st Battalion, 7th Cavalry conducts Air assault operations on area LIME (Ia Drang Valley) to search for and destroy the enemy. Operations will be concentrated on stream beds, river beds, and wooded high ground to a maximum height of 500 metres.

The warning order was issued late in the day at 5pm by his brigade commander. As the 1st Cavalry after-action report later recorded: "Few units that have a rendezvous with destiny have an inkling of their fate until the historical moment touches them." 1/7 Cavalry at the time was resting in a harbor south of Plei Me after three days of fruitless searches. By 10pm Moore had issued his warning order to his companies. The final orders group was held the following morning at 8.30am. Moore only actually saw the battlefield and selected an LZ two hours earlier in a dawn aerial reconnaissance in two helicopters.[138] It is known from the reconnaissance flight subsequently appended to Moore's after-action report that the pilot conducted a single loop, north to south, across the Ia Drang. Moore deliberately bisected a line indicated by a communications intercept leading to the Chu Pong. Somewhere on that line was the PAVN regiment, but Moore did not know where. Pressed for time, he selected the most promising area of open ground, along that flight path, close to the line of the communications intercept that would place his battalion in the vicinity of the enemy.

The orders group was concluded at 9.15am and H-Hour was set for 10.30am (it was a model of brevity – the transcript of Moore's orders were just two pages long). The speed of 1/7 Cavalry's operational procedures was also stunning; within minutes of the conclusion of the orders, the companies were preparing to mount up. But this slickness belied serious manning and logistic problems. Three of his companies (A, B, and C) were just over 100 strong (from an establishment strength of 164). D Company could only call on 80 all ranks. In total, Moore could only muster 431 troopers from a total strength of 633.[139]

Moore's chosen landing zone, LZ X-Ray, was located immediately east of the Chu Pong foothills. First, the surrounding area was "prepped" with a 20-minute fire plan. Due to last-minute positioning the guns only commenced firing at 10.17am, but "they were precisely where required and beautifully timed with the landing of the lead elements of the assault company."[140] The barrage was followed by aerial rocket artillery (helicopter gunships) that raked the treelines with machine gun fire. The assault was led by B Company under Captain John Herren, lifted by all 16 UH-1Ds, with Moore in the first lift. The first helicopter landed at 10.48am. "We landed and ran from the landing zone into the trees firing our M-16's [sic] at likely enemy positions," but there was no enemy. The helicopters returned to Plei Me to pick up the remainder of B Company and elements of A Company commanded by Captain Ramon Nadal.

Moore described the spot where the cavalrymen now found themselves:

The terrain was flat and consisted of scrub and trees up to 100 feet high; thick elephant grass varying in height from one foot to five feet; and ant hills throughout the area up to eight feet high with thick brush and elephant grass on and around them. Along the western edge of the LZ, the trees and grass were especially thick and extended off into the jungle on the foothills of the mountain.[141]

By around midday almost the entire battalion, less D Company, had been lifted into the clearing and a single prisoner had been captured; an unfortunate soul "dressed in dirty khaki shirt and trousers" who confessed to having eaten nothing but bananas for the last five days. More importantly he informed his interrogators there were three battalions hidden in the mountain overlooking the LZ "who very much wanted to kill Americans."

The lack of opposition had been deceptive and the noisy landing was detected. As the companies fanned out to explore the foothills they began to receive sniping fire. At 1.30pm, Herren urgently called Moore and informed him that his company was under heavy attack and that 7 Platoon, commanded by Lieutenant Herrick, was in danger of being surrounded. This enemy was elements of Dinh's 9th Battalion.[142] A Company was at once despatched to reinforce B Company and Moore ordered artillery fire, "walking" the fire from south to west to suppress the enemy assault. But almost immediately, confusion set in and nobody was really quite certain where the forward line of their own troops lay, complicating the delivery of the artillery fire.

1/7 Cavalry's confusion was equaled by the muddle on the communist side. When Moore landed, all the principal PAVN commanders were some distance from LZ X-Ray. The commander of 9th Battalion was conducting a reconnaissance on the banks of the Ia Drang with the commander of 66th Regiment. The two deputies were also elsewhere. An was unsighted but aware that something was afoot from the weight of artillery fire suddenly landing on the foothills of the Chu Pong.

In fact, what had happened was that B Company stumbled into 9th Battalion's 10 Company, co-located with the battalion HQ, and in the ensuing fight the PAVN almost collapsed. The stand-in commander, 9th Battalion's political officer, simply fled. The situation was saved by 11 Company, which launched a counterattack, later supported by 13 Company. It was these two sub-units that created the impression that B Company was in danger of being overwhelmed. The 9th Battalion commander raced back and re-joined his unit one hour later, but all accounts suggest that he failed to grip the companies and proved a weak leader.

At this point, it became a free-for-all. One platoon of A Company became disorientated and got lost. The remainder of the company bumped into a PAVN company (possibly advance elements of 7th Battalion) that was sneaking along a dry creek bed on the western edge of the clearing and a violent gunfight ensued. In the meantime, the cut-off platoon remained surrounded and efforts to make contact failed, although another platoon did manage to get within shouting distance before being beaten back. Even as these actions were developing, Captain Robert Edwards' C Company, which had only just landed, became embroiled in a desperate defense of the LZ as a wave of North Vietnamese attempted to overrun the site. The assault was determined and only finally petered out after an hour and a half of repeated attacks. Several departing helicopters were hit but none were downed.

The threat to the helicopters prevented the complete landing of D Company and the company commander Captain Louis Lefebvre (whose radio operator was killed while still on board the helicopter) found himself with just his mortar platoon and anti-tank platoon. He rallied these men and marched towards the sound of gunfire where A Company was fighting. In the ensuing gun battle he was then severely wounded, and command of the company passed to the anti-tank platoon sergeant with the survivors eventually placed under command of C Company, on the southeast corner of the LZ. By around 3pm, Moore had stabilized the battle and the balance of 1/7 Cavalry landed at LZ X-Ray amidst intermittent fire. It was obvious to everyone that the battalion had stirred a hornet's nest and had taken heavy casualties. At HQ 3rd Brigade, B Company of 2/7 Cavalry commanded by Captain Myron Diduryk was put on standby to reinforce the sister battalion if necessary.

The immediate emergency was over but the overall situation was far from satisfactory. 1/7 Cavalry's hold on the LZ was tenuous and B Company's cut-off platoon remained marooned on the hillside. At around 4.20pm, A and B Companies made a concerted effort to rescue the platoon, preceded by an artillery barrage. It proved a costly effort. Communist soldiers seemed to be everywhere: in the trees, in mouse holes, concealed in ant hills, and in hollows. Their camouflage was excellent and they displayed great fire discipline, waiting until the last moment before opening fire. The firepower thrown at them seemed to have little effect. The disorganized and largely leaderless North Vietnamese soldiers remained at their posts and sought whatever cover they could find, riding out the storms of shrapnel. The density of the vegetation beyond the relatively open scrubland of the clearing reduced visibility to yards, and the closeness of the bush encouraged the men to draw nearer, increasing the possibility of casualties if a group was caught by a burst of automatic fire. Command and control was further exacerbated by the visibility of the leaders and their radio operators, who necessarily had to stand to transmit successfully, or pass orders. All three A Company platoon leaders were killed. Four men were killed in the company HQ but somehow Captain Ramon Nadal dodged the bullets (his radio operator was killed). Even with this effort, the company was only able to make 150 yards before one of its own platoons became cut off and had to be rescued by saturating the area with white phosphorus shells. This seemed to catch everyone by surprise and there was a temporary abatement in the killing which allowed the dead and wounded to be retrieved, and enabled the isolated platoon to re-join the now greatly depleted A Company. To the right, B Company fared even worse. The company was unable to make 100 yards before aborting any further attempts to advance. At 5.40pm Moore called the whole thing off.

It would be wrong to conclude, however, that 66th Regiment therefore won this first bout. Later testimony revealed that the regiment paid dearly for the assault on X-Ray.[143] La Ngoc Chau, the political officer who took charge of the assault, reported that Dinh's 9th Battalion was considered "dismantled." Moore was not the only commanding officer dealing with heavy losses. Later testimony revealed that the communists had been totally confused by the events of the day.

As night fell, the exhausted troops were recalled to the landing zone. The dead and wounded were painfully recovered (as no one had anticipated mass casualties the battalion lacked stretchers and was also very short of medical equipment). Ammunition was resupplied, and water and food distributed. A perimeter defense was organized, reinforced by B Company 2/7 Cavalry, shocked by the scene of slaughter, and which arrived just before nightfall.

If Moore harbored private thoughts that the battle had run away from him, he might have been reassured to know that his adversaries were also suffering a crisis of confidence. 9th Battalion, rather than pressing its advantage, took the American withdrawal as a cue to break contact and scatter. In the meantime, Le Tien Hao, the 66th Regiment's acting commander, wandered off into the bush and was not seen for another two days. Only a handful of isolated platoons remained behind, it seems because they had no clue what was happening.

The cut-off B Company platoon was just 300 yards from the remainder of its comrades on the landing zone, but was far from demoralized. It had successfully beaten off every attempt to overrun the position and a spirit of defiance emboldened the trapped cavalrymen. Capture was unthinkable. They would have to be killed and they would exact a very heavy price if it came to this end. This remarkable platoon of 27 men had just seven unwounded soldiers. Another eight were wounded but could use a weapon in extremis. Twelve lay dead. Herrick the platoon commander, the platoon sergeant, and the weapons squad leader were all dead. Just seven fit men were holding off the persistent assaults. On that first night, three attempts appear to have been made to overrun the platoon and all were repulsed, the last by illuminating the area and calling in an air strike. Fear of infiltrators was so great the beleaguered soldiers spent the entire time prone, not daring to raise their heads lest they be picked off by sniper fire. In the event, it appears the North Vietnamese became as confused as the cavalrymen in the darkness and failed to capitalize on their advantage of greater numbers.

As well as the air strikes, the cavalrymen owed their survival to the UH-1D crews from 229th Aviation. This unit maintained the vital ferry service throughout the first hard-fought battle, often under fire. Pilot Charles Gentry remembered:

> I saw a lot of wounded Americans. I saw dead Americans ... resupply [was] going on all the time, even though there was firing going on. The trees in and around the landing zone, they were just devoid of any leaves. There were no leaves left. They were like sticks. So it was a very grim sight to see.[144]

The following month, the helicopter he was flying was badly damaged by machine gun fire. As he struggled to make a safe emergency landing,

> a bullet came through the bottom of the fuselage and up through, ricocheted through and hit me in the face, clipped through my flight helmet, right on the edge of it below my cheek. The pieces, by then shrapnel, or almost spent bullet ... hit me in the face and knocked me out.

The unconscious Gentry suffered a broken back on impact. Later he was told his helicopter had been holed 37 times.

Overall, 229th Aviation would fly 10,840 sorties over the course of the Pleiku Campaign (a remarkable total of 63,204 sorties was flown by the divisional aviation as a whole for a loss of just seven aircraft hit by enemy fire, four of which were recovered). In 229th Aviation, 14 helicopters were hit by ground fire, two helicopters were immobilized, but just two helicopters were actually downed and all were recovered.[145] As well as running the gauntlet of enemy fire the pilots had to contend with a fog at the bottom of the valley, created by the artillery barrages and air strikes. Landing by day was challenging. At night, with tactical lights, it was a feat of airmanship.

When dawn broke, Moore planned to rescue the platoon but he was preempted by a mass attack against the left-hand sector of C Company's perimeter that kicked off at around 7am. Unbeknown to Moore, this was the first move in a serious attempt to finish off 1/7 Cavalry led by Thuoc's 7th Battalion. The previous afternoon, the 66th Regiment Deputy Commander, Pham Cong Cuu, had gathered 7th Battalion and brought it forward to the high ground overlooking the clearing. He was later joined by the political officer La Ngoc Chau who had taken charge of the situation and led the aborted attacks the previous evening. That night Chau and Cuu hatched a plan. They would attack using a classic hammer and anvil ploy: two 7th Battalion companies and the survivors of 9th Battalion would assault the landing zone from one direction while 7th Battalion's weapons company poured fire from another.

The fighting that followed was ferocious. Fanaticism was met by firepower but often it was just raw guts that saved the day. 1/7 Cavalry's Forward Air Controller gave out the code word "Broken Arrow" – an emergency call that prioritized all available tactical aircraft in South Vietnam to this single battalion. As the battle raged, the fallen became intermingled. One American soldier was reportedly found with his hands around the neck of his North Vietnamese assailant. A dead platoon commander was retrieved surrounded by five dead communist soldiers. C Company held on tenaciously, reinforced by a platoon from A Company. All five company officers were either killed or wounded – the company commander himself was shot in the chest and continued to command his men for the next three hours before finally being evacuated. Among the company of surrounded cavalrymen was Sergeant Major Basil L. Plumley, a veteran of four combat jumps in the Second World War, a combat jump in the Korean War, and now on his third war. By the time the fighting abated, C Company had lost 42 men and suffered 62 wounded (from a total strength of 153 troopers who had landed at X-Ray the previous day).[146]

Just 15 minutes after this first assault, the hammer fell on the D Company sector, and within half an hour A Company was also being attacked. The entire clearing became a free fire zone with shell and mortar fire exchanged between the two sides. Throughout, Moore was forced to juggle command appointments as key officers or NCOs were killed or wounded. Sensing that a crisis moment was approaching, he alerted HQ 3rd Brigade that reinforcements would be required, but his call for assistance had already been anticipated and A Company, 2/7 Battalion, led by Captain Joel Sugdinis, was stood up. At around 9.10am this company was landed under fire and moved into line alongside its sister company from 2/7 Cavalry.

Soldiers fought for their lives against uneven odds. Moore wrote in his after-action report,

> One man of Company D who wound up in the C Company sector, was the only soldier left covering 50 yards. He personally shot 10–15 enemy

with his M-16 rifle firing from the kneeling position. The company radio operator picked off 15–20 from the Company C foxhole. The company commander killed several before he was wounded. The enemy fire was so heavy that movement towards or within the sector resulted in more friendly casualties.[147]

Some defenders wondered whether their enemy was "hopped out" on drugs. "Even after being hit several times in the chest, many continued firing and moving for several more steps before dropping dead."[148]

The situation then became desperate and Moore took a gamble, calling for close-in fires – essentially requesting artillery and air strikes virtually on his own positions. Shells did land within the landing zone, as did two napalm canisters dropped by F-100 Super Sabres, triggering a fire in an ammunition dump and wounding two soldiers. One of the burned men subsequently died in the same week that his wife gave birth to their first child.

The gamble, however, paid off. By 10am it was evident the attack was over. Moore waited a further two hours before ordering his men forward to clear the perimeters. What they found resembled a charnel house:

Dead PAVN, PAVN body fragments, and PAVN weapons and equipment were littered in profusion around the edge and forward of the perimeter. Numerous body fragments were seen. There was massive evidence e.g. bloody trails, bandages etc. of many other PAVN being dragged away from the area. Some of the enemy dead were found stacked behind anthills.[149]

The communist soldiers were so conscientious in recovering their wounded just two prisoners were taken.

Moore had not been alone fighting his battle. Colonel Brown, the 3rd Brigade commander, had played his part brilliantly throughout November 14, always staying one step ahead of the game and ensuring that Moore could concentrate all his efforts on commanding his battalion. In addition to warning off and despatching the two companies from 2/7 Cavalry, Brown had landed the entirety of 2/5 Cavalry under Lieutenant Colonel Robert Tully at an alternative landing zone code-named Victor, five miles southeast of LZ X-Ray, north of the banks of the river Tae. Marching at night through jungle would have been unfeasible so the battalion was forced to wait until dawn before marching to Moore's beleaguered men. It arrived shortly after midday. Map reading would hardly have been necessary given the towers of smoke created by the air strikes and artillery fire.

The arrival of these fresh troops finally created the opportunity to rescue B Company's cut-off platoon that had now spent 24 hours surrounded by the PAVN. Three companies were marshaled for this push: B Company 2/7 Cavalry, and A and B Companies of the newly arrived 2/5 Cavalry. The attack was supported by artillery and mortar fire and launched at 1.15pm. Just after 3pm contact was made with the surrounded platoon, now led by the aptly named Sergeant Ernie Savage. The ordeal was over. Healthy and wounded alike craved water by the time they were rescued. The dead were carried back down the hill. For both sides it was now time to draw breath.

An, at this stage, had become pretty confused as to what had actually happened at the landing zone. Obsessed with "frog-jumping" airborne American soldiers, the arrival of 2/5 Cavalry on foot had been entirely missed. The fact that the cut-off B Company platoon had been rescued was also missed. The heavy helicopter traffic at the clearing was interpreted as a retreat and the evacuation of casualties. An drew the flattering conclusion that 1/7 Cavalry had finally been beaten and began to organize the withdrawal of the remnants of 7th and 9th Battalion, leaving behind a small party to observe the area.

In one sense, An was right. 1/7 Cavalry, even with reinforcements, was in no position to continue the original search and destroy mission. The logical next move was indeed to withdraw the depleted unit from the area and to undertake a relief in place with the balance of 2/7 and 2/5 Cavalry, although this carried the certain risk of the UH-1Ds running another gauntlet of harassing fire. This is what Brown now planned. But first, the battalion would have to hunker down for another night at LZ X-Ray. This invited a last assault by 7th Battalion. It came at just after 4am and landed on B Company 2/7 Cavalry's position. For the next two and a half hours, B Company fought off the attack supported by four batteries of guns firing directly into the North Vietnamese assault lines. It was butchery, illuminated by star shells. Later, a pair of A-1E Skyraiders dropped anti-personnel mines. Private First Class Jack Smith thought the falling ordnance reminded him of green confetti. The following day he was wounded in the legs and horrified by the number of ants attracted to his bloodied limbs. The company suffered not a single fatality – in this latest exchange of blows, the American force had clearly got the upper hand.

What had changed An's mind? Again, it appears that An became confused over the exact dispositions of his enemy. Aware that the American soldiers were being supported by artillery fire from a second nearby landing zone, An ordered 33rd Regiment elements to find and destroy the guns but the commander got lost. He simultaneously ordered the survivors of 7th Battalion to launch a second attack against the clearing late in the evening, but this ad hoc unit also became disorientated and it was not until the early hours of the morning that the attack took place. This was the attack that fell on B Company that was easily beaten back.

Moore then ordered his companies to clear their perimeters by spraying the surrounding bush with fire – a standard procedure after an attack – and A Company 2/7 Cavalry appeared to inadvertently provoke a concealed PAVN company into launching a suicidal attack. This "mad minute," as Moore described it, resulted in most of the North Vietnamese being killed or wounded within 20 minutes. An had rolled his dice and now Moore rolled his, for the last time, ordering a probe 500 yards forward of the clearing at 10am. It got nowhere and the troops withdrew under fire. About the only substantial achievement was the recovery of three more dead who had been missed in earlier trawls. As on the previous day, the cavalrymen were amazed by the carnage surrounding their position (they claimed to have killed another 27 North Vietnamese soldiers just undertaking this limited action). By the end of this fight, 1/7 Cavalry had effectively written off 7th Battalion, adding it to the scalp of 9th Battalion which had been defeated on the first day.

2/7 Cavalry began arriving at just after 9.30am and Moore received his orders to withdraw to Camp Holloway at Pleiku, via an LZ Falcon, at 10.40am. B Company 2/7 Cavalry, having suffered a heavy toll of casualties, would also be evacuated with 1/7 Cavalry, along with one decimated platoon from A Company. The evacuation was complete by 3pm and the troops reached the safety of Camp Holloway three hours later.

Moore lost 79 men and suffered 121 wounded – a staggering 30–40 percent casualty rate, depending on whether the reinforcing companies are counted.[150] The fact that unit cohesion held was testament to the fighting spirit of the "Air Cav," and especially to the personal leadership of Harold Moore (a ten percent casualty rate is generally sufficient to provoke the surrender or flight of average troops). Moore had proved an outstanding commander: energetic, quick-thinking, and never beaten however dire the situation appeared. He later claimed 634 enemy killed by body count, but reckoned that over 1,200 PAVN had probably been killed or wounded. Over one hundred rifles, machine guns, and rocket launchers were captured or destroyed in situ.

The battle may have been over for Moore but it was not for his replacement, and the PAVN regiments were far from beaten. The baton passed to Lieutenant Colonel Robert McDade, the commanding officer of 2/7 Cavalry who had only taken over the battalion in the previous month from an experienced Korea veteran. A whispering campaign would subsequently be mounted against McDade. Whether or not justified, McDade was not of the same mold (Moore would be promoted to general rank). From An's perspective, this was now clearly an American retreat and he schemed to finish off the remaining cavalryman. On the communist side, 8th Battalion commanded by Le Xuan Phoi took the lead. An also ordered the lost remnants of 33rd Regiment to join the fray.

For Thomas Brown, the 3rd Brigade commander, the game was effectively over at LZ X-Ray. Rather than waste more lives trying to flush out the enemy, a decision was taken to flatten them with a massive bombing run, the first tactical use of B-52s in the war under the so-called Arc Light raids mounted from Guam (on the previous two days there had been B-52 sorties immediately north of LZ X-Ray). Pilot George Thatcher who flew the first of these 12 hour missions described them as "the definition of flying hours and hours of boredom."[151] For safety reasons, a two-mile exclusion was imposed for high-altitude bombing (the physics of a free fall bomb did not change and a 750lb bomb was as inaccurate in Vietnam as a bomb dropped by a Liberator in the Second World War). This implied that 2/7 and 2/5 Cavalry would have to vacate the area. Two alternative landing zones were quickly selected – Albany and Columbus – both to the northwest of X-Ray. 2/5 Cavalry would extract from the latter and 2/7 Cavalry from the former. The choice of landing zones was questionable – both battalions would be marching towards, not away from possible enemy positions. The better option would have been to march southeast, away from the Chu Pong and back to the clearing where 2/5 Cavalry had originally landed.

The bombing run went ahead as planned. Each B-52 flying in from Guam carried 51 750lb bombs. In total, over a five-day period, there would be five B-52 missions of 96 sorties with a total payload of 200 tons of high explosive.[152] Based on PAVN maps showing the dispositions of units, it is entirely conceivable that no enemy concentrations were hit. An would later state that he ordered units to deliberately move into areas just bombed by the B-52s following the not illogical reasoning that the next bombing run would land elsewhere on the Chu Pong. An himself narrowly missed being caught by a B-52 strike and joked about the incident. In fact, 33rd Regiment had already moved away into the valley and the other two regiments (32nd and 66th) were located at least two miles north of the beaten zones. The often quoted 2,000 enemy kill count appears grossly exaggerated and the available evidence (from the bomb target mapping which has survived) suggests the B-52 strikes on the Chu Pong massif were probably a fruitless exercise in deforestation. The psychological effect of the B-52s was, however, significant, with the North Vietnamese avowing that their appearance over the battlefield "struck terror in their hearts."[153]

2/5 Cavalry led the march away from LZ X-Ray at 9am. Two and a half hours later the column reached LZ Columbus, covering a distance of just over two miles. Short of Columbus, 2/7 Cavalry split off to the northwest to continue for another mile and a half to LZ Albany. At this stage the cavalrymen had been on their feet for over 48 hours and some were tiring. The order of march in the column was A, C, and D Companies with

A Company of 1/5 Cavalry bringing up the rear. McDade positioned himself near the head of the column that stretched for over 500 yards. Immediately short of the LZ, at midday, A Company stumbled on two North Vietnamese soldiers who were promptly seized as prisoners.

The controversy over the battle at Albany starts from this moment. The unexpected capture of two soldiers should have alerted McDade that there was a PAVN unit in the vicinity (even if, as was later reported, the prisoners implausibly claimed that they were deserters). The presence of North Vietnamese soldiers implied that the proposed landing zone was probably compromised and no longer safe. Aborting Albany and marching back to Columbus would have been a highly unpopular decision at the hottest time of the day, but it would have been the right decision. Instead, McDade called forward his company commanders for a conference, denuding the companies of their commanders. By then, the Recon Platoon had moved to the north corner of Albany and found another four sleeping North Vietnamese soldiers.

Now the cavalrymen let themselves down. The track they had been following was hemmed in on both sides by thick elephant grass. In such an obviously vulnerable and strung out formation, the companies should at least have posted sentries and adopted positions of all-round defense. Instead, many flopped on the track, removed equipment, started to cook, or dozed. Unbeknown to the soldiers, on the other side of the elephant grass were elements of two PAVN regiments that had been shadowing the noisy American column.

The attack, when it came at around 1.20pm, was a complete surprise. Elements of 33rd Regiment fell on the rear, and Phoi's 8th Battalion sprung on the head of the column. The attack was signaled by a salvo of mortar rounds on the landing zone. 33rd Regiment was actually still somewhat disorientated in the close bush but reacted to the sound of gunfire and joined the fight that 8th Battalion had already started, creating the impression of a coordinated pincer movement.

Within the space of a few minutes, 2/7 Cavalry was decimated. Sugdinis's A Company was cut off and cut up. Men cried out in fear. One survivor, Jack Smith, a bespectacled teenager at the time serving as a supply clerk in Captain John Fesmire's C Company, recalled that at least 20 of his comrades were dead within seconds. Smith later recollected following his executive officer through the bush in an attempt to reach safety.[154] The soldier closest to him was shot in the heart and died with a moan. The executive officer was shot in the back and then in the foot, the round taking off all his toes and leaving him screaming in agony. A soldier to his right was then shot in the arm and side, causing blood to pour out of his wound in spurts. An enemy machine gunner was so close Smith stuck out his M-16 and blew his head off. A grenade then felled a soldier to his right, who looked like he had been splattered with red paint. Later Smith played dead and a communist machine gunner used him as a sandbag. Smith recalled that this North Vietnamese soldier, also a teenager, was trembling with fear and failed to realize that the body he was using as cover was still alive.[155] The civilian Smith would later celebrate what he called "the miracle of life."

D company led by Captain Henry Thorp somewhat managed to recover the situation. The commanding officer of A Company 2/5 Cavalry, Captain George Forrest, ran the whole length of the column to re-join his company, surviving unscathed but losing both his radio operators. In this close-quarter battle there were many actual and suspected friendly fire incidents. It is inconceivable that there were not moments of outright panic. Several soldiers may have shot themselves with their .45s rather than allow themselves to be captured. The North Vietnamese took no prisoners and killed in cold blood any wounded Americans they found. The screams of the wounded unfortunately only served to hasten their end. Survivors chillingly recalled wounded cavalrymen pleading for their lives and the excited babble of North Vietnamese voices before a rash of gun fire signaled that the unlucky wounded soldier had been summarily executed. This happened within yards of other wounded soldiers who kept perfectly still and survived. The gun battles raged for the rest of the afternoon, the pressed cavalrymen supported by bombing runs led by A-1E Skyraiders dropping napalm and 250lb bombs. Some of these bombs unfortunately killed and wounded cavalrymen who had concealed themselves in the grass.

Eventually two defensive circles were formed at the front and rear, but between these two havens lay isolated groups of soldiers, many dead, many dying, and many just trying to survive. This was where the worst casualties were experienced as An sought to split the force by cutting through the middle of the column. As night fell, in desperation, the unlucky B Company that had been evacuated from LZ X-Ray along with 1/7 Cavalry now found itself reinserted into the beleaguered LZ Albany. One soldier recalled that he was in the men's club downing a beer after the hell of the previous two days when he received the order to mount up again.[156] Over the course of the night, a handful of soldiers attempted to escape to Columbus. Others were jumped on by gangs of North Vietnamese seeking out the weak and isolated. The battalion was unquestionably saved by a non-stop six-hour artillery barrage with illumination rounds, a feat of human and mechanical endurance. By the morning of November 18, it was all over and the North Vietnamese withdrew. It took a further 24 hours to recover the dead and wounded.

Albany cost 2/7 Cavalry 151 killed and 121 wounded. Four soldiers, or their remains, were only finally found five months later. A Company suffered 50 percent casualties, the majority taken in the first few minutes of the battle.

C Company suffered an astonishing 93 percent casualty rate (45 killed and 50 wounded out of 112). The claimed 430 enemy body count was irrelevant and probably pure invention. The battle had been a fiasco. But for the support firepower and undeniable courage of the cavalrymen, an American battalion would have been wiped out.

An inquest soon followed, but everyone wanted to see the good aspects of the battle. Westmoreland visited and congratulated the troops. Kinnard viewed the engagement as vindication of the air mobility concept. The 1st Cavalry after-action report enthused:

> Besides the other firsts, this campaign was the first real test, not only of the "First Team," as a unit, but of the airmobile concept in combat. I believe that both the division and the concept came through with flying colours.

The battle at X-Ray was elevated to heroic status but Albany was buried. Shamefully, 2/7 Cavalry's battalion journal for November 16–22 was deliberately destroyed which means that no historian will ever be able to piece together the events accurately from primary evidence. The cavalrymen were sacrificed and then were wiped from the record by a nervous hierarchy desperate to bury bad news. News reports told of the grit of the cavalryman. These were, after all, descendants of Custer, but they had escaped the fate of the antecedent 7th Cavalry.

Important points passed without critical analysis. It had taken 741 close air support missions, each averaging two tons of explosives and 96 B-52 sorties, to save the two battalions. This implied over 1,000 tons of high explosives, or the equivalent of a tactical nuclear strike. This was twice the tonnage expended by the Luftwaffe to destroy the city of Coventry in the Second World War. All available tactical aircraft were prioritized to save the battalions at Ia Drang. The effort to support Kinnard's men had swallowed 16 percent of the entire helicopter airlift workload in South Vietnam. Over 33,000 artillery shells were expended. Did all this make sense? Was air mobility the royal flush of modern warfare, or had old-fashioned saturation bombing been the ace of spades? The claimed 10:1 kill ratio was also problematic. Even if it was accurate, the arithmetic did not stack up. MACV would have to fight another hundred such battles to wear down the People's Army. Was Westmoreland, or anyone else, suggesting that this was the necessary and justified sacrifice? What if Hanoi did not fold and it took another hundred battles? Where exactly on the graph of attrition warfare was the victory moment?

It is also legitimate to ask what would have happened if 2/7 Cavalry had been wiped out at Albany. Would American public opinion have turned against the war, barely in its infancy, as it would do three years later? Or would the ire of a nation have been stirred? The narrative stated that 1st Cavalry beat off the People's Army in its first conventional stand-up fight, albeit at a very high cost that pushed US fatality numbers over the symbolic 1,000 threshold. Westmoreland won the Pleiku Campaign.

This was the view in Saigon, but it was not universally shared in Washington or by independent observers. Journalists smelled a disaster and the 1st Cavalry press conference held in the immediate aftermath of the battles at Camp Holloway descended into a shouting match. McNamara happened to be on an overseas trip during the ordeal at Ia Drang. Johnson reeled him in and despatched him to Saigon. After conferring with the re-appointed Ambassador Lodge, he flew to An Khe to hear the story from Kinnard (hardly an unbiased interlocutor), and the resting Moore. Coincidentally, Lodge had invited another personality to undertake a fact-finding mission at the same time – a little-known Harvard professor who had mostly specialized in Cold War strategy – Dr Henry Kissinger. This was Kissinger's first trip to Vietnam (he would revisit in July and October 1966). He wrote in his diary: "I am impressed by the fact that no one could really explain to me how even on the most favorable assumptions about the war in Vietnam the war was going to end."[157] Even as personalities like Kissinger were undertaking unofficial fact-finding missions and raising troubling questions, Westmoreland and DePuy, the MACV Deputy Chief of Staff for Operations, were promoting Ia Drang as the model for future victories. As would happen so often over the next few years, it was the misleading and unconfirmed body count numbers that appeared to dazzle everyone.

1st Cavalry – the glamor division – was always bound to attract the press pack. But this was not the only division undertaking offensive operations. Further south, in III CTZ (the Saigon area), all formations had been placed under 1st Infantry, commanded by Major General Seaman, in what was effectively a "super-division" level command (the others fell under Larsen in Task Force Alpha). This implied that along with the Marines in I CTZ, MACV was now responsible for three separate commands, burgeoning to corps size.

These formations were deploying within existing ARVN territorial and command arrangements. In III CTZ, the ARVN commander was Lieutenant General Nguyen Bao Tri, a Northerner from Hanoi who would author several books on Vietnam and its peoples. He commanded three divisions: 5th ARVN Infantry Division to the north of Saigon in Binh Duong Province; 25th ARVN Division to the west in Hau Nghia Province; and 10th ARVN Infantry Division to the east in Long Khanh Province.

Facing these were around 21,000 regular soldiers of the communist B2 Front under overall command of General Nguyen Chi Thanh, but with operational command delegated to the hard-line Major General Tran Van Tra. This force comprised two divisions: 9th PLAF Division which mainly operated in Binh Duong, Binh Long, and Tay Ninh Provinces; and 5th PLAF division which was based east of Saigon in Bien Hoa, Long Khanh, and Phuoc Tuy Provinces (People's Liberation Armed Forces "PLAF" units were "regular" Viet Cong units).[158]

1st Infantry and 173rd Airborne threw themselves into the task of securing the all-important corridor of Route 13, northwest from Saigon, with fresh energy. In the last three months of 1965, 1st Infantry, now fully deployed with three brigades, launched 59 battalion-level operations north of the capital, although only two resulted in substantial battles. For Captain Larry Burke, "My first impression was the pressing heat ... The thing I remember about Vietnam is the heat, the humidity, the smell, that swampy, mildew, wet smell."[159]

The first action took place on November 4, near a hamlet named Bau Bang on Route 13. Mounting what was intended to be a routine route security operation, 2/2 Infantry commanded by Lieutenant Colonel George Shuffer found itself under a concerted assault from 272nd PLAF Regiment, supported by other elements from 9th PLAF Division. Following a violent two-hour confrontation, somewhere close to 200 soldiers lay dead, 20 of them American. Bau Bang, where a civic action program had been planned, was reduced to a smoldering ruin.[160]

The second took place at the conclusion of Operation *Bushmaster* in the Michelin Plantation, a long-established insurgent redoubt from the period of the First Indochina War, some 50 miles northwest of Saigon. The rubber plantation had been established in 1925 and with its 12,400 hectares remained the largest in Vietnam. In a modus vivendi of pure convenience, three parties continued to benefit from its existence: the Michelin Company, the South Vietnamese government that collected taxes, and the Viet Cong that extorted illegal taxes. The only loser in this arrangement was MACV that paid compensation to Michelin when it destroyed the valuable trees in its operations.

The unlucky unit in this case was Lieutenant Colonel George Eyster's 2/28 Infantry which departed the area in a road convoy and was ambushed near a hamlet called Truong Loi by 4th Battalion, 272nd PLAF Regiment. The Viet Cong may have believed the American column offered easy pickings on a single muddy track but did not count on the storm of napalm and artillery fire summoned to rescue the ambushed battalion. By the time the fight was over as many as 142 Viet Cong were believed to have been killed. Eyster lost just six soldiers and a further 38 wounded.[161]

This, naturally, did not end the fighting in the plantation. Following an attack on 7th ARVN Regiment which decimated this formation, Seaman ordered a second Operation *Bushmaster* at the beginning of December. Once again, it was Shuffer's 2/2 Infantry that bumped the enemy near a hamlet named Nha Mat, located just six miles from their last battle at Bau Bang, and once again his adversary was 272nd PLAF Regiment. Like the first battle, the encounter proved a bloody affair: Shuffer lost another 39 soldiers but reckoned he had killed seven times this many enemy. Given the weight of fire that was expended to support 2/2 Infantry, including 175mm guns from 23rd Artillery Group, this may not have been a great exaggeration. Following the scrap, 272nd PLAF Regiment vanished from the Viet Cong order of battle for several months, suggesting that it had been badly worsted.[162]

173rd Airborne mostly operating to the east and northeast of the capital, mounted 14 large operations, one of which led to a significant battle. This took place on November 7 during Operation *Hump*, just 14 miles north of Bien Hoa, at the confluence of the Song Be and Dong Nai Rivers in War Zone D. Acting on partial intelligence, General Williamson pitched 1/503rd Infantry and 1st RAR against the presumed headquarters of 272nd PLAF Regiment and its affiliated battalions skulking in plantations. In fact, the soldiers stumbled into a different Viet Cong battalion near a feature known as Hill 65. In the ensuing fight 1/503rd suffered 49 killed and 83 wounded – by far the biggest casualty bill suffered by 173rd Airborne to date. A claim was made that 3rd Battalion, 271st PLAF Regiment had lost between 400 and 600 men, but this was a wild guess.[163] Williamson was clearly disconcerted by these casualty figures – indeed, at this point in the war, no US battalion had suffered so badly in a single fight – but the sobering lesson was quickly buried by the dramas that unfolded later that month in the Ia Drang Valley.

In late November, fearful that its more ambitious demands would likely be rejected by the White House, the JCS revised its number of desirable troops to 112,430.[164] CINCPAC, collaborating with MACV, continued to scope contingencies that all pointed skyward. By the end of the year, the numbers had been revised upwards several times, finally reaching 443,000, a target to be reached by December of the following year. Remarkably, all these figures were largely derived from simplistic force-ratio studies heavily influenced by the totemic and desirable 10:1 ratio, setting aside more significant factors that would probably decide the outcome of the war – the most important of which was who had the will to win. The Joint Chiefs need not have fretted. Like a junkie now hooked on war, the White House had fallen into the habit of acceding to every troop request. "Do you know how far we're going to go?" a miserable Johnson asked McNamara, "Or do the Joint Chiefs know? ... what human being knows?"[165]

Ironically, a parallel debate was taking place in Hanoi. Fearful of incurring heavy casualties, questions of force ratios were also posed, provoking withering censure from Nguyen Chi Thanh, commander of the Central Office of South Vietnam (COSVN):

> As a result, one turns his attention to looking for new factors in the formulas that exist in books…For instance, on learning that the enemy has just increased his troop strength, and without conducting a proper inquiry and studying the practical situation, one hastily jumps to such conclusions as: … to annihilate one American battalion … we must have a superiority in strength of at least seven to one or nine to one, and so forth. In fact, this is a kind of "divination," not scientific calculation, and usually the "diviners" are inclined to take regressive steps.[166]

The astute McNamara did not fall for divination, capitalist or communist. He listened, he pondered, and he then committed his thoughts to paper on November 30, following another fact-finding mission to Saigon, on the flight back to Washington.[167]

Johnson's stalwart of the Defense Department was returning in mourning dress. The strategy of Pacification had failed. There was no permanent security anywhere in South Vietnam and no guarantee this could even be achieved. The Viet Cong were as strong as ever; as many as 83 battalions now dominating the countryside. The guerrillas had been joined by 27 regular army battalions from North Vietnam. Roughly 9–12 North Vietnamese battalions were now making the journey down the Ho Chi Minh Trail and infiltrating into the south. At the rate both these forces were recruiting, it was not inconceivable that 16 enemy battalions would be added to the enemy order of battle every four weeks. Over the year, some 26,000 infiltrators had crossed the border. POW reports suggested that nine percent were ethnic North Vietnamese.[168] It seemed likely that enemy casualties and desertions would be more than compensated by this conveyor belt of fresh troops. The increased number of enemy was reflected in Viet Cong attacks: 2,287 at the beginning of the year rising to 3,349 by the end of the year.[169] The assumption that the deployment of US forces would stop the backward slide – the central plank upon which Westmoreland had based his Commander's Estimate – was not reflected by the numbers.

And how did the build-up of US forces measure up against this escalation? Not well. With the so-called Phase I deployment almost complete, MACV would have 34 fighting battalions and 365 aircraft in South Vietnam (an overall total of 220,000 servicemen in the Indochinese theater). Close to 2,000 special force soldiers from 5th Special Forces Group were in-country, including

62 "A" Detachments.[170] Several covert programs had been started – Apache Force, Mike Force, Delta Force, and Shining Brass – with mixed results. The 130 ARVN battalions hardly counted. Only elite units such as the rangers, paratroopers, and marines were reliable. The nine South Korean and one Australian battalions were small, and in the case of the Koreans, troublesome. Even with a proposed Phase II deployment of another 28 battalions (112,000 men) in 1966, the likelihood was that US forces would only be capable of holding on to their current gains. In other words, it was a grand stalemate.

Johnson – who had slain the "get out or get in" dilemma – was now once again faced with two choices, both bad. The President "pursued by two packs of hounds" was still being chased.[171] Scale down the ambition of what was achievable in South Vietnam and turn off the tap of further significant troop deployments. Or, ramp up the war. This would imply 400,000 soldiers and marines committed to South Vietnam by the end of 1966, and a further 200,000 by the end of 1967. If the President drew his breath at these numbers, he probably gasped when he read McNamara's concluding assessment. Even with the deployment of this force of over half a million men, McNamara could not "guarantee success." What Washington was embarking on carried "terrible risk and terrible cost." In a December 2 telephone conversation he openly described the present course as "suicide" and warned Johnson that the budget for defense needs would exceed $60 billion within the next two years.[172] Setting aside the cost in treasure, there was a good chance the government would have to explain to the American public a death toll exceeding 1,000 a month. American losses had already reached 1,378 by the end of the year. Over 350 aircraft had been shot down or damaged and 17 pilots were now languishing as POWs. On the pessimistic former score, McNamara was in fact wrong. The toll of US dead would actually hit a peak of 3,000 per month.

Johnson was displeased with this message. With the festive holidays fast approaching a meeting of the National Security Council was convened. Luminaries like Dean Acheson and Averell Harriman were invited, as well as fixers like Abe Fortas. The skeptic George Ball, who had warned both Kennedy and Johnson against military adventures in Indochina, was also present. Clifford Clark, McNamara's future successor and at the time Chairman of the President's Intelligence Advisory Board, joined the group. Clark was portrayed as a hawk but he would later harbor grave misgivings over the war, doubts that would surface with a vengeance when he assumed the post of defense secretary.

The President strode into the room clutching McNamara's November 30 memorandum and asked bluntly whether his secretary was advising him that no matter what strategy he pursued, America could not win the war. The truthful McNamara replied yes. On this gloomy note, the meeting convened and sat for two whole days debating the options. Giving up was not Johnson's style and no courtier has ever found favor by proposing surrender. Johnson had trapped himself like a poker player stacking up the chips too quickly and too early. The war had provoked an instant and intense domestic and international reaction. His closest advisor was predicting defeat not victory.

The deliberations were concluded with a vote. In a show of loyalty but not of wisdom, the vote went unanimously in favor of ramping up the war. In one respect, the wise heads were doing no more than reflecting the mood of the nation: notwithstanding the peace marches and draft-dodging, a majority of Americans supported the war. Less than one in ten wanted their President to quit.[173]

The pessimism in Washington contrasted with the self-belief in Hanoi. While Johnson conferred with his wise heads, the Politburo had similarly convened a gathering – the 12th Plenum of the Party Central Committee, "On the New Situation and Our New Responsibilities." It drew a quite different assessment to McNamara's gloomy prognosis: "Our people will certainly succeed in defeating the American imperialist aggressors and their treasonous lackeys. In the end, the great people's war fought by the entire Vietnamese nation is certain to defeat the American war of aggression."[174]

The war did ramp up. In November, the PAVN scored a cheap victory, overrunning 7th ARVN Regiment near the Michelin Plantation, and in Saigon a truck bomb outside the Metropole Bachelor Enlisted Quarters left eight American dead and 100 injured. In festive Hawaii, yet another US Army formation, 3rd Brigade, 25th Infantry Division, was packing its bags. By December, the navy had racked up 37,210 sorties and the air force 48,150.[175] Over 100,000 tons of bombs had been expended (or around 500 times the tonnage dropped on Monte Cassino). On the ground, MACV's strength had risen to 184,314 men in just nine months. There could be no doubt that America had joined battle.

Chapter 2

A GALLOPING YEAR,
JANUARY–DECEMBER 1966

Westmoreland – *Time* magazine's "Man of the Year" in 1965 – had a plan. Like all military plans it was divided into phases. Unlike many military plans, the phases were rolled out more or less on time and in sequence. The cliché that no plan survives contact with the enemy did not apply to the American juggernaut that hit South Vietnam.[1] Whether or not the plan was good or bad became sophism relegated to a side chapel. At the high altar, all genuflected. Pacification, Clear and Hold, Search and Destroy. There were, in the end, no other creeds to follow.

The men who would propel this machine arrived with the naivety of all soldiers entering a new war. Second Lieutenant David Christian landed in Vietnam self-confessedly "a young romanticist."[2] His cultural inheritance was "John Wayne movies and all that." He believed, "I was gonna kill the Commies, and I was going to come home." By the end of his service he concluded that he had learned two things: first, that he and his comrades had been used as "a political football in a crazy Asian war," and second, "Our leaders, our family leaders, the great elected politicians, betrayed us." Puerto Rican Calixto Cabrera joined the marines fortified by similar sentiments: "I thought it was like the thing to do if you're young, you're tough, you're a man. You go fight a war for your country. Go kill a bunch of commies and that's that. It was just a given."[3]

Marine Chuck Sawyer was motivated by a sense of guilt – he came from a service family that fought in the Second World War and Korea – but also curiosity: "being a history major, I also decided I want to be part of history, not just off to the sidelines reading about it."[4] He found his history, serving in the ill-fated 1/9 Marines "The Walking Dead." Later he recollected that he deployed to Vietnam a 21-year-old naïf, but "I came back as almost like a forty-year-old man who'd been around a bit."

For many, it was simply a question of not missing out. "Well, I was young and single and stupid," confessed marine gunnery officer Charles Allen, "I didn't want to be the only guy in my class in Quantico not to go to Vietnam."[5] Thirty years after the war, retired marine general John Arick was asked the same question: "Why did you want to go to Vietnam?" "Because that was the thing to do," he replied.[6]

The switch in feelings happened quickly. At the beginning of 1966, *Life* magazine ran a feature on the Vietnam War.[7] The mood had soured, bombing had resumed, and public opinion was worryingly swinging against the war. The editorial, written by Hedley Donovan, the editor-in-chief of Time Inc., called on Americans to hold their nerve. Using a metaphor the average American could relate to, Donovan argued that the first installment of victory would come within the next two years. The military build-up had only just been accomplished. The din of the first big battles had only just quieted. It was too soon to give up and come home. Donovan elaborated his analogy with the promise of a second installment, by which time victory would be achieved but "probably not before the early 1970s." Whether or not Donovan truly believed this prediction, could America stand such a long war? At the beginning of 1966, with the machine in motion, nobody was posing the question.

Phase I of Westmoreland's September 1 "Concept of Operations in the Republic of South Vietnam" had been completed by the end of the previous year. This was the force build-up that simultaneously witnessed a rapid transformation from air base security operations, to holding enclaves, to conducting offensive operations. The intent of this phase was to "stop losing."[8] Phase II was "the phase needed to start winning it" with special emphasis given to areas around Saigon, the Delta and to the Viet Cong-controlled provinces in the Central Highlands and the North.

Hanoi, naturally, had attended every development, filtered through the language of revolution and a liberation struggle. At the 13th Plenum of the Central Committee of the Vietnamese Communist Party, held on January 23, Foreign Minister Nguyen Duy Trinh dismissed Washington's switch from "special war" to "limited war" as an act of desperation:

Since they shifted to their new "limited war" policy in South Vietnam, however, the American imperialists have increasingly become bogged down and have suffered a continuous series of defeats. During the 1965–1966 dry-season campaign, during the recently ended rainy season, and during the early days of the current dry season, they had suffered painful defeats.

The puppet army has continued to disintegrate. The puppet government is in turmoil and is deeply divided.[9]

The portrait was delusional but in Hanoi reverie was fueling zeal. In Washington, it was beginning to take on the aspect of an acid trip.

1966 was the Vietnamese Year of the Horse, or as Westmoreland joked with his staff in an end-of-year address, it would be a "galloping year."[10] Under this phase, which would later be loosely referred to as the "10 April Plan," US strength in South Vietnam would rise to 70 battalions and 383,500 men.[11] Phase III would witness the destruction of VC forces everywhere, by the end of 1967. This would require the deployment of around 429,000 men by the summer of that year. None of these figures were actually authorized; they remained planning figures. But following McNamara's guidance, the JCS and MACV were urged to assume authorization in their future strategy. The thorny question of reserve call-ups, which would be needed to generate the necessary force levels, was simply deferred.

The brain controlling this gigantic assembly of forces was the MACV headquarters, at first based at the site of an old RVNAF Camp on Petrus Ky Street in a western suburb of Saigon. In August 1965, the whole shebang moved to Westmoreland's preferred location at Tan Son Nhut air base (against the wishes of Premier Ky who fancied building a hotel at the site, "after the war").[12] By the end of 1965, over 2,000 staff officers were beavering away in this headquarters, or more servicemen than the combined Australian, New Zealand, Thai, and Philippine contingents.[13] Under 300 were airmen and as a few as 50 were marines, confirming the army bias and Westmoreland's primacy. As many as 17 generals jostled in this space and all were army men except Moore (Deputy COMUSMACV for Air), and Youngdale (USMC Assistant Chief of Staff, J2). They had been forged by the experience of the Second World War, but now found themselves commanding kids being fashioned by the transformational sixties. As with all headquarters, the stream of visitors was a constant intrusion. In its first year HQ MACV hosted over 4,800 official visitors, representing a considerable drain on everyone's time and concentration.[14] A full third were brigadier generals or above, including 76 senators and representatives. These could not be deflected with a junior officer's brief.[15] Bullshit and protocol abounded.

Tan Son Nhut was soon transformed into a little America of low, tin-roof buildings and tree-lined avenues, complete with a Dodge City Mess, theater, steeple chapel, swimming pool, and tennis courts. Across Saigon, in over 70 buildings, another 36,000 US service personnel labored in various capacities. These "Saigon Commandos," as they were derisively known, had to be moved outside the capital – but where? Operation *Moose* (Move out of Saigon

Expeditiously) mutated into *Goose* (Get out of Saigon Eventually), and was only finally completed three years later. Most ended up in an expanded Tan Son Nhut with the remainder parceled out to Long Binh, Bien Hoa, and Cam Ranh Bay.[16] This army of REMFs ("Rear Echelon Mother Fuckers") produced paperwork more expeditiously than it relinquished the charms of downtown Saigon. By 1967, MACV would be churning out over 400 daily reports. The document exploitation team in the Combined Intelligence Center alone was producing over one ton of reports *every day*. The CIA complained, "The number of Viet Cong documents falling into Allied hands during a given month sometimes runs into the hundreds of thousands of pages."[17] Not even the most determined reader could get his head around this Niagara Fall of statistics and assessments. The most advanced computer at the time – an IBM 360 model – was eventually installed in HQ MACV to cope with the information overload.[18] Automation helped by speeding up processes, but it also perniciously contributed to the paper deluge by multiplying productivity several fold.

At the epicenter sat Westmoreland, who was more than just Commander US Military Assistance Command Vietnam (COMUSMACV). Like a Roman consul his power spanned lands and seas. In addition to his Vietnam command he was simultaneously Commander US Forces in Southeast Asia (COMUSEASIA), and Commander Central Region SEATO Field Forces (CCRSFF). The scale of the task he faced was daunting. As well as receiving, assigning, and deploying tens of thousands of US reinforcements he had to transform his headquarters from an advisory to operational role, while simultaneously extending the advisory effort. He also had to lay the logistic foundations for further massive ground reinforcements, and integrate the air, naval, and USMC elements into a joint command, all against a background of intense inter-service rivalry.

From Westmoreland's perspective what he did not command loomed larger in his mind. The obvious military solution in Vietnam was to create an overall Far East Theater command, in the manner of the wartime commands. This was rejected for reasons of political and military rivalries. US diplomatic missions in neighboring Laos, Cambodia, and Thailand balked at falling under a supra-regional command headed by Westmoreland. In Hawaii, Sharp was set against diluting PACOM's span of command (specifically, losing control of *Rolling Thunder*). The principal outcome of maintaining separate centers of power was the requirement for operational and tactical compromises, not uncommonly a fatal factor in wars. The other was a need for a consensual approach. Westmoreland had a natural talent for consensus, finely calibrating his arguments to suit the audience. What was striking about this general's stance on so many of the contentious questions that followed the decision to go to war was not his dogmatism but rather his willingness to accept the decisions of others, even if he judged them harmful to the campaign.[19] This was not born from an ingratiating or weak personality. Outside interference, while unwelcome, did not derail him from the mission. As he later professed, it only slowed progress to what he believed at the time to be an inevitable American victory.

This confidence still had to overcome formidable challenges, especially the logistics of the build-up. The US war machine gave the impression of irresistible majesty, but under the bonnet the engine strained. For most units deploying to Vietnam, the experience was rushed and chaotic. Battalion officers were advised to take everything – literally to strip their home barracks – because resupply and spares could not be guaranteed. Critical manpower problems could only be overcome by stealing officers and men from other units, with knock-on effects to morale (and marriages). In-country, there was no secure rear area in the conventional sense. The logisticians were building an infrastructure in the middle of a war zone with no fixed front lines. For historical reasons, 16 separate and stove-piped supply chains had developed in South Vietnam.[20] These duplicated effort, failed to coordinate effectively, and contributed to the general waste. This was manna for black market merchants, but misery for a quartermaster on the front line trying to order a spare part for a jeep. With just one international airport and 12 deep-draft berths, South Vietnam lacked the civilian sea and airport facilities, let alone military infrastructure, to accept the biggest and swiftest deployment of US forces since the Second World War.

The voracity of the military machine overwhelmed capacity. Routine MACV logistic demand was so great – two cargo ships daily – that units were ordered to deploy to Vietnam with sufficient organic spare parts to support six months of operations without recourse to in-country resupply.[21] By the beginning of 1967, Defense had reactivated 161 ships in the National Defense Reserve Fleet, chartered a further 227 merchant ships, and maintained a nucleus of 158 vessels in the MSC (Military Sealift Command) fleet.[22] Every month, MACV was demanding or expending 850,000 short tons of supplies, 10 million field rations, 80,000 tons of ammunition, and 80 million gallons of petroleum products. The individual soldier was consuming 96 pounds of supplies daily.[23] Soldiers ran out of 40mm grenades and pilots ran out of 1,000lb bombs. Both Shell and Esso were (lucratively) co-opted into the war effort. In such circumstances, commanding officers were bound to take the kitchen sink, adding to the groaning supply system. By the end of 1965, shortages were being reported in 105 critical areas, from boots to aircraft components. In the entire country there were just two refrigerated barges (Cam Ranh Bay and Qui Nhon) and one refrigerated ship (Da Nang).

The urgency and scale of the American reinforcement distorted local land ownership and provoked rushed deals. Two weeks before US marines were due to land in Chu Lai it became apparent there was simply not enough land to squeeze all the men and their equipment into the existing military facility. Two officers of captain rank, an engineer and a finance officer, were rushed north and set about trekking over a 15-square-mile lease deemed necessary to accommodate the troops. Over several days, they counted "each fruit tree, each banana tree, each paddy, thatched hut and grave." Assisted by local officials they negotiated with 1,600 farmers, and handed out $620,000 in compensation claims. With some more haggling, the marines got their base.[24]

This turned out to be the start of a land grab: over 1965–66, the construction funding appropriation for South Vietnam reached an astronomic $696 million ($5.2 billion in current prices). Most expected it to exceed the billion-dollar mark. This proved to be an underestimate. By January 28, 1966, over the course of a Honolulu conference, it had risen to $2.5 billion, a figure that displeased the cost-conscious McNamara.[25] Whether or not America was invading South Vietnam, it was certainly leasing and building on extensive lots of real estate. This provoked a bonanza for firms like Brown-Root-Jones and Raymond-Morrison-Knudsen (22,000 workers in-country alone) and demanded the full efforts of 15 engineer battalions.

Other firms were sucked into the war effort: The Alaskan Barge and Transport Company (stevedores and coastal transportation), Philco-Ford (equipment yards), Vinnell Corporation (power plants), and Pacific Architects & Engineers Inc. (repairs and utility support).[26] By the end of 1965, half the US Army's worldwide construction projects were being undertaken in South Vietnam. This surge engendered corruption but also a culture of dependency: "They [the South Vietnamese] couldn't think that the Americans once having committed their troops in Vietnam, having spended [sic] so much money in Vietnam could one of these days leave everything behind and call it quit [sic]."[27] Bui Diem's naive belief, then serving as ambassador in Washington, was widely held.

The logistic and administrative challenge of rolling out the Phase II deployment could not act as a brake to military operations. As units arrived, so they were fed into the fight. But the scale of what was being attempted, notwithstanding the immense resources of American industry, meant that 1966 was always going to be a year when the horse kicked rather than galloped. Johnson's decision against a general mobilization of reserves also contributed significantly to the slowdown of the military build-up. As the fighting escalated, four wars began to emerge in the four corps zones, each faced with the particularities of the terrain, the civilian population, and the enemy. In each of these there were many sub-plots, which units had to master and adapt to, mostly by trial and error.

First, this military symphony needed a political opening chord. This was provided in Honolulu, where all the major protagonists met in late January and early February to agree on the war strategy, in the wake of a 37-day bombing pause. For Johnson, this was the first fact-finding mission of his full presidency, deliberately timed to avoid the troublesome, televised senate committee hearings on the war organized by Senator J. William Fulbright. It would also be the only Honolulu conference in which every important actor attended. For Johnson, the February 1966 Honolulu Conference was the most important of his presidency. If there was hope of rescuing the war and stamping his authority on a conflict he had now taken responsibility for, it was now, or probably never.

Wheeler, Sharp, and Westmoreland represented the military, corralled by McNamara. On the civilian side, Rusk led a team that included Ambassador Lodge, Special Assistant for National Security McGeorge Bundy, John Gardner, the Secretary of Health, Education and Welfare, and Orville Freeman, the Secretary of Agriculture. Prime Minister Nguyen Cao Ky brought a 28-strong delegation, which included his rival Chief of State Nguyen Van Thieu.[28] As many as 80 delegates were squeezed into a drab, high-ceilinged dining hall room, decorated with pictures of aircraft, and over-watched by a row of seven clocks. Conspicuous in the album of photographs bequeathed by this conference was the central presence of Johnson, always leaning forward, always gesticulating. Opposite the President sat a battery of impassive South Vietnamese faces, some smoking.

Perhaps giddy from the sight of so many medal-decorated chests, Johnson made his infamous remark that he wanted the generals to "nail the coonskin to the wall," an instruction that no doubt animated the brass. But what Johnson really wanted was a "Great Society" planted in South Vietnam. This was why he brought his agriculture and health secretaries, as the *Washington Evening Star* quickly noted, and why he fingered Ky on the vital importance of establishing a credible democracy as well as undertaking real, rural reform in South Vietnam.[29] The *New York Herald Tribune* editorial did not miss this point either: "President Johnson is bidding for them by offering some of the benefits of his Great Society program to the South Vietnamese. It will not be easy, in time of war, [but] they must be pursued with the same vigor as we press the war on the battlefield."[30]

But if Johnson hoped for a political dividend from this conference, he was sorely disappointed. Most commentators found his belated discovery of "the other war," championed somewhat inaccurately as the "Lodge-Landsdale formula," an act of clutching at straws.[31] Many wrote negatively about the "pulverization of American occupation," "false starts," "confusion," and "a cruel deception for Americans."[32] The *Baltimore Sun* concluded:

Unless there was more substance to the Honolulu Conference than meets the eye, it could be summed up as much ado – not much ado about nothing but simply much ado. It was all spectacular and diverting but so far as we can see the problem of the war is where it was before the burst of activity began.[33]

Johnson's hopes were dashed because Westmoreland, less concerned with butter, sought more guns, which he got. In a dramatic jump, it was announced that the troop ceiling would rise to 429,000, a number MACV would reach by the end of the year. But the aspirations of Honolulu were also foredoomed because the South Vietnamese government was unable and unwilling to transplant American notions of democracy and good governance into its ancient paddy fields. On these two rocks did Honolulu founder.

General Walt's III MAF in the northernmost I CTZ had some claim to being the most experienced formation in South Vietnam. There were now some 41,000 marines in I CTZ, based on 3rd Marine Division and 1st Marine Air Wing, soon to be joined by 1st Marine Division. This force would almost double in size and for all practical purposes III MAF was an independent command. Relations between Westmoreland and Walt were scrupulously professional if tensely polite. The main difference between the two men was one of emphasis: the marines tended to view pacification as their main effort where Westmoreland sought open battle with the People's Army. This was partly driven by Westmoreland's concern that US forces would fall for the temptation of pursuing a coastal enclave strategy. The doctrinal disagreement was never allowed to become a wider and damaging inter-service spat, despite the stiffness of the relationship. Westmoreland also tended to overestimate enemy strengths, which may have been a ploy to force III MAF into big-unit operations. Westmoreland's bigger worry was the pocket-dynamo Lieutenant General Victor H. Krulak, a driven individual of Russian-Jewish heritage and now commander of the marine FMFPAC (Fleet Marine Force Pacific), which retained administrative and logistic control over III MAF. Krulak was an incessant counterinsurgency theorist and not shy of going behind Westmoreland's back to explain to anyone who cared to listen how the army general was getting it all wrong. The real war, he argued was "among the people," not chasing shadows in the boondocks. As in the case of many military families, a son – Charles – would serve two tours of duty in Vietnam. And like his father, Charles would also retire with general rank.[34]

There were other tensions: the Marine Corps' jealous husbanding of its aircraft inevitably conflicted with the Air Force's prerogatives; Walt did not hit it off with General Larsen in I Field Force, provoking boundary problems; and marine self-promotion in the media exacerbated relations with the Army.

There was also the thorny question of the Vietnamese allies. The marines were supported by 1st and 2nd ARVN Divisions whose reliability varied with the political situation and command personalities. Both initially fell under the popular Nguyen Chanh Thi, the former coup plotter who had strained relations with Saigon. In March, he was sacked and replaced by Brigadier General Nguyen Van Chuan, provoking widespread civil unrest across the north and creating another headache for III MAF.

Setting aside these spats and distractions, the military problem in I CTZ was twofold: holding the line of the DMZ, and challenging enemy pockets further south, principally in Quang Tin and Quang Ngai Provinces where elements of 1st and 2nd PAVN Divisions had infiltrated, soon to be joined by 3rd PAVN Division, also in Quang Ngai and in Binh Dinh Province. It was a huge area to cover: 70 miles wide and 265 miles from north to south. The western half of the CTZ was dominated by the spectacularly beautiful Annamite cordillera. Infiltration across the Laos border into this remote, jungle area was just too easy and impossible to prevent. The eastern coastal plain was interlaced by dozens of rivers. There were two important cities within the marine area of responsibility: the old imperial capital Hue, and Da Nang on the coast. Notwithstanding the quick build-up of forces, III MAF was still deployed in the original three coastal locations: Da Nang (3rd and 9th Marines), Chu Lai (4th and 7th Marines), and Phu Bai (2nd Battalion, 1st Marines).

The PAVN initially divided this area into two military regions: Military Region 4 on the DMZ, and Military Region 5 stretching down the northern neck of South Vietnam as far as the Central Highlands. Military Region 4 subsequently assumed responsibility for what became known as the Tri-Thien-Hue Military Region (encompassing Quang Tri and Thua Thien Provinces). An estimated 30,000 enemy had established their presence in I CTZ. Perhaps two and half million civilians lived in the five northern provinces, many of whom would become refugees.

As in the previous year, the operations were mostly conducted in the vicinity of the marine coastal enclaves. The New Year Operation *Double Eagle I* was followed by *Double Eagle II*, *Utah*, *Texas*, *Indiana*, and *Hot Springs*. In Thua Thien Province, Operation *Oregon* was launched in the late spring. In the An Hoa region, *Mallard* was mounted.

All these operations followed a similar pattern. Intelligence would be received, usually from South Vietnamese sources, of the presence of a Viet Cong or PAVN unit near a population center. In response, a search and destroy mission would be organized, commonly in haste and involving massive amounts of firepower. Mostly the marines became involved in fruitless skirmishes. The intelligence had either been poor, or the enemy simply fled the area, on occasions tipped off by sympathizers. In other engagements, marine battalions stumbled into entrenched and determined communist forces that exacted a heavy cost. "They were tough fighters," remembered Marine Calixto Cabrera, "but they scurried off really quick-like."[35] These operations could also have their comical moments. On *Double Eagle II*, Marine Don Cuneo adopted a puppy. While preparing a defensive position, with the puppy "bouncing around," his company came under mortar attack. "My first reaction was I grabbed my helmet and put it over the puppy."[36]

In all cases, distinguishing guerrilla from villager was difficult. Major Edward Banks recalled a popular cartoon which summed up the dilemma:

> There's a picture of [a] Vietnamese with pajamas, black pajamas and a hat on and the NCO ... he's pointing to that picture and saying this is the friendly forces ... In the next caption there's an identical picture of the same Vietnamese, same outfit and the NCO is pointing and saying these are the enemy.[37]

David Adcock, serving with 1/7 Cavalry, recalled the same confusion when he deployed to Pleiku. In training he had been taught "Charlie would be wearing black pajamas and these cone-shaped straw hats." To his surprise, on the bus from the airport, "There were people on either side of the road working in the rice fields that had on these black pajamas and cone hats. We thought, 'Whoa! Wait a minute.' As it turned out everybody in the country wore that kind of clothing."[38]

Operation *Utah* (March 4) offered a graphic of what could go wrong with this style of operations.[39] Good information was received on the location of 21st PAVN Regiment, about seven miles northwest of Quang Ngai city. The main enemy concentration appeared to be centered on a village called Chau Nhai, dominated by a feature annotated Hill 50. 2/7 Marines commanded by Lieutenant Colonel Leon Utter was selected for the mission, supported by 1st ARVN Airborne Battalion. The battalion's assistant operations officer later remarked that preparations for the deployment amounted to "nothing more than get on your horse and go."[40]

The operation began to unravel more or less from the beginning. An F-4 Phantom was downed along with one of the helicopter gunships (the F-4 crew nursed their stricken plane until they reached the South China Sea, at which point they elected to eject and await rescue). Despite the intense antiaircraft fire the helicopters continued to land. Eventually, half of the 20 UH-34s in the first lift were hit and damaged. Strong resistance on Hill 50 stalled 1st ARVN Airborne Battalion, a unit that became increasingly chary about getting involved in the fight, to the marines' disgust. 2/7 Marines in the meantime had secured two other hills. An attempt to assist the ARVN battalion turned into a fiasco. First, Hotel Company took heavy fire, then Foxtrot Company was cut down. Unbeknown to the marines they faced two battalions from 21st PAVN Regiment. Faced with this overmatching enemy the marines did the unthinkable and retreated to a night leaguer, losing nothing "but my pride" as Utter later recalled.[41] The following morning 3/1 and 2/4 Marines were rushed to the area as reinforcements. The fighting continued all day with 3/1 Marines eventually securing Hill 50 after a three-hour battle.

As in all close-quarter battles, there were lucky escapes. When Private First Class Don Reyerson opened his pack that night to eat his C-Rations he found beefsteak and potatoes scattered everywhere. A bullet had struck his entrenching tool, saving his life, but ruining his supper.[42] On the third day, 1/7 Marines reinforced but the enemy by now had withdrawn from the area. Just five prisoners were captured. 1/3 Marines claimed to have killed 101 guerrillas but only found five graves, explaining away the discrepancy with the suggestion that the remainder of the bodies were disposed of in a deep tunnel and could not be found. The total claimed kill count was over 600, a pure fiction. "Higher headquarters wants body counts," as marine officer Charles Allen later recalled, "So, screw it, you give them a damn body count. It'll make them happy."[43] The operation disproportionately cost the marines 98 dead and 278 wounded. The tunnel complex on Hill 50 was destroyed using five tons of C-4 explosives but it was only a matter of time before the Viet Cong would reoccupy the feature.

The huge amounts of firepower used on Operation *Utah* were largely wasteful. As 1/3 Marine's after-action report later conceded, 40 percent of the napalm bombs failed to ignite. The report concluded: "In regards to this massive [fire] preparation of the objective area, it should be noted that the fortification and entrenchments in the objective area were not destroyed and, in fact, were not appreciably affected."[44] The general intelligence had been accurate but the detail poor, resulting in the marines stumbling into well-concealed Viet Cong positions. A worryingly large number of the captured weapons were Chinese. Buried at the end of the report was the admission of civilian casualties: 23 "non-hostile casualties" attended by the Medical Officer, and "several children" treated for napalm burns. Battles of this kind changed nothing on the ground. Quang Ngai Province was where the My Lai massacre would be perpetrated two years later.

From III MAF's perspective, actions like Operation *Utah* were "victories" and nothing less. Search harder and destroy more – what else? Operation *Texas* duly repeated the experience of *Utah* and cost the marines another 99 dead and 212 wounded. At one point, a company ran out of ammunition and resorted to a risky bayonet charge. In another incident, a UH-34D was shot down and exploded spectacularly in a paddy field. A second pilot, Bill Dinwell, who witnessed the crash, would be haunted by the scene "36 years after I returned home from my '67 tour."[45] The helicopter had been carrying four crew and seven passengers. Only the door gunner survived, but in a critical condition. In a third incident, First Lieutenant W.H. Luplow, making a low-level napalm run-in an A4C Skyhawk, scraped bamboo trees and crashed. Remarkably, he stepped out of the wreckage uninjured.

As in the earlier operations, a misplaced reliance on firepower was evident, commented on by Lieutenant Colonel "PX" Kelley of 2/4 Marines:

> The overriding problem in Operation *Texas* was … how to inflict maximum loss of life on a determined, well-entrenched enemy with complex defensive positions. In the case of Phoung Dinh over 2,500 rounds of artillery and innumerable air strikes and napalm and heavy ordnance were called. The net result, however, indicated that the enemy … was not appreciably hurt by our preparatory fires and had to be killed in his positions by infantry actions at close quarters.[46]

Nineteen-year-old marine Joe Carey observed that his company had started with 247 men; by the beginning of February just 129 were standing; and on Operation *Texas* only around 90 were fit for battle. His war ended when a bullet struck his hand, which felt like someone had smashed his funny bone with a sledgehammer. The compensation was 62 days' recuperation in Guam, which Carey reflected would always remain one of his favorite places in the world. The higher price was being paid by Vietnamese peasants, caught between "a hammer and an anvil," unwilling to leave their fields and the land of their ancestors.[47] In the course of Operation *Texas*, the hamlet of Xuan Hoa was "almost totally destroyed."

By late spring familiar patterns were being repeated, and disasters. On May 12, during Operation *Georgia*, a 14-man squad from B Company 1/9 Marines vanished shortly after reporting an encounter with a water buffalo. The following day, the bodies of 12 of the missing marines were found. The squad had been ambushed and slaughtered. Colonel Carrington observed that, during this month, every single significant action was initiated by the enemy. It was the guerrilla who was choosing when to strike or withdraw. That month 9th Marines suffered 75 fatalities and 328 wounded, half by hidden explosive devices, pointing to another problem.

"Big unit" battalion operations may have attracted headlines but the daily routine consisted of endless patrols; by the height of the summer, some 2,900 per month. The drain on manpower was severe and the return limited. 9th Marines reported that, overall, 70 percent of their casualties were caused by mines and booby traps encountered on patrols.[48] A Delta Company from the same regiment suffered 68 casualties in just five weeks, all but three claimed by mines. This toll included five platoon commanders, three platoon sergeants, nine squad leaders, and six fire team leaders. Just four of the wounded were returned to unit.[49] This implied that the remainder had been maimed, as the rule with the marines was that you had to be wounded three times before you would be sent home. One marine recalled a comrade returned to the line with the stitches from a chest wound still in place, such were manpower problems.[50] Fear of these concealed menaces was exacerbated by a suspicion that the locals knew where they were buried but were not informing the marines. In June, 1st Marine Division reckoned that thousands of patrols had accounted for a mere 72 guerrillas.[51]

Novel tactics were attempted but rarely. In Operation *Kansas* (June 17–22) a screen of six concealed patrols from 1st Reconnaissance Regiment was used to disrupt PAVN and Viet Cong concentrations in the Que Son Valley, south of Da Nang. In total, 1st Reconnaissance Regiment's patrols made 141 sightings of presumed enemy who were engaged by aircraft, artillery, and even naval gunfire from the USS *Morton*. However, the sightings were not always accurate. Among the casualties of *Kansas* were 40 Asian elephants.[52] The newly arrived 1st Marine Division also mounted the first night parachute drop of the war: a 13-strong reconnaissance team dropping from the daringly low height of 600 feet from an Army CV-2 aircraft. Unfortunately a woodcutter's dog sniffed out the concealed parachutes. It was only a matter of time before Viet Cong began to converge on the area. The team leader requested helicopter extraction. Over the 24-hour period the marines had been on the ground they made seven separate sightings of guerrillas.[53] In a separate incident a patrol fought a desperate battle for survival on a feature named Hill 488, before being rescued. At one point, the guerrillas were so close they were able to yell at the Americans: "Marines you die within the hour!"[54]

The operation, however, little changed the facts on the ground. By August, the marines were back in the Que Son Valley. This second operation (*Colorado*) was opened with a bombardment in which 30 tons of bombs and eight and a half tons of napalm were dropped, an unheeded illustration of the futility of trying to "clear" the valley of enemy.[55] *Colorado* was remembered for the extremely confused nature of the fighting, as well as a surprise visit to the battlefield from the USMC Commandant, General Wallace Greene. When the general turned to a marine and asked what happened after they encountered the enemy, he received a perfunctory reply: "We killed them."[56] This may have appealed to the old man, but it wasn't true. In April 1967 the marines would return again to repeat the exercise. Grunts entering villages would find they had emptied: the very people they were supposed to be saving from communism were fleeing their professed saviors.

Not uncommonly, the only purpose of the operations was to generate favorable statistics. When it came to the notice of HQ MACV that III MAF was not racking up as many "battalion days in the field" as Army units – a quite meaningless measure of success – Colonel Francis Parry helpfully suggested that the marines play the statistical game: "[Three of the four Phu Bai battalions] should be considered on operations at all times ... [this] may seem a little dishonest, but it is something we have to do in self-defense. As long as we are in a statistical war ... we have to put ourselves in as favorable light as possible."[57] Thus did the upward gradient of claimed operations intersect with the downward gradient of truthfulness.

Operations in the hinterlands of Da Nang or Chu Lai were draining, but the real fight for the marines was shaping on the DMZ. There were skirmishes at a special force base at Khe Sanh (Operation *Virginia*), and a dozen operations to keep the coastal Route 1 open, north and south of the imperial city of Hue. By the summer it was clear that elements of 324B PAVN Division had infiltrated across the DMZ and were poised to strike in the area of Dong Ha city where the marines held a small base. In separate actions, 4th Marines chased off PAVN 802nd, 806th, and 812th Battalions, the latter an inexperienced unit that was virtually annihilated. This setback did not stop the infiltrations. As one officer later recalled, "[Every patrol] encountered armed, uniformed groups and no patrol was able to stay in the field for more than a few hours, many for only a few minutes."[58]

Another showdown was imminent. Earlier in the year a special force base at A Shau had been overrun amidst acts of astonishing heroics by helicopter crews who scrambled to save the surrounded defenders. A UH-34 piloted by Captain Wilbur C. McMinn, Jr. returned with 126 bullet holes. Of the 24 marine helicopters, 21 were eventually replaced from damage sustained in the dramatic three-day evacuation operation. Panicked South Vietnamese were shot by American soldiers. "It was either that," one confessed afterwards, "or sacrifice everyone."[59]

Waiting to be overrun was not a winning tactic, so the fight would be taken to the enemy. In the long term, this would prove a disaster for Quang Tri Province. Both cities in this province, Dong Ha and Quang Tri would be reduced to rubble, and just 11 out of 3,000 pre-war hamlets would remain inhabited. The entire province became a virtual free fire zone and one of the most blasted places on earth.

The big clash finally took place in the last two weeks of July (Operation *Hastings*). Four marine battalions were committed as a composite Task Force Delta against 324B PAVN Division.[60] The majority of the fighting took place in the remote Song Ngan Valley, a feature the marines nicknamed "helicopter valley" after four helicopters crashed or were downed by ground fire. This was an area of steep-sided hills and dense jungle dominated by a 700-foot spiky hill known as "the Rockpile" that would become notorious in later actions. Chinese-style human wave attacks were experienced, signaled by bugle calls. Staff Sergeant John McGinty laconically observed that "we just couldn't kill them fast enough."[61] By the time the action was over, McGinty's platoon of 32 men had been decimated: eight were dead and 14 wounded. K Company had been reduced to 80 men from 130 starters. Both McGinty and his company commander – Captain Robert J. Modrzejewski – were awarded Medals of Honor.

The fighting then became fragmented and disorganized. A battering from typhoon Ora made conditions worse. A fight for Hill 362 turned into a bloodbath. India Company 3/5 Marines began with 180 fit men and finished with just 68 standing. Wounded marines were executed by roving North Vietnamese. Lance Corporal Richard A. Pittman played dead to save himself. The North Vietnamese were "shooting anyone who moved." "It was darn near like a massacre," he later recounted, "I pretended I was dead when they got to me. They took my cigarettes and my watch, but they didn't shoot me."[62] Executive Officer Edward Conti later avowed it was the single most moving event of his life: "I had never experienced such devastation. But the worst part was the looks on the faces of the survivors of India Company. Their expressions were trance-like. They'd been to hell and back, and it showed."[63]

Massive amounts of firepower were used to scatter the North Vietnamese soldiers. In total, 34,500 artillery shells were fired and marine jets flew 1,677 tactical sorties. The skill of the gunners bringing down accurate fire over featureless jungle terrain, particularly at night, was impressive but the key was the helicopters. Over 10,000 helicopter sorties were flown – it was this factor that allowed the marines to stay one step ahead of the PAVN and to maintain an unrelenting pressure on their adversary. Even so, companies advanced at crawling pace. Captain John J.W. Hilgers, the H Company commander in 2/4 Marines, later recalled "the problems we were having negotiating the terrain, particularly the vegetation. Though we knew our location, we could not see where we were going; trusting only to our compasses. The heat with no breeze and unlimited humidity was devastating."[64]

Hastings cost Task Force Delta 126 killed, but the marines were certain that the communists had "died by the hundreds." The after-action report claimed 929 "KIA (PROB)" but only a suspiciously low 114 rifles were found.[65] Whatever the real figures, 324B Division's sanctuary had been temporarily dismantled, which felt like success.

General Walt summed up well what was the largest marine operation of the war up to that point, involving 8,000 marines and 3,000 ARVN: "We found them well equipped, well trained, and aggressive to the point of fanaticism."[66] This was not an enemy that should be underestimated.

Over the first half of the fall, the two sides continued to play a game of hide and seek. This was when the first serious disagreements began to emerge between HQ MACV and III MAF, with the former consistently inflating the enemy threat. The response to this supposed mass infiltration was the first phase of Operation *Prairie* (August 3–September 18). Much like *Kansas*, *Prairie* relied on covert patrols, so-called Stingray Teams, to report on communist units. The main outcome of these patrols was to pull 3rd Marine Division inexorably northward. Whether or not Westmoreland was accurate in his estimates, the PAVN infiltrations were becoming a self-fulfilling prophecy.

This happened for two reasons. First, enemy sightings encouraged search and destroy operations. The marines' speed of action amplified this response: in Operation *Macon*, a divisional-level mission, the orders were flying out of HQ III MAF within 24 hours of the first contact. This was alacrity no other military force in the world could match, with the possible exception of the Israeli Defense Force. It was also typical of these operations that for all the speed, *Macon* was only finally concluded 117 days later, each action provoking a chain reaction of more actions. And second, the perilous position of some marine sub-units commonly called for rescue missions. To assist an 11-man patrol on the Rockpile, 2/4 Marines launched an assault on an adjoining feature known as the Razorback which cost 120 casualties including 21 dead.[67] At times the fighting was desperate, with the communists concealed in a warren of caves. Five gallantry medals were awarded in this single encounter. The PAVN in turn could not resist trying to lure the marines into traps.

The doctrinal name given to these marine operations was "reconnaissance by force" but more often than not they amounted to blundering into the enemy. A commanding officer described the tactic thus:

> The idea was to probe slowly with the tip of the pen and then, when contact was made, retract the point into the pen's larger sleeve; that is, as soon as contact was made, supporting fire including napalm was directed onto the enemy positions.[68]

This was all well on paper, but it was not what was being played out in the bush. When Battalion Landing Team 1/26 was despatched to the Con Thien-Gio Linh area to winkle out elements of 90th PAVN Regiment (Operation *Deckhouse IV*), it sustained 203 casualties including 36 killed.[69] Analogies with ballpoint pens were barely adequate.

The root of the problem was cultural. The Marine Corps was imbued with an offensive spirit which it could not help but express by mounting aggressive operations. "You're dealing with a macho society, very, very macho," as Marine Calixto Cabrera put it.[70] There was "a lot of that testosterone gone crazy shit all over the landscape." A patient, smaller-scale, counter-guerrilla war was just not in the Corps' mentality (although it was in its Small Wars doctrine). The often-made argument that the marines in I CTZ sought to fight a cleverer war by emphasizing pacification over search and destroy was not reflected in their ethos or actions. Marine Chuck Sawyer summed up the mood of many of his brethren:

> The Marines' attitude seemed to be, well, we'll take them on and of course we did … We're gonna come and get you. We are going to take you out. We're going to take over part of the country, whatever. We don't care what our losses are.[71]

But whichever approach was taken, success remained elusive anyway, as thousands of foot patrols were amply demonstrating. Over a six-month period, III MAF conducted a staggering 68,000 patrols. The aim of this patrolling – pacification – remained a distant dream.[72]

The heat and difficult terrain made patrolling a grueling experience, but the principal threat remained the "gook," a far cannier enemy than subconsciously racist estimates suggested. When Captain Roger Ryman serving with 3/4 Marines took part in a bloody assault on a ridgeline known as the Nui Cay Tre heights, he was deeply impressed by the quality of the communist soldier:

> Their fire discipline remained excellent. Invariably they'd pick just the right piece of terrain, where it was so narrow that we couldn't maneuver on the flanks, and they'd dig in and wait for us in the bottleneck … Once, I heard a sudden snicker when one of our men slipped. The sound gave away a concealed enemy position a few feet away and started a fire fight. The NVA were damned clever.[73]

This action cost Ryman's battalion 20 fatalities. Captain Larry Burke recalled the cunning and devastation caused by VC ambushes. Clearing an area between Phuoc Vinh and Long Binh, soldiers were caught by "a huge explosion":

> One guy had his buttocks just sheared off, big pieces. Another kid by the name of Pennington was buck sergeant and a hell of a good soldier was laying there. His leg was just a mess, pulverized stuff … Another 19-year-old kid had his testicles blown off. Just a mass of goo between his legs. Gruesome stuff.[74]

Manpower became a problem. By the summer, both 1st and 3rd Marine Divisions were hollowing out. The authorized strength of a marine company was six officers and 210 enlisted men. The average in front-line companies was under three officers and 150 men. Even this number was misleading. "You might have 148 enlisted on the rolls of a rifle company," recalled Lieutenant Colonel Emerson A. Walker, a battalion commander in the Da Nang area, "but by the time you subtracted those sick, lame, and lazy, R&R, etc., etc., and etc., you were lucky to put 110 men in the field."[75] Companies were effectively taking to the field at half strength. Turnover exacerbated the problem. The same officer remembered that over a two-month period he lost 85 percent of his officers and 75 percent of senior non-commissioned officers.[76] It was this factor above others that rendered the proposition of pacification unrealistic. III MAF could not fight its war *and* engage in pacification – the arithmetic was impossible.

The same manpower draining experience was evident in army formations. In July 1966, 1st Infantry Division undertook an analysis of its 4,160 battle casualties to date. Infantry and armor soldiers had accounted for 3,244 of these casualties, representing a shocking 51 percent of the authorized strength of these categories. Half of all front-line soldiers were effectively becoming a battlefield casualty. By grade, the analysis brutally revealed the most dangerous rank bands: 37 percent of all E-3 private first classes were battlefield casualties, closely followed by their lieutenants at 36 percent. The war – like all wars – had swiftly become an exercise in culling young men in the junior ranks.[77]

It was not that American units were not getting the better of their opponents. They were. But the cost was too high and the ground too difficult to hold for any sustained period. Marine patrols soon followed the golden rule of never lingering in one spot, which de facto undermined Westmoreland's nationwide strategy of clear and hold.[78] One marine observed,

> World War II was about geography, you take it, and you hold it and you move forward from there. Now it's ours. Nothing was ever ours [in Vietnam] … "Go out there and search and destroy and kill it all. Break it all and come on back. Now go over here and do the same thing. Now go over there and do the same thing." I question the effectiveness of that strategy … It didn't seem to be working.[79]

The same paradoxes would beset a fresh generation of marines later in Afghanistan.

It was over this period that the humble Zippo lighter gained iconic notoriety. The unit involved was D Company 1/9 Marines. Fire had been received from a village known as Cam Ne. Squad Leader William R. Melton recalled asking his platoon commander what they should do if they were fired upon and receiving the blowhard answer, "if they fire on us we can destroy the village." The marine who then gained unwanted fame was called Marion

Pride. "The unfortunate part of it," Melton explained, "was that one of the men in our platoon used a Zippo lighter to set fire to one of the houses, and that got on television because we had Morley Safer of CBS News with us. Boy, he did us a job."[80] Melton seemed less preoccupied by the "job" done on the village and its inhabitants.

As a consequence of this footage, 1/9 Marines became known as "the Zippo battalion" (and later "The Walking Dead" following terrible losses). The Zippo had a perverse justifying logic, as one marine recalled: "we had orders to burn and kill everything if a Vill was deserted when we entered." As the spontaneous reaction of villagers was to flee at the approach of marines, thus converting villages into deserted settlements, "we burned most of them."[81] Another denied the troops were ever told this behavior was contrary to the protocols of the Geneva Convention,

> No, absolutely, positively not ... Not only were we not informed, this was well-known through the chain of command up to the colonel level that I know of because on occasions there were colonels in the field. They knew all this shit was going on. There's not doubt in my mind that the general corps also knew it ... So as standard operational procedure we participated in war crimes often, at least definitely that one.[82]

However, this was not the only war crime he participated in. The same marine openly confessed that he killed any wounded Vietnamese he came across. "Was that an official policy or was that your thing?" "No, that was me," he replied, "I killed a bunch of wounded people." Later, on a second tour, a fellow marine went further and shot a young woman with a baby:

> JC [Marine JC Barrera][83] had this woman. She was about eighteen or nineteen or something like that. They grow their hair real long, the women over there. He had just a full handful of her hair and he was just dragging her and she was screaming bloody murder and pulling back and resisting. She had this baby in her hands and JC just kind of let go of the hair and he shot her dead.

The reaction to this murder was "fury" that they might get into legal trouble and "a lot of resenting to have to cover up." "I realized that this was a war crime the minute it occurred. I didn't even put it in my journal. I was so afraid that my journal could be used to prosecute him and me ... I was just furious that he would have done this."

Tensions over the management of "the DMZ war" eventually came to a head in late September. The place in dispute, Khe Sanh, would become part of marine folklore and history would give reason to the skeptics. The tactical catch was identified right at the beginning by General Lowell English, the 3rd Marine Division ADC: "When you're at Khe Sanh, you're not really anywhere. It's far away from everything. You could lose it and you haven't really lost a damn thing."[84]

Westmoreland, however, did not see it this way. For COMUSMACV, envisioning Korean War-style sweeping movements of large enemy formations, Khe Sanh was an essential block to a possible outflanking movement by the People's Army. There was even wild talk of Hanoi mounting a three-division attack on the unsuspecting marines. Westmoreland got his way and 1/3 Marines was duly deployed to the isolated post at 12 hours' notice. At the time, III MAF had six battalions on the DMZ, which would have been more than enough rifles to stop an "invasion" given the overwhelming air superiority enjoyed by the marines. This would have been the best possible scenario, which was why the PAVN was avoiding such a confrontation. Westmoreland, unconvinced, prepared for the enemy prongs by ordering B-52 strikes, and lacing likely approach routes with mines and booby traps. These precautions proved unnecessary. By October all campaigning was washed away by the monsoon rains and the imagined communist offensive failed to transpire. The monsoon rains could not wash away what had already become a very toxic and hazardous landscape.

The year's end brought a stalemate and an acknowledgment that III MAF's primary pacification mission had stalled. The reasons for this were many and mostly insurmountable. There were too few troops in too large an area. What troops were available were being pulled away to mount search and destroy operations. By their very nature, these latter operations undermined, if not contradicted, the aims of pacification. How could you win hearts and minds when, say, just one battery of 3/12 Marines was firing off 28,600 shells in one month in the environs of Camp Carroll on the DMZ?[85] Could hearts and minds be won at all when a majority of marines openly disliked the enigmatic, sullen locals? "We're searching them, we're searching their village, we're rounding them up," remembered Marine Calixto Cabrera, "We've got all these guns pointed in their direction and then we're telling them we're there to save them. It's just like what's wrong with this picture? It doesn't compute."[86] US servicemen joked how friendly kids at the camp gates taught them how to count in Vietnamese: "dai, dah, doh, quok, me." The words actually meant: "Overthrow the American Imperialists."[87]

Following a series of murders of civilians involving servicemen, Walt conceded, "the general attitude toward the Vietnamese people is manifestly poor and must be changed," and he urged his commanders to get on top of ill-disciplined marines who "in a few minutes" were undoing months of effort through some thoughtless action.[88] Local corruption was also endemic: a weary Major Richard Braun observed that provincial politicians made "the mafia look like a bunch of Trappist monks."[89] The much-praised Combined Action Platoons (CAPs) depended too much on the unreliable local Popular Forces. The Golden Fleece program (rice harvest protection) was necessarily limited. "County Fairs" (hamlet visits), on occasions accompanied by Bugle and Drum Corps musicians to entertain the villagers, was another example of an enlightened program that offered more in idealism than in realistic hope of winning over the local population. Over 1966, 88 were conducted and 20,000 South Vietnamese were offered medical attention.[90]

III MAF was well aware that this was an inadequate number, but without more Vietnamese support there was little it could do to expand such programs. There were other examples of good intentions, but always on too small a scale and poorly supported by the ARVN. Marines from Echo Company, 2/5 Marines recalled how they eventually befriended farmers in the hamlet of Thanh My Trung by feeding the children:

> Gunnery Sergeant Jack R. Monters would bellow and rant and rave for order in his best Bronx manner. The children would giggle and swarm around him, intent only on the food. The cooks would try to dole out equal helpings to all. But so many small hands holding palm leaves would thrust forward that soon the entire affair resembled a mob scene from a silent movie comedy.[91]

In the end, the basic contradiction of offering help with one hand and swinging a punch with the other could not be overcome. A reflective First Lieutenant Marion Kempner sentenced the paradox with an observation that summed up the entire strategy being played out across South Vietnam:

> We must be really messing up these people's minds: by day we treat their ills and fix up their children and deliver their babies; and by night, if we receive fire from the general direction of their hamlet; fire generally will reach them ... I guess that just points up the strangeness of this war. We have two hands, both of which know what the other is doing, but does the opposite anyway, and in the same obscure and not too reasonable manner.[92]

He added, "it all makes sense, I hope." But hope was hardly the basis for a successful counterinsurgency war.

Marine operations in I CTZ were largely mirrored by army operations further south in the II Corps area. Here the fighting was mostly concentrated near Pleiku and Kontum in the Central Highlands, and on the coastal plains in Phu Yen and Binh Dinh Provinces. These were two quite separate wars. In the Highlands, General Larsen was facing the veteran 32nd, 33rd, and 66th Regiments, now organized as 1st PAVN Division and reinforced by 24th and 88th Regiments.[93]

Unbeknown to Larsen, enemy morale in the Central Highlands had collapsed. General Nguyen Huu An, the divisional commander, reported wholly inadequate stocks of 40 tons of rice to feed over 30,000 soldiers.[94] Units were under strict orders to plant a cassava plant (the staple in the Highlands) for every one they uprooted. Troops in jungle bases became pig farmers and raised chickens. Monkeys were shot out of the trees. Concerned by the lack of fighting spirit, "the Central Party Committee and Central Front Command organized the first political refresher course for 166 senior officials in the whole field ... including 13 regiment officials, 29 battalion officers, [and] 124 officers of regimental offices."[95] Participants were encouraged to take part in turgid, communist self-criticism sessions. At the end of the training, lists of "negative rightist ideology" were symbolically burned.

Fighting in the Central Highlands had little changed since the First Indochina War and revolved around control of the main arteries – the north-south Route 14, and the east-west Route 19 – as well as dominance of the provincial towns. In Binh Dinh on the coast, the struggle likewise had never really abated since the French campaign and it was contested over the same tracts of land. Phu Yen mattered because it encompassed the fertile Tuy Hoa Valley, an important source of rice for the insurgency that Westmoreland was determined to deny to the Viet Cong. In the coastal provinces the principal adversaries were 3rd and 5th PAVN Divisions respectively.

The rice protection campaign ran for three months. The main challenger here was 95th Regiment of 5th PAVN Division, a regular North Vietnamese formation that had infiltrated the range of mountains overlooking Tuy Hoa Valley and the coastal plain.[96] The mission to defend the vital crop was given to 1st Brigade, 101st Airborne. Keen to seize the initiative, Operation *Van Buren* was launched on January 15 and ran for almost six weeks. Mostly, the PAVN avoided the roving American battalions, but there were some sharp contests on the southern flank of the valley which cost the North Vietnamese some 300 dead, by 1st Brigade's reckoning. This was followed by *Harrison* (February 26–March 26), launched in the northern half of Tuy Hoa. No enemy were found, mainly because 95th Regiment was still lurking in the vicinity of the earlier clashes experienced in *Van Buren*. Acting on local intelligence, attention was switched south again, which led to a series of running battles at My Phu.

By the time the operation was halted, 95th Regiment, a "slippery enemy," had been completely broken up, suffering another 288 dead.[97] 1st Brigade lost 42 paratroopers with a further 234 wounded.[98] General Larsen ordered one more operation in Tuy Hoa (*Fillmore*, March 26–April 7) but with the rice harvest now ending, 1st Brigade once again switched its efforts to the north.

Following a month of fruitless patrolling, the break finally came in mid-June when it became apparent that a major communist attack was being prepared against Dong Tre, the location of a special force camp in the Trung Luong Valley. In response, Operation *Nathan Hale* was launched, led by 2/327th Infantry. Unbeknown to the Americans, the enemy was in fact a fresh North Vietnamese formation – 18B PAVN Regiment – which had marched south to reinforce 5th PAVN Division. *Nathan Hale* led to a fierce battle on a feature known as Hill 258 which resulted in the total annihilation of a PAVN company. By the time the operation concluded on July 1, over 450 enemy had reportedly been killed. 18B Regiment, in the usual fashion, simply vanished deeper into the hills.[99] From the perspective of HQ MACV, the Phu Yen operations had been a success – the granary had been denied to the enemy – but the military success bore an unintended civilian cost. By the summer, almost a fifth of the population had been displaced.[100] Rice filled bellies, but many more bellies now had to be filled in a string of refugee camps.

Nor was Phu Yen Province "secured" in any permanent sense. By the summer it was evident the province was once again slipping back under the influence of the insurgency. In response, General Pearson once again pitched 1st Brigade, 101st Airborne into the fray. Two major operations were mounted: *John Paul Jones* (July 21–September 5), and *Seward* (September 5–October 25). The North Vietnamese mostly refused to give battle but there were clashes with 18B and 95th PAVN Regiments. In an effort to outwit the elusive enemy, the brigade used stay-behind parties to lay ambushes, with mixed success. The biggest success came in *Seward*, where a body count of 239 was claimed, a result that Pearson described as "excellent."[101]

Fifty miles further north, in Binh Dinh Province, MACV not only faced an entrenched Viet Cong organized as 2nd PLAF Regiment, but also the 3rd PAVN Division (known as the Sao Vang Division). This was believed to comprise two regiments – the 12th and 22nd PAVN Regiments – which had infiltrated the previous year. Their only opposition had been the 22nd ARVN Division, a somewhat weak and demoralized formation.[102] Binh Dinh mattered, not only because of the coastal port of Qui Nhon, but also because it was here that 1st Cavalry had set up their base camp at An Khe, to dominate National Route 19 inland to Pleiku. To relieve the pressure, 1st Cavalry led three significant operations in the first half of the year: *Masher*, later renamed *White Wing*, which ran from the end of January to the first week

of March; *Davy Crockett* (May 4–16), and *Crazy Horse* (May 17–June 5). All
three operations unfolded in the contested Bong Son and An Lao Valley areas.
By August, 1st Cavalry would be joined by 4th Infantry Division, "The Ivy
Division," deployed to Qui Nhon.

Masher/White Wing attracted great media attention, partly because of the
controversial name which was changed at Johnson's insistence; partly because
it was such a large operation, and indeed it would prove to be the largest of
the 19 "big unit" operations conducted in 1966; and lastly because it was led
by the veterans of Ia Drang. Any 1st Cavalry operation was bound to draw
reporters from Saigon after the bloody clashes in the Ia Drang Valley.

By any reckoning, it was an ambitious undertaking. The operation took
place in a 19-mile box that included a mix of terrains: coastal plain, fertile
lowland valleys, and the steep, forested hills of the Central Highlands. In the
middle of the area was the dusty settlement of Bong Son, roughly five miles
inland, which stood astride the strategically important Route 1. Two valleys
forked from this town: An Lao, running almost directly north for 15 miles
before curling west around a mountain feature; and Kim Son, running
southwest for seven miles into a hilly catchment of seven twisting ravines.
The shape suggested a crow's foot, by which name it was known. Both
valleys were heavily populated with scores of hamlets and farms. The valleys
had been considered "lost" to the Viet Cong by the ARVN in December
of 1964, so this was the first time government forces would be entering
the area in over a year. The town Bong Son itself had grown on the banks
of the Song Lon River, at the confluence of several tributaries that flowed
from these valleys. Recognizing the importance of the location, the French
had built a road and rail bridge, encouraging the growth of the town.[103]
Dominating the entire area was Cay Giap Mountain, a massif rising from
the coast, southeast of Bong Son. This was also considered a guerrilla
stronghold.

The opposing sides viewed this difficult terrain from quite different
perspectives. For MACV, the valleys suggested traps. If the entrances could
be sealed, a classic hammer and anvil operation would surely result in the
destruction of the enemy. This, in essence, was the operational scheme of
Masher/White Wing. For the Viet Cong and PAVN, the valleys were corridors
down which they could withdraw, always one step ahead of their adversary,
drawing the cavalrymen deeper into the hills.

The area of operations was further complicated by the fact that it extended
across two provinces, Binh Dinh and Quang Ngai, as well as the boundaries of
I and II Corps (effectively the boundary between III MAF and I Field Force).
To tackle such a large area, a 20,000-strong force of American, Vietnamese,
and Korean units would need to be assembled.

Five generals got around the table on January 13 to hammer out a coordinated plan for the employment of this force: Larsen, commander I Field Force; Walt, commander III MAF; General Nguyen Chanh Thi, commander I Corps; General Vinh Loc, commander II Corps; and General Chae Myung Shin, commander the Korean (ROK) Capital Division.[104] As none of these commanders was willing to subordinate their forces under a unified command, it proved a recipe for a poorly coordinated scheme, reflected by the fact that each gave the operation a different code name. Formations committed to the battle included all three brigades of 1st Cavalry; four battalions from III MAF; the ARVN 22nd and 2nd Infantry Divisions, augmented by an airborne brigade and marine Task Force Bravo; and the majority of the ROK Division. The principal adversary was the known 3rd PAVN Division, but over the course of the fighting several new units were identified. These included the 18th PLAF Regiment supported by mortar, recoilless rifle, and antiaircraft companies, as well as 2nd and 210th PLAF Regiments. 22nd PAVN Regiment (7th and 9th Battalions), which had infiltrated from Gia Lai Province into the Kim Son Valley, also became heavily engaged.

The plan to deal with this enemy division was expressly based on proving "the validity of the tactic of 'Find, Fix, Fight, and Finish'," or what was now being called a "battle of annihilation."[105] In the logic of the lessons learned report:

> Combat experience in Vietnam has shown that good intelligence of VC units is difficult to obtain, placing a premium on swift reaction in order to take advantage of this information. Additionally, experience has shown that the enemy will not generally "stand and fight" when faced by a superior force aggressively employed, preferring to "fade away into the bush" in classic, guerrilla fashion. It then becomes obvious that to prevent this "fading away," in addition to aggressively attacking his force, we must fix the enemy by denying his routes of escape.

ARVN and ROK units would fix the valley entrances in the south, III MAF would fix the northern escape routes in the linked Operation *Double Eagle*, and Kinnard's 1st Cavalry would fight and finish the entrapped quarry. The coastal plain would be secured by additional ARVN and ROK units, and US Navy ships *Mason*, *Shelton*, *Orleck*, *Barri*, and *Spruston*. Or such was the hope.

Following some deception moves in Phu Cat, southeast of Bong Son, the main phase of the operation was launched on January 28. This opened on a somewhat downbeat note after a C-123 transport aircraft crashed, killing 42 cavalrymen. Bad weather and enemy action then conspired to unravel the plan still further. A Chinook was downed and this forced 1/7 Cavalry to abandon its original mission. Low cloud and heavy rain curtailed the deployment of the artillery guns to the firebases which prompted Hal Moore, now commanding 3rd Brigade, to abandon the plan altogether and order an improvised sweep of the plain.[106]

This was conducted by 2/7 Cavalry, flown to LZs 3 and 4 east of Objective Steel in a cavalcade of 100 aircraft. The landings proved hot. Five helicopters were shot down and 20 damaged.[107] Attempts to reinforce the cavalrymen failed and "contact in the LZ at the end of the day was still heavy, with the enemy located in well dug-in positions."[108] Commanding officer Lieutenant Colonel McDade later recalled, "Every time you raised your head, it was zap, zap, zap."[109] By the second day, 45 helicopters had been damaged and ten pilots killed. The troopers had bumped into a "hornet's nest" of defensive positions held by 22nd PAVN Regiment. They were "still under heavy fire" on the morning of January 30, although resistance was now beginning to wane as Moore fed reinforcements from 1/7 and 2/12 Cavalry into the fight. By now, four additional LZs had been secured – Tom, Romeo, Mike, and Dog – and the North Vietnamese were beginning to withdraw from the area. By February 3, the final Objective Gold had been secured "with negative enemy contact." Simultaneously, 3/1 Marines and 2/4 Marines, supported by South Vietnamese marines and infantry, staged an unopposed beach landing at Duc Pho. This was a huge operation involving 6,000 men and two thirds of all helicopters available to III MAF, but it proved an anticlimax. Whatever intelligence had suggested a strong enemy presence had been flawed – the marines flushed empty jungle.

The fight on the Bong Son Plain had been a bloody affair. 3rd Brigade reckoned it had accounted for over 550 communists. Over the course of the four-day battle, 7th and 9th Battalions from 22nd PAVN Regiment had been "rendered ineffective." But Moore had also suffered heavily: 123 cavalrymen and air crew had been killed and a further 200 wounded. Another battalion's worth of soldiers had effectively been removed from 1st Cavalry which was already suffering from manpower shortages.

After overcoming resistance at Bong Son, attention then turned to An Lao Valley. Kinnard reported:

> The Division was faced with the following choices: Continue to pursue the enemy, who it was felt had exfiltrated the MASHER area in a northwesterly and westerly direction; undertake operations in the Kim Song Valley, or initiate a campaign down the coast south of the Song Lai Giang River.[110]

He chose the first of the three options: with III MAF still in blocking positions in the north, the decision was taken to "locate and destroy enemy units which had successfully escaped from the coastal plain into the An Lao Valley and the hills between." By following this course, it was hoped the cavalrymen would "find possibly 210th VC" and perhaps "the Quyet Than (AKA 18th NVA) Regt."

The Bong Son Plain mission had involved one brigade. The second would involve two brigades and an additional six battalions of infantry. Marine units were used to block northern escape routes and 22nd ARVN Division sealed the southern exit. Persistent poor weather caused more delays but on February 6, 1st Cavalry mounted a five-battalion assault into the valley, drawing units from 2nd and 3rd Brigades. The division reported:

> The concept envisioned air assaults by battalions from both brigades … into the An Lao Valley … The brigades were to establish blocking positions east of the valley on the dominant terrain, assault three battalions west of the valley, and then attack East into and through the valley. The attack would then move south to clear the valley …

But once again, the plan was frustrated. The cavalrymen encountered some stragglers and uncovered a network of caches, but it was clear communist forces had disappeared into the hills. With the searching battalions reporting "negligible enemy contact," the scheme was called off.

Vexed by the lack of enemy, Kinnard now switched to his second option: scouring the Kim Son Valley. 3rd Brigade redeployed first, mounting an assault into the center of "Crow's Foot," an area believed to be held by 2nd PLAF Regiment. Here, resistance was stronger. In a series of actions, the troopers succeeded in overrunning 93rd Battalion of 2nd PLAF Regiment and captured a battalion commander. The captured Lieutenant Colonel Dong Doan proved a valuable catch, revealing the locations of more Viet Cong units.

Colonel Elvy Roberts' 1st Brigade was now brought into the action, relieving 3rd Brigade. Roberts deployed his three battalions – 1/8, 2/8, and 1/12 Cavalry – to comb the area, but with poor results. Acting on reports of suspicious movements, 1/12 Cavalry was despatched east to the Go Chai Mountain and had a fleeting encounter with 7th Battalion, 12th PAVN Regiment, but the enemy used the cover of night to evade its pursuers.

If 1st and 3rd Brigades were still experiencing frustrations in their efforts to entrap a slippery enemy, the sister 2nd Brigade led by Colonel William Lynch enjoyed better luck. This brigade had air assaulted into an LZ Pony, just east of the Kim Song Valley, acting on the intelligence gleaned from the captured Doan. With 2/12 Cavalry securing the landing zone, 2/5 Cavalry set up blocks and 1/5 Cavalry began to flush out the enemy.[111] 2nd PLAF Regiment was not so easily intimidated by this show of strength and resisted for four days in an area nicknamed the "Iron Triangle." On February 17, 1/5 Cavalry became heavily engaged and succeeded in overrunning the Viet Cong regiment's heavy weapons battalion. For the next three days, two companies from 2/12 Cavalry and 2/5 Cavalry joined their sister battalion in a series of assaults against the redoubt. This stubborn defense was only finally ended by B-52 strikes. Just 41 bodies and 13 assault rifles were subsequently found following an area search, suggesting that the majority of guerrillas had managed to evade. Nonetheless, the brigade assessed that it had killed 313 guerrillas and had effectively wiped out the 93rd and 95th Battalions.[112] By now, the operation was beginning to wind down, in part because of the cost to men and machines, but also because of the absence of a worthwhile enemy. The division with some frustration reported, "The enemy, by breaking contact and dispersing in small groups, intermingling with the population and moving at night and during bad weather, avoided further contact."[113]

The final act, code-named *Black Horse* after the divisional motif, was the clearance of the Cay Giap Mountain overlooking Bong Son. MACV was convinced that the North Vietnamese 6th Battalion, Quyet Thang Regiment was using this as a sanctuary, but the dense forest barred a conventional air assault operation. This problem was overcome by carpet bombing the feature and rapelling into the blasted spaces in the jungle canopy from Chinook helicopters. Few Viet Cong were killed but a larger number of "suspects" was rounded up at the base of the mountain. The operation was finally called off on March 8. After sweeping the mountain it was concluded anti-climactically, "there was no evidence that this area is used by regular VC units on a recurring basis nor is there any evidence of extensive supply caches."[114] *Masher/White Wing* had cost 1st Cavalry 288 dead and over 800 wounded – a casualty rate comparable with the Ia Drang battles. American public opinion barely registered these numbers in a war that still felt remote. A bigger commotion was caused by John Lennon who four days previously had declared the Beatles more popular than Jesus.

Kinnard dubbed the 41-day operation "the Bong Son campaign" in his after-action report.[115] Drafted just four days after the close of the operation, his account of the exploits of "The First Team" was self-deceiving. Perhaps the biggest transgression was his mendacious account of the treatment of the civilians in the An Lao Valley:

> We simultaneously informed the people living in the valley that we would not be remaining and offered them the chance to leave the valley if they chose to do so. About 4,500 out of a total population of around 8,000 inhabitants did elect to leave their homes on the valley … we flew over

> 3,300 of these people to freedom in our aircraft ... 2nd Brigade protecting
> this exodus while continuing to clear the enemy ...

The purported exodus of freedom-loving Vietnamese peasants was a gross misrepresentation of the facts. The farmers had no desire to leave their ancestral lands and they were forced into vacating their hamlets. The displaced families were then dumped in inadequate camps on the coast where they soon attracted reporters keen to tell the story of the plight of these refugees. A greater tragedy unfolded in three hamlets at Tay Vinh, Binh An, and Go Dai. Here, out-of-control Korean troops from the ROK Division massacred 1,108 villagers in cold blood, the first of several massacres these troops would be implicated in over the course of the war.[116] Families that had sought shelter in tunnels were wiped out by soldiers who lobbed tear gas into the shelters and then shot anyone emerging for air. At Go Dai, not a single villager survived. At Tay Vinh, 15 separate massacre sites were found. A survivor recalled: "There were lots of people on the paddy. The soldiers made people bury their faces in the ground and lie down on their stomachs. Around 3 p.m. they started shooting magazine rifles and throwing hand grenades."[117] A survivor of this massacre, Nguyen Tan Lan, witnessed the death of his sister. His mother survived but both her gangrenous legs were amputated. The final tally revealed that 166 children, 231 women, and 88 elderly had been murdered. Eight entire family groups were killed.

Marine Anthony Goodrich recalled "we would capture people, send them to the Koreans, they would basically interrogate them, then kill them. I saw that happen at least three times that I remember. They would interrogate them and then shoot them in the head."[118] When asked how he reacted to these war crimes, Goodrich replied, "Well, to be perfectly honest with you, we laughed."

It is inconceivable that senior US commanders were unaware of the massacres because US marines had to clear the mess and took photographs. Westmoreland ordered an investigation, which was deflected by the ROK Division commander. These bloodbaths were not mentioned in the after-action report that instead made the outlandish claim that the operation had made it possible "to return 140,000 Vietnamese to GVN [Government of Vietnam] control." This was a lie. Whatever chances had existed of winning over the population in Binh Dinh were entirely wrecked by Operation *Masher/White Wing*. An Lao and Kim Son were not pacified, and never would be. The two valleys became accusing fingers pointing at the US army base subsequently built in the lee of Bong Son.

The boasts became more exaggerated. Kinnard bragged, "We rendered five of the nine battalions of their three regiments ineffective." Even allowing for the claimed enemy kill count of 1,469 this did not suggest five battalions scrubbed from the enemy order of battle. A cursory examination of the battle statistics suggested that this figure had to be inflated. It was reported that a further 2,000-odd "enemy" were captured, detained as "suspects," or gave themselves up as ralliers. This gross tally of dead and captured enemy yielded just 203 individual weapons. Either the People's Army really was using sharpened bamboo sticks as weapons, or the claims were just that and not credible. The statistical elasticity was further undermined by an assessment that "as a result of this severe damage done to their units, the Sao Vang Division can be expected to be ineffective for a period of several months." Within a week of the cavalrymen riding back to their base at An Khe in a triumphal procession of 100 helicopters, 3rd PAVN Division had re-infiltrated the valleys.

Masher had always been the appropriate name and air mobility was again the questionable rather than the winning tactic, if MACV had not been so dazzled by its own propaganda. The helicopter crews incontestably performed miracles (and paid the price). Leaving aside the impressive battalion lifts, over the course of the operation there were 57 battery lifts of the divisional artillery – the first of the war involving the heavy 155mm guns – each of which on average required 12 CH-47 sorties to manhandle the heavy guns and ammunition loads. But once on the ground, the overladen troopers were no match for the nimbler North Vietnamese and Viet Cong, and the intelligence had always been poor.[119] Kinnard, in fact, launched the second operation knowing full well that there was "an absence of information" and that he was searching for "three unidentified, unconfirmed battalions" based on inconclusive sightings.[120]

Faced with the frustration of chasing an elusive foe, Kinnard's First Team had not so much cleared the valleys as blasted them intemperately. Mobility was supplanted by massive and purposeless destruction, rubbishing the claim that "[we] did remarkably little damage to the friendly or potentially friendly inhabitants of the area." The operation was supported by 1,352 air strikes that dumped 1.5 million pounds of bombs including almost 300,000 pounds of napalm. B-52s were used to decapitate Cay Giap Mountain. The combined artillery batteries fired off 141,712 shells, which included barrages from 8-inch guns. The Navy, unwilling to be left out of the action, added another 3,213 5-inch shells to the count. To put this in perspective, the weight of fire amounted to roughly one tenth of the shells fired at German positions in the battle of the Somme.

In fairness to Kinnard he was one of a handful of senior officers who later came to appreciate and acknowledge the quagmire in which the US Army had fallen – and the heart of the problem. "I really knew nothing about the background," he belatedly and frankly confessed. "I didn't understand the enemy we were dealing with, I didn't understand the allies … It was a total lack of understanding of the situation we were involved with."[121] The same lament – "we lacked understanding" would be repeated in the later American wars in Iraq and Afghanistan.

By May 5, 1st Cavalry was back on Bong Son Plain, now led by General Norton and with Kinnard promoted to Acting Commander of I Field Force. The resumed effort – Operation *Davy Crockett* – ran until May 16. In the first week, the 9th Battalion of 22nd PAVN Regiment was virtually wiped out in a clever three-battalion ambush, conceived and executed by Moore's 3rd Brigade. In the second week the search area was shifted to the Kim Son and Suoi Ca Valleys with few results. This mission was followed by *Crazy Horse* (May 16–June 5) involving 1st Brigade in the Vinh Thanh and Suoi Ca Valleys. In a series of running battles – some desperate – 2nd PLAF Regiment was mauled. Close to 400 guerrillas were believed to have been killed, but 1st Brigade suffered another 83 dead.

However, the failure to stifle the insurgency became most evident in the late summer when 1st Cavalry was forced to mount what became known as the Binh Dinh pacification campaign. All the enemy battalions purportedly destroyed in the previous battles made a reappearance: 2nd PLAF Regiment in the south of the province, 12th PAVN Regiment east of the Kim Song Valley, and 22nd PAVN Regiment on the Bong Son Plain. Far from defeated, in early September, the communists mounted their own offensive: 22nd PAVN Regiment assaulting three bases of 40th ARVN Regiment, and 2nd PLAF Regiment ambushing two battalions of 41st ARVN Regiment. Faced with this resurgence, three major operations were mounted: *Thayer* (September 13–October 1), *Irving* (October 2–24), and *Thayer II* (October 25–February 12, 1967).

The intent of *Thayer* was to throw a giant horseshoe in the Kim Son Valley and squeeze the insurgents into a trap, regardless that this gambit had failed in the past. Five battalions were airlifted into the valley following two days of B-52 strikes: 1/12 Cavalry, 2/8 Cavalry, 1/5 Cavalry, 2/12 Cavalry, and 1/8 Cavalry. Awkwardly for Norton, 2nd PLAF Regiment had long vacated the valley and replied by mounting a surprise attack with its 95th Battalion on LZ Hammond, the logistic hub of *Thayer*, 19 miles southeast of the valley. To add to the confusion, 7th and 8th Battalions of 12th PAVN Regiment sprang an attack on 41st ARVN Regiment in Cuu Thanh six miles to the east of Kim Son. 1st Cavalry quickly repositioned to catch the communist forces, and a further two battalions were positioned to act as cut-offs, but it was all too late. One week later, *Thayer* was brought to a close. A claimed body count of over 200 was little consolation for what had amounted to a divisional-level wild goose chase.[122]

However, the failure of *Thayer* laid the foundations for the partial successes of *Irving*. The key intelligence insight that fell out of the former operation was that the Viet Cong and PAVN were probably not in the mountains at all. Compelled by necessity, the battalions had infiltrated further east, not west, and were now skulking between Highway 1 and the coast. If this was the case, they faced entrapment and annihilation, if Norton could find them. Faced with such a large search area, an ambitious operation was conceived involving 22nd ARVN Division (Operation *Dai Bang 800*), the ROK Division (Operation *Maeng Ho 6*), and 1st Cavalry. The American area of operations would comprise a rough triangle bounded by the Kim Son Valley, the Mieu Mountains on the coast, and the inland town of Phu My on Route 504. Both 1st and 3rd Brigades would be committed on what was now their fifth major operation in Binh Dinh since the spring.

Now, the luck rolled with the Americans. Acting on intelligence from a deserter, 1st Brigade sealed the hamlet of Hoa Hoi at the northern end of the sandy Hung Lac Peninsula, trapping a battalion's worth of North Vietnamese from 12th Regiment. Unwilling to surrender, a two-day battle followed in which 233 enemy were killed for the low cost of six American dead. Buoyed by this early success the soldiers continued to scour the area, but found no enemy. Attention then switched to the Suoi Ca Valley, midway between Kim Son and the coastal plain. Unwilling to repeat the fruitless experiences of the past few weeks, Norton resorted to a uniquely desperate and utterly wasteful action. A strip of the valley approximately one mile by two and a half miles long was declared a free fire zone and subjected to an eight-hour artillery and aerial bombardment. When a platoon subsequently entered the area, not a single enemy soldier was found, dead or alive, or indeed any living thing.[123]

At the conclusion of *Irving*, quite preposterous claims were made. The combined American-Korean-Vietnamese sweeps on the coastal plains, it was reported, had resulted in over 2,000 communist dead and almost 1,500 prisoners. 1st Cavalry claimed 681 of this total, while suffering just 19 dead. 95th PLAF Battalion had been destroyed (for the third time); and 12th PAVN Regiment had been decimated. Both the Korean and ARVN statistics were plainly exaggerated, leaving aside MACV's numbers that did not stand scrutiny either. And once again, a renewed round of fighting had simply exacerbated an already dire refugee problem. By the end of October, another 40,000 farmers had been displaced, raising Binh Dinh's total to 152,000 – or one in ten of all South Vietnam's refugees. As significant as this suppurating cost in lives and misery for the peasants hung the open question: was Binh Dinh Province any more secure as a result of these operations?

With so much manpower thrown at securing the coastal Phu Yen and Binh Dinh Provinces, Larsen was forced to fight economically in the Central Highlands. The task of holding the line fell to the newly arrived 3rd Brigade, 25th "Tropic Lightning" Infantry Division. This formation was commanded by Colonel Everette Stoutner and comprised 1/35, 2/35, and 1/14 Infantry Battalions, later joined by 1/69 Armor. The logistic operation to redeploy the brigade from Hickam Air Force Base in Honolulu to Pleiku – Operation *Blue Light* – was the biggest of the war to date. In a matter of one month, 4,000 men and 9,000 tons of equipment were shifted to the Central Highlands.[124] The greenhorns arrived with M14 carbines, immaculate uniforms, and great expectations. They joined the veteran 1st Cavalry that continued to act as the fire-fighting formation in II CTZ.

From February to May, Larsen mounted six major operations in the Central Highlands: *Taylor* (February 5–8); *Garfield* (February 25–March 25); *Lincoln* (March 25–April 8); *Mosby I* (April 11–17); *Longfellow* (April 17–May 1); and *Mosby II* (April 21–May 3). There were clashes with 32nd PAVN Regiment north of the provincial capital of Ban Me Thuot, and a sharp fight broke out with 18B PAVN Regiment near the Chu Pong massif – the scene of the Ia Drang battles – but elsewhere the sweeping battalions mostly uncovered evidence of enemy occupancy but few enemy soldiers. For the time being at least, it appeared the People's Army B3 Front was biding its time and rebuilding its combat strength.

This scenario changed in the summer, by which time 2nd Brigade, 4th Infantry Division had begun to arrive in Pleiku. Some 30 miles west of the city, in a broad arc hugging the Cambodian border, as many as four North Vietnamese units had re-entered the line: the 32nd, 33rd, 66th, and 88th PAVN Regiments. In response, General Norton mounted *Paul Revere I* and *II* (May 24–August 22), which were more a continuous series of opportunistic actions than a closely defined operation. The fighting ranged from the special force camp in Plei Djereng in the far north to the Chu Pong massif in the south. With the exception of one clash at the beginning of August, at Landing Zones Pink and Orange south of Highway 19, virtually all the other engagements took place within a few miles of the border. There were desperate actions – at a landing zone named Ten Alpha where B Company from 2/35 Infantry found itself surrounded, and a second on a feature known as Hill 534 – but mostly the encounters with communist forces confirmed the primacy of American firepower. By the end of the operation, Norton dubiously reckoned that 1st Cavalry had accounted for 861 enemy for the loss of 90 soldiers. More realistically, he had established a psychological ascendancy over the B3 Front. 1st Cavalry's relentless pace of operations had almost certainly spoiled whatever plans had been hatched for a monsoon offensive.

Helicopter pilot Brian Glaspell who flew the medevac missions from the fighting at Plei Djereng had a different recollection:

Here are all these beds with white sheets with all these GIs missing arms and legs, with stumps and they're just kind of patched together. Blood everywhere … It was like a horror movie. It was like walking through this [field hospital] corridor and you didn't want to step off on either side or you might become part of that horror movie.[125]

Further north in Kontum Province, good intelligence had revealed that the 24th and 88th PAVN Regiments were converging on Highway 14 with the probable intention of overrunning a special force camp at Plei Djereng. The response to this threat was Operation *Hawthorne* (June 2–20) which involved 1/237th Infantry, and two South Vietnamese battalions, 1/42 Infantry and 21st Ranger Battalion. The intelligence proved accurate and there was a series of clashes along a six-mile stretch of the subsidiary Route 610 which traced the line of a valley leading to Dak To. Having disrupted the enemy, a decision was then taken to chase the retreating PAVN out of the valley. This pursuit resulted in further clashes at the northern end of the valley which persuaded General Pearson to fall back on what was becoming the standard answer to an elusive enemy – massive aerial bombardment. On June 14, B-52s dropped 648 tons of bombs in a two-and-a-half-mile box north of a hamlet called Dak Pha. A claim was made that the strike killed 200 enemy but there was no proof of this whatsoever. Hawthorne indisputably spoiled 24th PAVN Regiment's plan but the claims made for the operation were wild. For the cost of 48 American lives, it was reported that a grand total of 1,246 North Vietnamese had been killed.[126]

MACV arguably faced its biggest challenge in III ARVN Corps (the American III CTZ). By March, Seaman's II Field Force Vietnam based at Bien Hoa had been activated to control III CTZ, with Larsen's command in Nha Trang becoming I Field Force. The former was subsequently moved to Long Binh still under command of the promoted General Seaman, with Major General William DePuy assuming Seaman's old post as commander of 1st Infantry Division.[127] Over two decades, an insurgent infrastructure had grown surrounding the capital with a network of caches, tunnels, and hides. Away from "secured" areas, which mostly meant the web of routes leaving the capital, the Viet Cong operated with virtual impunity. It is arresting that the majority of American operations took place within a broad arc barely 20 miles from Saigon city center. The capital was ringed by a sea of rural hatred directed at the denizens of the Gia Long Palace, if only MACV could see it. The major unit in III CTZ was 1st Infantry Division, at first supported by one brigade from 25th Infantry Division. The short and even shorter-tempered DePuy was no stranger to desperate battles, having fought from Utah to Bastogne in the Second World War.

Like so many of his generation, DePuy was seared by his wartime experience. If DePuy seemed ruthless, it was because war had taught him to be so for the sake of his soldiers:

> In the six weeks in Normandy prior to the breakout, the 90th Division lost 100 percent of its soldiers and 150 percent of its officers. In infantry units, where these casualties were almost entirely concentrated, the rates ran at 300 to 400 percent – in just six weeks … That's indelibly marked on my mind. I told that story to General Johnson [Army Chief of Staff] … And, I told him that I couldn't change; I either would have to be removed or I would continue to remove officers who I thought didn't show much sign of learning their trade.[128]

Johnson kept DePuy.

DePuy, known by his call sign "Danger Seven Seven," would gain a reputation as one of the more aggressive commanders in South Vietnam, using massive amounts of ammunition to subdue "objectives." "I wanted a division that could pile-on," as he put it.[129] In this aim he was well served by Generals Paul Gorman, G3 at MACV, and William Le Gro, G2: "We based all of our operations on Bill Le Gro's intelligence. The Le Gro/Gorman team was unbeatable."[130] His canon was to waste ordnance not American lives, but like every other general, he did both. DePuy proved a fanatical and driven divisional commander, involving himself in every aspect of his command. He sacked 11 lieutenant colonels soon after assuming command (a pattern repeated from the Second World War where he was similarly quick to cull weak officers).[131] On another occasion he was sent a list of 24 lieutenant colonels and accepted just two. He promoted a search method that was later adopted by the rest of the army ("the clover leaf"); and he even found time to design a new infantry trench, duly named after him. His one-page tactical directive to his division was hailed as a model of succinct common sense, which it was, but in a war that lacked sense.

Some criticism was unfair and stung. Before quitting command of 1st Infantry Division, DePuy commissioned an analysis to determine which division was really blasting its way across South Vietnam. "The 25th Division fired more artillery than the 1st Division fired by a wide margin," it concluded.[132] This may have been true but others recalled the obsession with body counts. Private First Class Jerry Benson remembered a decent officer named Lieutenant Webster returning to the office one day in a foul mood.

> Boy he was mad. I'd never seen him so mad in all my life. He wasn't that type of personality. He just came from a meeting. The emphasis was that our battalion was not getting a large enough headcount [body count] in the field. Headcount was the emphasis of that meeting. That just irritated the heck out of him.[133]

DePuy's commitment to the soldiery extended in other ways. 1st Infantry Division became known as the formation that never left anybody behind (and indeed, under his command, DePuy recorded no "Missing in Action" – MIAs). On one occasion he committed two battalions to recover the body of Sergeant Nunez. Soldiers remembered such gestures.

Moving with customary energy, DePuy established five bases at Di An, Phu Loi, Lai Khe, Phouc Vinh, and Camp Cox, but insecure roads and the geographical separation of the units would pose significant problems for 1st Infantry, and the division was eventually forced to reorganize its dispositions to more effectively address the difficulties of operating in an insecure battlefield. By December, III CTZ would be reinforced by 9th Infantry Division, "Old Reliables."

The principal enemy in III CTZ were the 5th and 9th PLAF Divisions, led by General Nguyen Chi Thanh, overall commander of both the COSVN and the B3 Front. Here, there were as many as 61,000 Viet Cong, reinforced by three newly arrived PAVN regiments. The former division was mostly based to the east in Phuoc Tuy Province and comprised two units: 274th and 275th Regiments. The latter was split between War Zone C on the Cambodian border and Binh Duong Province in the north. This larger formation comprised 271st, 272nd, 273rd, and 101st Regiments. By the spring of 1966, these Viet Cong divisions had been joined by the 7th PAVN Division and the 70th Guards Regiment. MACV maps showed three enemy sanctuaries, virtually unchanged since the First Indochina War – War Zones C and D, and the Iron Triangle – but this was a misleading portrayal of Viet Cong presence. The truth was that government writ only existed tenuously on Route 13 along an 80-mile corridor from Saigon to Loc Ninh in the north (traversing Binh Duong and Bing Long Provinces). 1st Infantry's essential task was to keep this corridor open and push back against the encroaching insurgency.[134] The division was comfortably outnumbered by an enemy with long experience of fighting a guerrilla war in the hinterlands of Saigon.

The reinforcing 25th Infantry Division under Major General Frederick Weyand had begun arriving in December 1965 and was complete by March

1966. 3rd Brigade was despatched to Pleiku, with 1st and 2nd Brigades deployed to the area of Cu Chi, northwest of Saigon. This was where, in VC cadre Duong Long Sang's words, a "people's war" was under way, involving not just fighters, but children and the old who supported the insurgency in myriad ways.[135] MACV had six battalions to protect Saigon, and a total of 36,000 men in III Corps. More troops meant more operations – each designed to flush out and destroy Viet Cong units.

The year began with *Marauder I* (January 1–8) and was followed by *Crimp* in the Ho Bo Woods adjacent to the Iron Triangle (January 8–14). This operation was supported by 1 Royal Australian Regiment (1 RAR) with conspicuous success. *Crimp* proved a hugely significant operation, yielding a treasure trove of 7,500 documents that revealed in detail Viet Cong operations in Military Region 4. A single document from this find itemized the history of the movement from the 1950s to 1963 and became known as "the Crimp document," offering intelligence officers, and later historians, a unique insight into the communist insurgency.[136]

Crimp was followed by *Mallet* (January 28–February 1) mounted on Route 13 in Phuoc Tuy Province, between Bien Hoa and Vung Tau on the coast.[137] No significant enemy was found but a large cache and bunker complexes were uncovered, including the unusual find of a guitar which was confiscated by the searching soldiers. This operation was followed by *Ba Ria* (January 29–February 15), and *Rolling Stone* between Highways 13 and 16 in Binh Duong Province (February 11–March 2). Further west of these series of operations, *Mastiff* was launched in the Boi Loi Woods, seven miles south of Dau Tieng (February 21–25), followed by *Boston/Cocoa Beach* at the Lo Ke Rubber Plantation, west of Bau Bang (March 3–6). The majority of these missions provoked fleeting skirmishes. Whenever the Viet Cong elected to stand and fight, they were invariably worsted.

Enticed by a concentration of American troops so far north of Saigon, 271st and 273rd Regiments of 9th PLAF Division struck near a hamlet named Tan Binh. In the resultant brief battle, 142 insurgents were reported killed for the loss of 11 American lives.[138] This operation was followed by *Silver City* (March 7–March 23), a combined effort involving 1st Brigade, 1st Infantry Brigade and 173rd Airborne. The intent was to hunt down the units of 9th PLAF Division and destroy the B2 Front, Military Region I headquarters in War Zone D. Both objectives were more or less achieved, but more by chance than good intelligence. In the second week, 2/503rd stumbled on a base area and caches. The following day 271st Regiment made a suicidal attempt to dislodge the battalion that resulted in over 300 insurgents killed. Even if the kill count was exaggerated, this action near a hamlet called Bao Phung signaled the end of Viet Cong challenge to the American presence in the area.

In the first week of March, the attached 173rd Airborne Brigade had participated in Operation *Silver City* in Binh Duong. *Abilene* (March 29–April 11) revisited Phuoc Tay and resulted in a close fight near the so-called May Toa Secret Zone with the Viet Cong D800 Battalion. Southeast of Saigon, in the mangrove swamps of the Rung Sat Special Zone, numerous sweeps were undertaken under the banner of Operation *Lexington*, but with poor results. These operations ran concurrently with the divisional Operation *Birmingham* (April 24–May 14) in Tay Ninh, northwest of Saigon. The intent was to hunt down C230 and C320 PLAF Battalions. Over the course of the operation, large quantities of war supplies were discovered in the border area between Vietnam and Cambodia. The catch included 8,608 "pairs of pants" – an unusual sartorial haul. Between May and July, the division reported: "Three Main Force Viet Cong regiments were engaged in five major battles and in each the enemy forces were decisively defeated. The elite 272d VC Regiment was engaged in battle on two separate occasions."[139] By the summer, *El Paso II/III* had been launched in War Zone C, which resulted in clashes with all three regiments of 9th PLAF Division. The claimed body count for these operations was 825, for the loss of 125 soldiers.[140] July witnessed Operations *Cedar Rapids* and *Springfield II* on Routes 16 and 13 respectively, but the Viet Cong were now avoiding battle.

In contrast to DePuy's war, Weyand's 25th Infantry Division fought a quite different sort of conflict west of Saigon in Hau Nghia and Long An Provinces. Hau Nghia symbolized all that had gone wrong in Saigon's attempts to pacify the countryside. The province offered its own unique challenges: the eastern half comprised swamplands in the Plain of Reeds; the western half included the Filhol Rubber Plantation, Ho Bo Woods, and Boi Loi Woods. Less than one in ten of the hamlets were under government control and some had not seen a government official in years. Weyand was determined to reverse this poor history, not by hunting North Vietnamese main force units in the manner of 1st Infantry – there were none in the province – but rather by mounting a classic pacification campaign.

Frederick Weyand was one of those rare examples of a wartime officer who actually missed the war. Confident and bright, he briefly languished in defending San Francisco harbor, before being poached to serve in the War Department's Office of the Chief of Intelligence. In this regard his wartime career matched the two high-flyers who were now his political masters, McNamara and Rusk. Unlike the latter, he elected to pursue a career in the armed forces, where his expansive intelligence ensured a rise to senior rank. Weyand was both politically sharp and an organization man in a culture that venerated management as a science. Had he thrown his lot into the civilian market he might well have blossomed into a fifties industrial "whiz kid." His only combat command was a single year's service in Korea as commander of 1/7th Infantry Regiment.

This apparent lack of experience did not ill-equip him for tackling a stubborn insurgency. Unlike his peers, Weyand quickly understood that the conflict in Vietnam was politically rooted and had no military resolution. As early as August 1967, he confidentially told a CBS and *New York Times* investigative team that the war was stalemated and could last generations, a message that would have dismayed Westmoreland, and many fellow generals, who were still convinced that a righteous and rightful victory lay within their grasp.[141] Even if all the military effort was achieving "zilch," Weyand still felt compelled to try to win – what else do generals exist for? – but he determined to do it smartly. This enlightened approach unfortunately little profited the soldiers of "The Tropic Lighting Division." The formation was involved in all the major battles in an arc north of Saigon from 1966 to 1970 and 4,561 would be killed, one of the steepest tallies of any division.

The challenges Weyland faced were severe. Although the Viet Cong only maintained 165th PLAF Regiment in Hau Nghia, virtually every hamlet and village supported a guerrilla company and the local ARVN formation, also confusingly designated 25th Infantry Division, was hopeless.[142] Weyand also faced the constraint of operating with just two brigades, as 3rd Brigade had been committed to the Central Highlands.

25th Infantry opened its account on March 29 with Operation *Circle Pines* in the Filhol Plantation and Ho Bo Woods.[143] The operation lasted ten days with modest results. This was followed by *Maill* (April 26–May 12) in the vicinity of Bao Trai, around 22 miles to the west of Saigon. Weyand viewed this mission as a model for future effort, blending civic action programs and close cooperation with the demoralized South Vietnamese security forces. Operation *Wahiawa* (May 16–May 28) followed, returning to the Filhol Plantation, Ho Bo Woods, and Boi Loi Woods, but once again the Viet Cong refused to fight. Over June and July the division mounted three operations: *Fresno* (June 13–July 14), *Santa Fe* (July 13–14), and *Kokohead* (July 22). These included a mix of hamlet searches, ambushes, and platoon patrols with more deliberate actions supported by B-52 strikes. By September, 25th Division had got into its rhythm and launched three further operations in Hau Nghia and one in Long An. *Kahili* (September 17–November 14) ran concurrently with *Kamuela* (September 20–October 4) but neither proved productive. *Sunset Beach* (September 2–October 11) followed a similar pattern. *Lanikai* (September 15–November 5) was the last of the major divisional operations but the first serious foray into Long An.

Long An was Saigon's rice bowl. Both the South Vietnamese government and Saigon Embassy had been opposed to American military operations over this band of farming land southwest of Saigon, lest it imperil the capital's food chain, but by mid-1966 it was plain that security had badly deteriorated. In this zone, the ARVN contented itself with holding the line of the Song Vam Co Dong River at Ben Luc, a mere ten miles from Saigon astride Route 4. Here, 3/50 and 4/9 ARVN Battalions faced off 2nd Independent PLAF Battalion and 506th Local Force PLAF Battalion, but neither side had the strength to prevail. This was a totally flat area of dykes and rice paddies, some chest deep, which made patrolling extremely challenging. On many missions, boats substituted for helicopters.

Weyand saw *Lanikai* as an exemplar of pacification operations, but not all his subordinates agreed.[144] For some, the lack of action and the low body counts were indices of failure rather than success. And measuring success was proving as hard in Hau Nghia as elsewhere in South Vietnam. Over the course of its operations, 25th Division undertook 300 construction projects, offered medical care to 44,000 families, and distributed food aid to another 56,000.[145] Yet the number of Viet Cong attacks increased in both Hau Nghia and Long An, and the enemy strength grew from 3,200 to 6,000. It seemed to matter little whether Seaman's divisional commanders – DePuy and Weyand – waged a more aggressive campaign or engaged in pacification. The outcome was the same. The majority of the rural areas surrounding Saigon remained firmly in communist control. In fact, the differences between DePuy and Weyand were not so great: the former soon appreciated that the "other war" – or pacification – was part of the same, single "very big war." Acutely aware of the deficiencies of the ARVN, DePuy judged that his division had no choice but to engage in both wars simultaneously.[146]

A feature of all these operations – regardless of the area, enemy, or personal style of the American commander – was their inconclusive and open-ended character. In this respect, the military campaign of 1966 offered a near-perfect metaphor for Washington's open-ended political commitment to South Vietnam. A limited search and destroy operation would invariably expand, sucking in more units. What was meant to last one week would roll on for several. "Victory" would be declared when exhaustion set in, usually with the Viet Cong breaking contact. Nothing would really be won, or lost. "Notwithstanding these defeats," 1st Division warily observed, "there are no indications that the VC are any less determined to seek a victory or that they will cease to attack at a time and place of their choice."[147] Following El Paso II, 9th PLAF Division simply replenished its ranks and moved back into the area of the Michelin Plantation. There it clashed with a battalion of 196th Infantry Brigade which mounted a week-long operation (*Attleboro*) in the shadow of the Nui Ba Den, or Black Virgin Mountain. The fighting forced MACV to throw more units into the fray, in part because Brigadier General Edward H. de Saussure's performance was judged so poor; DePuy considered replacing him in the field, which he did at the beginning of November. It then became a signature DePuy operation.

By the time *Attleboro* concluded six weeks later, 22,000 soldiers from 1st Infantry, 4th Infantry, and 173rd Airborne Brigade had been sucked in. Over 1,000 air sorties were called, augmented by 11 B-52 strikes (a total of 16,000 tons of bombs). A whopping 70,470 shells were fired off "to soften areas in front of advancing maneuver elements." More than two and a half million PSYOPS (psychological operations) leaflets were chucked at the locals. II Field Force suffered 155 fatalities but reckoned it inflicted ten times this amount on the enemy. Prodigious caches of rice and ammunition were uncovered and it was likely that *Attleboro* succeeded in thwarting 9th VC Division's intended winter campaign. In Lieutenant P.J. McKeand's recollection:

> It was like bargain day at Macy's as the infantrymen raced up to the first cache and began carrying the rice and other supplies out to the landing zone ... They quickly located a second cache, then a third and a fourth. They discovered the area was a huge VC "supermarket" loaded with rice and salt and other free bargains waiting for the taking. And they did just that. By the end of the first day, the shelves had been cleared of more than 420 tons of rice. The shopping spree was extended another two days, to accommodate the GI bargain hunters.[148]

However, "Enemy units that are badly defeated cannot be considered deleted from the enemy order of battle," concluded the division's lessons learned document.[149]

The cacophonous accompaniment to all these operations, regardless of success or failure, was the tremendous expenditure of high explosives. In May alone, 1st Division recorded:

> 83,286 rounds (2,744 tons) of artillery were fired during a total of 19,318 missions in support of operations. Close air support sorties for the 1st Infantry Division totaled 967. Air delivered ordnance consisted of 461.3 tons of high explosive, 224.4 tons of napalm, 60.9 tons of fragmentation bombs, 19.5 tons of white phosphorus, 425 rockets, and 133 canisters of CBUs.[150]

This was the American way of warfare, underwritten by stupendous resources. By March 1967, MACV could count on 41 artillery battalions and it was always likely they would be used. Over the same period, fighter-bomber numbers in South Vietnam swelled to 338. This was more firepower than NATO allies on the Central Front could muster to face off the Soviet threat – all to chase an invisible enemy in jungle.

As in the two northern corps areas, blasting your enemy, or commonly empty forest, was becoming the modus operandi. This was an almost inevitable consequence of DePuy's tactical style "with emphasis on te [sic] OVERMATCH principle of fire and movement [capitals in the original]." When movement failed – as it inevitably did from the heat, the weights the soldiers were carrying, or the difficulty of the terrain – the most natural evolution was to fall back on fire.

The archetypal example of this type of operation was *Paul Revere*. Eventually, there were four *Paul Reveres*, each inexorably linked by the illusion that one more push would do the job. The intent of these operations was to intercept enemy forces infiltrating across the Cambodian border into the Central Highlands, a Sisyphean task. The first kicked off in spring and the last closed with the winter monsoons on Christmas Day. In total, the operation lasted 203 days, a record in US Army history.

On May 10, 3rd Brigade of 25th Infantry Division opened Operation *Paul Revere I* in the Chu Pong Mountains on the Cambodian border, the site of the Ia Drang battles of the previous year. The area of operations allocated to Brigadier General Glenn Walker measured 25 miles by 50 miles, a quite impossible area to dominate, comprising impenetrable forested massifs, scrubby plateau, and rolling jungle.

The brigade soon became embroiled in scruffy battles with fleeing communist soldiers. Its reports made tedious reading: at no time did the brigade encounter even a battalion-sized enemy unit. Commonly, village trawls were simply revealing the mixed and complex tapestry of Vietnamese rural society. Deserters, draft dodgers, individuals with false ID cards, former Viet Cong, political troublemakers on blacklists, ralliers on the run, suspected sympathizers, crooks, and genuine Viet Cong – all were netted. In the end, there were only four substantial "battles" over the course of the four *Paul Reveres*: "The Battle of Alpha" (May 28–30); "The New Battle of the Ia Drang" (July 31–August 2); a defensive battle on August 9; and "The Battle for Dragon Crater" (November 19). None was decisive in any way.

Paul Revere degenerated into a desultory rummage over ground where the quarry could always find another hole to bolt down. By the summer the operation had entered its third phase but little else had changed, although the PAVN was not having it all its own way. The uninterrupted tempo of operations meant that it could no longer establish large, secure sanctuaries in the Central Highlands. Both sides were suffering, but at a dribbling rate.

Was there any point to this? By the end of July, 1st Infantry reported 4,543 casualties from all causes (from which only one quarter were battle casualties; the remainder were non-battle injuries or had succumbed to illness and disease). The imbalance between officer and enlisted men casualty rates which later became contentious was already evident. Between May and July, 206 enlisted men were killed in action. Over the same period, just five officers lost their lives. In the same three months, 91 soldiers went AWOL from 1st Infantry.[151]

As in previous operations, firepower was the answer to every tactical problem. A RAND study of *Paul Revere II* observed:

> USAF operations … were absolutely essential to the success of PAUL REVERE II … Once in the field, Free World Military Assistance Forces (FWMAF) received massive tactical air support. The 1st ACD alone was supported by 145 Immediate and 452 Preplanned sorties which dumped 397.7 tons of GP, 52.8 tons of napalm, 37.7 tons of frag bombs, 48 tons of rockets and 134 canisters of CBU on enemy positions. Strike sorties for the entire operation totaled 823, delivering 660 tons of ordnance on enemy positions. B-52s responded with three Preplanned and two Quick Run (Immediate) strikes with 59/ a total of 27 sorties flown and 486 tons of ordnance expended.[152]

However, no lasting tactical gain was achieved and the 2,000 claimed kill count at the end of *Paul Revere II* was pure invention.

Operation *Paul Revere IV* eventually ran for three months and involved two brigades from 25th Infantry and 4th Infantry. These two formations added another 110 fatalities and over 500 wounded to their lengthening casualties lists.[153] Occasionally, there were sobering disasters such as the annihilation of an entire platoon by 101C Regiment. Some of the American soldiers had been executed after they had been wounded. By the end of the operation, just 104 AK-47s were found but the claim was made that over 850 enemy were killed. Were they armed with bows and arrows? By contrast, the brigades admitted to burning down or destroying 701 huts. This begged many questions. Who was being attacked? What was being destroyed? How did this serve pacification? Over the summer, 1st Division's civic action program was paltry: one school was renovated, newspaper subscriptions were bought for another, and a set of athletics suits were donated to a third.[154] Did anyone believe that Vietnamese hearts and minds were going to be won with these token gestures?

The individual courage of soldiers undertaking these missions is not in doubt. At the beginning of November, a search and destroy operation was mounted near the Nam Sathay River which resulted in three downed Chinooks. A door gunner in the first aircraft to go down decided to take his chances, leaping from the door as it struck the tree canopy.

> He later stated that several NVA stared up at him in amazement as he jumped into their midst. The enemy soldiers were apparently so astonished,

that the gunner was able to scramble into the trees and thereafter successfully eluded pursuit. The other crew members were all killed in the crash and their chopper subsequently burned.[155]

The aircraft had landed on top of a bunker killing several North Vietnamese soldiers and creating a distraction that allowed him to escape.

There is little doubt that the geographical span of the insurgency tested MACV. It was difficult to tell whether the fight was being taken to the enemy, as Westmoreland intended, or whether US Army units were simply engaged in fire-fighting. For some units, a tour of Vietnam was an experience in being shunted around the country in seemingly disconnected operations. The experience of 1st "Above the Rest" Battalion, 327th Infantry Regiment, 101st Airborne Division was typical of this pattern.[156] This was a unit with a long pedigree extending back to D-Day. It arrived with a reputation which it intended to enhance, and its sister second battalion would be the longest serving unit in Vietnam, finally leaving in April 1972.

The year began for 1/327th Infantry with Operation *Seagull* in Ninh Thuan Province. This was followed by Operation *Harrison* in which the battalion clashed with 95th PAVN Regiment southwest of Tuy Hoa. By the early spring, the unit had been pitched into Operation *Fillmore* in Phu Yen Province. The infantrymen then found themselves working the II and III Corps' boundary on Operation *Austin II*, a mission remembered for the dry terrain which forced the unit to carry water bags. In complete contrast, the battalion was subsequently despatched to the humid jungles of Quang Duc Province, north of Saigon, on Operation *Austin VI*. Here the unit was rested as I Field Force reserve in the "mosquito-infested lowlands of the Eapa River," at Cheo Reo. In June, the unit was glad to leave this muddy camp and decamp to the cooler highlands near Dak To. It was committed to Operation *Hawthorne*, the relief of a besieged outpost at Toumorong, then became engaged in one of its hardest battles that lasted a full six days. The matter was settled by 24 sorties of B-52s that carpet bombed the Dak Tan Kan valley where 24th PAVN Regiment had taken refuge. At the conclusion of this operation the weary infantrymen were delighted by an unannounced visit by actor John Wayne to their bivouac area. In Dak To, a victory ceremony was staged which involved a somewhat embarrassed honor guard of soldiers receiving garlands from local girls. As the fighting died down in Kontum, 1/327th Infantry was redeployed south again, returning to Tuy Hoa, to undertake Highway 1 clearance operations. In November, it took part in Operation *Geronimo*. There was one more excursion north and the battalion spent Christmas Day in Kontum. By New Year, it was back to where it had started in Ninh Thuan Province. In 12 months, this battalion had served in every corps area except the Delta.

The peripatetic tale of 1/327th Infantry included a sub-plot that revealed how quickly the war was diseasing the bloodstream of the army. The battalion formed a reconnaissance unit – Tiger Force, so-called for its distinctive camouflage – which was celebrated for its fighting prowess and later gained a Presidential Unit Citation. The unit was the creation of David Hackworth who would subsequently court controversy in his own right. Tiger Force reveled in its macho image. The platoon enjoyed stealing the limelight in the 101st Airborne Division newspaper, *Screaming Eagles*. Team photographs showed 20-year-olds dismissive of the protocols of military discipline, goofing and posing with an array of weapons, dressed to kill. A majority were small-town white kids, with a sprinkling of Latinos and the odd black. They were an elite group and you joined the club "by invitation only." "We were young and strong and vital," one soldier bragged. "These were young men who took the art of combat very seriously."[157]

The truth was more somber. The depraved face of Tiger Force would be uncovered 30 years later thanks to the detective work of a local reporter, Michael Sallah, working at the *Toledo Blade* (Major General Olinto Barsanti, Commander 101st Airborne, was aware of the atrocities at the time but chose to cover them up).[158] The allegations against Tiger Force related to actions of the platoon from May to November 1967, and specifically during Operation *Wheeler*. They ranged from the widespread practice of collecting ears to the murder and rape of peasant families. Killing prisoners became the unwritten rule, on occasions after torturing the individuals. Villages were cleared by killing anyone refusing to leave. In the most notorious incident, a baby was allegedly decapitated after the mother was killed. The battalion commander, Lieutenant Colonel Gerald Morse, urged his men to reach a 327 kill count score to match the regimental number and renamed his three line companies the Assassins, Barbarians, and Cutthroats. Sallah's research suggests that Tiger Force contributed significantly to the kill count but was indiscriminate over how it ratcheted up the score.

It would be exaggeration to argue the entire platoon was rotten; many Tiger Force soldiers were both impressively professional and uncommonly courageous. It was more the classic case of influential or strong individuals corrupting the remainder and enforcing a code of silence. Lieutenant James Hawkins gained a certain reputation for opening fire on innocent civilians, on one occasion going out on an ambush drunk. His attitude sickened at least one fellow subaltern, who quit the unit.[159] When Lieutenant Donald Wood complained of the behavior of some of the soldiers, he was curtly informed, "We're in the middle of a war, Lieutenant. And you want me to take our best unit out of action because a few guys are killing gooks?"[160] Another soldier, Private Sam Ybarra, was lauded in the Army newspaper *Stars and Stripes* for achieving the unit's 1,000th kill. Ybarra was later identified as one of the worst offenders, allegedly responsible for scalping a prisoner and raping a 13-year-old girl. The manner in which nefarious actions by some individuals were covered up, or not properly investigated, left as black a mark on the Army's hierarchy as the actions the soldiers allegedly perpetrated. This was the single US Army unit – from Sallah's research – that committed the most atrocities over the longest sustained period and not a single soldier was ever prosecuted.[161]

In other operations, it was an open question which side was being searched for and who destroyed. Charles Sabatier, drafted in May 1966 and later paralyzed by a bullet that severed his spine, recalled with some bitterness:

> As soon as I got there … it was almost like there were just a bunch of guys that got together and gone camping one afternoon that had never camped in their lives, this is what the whole thing was like. It was almost like the Keystone Cops – it was amazing the incompetency of the people …
> I probably saw a half a dozen dead Americans before I ever shot at North Vietnamese or Viet Cong, strictly from our own mistakes.[162]

A stocktake of the first full year of US military operations in South Vietnam left many questions unanswered. The principal question was: did Westmoreland's campaign plan amount to a winning strategy – 1966, after all, had been intended as the year when America would start "winning it" – or had waging battles simply become the strategy? At Johnson's insistence the reinforcement had been accelerated.[163] Westmoreland would have up to 79 battalions in-country, or around 395,000 personnel, by the end of the year. This would tip the war favorably – wouldn't it?

The deceptive way in which this question became muddled was reflected in a cable from Lodge at the mid-year point. As an illustration of insolvent strategic thinking, it was a masterpiece:

> We are "on the track" with regard to almost every aspect of the war and we are winning in several … but all of this is still not called "victory" … in truth we do not need to define "victory" and then go ahead and achieve it 100%. If it becomes generally believed that we are sure to win (just as it is now generally believed that we cannot lose) all else would be a mopping up. If there is "the smell of victory" we will be coasting.[164]

Setting aside the wishful generalizations, the notion that "victory" did not need to be defined would surely have raised eyebrows in Hanoi. In the communist capital, victory was precisely defined. And the side that exactly defined its war aim was always more likely to achieve that aim. The side that didn't was always more likely to smell the stink of defeat.

Westmoreland, unlike the ambassador, was more guarded. The enemy had been beaten but was far from defeated, he suggested.[165] This assessment was partly driven by his natural tendency to inflate enemy strengths, but also by political instinct. Only by talking up the enemy could Westmoreland keep open the tap of reinforcements. Sharp proved the most bullish, writing in terms that Hanoi would have approved: "We must be prepared to accept heavier casualties ... If greater hardships are accepted now we will, in the long run, achieve a military success sooner."[166]

Westmoreland's doubts, in fact, were well founded. Over 1966, there had been a 44 percent increase in "battalion days of operations"; a 25 percent increase in battalion-sized operations; and a 28 percent increase in small-unit actions. Air sorties had risen to 14,000 per month, and armed helicopter sorties had doubled to 29,000 per month.[167] Despite this level of effort, MACV could not kill faster than the enemy could replenish. As many as 8,400 PAVN were assessed to be infiltrating south, augmented by 3,500 Viet Cong recruits, every month. With the usual mathematical precision, it was assessed that although the enemy was losing 2,230 combatants per week, it was recruiting or infiltrating as many as 2,915 in the same period. The numbers suggested that for every 100,000 additional troops Washington added, it gained a meager return of just 70 additional enemy dead per week. In a candid admission, even this simple extrapolation was judged suspect. Only about one sixth as many weapons were being recovered as claimed enemy dead, unfortunately implying that for every six Vietnamese killed by American forces, five may have been civilians – or the body counts were being grossly exaggerated. Whatever the reasons, there was exaggeration over enemy body counts, and underestimation of the rate of enemy infiltration and recruitment. Attrition warfare was proving to be a dead end, literally.

When the CIA's Directorate of Intelligence published its 315-page top-secret assessment on the state of the war at the end of 1966, it was with good reason entitled: "The Vietnamese Communists Will To Persist." The tome was a parade of facts and numbers – for the diligent reader prepared to wade through the text. But the CIA was not arguing that Hanoi was winning. It was not, and the report itemized in painful detail the cost of the war to the communists. Rather, no matter how much pain, Hanoi was unlikely to be deflected from its strategy and goal of unifying Vietnam.

Once again, the malodorous vapors issuing from the South Vietnamese patient on his sick bed were pungently obvious to anyone with a keen nose. The salient point about the military campaigning of 1966 was that it had taken place against a background of almost total failure in most other policies and initiatives, and this became hard to disguise.

Domestically, the year had actually begun with the good news of a roaring economy, which helped to hide the war news. But with a federal budget of around $100 billion, Johnson was still managing to run a $7.5 billion deficit. The Great Society was now costing $44.7 billion, or more pointedly, this is what it was costing to run the federal government. Republicans fretted over big government and wondered where it was leading the country. The war was also deepening discontent. In 1966, the 2,000th fatality watershed was passed. Was Johnson sure this sacrifice was blood spilled on the road to victory? Many influential voices thought not. The formidable Senator Fulbright in the Foreign Relations Committee warned his compatriots of the arrogance of power and quipped that America was in danger of becoming a dragon eaten by shrimps in shallow waters. The influential writer Walter Lippmann turned against the very president who had awarded him the Presidential Medal of Freedom. Retired General James Gavin, always the most intellectual of the wartime paratroopers, spoke against the war, and he was joined by the veteran diplomat George Kennan who originally coined the term "containment." What all these men shared was a long and broad strategic perspective. They had lived through gestation of the Cold War (Lippmann popularized the phrase). Unlike the Johnson administration, they could see no vital interest in one corner of Southeast Asia. The domino theory, they argued, was bunkum. This was a civil and nationalist war in which America had no great stake. Good sense was flying out the window at the mention of the word "Communist." Couldn't the government see that interfering Westerners were unwelcome in Asia; that this was an immoral war; and that Americans were becoming embroiled in barbarity?

The government's counter-arguments were familiarly uninspiring: this was not a war about Vietnam, but about the future of Asia and the free world. America was not losing. But for the intervention, South Vietnam would have collapsed. And thanks to the intervention, the South Vietnamese government held the capital, all 44 provincial capitals and almost all 241 district capitals. The Viet Cong only held jungle and mangrove swamp. The war could be over by the following year, if Washington stuck the course. In reaction to his critics, Johnson staged a seven-nation conference in October, held in Manila, to flash "progress" at a skeptical media. "The peace and security of Asia and the Pacific and, indeed, of the entire world, are indivisible," the communique proclaimed.[168] He left with the soothing reassurances of Westmoreland and Ky and barked as parting advice, "Don't let the newspapermen divide us."[169]

The Joint Chiefs, paradoxically, sided with the critics but for different reasons. The war was drifting because it was being fought with "continued restraints," notably in the bombing campaign in the North, in cross-border operations, and in special operations. If America wished to achieve its objectives "in the shortest possible time and at the least cost in men and materials," these had to be lifted.[170] The Chiefs felt doubly handicapped by government policy barring call-up of reserves, a policy that Johnson could not possibly countenance without risking a backlash, and by an insistence on fully manning the CONUS (Continental United States) training base.

Secret skeptics like McNaughton were finding it increasingly difficult to disguise their feelings. In this he was reflecting an increasingly abrasive relationship between the civilians and the military in the Pentagon. Four days after returning from his seventh trip to Vietnam, McNaughton made an October 18 diary entry:

> I drafted Bob's report to the President on VN. It was pessimistic. We are doing fine in the "new (big) war," but no better or worse in the war for the people. No progress since 1961. I told Bob [McNamara] today that I was going to make my third try the next time the Vietnamese made public asses of themselves … Find a way out [underlining in the original].[171]

If the critics were right, what was the way out? Here there was a certain shared bankruptcy of ideas. The principal counter-strategy offered by critics revolved around granting the Southern communist, National Liberation Front (NLF) political legitimacy; holding coastal enclaves and the capital; and making it clear to Hanoi that Washington would not ship the troops home until a negotiated peace were agreed.

Attempts to start meaningful peace negotiations had been relentless. Over 1965, Dean Rusk made 190 diplomatic contacts on the subject, or practically one every other day.[172] In 1966, Johnson launched a peace offensive in 20 countries proposing negotiations on the basis of the 1954 and 1962 Geneva Accords, a truce, the withdrawal of troops, and free independent elections – but not the handover of South Vietnam to the communists. The same formula had been repeated at the Manila conference. His diplomatic team included many of the heavy-hitters: Vice President Humphrey, Ambassador Harriman, UN Ambassador Arthur Goldberg, Special Presidential Assistant McGeorge Bundy, and Assistant Secretary of State G. Mennen Williams. The caricature of a warmongering Johnson administration was quite wrong. Behind the scenes, the State Department was tirelessly seeking ways to coax the North Vietnamese leadership into dialogue. The problem facing Johnson was intractable – the enemy had no wish to negotiate an end to the war. The Politburo's position was unwavering. America should quit South Vietnam and the country should reunite under a communist government. There was nothing to negotiate.

In South Vietnam, the "fatal impact" of the rich and the strong on the poor and the weak, as Fulbright warned, was having deleterious consequences on the economy. Money supply rose by 72 percent and the cost of living by 92 percent. Severe devaluations of the piaster against the dollar were failing to cope with sopping up this accelerated monetary circulation. The "inflationary gap" was caused by an increasing piaster expenditure associated with the sudden US military build-up and civilian aid. US expenditure was estimated at 59.8 billion piasters. When combined with a South Vietnamese defense budget of 57 billion piasters, a domestic budget of 40.1 billion piasters and other spending, total monetary creation was likely to exceed 175 billion piasters. With monetary absorption running at around 130 billion piasters this created a "very disturbing" inflationary gap of around 45 billion piasters.[173] The US war effort was promoting the possibility of economic meltdown in South Vietnam through "wildcat soul destroying inflation."[174] Ultimately, it was grave concerns over this runaway inflation that convinced McNamara to cap force levels to 470,000 by the end of 1968, not military calculations. This was almost 100,000 fewer troops than requested by the less fiscally minded Joint Chiefs.[175] Even this manpower level was going to raise the cost of the war by $12.4 billion. Was it necessary for Hanoi to win in battle when it could wait for the "conflicting inexorables" of ARVN soldiers unable to buy a bag of rice, riots on the streets, and a collapsing Saigon government?

The failure of governance in South Vietnam continued to script a melodrama that wearied the most patient State officials. In April, Buddhist riots erupted again over the dismissal of the popular Lieutenant General Nguyen Chanh Thi (which caused unhelpful civic unrest in I CTZ), and Ky was forced to promise elections. Increasingly, the Buddhist block began to view itself as the ultimate power-broker in the country, able to change governments just by calling mobs to the streets. The protests continued throughout May, dramatized by the spectacle of more self-immolations. In Hue, the US Consulate was sacked and marines found their paths impeded by Buddhist altars strewn across the streets. Saigon was paralyzed by a dock strike, later copied by the stevedores at Da Nang. Profiting from the paralysis, the Viet Cong infiltrated Tan Son Nhut air base, knocked out the control tower and destroyed 36 aircraft. Seven American servicemen were killed and 140 others injured. ARVN units threatened to mutiny. Johnson retaliated by ordering the bombing of the Hanoi-Haiphong oil installations, a raid of over 100 aircraft led by USS *Ranger*, with just one loss. But a highly influential CIA/DIA (Defense Intelligence Agency) report made plain the failure to make any appreciable dent on the Hanoi war effort. All the justifications for *Rolling Thunder* – smashing the POL infrastructure; stopping the infiltration; cutting off supplies; eroding communist morale – nowhere could the evidence be found that these had come to pass.[176] One year after the start of the *Rolling Thunder* campaign and following a massive expansion of the war, infiltration along the Ho Chi Minh Trail had actually increased (to possibly 8,000 soldiers per month). In 1965, this route had been assessed to have a 234-ton capacity – easily enough, as a North Vietnamese soldier was estimated to require supplies of just 3.6 pounds daily.[177] Only the most myopic could see victory in this panorama – or the irrepressibly bullish like Krulak, who showered doubters with verbal shrapnel. Not only was America going to win, he thundered, but the war was being won now.

Following the failure of the Christmas 37-day bombing truce over North Vietnam, Johnson had ordered a resumption of the bombing post-Tet. There were now over 3,000 aircraft in-theater flying an average of 700 daily sorties. The Pentagon was predicting losses of 500 aircraft (in fact, around 350 had been shot down, the overwhelming majority in North Vietnam). Some pilots had already exceeded 500 missions – far in excess of the demands made on wartime pilots. A few, albeit rare, senior pilots were Second World War veterans, and had served in Korea. For this band of aviators, who had witnessed the remarkable transformation of air power in the jet age, this was the third time their country had asked them to chance their lives.

Against this backdrop, the September elections were "a particularly welcome miracle"; there was an 80 percent turnout to vote in 117 assemblymen, and the proceedings more or less transpired peacefully by Vietnamese standards. Johnson hailed this as a victory for freedom. The Buddhist boycott had not materialized and the Viet Cong were unable to thwart the process. But there were hundreds of security incidents across the country and changing legislators was not advancing the cause of good governance in South Vietnam.

It fell to McNamara – offering an honest perspective in an increasingly dishonest war – to give Johnson an accurate assessment of his war in an end-of-year memorandum.[178] This was delivered against the background of a rolling script of bad news. On December 2, eight aircraft were shot down over North Vietnam with 13 pilots killed or captured – both the highest numbes recorded to that date. Two days later, the Viet Cong again attacked Tan Son Nhut air base and damaged or destroyed 18 aircraft. One week later, in the worst friendly fire incident of the war, 17 marines were killed in an air strike. On Christmas Eve a transport aircraft crashed into a suburb of Da Nang killing over 100 Vietnamese civilians. Bob Hope had only arrived five days earlier to start his annual show. There was no Russian equivalent to Hope's bevy of dancing girls. More pragmatically, the Soviet Union donated 100 MiG-17 fighters to Hanoi in a morale-boosting, festive season gift.

McNamara began by reminding the President that a year ago he had warned of the unlikelihood of victory. Since that last Saigon visit, the communist momentum had been stalled, the enemy body count had climbed, and the North's infrastructure had been damaged. It all counted for little. "I see no reasonable way," he advised Johnson, "to bring the war to an end soon." Whatever advice he was receiving from Lodge, Westmoreland, or the Joint Chiefs, the facts were these:

> Enemy morale has not broken – he apparently has adjusted to our stopping his drive for military victory and has adopted a strategy of keeping us busy and waiting us out (a strategy of attriting out national will). He knows that we have not been, and he believes we will probably not be, able to translate our military successes into the "end products."

Attrition was a flawed strategy; no matter how many enemy were killed "he can more than replace his losses by infiltration from North Vietnam and recruitment in South Vietnam." There were now, McNamara warned the president, 63 more enemy battalions in the South than in the previous year.[179] Pacification was a "bad disappointment" that had "gone backward." The Viet Cong controlled the night, full security existed "nowhere," and "we control little, if any more, of the population." It was a shocking fact, McNamara continued, that "in almost no area designated for pacification in recent years have ARVN forces actually 'cleared and held' to a point where cadre teams could have stayed overnight in hamlets and survived." The notion that government forces were clearing and holding was a fiction. The ARVN lacked "dedication, direction and discipline." One fifth had deserted. Corruption was endemic. *Rolling Thunder* had not cowed Hanoi. "We find ourselves," he concluded in this depressing litany of failures, "no better, and if anything, worse off."

What McNamara could not bring himself to say was quit, which is where his tormented conscience lay. In an unguarded moment, McNamara had confided with an equally skeptical McNaughton, "I want to give the order to our troops to get out of there so bad I can hardly stand it." [180] But even if he had advised quitting, a now committed Johnson could not have countenanced liquidating the war so abruptly, just one year after authorizing a massive reinforcement of the South. The grand old Duke of York marching ten thousand men to the top of hill, and then back down again, was a nursery rhyme, not a guide for foreign policy. McNaughton sensed a president grasping for the "specter of victory," for that was what it had become. He wrote:

> I'm afraid the President will decide to kick the bejesus out of North Vietnam in an effort to end the war quickly. While this might do some good, I doubt it – because we haven't come near to a winning combination in the South.

Furthermore, a cinderizing campaign against the North would not only run a high risk of enlarging the war (via China or Russia), but also convince the whole world that we were a thorough-going bully. But what can we do?! There is no quick way out.[181]

Cognisant of the snare in which his president now found himself, McNamara instead recommended a strategy of limited war, or "a military posture that we credibly would maintain indefinitely," a lukewarm and doubtful scheme that offered no end, or even satisfactory conclusion. The advice boiled down to three principles: cap the troop levels, limit the bombing campaign, and focus on pacification. Even doing all of this, he warned:

> The prognosis is bad that the war can be brought to a satisfactory conclusion within the next two years. The large-unit operations probably will not do it; negotiations probably will not do it. While we should continue to pursue both these routes in trying for a solution in the short run, we should recognize that success from them is a mere possibility, not a probability.

Now, was the President listening?

Chapter 3

THE BIG-UNIT WAR,
JANUARY 1967–JANUARY 1968

On January 24, 1967 a self-satisfied Major General DePuy wrote to Joe Alsop, the well-known if controversial columnist who, unlike many of his peers, supported the war. Alsop was on FBI files for having sex with a KGB agent in a Moscow hotel, but this "scrupulously guarded homosexual" was useful to the administration.[1] "Dear Joe," the general wrote:

> We have just concluded an operation which I believe represents THE turning point in the war. This operation has virtually destroyed Military Region IV Headquarters, which used to be the Saigon-Cholon-Gia Dinh Special Committee. This is the Headquarters charged with winning the war in the Saigon area.[2]

He might have garnished his triumphal missive with the fact that MACV had conducted a staggering 341 "large unit operations" up to January, announcing the New Year with a bang.[3] Adding gloss to the news, that same month Hanoi had unwisely despatched its MiGs to intercept American bombers and in a single day lost seven aircraft.[4] To avoid destruction on the ground Peking was allowing Hanoi to base its jets in the sanctuary of Mong Tu Air Base, across the border in Yunnan province, but this had not saved them from destruction in the air.[5] The letter was a piece of pure DePuy bravado in what would be his last operation in command of 1st Infantry Division. Unfortunately, it was far from the truth.

While the generals were talking up the war, a morose Secretary of State Dean Rusk visited Vietnam on a rare fact-finding mission. With simmering discontent at home, he faced a growing "credibility gap," a phrase that was beginning to haunt the Johnson administration. A division of views between State and Defense had killed off a proposed NSAM articulating Washington's war aims. As damagingly, the Joint Chiefs were now in open rebellion against McNamara after his pessimistic end-of-year report. In response to the Secretary's proposal of a limited war, the JCS recommended more troops and accelerated bombing, dramatizing their requests with the far-fetched claim that "the next sixty days can determine the outcome of the war."[6] The CIA demurred. In a January 9 memo, the agency offered: "At present, we think the only safe estimate is that the struggle, if it is aimed at the creation of a peaceful South Vietnam state which can stand on its own feet, will still be long and costly."[7]

The incremental cost of the conflict had risen to over $20 billion with the defense budget leaping to $78 billion (who could believe that under Eisenhower it had stood at a paltry $10 billion, and this expenditure had incited anxieties over the growth of a "military-industrial complex"). Bob Dylan's "Masters of War" were doing rather well out of the Johnson administration. The air war alone had provoked one of the biggest infrastructure construction programs in the world. Vietnam now boasted nine new air bases with 10,000-foot runways. Where pilots once struggled to land their helicopters in paddy fields, they now had a choice of 282 air strips. Raymond Morrison-Knudsen, Brown and Root, and J.A. Jones were awarded the biggest construction contract in history, worth around one billion dollars. At Long Binh alone, a base was being constructed with a capacity for 60,000 troops. A permanent queue of over 150 cargo ships waited daily to unload war materials in South Vietnam's clogged ports at Saigon, New Port and Cam Ranh Bay. There were now 68 American generals in-country commanding a force of 102 battalions, up from 45 in the previous year.[8] Combined with the Free World Military Assistance Forces (FWMAF) – the hodgepodge of allies propping up Saigon's rickety government – the total comprised 265 battalions, and the number would climb higher over the course of the year.[9] Lodge, seemingly hypnotized by the numbers, gloated "allied forces will make sensational military gains in 1967."[10] It was the beginning of the end game, or was it?

Hanoi's resolve had hardened not weakened. The *may-bay-my* (American aircraft) were no more breaking the determination of the North Vietnamese than the Luftwaffe broke Londoners, or the devastating Allied bombing campaigns succeeded in bringing the German or Japanese civilian populations to their knees. The very timidity of the bombing undermined its purpose, or at least its war-winning purpose. As the controversial *New York Times* reporting of Harrison Salisbury indecently exposed, the bombing was rather too often destroying non-military targets and increasing the sense of resistance in the North.[11]

Salisbury was the first American journalist permitted to visit the North. His brief and staged tour in the second half of 1966 nonetheless represented the only ground view of a war in the North available to Americans. When he pointed out that the city of Nam Dinh had been bombed 65 times in six months, in raids that inevitably resulted in destruction of civilian areas, he received a sharp rebuke from the Pentagon for his "misstatements of facts." On the same day, 100 colleges and universities petitioned Johnson to reconsider the war and threatened civil disobedience.[12] Twenty of Salisbury's 24 in-depth pieces on Vietnam became front page news, and for a period of three months he was widely sought by television channels. Over the same period, UN Secretary General U Thant, leading international condemnation, appeared to some to have become a spokesman for the North Vietnamese government.

In his January State of the Union address a sweating Johnson offered no new ideas. His policy could be summed thus: keep going until the infiltration ends (a reverie); or until the fighting dies down (it was manifestly escalating); or until the North Vietnamese agreed to an "honorable peace" (Hanoi had given no indications that it had any interest in engaging in peace talks). The President could only offer a vision of national masochism – "the necessity of choosing a great evil." Let there be no doubt, he warned the senators, that "we face more cost, more loss, and more agony." And, somehow, Congress accepted the whipping. Some begged for more, or at any rate, more bombing. Even anti-war protestors ran out of momentum over the winter, becoming somewhat distracted by the case of a Captain Howard Levy, an Army doctor who, citing the "Nuremberg defense," refused to teach Green Berets on the grounds that he believed they were committing war crimes.[13] Johnson invoked the lofty phrase "this time of testing" in his Texan drawl, and less loftily slipped in a six percent tax surcharge to finance a war that was now costing $17 billion annually. This was hardly the answer.

For Westmoreland, 1967 would be the year when his grand strategy would come to fruition, a somewhat premature hope.[14] He wrote: "The growing strength of US/FW forces will provide the shield that will permit the ARVN to shift its weight of effort to an extent not heretofore feasible, to direct support of RD [Revolutionary Development]."[15] Thus would the powerful shield of MACV hold the barbarians away from the gates of pacification, swatting the hordes in search and destroy missions, while the South Vietnamese built in the cleared areas (the "Revolutionary Development"). Invoking the analogy of a boxer in his memoirs, an American fist would strike offensively while the South Vietnamese fist held its guard.[16] This was Combined Campaign Plan 1967, which looked good on paper, but it remained paper thin. "Without sufficient forces," a later author of the Pentagon Papers opined, "the task was prodigious … to attempt to 'shield' without adequate forces to 'shelter' [the

ARVN] was bound to be precarious."[17] In the usual way, inputs and plans did not add up to outputs or results, but the protagonists were reluctant to accept this reality.

The "other war" – Pacification in American parlance, and Revolutionary Development in the hyperbolic language of the Saigon government – was not going well. By 1966, $600 million had been spent on aid, or $39 spent per citizen (compared to $1,400 per capita spent on the military effort). But corruption sucked the life out of aid efforts, however well-intentioned and evangelical its dispensers. Units routinely reported the disappointment of seeing items handed out as charity (soap was a favorite) reappearing on the black market. Other units, in gestures of goodwill, set up home charities, forwarding toys and other goods to Vietnam to be distributed by the troops – the "junk" sitting in tens of thousands of American garages – only to find that these gifts also ended up on street stalls.

Much was made of the Marine Combined Action Platoons (CAPs) in I Corps Tactical Zone (I CTZ), but this initiative was oversold both during the war and zealously after the war when recriminations began.[18] General Walt was a CAP enthusiast, which he credited to Captain John Mullen, who in turn appeared to have derived his ideas from the British experience in Malaya. Proto-CAPs seemed to have started in June 1965 – before the term was coined – by a company commander in 3/4 Marines serving in Phu Bai, who sought to overcome the limitations of numbers by joining forces with Vietnamese Regular Force platoons. This made eminent sense, especially as the marines were struggling to interact meaningfully with locals whose language and culture they did not understand. The local 1st ARVN Division commander was so impressed by the experiment that he placed six of his platoons under marine command – thus, it seems, the CAPs were born. For Walt, the CAPs served a political as well as military purpose; through them he hoped to show how the marines, unlike the army, understood the exigencies of modern, counterinsurgency warfare. But the fact was that Westmoreland was also an enthusiast, and the problem was not a matter of doctrinal dispute, but simply numbers. By the end of 1965, there were just seven CAPs. Over two years, III MAF raised a further 75, but there were thousands of hamlets in Vietnam's northern provinces. Extending goodwill to handfuls of hamlets in government-controlled areas was not addressing the problem of the scores outside government control, or that had no wish to see American soldiers in their fields, whatever their intentions.

With inevitability, the collection of statistics spread to the hamlets. The program was known as the Hamlet Evaluation Scheme (HES). This was meant to shed light in the darkness, but the lamp of data dazzled as much as it illuminated. Every US sub-sector advisor was instructed to fill a weekly spreadsheet listing 18 points, eight problem areas, six factors, and three indicators. This information was then forwarded as a votive gift to Saigon where a big picture map of the status of rural Vietnam was compiled. Gathering information on the hamlets was essential; the problems lay in interpretation and the temptation to use problematic indicators as measures of success. Positive percentage signs too easily substituted for real gains. Changes in accounting criteria created illusions of progress which were then reversed after more rigorous criteria were applied (as happened in 1968 when it was determined that around two thirds of the reported "gains" in the previous year had simply been the result of changes in the manner in which the data was being recorded). What mattered was reporting "progress" to Washington and to a skeptical electorate. This pernicious statistical game, of course, would be repeated in Iraq and Afghanistan in later years.

The moot point was long-term commitment, exactly the same problem experienced in the latter wars. A village chief in Chu Lai spoke for every villager in South Vietnam. "I will cooperate with you," he assured a Lieutenant Colonel Warren P. Kitterman of 2/7 Marines, but "what happens to me when you are gone?"[19]

At the February 1966 Honolulu Conference, Johnson had attempted to implant the virtues of the Great Society into his war-hungry Joint Chiefs. "Preserve this communique, because it is one we don't want to forget," he warned. "Bear in mind that we are going to give you an examination and the 'finals' will be on just what you have done."[20] The examination was not on how many battles had been won, hills seized, or enemy killed but on "how you have built democracy in the rural areas." But he had also memorably quipped that he wanted to see "coonskins on the wall" and the latter was locker room language the Joint Chiefs more readily comprehended.

The vexed question that had still not been properly addressed was who should lead? At the time, civil affairs were led by the US ambassador and delegated through his deputy to the Office of Civil Operations (OCO). The ineffectiveness of this arrangement in Vietnam, for a range of reasons, led to all pacification programs, civil and military, placed under command MACV by mid-1967. This was CORDS, or the Civil Operations and Revolutionary Development Support, an unhappy amalgam of the American and Vietnamese programs. As a political sop to State, day-to-day management of CORDS was invested in a civilian deputy to Westmoreland (the newly arrived Robert Komer), with the also newly in-post Ambassador Ellsworth Bunker acting as *primus inter pares*. The pipe-puffing "Blowtorch" Komer seemed suited to the job, energetic, unafraid of confrontation, and not intimidated by the generals at HQ MACV. Like every other skillful operator in Saigon, not least Westmoreland, he soon developed his own back channels and became artful in bypassing chains of command. Johnson had always hated OCO anyway, putting it "on trial," and was pleased that at last the program had been placed within a firm institutional structure, or so he imagined.

The second question was who should undertake pacification, and this proved the Achilles heel. If US forces were employed for offensive operations, then it naturally fell to the ARVN to undertake pacification. The task was thus passed to the South Vietnamese, supported by US advisors lumbered with the unhappy task of trying to "persuade, cajole, suggest, or plead" against a background of "corruption, antique administrative financial procedures, and widespread lack of leadership."[21] It was an impossible task. The quagmire that sank all good intentions was corruption. In the sobering analysis of a 1967 review of the CORDS program: "Even the best conceived and executed RD [Revolutionary Development] program will result in failure in terms of gaining the allegiance of the people as long as such extensive corruption prevails."[22]

This reality was not recognized by MACV. CORDS was formally agreed between Westmoreland and General Vien the Chief of the Joint General Staff, and formally incorporated into the overall scheme of the war:

> In the 1967 campaign plan, we propose to assign ARVN the primary mission of providing direct support to RD [Revolutionary Development] and US/FW Forces the primary mission of destroying VC/NVA main forces and base areas. Agreement has been reached between General Westmoreland and General Vien that, in I, II, and III Corps areas, ARVN will devote at least 50% of its effort directly in support of the RD program. In IV Corps, where there are no US forces, it was agreed that ARVN might have to devote up to 75% of its effort to offensive operations.[23]

A strategy of clearing and developing placed great and unrealistic emphasis on the ARVN, who had to coordinate with Regional Forces, Popular Forces, the National Police, and district and provincial chiefs. This had never been achieved in the past – why did anyone believe that this history of failure could somehow now be overturned?

The campaign plan raised other indigestible questions: if US forces were to take over offensive operations then, logically, it was American units that were going to suffer the heaviest casualties. A more politically acceptable solution would have been to share the burden, but if US advisors led in pacification, Washington feared an American takeover of this effort as well. As a consequence, the Combined Campaign Plan, finally issued on November 7, 1966, was a compromise that in reality was soon diluted. As many as 53 ARVN battalions were assigned to pacification, and the number of US advisors was deliberately restricted to allow the South Vietnamese to take the lead. This barely lasted a year. By October 1967, there were 10,437 advisors, with more than 1,000 at corps level and 800 at divisional level.[24] Americans were assuming control of South Vietnamese command structures, as much as the French, even if they would have balked at being told so.

Staggeringly, only around four percent of this pool was allocated to training establishments. The MAAG began its mission as a conventional training team in 1955, but a decade later, under the MACV, the effort had clearly drifted away from this original concept to the point where the Pentagon had effectively stopped trying to train the RVNAF on any scale or purposeful manner, and had simply taken over the war. A year earlier, in his diary, McNaughton had written: "McNamara this morning, while talking with Cy (Vance) and me, said that 'there is not a piece of paper – no record – showing when we changed from an advisory role to a combat role in Vietnam.'" In the intervening period, this relentless process of "Americanizing" the war had "gained even more momentum."[25] He was right.

Implicit in Westmoreland's strategy was a reaction to the gravitational pull of the enemy's bases and sanctuaries. This meant taking the war away from the population centers and marching off towards the border areas, first in the south, then to the DMZ, and finally in the Delta. Find, Fix, Destroy – this was how the war would be won.

The first swipe of 1967 took place in the so-called Iron Triangle, just 20 miles north of Saigon. It was the biggest search and destroy mission of the war to date and it was given the inappropriately pastoral name Operation *Cedar Falls*. This was the operation that DePuy crowed about in his letter to Alsop.

There was a continuous narrative to *Cedar Falls* stretching back to Operations *Birmingham*, *El Paso II*, and *Attleboro*, all undertaken in the previous year. In these earlier missions, MACV had sought to disrupt enemy sanctuaries in War Zones C and D. This was where the COSVN (Central Office of South Vietnam) was believed to be located, which ultimately controlled the guerrilla war in the South. It was also where an underground infrastructure had taken root from the First Indochina War, which MACV was especially keen to dismantle. The planning for *Cedar Falls* began in early December 1966 but was intended to follow a twin operation, *Junction City*. In the event, the order of the operations was reversed and it was the former that kicked off in the New Year.

The Iron Triangle, described as a dagger pointing at the heart of Saigon, was the location of the headquarters of VC Military Region IV, along with its 1st and 7th Battalions, both subordinate to 165th VC Regiment. Elements of 272nd VC Regiment and other miscellaneous sub-units were also believed to be in the area. Bounded on two sides by the Saigon and Thi Tinh rivers, and backed by the immense Thanh Dien forestry reserve, it offered a perfect sanctuary to interdict the radial routes proceeding northwest from the capital. Much of the roughly 60 square miles of the Triangle was covered with thick forests. More open areas of rice paddy fields could be found in the vicinity of settlements. The village of Rach Bap sat in the middle, astride Route 14. The two northern corners of the triangle were anchored by the villages of Ben Suc and Ben Cat.

Over 1966, operations had usually been triggered by single-source intelligence, generally human (HUMINT), or from intercepted communications (SIGINT). Operation *Cedar Falls* was the first major operation that benefited from multi-source intelligence fused as "pattern activity analysis."[26] It was the high quality of the pattern activity analysis in the area of the Iron Triangle that persuaded Seaman, still commanding II Field Force, to reverse the order of *Cedar Falls* and *Junction City*. This was the fruit of the US Army's indisputable intelligence genius, Brigadier General Joseph McChristian, "an all business, no nonsense officer," who revolutionized the manner in which the army collected, collated, and analyzed intelligence in South Vietnam. When intelligence personnel first deployed to Saigon, they discovered they could not even get hold of chemicals to develop film, and the amateurish advice was "bring over as many household refrigerators as possible" (for beer).[27] McChristian galvanized the disparate service organizations and established a formidable intelligence network. Later, his awkward commitment to establishing the objective truth would lead to his demise in an organization that became increasingly uncomfortable with unpalatable facts.

Cedar Falls was intended as a classic "anvil and hammer" operation but is better described as a vice. Blocking positions were established along two sides of the triangle (Yankee to the west, and Zulu to the east). These followed the natural obstacles of the Saigon and Thi Tinh rivers. The vice was then squeezed from the open northern side of the triangle with a combination of air assault and ground attacks.

Major units that took part included DePuy's 1st Infantry Division, 11th Armored Cavalry Regiment (ACR), and 173rd Airborne Brigade (code-named Task Force Deane after its commander, Brigadier General John Deane). Elements from Weyand's 25th Infantry Division and 196th Light Infantry Brigade assisted in forming the blocks, supported by ARVN units from III Corps. In total, 28 battalions took part, supported by 3rd Tactical Air Wing and II Field Force Artillery.

There would be three phases to the operation. On D-day, January 8, 2nd Brigade, 1st Infantry, commanded by Colonel James Grimsley, would air assault on Ben Suc. The following day, 11th Armored Cavalry Regiment under Colonel William Cobb would sweep west from Ben Cat, supported by further air assaults along the northern boundary of the Triangle mounted by 3rd Brigade and 173rd Airborne. These formations were commanded by Colonels Sidney Marks and Deane respectively. Lastly, all the battalions would drive south, clearing the Triangle as far as the confluence of the two rivers. Four officers of general rank commanded the operation, a sure sign that *Cedar Falls* was "a big one."

The task of seizing Ben Suc fell to 1st Battalion "Blue Spaders," 26th Infantry. At the time, the unit was commanded by future NATO Supreme Commander and later Secretary of State, the 43-year-old Lieutenant Colonel Al Haig. His mission, simply, was to root out any guerrillas, remove all civilians from the area, and flatten the village. This was, if nothing else, an impeccable interpretation of the concept "search and destroy." Haig later recalled that in his first interview with the bellicose DePuy, he was advised, "I want you to remember that the United States is a very rich country. We have lots of ammunition. Use it on the enemy, and to hell with anyone who doesn't like it."[28] DePuy could not have been more explicit if blood had been dripping from the corners of his mouth. Like every other commanding officer in awe of the general, Haig dutifully complied.

The village of Ben Suc was home to around 3,500 inhabitants. Another 2,500 were reckoned to live in the adjacent hamlets of Rach Kien, Ap Bung Cong, and Lam Vo. In fact, there were as many as 18 hamlets in a six-mile box around Ben Suc. A later edition map sheet of the area showed that every single hamlet was destroyed (reflected in the after-action report which unembarrassedly described the operation as a "destruction mission"). Two enemy units were believed to be based in these settlements: a 61st Local Force Company, and 7th Battalion of 165th VC Regiment. This did not necessarily make Ben Suc a hotbed of terrorism. Like many villages of its type, the majority of peasants were more concerned with continuing their traditional way of life, and less concerned with ideologies. This life was tending the paddy fields south of the village, in the U-bend of the river, as well as harvesting the extensive mango, jackfruit, and grapefruit orchards north of the hamlets. Ben Suc was a modest village, boasting a single pharmacy, hairdresser, and bicycle repair shop. The settlement had no electricity.

At precisely 8am, the "Blue Spaders" descended on Ben Suc in 60 helicopters arrayed in two giant "V" formations. Frank Castro, an army correspondent traveling with the cavalcade, reported that "total confusion erupted" in the village.[29] For the soldiers, there was total exhilaration as 420 men were disgorged in less than 90 seconds to the north, east, and west of Ben Suc.[30] Five minutes later, artillery and air strikes rocked the orchards north of the village to deter anyone attempting to escape. All the while a helicopter circled the village broadcasting the message: "Attention people of Ben Suc. You are surrounded by the Republic of South Vietnam and allied forces. Do not run away or you will be shot as VC. Stay in your homes and wait for further instructions."[31]

It was all over in two and half hours and there was practically no fighting. The villagers were rounded up in the vicinity of an old school house. An attempt to show the kind side of American soldiers led to surreal scenes. A chow tent was set up offering the rounded-up farmers hot dogs, crackers, and bottles of Keen. Less than 100 accepted the offer. Following interrogations and screenings, 106 males were detained and 28 were classified as Viet Cong (some North Vietnamese were also detained, including a former mathematics professor).[32] Much was later made of the discovery of 7,600 enemy uniforms, but this bald statement was misleading. The unit after-action report included a sketch map showing the location of all finds.[33] The stash of uniforms was actually found south of Ben Suc, on the banks of the Saigon River. It may well have been a consignment from factories in Cambodia where the uniforms were made. The tunnel complexes and "base camps" were all north of the village. Nothing of any significance was found at Ben Suc.

For the inhabitants of Ben Suc, the operation was an incalculable personal disaster. Villager Le Ban Va was working in fields when Haig's men arrived. Strafing helicopters wounded one old man, and killed five others who were left in a "bloody mess." He recalled:

> While we were being herded, the cattle and buffaloes which we shut up in the pens and compounds were all shot and killed. Then within the first few days, they herded us … My wife and the rest of the family were taken away, leaving all the belongings behind. They did not allow us to take anything along with us at all.[34]

Va had to carry his 90-year-old mother on his back. Two days later, the family found itself in a tented refugee camp in Binh Doung. One year later, he escaped with his family and returned to his ancestral lands, only to be caught in the Tet Offensive. "I was again herded away during a search and destroy operation." But for a second time he escaped and returned. In 1972, the rebuilt hamlets were bombed for a third time and "that time they removed everybody and then bulldozed the whole place flat." Va's experience was not unusual. It was that of tens of thousands of peasants over the course of the war whose "hearts and minds" US operations were trying to win over. "It didn't seem like we were winning hearts and minds," one marine later commented, "we were putting bullets through both of them."[35]

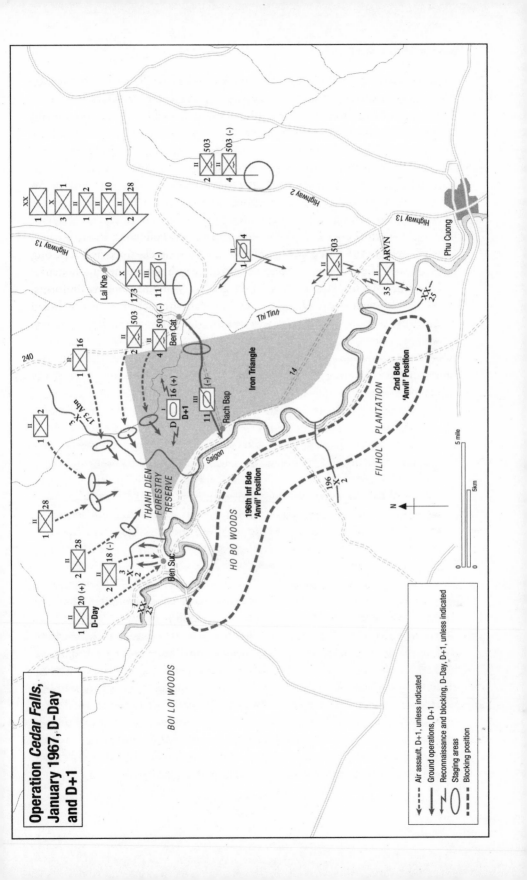

Operation *Cedar Falls*,
January 1967, D-Day
and D+1

According to Haig's account, 40 "presumed Viet Cong" were killed in Ben Suc and the adjoining hamlets. The presumption was weak. They included a man and a woman who had been eating in fields and who ran away from an armed helicopter, three men in a raft on the river, another three hiding in reeds, and a man who hid in a tunnel, then panicked and ran away from approaching soldiers. All the dead were unarmed.

The gunners of 1st Aviation Battalion were responsible for the majority of the shootings. As a gunner in the doorway of a Huey was hardly in a position to make a judgment on whether a fleeing figure was Viet Cong or an alarmed peasant, this suggested a casually amoral attitude to killing Vietnamese.[36] Indeed, the principal engagement rule for opening fire appeared to have been to shoot at anyone running away. As this was exactly what a Vietnamese peasant was likely to do at the approach of an armed helicopter, or a platoon of soldiers, the cull was predictable.

After the war, Marine Calixto Cabrera acknowledged that a farmer could be running away for any number of reasons, "but as far as we were concerned there was only one reason. They're VC. Most of the time we would open fire on anyone who ran away. Thirty percent of the time we hit them."[37] So these people were fair game? he was probed. "Yeah," he replied, "it was fair game." Nineteen-year-old helicopter door gunner Alfred Alvarez, son of a Second World War veteran, remembered his first "kill" in these terms:

> I saw this one guy and it seemed that he took off from the bushes and he made himself seen. He was out there in the open area. So I opened fire on him and I could see my rounds all around him and I could see all the red on his black pajamas as he fell down. When that day was over with at first I felt kind of bad because, I guess, through my Catholic religion, you know it's a sin to kill.[38]

Later he remembered taking part in an operation in which defenseless Vietnamese attempting to flee by swimming across a river were shot "like ducks in the water" by hovering American helicopters.

The total number of weapons captured was just three, a submachine gun and two old rifles, all found in caches dating from the First Indochina War (the unit after-action report stated 12 rifles and one machine gun; but Haig, in his memoirs, claimed that 447 weapons and 1,087 grenades were recovered, a huge haul which he deceivingly conflated with the total haul from Operation *Cedar Falls*).[39] The Viet Cong foot soldiers, anyway, escaped. The subsequent destruction of Ben Suc belonged to an annal from ancient warfare, with Haig's men playing the role of Roman legionaries, utterly razing a barbarian settlement. The hooches were first burned with gasoline. Then bulldozers pushed mounds of earth over the smoldering ruins. To collapse tunnels, ten tons of high explosives were detonated in a large hole dug in the center of the area. Lastly, air force jets bombed the smoldering ruins, just to make sure.[40]

In total, 5,987 villagers were forcibly removed (582 men, 1,651 women, and 3,754 children). The uneven gender balance suggested that a proportion of the men had fled, or escaped in the tunnel systems. The Noah's Ark of animals that joined this human exodus included 247 buffalo, 225 cattle, and hundreds of pigs and chickens.[41] As in previous operations of this type, the resettlement of the 6,000-odd villagers and their animals turned into a fiasco. For reasons of secrecy, the Binh Duong provincial governor had been given just 24 hours' notice of the arrivals. The shell-shocked "hostile civilians" – as they were termed on the battlefield – became "refugees" by the time they arrived at Phu Loi. They found themselves in a barbed wire encampment, living in ten-foot tents, with a ditch for latrines, and suffering chaotic food distribution.[42] Each household was awarded a compensation payment of 5,000 piasters (roughly $38). This amounted to an average two-month salary in South Vietnam, hardly fair compensation for the brutal eradication of their livelihoods and lands without warning or reason.[43]

The day after Ben Suc suffered its extinction, 3rd Brigade prepared for the next phase that would eventually see five battalions landed in the Thanh Dien forest. This was DePuy's "hammer." Each landing was preceded by artillery and air strikes, giving any guerrillas ample warning to escape. Small camps and caches were found, including one haul of 135 rifles.[44] Simultaneously, 11th ACR set off from Ben Cat, meeting little resistance in its four-mile march across the southern boundary of the forest. For the soldiers involved, the enemy proved elusive if not invisible. It was not easy to hunt down the Viet Cong when each man was laden with 400 rounds of ammunition, grenades, mortar bombs, water, and three days' worth of C-Rations. "I had done some hard work," remembered draftee Stephen Dant who served with 5/46 Infantry, "but I had never worked this hard carrying this much weight through that much crap in all my life."[45]

Vietnam is remembered for the excessive use of firepower, but the opposite experience was also not uncommon. Jerry Benson, serving as a humble infantryman in 1/18 Infantry, avowed: "I personally never fired my rifle, which was the case with a lot of guys in our company."[46] There was no reason to when you could not find, still less see, your enemy. Captain Larry Burke, an infantryman with Ranger tab serving in 1/2 Infantry, was equally honest: "I never saw a VC. I mean I didn't see them ... hell you never saw them because of the vegetation ... as far as seeing a guy raising up and shooting at you or something, man I didn't [and] I was in a battalion for six months."[47]

"I've been in-country like five or five and a half months and I've yet to fire my rifle," read the diary entry of one marine at Firebase Baldy on the DMZ.[48]

Despite the elusive enemy, McChristian's pattern activity analysis proved accurate. 11th ACR eventually uncovered 177 enemy caches or other facilities. Almost 90 percent were located within less than half a mile of where they had been predicted, and the average distance was 200 yards – a stunning intelligence coup.[49] 196th Light Infantry made the most significant discovery when it uncovered 40 pounds of documents – half a million in total – in tunnels that took six days to search. In the depths of the Thanh Dien forest, 1/2nd Infantry were amazed to discover an underground hospital, complete with 100 beds.

Cedar Falls continued for another 16 days. There were no major clashes but there was plenty of destruction. The battalions that swept through the area were faithful to their orders, and the Zippo lighter proved as useful as the M-16. Guerrilla Dang Xuan Teo, serving in a reconnaissance company of the Saigon-Gia Dinh Military Command recalled: "The Americans used all war making means such as B-52s, fighter bombers and artillery to bomb and shell ... until not a tree or a blade of grass was still left standing on the ground."[50] Pressed by the relentless 3rd Brigade, Teo spent days living underground: "[we] were forced to eat banana roots and leaves in order to survive."

Anything or any structure that might be of use to the Viet Cong was burned down and destroyed. In practice, this translated into the destruction of any manmade object. Over 500 buildings were destroyed, along with 1,100 bunkers and 525 tunnels.[51] In many respects, the operation became a showcase for grinding, mechanical American technology, re-landscaping the topography if necessary. It had always been appreciated that the forest offered refuge to guerrillas. The answer to this problem was mass deforestation. Fifty-four bulldozers were employed to uproot trees. By the time they finished their work, seven square miles of forest had been uprooted, or roughly ten percent of the area. The problem of the tunnels was addressed with a mix of acetylene and high explosives administered by the "tunnel rats" of 242nd Chemical Detachment. Bunkers were vaporized by flamethrower platoons from 1st Squadron, 4th Cavalry. To flush out suspected guerrillas, 55-gallon barrels of CS gas were lobbed from helicopters. Where no tracks existed, these were made by tank dozers and Rome Plows.[52] Even the swirling Thi Tinh, the "garden river," succumbed to this technological juggernaut: 1st Engineer Battalion simply threw a 160-foot Bailey bridge over the watercourse to allow the tanks to roll into the Triangle.

At midnight, on January 26, the operation was officially declared closed. Seventy-two soldiers had been killed and 337 wounded.[53] DePuy's units reckoned they killed 750 Viet Cong, in addition to rounding up over 1,000 ralliers and "suspects." But an unanswered question hung over *Cedar Falls*: had the scorched earth policy won the Iron Triangle for the government, or turned more peasants against the government? Setting aside the not inconsiderable moral question weighing over what amounted to punitive punishment of entire hapless communities caught in the fighting – niceties that MACV did not raise, or would have even considered raising – was there any point to this wanton destruction? DePuy boasted of a turning point in the war, "a blow from which the VC in this area may never recover," but he was utterly deluded.[54] The majority of Viet Cong escaped. The destruction to the guerrilla infrastructure – a serious blow – was made good. There was in the end no Revolutionary Development in the area because there were no civilians to win over. Instead, the Iron Triangle became a deathly, wrecked strip of land swiftly reoccupied by communist forces. Within two days of the termination of the operation, Assistant Divisional Commander Brigadier General Bernard Rogers flew over the area in a helicopter and was dismayed to see a Viet Cong platoon cycling back into the Triangle. Within two weeks "the Iron Triangle was again literally crawling with what appeared to be Viet Cong."[55] Guerrilla Teo recalled: "Before this time [Operation *Cedar Falls*] we only had a company of regional forces. But by [the end of 1967] we already had a battalion. And by 1968, we had a company in every village."[56] *Cedar Falls* had acted as a recruiting sergeant for the guerrillas. Within a year, the communist Tet Offensive would be launched from this very "cleared" area. If *Cedar Falls* offered an augury for Westmoreland's campaign plan, it was anything but "THE turning point of the war."

Cedar Falls had ambitiously attempted to clear 60 square miles of forest and cultivations with just over 20,000 soldiers. *Junction City*, the subsequent operation, raised the level of ambition wildly higher. Seaman had been instructed to "think big."[57] This he positively did. Thirty thousand men would be used to draw a noose around 2,500 square miles in War Zone C, in northern Tay Ninh Province. To achieve surprise, one battalion would be parachuting into battle. Given that one square mile of jungle could easily swallow a single battalion, and given the experience of *Cedar Falls* – if MACV had not been so deluded by its own propaganda – the chances that *Junction City* would succeed in its aim of entrapping the Viet Cong were slim.

The major events of the operation took place in a 30- by 50-mile box. This was bounded in the south by an imaginary line drawn between the villages of Ben Cat and Tay Ninh; to the east by Highway 13; and to the north and west by the Cambodian border. Running through the middle of the area was Route 22. This old colonial road joined Tay Ninh with the village of Ap Trai Bi and ended on the Cambodian border. Forking right and just north of Tay Ninh was Route 4 that passed by Katum and "the French Fort," in fact a village called Prek Klok where a special force base was built. There were two major rivers in the area, the Saigon and the Vam Co Dong, as well as numerous, treacherous tributaries. The lowlands to the south were generally marshy with some rubber plantations. Further north the land became more hilly and forested. In the far north, on the Cambodian border, the ground opened up again. It was difficult country for vehicles and heavily laden soldiers but ideal for guerrillas.

Like the predecessor operation, *Junction City* had origins in the search and destroy missions of the previous year, notably *Birmingham*, the operation that confirmed MACV's estimate that the COSVN was located somewhere in War Zone C, near the Cambodian border. Such a lucrative target could not be resisted. In the course of the operation it was also hoped to destroy the 9th VC Division and 101st PAVN Regiment. Good intelligence made it possible to precisely establish the locations of the various units: HQ 9th PAVN Division in the eastern half of War Zone C; 101st PAVN Regiment in An Loc and Loc Ninh to the northeast astride Route 13; 271st VC Regiment to the northwest at Lo Go near the Cambodian border; 272nd VC Regiment in the Michelin Plantation at Dua Tieng; and 273rd VC Regiment in Tan Uyen, north of Saigon. The latter two regiments had in fact drifted out of War Zone C.

However, what otherwise good intelligence analysis had failed to appreciate was that PAVN units, and to a lesser extent their VC hosts, were mostly depleted if not exhausted. Daily survival was an all-consuming preoccupation. It is striking how many references to food can be found in North Vietnamese memoirs of this period.[58] The next meal became an obsession. Managing debilitating illnesses, principally malaria, was another. The enemy DePuy anticipated fighting were ragged collections of demoralized Northerners, far from prepared to engage in battle.

The scheme for *Junction City* was described in the melodramatic opening sentence of the 1st Infantry after-action report: "On 22 February 1967, a gigantic military horseshoe was pitched into the pit of War Zone C and the largest operation of the Vietnamese war underway."[59] The western and northwestern half of this horseshoe was created by Weyand's 25th Infantry Division, supported by 3rd Brigade, 4th Infantry Division and 196th Light Infantry Brigade. The other half of the horseshoe was completed by 1st Infantry Division and 173rd Infantry Brigade. 1st Infantry was now commanded by Major General John Hay and 4th Infantry by Major General William Peers respectively. Once in place, the plan was to drive north through the open base of the horseshoe using 2nd Brigade, 1st Infantry, and 11th ACR, destroying any Viet Cong or infrastructure encountered.

1st Infantry kicked off the operation, conducting three heliborne assaults. The objective was seizing the un-metalled Route 246 that meandered parallel to the Cambodian border. To prevent enemy units slipping the trap, this route would have to be severed. The three units involved were: 1st Battalion, 2nd Infantry "Black Scarves," a mechanized infantry unit that took its nickname from the Viet Cong's black uniforms; 1st Battalion, 26th Infantry (Haig's battalion); and 1st Battalion, 28th Infantry "The Black Lions," a veteran unit from Utah Beach. The division would later be augmented by 1st Brigade, 9th Infantry, tasked with keeping Route 13 open. Sequentially with these assaults, 1st and 4th Battalions, 503rd Infantry staged further heliborne assaults on Route 246. The remainder of the eastern horseshoe was completed by 4th Cavalry, who had taken part in *Cedar Falls*; 2nd Battalion, 2nd Infantry, a sister battalion of the "Black Scarves"; and 1st and 2nd Battalions, 16th Infantry. It was an impressive feat of organization, transport, and logistics. In a matter of a few hours, II Field Force successfully mounted a total of eight battalion-level heliborne assaults and a parachute drop. Just four American soldiers were killed.

The parachute jump – the first major drop of the war – was mounted from Bien Hoa by 2nd Battalion, 503rd Regiment. Accompanying the 845 paratroopers on their 35-minute flight was a diminutive 22-year-old former convent girl, the pony-tailed French reporter Catherine Leroy. Leroy would subsequently gain a reputation as a fearless photojournalist, ending her smoky days where else but in the Chelsea Hotel, refuge of the eccentric and rootless. By the time the fleet of 16 C-130s began the run-in near the village of Katum, the heat of the morning was already creating stifling conditions in the back of the cramped aircraft. Some paratroopers elected to jump with rolled-up sleeves, and many were attired with buttons stolen from a popular Avis advertisement, "We try harder." [60] The green light was given exactly on time at 9am, as the lead C-130 passed over the drop zone, two and a half miles north of Katum. The drop length was 26 seconds requiring two passes. Chief Warrant Officer Howard Melvin, a veteran of Salerno, Saint Mère-Eglise, and Nijmegen, was on his fifth combat jump – this would definitively be his last leap into the unknown in a career of wars. In the tradition of airborne units, the first out the door was the 40-year-old brigade commander, Brigadier General John Deane, a wartime lieutenant who rose to battalion commander in just two years fighting in Belgium and Germany. For all the risks entailed in a parachute operation, the jump went well – all paratroopers were down in ten minutes and barely a handful hung in trees (one luckless individual spent seven hours dangling from a tree before he was rescued). The heavy drop followed exactly half an hour later, delivering howitzers, mortars, ammunition, water, and rations. It was a model operation executed flawlessly.

The excitement of the opening gambits of *Junction City* soon gave way to the exertion of beating through close terrain in soaring temperatures. There were few engagements of any size until 1st Battalion, 16th Infantry "The Rangers" bumped into elements of 101st PAVN Regiment six days later, near Prek Klok. Following a fierce fight, the North Vietnamese retired from the battlefield leaving behind a reported 167 dead. This action cost B Company 25 dead and 28 wounded in a desperate action. On March 10, there was a second battle when an attempt was made to overrun the fledgling camp at Prek Klok, now held by 2nd Battalion, 2nd Infantry. This was beaten off with 197 Viet Cong fatalities attributed to 272nd VC Regiment.

For the most part, however, *Junction City* mutated into a phony war. Camps and caches were discovered, some substantial and rich in intelligence material, but there were no major engagements. The press pack began to hint that the whole business had been overblown and the soldiers were fruitlessly bashing the jungle long after the North Vietnamese and Viet Cong had scooted over the border. However, this does not appear to be what happened. Rather, the enemy scattered at the show of force, watched, waited, and then struck when the odds were more in their favor.

The pot began to boil after March 17 when Phase I of the operation was declared over. This led to the withdrawal of several units and perhaps sent a signal to the Viet Cong to attack. In yet another change of command, Seaman bowed out and the Texan wartime veteran Lieutenant General Bruce Palmer took over as commanding general II Field Force.

Junction City II shifted the emphasis eastwards towards Katum and Route 13, an area never previously entered by US forces. Over the next four weeks, 1st and 25th Infantry Divisions mounted multiple search and destroy missions. There were three major battles: Ap Bau Bang II, Suoi Tre, and Ap Gu. All were initiated by the Viet Cong.

The first involved 3rd Squadron, 5th Cavalry Regiment, a sub-unit equipped with six tanks and 20 M-113 armored personnel carriers (APCs) tasked to secure a temporary position named Fire Support Base 20. The Viet Cong attack fell just before midnight on March 20 and was heralded by a herd of belled cattle driven towards the firebase as a distraction. Following a salvo of mortar and rocket fire, 273rd VC Regiment made an attempt to overrun the surrounded cavalry squadron. Several M-113s were destroyed and damaged and for a brief moment, a Viet Cong section sought to strip a captured APC of its weapons. In one desperate incident, the battened down crew of Track 10, swarming with guerrillas, asked to be engaged by friendly fire. After some hesitation, Track 17 commanded by Staff Sergeant Dorren opened up with canister shot on the carrier, killing the assailants. To Dorren's dismay, Track 10 then received a direct hit from a mortar round and burst into flames. All but one crew managed to escape.

The attacks continued throughout the night but were held at bay by artillery fire (3,000 rounds), air strikes (29 tons of bombs), as well as by the determination of the cavalrymen. By dawn, 63 soldiers were wounded and three dead. Eventually, 227 enemy dead were found and buried, the majority killed by the artillery and air strikes. General Hay was so disgusted by the performance of the communist commanders, whose suicidal attacks he disdained, he was moved to send a letter, translated into Vietnamese, to the 9th VC divisional commander. In it, he bluntly informed his counterpart that the Viet Cong battalion commanders had "disgraced themselves by performing in an un-soldierly manner."[61]

The second battle – Suoi Tre – took place on March 19 at a proposed Fire Support Base Gold, a position intended for 3rd Battalion, 2nd Infantry. This new firebase was located just two miles from the scene of the battle of Ap Cha Do (Operation *Attleboro*), and it was evident that 272nd VC Regiment had never really vacated the area. As the first wave of helicopters landed, sentries set off pre-prepared charges and mines, destroying three of the machines and damaging another six. Within minutes, 15 soldiers had been killed and 33 wounded. Despite this setback, the position was occupied and later reinforced by 2nd Battalion, 12th Infantry in a lift that resulted in seven more damaged helicopters. For the next 24 hours the bush fell silent, suggesting that the guerrillas had left the area. Then, on the morning of March 21, a barrage of 650 mortar rounds crashed into the perimeter and a series of human wave attacks erupted across the line. First B Company in the southeast quadrant reported that a platoon position had been overrun, then it was the turn of A Company in the northeast quadrant. Within two hours the entire eastern half of Gold had collapsed back to an inner perimeter. Soon the battalion HQ found itself in hand grenade range of the assaulting Viet Cong, but by 9am, reinforcements had broken through to Gold. These included elements from 2nd Battalion, 12th Infantry, 2nd Battalion, 22nd Infantry, and some handy tanks from 2nd Battalion, 34th Armored. An hour and a half later it was all over, with the guerrillas retreating in disarray. This reckless attack resulted in the decimation of 272nd VC Regiment. Some 647 bodies were recovered along with 65 heavy weapons. American losses were 31 dead and 109 wounded. For the Viet Cong it was an outright defeat if not a disaster.

The third battle, Ap Gu, took place on March 31–April 1 and involved Haig's Blue Spaders. The scene was Landing Zone George near the Cambodian border. As in the previous battles, an American battalion secured a pocket in hostile territory and then found itself under attack, in this case by 271st VC Regiment and elements of 70th Guard Regiment. The fighting kicked off when the Reconnaissance Platoon and B Company strayed into an enemy position and were worsted. A Company was eventually used to assist in the withdrawal but, by the end of the day, seven soldiers had been killed and 38 wounded. In the meantime, 1st Battalion, 16th Infantry had been despatched to George as reinforcements. The following morning, the entire force was subjected to a mortar bombardment which sounded to the surrounded soldiers like continuous, heavy machine gun fire. Miraculously, just 12 soldiers were wounded, the men undoubtedly saved by the fox holes they had dug when the position was first occupied. The attack occurred just seven minutes after the last mortar bomb fell and C Company's position in the northeast was quickly overrun. For three hours the battle raged. This involved hand-to-hand fighting before the company managed to restore its line, in no small part thanks to airstrikes that arrived in 15-minute intervals. Over 100 tons of bombs were dropped on the Viet Cong in 115 sorties. This firepower was augmented by 15,000 artillery shells. Eric Woods, a soldier serving with the Reconnaissance Platoon, recalled seeing dead bodies bounce in the air from the impact of the bombs, and the pyrotechnic display reminded Haig of Fourth of July fireworks.[62] Sergeant Puckett wrote that it all seemed like a bad dream, filled with dismembered bodies. In the subsequent trawl, 491 enemy dead were discovered. Haig lost nine men with another 32 wounded.[63] It was, as one officer put it, "a damn good score."[64] But not everyone was impressed. A fellow officer thought Haig was "a glory hound and he knew the right buttons to push."[65] The same officer wondered if the high-flyer exaggerated his own achievements.

Operation *Junction City* did not quite close with these actions. Phase II was declared over on April 15, but a decision was taken to extend the operation under 25th Infantry Division. This last phase ran for another 20 days and ended on May 14. The badly battered Viet Cong offered no further major challenge. It was now time to do the arithmetic, and how pleasing the sums must have appeared to MACV. A grand total of 2,728 Viet Cong and North Vietnamese were reportedly killed.[66] American losses were 282 killed and 1,576 wounded. Ten enemy soldiers were being killed for every American soldier: the Holy Grail ratio had been achieved.

War Zone C had unquestionably been trashed. Five thousand structures of one type or another were destroyed, over 500 weapons were captured, and 850 tons of foodstuffs were spoiled. The most insightful hauls were the captured foodstuffs and equipment which opened a window into life in a guerrilla camp. The guerrillas were subsisting on a lean diet of beans and rice, supplemented with dried fish (ten tons) and peanuts (200 pounds). Personal equipment included sandals (7,914 pairs) and uniforms (716). Everything needed to maintain jungle workshops was uncovered: amp meters, bolt threaders, drill bits, generator brushes, solders, saws, shovels, and sewing machines.

Firepower won the day, but the courage of the common soldier also counted. It was indicative of the mismatch between the forces that just 79 enemy artillery shells were found: this amounted to two minutes' worth of fire. American batteries, by contrast, had fired off hundreds of thousands of shells. Even accounting for this gross imbalance in firepower, the Viet Cong proved fanatical and wasteful. Every major engagement ended in resounding failure. In a contest between waves of humans and storms of shrapnel, the humans were always going to lose.

In *Junction City*, the tactical victory had been won, not so much because of the plan but in spite of the plan. The COSVN and 9th VC Division had not been trapped. Search and destroy was a dubious tactic at best when, as the Systems Analysis Office was pointing out, 90 percent of major engagements were being initiated by the enemy, and in over 80 percent of cases, there was evidence that the engagement was preplanned.[67] Just 5.4 percent of engagements were being conducted in conditions where "the U.S. tactical commander has reasonably accurate knowledge of enemy positions and strength before committing his forces." American battalions were not so much searching and destroying as blundering and getting entangled in surprise confrontations with an enemy whose presence they had not even reckoned.

The same query that arose uncomfortably in 1966 remained unanswered: who was truly doing the searching and destroying? All the evidence suggested that, despite the massive advantage enjoyed by US forces, it was the Viet Cong that was succeeding in locating its enemy and then engaging that enemy, albeit to its great cost. Every single battle in *Junction City* had followed this pattern. The reason why MACV walked away the runaway winner was because too many Viet Cong units foolishly chose to attack American units in the mistaken belief that these could be overrun. Even after it became apparent that this was a doomed tactic, the suicidal attacks persisted.

The perverse problem facing Westmoreland was that he could not convert these tactical wins, handed to him by a reckless enemy, into strategic victory. As in *Cedar Falls*, Viet Cong were observed reoccupying War Zone C within days of the withdrawal of US forces. The characteristically blunt Komer, no soldier but an acute observer of the military stalemate, distilled his feelings in a downbeat prognosis of the war. America was now "winning," he wrote, but this was "a far cry from saying, however, that we're going to win it – in any meaningful sense."[68]

The attention gained by *Cedar Falls* and *Junction City* somewhat distracted from other operations undertaken by MACV at the beginning of the year. In Binh Dinh Province (II CTZ), 1st Cavalry mounted the ambitious Operation *Thayer II* (the scene of Operation *Masher* in the previous year), which reported a whopping and implausible 1,529 enemy kill count. For the soldier on the front line, the inescapable nihilism of "search and destroy" was more prominent. Mark Smith recalled seeing an old man pointlessly machine-gunned:

> What affected me about the old man and the village as a whole, that operation as a whole, was that the incident with the old man, shooting him down seemed representative of the way we conducted operations. There was no reason on earth to shoot him ... Nevertheless, everything that wasn't destroyed in that village, we destroyed right down to the wicker baskets and pots. We shot the cattle. We shot everything that was living except civilians and some of those got shot too.[69]

Was it surprising that "all we saw were people staring at us like we were from Mars"?

At the conclusion of this operation it was reckoned that 18th PAVN Regiment had been rendered "ineffective." *Thayer II* tested men and machines to the limits. Some units lived rough for 45 days. Sixteeen inches of rain fell in the last week of November, washing away temporary bases and equipment. Fatigues and boots were literally falling apart, requiring a refit in An Khe. For trooper Robert Powers, it was "like heaven to be clean again."[70] Freshened up, he headed off to the fabled "Sin City" of An Khe, with some buddies armed with condoms, but the experience was disillusioning. Sin City proved to a collection of 50 odd buildings set in a circle, surrounded by barbed wire and Military Police. The girls could barely speak English. It was evident that the presence of American forces had thoroughly corrupted the town. Deciding that this was not his idea of sex, the chastened cavalryman returned to Camp Radcliff, but not for long. *Thayer II* naturally led to Operation *Pershing*, which witnessed the cavalrymen revisiting Bong Son and scouring more or less the same hills that had been searched on *Masher*.

Helicopter pilot Brian Glaspell recalled a similarly chastening experience in Pleiku's "sin city":

> I remember going to a bar, picking up a girl. She took me to her home and as soon as we walked in the door here's this family with small children. I'm with this girl who's sixteen, seventeen years old. Probably their major income is coming from her. I remember thinking, being struck by that. What are these people being forced into? ... It was my first awareness of what happens in a war.[71]

Big-unit operations on the Cambodian border or in the Highlands made great copy for *Stars and Stripes* magazine, but they brought Washington no closer to a political solution, and as the White House was well aware, only a political solution would prove durable. It was in search of this elusive prize that President Johnson arrived in Guam, amidst great fanfare on March 20, to meet Premier Ky and Chief of State Thieu. This was the base from which the B-52s had been flying, soon to be redeployed to Thailand where their transit time to Vietnam would be reduced to two hours, automatically tripling the sortie rates. There was little that could be done to manage the disparity in heights between the tall Texan and the diminutive Vietnamese, and still less their mutual dislike. In tow, like three funerary assistants, were the newly appointed Ambassador Ellsworth Bunker, Deputy Ambassador Eugene Locke, and Robert Komer, in his capacity as head of the Pacification program.[72]

The backdrop to this third heads of state summit (following Honolulu in February 1966 and Manila in October 1966) was increasing domestic discontent. In February, 1,500 American scientists, including 17 Nobel Prize winners, had made the unprecedented gesture of protesting against the use of chemical weapons in the Vietnam War. Less distinguished but noisier, thousands of women besieged the Pentagon in a modern, outdoor production of *Lysistrata*. "You are ruining Greece with your mad wars," Aristophanes' heroine cried, and much the same chant was directed at McNamara on his way to work. In the Senate, personalities like James Gavin, ever critical of the management of the war, agitated in the Senate Foreign Affairs Committee. Robert Kennedy, preparing his challenge for the Democrat nomination, added his voice to the anti-war – or at least, anti-bad-war – chorus. To add to Johnson's woes, all the big guns of the East Coast press seemed to be turning against the administration, alarmed by the only statistic that really mattered: in the first week of March, MACV suffered a record number of casualties including 232 killed and 1,381 wounded.[73] How was this all pointing to victory?

Bunker, a sugar magnate turned diplomat, was as hawkish as his predecessor and convinced of the necessity for strong military action. But he also understood that his mission was to accelerate the training of the Vietnamese, to create the ultimate conditions for an American disengagement. These were the seed beginnings of the policy of "Vietnamization," or transferring the war back to the Vietnamese, a program reinforced by the appointment of General Creighton Abrams as Westmoreland's deputy in May.[74] On his deployment to Vietnam, a *New York Times* piece coined the phrase "the patience of Bunker," and he would certainly demonstrate this quality, eventually serving for six years in Saigon.[75] His appointment had in fact come out of the blue. Married the previous month in Kathmandu, he was summoned to see Johnson at his Texas ranch, offered one plane to tell his bride Carol of their new marriage circumstances, and a second to fly him from Kathmandu to Guam. To ease the separation, Johnson promised him a monthly liberty run to Kathmandu, a promise that was kept, and which Bunker later described as "a very popular flight."[76]

At Guam, a military assessment of the situation was abbreviated to two short sessions. Westmoreland used the opportunity to impress his political masters with positive statistics: enemy losses had doubled; enemy prisoners had quadrupled; enemy weapon losses had almost tripled – all the indicators were pointing in the right direction.[77] There was even fanciful and seductive discussion over reducing the US military presence by 100,000 in the following year, if current progress were maintained.[78] That the numbers were bound to be bigger, given that MACV was mounting scores more operations than the previous year, did not appear to be raised. Nor did the protagonists question whether this arithmetic of attrition actually implied that enemy losses were now out-running enemy gains. Numerous recent reports had indicated that this was not the case. The numbers in the end were for political digestion, and no one was in a mood to ruffle the public show of unity in "upbeat" Guam – except Hanoi. On the flight back, the Politburo leaked that even as Johnson had been conferring with Ky and Thieu, he had also secretly been opening communication channels with the North Vietnamese government.

Westmoreland's superficial account of the war at Guam belied that just two days previously he had submitted a highly detailed analysis of force requirements for 1968. This argued for an "optimum force" of 671,616, and an "essential force" of 555,741 (the latter was the original number from the so-called Program 4 package that was eventually cut to a ceiling of 470,366 because of McNamara's fears over provoking runaway inflation in South Vietnam with the American spend).[79] Knowing that such gross numbers would cause consternation in Washington, Westmoreland held out the bait of a quick war, a theme that enjoyed some currency in government circles.[80] His notions of "quick," however, remained incompatible with electoral cycles or American public opinion. When pressed by Johnson the following month, Westmoreland offered that the "optimum force" might win in three years, and the "essential force" in five, an assessment that left the President flummoxed.[81]

Setting aside whether another 100,000 troops would make the decisive military difference – a question that was not being addressed rigorously enough, or at all – Westmoreland's estimate of the situation on the ground was not unrealistic. The stumbling block with Westmoreland's request – specifically the "optimum force" – was that America was fast running out of soldiers. It was calculated that if the continued rate of deployment were maintained, the armed forces would run out of reserves by 1972. Westmoreland's submission was only feasible if reserves (currently on a 24-month liability) were held for the duration of the war, *and* if regular force tour lengths were extended. Both would require Congressional approval. In other words, Westmoreland's plan, all along, was completely unrealistic.

Nowhere had this plan been more badly received than in McNamara's own Systems Analysis Office. Headed by Alain Enthoven, the response was one of "surprise and incredulity."[82] Unlike the military chiefs, Enthoven saw no reason for optimism in pursuing a war of attrition, and neither was he that impressed by the claims made for search and destroy. In a discerning preface, replying to Westmoreland's troop requests, Enthoven pretty accurately predicted the likely and unhappy drift of the war:

> Despite considerable progress in the Vietnam conflict during the past year, an end to the conflict is not in sight … Hanoi is willing to wait … Additional forces, added burdens on the US economy, and the calling up of reserves will only serve to increase DRV's [Democratic Republic of Vietnam] belief that the US will not remain in SVN [South Vietnam] … Additional forces make it appear that we are trying for the "quick kill."[83]

In direct challenge to Westmoreland, Enthoven added that Hanoi well knew that Washington could not possibly achieve such a quick win. Faced with this frustration, domestic support for the war would collapse. "We should be seeking for ways to ease the burden," he wrote, "rather than making the war more costly." What were the minimum military goals – this was the question MACV should be posing – not how can we widen the war. Enthoven acknowledged the enemy could not win either, and "they've taken heavy losses trying," but their determination to win was undiminished. This was effectively the dilemma that would underwrite the Tet Offensive, now only months away. America did not have to "start winning," in Enthoven's estimation a probable impossibility. This strategy was too costly. Washington just had to stop Hanoi winning, a far easier and alluring option within existing resources. To date, the People's Army had failed to overrun even a single US company. Why was Westmoreland demanding a half-a-million-strong army to defeat this enemy?

Enthoven was not the only dissident voice in McNamara's circle. McNamara's most agitatedly intelligent and fiercely ambitious aide, John McNaughton, in a May 6 memorandum, similarly articulated grave doubts over the military's call for more troops.[84] As far back as the previous December, McNaughton had been mulling over his own future, which he viewed as intertwined with the Vietnam War. "The question may come soon when I can't be a part of it anymore," he wrote in his diary. "The trouble is, it does no good to 'resign from the human race.' And I would not make a noisy resignation, so there would not even be that effect."[85]America's strategy, he argued in his memorandum, was based on a "fatal flaw" that had ensnared policymakers for the last three years. Adding more troops to the bonfire while "only praying for their proper use [underlining in the original]" was no strategy at all. Doubtless, Westmoreland would have taken exception to his strategy described as wishful prayer, but McNaughton's dissection of the military mentality was sharp, and he was not so easily fooled by MACV's statistics purporting progress. A firm and emphatic "no" was needed from the President. Anything less would lead to ceaseless interdepartmental scheming, a game at which McNaughton himself was something of a grandmaster. In another instance of official prescience drowned out by the unremitting drum roll of war, McNaughton captured the mood that would engulf America by the following spring:

> A feeling is widely and strongly held that "the Establishment" is out of its mind. The feeling is that we are trying to impose some US image on distant people we cannot understand (any more than we can the younger generation here at home), and that we are carrying the thing to absurd lengths.[86]

McNaughton then set about unpicking every one of MACV's assumptions with forensic precision. The notion that the campaign was reaching its "cross-over point" when enemy deaths exceeded enemy infiltration was nebulous at best. "In any event," he correctly concluded, "there is no suggestion that the added deployments will end the war in less than two years and no assurance that they will end it in three, or five, years." The answer was "Course B," a more limited war, much like Enthoven's recommendation, based on denying Hanoi victory and using existing forces more effectively. Both men, of course, were preaching to a convert, but could McNamara convert the Joint Chiefs, or the White House?

It may have surprised all these officials (and certainly Westmoreland) to discover that Hanoi, far from assessing that it could not win, judged that it was already winning. Even as the White House agonized over the right strategy, Hanoi was making preparations for the final push – the grandly named "General Offensive and General Uprising." In May, the Politburo, in conjunction with the Dang Lao Dong Viet Nam (North Vietnamese Communist Party), issued instructions to the Central Party Military Affairs Committee to prepare plans for a decisive offensive. In June, the Central Committee ratified this strategy. Deliberations continued well into the fall, by which time a date was set for D-day: January 30–31, 1968. This marked the beginning of the Tet lunar New Year holiday, a period when it could reasonably be expected that as many as half of South Vietnam's soldiers and policemen would be on holiday. The planning then continued against a rushed timetable to the end of the year. At the 14th Plenum of the Vietnamese Communist Party Central Committee, held in December, the forthcoming "general offensive and general uprising to secure a decisive victory in a relatively short time" was formally endorsed.

Central Resolution 14 was issued on January 1, by which time almost all the preparations for the offensive were in place.

Unaware of Hanoi's secret plan to end the war in 1968, MACV continued to be fully preoccupied with meeting its own rushed timetables and schedules. In this respect, 1967 was a tale of two opposed, military machines hurrying to build up manpower and material, but with one side completely unaware that the other was doing so not to grind out a war of attrition, but to secure a quick and decisive victory.

As early as November 1965, a mistaken consensus had been established that: "The Communists apparently recognize that the chances of a complete military victory have disappeared."[87] It was a measure of MACV's self-confidence – a confidence widely shared outside military corridors – that the possibility of Hanoi actually attempting to win on the battlefield was not seriously countenanced. How could it be? On every occasion the communists took on US units, they lost, usually comprehensively. It would have taken a huge leap of imagination, or madness, to suggest that the North Vietnamese Politburo was secretly preparing to defeat the armed forces of the United States in an open and conclusive confrontation within the next few months. It would have been madness because the planned Tet Offensive was, ultimately, a sort of collective madness inspired by abstract communist ideologies, far removed from the realities of South Vietnam.[88] General Tran Van Tra later described the plan as "an illusion based on our subjective desires" but "delusion" would have been the better description.[89] Saigon was rotten to the core, but she was no more ready to yield to dour communists than a prostitute working in a Cholon "House of a Rising Sun" was ready to get to a nunnery. McNaughton's fear that the establishment was out of its mind applied equally to the other side.

By the spring, MACV's focus returned to the DMZ, agitated by reports that the 324th and 341st PAVN Divisions had re-infiltrated into the South. This had two important consequences. Westmoreland's perennial fretting over the vulnerability of the northern border – a concern not shared by the marines holding the line – led to the creation of an ad hoc division, formed by stripping brigades from I and II Field Forces. The "stolen" formations included 3rd Brigade from 25th Infantry, 1st Brigade from 101st Airborne, and 196th Light Infantry Brigade. Provisionally designated Task Force Oregon, this formation was eventually redesignated the 23rd Infantry (American) Division on October 25 (the peculiar name was derived from the conflation of American and New Caledonian, where the wartime division was raised). It was later built around 11th, 198th, and 199th Infantry Brigades. The Americal would gain an unfortunate reputation, but would also count among its officers the future distinguished Colin Powell and Norman Schwarzkopf. At first, the new division was based in Quang Tin and Quang Ngai, allowing 1st Marines to concentrate all its forces on the DMZ. 3rd Marines in turn withdrew south to Da Nang. Still unsatisfied, Westmoreland would continue to play with the idea of deploying 1st Air Cavalry in its entirety to I CTZ. Even without such a drastic move, by the end of 1967 I CTZ would swallow 42 percent of all battalions available to MACV.

The second consequence was the great barrier debate, an ultimately futile exercise in border control.[90] To its proponents, a barrier on the DMZ seemed an attractive option despite unanimous opposition from the Joint Chiefs. The sticking points were the sheer scale of what was being proposed; the resources that would be required to build and guard such a barrier; and doubts over its effectiveness in Saigon.

The "McNamara Line" project was eventually placed in the hands of the unfortunately named Lieutenant General Alfred Starbird, an officer who was prodded into selling the idea to a resistant Westmoreland.[91] The marines were scathing over the whole project, one remarking: "With these bastards you would have to build the zone all the way to India ... even then, they would probably burrow under it."[92] Another III MAF staff officer tasked with implementing the scheme wrote: "They must be smoking hashish." After much horse-trading, Westmoreland got his way on the DMZ (essentially, an acceptance that the northern defense of the border would be largely based on strongpoints, rather than a physical barrier), but some of the more technologically innovative ideas, such as sensors, were used on the Laotian panhandle. By the end of the year the barrier was effectively abandoned, but not before provoking even more acrimonious sniping and shelling between III MAF, Westmoreland, and a disgruntled McNamara.

The very American fascination with technological solutions to military problems had a darker side. Without doubt the most controversial aspect of America's air campaign in Southeast Asia was the use of herbicides, or in the eyes of critics, chemical warfare. The world had last witnessed chemical warfare in the First World War and was quite unprepared for the country posing as idealistic beacon to mankind resorting to what was universally regarded as a base form of warfare. From the Pentagon's perspective, spraying jungle canopies with herbicides did not amount to chemical warfare, just accelerated defoliation. Stripping leaves from trees harmed no one and deprived the Viet Cong of cover.

In Vietnam, four herbicides were used, identified by the colored band painted on the containers: orange, white, blue, and purple.[93] The most well known and controversial was Agent Orange.[94] What provoked concern with this particular herbicide was the teratogenicity of the mix (the potential to deform fetuses) caused by the presence of the highly persistent and toxic dioxin "TCDD."[95] Most military stocks were supplied by Monsanto, a firm that would court controversy with the pesticide DDT and later with the development of genetically modified crops. In civilian use, Agent Orange was diluted with water or oil. This procedure was not adopted in Vietnam because the military feared that the dilution would reduce the effectiveness of the agent. One of the undisputed effects of this campaign was to accelerate the migration to the cities of peasants abandoning spoiled croplands, which contributed to the growth of slums in Saigon.[96]

The first large-scale use of herbicides was in early 1962 under the code name Operation *Ranch Hand*. The missions were flown by the 12th Air Command Squadron and 12th Special Operations Squadron which counted on 25 aircraft at its peak in 1969. The first mission, undertaken under conditions of great sensitivity, was authorized by Kennedy on August 10, 1961, actually by a South Vietnamese H-34 helicopter to avoid tainting Washington.[97] All subsequent missions for the next year had to be authorized by the presidential office. Authority was then delegated to Commander MACV and the US ambassador.

In the beginning, the missions were all about protecting vulnerable routes. Much like the British in Malaya who sprayed the sides of roads from converted water bowsers, trials were conducted in the Central Highlands and later in III CTZ to assess the utility of defoliants as an anti-ambush measure. Only later did they become a weapon for widespread defoliation and attacking supposed insurgent croplands. At first, most Americans were skeptical of the value of the operations (the ever-sharp MacNamara questioning the numbers). Fear of reputational damage was a constant concern. Operation *Ranch Hand* ultimately expanded because the war expanded, but not with great enthusiasm.

Between 1962 and 1966 defoliant missions increased incrementally, with the peak years in 1967–1969. Thereafter the missions dropped sharply with the last fixed-wing mission recorded on January 7, 1971 and the last helicopter spraying operation flown on October 31 of the same year. In total, 18,850,000 gallons of herbicides would be dispensed, of which over 11 million gallons was Agent Orange.[98] According to USAF records, 6,542 spraying missions were conducted and the total acreage covered was in the order of 3.6 million, of which two thirds was sprayed once and just over ten percent was sprayed three or more times (a higher figure of 5 million acres or 12 percent of South Vietnam is also widely quoted by critics of the program). The most sprayed areas were CTZs I and III and the most affected areas were the Long Mountains of Truong Son and the Vietnamese-Cambodian border. There was no official South Vietnamese opposition to Operation *Ranch Hand*, despite the deleterious consequences suffered by peasants forced to abandon lands.

South Vietnamese complicity in the use of herbicides was much deeper than reported and American reticence more vocal. Kennedy was very wary of the proposal from the beginning, consulted widely over the legality of using herbicides as an instrument of war, and would not sanction the use of herbicides against croplands. It was Diem, with some arrogance, who pushed for crop spraying, telling US advisors that he knew perfectly well which croplands were being harvested by the Viet Cong. Herbicides would save Vietnamese work gangs the effort of slashing and uprooting the crops. In fact, Diem's "knowledge" was more a casual expression of Vietnamese racism towards minority rural populations, especially the Montagnards.

The Department of Defense sided with Diem, seeing the potential of another weapon in the armory. The State Department, led by the veteran voice of W. Averell Harriman and Roger Hilsman, was appalled at the notion of America denying food supplies in such an indiscriminate fashion and opposed the proposal. Presciently, Harriman argued that the use of herbicides would hand the North Vietnamese a propaganda victory and result in a massive public relations fiasco. Perhaps guided by this wisdom, Kennedy authorized crop spraying missions on October 2, 1962 but only in South Vietnamese aircraft. The switch to US aircraft and pilots happened after the Tonkin Gulf incident when American attitudes hardened, but even then USAF aircraft were obliged to fly in the livery of the South Vietnamese Air Force.

Nor did international opinion react to the use of herbicides. It was well known by 1962 that herbicides were being used because the unholy trinity of Radio Hanoi, Radio Peking, and Radio Moscow were all loudly protesting and telling the world of this perfidy. It is almost certain at this stage that Washington would have reacted to international condemnation but there was none. The protest, typically, came from America's conscience. In February 1963, Richard Dudman, a foreign policy commentator, wrote a series of articles on the use of herbicides, published by the *St Louis Post-Dispatch*, which raised concerns in Congress. The following year in May, a staff writer called Jim G. Lucas wrote an article describing the destruction of crops in a friendly village called Cha La in the Mekong Delta. The *Washington Post* published the story and ran an editorial condemning the use of herbicides and calling for the immediate cessation of crop-spraying operations.

This media protest was supported by academic works. At the height of Operation *Ranch Hand*, in 1967, the RAND Corporation published two reports on crop spraying that once again raised doubts over the entire rationale for the program. Just over 200 captured Viet Cong were interviewed, who claimed that the herbicides were having little effect on their food supplies but they were succeeding in alienating the population. In other words, *Ranch Hand* was acting as another recruiting sergeant for the enemy. McNamara was sufficiently disturbed by these reports to direct the Joint Chiefs to respond to the criticisms. With a certain pig-headedness, the Chiefs countered that any supposed innocent peasants in the sprayed areas were probably alienated anyway, and the evidence that crop spraying was not significantly disrupting food supplies was simply discounted. Protest also began to be voiced by the scientific community, led by the Federation of American Scientists. In January 1966, 30 Boston scientists protested against the indiscriminate nature of herbicidal warfare. A year later a much more serious protest was mounted by 5,000 scientists, including the 17 Nobel laureates, who sent a petition to Johnson's Science Advisor calling for the end of the use of herbicides.

By the following year Ambassador Bunker appointed a committee to review the effects of Operation *Ranch Hand*. Then Nixon killed off the program following the December 1969 ratification of the Geneva Protocol on chemical and biological weapons, which included riot control agents and herbicides within the convention.

Setting aside exaggerated postwar claims, it is unquestionable that the effects of nine years of herbicidal warfare over South Vietnam, eastern Laos, and Cambodia were pernicious. The sensitive ecological balance of jungle areas was undermined, and in some parts destroyed, through resultant soil erosion. This was especially true of areas that received triple spraying. In other areas, invading species like cogon grass and especially hardy bamboos made it very difficult for the forest to regenerate. Mangrove forests, because of their extremely delicate ecology, had been most devastated. Around 36 percent of South Vietnam's mangrove forests were destroyed and it is estimated that full regeneration will take a century under protected conditions.

The military advantages gained by the use of herbicides will always remain a matter of debate. The effects on human health have proved notoriously hard to prove, although possible correlations with a range of illnesses were eventually conceded and enshrined in the 1991 Agent Orange Act. Relations between the Federal Government and the Department of Veterans Affairs soured. Liberal American opinion, strongly influenced by books such as *Silent Spring* and strumming along to Neil Young's lyrics about Mother Nature on the run, found another reason to hate Washington. Across the world, America suffered great reputational damage. For many, Agent Orange came to symbolize everything that was wrong and immoral about America's dirty war in Vietnam.

For marines on the DMZ not fighting internecine wars, there was the real war. 3rd Marine Division faced four People's Army divisions across the border: the 304th, 320th, 324B, and 325C, all subordinated to the communist Military Region 4. In the so-called Tri-Thien-Hue Military Region further south, the PAVN had infiltrated two divisions: 2nd PAVN Division (also confusingly designated 620th), operating in Quang Ngai and Quang Tin; and the durable 3rd PAVN Division deployed in Binh Dinh, Quang Ngai, and Kontum. These were supported by two "main force" Viet Cong regiments and a well-established support infrastructure. The marines, of course, could not pursue and destroy their enemy over the border. This meant 1 CTZ would always be fighting with one hand tied behind its back. The advantage to Hanoi was incalculable.

At the start of 1967, 3 MARDIV opened its account with a continuation of the *Prairie* series of operations. These ran from January to May. In total, 24 major operations were launched, 14 of which were classed as "significant" (an operation that resulted in more than 100 enemy dead). This was the hot war. *Prairie I* was closed on January 31. The claimed enemy kill count was over 1,300 but the marines also suffered 239 killed. When *Prairie II* concluded, it was claimed that a further 700 communist soldiers had been killed. The fighting, at times, was desperate. At one point, bereft of reserves, elements of 2/3 Marines that were already embarked for their return to Okinawa were thrown into the fight. The G Company commander – Carl E. Bockewit – had been assured the night before that his combat days were completed. "That's good," he said, "Last night I had a dream that if I went north of the Cam Lo I would die."[99] The following day he was shot and killed near a feature named Hill 124, caught in a two-sided communist ambush. *Prairie III* followed without pause. Marine losses were a further 56 killed and 530 wounded.

Prairie IV proved even hotter. Only four days after the launch of the operation in the third week of April, an observation post on a Hill 861, five miles northwest of Khe Sanh, was jumped by a large enemy force. Reinforcements were scrambled to the area, but the PAVN had dug in on two hill features. There followed a six-day battle in which both sides displayed grim determination to hold on to their gains, whatever the price. This proved high: in a wave of assaults, 155 marines were killed and 425 wounded. Effectively, a battalion had been wiped out. PAVN losses were reported as 940 killed.[100] Marines urinated on mortar tubes to cool them. Adversaries stumbled into each other in the hilltop fogs. On Hill 881S alone the marines subsequently counted over 250 well-concealed enemy bunkers. Attempts to blast these with support fire had failed.

Marine Dave Crawley remembered the stupidity of the tactics:

Well, unfortunately first they called in the 9th Marines and they went through a couple companies of the 9th Marine Regiment, killing and wounding everybody. Then they sent India Company up and they killed and wounded that company. Then they sent Kilo Company up and by this time they'd killed enough of them that we fought our way to the top. So, it seems to be the practice of the Marines. They just keep throwing in Marine outfits and when one got decimated they'd pull it back and throw in another one.[101]

Captain Michael Sayers, a B Company commander with 9th Marines, recalled the grim task of recovering the bodies:

We were carrying KIAs and WIAs in ponchos [borne by] four men to a litter. The heat deteriorated the bodies rapidly and they bloated fast. Almost impossible to carry in the dark, the mud, and the rain. Many times we stopped our march to retrieve a body that had fallen out of a poncho and rolled down a hill.[102]

The cost to civilians was equally steep. 1st Marine Aircraft Wing dropped 518,700 pounds of ordnance on the target area. The nearby village of Lang Vei – a friendly settlement hosting a CIDG camp – was mistakenly bombed. One hundred and fifteen villagers were killed and twice the number was horribly wounded. As many as 140 buildings and structures were flattened.

By the end of May the battle swung to the eastern flank of the DMZ to Con Thien and Gio Linh, and the infiltrations did not stop. Over June and July, 3rd Marines ran continuous operations across the northeast quadrant of Quang Tri Province (Operations *Cimarron*, *Buffalo*, and *Kingfisher*). Mostly, the PAVN refused the fight. On occasions, a successful combination of accurate intelligence and rapid concentration of firepower exacted a heavy price on the infiltrators. Counting body parts was such a repulsive and inexact chore the marines learned to count enemy waterbottles instead, to assess how many had been killed. Tanks were used but these were vulnerable to well-concealed RPG teams. By the spring, several battalions were on their second commanding officer, the first killed or wounded. In the case of a personality like Lieutenant Colonel "Spike" Schening, commanding officer of 1/9 Marines, this was the third time he had been wounded, having previously received injuries in the Second World War and Korean War. All these actions were warm up acts to the main performance that struck Con Thien at the beginning of September.

Con Thien meant "Hill of Angels," an irony that escaped no one. There were, in fact, three low-lying hills clustered together in the shape of a swollen pear. The French had built a fort at this location which was later abandoned and became derelict. The CIDG took it over in 1965, supported by a special force detachment. Con Thien was just two miles from the DMZ and the central anchor to the porous McNamara Line. It was a dust bowl in the dry season and a mud bath during the winter monsoon.

Over the summer and fall of 1967 the hill gained a symbolic significance and butcher's bill far in excess of its military worth. The justification for holding Con Thien was that it enjoyed "a commanding view of the terrain for a dozen miles in all directions."[103] This was true but this advantage did nothing to stop the infiltrations. By the time the battle started, PAVN units subordinate to 324B PAVN Division had bypassed Con Thien and were establishing their own jungle bases further south. During Operation *Prairie III*, in March, 1/9 Marines had discovered a substantial bunker complex southeast of the base. Whatever Con Thien was achieving, it was not stopping the infiltrations, any more than the McNamara Line with its ground sensors and mines. For the North Vietnamese, the significance of Con Thien was that it provided a perfect aiming point for its artillery. Like so many other featureless hills in wars, mere possession became its *raison d'être*. As ever, the possession came at a price.

The first attack fell on May 8. It came as a complete surprise. Following a barrage of 300 mortars and artillery shells, sappers from 812th PAVN Regiment attempted to break into the perimeter with satchel charges and flame throwers. The assault was repulsed with heavy losses on the enemy side but it cost 1/4 Marines 44 dead. As a consequence of this attack, all civilians were moved south of the Ben Hai River in Operation *Hickory*, and the area between Con Thien, Gio Linh, and Dong Ha was declared a free fire zone (in total, 11,000 villagers were moved). On a map, the so-called "Leatherneck Square" looked solid enough, but the solidity was entirely illusory.

Leatherneck Square became a chessboard where each side attempted to outwit the other, with feints, sacrifices, and over-hopeful checks. Over the course of *Hickory*, 2/26 Marines, 2/9 Marines, and 3/4 Marines mounted a succession of assaults on bunker systems across the frontage of Con Thien. These were supported by A and B Companies from 3rd Tank Battalion, a rare instance when the M-48A3 tanks could be used relatively freely across open ground. It was evident from these engagements that the People's Army was openly violating the DMZ and deploying entire units into well-concealed harbors on the South Vietnamese side of the border.

Hickory cost another 142 dead and 896 wounded but the marines could not stop the infiltrations. In May, 3/4 Marines discovered an enemy unit southwest of Con Thien, on a feature called Hill 174. A three-day battle followed and the hill was pummeled with artillery and air strikes. It was eventually taken on May 31, but at the cost of another 164 dead and 1,240 wounded. Over the course of Operation *Buffalo* in July, B Company of 1/9 Marines was caught in an ambush just over a mile from the base. A shocking 84 marines were killed – the worst single toll of any marine unit – and 190 were wounded. Only 27 marines escaped uninjured. When reinforcements arrived, Staff Sergeant Burns from 1st Platoon, B Company was asked where the company was. "Sir," the NCO replied, "this is the company, or what's left of it."[104] Burns was subsequently awarded the Navy Cross.

This episode earned the survivors the nickname "The Walking Dead" (from a Ho Chi Minh speech in which he described the marines as "*Di bo chet*"; Radio Hanoi subsequently taunted the unit by playing the Martha and the Vandellas' song, "Nowhere to run to, baby, nowhere to hide"). Some avowed 1/9 Marines was jinxed. The PAVN had dressed in American uniforms, a trick the North Vietnamese would repeat over the summer. *Buffalo* cost a further 159 dead and another 345 wounded. The claim that 1,200 communists had been killed was exaggerated cover for a poor sequence of operations.

1/9 Marines had already been ravaged by operations on the DMZ before the fiasco on *Buffalo*. Earlier in the year, an engineer wire running line had been captured, tortured, and mutilated. "It seems from that day forward, all illusions of codes of conducts and humanity seemed to end. The sweeps to find Charlie became very vicious," recalled a marine, "it semed like we lost a couple of our friends everyday. We were all insane with fear and hatred."[105] On *Buffalo*, the People's Army had unusually used flamethrowers to force the marines out into the open. Both sides had exchanged massive amounts of firepower, with Marine aircraft alone dropping 90 tons of bombs in just the first few hours of the battle. It took three days to recover all the dead and body parts. To add insult to injury, two days later, 1/9 Marine's command bunker at Con Thien received a direct hit from a 152mm shell. The projectile penetrated five feet of sandbags and timbers, killing 11 marines and wounding another 18, including the aforementioned commanding officer, Lieutenant Colonel Schening.

Revenge was exacted on September 4 by I Company, 3/4 Marines, which decimated a communist unit south of the base. Three days later an even bigger battle ensued between I Company, 3/26 Marines and another infiltrated PAVN unit. This also took place south of Con Thien and ended in a draw. By the end of the five-hour battle, over 50 North Vietnamese had been reportedly killed, but 3/26 had suffered 20 fatalities. The skirmishing continued for the next week without resolution. On September 10, 3/26 Marines clashed with 812th PAVN Regiment. This proved a desperate affair. The marines faced human wave assaults which they repulsed with heavy casualties. Another 34 marines were killed and another 192 wounded (by this stage 3/26 Marines had suffered 40 percent casualties). The PAVN also suffered grievously from reckless tactics that left 144 of their own number dead on the battlefield.

Con Thien was clearly surrounded, but would it be assaulted? This question seemed to be answered on September 12 when a probing attack was made against the perimeter. It failed miserably but, taking no chances, 3/9 Marines was reinforced by 2/4 and 2/9 Marines on the flanks, to protect the vital supply Route 561 from Cam Lo. These became involved in skirmishes with 90th PAVN Regiment at Phu Oc (September 21), at "Washout Bridge" (October 14), and on Hill 48 (October 25). At the latter, 3/26 Marines was caught in especially bitter fighting with 812th PAVN Regiment. From these actions, it appears the PAVN either never intended to mount an all-out assault on Con Thien, or decided the easier option would be to bombard the hill from the sanctuary of bases north of the DMZ. So began "The Siege of Con Thien."

In fact, Con Thien had already been subjected to artillery bombardments earlier in the year, in February and March. The latter bombardment had lasted two weeks. By the fall, the PAVN had managed to range a variety of weapons against the base: 82mm and 120mm mortars, 152mm artillery pieces, and 122mm rockets. The high point came on September 25 when over 1,000 shells landed on the base. By now, monsoon rains had transformed the hilltop into a quagmire of red mud, scattered debris, and half-flooded trenches. In just one 48-hour period, 17 inches of rain fell on the hill.[106] The heavy rain made Route 561 impassable, forcing all resupply to go by helicopter – an unsatisfactory situation that left the defenders on the hill on short rations for a period. The only consolation was that enemy shells were now swallowed by the knee-deep mud, sending geysers of shrapnel upwards but not sideways. When a tank platoon attempted to cross flooded fields south of the base, two tanks bogged down. The platoon leader advised the infantry commander that the fields were impassable, at which point the captain pulled out a pistol and threatened: "You get in there and get those tanks out of there or I am going to blow your ___ head away."[107] The lieutenant complied and all five tanks got duly stuck. Another marine remembered "a gook" whose entire upper body had been blown away but whose two legs remained upright, stuck.

For the beleaguered marines, Con Thien became "the Meat Grinder." They shared their hill with a plague of rats, "nervy, scummy creatures" that foraged in the bunkers for scraps of food and body parts.[108] The "blue-gray caste" of death became too familiar. The communist barrages provoked one of the biggest retaliatory air strikes in history: 1st Marine Air Wing alone dropped 2,587 tons of high explosives.[109] It was joined by naval gun fire, B-52 strikes and counter-battery fire from marine artillery units. Over 10,000 shells a day were being lobbed back over the border. This failed to silence the well-dug-in enemy guns.

Con Thien prefaced the more famous Khe Sanh as a magnet for journalists keen to relay the experience of war with grit between their teeth and mud on their boots. Both *Time* and *Life* covered the story with gripping narratives and superb photography. The former inflected its report with the subtitle "Rising

Doubt About the War." No American father or mother wanted to see a picture of their son, curled like a fetus at the bottom of a muddy hole, on the cover of a national magazine. Mike Wallace of CBS News got a scoop with "The Ordeal of Con Thien," broadcast from the front line. "You can't be saved, you can be lucky," a marine told John Laurence, the CBS reporter on the spot. Another declared that if he lived another 100 years, he would be unable to tell the true story of Con Thien. Harrowing footage showed young Americans, white and black, cowering in mud, smoking, joking, and dressed informally (only helmets and flak jackets were de rigueur). "We are just occupying ground," a young officer wearily complained. "Futile and frustrating" was another's verdict. The Wallace broadcast carried an unmissable message: Con Thien was a microcosm of a stalemated and pointless war. With some exactitude, Westmoreland commented that the aim of the battle had not been to defeat the marines militarily – the PAVN could not hope to achieve that – but to defeat America psychologically.

The 34-day siege finally ended in early October. 3/9 Marines were pulled off the hill having suffered 27 fatalities and 600 wounded from the artillery and rocket fire. Lance Corporal Jack Hartzel recalled deploying with a platoon of 45 men and leaving the hill with just 12.[110] Lieutenant James Coan, an M-48A3 Patton tank commander, was especially impressed by the bravery of the "cannon cockers," or artillerymen, who would return fire even as shells were landing in their midst.[111] "I got real religious," he remembered, "I had a pocket Bible and I started reading that frequently, particularly the Psalms." Over the course of September, across the sector, a further 196 marines had been killed and 1,917 wounded. These losses were a fraction of those suffered by the North Vietnamese, who had committed troops to their own sort of "meat grinder" in hopeless assaults against the marine strong points.

The "Border Battles" were only one course on General Robert Cushman's menu of cold dishes. III MAF was simultaneously struggling to pacify the southern half of I CTZ, with as little success. This offered an opportunity for the army to take the strain, show its mettle, and offer its dead. Over the spring, as we have seen, Task Force Oregon had been stood up. The omens for this formation were not good. It was widely recognized that MACV was cobbling together disparate brigades with few common bonds. The task force lasted just five months before 3rd Brigade was chopped to 4th Infantry Division in the Highlands, and 1st Brigade returned to its parent division. This only left 196th Infantry, which became the nucleus for the weakest division fielded by MACV – the 23rd American Division. To make up the numbers, 198th Infantry Brigade was shipped over from the Dominican Republic, later joined by 11th Infantry Brigade, a Pacific reserve unit based in Hawaii. Both brigades were undermanned and undertrained. The divisional commander, Major General Samuel Koster, seemed a good choice, having led Eighth Army's anti-guerrilla operations in the Korean War. But the pattern of this dirty war was repeated in Vietnam. His career would end in the disgrace of the My Lai massacre. Humiliatingly, Pete Seeger immortalized him in the protest song "Last Train to Nuremberg."

Task Force Oregon undertook its first operation – *Malheur I* – against 2nd VC Regiment near a town called Duc Pho, in the southeast corner of Quang Ngai Province.[112] The operation was led by Brigadier General Salve Matheson's 1st Brigade, 101st Airborne, and involved 1/327 Infantry, 2/237 Infantry, and 2/205 Infantry. *Malheur II*, mounted in July, shifted the effort to the Song Ve Valley area. As the mission expanded, the brigade encountered elements from 3rd PAVN Division, 1st VC Regiment, and 2nd PAVN Division, as well as numerous local sub-units. A feature of both operations, which eventually extended over three months, was an absence of any significant engagements. The after-action report instead listed a relentless roll call of daily "light contacts." Most were against "two to five enemy." It seemed that wherever the soldiers patrolled they were met by sniping fire, or an ambush, booby traps or gravel mines. As the brigade soberly warned: "Training in identification of VC mines and booby traps must be continuously stressed despite the fact that enemy mines and booby traps may appear to be absent in the current area of operations. These devices are almost always present."[113]

Despite failing to encounter any large Viet Cong unit, the brigade still called 27 B-52 sorties and 1,055 tactical air sorties, against what targets can only be speculated.[114] *Malheur* had become the evil hour. At the conclusion, Matheson claimed 914 enemy killed and 295 captured weapons for the loss of 104 paratroopers and 575 wounded.[115] The losses to malaria, fever, and "other" causes were far greater. The divisional medical company handled 3,288 patients, "the highest number of casualties since arriving in Viet Nam," further draining manpower. The range of captured weapons revealed a continuous narrative of fighting since the First Indochina War. The haul included 7.5-caliber Chatelleraults, Mosin Nagants, and even a German M-42 machine gun. Resignedly, the brigade observed, "Once again the enemy appeared to return to an area within 48 hours after US troops had passed through."[116] The words might have been written by a colonial French commander.

Task Force Oregon and later the redesignated American Division then took over the fight from 1st Marines in Quang Nam and Quang Tin Provinces, in the hinterlands of Da Nang. There were several major operations – notably the marine-led *Union* and *Swift*, and the army-led *Wheeler* and *Wollowa* – and each confirmed that the great hubs of Da Nang and Chu Lai remained islands marooned in Viet Cong-dominated ground.

Union cost 5th Marines over 300 casualties. One of the more common abbreviations in the operation's after-action report was "PROB" signifying

"Probable." It was annotated after claimed "VC KIA" ("Viet Cong Killed in Action"). Typically, the marines were doubling their kill count score with this self-deluding abbreviation. Operation *Swift* – whose intent was to write down 2nd NVA Division – cost the same formation another 127 fatalities. Instances of bravery and self-sacrifice, on both sides, were common. Over the course of the operation, the 3rd Battalion's chaplain, Lieutenant Vincent R. Capodonno, was twice wounded recovering casualties, but refused medical attention. The third wounding killed him. Capodonno was the first Navy chaplain killed in action in Vietnam. He was awarded a posthumous Medal of Honor. In *Union II*, Corpsman Larry Casselman recalled an unusual truce. Tasked to retrieve bodies and body parts, he noticed, "the North Vietnamese were doing the same thing on the other side of the rice paddy and we both saw each other. They saw us, we saw them. Nobody started shooting ... they picked up their dead, we picked up ours and they disappeared."[117] Casselman's company had started with 180 marines. Just two platoons were standing by the end of the operation. *Swift* he remembered as "that horrendous operation." Rushing to give aid to a marine injured in a mortar attack,

> I reached down and I felt his helmet and his helmet was mashed in and it was all slimy with blood. It was one of those sickening moments ... I couldn't even get his helmet off. I couldn't do anything about his wound. I mean, it just landed right on his head.

During this run of actions an incident occurred which added to simmering controversy over the newly issued M-16 rifle, provoked by the fighting at Khe Sanh earlier in the year. Following a village assault by H Company, 3/5 Marines, led by Captain Gene W. Bowers, nine marines were killed, six immediately forward of enemy positions in paddy fields. In 1981, Bowers wrote: "[They] were found, with their M-16 rifles broken down in an attempt to remove cartridges jammed in the chambers." Each had "powder-burned bullet holes in their heads."[118] The Viet Cong had fallen on the defenseless men and executed them. Marine Calixto Cabrera had a similar hairy experience when first issued with the new rifle:

> Well, lo and behold we're setting into this place and are starting to take sniper fire. We start returning fire with these M-16s and it was like you shoot the round, you take out your cleaning rod, you knock out the cartridge, you chamber another one, you fire it, you take your cleaning rod – it was jamming. It was just like, "What the hell do we have here? It doesn't work. It doesn't work."[119]

The furor over the M-16 prompted a Congressional enquiry. The marine hierarchy, led by General Metzger, dismissed the complaints of marines as "hogwash" and attributed round extraction problems to dirty rifles. Investigation concluded that reason lay with the marines. The original chamber assemblies were replaced with new ones manufactured with a more durable chrome coating, and the buffer group was modified to reduce the cyclic rate of fire. Even with these modifications the rifle experienced teething problems and a final solution was not implemented until 1968. In the meantime the marines soldiered on with a weapon they did not fully trust.

The Que Son Valley and surrounding areas were revisited multiple times. The level of destruction was immense. Over September, 2/11 Marines fired off 33,869 high explosive shells in support of 5th Marines. Roughly 85 percent of the missions were unobserved, or "H&I" ("Harassment and Interdiction") missions.[120] These, by definition, were indiscriminate. By the end of the year, III MAF was being supported by an astonishing 49 artillery batteries. Yet at the conclusion of each operation, the "cleared" areas were simply re-infiltrated. The deadly *Wheeler-Wollowa* was extended and only finally closed at the end of May 1968. The Americal Division recorded 682 fatalities and made the extravagant claim of over 10,000 enemy dead.[121] Whatever the true numbers, hundreds of casualties were being suffered by both sides, without conclusive results.

By December, 1 CTZ had recorded over 3,600 fatalities (from a total force of just over 103,000). Improbably, it was claimed that 25,452 enemy soldiers had been killed and 23,363 probably killed.[122] These numbers were both exaggerated and irrelevant. The DMZ remained porous and contested. The southern provinces had not been pacified.

For 3 MARDIV, the year would end on a sour note. On November 14, the UH-1E carrying the division's commander, Major General Bruno A. Hochmuch, crashed near Phu Bai. He was replaced by Major General Rathvon McC. Tompkins. Hochmuch was the first of 11 general grade officers killed in Vietnam, the last Major General John A.B. Dillard, Jr., killed in 1970. With the changing nature of warfare and bureacratization of generalship, over 40 years would elapse before another American general was killed in action: Major General Harold Greene killed by an Afghan soldier in an insider attack in Afghanistan in 2014.

Elsewhere, in II CTZ, the fighting continued where it had left off in the previous year: on the coastal plains in northern Quang Ngai Province, and in the Kontum-Pleiku region. *Thayer II*, which was initiated in October 1966, finally closed during the 1967 Tet truce (February 8–12, during which period there were no less than 272 violations). Over the course of five months 1st Cavalry, supported by 3rd Brigade, 25th Infantry, dubiously claimed 1,757 enemy killed.[123] This was followed by *Pershing*, which revisited the Bong Son Plains. *Pershing* became an open-ended operation that continued for the next ten months of the year. No amount of killing (and being killed) made a difference to the overall balance of power in Quang Ngai, which remained a Viet Cong-dominated province. Over the course of the summer, the fighting waxed and waned. Air support was prodigious (3,534 close support missions, not counting marine air and B-52 strikes). The cavalrymen eventually claimed an enemy body count of over 5,000.[124]

In the Central Highlands, 4th Infantry Division, commanded by the cigar-chomping Major General William Peers, faced 1st and 10th PAVN Divisions. These formations had established a chain of hilltop defensive positions along the border which proved hard to find and even harder to dislodge. The division opened its account with Operation *Sam Houston* on the Cambodian border, an operation that finally closed at the beginning of April with 733 reported enemy losses. Inexperience or poor tactics led to bloody setbacks. On February 15–16, 1/12 Infantry and 2/8 Infantry both got caught up in sharp, close-range gun battles and suffered heavy casualties. The green division reported what every veteran could tell: "The most difficult tactical problem in fighting the NVA in large areas of difficult terrain is finding the enemy. That is, finding him without having tactical units shot up and pinned down by automatic weapons and snipers … at close range."[125] This was followed by the inconclusive Operation *Frances Marion* that would dribble on until October. The division experienced eight battles but none were decisive. In late April 2/8 Infantry clashed with 2nd Battalion, 95B PAVN Regiment close to the Ia Meur River. On May 18, B Company of 1/8 Infantry was caught by K4 Battalion, 32nd PAVN Regiment. Twenty-nine soldiers were killed and 31 wounded.[126] Two days later the same unit was attacked by K5 Battalion in an ambush and again suffered heavy losses. 3/12 Infantry which came to their rescue was jumped by 66th PAVN Regiment and bloodied. On July 10, south of Duc Co, 1/12 Infantry was caught in another melee with 66th PAVN Regiment. On July 23, 3/12 Infantry clashed with 32nd PAVN Regiment. As in the past, this sparring was a certain indicator that the People's Army was squaring up for a decisive confrontation, but nobody was quite sure where or when it would fall. The two adversaries finally came to blows at Dak To, at the beginning of November, three weeks into Operation *MacArthur*. If his spirit was watching, what would he have made of it all?

Dak To was a CIDG camp and air strip located in a valley two and a half miles west of a modest settlement called Tan Canh. The name meant "Hot Water," after nearby springs. The camp itself was built astride the secondary Command Route 512 that led to the Laotian border 12 miles to the west. Immediately south of the camp, across the Dak Po Ko River, was a range of forested mountains rising to over 4,000 feet. "The jungle is laced with vines and thorns," wrote Robert Barr Smith for *Vietnam* magazine, "and in it live diverse snakes, a million leeches and about half the mosquitoes in the world."[127] The most prominent feature was Hill 1338 with commanding views across the entire area. West and north of the camp the ground consisted of hilly jungle, interspersed by ravines. It was one of many such isolated camps constructed early in the war to monitor cross-border infiltration.

Tan Canh was the last major settlement on National Highway 14. The only trafficable corridor from Laos to Kontum was via Highway 14. Tan Canh therefore was the doorway to this area of the Central Highlands, and Dak To the key.

For many months, the PAVN had not so much pushed against this door as entirely bypassed it, gradually building a network of hilltop defensive positions to the southeast of Dak To that threatened to cut off the lifeline of Highway 14. The operations at the beginning and middle of the year had stumbled across this gradual eastward encroachment, but had been incapable of halting the tide. As casualties mounted, Peers fretted. In June, two battalions from 173rd Airborne Brigade were redeployed from the Saigon area to reinforce the pressed 4th Infantry (2/503rd and 4/503rd). The subsequent "Battle of Dak To" has its foundation in this decision.

173rd Airborne had been the first army unit to deploy to South Vietnam in the summer of 1965. Then commanded by the over-confident Ellis Williamson, the brigadier general had boasted he would see off the Viet Cong by Christmas (the upbeat Williamson later entitled his autobiography *Forty Years of Fun in the Army*; some of his soldiers may have disagreed). After two years of desultory fighting, mainly in III CTZ, the paratroopers were no closer to home. Dak To was the formation's 38th major operation since arriving in-country.[128] By then, the experienced troops had been replaced by fresh recruits and the casualty list had lengthened. One company commander recalled that he was assigned three brand new second lieutenants on the eve of battle, and that none of his senior NCOs were of the required grade.[129]

The veterans of *Cedar Falls* and *Junction City* were now under the command of Brigadier General John Deane when they were ordered north. As the only independent airborne brigade in the army, they felt themselves to be an elite formation. 4th Infantry were less impressed and felt that the new arrivals in Kontum were not heeding their warnings over the quality of this regular enemy. Dak To would end Deane's command in controversy. His replacement – the bespectacled Brigadier General Leo "Hank" Schweiter – was another Second World War and Korea veteran who had commanded 5th Special Forces Group. He too would be severely tested.

Ranged against the paratroopers was 1st PAVN Division, including elements from 24th, 32nd, 66th, 174th, and 320th PAVN Regiments. 40th PAVN Artillery Battalion was also confirmed in the area. Thanks to a rallier called Sergeant Vu Hong, who defected on November 2 just as 173rd Airborne was deploying to Kontum, Peers was fully cognisant of the enemy plan. Vu Hong had been serving with a reconnaissance unit in 66th Regiment. His knowledge of the battle plan was good – so good there were doubts whether his defection was all part of an elaborate deception plan.[130] The overall intent was to "annihilate a major U.S. element in order to force the enemy to deploy as many additional troops to the Central Highlands as possible," or what the communist commander dubbed "a provocative battle."

Hong's intelligence was confirmed by "Snoopy," an aircraft that detected human scent, and by Red-Haze, another aircraft that used infra-red sensors to detect camp fires through the triple-layer jungle. In total, there were perhaps 7,000 North Vietnamese soldiers converging in the Dak To area. These had been infiltrating the area over several months and had built substantial defensive positions, including well-concealed bunkers.[131] This was known as Sector B3 and was commanded by a Dien Bien Phu veteran, Major General Hoang Minh Thao, whose real name was Ta Thai An.[132] Thao was born in 1921, the son of a tailor from Hung Yen province. He was sent to a private school in Hanoi where two teachers were Vo Nguyen Giap and future prime minister Pham Van Dong. Arrested by French police for owning a book entitled *The Death of Capitalism*, he joined the communists and turned against the colonial masters. From the air, Dak To indeed looked very much like another Dien Bien Phu, except that it could be readily reinforced and the PAVN had no realistic hope of overrunning the base.

MACV's battle plan was also ropey. To interdict the infiltrations, Westmoreland ordered the building of more Fire Support Bases (FSBs), supported by a larger base on a feature called Ben Het. These would be used to launch search and destroy missions on the communist regiments. Peers' immediate commander was the newly appointed Lieutenant General William Rosson, Commander I Field Force, an officer with long experience of Indochina dating back to the 1950s. Between them, the two generals commanded 16,000 men including six ARVN battalions drawn from 42nd Infantry Regiment and an airborne outfit, as well as two brigades from 4th Infantry, and a brigade from 1st Cavalry.

Peers dubbed the campaign "the Battle of the Highlands." The logic that bound his plan was the expectation of finding and hammering 1st PAVN Division. This was largely achieved, but at a terrible cost. In the usual fashion, the ensuing "Battle of Dak To" was not one but several operations. In total, there were three: *Stilwell* "The Battle of the Slopes" (June 18–22); *Greeley* (September 18–October 14); and *MacArthur* (November 1–December 14). These became synonymous with hill features – Hills 664, 830, 823, 882, and 875 – pimples on Map Sheet 6538-2 where the 503rd battalions were bled. The other contested hilltops were Hill 724 taken by 3/8 Infantry, and the pinnacle of Hill 1338, fought over by 3/12 Infantry. In the valley itself, Dak To was only really threatened by barrages of mortar bombs, and only on two bad days (November 12 and 15). However, these succeeded in causing widespread damage. The second attack triggered numerous secondary explosions; 1,100 tons of ammunition was destroyed and the runway remained unusable for five days. The detonation of one dump left a 40-foot-deep crater and the blast wave was felt a mile away. One soldier wondered whether "Charlie had gotten hold of some nuclear weapons." Coupled with the unforgiving terrain, this setback created huge logistic challenges for the defenders.[133]

The fighting started with a disaster on the American side and ended with a bloody sacrifice on Thanksgiving Day. The same unit, 2/503rd, was involved in both these events. The first took place in the third week in June when A Company ran into 24th PAVN Regiment. In the subsequent brawl, which drew in C Company, 76 paratroopers were killed. Many of the wounded were executed by a shot in the back of the head.

The second took place on Hill 875, a place of glory, or perhaps madness. By the middle of November, 2/503rd was an understrength unit with just 290 paratroopers. One soldier joked with a reporter that there was no longer a problem with spares in the battalion. Hill 875 was held by 174th PAVN Regiment, dug in behind three trench lines. No attempt was made to recce the enemy position, and indeed there was no firm intelligence on who might be at the top of the hill and in what strength. Instead, there was a grossly misplaced assumption that some preparatory fires and a bit of shoving would yield the position. C and D Companies duly marched up the northern slope, in column, and were decimated. Seventy-one paratroopers were killed and A Company survivors were lucky not to be massacred by an outflanking PAVN unit. Hill 875 was eventually captured, following reinforcement by 4/503rd and 1/12th Infantry, but by then the communist soldiers had slipped away from the hill.

The fighting was close range and vicious. In some places the bamboo was "5 to 8 inches thick." Soldiers doubted their M-16 rounds were penetrating the foliage. Hilltops were blasted clean by high explosives, and hillsides were razed with napalm. Soldiers used their helmets or discarded ammunition boxes to dig shelters from the metal storm. After one skirmish, six American bodies were found on one side of a log, and four dead North Vietnamese were found on the other side. Anyone who stood up risked a bullet between the eyes. One soldier recalled decapitating a communist soldier by firing an M79 grenade at point-blank range into his face. Another remembered finding his buddy with both feet facing the wrong way. He was still alive but in agony. Grenade exchanges across bomb craters became commonplace. The wounded could not be extracted and continued to be executed by roaming North Vietnamese patrols. In one of the worst friendly fire incidents of the war, a Sky Raider dropped a bomb at dusk that killed 42 paratroopers at a company aid post at the foot of Hill 875. This attack killed the unit commander and spread body parts across a wide radius. "Panic and despair spread like wildfire," recalled one survivor.[134] There were no tactics beyond frontal assault, for which the battalions paid dearly. One veteran later averred that it all amounted to "just plain incompetence."[135]

The killed-in-action count told its own story: November 6 (17), November 11 (20), November 12 (11), November 13 (25), November 18 (15), November 19 (44), and November 20 (65). For 2/503rd the total casualties from November 19 to 22 alone were 86 KIA and 130 WIA. A and C Companies ceased to exist as effective fighting units. Overall, the paratroopers lost 191 killed, 642 wounded, and 17 missing in action. One quarter of the 3,200-strong airborne brigade was written off – it was an unmitigated disaster. The rifle companies suffered worst with over 50 percent losses. Forty helicopters were damaged or destroyed, along with two C-130 transports parked at Dak To (Peers happened to be airborne when the aircraft were hit and witnessed their conflagration). The enemy kill count was 715, but a suspiciously low nine prisoners were captured.[136] This gross number was raised to 1,227, then 1,644, including ARVN claims.[137] In one notorious episode involving 1/503rd, the commanding officer ordered a recount of the enemy dead because it was insufficiently high. The initially reported 80 enemy KIA was duly bumped up to a more impressive 175 dead. In another, paratroopers found just 15 dead North Vietnamese. By the time the number was recorded in 173rd Airborne's after-action report, the number had multiplied to 513 dead.

The big clashes grabbed the headlines, but Dak To had been a continuous series of small-unit engagements in close terrain in which neither side was able to achieve a decisive outcome, and both suffered inevitable attrition. This was not a style of warfare in which the Americans had the advantage. The soldiers were too noisy and significantly weighed down. The light-footed PAVN could always take the option of disappearing further into the hills, which they did when put under sufficient pressure. In the end, firepower had been the deciding factor. There were 804 close air support sorties, delivering 981 tons of high explosives. B-52s flew 135 sorties and undertook the saturation bombing of 30 square miles of jungle, delivering a further 3,348 tons of bombs.[138] Artillery units fired off an overwhelming 46,427 shells into the hills. No wonder 1st PAVN Division scooted back across the border.

Had there been any point to capturing "that goddamn hill"? If anyone had asked the surviving paratroopers, the answer would have been predictable and profanely expressed, but nobody did. Westmoreland hailed Dak To as the beginning of "a great defeat of the enemy" (Hoang Minh Thao naturally also described it as "the most effective campaign against the US Army up to that time").[139] The editorial of the *Washington Post*, in a rare break for Johnson who was more used to being the butt of criticism from this broadsheet, celebrated:

> It can no longer be argued that we do not have a plan and a timetable and a grand strategy ... . The program laid out by General Westmoreland last week is nearly overpowering in the precision of its promises and the almost total absence of qualifications or doubt. The strategy, quite simply, is to "weaken the enemy." ... It points persuasively to a time when the war will wither away.[140]

But then, Hanoi also claimed the same.

In a secret presentation to MACV commanders delivered on December 3, Peers was more matter of fact. "We had to blast them out," he conceded. The truth was that both adversaries withdrew to refit and the twisted, charred stump of Hill 875 was returned to nature on December 1. It was never revisited by either side.

By the height of the summer, MACV was winning its battles. This seemed incontrovertible. But was it winning its war? In a strategy of attrition warfare, answering this question necessarily implied assessing how many enemy units were out there, how many were being taken off the battlefield, and how many reinforcements were being added to the battlefield. This required an accurate assessment of the enemy order of battle. Over the summer and fall of 1967, determination of the enemy order of battle provoked one of the great, acrimonious, and ultimately unresolved debates of the war. It only added gall that this debate coincided with another quite different war in the Middle East. Over six days in June, Israel stunningly demonstrated how to wage and win a military conflict. How far removed was this lightning war from the dour killing match being waged by MACV.

There was no single estimate because there was no single, overarching intelligence agency. Rather, there was a competition of agencies, each using different criteria and jealously defending different methodologies. The Defense

Intelligence Agency (DIA) was responsible for producing the Department of Defense (DOD) assessment, but MACV and J2 at PACOM also produced their own independent estimates. Several civilian intelligence agencies added to the debate including the CIA, the National Security Agency (NSA), and the State Department's Bureau of Intelligence and Research (INR).[141] The Federal Office of National Estimates played a role as central, interagency arbiter but enjoyed no executive powers over the various intelligence staffs. The strength of this system was that it fostered independent examination (the "competitive analysis" philosophy favored in the United States). The weakness was that it was capable of generating bitter dissent, especially if the intelligence became politicized. The lack of a single, agreed set of numbers was a well-known problem, so much so that a conference was held in Honolulu from February 6 to 11, attended by all the intelligence agencies. In an endorsement of Westmoreland's Assistant Chief of Staff of Intelligence, Brigadier General Joe McChristian, it was agreed that the total enemy force would be counted as the sum of the combat units, administrative and support units, irregular units, and political cadres.[142] This should have settled the debate, but for the matter of personalities.

The debate was complicated by several actors appealing to different audiences. Johnson needed to demonstrate to a skeptical American electorate that Hanoi was weakening, not strengthening. Westmoreland also needed to prove that the North Vietnamese and Viet Cong were being worn down faster than they could reinforce – otherwise, what was the point of his attrition strategy that was beginning to add American corpses like matchwood to the body count? On April 28, 1967, he had addressed a Joint Session of Congress in which he delivered a politicized and positive assessment of the war.[143] This address received a long ovation, and Westmoreland cherished it as one of his proudest moments. But the press heard humbug and was soon unpicking the contradictions in his promise that a "cross-over point" may have been reached. Westmoreland compounded this false narrative with a tendency to judge that "the people in Washington" were not sophisticated enough to digest the numbers. This encouraged him (and his staffs at the Operations Analysis Branch in Saigon), to select and nuance statistics, and as damagingly to sin by omission. He sat his own government as well as the press at this table of unsophisticated diners.

The problem was that these two conjoined partners – Johnson and Westmoreland – were in violent disagreement with virtually every other actor, including McNamara at Defense and McChristian in Saigon. Inevitably, middle-ranking officials were sucked into this battle of titans, and they were less circumspect or political. Some were downright indignant and spoke out: Sam Adams, a rigorously honest CIA analyst; a George MacArthur, who claimed that his high estimates were deliberately cut back by superiors in the MACV intelligence chain; Colonel Gains Hawkins, who reportedly quoted low figures against his better judgment to conform with MACV's measurements of progress, a charge he later denied; a dissenting George Hamscher, also serving in Army intelligence; and Colonel Everette Parkins, who was allegedly sacked for disagreeing with Westmoreland. The popular and able McChristian also departed in the summer under a cloud. The coda would be played out in an unseemly three-year courtroom battle and $120 million lawsuit against *CBS News*, following the 1982 broadcast of "The Uncounted Enemy," a program that insinuated dishonesty in Westmoreland's conduct.

Counting "the enemy" was not straightforward for a number of methodological and technical reasons. Even if all the agencies had been in broad agreement, there would have been disparities. At the heart of the dispute lay the count of the Viet Cong Self-Defense Forces. These were villagers that provided support to the fighters, but did not necessarily fight. An old woman sewing uniforms counted as a member of the Viet Cong Self-Defense Force, as did a child sharpening panji sticks. Nobody knew with any certainty the strength of these village support networks, and in this respect it was a bogus debate. Other than providing a rough index of rural support for the guerrillas, the numbers did not matter anyway. The war was going to be won or lost by the regular forces. As early as 1964, Westmoreland had voiced to a pack of correspondents that he could not foresee the Viet Cong defeating the ARVN.[144] In this assessment, he had always been correct.

The matter came to a head on May 18 when McChristian – soon to return home – presented Westmoreland with the latest enemy force estimates. This was the fruit of several weeks' work by the Combined Intelligence Center in MICV ("Military Intelligence Command Vietnam"). There was no better set of numbers. According to the revised numbers there were an estimated 60,750 Viet Cong, 101,150 Self-Defense Forces, and 23,400 "secret" Self-Defense Forces. In total, this implied 185,300 irregular forces. Political cadre numbers were also revised upwards from 40,000 to 88,000.[145]

Westmoreland was appalled. In effect, his intelligence chief was telling him that MACV had been routinely underestimating the enemy strength by as many as 120,000 personnel. As Westmoreland had only just returned from his public relations trip to the United States, the political implications of these numbers did not escape him. He refused to sign off the study and forbade McChristian from passing on the findings to PACOM, or the JCS.

Westmoreland did not so much cook the books as re-order the menu. The study was sent back to the MICV for further revision. Westmoreland was not alone in his fears that a substantial and retrospective hike of enemy numbers would be seized upon by the press and be misunderstood in Washington, with disastrous public relations consequences. It was obvious to everyone involved in the numbers game that wild swings in enemy force estimates were unhelpful and as likely to mislead as illuminate. Following a month of deliberations, during which period the numbers leaked out anyway, a decision was taken to republish the study. In this second publication, Self-Defense Forces and political cadres were acknowledged but not counted as part of the overall enemy total. This ran against the February Honolulu agreements, but made less alarmist reading.

Here again the matter may have rested, except that in early June, Johnson tasked CIA Director Richard Helms to coordinate the promulgation of a fresh estimate of communist forces in South Vietnam – Special National Intelligence Estimate (SNIE) 14.3-67 – using the offices of the Board of National Estimates. This body was dominated by the CIA, whose estimates were largely based on the work of a now angry Sam Adams. When the various agencies met on June 23 there were fireworks. Adams insisted on a high figure of half a million, and the DIA, backing MACV, would not shift from its low estimate of 300,000. The NSA and State Department both defended the CIA position. Faced with an impasse, the meeting broke up without resolution.

At this stage, two characters entered the story who contributed in no small measure to Westmoreland's reputation as a dishonest general. The first was Major General Phillip Davidson, Chief of Intelligence at US Army Pacific, who took over from McChristian. The second was his enforcer, Colonel Daniel Graham. Both men were dismissive of McChristian and set about undoing his legacy in unpleasant, bullying, and on occasions dishonest ways. Their behavior and attitudes appalled the long-serving J2 staffs who felt strong loyalty towards their old boss. If analysts refused to revise enemy numbers downwards, the Head of MICV's Order of Battle Branch, Colonel Gains Hawkins, arbitrarily took it upon himself to make the changes. He later conceded that although he never received a direct order to do so, he did feel under strong pressure to generate more optimistic assessments. This was intelligence work at its base worst and morale in J2 collapsed.

The agencies met again in August, and once again the mood turned sour. MACV would not budge from its politically acceptable estimate – an estimate explicitly offered to avoid provoking negative headlines in the media.[146] PACOM and the DIA loyally supported MACV's stance, at least at senior officer level. Mid-ranking officers privately conceded to CIA and State Department officials that the numbers were being deliberately downplayed against the assessments of Saigon's own analysts. In the words of Colonel George Hamscher, serving at PACOM: "It progressed from unprofessional to wrongful; and it amounted to falsification of intelligence."[147] Westmoreland never ordered or even explicitly encouraged this dishonest behavior, but all the MACV participants strongly felt they were defending the implicit wishes of their commander. Faced with this intransigence, the media was conveniently furnished with a CIA leak quoting the higher numbers. A wrong-footed MACV reacted immediately by warning the White House that endorsement of the CIA estimate would constitute a public relations disaster. Unable to reconcile the quarrelsome parties, the meeting concluded with an agreement to reconvene in Saigon the following month.

By the time the agencies met again on September 9, insults were being openly traded. The sticking point remained the Self-Defense Forces and secret Self-Defense Forces. MACV refused to count these within the aggregate enemy force estimate because these elements would automatically add 120,000 men to the total.

In the end, it fell to the CIA's George Carver to make the necessary compromises – and what a fudge it was. SNIE 14.3-67 quoted the low number of 223,000–248,000 but counseled that the totality of elements – regular, irregular, political, and Self-Defense Forces – better represented the "effectiveness" of enemy forces. In a contradictory statement, the estimate separately added that summing all the components of enemy force would, however, be "misleading." MACV conceded that Hanoi could continue on the present path of attrition "for at least another year," but the CIA and State Department gave way on the reported decline in Viet Cong strength. The weasel wording pleased no one, least of all the CIA men who felt their professional integrity had been compromised to mollify MACV.

SNIE 14.3-67 was finally published on November 17, following seven wearying months of acrimony. Even at the eleventh hour, the two irreconcilable sides attempted to out-maneuver each other with the wording of the accompanying press statement. Irritated by these shenanigans, the CIA quit the stage and refused to take part in the public presentation of the document. It fell to a Colonel Elmer Martin to condemn the whole shoddy business:

> I came to believe that General Westmoreland had authorized his MACV intelligence staff to intentionally falsify intelligence information about enemy strength … to give the erroneous impression that we were winning the war. I viewed this as a conscious effort or conspiracy on MACV's part to distort crucial intelligence on the enemy we faced in Vietnam.[148]

The manifest irony was that SNIE 14.3-67 had become a quite irrelevant document. If there was rejoicing at MACV, it would be short-lived. Saigon was now less than two months away from being visited by the typhoon of the Tet Offensive. Counting the dead, not the living, would be the order of the day.

Compared to the newsworthy dramas being played out on the DMZ or the Central Highlands, the Delta seemed a flat, oppressive backwater of uninspiring and unglamorous operations. Holding over a third of the country's population and producing half of its agricultural produce, it was inevitable the war would move to the Delta. But few journalists were keen to follow the soldiers into this triangle of mud and mosquitoes. There was no underpinning narrative because the Viet Cong, it seemed, were everywhere and nowhere.

In reality, there were two deltas, created by tributaries of the Mekong ("Seven Dragons") river. The larger was formed by the Tieng and a second by the Hau, both entering South Vietnam across the lawless and remote Cambodian border. This geographical pedantry would have passed by the average soldier on patrol. This was an area of nine million acres of half-submerged paddy fields; a steaming, marshy, impossible terrain for vehicles, and no kinder to soldiers on foot. During the wet season – May to October – much of the Delta was inundated and what roads existed impassable. Tidal fluctuations could range up to about four yards.

Here, government statistics were meaningless. Everyone knew the guerrillas effectively controlled this vast region, from the inaccessible border area of "Three Mountains" through the Plain of Reeds and south to the U Minh Forest and Ca Mau peninsula. ARVN and later American units leased tracts for the duration of operations, but then handed the land back to its rightful owners. The US Corps of Engineers rose to the seemingly impossible challenge of erecting anything substantial on this water world by building a brigade base, Camp Dong Tam ("United Hearts and Minds"), near My Tho. This was where a French SAS battalion had landed in October 1945, the first town to be re-invested by Leclerc's expeditionary force.[149] A second, Camp Bearcat, was built at Vung Tau on the coast, but the fresh and seawater tides claimed everything else. So unappealing were the riverine operations, they were the first restored to the South Vietnamese, with the US force handing over to a Vietnamese Navy Amphibious Task Force 211 in August 1969.[150]

This was where 9th Infantry Division "Old Reliables" deployed, under Major General George Eckhardt, an officer with a prominent chin and sharp mind, who would serve in Vietnam over four years, concluding his wartime career as a Special Assistant to the MACV Deputy Commander.[151] His division would suffer 2,604 fatalities over the same period, with the province breakdown revealing where the heaviest fighting took place: Long An in the north (761), Dinh Toung (654), and Kien Hoa (333).[152] He counted among his soldiers a future Defense Secretary Chuck Hagel, then a 21-year-old sergeant. Patrolling the rivers was future Secretary of State John Kerry, a naval lieutenant. The division proudly described itself as Hitler's nemesis, but over the course of its service in the Delta it would become the nemesis of countless innocent Vietnamese.

Policing the 4,000 miles of waterways required a riverine force. MACV had originally founded a Mekong Delta Afloat Force, a successor to the French Dinassaut (*Division d'Infanterie Navale d'Assaut*). This developed into the Mobile Riverine Force (MRF), which in the usual way provoked internecine squabbles over command and control.

This "brown water navy," in many ways, was a matched cultural facsimile to the land forces. Faced with the enigma of war, America turned to technology and especially to its unnatural spawn, firepower. Standard river patrol boats were too vulnerable in the treacherous Delta, so a flotilla of vessels was invented, or re-invented, to cope with the unseen enemy in the mangrove forests.

Civil War ironclads provided the inspiration for the "Monitors" (the name originated from the earlier French gunboats built at the Saigon Arsenal). These waddling monsters displaced 169,000 pounds, and were armed with machine guns, 40mm cannon, grenade launchers, and 81mm mortars. A small team of engineers and draftsmen was given just four months to design and build the vessels. Working 60-hour weeks, they completed the job in three.[153] Later, 105mm guns were added to the bows of converted barges, "which got Charlie's attention in a big way."[154] Troops were transported to their objectives in converted world war landing craft, the "Tangos," or Armored Troop Carriers (ATCs). The hovercraft also made its war debut with 39th Cavalry Platoon (Air Cushion Vehicle).[155] Soldiers riding these platforms risked losing kit in the lift fans intakes. In November 1968, an entire soldier vanished into a lift fan, an experience he did not survive. Two armed hydrofoils were also deployed, propelled by powerful Rolls Royce gas turbine engines, but the experiment proved a disappointment.

Other landing craft were converted into flamethrower boats, or "Zippos." It was said you could identify a sailor working the Zippos because all the hairs on his forearms were burned away. The first successful operational launch of the scalding napalm mix was recorded on October 4, 1967. A sailor serving on Zippo 4 fondly remembered the "Sunday specials": "We'd get to an area just after dawn and hold Reveille on 'Charlie' by way of the Zippo Boat. We found this a pretty good way to start a fight."[156] In total, 23 different classes of river boats saw service with Navy Task Force 117 and the coastal divisions, the majority based at Camp Dong Tam, along with 2nd Brigade, 9th Infantry under Colonel William B. Fulton.[157] For the sailors engaged in the risky business of Delta operations, there was always "a healthy regard for the danger involved and an appreciation of the VC will to fight and of his cleverness."[158] As one remarked, "One thing we learned quickly was that someone was definitely trying to kill us."[159]

With the remainder of the division based at Camp Bearcat, 2nd Brigade and the MRF officially began operations on June 1, 1967.[160] This was the *Coronado* series which ran all the way to July of the following year. Overall, there were 11 operations and none was decisive. The area was too big, the terrain too challenging, and the enemy too elusive. From a soldier's perspective the missions could seem pointless and deliberately mounted to provoke a reaction. Rifleman Tom Hain, serving in Bravo Company 4/47th Infantry, observed,

> If anything did happen there were three ways of dealing with it; (1) Shoot back and keep going, (2) Shoot back until the incoming fire stopped, or (3) Shoot back and unload the troops to go after them. More often than not it would be choice #3.[161]

When they were not engaged in fighting the near-invisible Viet Cong, the river patrols could find themselves fending off locals trying to sell goods from sampans on the river banks. The 21-year-old Hain recalled the locals had a way of tracking down the patrols, even when they moved camps. The most valued commodity on sale was a "cold '33'," which Hain would guzzle even if, or perhaps because, the alcohol dulled the senses. Most of the time, patrolling simply involved monotonous trudging in muddy fields, weighed down by the shoulder-sapping "basic load." This might include three days' worth of rations, four water bottles, a radio, and 25 pounds of weapons and ammunition. A packet of cigarettes per day was normal, with an extra packet in reserve. Delta soldiers were instantly recognizable because they learned to stow their precious cigarettes under their helmet bands, the only place likely to remain dry if they had to dive into the flooded fields.

One of the most unpleasant places to fight, "a special kind of hell," was the so-called Rung Sat Special Zone. With masochistic candor, the *Army Times* described it in these words:

> Dark at night, malodorous, eerie and silent, covered with a crusty mud that may give way in any instant to plunge the unwary into a fetid pool of muck, the Rung Sat Special Zone spreads over 400 square miles in South Vietnam between Saigon and the South China Sea … Neither land nor sea, the Rung Sat is a tangled maze of mangroves dotted with bamboo thickets that always seem to be dying, never growing. The swamp is interlaced with sluggish salt rivers that appear incapable of supporting life … The smell of decay permeates the humid stale air. It is an odor the soldiers never quite become accustomed to. It is putrid, acrid, primeval.[162]

During the day the soldiers had to fight off "galaxies of mosquitoes" and at night they were tormented by giant red ants. The leeches were "huge" and unavoidable. The intertwined vegetation reduced visibility to yards, and the sludge slowed platoons to a slow crawl. Everyone suffered from immersion foot after 48 hours. The foot disease incident rate soared to 35 percent after five days in the field.[163] Wounds quickly turned septic. It was monotonous hot work and contact with the enemy was rarely made. "I hate it, all that mud," opined a Specialist Charles Rock to *Army Times*, probably speaking for every soldier.

Between these extended periods of monotony, fighting on the Mekong Delta could be a highly treacherous business. On June 19, A Company, 4/47th Infantry, a sub-unit operating as part of 2nd Brigade's "River Raiders," set off on a mission in the eastern sector of Long An Province. The "Spearheaders" were commanded by Lieutenant Colonel Guy Tutwiler, an officer keen to get to grips with the hitherto unseen enemy. "For nearly two months," the divisional newspaper reported, "the men of 4th Battalion, 47th Infantry had trudged the oozing tidal lowlands of the Rung Sat Special Zone without significant contact with the enemy."[164] All the while they continued to take casualties and the frustration mounted.

On this day, the battalion was ferried to its target area – a bend on the Rach Gia River known as "Snoopy's Nose." The soldiers traveled on Task Force 117 "Tangos," the small flotilla preceded by Monitors. The mission was intended as a routine search and destroy operation. By the time it concluded the tide had risen and fallen three times, and with it a horrendous butcher's bill.[165] The operation had been conceived by Colonel William Fulton, the 2nd Brigade commander, and Captain Wade Wells, commander of River Assault Flotilla One. They baptized it *Concordia*, and it was in fact the first mounted in the area by 9th Division. A more inappropriate name could hardly have been chosen. The *Los Angeles Times* carried the shocking news one week later – "Vietcong Destroy 134-Man U.S. Unit" – allowing sufficient time for the Defense Department to inform families of the deceased before the news broke.

Unbeknown to the American force, A Company had stumbled into the veteran 5th Nha Be Battalion, which had relocated to Can Giuoc District, 40 miles south of Saigon, precisely because this inland peninsula of dense mangroves was impenetrable to foot patrols and a potential death trap to intruders. The local ARVN unit, 46th Regiment, 25th Division, avoided it altogether, confirming its status as a Viet Cong sanctuary.[166]

The intruding riverine force was hardly stealthy; *Time* magazine lyrically described the Monitors as gunboats that "slither along like water moccasins," but they were more properly clanking, riverine cruisers, billowing diesel fumes, each noisy boat surmounted by a cluster of antennae, and typically a prominent, flapping Stars and Stripes.[167] They practically invited being shot at.

A total of five companies were landed one and a half miles south of a village called Ap Bac in a cacophony of preparatory fires laid on by the Monitors, thereby alerting the Viet Cong of the presence of the force. Fanning out, the companies began to sweep the area in cloying mud that was waist deep in some fields. "We might as well be whistling *Dixie*," joked a bored aerial observer, watching the ant-like lines of soldiers undertaking what seemed another futile clearance of empty paddies.[168]

At just after 11.50am, Captain Robert Reeves' A Company stumbled into a carefully laid L-shaped ambush, near a feature called the Rach Nui Canal. Sergeant Michael Lethcoe spotted a blue wire that led to a large, improvised claymore mine. Someone shouted "hit the dirt" just as the mine detonated.[169] An instant later, the Viet Cong, who had waited until the soldiers were within 50 yards of their concealed bunkers, opened up in a devastating fusillade. Private First Class Frederick Haag, one of the men caught in the volley, helplessly remembered, "We had nowhere to go." Like the rest of his comrades, he dived into the brackish paddy, only keeping his head above water, and waited to be picked off.

As the tide rose later in the day, the wounded drowned, and survivors found themselves up to their necks in water. Medic Michael Snider wrote, "Our men in the middle of the rice paddies didn't have a chance and 75 percent of Alpha Company was wiped out in the first 5 minutes of the battle." He was hit in the back by an AK-47 but his flak jacket deflected the bullet.[170] Tutwiler's after-action report recorded somewhat more prosaically, "I received a call from the commander officer of Alpha 4/47 saying that he was receiving heavy fire from the vicinity of Objective 18 and that he had received a number of casualties from the initial fire. He indicated that he had lost contact with his platoons." Only later was Tutwiler apprised of the reason for the collapse of control; the shaken Reeves "estimated his casualties at 75% to 80%."

What followed was a desperate action to save A Company from annihilation. The Monitors, led by Commander Chuck Horowitz, broke all the rules and risked boats to provide close-in support fire. The charismatic task force chaplain, Raymond Johnson, leaped into the river to recover wounded soldiers, and was himself wounded in both legs. Struggling on, he was then injured again by an explosion that "felt like the wallop of a baseball bat."[171] A piece of shrapnel, he later discovered, had embedded itself in a New Testament he carried under his flak jacket. He was joined in the rescue attempt by an engineman and boatswain. A total of 15 sailors would be wounded, including Horowitz, who repeatedly exposed himself to enemy fire. An artillery battery entered the contest lobbing over 2,000 shells, but rounds fell short. Signaler Sonny Castellano later recorded, "Every time a shell went off we were showered with shrapnel."

Helicopter gunships were then scrambled to the scene. "My God," uttered one of the pilots, Captain Sam Slaughter, as he circled the stricken company. "The troops are in awful trouble." He would continue to fly his bullet-holed machine for the next two days and one night, barely shutting down during the entire period, even when refueling and re-arming.[172] Medevac helicopters struggled to land amidst the cross-fires, and four were shot down, one rolling spectacularly in mid-air. Just one succeeded in making the hazardous transaction of casualties.

In the meantime, B Company fought its way to the north of the trapped men followed by C Company, 3/47th Infantry. These reinforcements were unfortunately dropped on the wrong side of a deep tributary, which they only finally crossed after the soldiers commandeered two sampans. However, the Viet Cong was "so heavily entrenched they had everyone pinned down," and the additional companies were unable to make any headway.[173] When nightfall arrived, A Company was still entrapped. Following normal procedures, the wounded Horowitz ordered his boats to retire from the area to avoid ambush, provoking a furious response from Fulton. Whether or not the gunboats would have made any difference, the guerrillas used the cover of darkness to elude the closing circle of American troops.

A Company had suffered 21 killed and 53 wounded: effectively, the company had been wiped out. The total American casualty toll was 48 killed and 143 wounded.[174] A subsequent sweep discovered 98 corpses, and a later captured document suggested that as many as 170 guerrillas may have been "lost." As always, the weapon haul was trivial; just six weapons were found, and 13 bunkers were uncovered.[175] This raised suspicions that some of the "enemy" dead may have been civilians – indeed, moments before the ambush was sprung, A Company was denied an artillery fire request because of the presence of farmers in the area. Subsequent claims that 5th Nha Be Battalion was removed from the enemy order of battle proved empty.

The real consequence of the battle of Rach Nui Canal was a hardening of attitudes in the blooded 47th Regiment. One veteran later wrote, "In the days and patrols following that battle of June 19th, I did some dark things that I am not proud of, as I was not in my right frame of mind."[176] The "Old Reliables," like too many other formations deployed to Vietnam, became rotten, and later, murderous. By the time this division was withdrawn from Vietnam in 1972, it had gained the unhealthy reputation of being the most obsessed with body counts, and the formation manifesting the lowest ratio of captured weapons to enemy killed.

Most notoriously, over the course of Operation *Speedy Express* (December 1968–May 1969), 9th Division claimed to kill 10,899 guerrillas for 267 own losses, and only retrieved 748 weapons, a quite unbelievable proposition. These outrageous claims piqued the suspicions of *Newsweek*'s Saigon Bureau Chief, Kevin Buckley, whose investigations pointed to the repugnant truth that the division – now under the command of the cold-hearted Major General Julian Ewell "butcher of the Delta"– was killing Vietnamese civilians indiscriminately. An anonymous sergeant wrote a confidential letter to Westmoreland claiming the division – Westmoreland's old division from the Second World War where he commanded 60th Infantry – was committing a My Lai massacre every month of the year.[177] Westmoreland would later profess every allegation of atrocities was investigated, an utterly feeble defense. Creighton Abrams went as far as describing the "Old Reliables" as magnificent.[178] But 9th Division's unhinged behavior, encouraged by its commander, was widely known at the highest levels. Not a single individual was prosecuted.

There was an inland correspondence to the Delta labyrinth and it was in Cu Chi. This territory mostly fell within Frederick Weyand's 25th Infantry's area of responsibility, a division that was handed the impossible task of securing a much larger region stretching from the Parrot's Beak on the Cambodian border, across the spans of War Zones C and D, and including the Iron Triangle, scene of Operation *Cedar Falls*. In total, the division was responsible for the 11 provinces surrounding Saigon. Cu Chi was just 30 miles from the capital; in this sense it was an open back door that could not be ignored.

Nowhere was Weyand's enemy more entrenched than in the area of Cu Chi, not so much terrain, in military parlance, as an entire subterranean world. This was an extremely fertile tract of land, a garden paradise of "mangoustine, *chom chom*, everything," which is why the French appropriated the lands, turning the farmers into indentured serfs and building vast commercial plantations.[179] The US Army had experienced tunnel warfare during the Pacific War, and two major operations had already been mounted to destroy the Cu Chi tunnel networks (*Crimp* in January 1966, and *Cedar Falls*, January–February 1967), but neither was successful.

The problem simply was the scale. Today, a claimed 75-mile complex of tunnels survives as a national monument and tourist attraction. During the war, the full extent of the tunnels may well have doubled this distance, covering an area of several hundred square miles. This encompassed many of the place names that would become wearily familiar to American soldiers serving in III CTZ: Boi Loi Woods, Ho Bo Woods, Fil Hol, and the Michelin rubber plantations. Despite the obsession with the latter, it appears the nucleus of the tunnel system was located in the horseshoe formed by the Saigon River navigating around Ho Bo Woods further to the north. It then extended for a distance of about 25 miles southeast to Fil Hol.

There are no accurate maps of the network so it is difficult to separate facts from the mythology. A majority of the "network" may have been no more than bolt holes, unconnected, and serving as bomb shelters for hamlets. Larger complexes were four storys deep and included dormitories, field hospitals, and headquarters. Scarce medicines were pilfered from US bases riddled with Viet Cong sympathizers, or obtained by bribing corrupt local officials. Blood transfusions were performed with bicycle pumps and plastic bottles. Herbal remedies proliferated and amputations were performed with plumber's tools. At least one baby was born underground, to the singer and part-time guerrilla Dang Thi Lanh, in the middle of an air strike.[180]

To what extent the tunnels were used to shift troops unseen from one part of the battlefield to another, as was claimed, is difficult to determine. Crawling underground laden with equipment in a narrow tunnel, even for a few hundred yards, is exhausting. Living underground for any length of time was very unhealthy and there was a high incidence of illness amongst the tunnel dwellers. One peasant woman recalled living for two weeks underground, but this seemed the exception.[181] Long exposures underground left the villagers partially blind and unable to stand when they emerged to the surface. The notion that Viet Cong battalions effectively marched underground over great distances seems highly implausible, especially as there was no need to. Hau Nghia and Binh Duong Provinces, where the majority of the tunnels were located, largely belonged to the guerrillas. Security operations were transient storms. Mostly the tunnels seemed to be used to evade the sweeps and avoid bombs (unsuccessfully in some areas hit by B-52 strikes that were sufficiently powerful to expose or collapse tunnels). Cu Chi was turned into a blasted, desolate wasteland, and the tunnels then became the only place where families could live in ancestral lands they were unwilling to abandon. Families starved or ate roots, chewed lemon grass or caught frogs, but adamantly refused to surrender the soil. Discarded American C-Rations were also eaten, tinned foods exercising a particular fascination with Vietnamese peasants who had never tasted such exotica.

What made the tunnels possible was a soil similar to laterite clay that was easy to dig in the monsoon season, and which dried into a hard and stable consistency in the dry season. The roots of bamboo trees, abundant in the area, served to strengthen the roofs of the tunnels. What began as a ruse to avoid French or Japanese troops during the war became an industrial, collective effort. There were perhaps 20 miles of tunnels at the end of 1945.

Over the next 20 years, families dug their own shelters, joining these with those of neighbors, all linked by a spine of "connector tunnels" that ran between hamlets.

The back-breaking work was remarkably recorded in an album of images taken by the National Liberation Front photographer Duong Thanh Phong. They showed half-naked peasants with hoes and wicker baskets, carving out their underground worlds with requisite, revolutionary smiles. Men and women shared the labor. In the beginning, before the bombing destroyed the forests, timbers were used to support walls and ceilings. A large room might measure 15 foot across and have a six-foot ceiling, but most were cramped, insalubrious spaces. Asphyxiation was a real possibility, despite the air vents, and on some occasions tunnel dwellers had to lie flat on their stomachs to breathe the only available oxygen. Whether or not the tunnels served great military purpose they bore testament to an astonishing well of local resistance, and they sufficiently aggrieved a MACV that elevated their existence to mortal threat.

The extent of the tunneling was first explored by soldiers from 1st Battalion, Royal Australian Regiment on Operation *Crimp*, some of whom paid for their curiosity with their lives. The tactical problem was then passed to 2nd Brigade, 25th Infantry, and individually to 1st Battalion, 5th Regiment whose motto was "I'll try, Sir." When the unit first deployed to Cu Chi it had to rely on 20-year-old French maps. By the time it withdrew, it had suffered 175 fatalities. The heaviest fighting took place in the winter and spring of the previous year when the brigade was engaged in 66 days of continuous operations to establish what would become known as Cu Chi Base Camp. With self-defeating historical ignorance, 2nd Brigade then set about attempting to pacify a region which had implacably resisted foreign soldiers for a generation, and which had no truck with the corrupt Saigon government. "My father and my sister died under the French," one farmer impassively explained. "When the Americans came and started bombing they killed my wife, my children, my relatives, and my countrymen."[182] The Americans, another observed bitterly, "destroyed everything."

Defeating a tunneling enemy spurred technological solutions: lachrymose gas, improvised oxyacetylene bombs, ammunition boxes filled with napalm and primed with white phosphorus grenades, and explosive charges designed to collapse walls. But mostly, it was about nerve. Burying your adversary alive was not as rewarding as gathering intelligence, and prisoners if possible. This task fell to the "tunnel rats," soldiers small enough and plucky enough to venture into the tunnels. At first, only volunteers were accepted. The preferred weapon was a pistol, but it was found that the standard issue .45 Colt deafened and some resorted to buying their own handguns. As well as facing chance encounters with the enemy, tunnel rats had to hazard booby traps and a range of verminous or poisonous animals, including snakes and spiders. The bamboo viper and banded Krait were especially feared because of the strength of their venom. On occasions, "chambers were crawling with a thick black mass of tiny spiders the size of a thumb nail, giving the illusion that the walls were moving."[183] Roosting bats were another unwelcome denizen of the holes. All this served to elevate the aura of the tunnel rats and their underground war in Cu Chi.

While undeniably very real to the soldiers who ventured underground, this war was completely marginal to the wider campaign over ground. The intelligence coups, although spectacular, were also rare. Mostly, soldiers found bunkers which they blasted with automatic fire or hand grenades, not elaborate tunnel systems. Often, the villagers could hear the American soldiers above them, and waited until the unit had left the area. There are no reliable numbers for how many Viet Cong were killed in the tunnels, or even how many used the tunnels. Certainly hundreds and probably thousands of civilians perished. North Vietnamese propaganda nurtured a national myth that has been reciprocated by Western veterans. Both have been leveraged by the tourism industry. In this competition of revolutionary heroism versus gritty tunnel rat the civilian has been entirely obliterated. It is not unlikely that this perfectly reflects the truth of the tunnels; that they mostly served as the graves of frightened peasants fleeing army operations or aerial bombardments, and not as Satanic chambers of communist fighters.

American soldiers were now fighting and dying in tunnels and in mangrove swamps, in the forests of the Central Highlands, and on the shell-blasted DMZ – but was this bringing South Vietnam any closer to the political stability it so desperately needed? It was with some apprehension that the Saigon embassy watched the September 3 presidential election unfold and with even more relief when it concluded. *Di bau* ("Go and vote") day – to everybody's general surprise – turned into a huge success. Even allowing for some tampering of the electoral rolls, there was an 83 percent turnout, scotching fears that the winner would lack a strong mandate. Viet Cong intimidation was largely contained. There were 171 attacks that left 55 dead and 267 wounded – a spike that barely registered in the daily round of violent incidents across the country. In one such attack, at a polling station at Long Thanh District School, a mortar bomb fell plum through the roof, blowing a hole in the flimsy wooden beams. The voting continued regardless. There was almost a carnival mood in parts of Saigon.

Cynics pointed out that many Vietnamese voted because a stamped voting card was a prerequisite for extracting later favors out of government officials, not least the rapacious class of rural tax collectors. But it was also the case that a voting card could mean a death sentence if the carrier was stopped by the Viet Cong. Against this background, the mettle of the South Vietnamese voter had to be acknowledged. There was a yearning for political change and desperation for peace; 4,735,449 voters made that quite clear. In total there were 11 presidential ballots and 48 congressional ballots (a voting complexity that baffled too many illiterate voters), but it was always certain there would only be one winning ticket. This was held by South Vietnam's two military proconsuls: Nguyen Van Thieu and Nguyen Cao Ky. When the counting was done, it emerged that the main opposition candidate, a lawyer called Truong Dinh Dzu, had run the soldiers close, but not close enough to derail the Thieu-Ky ticket. The army vote – there were over one million men in arms in regular or militia forces – was instrumental to the military victory. Notwithstanding some evidence of vote rigging it was clear that South Vietnam's junta had won a strong vote of confidence, and the communist National Liberation Front had been marginalized. Upper and Lower House elections were similarly acceptably concluded, laying the foundations for a new constitution submitted to the renamed National Legislative Assembly.

It may have appeared to an old hand weary of Saigon's political merry-go-round that the foundations for stable governance were finally being laid, but this was far from the truth. The Thieu-Ky ticket was riven with tensions and rivalries. Washington's preferred candidate – and probably the only personality capable of effecting the political and social revolution that the South Vietnamese needed – was the air force general Ky. But by pursuing a policy of neutrality, rigorously enforced by Ambassador Bunker, a tactical opening was created for Thieu. Cognisant that the Saigon Embassy would not publicly declare for Ky, Thieu manipulated the generals arguing that American silence signaled tacit approval for his continued leadership. As only one military candidate could be submitted for the presidential nomination, Thieu stole the slot, mollifying Ky by offering him the position of running mate. Under Thieu, South Vietnam had little hope of bringing about a social transformation to confront the ideological challenge from the North. Ky held that key, but was not allowed to pass through the door. CIA analyst George Allen was surely right in his post hoc judgment:

By pursuing Bunker's strict policy of remaining aloof from the electoral process, the United States lost its last real opportunity to undergird our war effort in Vietnam with a well-organized political base. In itself such a base would not have guaranteed victory, but without one, defeat in the long run was inevitable.[184]

The conclusion of the presidential elections set the scene for the second heads of states conference held in Manila in October 1967. Prior to the conference, McNamara made a fact-finding mission to Saigon. Nobody in the party knew this would be his last trip to Vietnam, but equally, no one was greatly surprised when the news eventually broke that he would be leaving Defense in the New Year, to assume the presidency of the World Bank.

Robert McNamara served in the seven most difficult years of any modern American defense secretary. By the end of 1967, he was a tired man. His closest aide, friend, and ally, Deputy Defense Secretary John McNaughton, had been killed in an air accident in October. It was rumored that his wife was unwell. McNamara was elevated to a public service career as a Kennedy protégé – a gamble as Kennedy had barely known the industrialist – and he had continued to serve his successor with unswerving loyalty. It was McNamara's unshakable loyalty – a quality never acknowledged by heckling critics, then and later – that led him down thorny paths, not gross misjudgments or deliberate deceit. He was in the end no more slippery with events than any other government or military official, or the President, and unlike the majority of his peers, he singularly and with impressive depths of energy actually sought to confront the facts. McNamara was hated by strident liberal activists, by southern conservatives, and by thick army officers who appeared even duller set against the corona of his sharp brain. With such enemies, he needed every friend.

He believed in the domino theory, but so did everyone else. He limited the bombing war in North Vietnam because he feared a Third World War, and avoiding this denouement, he judged, was the first responsibility of any American defense secretary. For this stance, he earned the eternal enmity of the airmen who were convinced they could bring the war to a swift conclusion if only he would let them flatten the North. Thousands of North Vietnamese civilians probably owed their lives to Robert McNamara. The concentrated exactness of his mind was almost intimidating: it is difficult to find declassified minutes of NSC meetings from this period in which McNamara's interventions do not jump out as the most intelligent and incisive in the room. It was not surprising that Johnson was in awe of "Mac." He may have come across as reason incarnated, but his voice also cracked easily, betraying emotion. McNamara was a rare example of a public servant who combined metaphysical subtlety with the most rigorous empiricism; the Janus face of good and evil fascinated him as much as a budget spread sheet.

There are few more agonized accounts of why America lost Vietnam than his *In Retrospect: The Tragedy and Lessons of Vietnam*. Those lessons are still true in today's wars, and ignored. Out of office he maintained a dignified silence to the end of his long life. Above all, and despite the meritless and exaggerated "monstrous McNamara" opprobrium that was thrown at him, it was never McNamara's war. This is capstone fact. From the winter of 1965, McNamara stopped believing the war was winnable and became the reluctant servant of a president who had trapped his country in Southeast Asia. That he told his master so made his departure inevitable and whether he resigned or was sacked is irrelevant. The relationship would never have survived. Rationality, as he eloquently put it, will not save us.

In a rational war of charts, graphs, and tables, there was one indisputable statistic that all of Washington's policymakers could agree on: how much it was all costing. After seven years, the dollar trend line was pointing determinedly upwards: 1960 (250 million), 1961 (258 million), 1962 (313 million), 1963 (291 million), 1964 (362 million), 1965 (559 million), 1966 (737 million), and 1967 (755 million).[185] The government of South Vietnam was contributing roughly half again. *Life* magazine calculated that it was costing $400,000 to kill a single guerrilla, or 75 bombs and 150 shells per corpse.[186] Could a war be won by spending yourself to victory? Was this extravagance justified?[187]

It would have been tempting to make the banal observation that the rising cost of the war was the inevitable consequence of more troops, more aircraft, and more ships. But this would have been to focus cost on the inputs and not the outputs. The war was not getting any bigger. More men and materials were simply being shoveled into the same space. The Vietnam maw was never satisfied because of the manner in which the war was being prosecuted. The principal inflationary pressure was the single index by which progress to victory was being measured: enemy attrition. In a bond market of body counts, MACV really only had one option – to keep issuing the debt of its own dead.

This mountain of human and financial debt only made sense if it succeeded in outstripping the enemy's capacity to restore its balance sheets. Westmoreland thought it could, but an overwhelming body of evidence had grown by this high point in the war to suggest that he was quite wrong. To win a war of attrition required controlling and imposing a rate of attrition on the enemy. This was not happening. The rate of attrition was being determined by the enemy's decisions and actions, not by MACV. The JCS observed, with some concern, that three quarters of battles were taking place at the enemy's choice of time, place, and duration. A CIA study had revealed that less than one percent of nearly two million small-unit operations conducted over two years had resulted in contact with the enemy. The enemy was suffering attrition – this was undeniable – but mostly because of his own poor tactics and misjudgments. An analysis of battles from late 1965 to early 1966 showed that 88 percent were started by the enemy, 46 percent began as enemy ambushes, and 63 percent of infantry targets were well-concealed and protected enemy in trenches and bunkers.[188] And the enemy was reserving the right to withdraw when the costs became steep and the rewards poor. Green Beret Brian Jenkins, writing towards the end of the war, captured the dilemma perfectly:

> Most importantly, it has been demonstrated statistically that the enemy initiates contact most of the time and avoids it when he desires. He thereby controls his own rate of casualties, negating any strategy based upon attrition. The enemy has been willing to suffer losses at a far greater rate than our own, but he has not accepted these losses as decisive and refuses to sue for peace. Instead, he prolongs the conflict, which nullifies our claim to Victory. We *are* winning, but we must keep winning indefinitely … our military strategy may be, as I believe it is, irrelevant to the situation.[189]

A question, then, hung over MACV: was there sufficient evidence at the time, at least by the end of 1967, if not earlier, to have come to the same unhappy conclusion?

The beating conscience of statistical probity resided in one organization: McNamara's Office of Statistical Analysis. The deductions it drew were all poor. There were well-understood problems with statistical analysis; the raw data was seldom totally accurate or verifiable and this was especially true of data provided by South Vietnamese sources. But an obsession with numbers was clouding judgments of "intangibles" and even hawkish personalities like Sharp lamented, "We have trapped ourselves because of our obsession to quantify everything."[190] This was true, but the numbers, however flawed, were the only measure available in an amorphous war, and more importantly, the only counter-banner which the White House could wave in the face of protestors. It was inevitable that "statistics and their analysis became not management tools, but weapons in public relations campaigns and policy battles."[191] "All of our estimates of enemy strength and variations in it contain very great uncertainties," a November 1 McNamara memorandum argued. "Thus, any conclusions drawn from them must be considered to be highly tentative and conjecture. Nevertheless, the data suggest that we have no prospects of attriting the enemy force at a rate equal to or greater than his capability to infiltrate and recruit."[192] With the almost certain knowledge that this would be his last major paper on the war, there was little restraint and every incentive to issue a last rallying call for good sense.

US marines make their staged landing at Red Beach, Da Nang on March 8, 1965. They were met by a reception party of local girls with floral wreaths. (Bettmann / Getty Images)

November 1965: cavalrymen are dropped off by UH-1D in the Ia Drang battles. (US Army)

Every war has its moment of innocence: here Brigadier General Frederick Karch is welcomed to the "splendid little war" at Da Nang by General Nguyen Chan Thi in March 1965. (Photo by Larry Burrows/The LIFE Picture Collection via Getty Images)

Chemical warfare: over the course of Operation *Ranch Hand* (1962–71), nearly 19 million gallons of herbicides were dispensed over South Vietnam, creating a long-term toxic legacy. (Bettmann / Getty Images)

An Australian soldier examines a Viet Cong tunnel during Operation *Crimp*, January 1966. (US Army)

Lieutenant Colonel "Hal" Moore: an outstanding field commander and undeniable hero at the battle of Ia Drang. (SAI/Shutterstock)

Operation *Masher* (January–March 1966). At Johnson's insistence the name was changed to "*White Wing*" but it made no difference. *Masher* was the fitting name. (Bettmann / Getty Images)

Civilians paid the heaviest price in Vietnam's interminable fighting.
(Bettmann / Getty Images)

Phuc Tuy Province (June 1966): soldiers from 173rd Airborne resume the march after a resupply. (Photo by Hulton Archive/Getty Images)

Hitting an invisible enemy in triple canopy jungle was always a challenge: here a USAF A-1E Skyraider launches rockets against a suspected Viet Cong position during Operation *Thayer*, October 1966. (Photo by Underwood Archives/Getty Images)

Weighed down: the average GI could not outmaneuver his more nimble guerrilla enemy.
When maneuver failed, firepower took over.
(Photo by Rolls Press/Popperfoto via Getty Images)

A Viet Cong propaganda image: guerrillas patrolling the Delta waterways.
(Photo by Keystone/Getty Images)

Fighting in the brush with limited visibility and fields of fire was treacherous and confusing.
Here paratroopers from 101st Airborne open fire on suspected enemy during Operation *Wheeler*,
September 1967. (Bettmann / Getty Images)

Search and totally destroy: the astonishing landscape left in the wake of Operation *Cedar Falls* (January 8–24, 1967). In the centre of the image was the village of Ben Suc, razed to the ground by future NATO Supreme Commander and Secretary of State Al Haig, then commanding officer of 1/26 Infantry, "The Blue Spaders." (Photo by Dick Swanson/The LIFE Images Collection via Getty Images)

The start of the long journey home. Here soldiers use an improvised stretcher to carry a wounded comrade during Operation *Junction City*, February 1967. (Bettmann / Getty Images)

November 1967: marines take cover at Con Thien. The name meant "Hill of Angels," an irony that escaped no one. (Bettmann / Getty Images)

Operation *Pershing* (February 1967–January 1968): 1st Air Cavalry search and destroy. (Photo by Patrick Christain/Getty Images)

The Ho Chi Minh Trail as communist propaganda would wish to portray it in 1968. The reality was different. (Photo by Sovfoto/Universal Images Group via Getty Images)

The gold star of the Viet Cong in the ascendant, 1968.
(AFP via Getty Images)

Like Roman legionnaires burning barbarian settlements: scorched earth was a self-defeating tactic. Operation *Pegasus*, 1968. (Photo by Larry Burrows/The LIFE Picture Collection via Getty Images)

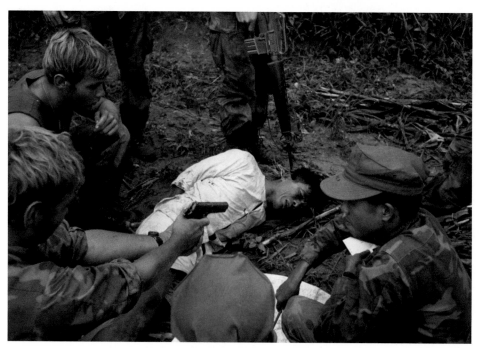

Interrogation at gunpoint – but no amount of ill-gotten intelligence could solve an unsolvable war. (Bettmann / Getty Images)

My Lai, 1968. To the right, Do Thi Can buttons her blouse after resisting rape by soldiers from Charlie Company; Pham Thi So is at the front grimacing; to the left is "the balding lady" "Phu" comforting Do Thi Be. Moments later, they were all gunned down. (Photo by Ronald S. Haeberle/The LIFE Images Collection via Getty Images)

A soldier from 1st Cavalry rushes between rubber trees in the Michelin Plantation. Possession of this area was contested throughout the war. (Bettmann / Getty Images)

Sergeant Gerald Laird, 1/502 Infantry, 101st Airborne, manning an M60 machine gun. The ability to lay down high volumes of fire was crucial to winning small-unit actions. (USAHEC)

Marines take cover behind tanks during street fighting in Hue, February 1968.
(Bettmann / Getty Images)

"I don't want no Dinh Binh Phoo." President Lyndon B. Johnson examines a sand model of the
besieged Khe Sanh with Special Assistant to the President Walt Rostow in 1968. (NARA)

Khe Sanh, just ten miles from the Laotian border. Giap said the battle was unimportant to him, but several thousand of his soldiers still died pointlessly besieging this marine base. (Bettmann / Getty Images)

The numbers, as ever, simply did not stack up.[193] American air power was blasting corners of Indochina to smithereens. Every month, allied forces were engaging in an average of 35 battles with Viet Cong or PAVN battalions, which they always won. None of this was making an impact on the North Vietnamese war effort, or at any rate, the impact that Westmoreland's strategy implicitly demanded. By this stage in the war, scores of CIA reports had been making this inconvenient point.[194] Over the course of the last 12 months, Viet Cong battalions had increased from 74 to 94, and PAVN battalions from 43 to 86. The estimated weekly rate of infiltration into the South had also increased from around 500, to almost 2,000. MACV was swatting mosquitoes that reproduced far more quickly than it could swat.

Furthermore, "winning" on battlefields was utterly irrelevant to what everybody agreed was the core task: Pacification. To ensure no casual reader missed the point, McNamara wrote: "The pacification program has been stalled for years; it is stalled today. The situation in this regard is no better – possibly worse – than in 1965, 1963 and in 1961. [underlining in the original]"[195] Elaborating the theme with a candor entirely missing from MACV reporting, he explained:

> Physical security must come first and is the essential prerequisite to a successful revolutionary development effort. The security must be permanent or it is meaningless to the villager, and it must be established by a well-organized "clear and hold" operation continued long enough to really clear the area … So far this prerequisite has been absent. In almost no area designated for pacification in recent years have ARVN forces actually "cleared and held."[196]

The war would not come to a successful conclusion until a way was found to succeed in this task, "our task all along," as McNamara sternly reminded his readership.

Johnson must have had an inkling of his defense secretary's doubts as, on the same day that McNamara delivered his report, he convened a meeting of the so-called "wise men."[197] The idea was in fact Rostow's and the membership of the colloquium was stellar: Omar Bradley, Matt Ridgway, and Maxwell Taylor; Arthur Dean, chief negotiator during the Korean War, Dean Acheson, Eisenhower's secretary of state, Douglas Dillon, John McCloy, Robert Murphy, all officials who had served under either Eisenhower or Truman; and the usual Vietnam crowd, Wheeler, Lodge, McGeorge Bundy, and Rostow. If this was a gathering of wise men, George Ball did not think so. "You're like a flock of buzzards sitting on a fence," he caustically swiped at Acheson. "You ought to be ashamed of yourselves."[198]

Wisdom seemed to be sacrificed on the altar of patriotic denial and the outcome was a good deal of foolishness. A doddery Bradley offered that GIs were eating ice cream three times a week, as if the war might be won on a gastronomic satisfaction count. Acheson blamed the "dilettante" head of the Senate Foreign Relations Committee J. William Fulbright; McGeorge Bundy blamed "the communications people in New York"; Abe Fortas blamed "so-called intellectuals"; and Clark Clifford appeared to suggest that "public opinion" was at fault. In the ritual way, missives from Ambassador Bunker were read out indicating that "progress," much like fool's gold, was detectable in the alchemical laboratory of Vietnam. McNamara alone was prepared to state the truth: America's efforts since 1961 had amounted to "failure." But when the conferees were asked the inevitable question – should, then, America withdraw from Vietnam – the chorus of disapproval was unanimous. Unthinkable, undesirable, absolutely not – such was the sum of wisdom.

McNamara was not the only dissenting voice. In October, Vice President Hubert Humphrey visited Vietnam. His testimony to the Committee on Foreign Relations was bleak. America, he told the Congressmen was "throwing lives and money down a corrupt rat hole," and "the American people would not stand for this involvement much longer."[199] The erosion of morale on the home front was a phenomenon that generals wrapped up in the war could not share, partly because their profession viewed low morale as a disease, but also because they were not experiencing it. McNamara had been seared by the horrific sight of Norman Morrison, a pacifist Quaker, committing self-immolation outside his Pentagon Office. Norman Mailer had harried Johnson with hysterical invectives. "It will hound you," he hollered. "They will go on marches and they will make demonstrations, and they will begin a war of public protest against you which will never cease. It will go on and on and it will get stronger and stronger." He was proved right.[200] By 1967, not a single month passed without a major anti-war protest witnessed somewhere in the United States.

The year's protests had begun with a fashionably hippy "Human Be-in" in San Francisco's Golden Gate Park, which attracted as many as 30,000 flowery protestors, and ushered in the New Year with a 5,000-strong all-woman rally in the capital. "War is not healthy for children or other living things," read the polite and pragmatic slogan of "Another Mother for Peace," but other protests turned abusive and violent. The Pentagon was marched on five times. In the largest of these demonstrations, on October 21, there were scuffles and 647 arrests. The New York Times printed a three-page anti-war advertisement; Christian groups staged nationwide fasts; and the group "Vietnam Veterans Against the War" (VVAW) was born. America was already perilously fractured before the Tet Offensive, and this rending of the national fabric could hardly be ignored by officials negotiating their way to work past placards accusing them of murder. In July 1967, for the first time, the Gallup Poll showed a majority of Americans viewed the Vietnam War as a mistake. Support for the war never recovered.

Secretly, Johnson was in despair. At the end of 1967, Bill Moyers, his loyal Special Assistant, decided to stand down. The two men spent seven hours alone driving around Johnson's ranch.

> We sat for a long time as the sun was disappearing over the far horizon of the LBJ ranch and we talked about Vietnam. He said, "If history brings me out ... that is, if the Communists don't take over South Vietnam I will be considered by posterity a great man who took a great risk and won, and it'll all be all right. If it doesn't come out," he added, "if the Communists wind up running South Vietnam I will be considered an obscure footnote, a man who gambled all he had, and lost."[201]

For Westmoreland, the year's end came with the knowledge that his tenure as COMUSMACV was nearing an end. In November it was indicated to him that he was being slated as Johnson's replacement in Washington as the Army Chief of Staff, a posting confirmed in a private letter in December.[202] Cognisant of his legacy, he continued to talk up the war. Against a growing consensus of stalemate, if not failure, in Washington, Saigon persisted in reporting progress. Total enemy losses were averaging 14,600 per month Westmoreland claimed, or as many US soldiers as killed in the entire war. How could this industrial output not be progress?[203] For Johnson, now burdened with a war he knew he could not win, limitation, not expansion, became the policy imperative. A week before Christmas Day, with another bombing truce rumored, the President pronounced.[204] MACV's strength would be capped at 525,000 and there would absolutely not be a reserve call-up. There would also be no ground extension of the war into neighboring Laos or Cambodia. *Rolling Thunder* would be constrained to its current levels and there would be no relaxation of the list of no-strike targets, including Hanoi and Haiphong. In his December 18 "memorandum for file" Johnson effectively conceded the war, but hoped to still win the peace.

Even as he deliberated on how to bring the war to an honorable end, his oiled war machine continued to rotate troops through Vietnam. In December, the remainder of 101st Airborne Division deployed from its home base in Fort Campbell to Bien Hoa. 11th Light Brigade joined the Americal Division in Chu Lai. For the first time, there were now more American soldiers in combat than during the Korean War. A half-hearted Christmas truce was entirely ignored by the Viet Cong. On Christmas Day there were 40 major attacks. The New Year was greeted by 63.

Chapter 4

TET, JANUARY–DECEMBER 1968

After the gloom that seemed to fall like a pall over Washington at the end of the year, 1968 began in a mood of cautious optimism. Westmoreland had secured his uplift of 525,000 personnel and there were now nine US divisions in Vietnam, including the two marine divisions.[1] Just short of half a million men, this land force was supported by 1,700 aircraft, not counting the vast helicopter fleet. The South Korean contribution included two divisions in II CTZ and a marine brigade in the north. A combined Australian-New Zealand brigade was operating in III CTZ, with some effectiveness, and Thailand had boosted its contingent to a light division. The Free World forces now numbered 60,000 strong, including a Philippines civic action brigade.[2] When combined with the Republic of Vietnam Armed Forces (RVNAF), the allies could now field over one million men.[3]

The rotten plank on this boat remained the South Vietnamese Army. An American assessment of their principal ally made depressing reading. 9th Division at Sa Dec was nearly useless. 5th and 7th Divisions at Lam Son and Can Tho respectively were barely better. 22nd Division at Ba Gi and 23rd Division at Ban Me Thuot were more proficient, but suffered from unreliable subordinate regiments. 25th Division at Duc Hoa had improved with an issue of M-16 rifles, and 21st Division at Bac Lieu was considered one of the better Saigon divisions. In the north, 2nd Division based at Quang Ngai was a write-off. The only regular army formation MACV could fully trust was the 1st Division at Hue. In reality, the burden of the fighting was being undertaken by the Airborne Division and Marine Brigade, supported by the Ranger battalions. The remainder of South Vietnam's army largely remained a static, territorial, and marginally usable force.[4]

Whether accepting MACV's lower estimate of a 300,000-strong enemy, or higher estimates that suggested as many as half a million, it was incontrovertible that America and her allies had finally won the war of escalation. This did not imply that the war of attrition was being won – it was not – but it highlighted that a simple numerical comparison of forces was inadequate. Notwithstanding the continued and consuming obsession with infiltration, it was estimated that barely 50,000 PAVN had made the march south, and the hard-core Viet Cong possibly numbered 66,000 strong. The remainder was made up of the contentious Viet Cong Self-Defense Forces and support elements that no one could tally with any accuracy.[5] It later transpired that in fact just over 30,000 PAVN had infiltrated into South Vietnam over the course of 1967, along with 6,500 tons of supplies, or roughly what a US division was expending in a week's combat.[6]

All of which makes the events that followed even more remarkable. Why, when Hanoi stood no reasonable chance of defeating the South in one bold offensive, still less the guarantor of American firepower, did the North precisely attempt to do this? The 1968 General Offensive (*Tong Cong Kich*) and General Uprising (*Tong Khoi Nghia*) was the great pivot of the war – there is no debate on this matter. At the beginning of year, the two adversaries clashed in what proved to be the decisive military encounter in the American war. Yet it came about from miscalculations and delusions on both sides. The Tet Offensive was not so much David versus Goliath as utter recklessness.

In Vietnamese Marxist ideology, a general uprising or *khoi nghia* held mythical stature; it was the natural culmination of the great political struggle or *dua tranh*. Ho and Vo Nguyen Giap had anticipated a general uprising against the French in 1945 and were in fact surprised that it did not materialize.[7] In 1954 the Viet Minh won, not because they incited popular revolt, but because they achieved a "decisive" victory, a very precise phrase that implied not the total defeat of your enemy, but an outcome that made the war no longer digestible for your enemy. This was how the French had been beaten, on the battlefield at Dien Bien Phu, but also in every home in France. In 1960, a general uprising against Diem had also flopped, but once again the Hanoi leadership sidestepped this inconvenient truth.

Whatever post-facto justifications and embellishments were made for Hanoi's gamble to similarly end the war in 1968, there can be few uncertainties over the original plan or intent. A copy was captured by US forces, and key communist protagonists belatedly revealed the opaque maneuverings of the Hanoi Politburo.[8] The primary goal was not to stir a hornet's nest of widespread violence, lengthen the butcher's bill of casualties, and precipitate a collapse in American national will, although this was anticipated as a dividend. It was to comprehensively defeat South Vietnam's armed forces, forcibly remove the "puppet government," and present Washington with the fait accompli of an alternative government. Riding this crest of battlefield success, Hanoi expected to incite a mass uprising. So confident (deluded) were some heads in the Politburo, that on the eve of the offensive, Hanoi instructed the COSVN to announce a new party, the Alliance of National, Democratic, and Peace Forces (*Lien Minh Dan Toc Dan Chu va Hoa Binh*), which would be presented to South Vietnam as the new government.[9] A flag was even designed. The General Offensive-General Uprising had no hope of militarily defeating the "imperialist" Americans. Hanoi knew this but it hoped to draw, distract, and bleed US forces away from the population centers, or fix them, long enough to accomplish its goal.

Writing after the event, *Hop Bac*, Hanoi's propaganda rag, described the aims of the Tet Offensive thus:

[The] Uprising of the South Vietnamese army [PLAF] and people was designed to annihilate and disintegrate the puppet army, to smash the machinery of the puppet government, to destroy American manpower and collapse the aggressive will of the U.S. pirates, [and] to topple the U.S.-Thieu-Ky regime.[10]

This, it was anticipated, would lead to a situation of "fighting while negotiating" or *danh vua dam*, first articulated in the Lao Dong's 12th Resolution of December 1965.

The North was fully confident that it could defeat the weaker ARVN in the 250 districts it controlled, but was less sure of winning in the 15 districts in which US forces held sway.[11] This little mattered: with the weaker leg pulled away, the American stool would topple over. Predominantly employing regular PAVN formations, Hanoi would suck US forces into fruitless actions on the DMZ, as well as on the Laotian and Cambodian borders. Historians who have argued the Tet Offensive really began in the border battles of the previous fall and winter have done so with manifest reason. With US forces committed and distracted, a combined PAVN-Viet Cong offensive would then be unleashed simultaneously across every province, with the intention of seizing all the main cities and towns, and riding a bow wave of imagined popular support. By the time MACV responded, it would be too late, so the plan envisioned: a revolutionary government would be installed in Saigon and the game would be up. Just as in 1954, Hanoi would hold the winning hand in the negotiations. With their southern ally dismembered on the battlefield, and a provisional government in place, why continue the war? What would be the point of American soldiers fighting for South Vietnam, if it had effectively crumbled as a political entity?

The Politburo plainly kept a canny eye on the forthcoming US presidential election, and was well aware of growing American discontent with the war, but the principal aims of Tet were not to foment the latter, but rather to reap waning American morale as the inevitable bonus of a communist *coup d'état*. This would force Washington to eat "with chopsticks," in the gastronomic analogy invoked by the COSVN's deputy chief of staff and member of the Politburo, Lieutenant General Nguyen Van Vinh. In retrospect, what is striking about the Tet Offensive is that it failed to achieve strategic surprise or any of its tactical objectives – the preconditions upon which Hanoi's hopes rested for a collapse of American will – but that collapse happened anyway.

Ultimate responsibility for the General Offensive-General Uprising should have rested with the Commander-in-Chief of North Vietnam's armed forces, Vo Nguyen Giap. But Giap's role remains shrouded in some mystery. Contemporaneous CIA interrogation reports of captured Viet Cong seem to indicate that Giap was responsible for the overall scheme which comprised three phases. In the reporting on one such report:

> Phase 1 called for a general offensive against the cities. If this failed, Viet Cong troops during Phase 2 would besiege the cities and, at the same time, lure U.S. troops into the Khe Sanh area. Phase 3, which was expected to coincide with the establishment of a coalition government, would involve a decisive battle in the Kontum-Pleiku or Saigon area.[12]

Yet over the five months when the Tet Offensive was being planned, it appears Giap may have been living in Hungary, and was only summoned back to Vietnam two days before the offensive was launched, on a Chinese aircraft.[13] American intelligence had some inkling that Giap may have fallen from favor because he disappeared from news items. In fact, over this period, Giap was only mentioned once in official statements, and then in relation to attending the October parade in Moscow. At the December 25, 1967 anniversary celebrations of the founding of the North Vietnamese Army, Giap was still notably absent.[14] If it is the case that he was in temporary exile, then the "architect of Tet" epithet that has accompanied Giap stands on shaky ground. He could not have contributed to the planning in any meaningful sense, or even to the previous border battles. The long foreign sojourn was ostensibly for medical treatment, but more recent research suggests that Giap's absence may have been more related to grave doubts over launching a general offensive, and in this sense represented a punitive exile (Ho Chi Minh also spent lengthy periods in China over this period for medical reasons; and he also held grave reservations over the proposed plan).[15] Far from being the architect, it appears Giap may have been the reluctant and estranged partner in a strategic misadventure concocted by Party Secretary Le Duan and General Van Tien Dung, presented to the Politburo on July 18–19, 1967 with Giap safely exiled.[16] A plausible explanation for his return would appear to be that the regime needed its most famous figurehead general at the critical hour.

What American intelligence had mostly missed in the summer of 1967 was that the Hanoi Politburo – in a mirror reflection of Washington – was divided between the so-called moderates led by Giap, and a hard-liner faction.[17] The fault-line went further back to the origins of the revolution between the "North Vietnam Firsters," Giap, Truong Chinh, and Pham Van Dong, and the "South Vietnam Firsters," Le Duan, Le Duc Tho (Kissinger's later nemesis), and Nguyen Chi Thanh.[18] A third group, known as "the Centrists" then emerged, prominently led by Ho Chi Minh, Le Duc Tho, who appears to have cooled his views, and Foreign Minister Nguyen Duy Trinh.[19] These divisions were exacerbated by the Sino-Soviet split, with supporters and detractors of the two great communist powers divided evenly within the Politburo.

In the North, resistance from moderates was squashed by arresting hundreds of dissenters in July 1967, in what came to be called with typical communist primness the "Revisionist Anti-Party Affair."[20] This culling of "revisionists" echoed an earlier putsch following the 9th Plenum in December 1963, in which a number of moderates were arrested. Giap may have been a casualty of this internecine warfare. These detentions were followed by further waves of arrests in October and December, on each occasion immediately preceding an important Politburo meeting and aimed at stifling dissent. In the South, far from being galvanized, the plan for a General Offensive-General Uprising provoked a bout of intense internal debate, if not "disbelief."[21] In a reflection of MACV, these pessimistic broodings, in fact any defeatist reports, were being carefully filtered so that Hanoi, like Washington, only heard what it wanted to hear. Between July and October 1967, a series of meetings were held between Northern and Southern representatives which papered over the misgivings but did not resolve them. The hard-liners carried the day because no party member wished to be labeled a "revisionist," not because there was unanimous belief in the plan.

The original idea for a decisive dry-season offensive in 1968 appears to have first been mooted by Thanh, then heading the COSVN, in January 1967, but his untimely death from a heart attack, apparently following a heroic drinking spree, ended his revolutionary career (there is a suggestion that Giap may have poisoned Thanh, whom he disliked).[22] In fact, a similar plan to the Tet Offensive had long been in gestation. As far back as 1963, a faction in the NLF, again led by Thanh, argued for a general offensive as a response to America's "special war."[23] The following year, Tran Bach Dang, chief political officer in Saigon and member of the NLF Central Committee, was advocating a similar scheme.[24] The baton then seems to have been taken up by the hard-liners led by Communist Party Secretary Le Duan, and General Van Tien Dung, Giap's chief of staff: "The U.S. imperialists can land men on the moon but they will be absolutely incapable of resisting the laws of social development."[25] This communist "social development" was nothing less than the "logical" law of an inevitable popular uprising, assumed in the minds of Duan and Dung. This became known as "Plan X" but was stalled by Johnson's intervention in the spring of 1965. Whereas the moderates and centrists argued for patience and a protracted guerrilla struggle, Duan and Dung believed that Saigon's "puppet" government and troops were ripe for a fall – they just needed to shake the tree vigorously enough. The via dolorosa of revolutionary victory should be paved with the bloody cobbles of the sacrificed, ten million dead if necessary, as Ho once remarked, but never meant.

Tet was thus born from an over-vaulting communist fantasy that hoped but failed to catch with its surcease, success. But it also seems to have been engendered from a suppressed desperation. There is abundant evidence that points to weakening communist morale in the South and a growing sense that the war, as Westmoreland claimed, was actually reaching a "cross-over point." There were also the deep and irresolvable divisions between the Northerners and Southerners. In a secret Saigon CIA cable despatched on December 19, 1967 it was reported that NLF head Nguyen Van Tien had told a source that Hanoi and the NLF were riven with major policy differences, chief of which was the latter's intent to form a government embracing "all major religious and intellectual groups" and to promote an economy with "capitalists and private landholders." Or, in other words, the NLF and Hanoi were fighting for completely opposing war aims. The campaign demanded a unified, synchronized plan between North and South, but the practical difficulties of coordinating between Hanoi and the NLF had further split the effort. The Southern plan was staffed by Pham Hung, a deputy of the deceased COSVN commander Thanh. The Northern plan was prepared by Dung.[26]

Formal approval to launch the Tet Offensive was only obtained at the 14th Plenary session of the Party Central Committee on January 1, 1968. Ho Chi Minh abstained in the vote to signal his displeasure. Giap was not even present. The final, confirmatory order seems to have been delivered as late as January 21, just one week before the attack, and many units received their orders just 72 hours before the offensive.[27] That the offensive only gained formal authorization one month before its launch suggests reservations over its wisdom, which is exactly what was besetting the entire scheme, especially in the South.

The triumph of the hard-liners had not resolved differences. The very title of the scheme – General Offensive and General Uprising – eloquently testifies to the fact that there were two conceptions, conjoined in communist theory, but in practice reflecting irreconcilable camps. One bad plan is unfortunate, merging two is a disaster. In private, it seems Giap believed neither stood much chance of success – indeed he had long-harbored misgivings over confronting North American military might – and remained anxious to preserve the military resources of the North. As early as the winter of 1965, following the Ia Drang battles, he had become critical of costly confrontations, provoking disagreements with Thanh who was much less confused by the attrition bill, and who viewed Giap as a follower of "old customs."[28]

The burden of the fighting was thus passed to the NLF and Viet Cong, probably cynically, who paid the highest price. That they were led disjointedly by six generals – Tran Van Tra, Mai Chi Tho, and Le Duc Anh in the northern half of the country, and Vo Van Kiet, Tran Bach Dang, and Huynh Cong Thanh in the south – somewhat doomed the scheme to failure. These were survivors with impeccable communist credentials, but thin competence in general command.

Muddying the conception, Hanoi's final plan actually predicated three phases running from January to August. Tet would be "a process" rather than a single blow. In the words of the Politburo's January 1 directive, "The upcoming general offensive/general uprising will be a period, a process, of intensive and complicated strategic offensives by the military, political and diplomatic means." This was the "strike and talk" strategy previously articulated in Resolution 13 of January 1967 by Foreign Minister Trinh and General Dung. Le Duan had been making the same arguments in December 1965. The aim of this supreme revolutionary effort would be the "decisive victory" that would force "the United States to enter negotiations to end the war."[29] Decisive victory did not imply bringing your opponent to his knees, just pulling the rug from under his feet, as had happened with the French. This, in fact, was the CIA view: "In the final analysis, we believe the Communists view their military effort in a political-psychological context that is not always compatible with Western precepts. 'Victory' for them can be simply avoidance of defeat...and thereby 'defeat' – the aims of their opponent."[30]

There were two glaring problems with this phased plan. The first is that Hanoi clearly encouraged the NLF and Viet Cong to make a supreme effort with the hope that the first phase of the offensive/uprising would be successful, quick, and decisive. The assigned missions and formation of an alternative government do not make great sense otherwise. Doctrinaire communists may well have believed in this fantasy, but it appears more likely that a majority of the Politburo knew perfectly well that they faced resistance not welcome in the South. Indeed, the Politburo's relations with the NLF had become strained by this stage. In this respect, phase one of the Tet Offensive can only be viewed as a cynical act.

The second problem with this contingent scheme was that no general can confidently predict the outcome of one phase of a major operation, let alone predict subsequent phases many months ahead. Hanoi tacitly acknowledged the first phase might fail – then what? The manner in which the Southern generals improvised against mounting losses suggests muddle and post-facto justification. A fear of reporting the truth – the utter failure of the uprising – meant that each of the subsequent phases was based on false information and fantastic assumptions.

Western debate over what these plans actually intended to achieve, based on the perspectives of the party leaders and commanders, perhaps somewhat passes over what the ordinary foot soldier or guerrilla believed he was fighting for. Here, there was even more confusion. General Tran Van Quang, the Party Secretary of Tri Thien Regional Committee, warned his soldiers, "The General Offensive/General Uprising is a process. I repeat, a process." But it appears that this directive was not heeded or understood.[31] Testimony and actions seem to point overwhelmingly in one direction: for the sacrificial Viet Cong, distant from the politicking and ideological reveries in Hanoi, the Tet Offensive was about "going for broke" and ending the war. What they were asked to do made little sense otherwise. Bui Tin, PAVN Colonel and veteran of Dien Bien Phu, similarly reflected the confusion over the Tet Offensive's ultimate aims. In his later justification, the mission was to create mayhem and widespread damage, over many months, adding,

> Of course, at the lower echelons there has been a misunderstanding or an imprecise understanding of the directives of the Central Committee. Therefore, there have been some people at the lower echelons who understood this as the final battle. But this was not the idea.[32]

On the ambiguity of "the idea," many were fated to sacrifice their lives in futile gestures.

Militarily, the Tet Offensive was already compromised thanks to MACV's intelligence breaks and early capture of plans. By the summer of 1967, the general consensus was that Hanoi was going to play a waiting game, bleeding US forces, with the knowledge that Johnson faced the challenge of a presidential election the following year. For all the secrecy, Hanoi's scheme was transparent, well-signaled, and correctly deduced though underestimated by Westmoreland. By the end of the year, several documents had been captured which revealed the framework of the forthcoming offensive.[33] Even without these intelligence breaks, the reality was that the Tet Offensive stood little chance of success, for a single and uncomplicated reason – North Vietnam's military commander-in-chief, Vo Nguyen Giap, did not believe in the plan.

Forced to implement a scheme he doubted, Giap did everything in his power to preserve his army from possible destruction. Far from betting all his counters, Giap jealously guarded his stock and allowed the NLF and Viet Cong to commit suicide.

Politically, the entire scheme was compromised with the arrest of Ba Tra, a Viet Minh veteran and senior member of the Saigon Viet Cong cadre, in May 1967. Tra's role was to form the so-called Alliance of National and Peace Forces that would announce itself as a legitimate coalition government – the Provisional Revolutionary Government (PRG) – comprising a mix of "neutralists" and communists.[34] Tra revealed all the names of the plotters, and in the usual way Saigon became a cockpit of conspiracy theories. Subsequently rounded up in the net was the wife of Tran Bach Dang, the NLF Party Secretary for Saigon, and one of the generals who would lead the assault on the city. A later capture of Truong Nhu Tang, a comptroller of the shadow Saigon government, who revealed more names, was a further crippling blow. These catches led Saigon's generals to in fact believe that the Alliance was an American plot, concocted to find a way out of the war, a popular myth that would re-surface when the shooting started. Regardless of these wild fancies, without a credible alternative government in place the General Uprising stood no chance: to whom were the imagined revolutionary masses supposed to turn?

The entire scheme was further compromised by a last-minute change of timings. Westmoreland's intelligence chief Davidson guessed correctly that "N-Day" would be set for the night of the February 4/5, at the end of the Tet festivities. Westmoreland's wily rejection of a proposed seven-day truce over this period completely threw the communist plans. Hanoi scrambled to rescue the situation by ordering N-Day on the Tet lunar New Year but made the elementary error of confusing dates. For Southerners, this fell on January 30, for Northerners, a day later. This meant that some units began their attacks a full 24 hours before the main offensive, compromising surprise. More seriously, far too many Viet Cong regular battalions had counted on the extra days to marshal their men and infiltrate to their battle positions. When the offensive launched they were out of place and unable to contribute to the fighting. In Saigon, just eight battalions were able to enter the fray in support of the sappers who had undertaken the first assaults, and these failed to link up.[35]

Some preparations were amateurish. When Dang Xuan Teo went to retrieve rifles secretly concealed 200 yards from the national radio station, he discovered, "most of the weapons had been eaten by termites. Only the steel parts were left."[36] The assault group nonetheless managed to seize and hold the station for a day, before his surviving men "detonated the explosive, destroying the entire radio station complex and sacrificing themselves as a result." In other instances, units moving too early walked into ambushes. "There was nothing but arms, legs, brains, blood," remembered Norm Gardner, "I had never seen such carnage in my life. They [40-odd Viet Cong] walked right into this ambush and it was just awful."[37] A consummate irony and measure of the failure of the Tet Offensive is that hopes that it might just succeed were effectively over by February 5, the original attack date. Out-gunned, uncoordinated, and dispirited, Viet Cong survivors were ordered to withdraw, which they did in some disarray, harried by ARVN and US units.

Tet was a contingent "decisive victory," but not for the reasons commonly given. What the General Offensive-General Uprising provoked was a situation in which both sides became locked in the embrace of their own particular failures. Both the Politburo and the Johnson administration needed to demonstrate they had won their defeats. Tet exposed the fact that Hanoi could not successfully coordinate a strategic campaign between the People's Army and Viet Cong; that it could not take on America in a "big unit war" without suffering crippling and unacceptable losses; and that it did not command the popular support of Southerners. But Tet also exposed the fact that Washington could not ask for more sacrifice to win an unwinnable war. Westmoreland quickly parried and then beat back the communist offensive, for which he has never received sufficient credit, but this did not amount to winning.

Tet became a "decisive victory" because it marked the end of the period when the United States attempted to win the war militarily, and it ushered in the period of withdrawal and "Vietnamization." Even so, no longer seeking to win the war did not imply that Washington was prepared to give up on South Vietnam and hand it over to the communists. The fatal miscarriage lay in the hollowness of Vietnamization, as well as in the intractable difficulties facing the strategy of rural pacification, not in the events that preceded it. And victory for the communists still lay seven years hence, by which time the Tet Offensive was an insignificance. A new American president was in the White House and a whole new set of geopolitical circumstances had emerged. The peace talks announced with such fanfare at the end of the Johnson presidency had to start all over again, from base foundations. The "talking while fighting" in fact achieved nothing. The "process" simply became an industrial process for turning Viet Cong into cadavers. The probability is that a Vietnamized war would have ended as it did anyway, without the terrible sacrifice demanded by a reckless Hanoi at the beginning of the 1968 Tet lunar New Year.

The second great debate over the Tet Offensive rages over whether it represented an intelligence failure. The fulminations started almost immediately in a nation acutely sensitive to the strategic shock of a surprise attack. On February 6, at a Democrat congressional leadership breakfast, Johnson found himself assaulted by Senator Robert Byrd concerned with "the poor intelligence."[38] The phrase has stuck ever since but the debate has largely been viewed through the prism of the popular trauma the offensive provoked, rather than what was known at the time.

There were "only" two intelligence failures, one related to the timing, and the second to the scale. Westmoreland thought the offensive would probably start before Tet, and Davidson reckoned it might fall immediately after the holiday. Davidson guessed right, but in the event both were wrong by a matter of days, thanks to Westmoreland's rejection of the communist proposed truce. This hardly grades as a gross intelligence failure; attacking on Tet – a sacred feast – would have been an affront to Vietnamese sensibilities, which it was. Regardless of this uncertainty over timings, Westmoreland did take the sensible precaution of rejecting the duplicitous seven-day Tet truce proposed by the NLF. Taking the initiative, he consulted with President Thieu, controversially bypassing both Ambassador Bunker and the White House, and he reduced the proposed ceasefire to 36 hours. In I CTZ, all truce arrangements were entirely canceled. MACV was not fooled by the communist ruse; Westmoreland anticipated and prepared for the double-crossing. The single measure of shortening the ceasefire period provoked Hanoi into accelerating its plans and condemned the communist offensive to a poor start before a single shot had been fired.

The second failure relates to underestimation of the enemy. This is more important. Although MACV appreciated this would be a big offensive it underestimated the scale, a miscalculation that Westmoreland excused because as he put it nobody would have believed such a "preposterous" idea. This is only a partial truth. MACV correctly estimated that an all-out offensive could not possibly succeed, but this did not imply the very notion should be dismissed. It was dismissed not only because it was "preposterous" but because a military and political leadership had entrapped itself in its own rhetoric and divisive debates over the foredoomed strategy of attrition warfare. In the impeccable judgment of historian Ronnie Ford:

> While the North Vietnamese were busy analyzing, debating, adapting, disseminating, explaining, testing and implementing their strategy to win the war in South Vietnam, the United States intelligence community became embroiled in a debate over how long it would take for the Communists to lose. This is why the United States was surprised at Tet.[39]

This argument had manifested itself most bitterly in the great order of battle debate of 1967. It mattered not only because "proving" enemy attrition had become the only way MACV could demonstrate progress, but more importantly, it had become the single measure Johnson could fire back at an increasingly skeptical press corps and electorate. Like the famously posed photograph of marines on Mount Suribachi in Iwo Jima, Johnson urgently needed to plant a flag of victory, and the only mountain on offer was a pile of "VC kills" and a rather frayed Old Glory sub-titled "Attrition Warfare." Obsessed with numbers, the more decisive question of communist intentions, however foolhardy, fell from the table.

As early as the previous fall, both American and South Vietnamese intelligence agencies had discerned that Hanoi was preparing a significant push in the New Year. The obsessively secretive communist leadership had no reasonable hope of keeping the plan entirely secret; it could only hope to spring the surprise at the moment of its own choosing. Captured documents, prisoner interrogations, and astute analysis of Hanoi's press and radio all offered credible indicators of the impending communist offensive.

By the beginning of the New Year, the White House became increasingly concerned with the convergence of possibly as many as 20,000 PAVN on the isolated marine base at Khe Sanh. Whatever disagreements existed over the overall communist strategy, there was unanimity that the base faced a serious threat. Westmoreland had long fretted over a major PAVN offensive on the DMZ, commonly in the face of marine skepticism. Incontrovertible evidence that a big battle was brewing triggered a preplanned, contingency reinforcement and reorganization. A MACV Forward HQ under Abrams was established in I CTZ, in anticipation of the clash. This would eventually lead to the foundation of an entire new command: XXIV Corps. 1st Cavalry was redeployed between Hue and Phu Bai, augmented by a brigade from 101st Airborne. Elements from the American Division relieved III Marine units, and an ROK marine brigade was similarly ordered north, allowing 1st Marines to shift the balance of its combat battalions closer to the DMZ. Khe Sanh itself was reinforced with two more marine battalions and a South Vietnamese Ranger battalion. Hue, an obvious prize in any forthcoming battle, was secured by paratroopers. All this of course played into the hands of Hanoi. On the eve of the Tet Offensive, half of all available US combat units were deployed in I CTZ, or as far away as possible from the real communist objective, Saigon. At least this part of the plan did succeed; the Politburo could hardly have hoped for a more favorable disposition of forces.

Few could agree, however, what this northern build-up of forces meant. Was it the prelude to an invasion? Was it another Dien Bien Phu? Or just a distraction? In the heart of the CIA station in Saigon, three young analysts, Rob Layton, Jim Ogle, and Joseph Hovey, unencumbered by political considerations and attuned to the signals, believed they had exposed the strategy of the General Offensive-General Uprising.[40] In their excitement they pushed out a report in November 1967 in which they argued that the border battles were a deliberate diversion from a main assault on the cities, an assessment that Westmoreland in fact shared.

In December, they refined the analysis and wrote that the forthcoming military and political offensive was intended as the turning point in the war, which would determine the course of the rest of the conflict. In the words of the report: "the war is probably nearing a turning point and the outcome of the 1967–68 winter-spring campaign will in all likelihood determine the future direction of the war."[41] These words were copied to Johnson. However, the Saigon analysts also made a gross error: the prediction that if the offensive failed, Hanoi would likely "scale down the war." CIA in Washington strongly and rightly disagreed – the war would go on regardless. Both concurred with some prescience that "having gotten the Viet Cong to accept these months as 'decisive' ... this situation could have serious effects on Viet Cong morale ... if the campaign fails."[42]

There has been an attempt to portray this episode as an example of Washington – specifically the CIA – not heeding the warnings of its own analysts. However, this interpretation is searching for an intelligence scandal where none exists. Notwithstanding differences in views, *all* sides of the argument were forwarded to Johnson through the office of Walt Rostow on December 15, 1967. There was no censorship on the part of the CIA's Office of the Special Assistant for Vietnamese Affairs, led by George Carver. Like virtually every other intelligence agency, the CIA struggled to believe Hanoi would act in a reckless manner. Viewed through a rational American intelligence lens, CIA analyst George Allen later wrote, "We did not think the Communists believed the time was propitious for a general uprising. Their evolving strategic scenario reflected an unrealistic assessment on their part of the prospects for success."[43] But this did not incline the agency to gag its own analysts as some have suggested. Layton, Ogle, and Hovey emerge almost as seers because they alone pressed the idea that 1968 was intended as the decisive year in the war. In this regard they were correct, and not ignored.

The problem more lay in MACV where the new double act at J2, Major General Phillip Davidson and Colonel Daniel Graham, were dismissive of the CIA hypothesis and clung to the orthodoxy that the enemy was too weak and only committed to a drawn-out guerrilla war. Saigon may have cried wolf too many times, but it appears more likely that neither Davidson nor Graham, smarting from the bitter summer arguments with the CIA, were willing to countenance an assessment that might re-ignite the feuding. Sharp agreed with MACV J2, judging the chances of a major offensive remote, but Westmoreland, trusting his perennial suspicions of North Vietnamese intentions, was not so sure.[44]

If the CIA did not fully agree with the young analysts in Saigon, what was its official position on the eve of the offensive? On January 18, only days away from the deluge, the CIA Office of National Estimates submitted its

"Alternative Interpretations of Hanoi's Intentions," signed off by Carver. The 20-page estimate was a masterpiece of intelligence sophistry:

> In the present circumstances it is true that a multitude of things <u>could</u> happen, at almost any time. Hanoi <u>could</u> quit tomorrow, or at any time thereafter; the Chinese <u>could</u> enter the conflict with their own armed forces in greater number; China <u>could</u> collapse in total chaos; the Soviets <u>could</u> take a far more active role, either in support of Hanoi to continue the war or in withdrawing such support; the South Vietnamese government and polity <u>could</u> disintegrate; the Sino-Soviet controversy <u>could</u> become more or far less acute than it is, and this change the context of the Vietnam struggle; the policy of the US government <u>could</u> change in any number of ways, and so on [underlining in the original].

Unfortunately, every "<u>could</u>" was completely wrong (except, of course, that US government policy did indeed change, but not in a way that CIA analysts would have predicted at the beginning of the year).

Faced with this baffling array of possibilities the CIA estimate suggested three hypotheses for Hanoi's likely intentions in 1968, but in truth they were Goldilocks options. Either Hanoi would end the war; or it would continue the war until it gained advantage; or it would continue to fight hard in the coming months (the annual winter-spring offensive) but search for compromises to end the war. The last option was actually very close to the Saigon position.

In the single paragraph where the intelligence assessment came within touching distance of the truth ("one may conjecture that Hanoi's postulated confidence rests in some factor or event which is not yet apparent to the US, such as a major escalation by the Communists"), the report went on to outline wholly spurious scenarios such as an attack on Laos, or Chinese "moves in Vietnam or elsewhere in the periphery." Nowhere in the paragraph or elsewhere in the estimate was the prediction that the "major escalation" would be precisely in South Vietnam. Nowhere was it suggested that Hanoi might actually try to win the war.

This real intelligence failure was compounded by presentation, and the consequent media backlash. The "credibility gap," however, was dealt a fatal stab not in the first week of February 1968, or even in Walter Cronkite's requiem Tet broadcast, but in the last two weeks of the previous November when Johnson – it appears encouraged by Bundy, and intimates Fortas and Clifford – decided to launch a propaganda offensive. Few have been so clumsy and so emphatically rejected.[45] At a National Press Club address, Westmoreland advised, "The end begins to come into view." The enemy was "certainly losing" and Hanoi knew it. The Viet Cong strength was "declining at a steady rate" and the enemy had not "won a major battle in more than one year." In a later joint press conference held with Ambassador Bunker, the message was repeated: the war of attrition was being won, the rate of progress would now accelerate, and it was conceivable the war could be handed over to the Vietnamese within the next two years. This panorama of progress was met with universal skepticism. The *New York Times* accused the administration of stirring unease with its positive statistics. Don Oberdofer in the *Washington Post* more brusquely wrote: "Statistics on War Fail to Prove Real Progress."[46] But it was Ward Just, also writing for the *Post*, who identified the real issue; the war strategy had metamorphosed into a media strategy, or in other words, it was no strategy at all. When Tet burst it was no wonder there was a furor – if this was winning, what was losing?

The Tet holiday in South Vietnam ran from Monday January 29 to Wednesday 31. At the beginning of the year The Beatles had released the "Magical Mystery Tour" album. It had shot to the number one slot and would stay there for the duration of the communist offensive, the perfect musical accompaniment to the psychedelic blitz that was about to unfold.

On the preceding Friday, sufficient intelligence had been acquired indicating that the bomb of the General Offensive-General Uprising was about to detonate. An ARVN patrol captured an NLF commissar named Colonel Nam Dong, who revealed the entire plan, including the launch date – but this information was not passed to MACV. Riven with suspicions, it appears that South Vietnamese intelligence was still convinced the US Embassy was covertly colluding with the communists. In these circumstances, the ARVN was unwilling to let on to the Americans that the secret plan had been uncovered.[47] Two days before N-Day, NLF tapes were captured proclaiming the liberation; again this intelligence was not shared, but it did serve to place II ARVN Corps on alert. More guerrillas were captured with tapes intended for broadcast on Saigon radio. Prisoners under interrogation told of their role to guide units into the capital. Other apprehended Viet Cong confessed that they had orders to assault cities across South Vietnam. None of this intelligence gathered by South Vietnamese units was passed to MACV.

Even if it had been, there was still a sense that it would have been dismissed as alarmist. In III ARVN Corps, ex-special forces soldier and now CIA operator Norm Gardner recalled, "we knew that something was going to happen."[48] An opium-smoking "but extremely bright intelligence officer" named Colonel Kung had briefed the CIA men on 43 items of intelligence he had received. When asked what it all meant he replied, "They're going to attack Saigon." This good intelligence was briefed to HQ MACV "but nobody really believed this." At the eleventh hour, all eyes were still fixed on Khe Sanh and I CTZ, and the most probable scenario remained an attack after the Tet holiday.

The first attacks fell in II CTZ in the Central Highlands, and in the southern half of I CTZ, shortly after midnight on January 30. Tet had launched 24 hours before N-Day. After six months of planning what was intended as a simultaneous offensive across the territory of South Vietnam failed spectacularly, thanks to the misunderstanding over the start of the Lunar New Year. By the time MACV staff officers were at their desks at Tan Son Nhut that morning, Westmoreland's intelligence chief was telling his boss "this is going to happen tonight and tomorrow all over the country."[49] Strategic surprise, such as it existed given that MACV was aware that something big was afoot, had been compromised. By 11.25am a flash message had been forwarded to all MACV units placing them on high alert. This provoked some minor readjustments of dispositions in the Saigon Military District, a few conversations between commanders, but little else.

An arresting aspect of the events of January 30 is that neither MACV, nor the South Vietnamese Joint General Staff, reacted to the developments in anything less than a complacent manner. It was as if the Wermacht had crossed the Belgian border in 1940, and the Allies had spent the remainder of the day pretending it had not. Westmoreland found time to give an interview to a *Time-Life* correspondent, and to play some afternoon tennis.[50] He informed Sharp with culpable over-confidence that the situation was "well in hand," and cited a large enemy body count as proof that the enemy offensive in II CTZ had roundly failed to get off the ground.[51] Weyand in III Corps discussed contingency plans with his counterpart Lieutenant General Le Nguyen Khang, but the conversation was about actions to take if, not when, a general attack should fall. The instant recall of all personnel on leave did not happen. Main routes to Saigon were not sealed. The guards on prominent buildings were not increased. The police did not step up their security measures. Units did not muster, open armories, warm up vehicles, or prepare weapons. Military personnel in the capital were not confined to barracks. US civilian agencies took no additional security measures. Many of the thousands of Americans working in the capital district, military and civilian, were only vaguely aware of a general alert – but how many such alerts had they lived through before anyway? Nobody believed the North Vietnamese could, still less attempt, to win the war. The shrimp did not attack the dragon, to invoke the Chinese saying. But perhaps in shoals, it did. On the January 30, 1968, the debt of years of positive reporting, false and misleading statistics, assessments of progress where no progress

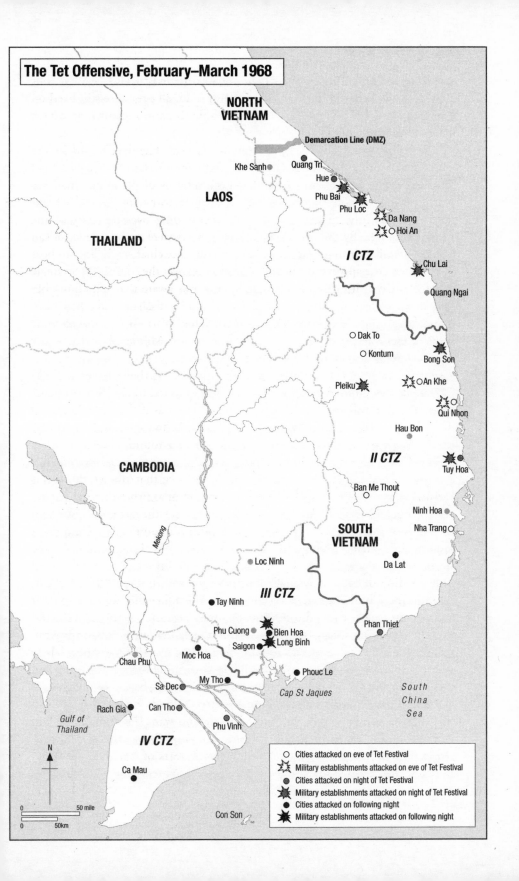

The Tet Offensive, February–March 1968

NORTH VIETNAM

Demarcation Line (DMZ)

LAOS

THAILAND

Khe Sanh
Quang Tri
Hue
Phu Bai
Phu Loc
Da Nang
Hoi An

I CTZ

Chu Lai
Quang Ngai

Dak To
Kontum
Bong Son
Pleiku
An Khe
Qui Nhon

Hau Bon

II CTZ

Tuy Hoa

Ban Me Thuot

CAMBODIA

Ninh Hoa
Nha Trang

SOUTH VIETNAM

Loc Ninh
Da Lat

III CTZ

Tay Ninh

Phu Cuong
Bien Hoa
Saigon
Long Binh
Phan Thiet

Moc Hoa
Phouc Le

Chau Phu

Sa Dec
My Tho
Cap St Jaques

Rach Gia
Can Tho
Phu Vinh

Mekong

South China Sea

Gulf of Thailand

IV CTZ

N

Ca Mau

0   50 mile
0   50km

Con Son

○ Cities attacked on eve of Tet Festival
✶ Military establishments attacked on eve of Tet Festival
● Cities attacked on night of Tet Festival
✶ Military establishments attacked on night of Tet Festival
● Cities attacked on following night
✶ Military establishments attacked on following night

was being made, of propaganda fed to the media – the entire narrative of a game "well in hand," to use Westmoreland's complacent phrase – was finally paid.

———

The facts of the subsequent communist avalanche are well known. Over the next 24 hours, around 80,000 People's Army and Viet Cong attacked more than 100 towns and cities, including 36 of the 44 provincial capitals, five autonomous cities, and 72 of South Vietnam's 245 district towns. Every major US Army and air base was attacked.

A CIA assessment published on February 21 somewhat refined this rough sketch.[52] It estimated, "field reporting since the start of the current Communist offensive indicates that approximately 58,000 Communist main and local forces were committed in attacks on urban areas and military installations through 13 February." Of these, roughly four in ten were Northerners; a third were VC main forces; and the remainder were local forces. Strikingly, the granularity of American intelligence was so fine by this stage in the war the CIA report was able to include an annex listing every communist unit and sub-unit that had taken part in the fighting.

In the first two weeks of fighting it was estimated that more than 30,000 enemy had been killed, or over half the force. Five thousand had been captured. It had been a disaster by any reckoning, notwithstanding the exaggerated body count. Communist morale plummeted, although this could not be admitted. MACV had suffered just over 1,000 fatalities over the same period. The CIA report, however, cautioned that the psychological impact had been huge: "The Vietnamese populace appears to be dismayed at the apparent ease with which the Communists were able to enter the cities in strength and attack key installations."

In I CTZ, Da Nang was assailed by a regiment from 2nd PAVN Division but driven back by 3/5 and 2/3 Marines. Quang Nam, Hoa Vang, and Chu Lai were all assaulted and stoutly defended by a hotch-potch of ARVN units. Assaults on Quang Ngai, Tam Ky, and Quang Tri similarly failed to make an impression. Further south, assaults on An Khe, Ninh Hoa, Nha Trang, and Qui Nhon were comfortably repulsed. At Ba To, an attack was launched with spears and knives.[53] In the majority of cases the attacks were over in a matter of hours. Some lasted more than a day. At the end of the first day, the communists could only point to success in the imperial city of Hue.

Some of the more desperate actions were experienced in the Central Highlands (II CTZ), in Pleiku, Kontum, Ban Me Thuot, Dalat, Phan Thiet, and Ban Tre.[54] Even in these towns, the communists struggled to hold on to their gains once reinforcements arrived. In Kontum, scene of some of the fiercest fighting, 24th PAVN Regiment, 304th PLAF Battalion, and 406th Sapper Battalion swept aside Montagnard scout companies. But this was their only success. Within 24 hours, elements from 7/17 Cavalry, 1/22 Infantry, and 1/69 Armored had piled into the town and were evicting the aggressors.[55] In Phan Thiet, 482nd Local Force Battalion and 840th Main Force Battalion proved stubborn, but in the end were no match for a combination of 3/506 Infantry and 44th ARVN Regiment.

In III CTZ, Ben Cat, Duc Hoa, Cu Chi, Ba Ria, Xuan Loc, and Tay Ninh were all subjected to significant assaults, but all failed. In Saigon, the plan broadly envisaged a surprise attack by assault teams, exploited by over 20 Viet Cong battalions, and reinforced by three PAVN divisions. As in the north, coordination was abysmal and the advantage gained from the initial tactical surprise was swiftly overturned.[56] The designated targets for the assault teams unambiguously led to a conclusion that the Southern generals were trying to win the war in a single blow and little understood Hanoi's vague notions of a "process." The objectives included the Presidential Palace, the national radio station, the national police headquarters, the Saigon Central Command, and Tan Son Nhut airport. This was a blueprint for a *coup d'état* – why else would you throw everything at these well-defended symbols of power, if you did not intend to usurp power?

In IV Corps, the Viet Cong enjoyed some significant early successes, but this was largely due to the absence of any meaningful security presence in the Delta. Route 4 was interdicted in 62 places, six bridges were demolished, and 13 of 16 province headquarters were attacked.[57] My Tho held against a sustained assault by 261st, 263rd, and 514th PLAF Battalions. 9th ARVN Division redeemed itself in Vinh Long, defeating the 306th, 308th, and 857th PLAF Battalions. 21st ARVN Infantry Division stood firm at Can Tho and Soc Trang. Across South Vietnam, Tet effectively collapsed within the week, although some tardy units launched forlorn attacks as late as February 10.

The Southern failure to win in a single blow meant that the communists had to fall back on the dubious strategy of "process" and "talking with fighting" – or admit that the whole business had been a shambles and a failure. Regardless that the NLF was now in a position of grave weakness, and that there had been no general uprising, the Vietnam Alliance of National Democratic and Peace Forces was duly announced as an alternative neutralist government. This was based on the Cambodian border in the area of the "Parrot's Beak." It comprised figureheads no Southerner had heard of and governed little more than a few acres of jungle. This was the prelude to the talking, but first there had to be more fighting. From May 5 to June 18, Hanoi ordered a "mini-Tet," which proved a suicidal experience for the Viet Cong soldiers attempting to break through the now well-prepared defenses of Saigon. Nonetheless, this nudged both sides into announcing, in May, that peace talks were on the table, if the shape of the table could be agreed. There was a last throw of the military dice in August, which proved equally disastrous, by which time the sacrificial lamb of the "South Vietnam People's Liberation Army" was looking like a decidedly poor offering to the ideological gods in Hanoi. Decimated Viet Cong regular units withdrew across the border to refit, and unprotected guerrilla units were pushed back, losing ground they had encroached over the previous two years. The peace talks did finally take root in November; the NLF was granted participant status; the great table debate was resolved by joining two rectangular tables to a central circular table; and the outgoing Johnson ordered a bombing truce. A sort of victory had been won, perhaps the "decisive victory," or so Hanoi could claim.

Little of this, however, is remembered. It passed like a typhoon, lifting roofs and tossing telegraph poles, before returning the landscape to relative calm. At least in the Western narrative, the Tet Offensive is remembered as a play with three acts that took place in Khe Sanh, Saigon and Hue. Each, in their own way, seemed to encapsulate the follies of a war that had lost all rhyme and reason.

The iconography of the war was important. At the height of the Tet Offensive, 90 percent of US news coverage was devoted to the war, and some 50 million Americans were tuning in to watch the drama.

In the deep and far north, 500 miles from the cockpit of Saigon, a quite different battle was fought. No other clash in the Vietnam War attracted as much criticism, or as much pyrotechnic prose, most vividly in Michael Herr's *Dispatches*.[58] From February to March, 38 percent of all Vietnam reporting by Associated Press covered this battle, and it filled a quarter of all television news stories.[59] Much of this was the fault of Westmoreland, who reversed his earlier hunch and promoted a theory that all the action in the south was merely a distraction for the main action that was about to take place on the DMZ. In his foreword to the later battle write-up he argued, "There is also little doubt that the enemy hoped at Khe Sanh to attain a climactic victory, such as he had done in 1954 at Dien Bien Phu," a claim denied by his adversary Giap. Westmoreland compounded the error by asserting that the overall intent was to seize the two northern provinces to establish a "liberation government." There was no intelligence supporting this thesis.

Khe Sanh, more than any other battle, strained relations across the military and political hierarchies. Everybody seemed to lose their heads. No other encounter provoked Johnson into demanding a sand table be built in the White House. No other battle kept the President so awake, demanding situation reports in the dead hours of the morning, and a written pledge "signed in blood" from the Joint Chiefs that they would not fail, or so the popular myth went. Westmoreland spent the entire period sleeping near the Combined Operations Center rather than in his quarters. From here, he received a call from the White House every afternoon demanding updates on the situation. Westmoreland in turn felt let down by a lack of trust in Washington fanned by media hysteria. No other battle provoked MACV into contemplating a tactical nuclear strike in the charmingly named Operation *Fracture Jaw*. The communists would never again concentrate such a large military force against the American foe, and the full might of American military prowess would never again be called upon to win a single battle.

And yet no other battle provoked so much disagreement over why it was being fought at all. To Westmoreland, as we have seen, it was clear as daylight. To his enemies and skeptics, it was lunacy. The three services fell out like quarreling siblings, and Washington surrendered rationality. Most damagingly, relations between Westmoreland and I CTZ Commander marine Lieutenant General Cushman hit a nadir. Such was Westmoreland's paranoia over the war in I CTZ that he took the "unpardonable" decision to establish the four-star MACV Forward HQ commanded by Abrams, to the chagrin of the marines.[60] By February 5, 366 officers had set up MACV's Trojan Horse in Phu Bai.[61] The deployment changed little as Cushman retained tight control of tactical decisions affecting his marines in III MAF, and Abrams, who actually shared Westmoreland's misgivings over the performance of the marines, was too relaxed a character to provoke inter-service battles. In an inflammatory message to Wheeler, Westmoreland asserted, "The military professionalism of the Marines falls far short of the standards that would be demanded of our armed forces." He added, in a pompous, sweeping generalization, "Their standards, tactics, and lack of command supervision throughout their ranks requires improvement in the national interest."[62] Cushman was incensed. The breakdown in relations then extended between Westmoreland and his air chief Momyer. "Spike, if I lose Khe Sanh," Westmoreland threatened Momyer, "I am going to hold the United States Air Force responsible."[63] This was supreme ingratitude from an army commander towards an air force that would in fact save the besieged marines.

Hanoi never properly understood why it fought the battle, and it has never been honest in its accounts since. In the end, it all amounted to so much death for the possession of a slight plateau measuring roughly one mile long and half a mile wide, near an old French coffee plantation. Over 5,000 North Vietnamese soldiers were killed contesting this space over a two-month period.

Then, as if disenchanted by the play, both sides quit, the Americans eventually never to return.[64] Nobody could even agree on the name of the place. To the communists it was Ta Con. On the 1:50,000 scale map sheet TL 7014-6342-2 it was annotated Xom Con. To the marines holding the place it was simply Khe Sanh, named after a nearby village three miles to the south.

Khe Sanh Combat Base – to give it its full name – was strategically located in the mouth of a valley, immediately north of a key junction on Colonial Route 9 and a short drive from the Laotian border. Any invader from the north seeking to bypass the heavily fortified DMZ had to pass through this natural constriction. This was why a special force camp had been built here, along with a second camp six miles to the southwest at Lang Vei. Immediately east of the base was the Rao Quan River, cutting a very steep, wooded ravine, which effectively acted as a barrier to any assaults from this direction. North of the base was a ring of hills, only known by the spot heights – 758, 881, 861, 556, 950, and 1015 – and this is where the comparisons with Dien Bien Phu were made. Many of these features had been contested in the previous year, on occasions in desperately close fights.

And yet for all Johnson's horror that Khe Sanh might unravel into another damn "Dinbinphoo" (Dien Bien Phu) it was precisely the topography that dictated this would never happen. In the latter battle, the French base had been ringed by hills from which Viet Minh sappers had been able to dig approach trenches to the very edges of the defended strong points. The lie of the hills had also permitted Giap to build bunkers to conceal artillery guns used to batter the besieged French. Not only was Khe Sanh not ringed by hills, but the nearest dominant feature, the long spur of Hill 881, was a good two miles from the northwestern perimeter of the base, a quite impossible distance to close. The People's Army did dig approach trenches to the south and west but they were not on the scale of the earlier siege. Repeating the tactics of Dien Bien Phu would have taken many months, and a prohibitive manpower bill. There was only one viable avenue of approach to the base and this was from the north, along the ungraded subsidiary Route 608. This route traversed open and in some places marshy terrain. Unless the communists attempted to squeeze a Soviet-style, armored thrust down the valley, which they were quite incapable of orchestrating, Khe Sanh was not going to fall. The only other viable approach route was from the Laotian border to the west, hand-railing Colonial Route 9. This axis was blocked by the special force and CIDG camp at Lang Vei, which represented the easier and tempting target.

The Dien Bien Phu comparison was always exaggerated. Major General Rathvon McC. Tompkins whose men were based at Khe Sanh thought so, as did the base commander, who pretended he had never heard of Dien Bien Phu.[65] Setting aside the topography, the differences between the two battles were

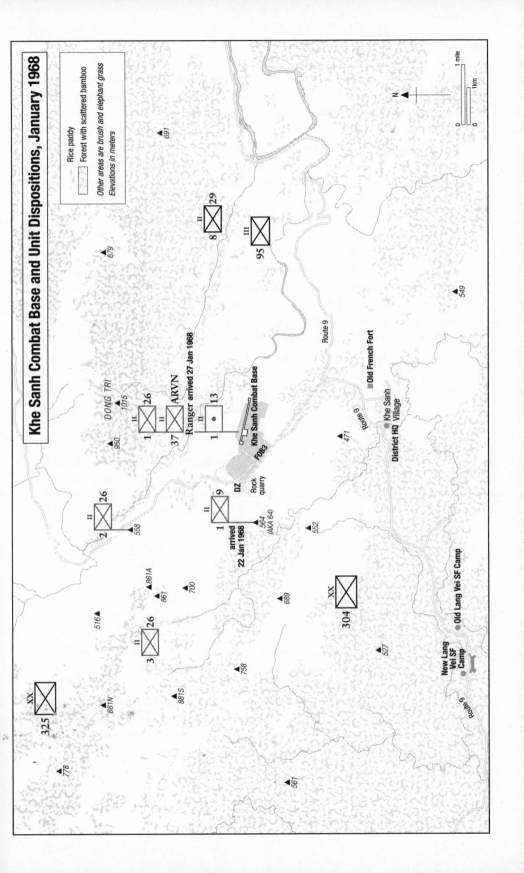

Khe Sanh Combat Base and Unit Dispositions, January 1968

Rice paddy

Forest with scattered bamboo

Other areas are brush and elephant grass

Elevations in meters

N

0 ___ 1 mile

0 ___ km

691

679

III 95

II 8 29

549

DONG TRI

1015

950

ARVN

Ranger arrived 27 Jan 1968

II 26 1

II 37

II 1 13

Route 9

Old French Fort

Khe Sanh Combat Base

FOB3

DZ

Rock quarry

471

Route 9

Khe Sanh Village

District HQ

II 26 2

558

II 9 1

arrived 22 Jan 1968

564 (AKA 64)

552

689

XX 304

861A

861

700

527

New Lang Vei SF Camp

Old Lang Vei SF Camp

Route 9

516

II 26 3

758

881S

XX 325

881N

778

561

manifest. The principal vulnerability at Khe Sanh was actually the single water point located outside the camp perimeter, which the PAVN failed to destroy. The lack of deep underground bunkers also struck visitors, a failure attributed to marine bravado. But these were minor weaknesses and other comparisons fail. Unlike the marines, the French garrison had been truly, almost madly, isolated. There had been no hope of relief by a ground force. The entire French gamble had rested on its weak air force and even a cursory comparison of the balance of air power in the two sieges revealed wide disparities. Ten times as many aircraft were committed to the defense of Khe Sanh, eventually dropping a bomb tonnage equivalent to five Hiroshimas – the PAVN stood no chance. At Dien Bien Phu, the cunningly sited Viet Minh artillery guns dumped thousands of shells on the trapped defenders. At Khe Sanh, at the height of the siege, around a hundred shells were landing daily on the camp. This was grossly insufficient. Just 205 defenders were killed over 77 days – a low rate of attrition that was not going to affect the final outcome of the battle. When the PAVN lobbed mortar bombs, the marines learned to count 21 seconds between the "thunk" and the "bang," or plenty of time to take cover. The French garrison suffered 14 times as many fatalities in one month and became swamped by the wounded that could not be evacuated. At Dien Bien Phu, the air force had been unable to resupply the garrison at anything approaching the level necessary to sustain a drawn-out fight. At Khe Sanh, USAF C-130s and C-123Ks landed or parachuted 12,000 tons of supplies. Army helicopters ferried a further 4,600 tons. Almost 20,000 passengers were shuttled in and out of the base, a measure of the failure of the communist attempt to close the runway.

Marine Tony Gleaton – flown in as one of those reinforcements – recalled the shock of arrival:

> as I looked out of the plane and looked down and it looked like a Hieronymus Bosch painting like, you know, it looked like hell. I mean there were explosions and craters … the mud … you'd be stepping in that shit and it could take a boot off if it's not laced up tight. We finally did, we finally got in. I think it took us almost a week to get there.[66]

His sojourn did not last long. Soon after arrival he was caught in an explosion and was on his way out again in a medevac helicopter.

However, Khe Sanh was never going to be another Dien Bien Phu, but nobody at the time could view the siege except through the lens of the earlier French defeat. When journalist Oriana Fallaci interviewed Giap one year after the battle, he asserted, "Khe Sanh didn't try to be, nor could it have been, a Dien Bien Phu. Khe Sanh wasn't that important to us. Or it was only to the extent that it was important to the Americans."[67] For Giap, if he is to be believed, it was all about American prestige. Washington could not afford to lose at Khe Sanh. Giap could take or leave the prize – either way, the result would be perceived as a symbol of the futility of the war in American eyes. When the base was finally abandoned in June, the symbol was stamped.

Despite obstinate communist opacity over the battle, a captured map has proved revealing both of PAVN dispositions and intentions.[68] Hanoi's intelligence, as ever, was accurate. Tran Quy Hai, the front commander, believed, correctly, that the base was being held by 26th Marine Regiment supported by 37th ARVN Ranger Battalion. Surreptitious reconnaissance had established outlying USMC and ARVN positions in nearby hill observation posts and in the village of Khe Sanh. Hai established a corps HQ in a village called Sar Lit, across the border, with two veteran formations under his command: 304th and 325th Divisions (also sometimes referred to as 325C Division). The former was "the banner unit of the People's Army of Vietnam," Hanoi's oldest division.[69] Victors at the battle of Route Coloniale 4 and Dien Bien Phu, 304th Division had some claim to being not only the senior but also the best formation in North Vietnam. 325th Division had been raised after the war, but was the first to enter South Vietnam, infiltrating between December 1964 and April 1965.[70] From analysis of over 2,000 captured documents it appears this division only deployed with its 18th Regiment, supported by 31st Regiment from 341st Division, and an unknown regiment from 324B Division.[71] For the first time in the war, a battalion of PT-76 light tanks was also deployed into South Vietnam, to the later considerable surprise of the defenders of Lang Vei.

By December 1967, the covert infiltration of all these units was complete. Khe Sanh was effectively encircled from the west and south, but never surrounded. Not one PAVN unit was located to the east of the base, the communists probably concluding that the Ran Quan River presented an insuperable obstacle.

Hai established two major artillery bases to support the forthcoming assaults. The first was built on Hill 881, roughly five miles northwest of Khe Sanh. The second remained on the Laotian border, about nine miles southwest of Khe Sanh but less than three miles from Lang Vei. These shared between them as many as 26 122mm rocket launchers and 24 105mm artillery guns. The logic of their placement suggests that Hai intended two axes of advance, one from the north and one from the west, as the ground naturally dictated, each supported by the firebases. The fact that the communists were able to establish these redoubts, undetected and within striking distance of Khe Sanh and Lang Vei, is testimony to the logistic stamina of the PAVN, as well as the difficulty the marines faced trying to staunch the infiltration of an enemy aided by the cover of a triple canopy jungle.

The hopelessness of Khe Sanh as a block to infiltration was more starkly evident in the disposition of the Hai's infantry battalions. 304th Division units were actually two miles south of Lang Vei, hidden in the spurs of Hill 663. Khe Sanh had already been bypassed. These included 66th PAVN Regiment that would mount the assault on Khe Sanh village, and 9th PAVN Regiment, to the east, that would seize the intersection on Colonial Route 9, immediately south of the base. The third regiment, the 24th, was further west on the Laotian border.

These were the dispositions, but what did the communists truly intend? Notwithstanding Giap's diffidence, Khe Sanh was the only battle in the entire Tet Offensive in which the People's Army appears to have made a concerted and sustained attempt to overrun a substantial American force, and yet, for all its local importance, it mattered not a whit to the overall outcome of the General Offensive-General Uprising. Abrams later confessed to being baffled by the battle and viewed it as a grand failure of Giap's strategic vision. "Look at Khe Sanh," he joked in a command meeting. "Poor old Giap ... I feel really sorry for him. He was a prisoner of his experience. And he kept at that thing, kept at that thing, and chewed those divisions up so there wasn't a damn thing left."[72] If instead Giap had trundled down the coastal plain, Abrams confessed, "I don't know how the hell we'd ever have gotten them out of there! We couldn't put another battalion in northern I Corps! There was a time we couldn't put another company in northern I Corps!"[73]

Abrams was right. Hanoi could hardly have picked a more distant and unimportant spot from the strategic prizes where the game was going to be won, or lost. Indeed, it is not implausible that Khe Sanh was picked precisely because it was the westernmost and most remote marine base, within walking distance of the Laotian border. An attempt would be made at dislodging the defenders at Khe Sanh. If it succeeded, Hanoi could claim a great victory – its first undeniable victory against American troops. If it failed, it could still claim that it had drawn American troops away from its real objectives. Either way, disaster could be avoided by scooting back across the border. A deserter would claim that the overall strategy had been to overrun all the marine bases on the DMZ, but this sounded like self-serving propaganda to rouse the troops, and no actions undertaken on the Route 9 front suggest that such a bold move was ever countenanced. Regardless, and on both counts, the strategy was a resounding flop. Hanoi never seemed to calculate the tremendous flexibility and weight of American air power and although Westmoreland "took the bait," there was no sufficiently decisive shift of US ground forces allowing the communists to seize their Tet objectives further south. From Westmoreland's viewpoint, it was the People's Army that took the bait. For 325th and 304th PAVN Divisions, Khe Sanh became a sacrificial altar, a "meat grinder" with no great purpose.

The marines had first entered the area in the ineffective Operation *Virginia* (April 17–May 1, 1966). Just one shot had been fired.[74] The first full marine battalion deployed to the base in late September – 1/3 Marines under Major Peter Wickwire – against the wishes of General Walt. By now Khe Sanh had become a busy outpost hosting MACV-SOG (Studies and Observations Group) teams and CIDG (Civilian Irregular Defense Group). These routinely made incursions into Laos, supplying intelligence highly rated by Westmoreland (the *Shining Brass* and *Prairie Fire* missions). In the short term, the marines were tasked to remain at Khe Sanh to protect the productive special force operations. In the longer term, Westmoreland harbored plans for a full-scale incursion into Laos. If this were ever to pass, Khe Sanh was indispensable. The pressure of the "DMZ battles" and an obvious political reluctance to expand the war meant that, by the beginning of 1967, the base had been reduced to a single company provided by 1/9 Marines.[75] By the end of the year, with the front stabilized, Khe Sanh was once again reinforced with a full regiment – 26th Marines.

When Tet erupted, the base was under the overall command of a Colonel David Lownds. He refused to be drawn in by all the hoopla, and responded to the drama by growing a bristly mustache. In the recent past, two marine bases at nearby Con Thien and Gio Linh had been similarly besieged. The besiegers had been annihilated by a combination of air strikes and counter-battery fire (in the perfectly named Operation *Neutralize*).[76] 1/26 Marines defending the base itself fell under Lieutenant Colonel James Wilkinson, a "well-regarded officer" whose battalion would serve the longest stretch at Khe Sanh. For the marines stuck in this outpost, Khe Sanh was a small island of olive drab tents and tin-roof huts, littered with piles of stores and oil drums, all surmounted by a forest of antennae. As the battle developed, the red clay became saturated with shards of shrapnel. The biggest discomfort was the rats, as big as "footballs," and attracted by human flesh.

The attack, when it came, was not a complete surprise. A PAVN deserter sneaked into the camp on January 20 to warn the marines that an assault would be launched that very night. Lieutenant La Thanh Tonc arrived waving a white flag and offering some surprisingly accurate intelligence.

Tonc's warning mostly unfolded as he described it. In a mass infantry attack reminiscent of the human wave attacks of the First Indochina War, 6th Battalion made a concerted attempt to overrun the marine outpost on Hill 861 but failed. The nearby village of Khe Sanh, however, was easily overrun (by 8th Battalion from 66th Regiment, 304th Division), but this had only been lightly defended by a Regional Force detachment and two marine platoons. An attempted rescue mission in the vicinity of a feature known as the Old French Fort turned into a disaster: 27 American pilots and crew and

74 Regional Force soldiers were either killed or went missing.[77] Despite this setback the majority of the marines and wounded were successfully evacuated and stragglers made their own way back, on foot, to the sanctuary of Khe Sanh Combat Base. The principal significance of this loss was that it doomed Lang Vei, which should also have been evacuated, but was not.

The failure to capture Hill 861 seemed to derail the planned assault on the main base. Instead, the North Vietnamese contented themselves with shelling Khe Sanh with around 100 mortar bombs and 60 122mm rockets.[78] This dawn salvo produced the only success on the communist side. One rocket landed on the main ammunition dump with devastating effect. Lance Corporal Seitz recalled that the resultant fireball "was like watching on the TV set."[79] In the order of 11,000 shells landed across a wide area. Marines who had taken shelter in trenches had to gingerly remove "glowing red," unexploded shells that had been lobbed into their refuges. Gallantly, C Battery of 1/13 Marines continued to offer counter-battery fire although the gun line was within 75 yards of the exploding dump, and even after a shell hit a gun pit. The battery commander, Captain William J. O'Connor, spent three hours picking up unexploded duds and carrying them away before they exploded. By the end of the morning, over 3,000 shells had been fired back, despite the battery taking casualties and losing all communications. The damage caused by this mortar and rocket attack was steep. Khe Sanh was left with just 4,000 shells; the airstrip and control tower were temporarily put out of action; and a dozen helicopters suffered varying degrees of damage.

Notwithstanding this coup, if this was the start of a serious attempt to capture Khe Sanh, it had got off to a bad start. Aside from seizing the village, the PAVN had failed to overrun any marine position and seemed to have lost momentum. On January 22, General Cushman flew in an additional marine battalion – 1/9 Marines, a unit that had endured the misery of Con Thien. The sister 2/26 Marines had already been deployed to the base the previous week. Five days later, the three marine battalions were joined by an ARVN ranger battalion. If a second assault were mounted, the PAVN would be facing many more defenders. Instead, at least at the base, it all went quiet. Predictions that a major assault was imminent came and went, but there was little action beyond intermittent shelling (no action of significance on the North Vietnamese side; III MAF responded with more than 300 daily air strikes).[80]

For all the sound and fury, the action at Khe Sanh became curiously anticlimactic, although clearly not to the marines taking cover in the scrapes. An attempt was made to overrun Echo Company on Hill 861A which cost the PAVN over 100 dead. Seven marines were killed and 37 wounded. Some communist soldiers had settled down to read copies of *Playboy* magazine, filched from captured trenches, such was their complacency. Others more pragmatically searched for American tinned rations. Then the marines counterattacked in what was later described as "a melee that resembled a bloody, waterfront barroom brawl."[81] Unable to recover their dead, the North Vietnamese corpses began to rot. Marines manning the hillpost resorted to wearing gas masks. Hundreds of bodies were eventually burned.

A week after the battle had been joined, 7th Battalion of 66th Regiment and 4th Battalion of 24th Regiment overran the CIDG camp at Lang Vei. This attack witnessed the first use of the PT-76 tanks, some of which apparently included female crew, or at least this is what the communist propaganda claimed. The stoutness of the defenders was matched by the ill-discipline of the attackers: looting seemed to preoccupy the North Vietnamese as much as finishing off the Americans. Remarkably, the majority of the two dozen or so Green Berets at Lang Vei managed to escape and evade, although virtually every man was wounded.[82] One of the fugitives – a Lieutenant Paul Longgrear – experienced such improbable escapes he later abandoned his atheism, converted to Christianity, and became a minister. Eventually, almost 250 of the indigenous troops also managed to straggle home. These were later joined by around 3,000 Laotians serving with the Laotian Volunteer Battalion 33 who had earlier been overrun at a border base and who converged on Khe Sanh. The PAVN also succeeded in cutting Route 9, but the monsoon was seeing to that anyway. An attempt was then made to dislodge 1/9 Marines from Hill 64 by elements from 101st Regiment, but this ended in a bloody failure. Twenty-four marines were killed defending this hastily prepared position, but many more communist soldiers were strewn across the hillsides.

After all the anticipation and arguments, this was the story of the siege of Khe Sanh. The mountain outposts were attacked, but resolutely defended and never overrun. Approach trenches were dug but the base was not encircled. The runway was regularly shelled but never closed. On the worst day, February 23, 1,307 shells fell on the base, killing ten marines. The unequal nature of the fight (entirely missed by the press that continued to portray a modern-day Alamo) was well illustrated by the artillery duels. Notwithstanding the lucky early strike on an ammunition dump, 1/13 Marines lobbed back 158,891 shells. On March 17 – St. Patrick's Day – the batteries even fired green smoke rounds on enemy positions in honor of the patron saint of the Fighting Irish.[83] Aircraft were sniped at but without the necessary density of antiaircraft fire to close the lifeline. In the entire siege, a single large-scale attack was attempted. This fell against 37th ARVN Ranger Battalion holding the western end of the runway, but was easily repulsed.[84] Seventy-eight bodies were later recovered huddled in trenches where they had died. The PAVN never seriously threatened to overrun the base. Had an all-out assault been attempted, it would have roundly failed. The marines at Khe Sanh were not going to capitulate.

The resupply of Khe Sanh proved the lifeline. This was mounted by 834th Air Division, supported by 152 Aerial Refueler Transport Squadron, and helicopters from 16 and 18 Marine Air Groups. The base needed around 235 tons of supplies delivered daily.[85] To meet this need, a daily average of 11 C-130 sorties was achieved. But such was the wear and tear on these machines the longevity of the tires halved from 40 to 18 sorties.[86] Although deliveries fell short on many days, the marines were never in a state of emergency. In Operation "*Cool It*," helicopter pilots even managed to deliver hundreds of Dixie-cups of ice cream to the luxury-starved marines manning the hilltop posts.

For the communist gunners, the larger "Herky Birds" proved an irresistible target. One pilot, Colonel Thomas Sumner, flew 20 sorties to Khe Sanh. On only one trip did he not return with a bullet-riddled fuselage. Another, Colonel Howard Dallman, managed the improbable feat of landing his aircraft on fire, turning it around, unloading it, and taking off on three engines, still taking ground fire. To save the pilots from an inevitable downing, air drops were attempted – 496 in total – delivering 8,100 tons of supplies, with an impressive 110 yards circular error probability.[87] Even so a disaster was inevitable. On March 6, a C-123 was hit and crashed, killing 43 marines and all the crew. In total, 26 transports would receive serious damage running the gauntlet at Khe Sanh, and virtually no aircraft managed the run unscathed.

Khe Sanh would never have fallen anyway because it was defended by an unprecedented bombing operation. This was given the codename *Niagara II*, so Westmoreland recalled, because he wanted a waterfall of high explosives to fall on the enemy. His wish came to pass. B-52s alone dropped 59,000 tons of high explosives, flattening tracts of jungle before the amazed stares of the besieged marines. With dark military humor the marines nicknamed the Arc Light raids "Number One on the hit parade." Communist soldiers were found wandering dazed with blood streaming from their noses and ears. Whatever damage was inflicted on the enemy, the devastation to the fauna was equally tremendous. This remote border area was populated by elephants, tigers, and other exotica. Pilots were instructed to avoid killing "friendly" elephants (animals not marked by the tell-tale red mud indicating they had been transporting communist stores down the Ho Chi Minh Trail), but B-52 strikes were not that discriminate. Westmoreland himself would later concede, "The thing that broke their backs was basically the fire of the B-52s."[88]

A high kill count was claimed for the bombing (over 10,000 enemy killed) but around 1,600 bodies were actually counted. 304th Division was in action again in May at Dong Ha, suggesting that the division had not been totally smashed by the bombers. 18th Regiment from 325th Division was also in action at Hue, suggesting that it too avoided the pummeling. Desertions and demoralization appear to have been the bigger problem on the communist side. Captured documents and prisoner testimonies revealed that the average communist soldier had suffered great hardships, hunger, and sickness, even before having to come to terms with the possibility of being blasted to oblivion by a B-52 strike.[89] Most units, it appears, were only at half strength anyway. When Pham Xuan, then serving with 66th Regiment, fell ill with malaria, he was literally brought back from the dead. "Thinking that I was dead," he recalled, "military comrades, took me to a private cellar to wait for burial." Fortunately, a comrade, Nguyen Van Du, realized he was still breathing and alerted the regimental doctors.[90] The DMZ was never a happy place to soldier. Regardless of the true enemy kill count (postwar Hanoi would state that around 2,400 soldiers were killed over a six-month period on this front), it is indisputable that the sheer weight of aerial bombardments conducted around Khe Sanh had the decisive effect on the outcome of the battle.

The most detailed study of the battle, conducted by authors Prados and Stubbe, has vividly quantified this explosive Niagara. Over 24,000 strike sorties were flown. At the height of the fighting, the skies over Khe Sanh resembled "a giant beehive" filled with shrieking jets. Every day of the siege, the equivalent of 1.3 kilotons of tactical nuclear weapons was dropped on the enemy, or imagined enemy. If a figure of 20,000 North Vietnamese soldiers is accepted, then the US government personally delivered five tons of bombs to each communist soldier. Or, viewed another way, each defender was protected by more than 15 tons of bombs.[91]

Notwithstanding that Khe Sanh was not going to fall, the marines could not be allowed to sit out an indefinite siege. Everybody knew that the base was going to be abandoned and "no one wanted to be the last person to get shot at Khe Sanh."[92] Operation *Pegasus*, the relief operation, was mounted from Ca Lu, and commanded by Major General John Tolson, commander 1st Cavalry. Unwilling to be "saved" by the Army, a marine contingent also took part, supported by engineers and an ARVN airborne brigade. It started on April 1 and it was all over in a week. The official handshake took place at 8 o'clock in the morning on April 8. To actually reach the base on the dilapidated Route 9, army engineers rebuilt nine miles of road and erected nine bridges. Even if the communists had broken through, they would not have got much further beyond Khe Sanh. General Lowell English had always been right: "You could lose it and you haven't really lost a damn thing."[93]

What if anything was achieved, by either side, in this costly encounter? Ultimately, the Khe Sanh Combat Base had not served its purpose. PAVN infiltration around Khe Sanh, the A Shau Valley, and further south in Hue and Da Nang was never interdicted. Some 5,000 marines were fixed in a remote base which ultimately required a vast amount of air force resources to keep them alive. The psychological attrition suffered by the Johnson administration was severe – Khe Sanh traumatized some senior American officials in Washington. Military commanders similarly became fraught and relationships were strained. Khe Sanh distracted from the main effort in Saigon and provoked hysterical media coverage. The poor, suffering marines became a national obsession, even if the besieged did not really share this perception of themselves. Critics never offered realistic alternatives, or only offered one – get out. But evacuation, for a number of reasons, was not feasible without a significant loss of stores and materials. This alternative also ignored the judgment of the marine command that saw no reason to capitulate. Khe Sanh was not going to fall – it was that simple for Tompkins – so why quit? The enemy would be defeated and suffer heavy casualties, which transpired.

A follow-up operation – *Delaware* – was conducted in the A Shau Valley in April and May. This was mounted by 1st Cavalry, 101st Airborne, and 1st ARVN Division, led by Lieutenant General William Rosson (now in command of XXIV Corps with Abrams reverting to his post as Westmoreland's deputy). This resulted in heavy fighting in Thua Thien Province, and in the destruction of a large quantity of enemy materiel. MACV judged the operation a great success. In Rosson's self-serving estimation it was "one of the most audacious, skilfully executed and successful combat undertakings of the Vietnam War."[94] It certainly served to send the People's Army packing, but its effects were only temporary. Within a short period, A Shau reverted to being an enemy sanctuary. Khe Sanh itself was eventually vacated on July 3, an operation as tricky militarily as it was politically. Strategically, the withdrawal meant little. The new anchor base was established at Ca Lu, a few miles further down Route 9 to the east. The front line, such as it existed on the previous DMZ, barely changed.

By 1968, Saigon had become the greatest jungle in Vietnam, where everything was for sale. The city was more a restless, broiling energy than a defined urban space. More than two million people were squeezed into central Saigon making it the most crowded city in the world.[95] Greater Saigon, which more than doubled the population, was a labyrinth of shanty towns which now extended 28 miles to the west, 20 miles to the south and 35 miles to the north. Its inhabitants lived with the sound of artillery fire and the rumble of B-52 strikes. At night, a midnight curfew restored some semblance of peace. The traffic was insufferable, with over half a million motorcycles creating a permanent smell of acrid, two-stroke fumes. There was a lack of reliable electricity and water. The drug trade and a black market in military ware, including weapons and ammunition, thrived. Street hawkers, conmen, and prostitutes all engaged in a frantic scramble for the American dollar. With as many as 25,000 American troops annually spending $200 million, mostly in the city, this dollar was not hard to find. It was estimated that the average bar girl was making twice the prime minister's salary. Saigon was a city being raped and now it was the communists' turn.

There were two iconic moments in Saigon, and both had everything to do with image and nothing to do with actuality. The first was the assault on the US Embassy by 19 members of C-10 PLAF City Sapper Battalion. It began in the early hours of the morning of January 31 with a massive explosion that tore a hole in the perimeter wall on Thang Nhut Boulevard. By dawn, after much confusion and some hairy close-quarter gun fights, it was all over. Eighteen of the assailants lay dead in the gardens like bloodied rag dolls. Just one survived, wounded, a slight young man dressed in shorts and plimsolls. Five Americans had been killed. But for the heavy, cherrywood doors of the Chancery, it could have been worse. When the attack fell, all the South Vietnamese guards fled and the Saigon First Precinct Police refused to help.

The audacious but ultimately suicidal attack was swiftly snuffed out, but not on the news wires, where the echoes of gun fire in a US embassy rung loud. The early evening news channels carried the story with all its drama – and exaggerated accounts – shocking an American public. How could the symbol of American power in Vietnam have been so easily attacked? How did the enemy penetrate the heart of Saigon with impunity? The attack on the US Embassy, more than any other event on the first night of the Tet Offensive, profoundly shook public confidence in the narrative promoted by the Johnson administration. The shocking television images did not look, smell, or feel like victory. They looked like a misbegotten war, plain in every American living room.

The second event took place at the northern end of Ngo Gia Tu Street in Cholon, and involved a rather weedy-looking Saigon police chief called Nguyen Ngoc Loan. Today, this is the site of "Cozy," an Italian sofa shop. The inoffensive Loan would end his days as a one-legged manager of a pizza parlor in a Washington suburb, but not before involuntarily offering perhaps the iconic image of the entire war.

There were two other elements to the story: a .38 Special Smith & Wesson, and a captured Viet Cong captain called Nguyen Van Lem. The unfortunate barefoot Lem, dressed in a red plaid shirt, knew he was in trouble from the moment he was hustled down the street, arms trussed and flanked by bullyingly triumphant ARVN soldiers. He had been found hiding near the An Quang pagoda, two hundred yards away, armed with a pistol. At the end of the street,

Eddie Adams, an Associated Press reporter, and Vo Su, an NBC cameraman, picked up their gear. After a fruitless morning, over the course of which neither had found a newsworthy story to report, here was some action, at last.

Lem was brought to Loan. Loan waved the soldiers to one side, lifted his .38 Special Smith & Wesson to Lem's head, and pulled the trigger. Lem fell like a stone, blood gushing from his insensible head. No words were exchanged. The banality of the miserable execution was mesmeric.

Yet Lem's abrupt demise was unremarkable. A similar scene had probably been played out a thousand times in Vietnam's endless wars. What transformed the execution was the camera. It is one thing to know that a war is immoral, ugly, and brutalizing, and quite another for it to be exhibited so matter-of-factly. Loan could have been stubbing out a cigarette on the pavement. It was "some guy shooting somebody" as Adams laconically recalled.[96] A child crossed the road to take a look. It seemed the most natural thing to do. The blood from Lem's brain ran away in three graceful rivulets, like a pattern on the Mekong Delta. Loan disappeared from shot, as if nothing had happened.

But something quite momentous had happened. Adams' famous photograph of the "few grams of lead that are caught forever between barrel and head" exploded in many more heads.[97] Every last, dumb patriotic cliché tumbled with the lifeless Lem. Was this really what Americans were fighting for? "It was clear at that point," CIA officer Norm Gardner later reflected, "that the Americans weren't going to stand for this crap."[98]

Truth also took a bullet to the head on that morning. Adams' photograph had international aftershocks – how could it not? Loan the executioner had to be redeemed, in some way, and Lem demonized. But how do you redeem a cold-blooded executioner caught on camera committing a war crime? By an inverted and perverse victimhood, characteristic of the wider exculpation of atrocities committed over the course of the war: Loan was the real victim, not Lem. So grew the stories that Lem had been responsible for throat-slitting; that he had murdered women and children; that he had been found at the site of a mass grave even. None of this was remotely true. The latter appear to have been conflation with an Associated Press story of a decapitated ARVN officer and his murdered family in a northern Saigon suburb – or nowhere near were Lem was found.

Adams was a former marine, a personal friend of General Lewis Walt, and later described Lem as "a hero" who should be mourned. At the time, as fellow photographer Horst Faas, then photo editor for AP News recalls, Adams was actually excited by his coup, felt no guilt, and pretended to be nonchalant. Adams' later sense of guilt over the image stemmed from the trouble Loan experienced in exile in America when the powerful engines of Congress and the Immigration and Naturalization Service combined to almost expel the former brigadier general as a war criminal, only saved by a personal intervention from Jimmy Carter. He was charged with "moral turpitude," a malaise shared with his excusers.

———

Of all the set piece battles fought over the course of the Tet Offensive, the battle for Hue was the most poignant. The very name sounded like a resigned sigh. What other outcome was likely when General Tran Van Quang, PAVN commander of the Tri Thien-Hue Front, gave the signal to assault the city in the early hours of the morning of February 1? The surprise was near complete, as was the destruction.[99]

Hue was the jewel in the Vietnamese diadem – an imperial city on a Perfume River. At the heart of the old city was a 19th-century citadel and palace. This complex mixed the vernacular of a Buddhist cosmogony with the stoutness of French military engineering. The result was three square miles of ornate buildings, narrow alleyways, and thick walls. Some of the fortifications were 40 feet thick. The moat was 90 feet wide. The Japanese had added to the French layout by building additional tunnels and bunkers. If serving no other purpose, the former capital of Annam had been built to withstand the most determined assault.

The old city had grown north of the river and comprised four quadrants. The northeast corner housed the headquarters of 1st ARVN Division, commanded by the able Brigadier General Ngo Quang Truong. The only other military unit in the old city was a company of "Black Panthers," the Hac Bao rapid reaction force also under the command of Truong. In reality, the defense of Hue lay in the hands of the provincial police – in the beginning it was always going to be a push-over for the PAVN and Viet Cong. The northwest corner of the Citadel also included a small air strip, Tay Loc Airfield, which would witness heavy fighting. The southern half was dominated by the palace itself with its 750-yard-long walls. Immediately east of the old city walls was the sprawling working-class Gia Hoi district. South of the river and connected by the six-span Nguyen Hoang Bridge was the modern, smaller city. This was where a 200-strong MACV American-Australian training team was housed in a large compound in Doc Lao Park, near the Tu Do stadium. Six blocks to the west was the modern administrative center where the Thua Thien Provincial Administration Center building was located. The modern city also housed Hue University, a US Consulate, a modern hospital, and a cathedral. One mile south of the MACV compound, past rows of cane fields, was a second waterway, the Phu Cam Canal, spanned by the An Cuu Bridge. Any force dominating the Nguyen Hoang Bridge effectively isolated the city from the south. Entry into the Citadel from the other three sides was via six gates, which would prove hard to take. Around 140,000 Vietnamese called Hue home on the eve of the Lunar New Year in 1968.

At 2:33am on February 1, the firing started. Nguyen Van, who was in the vanguard, recalled:

> We attacked simultaneously 30 different targets, concentrating our fire on the nerve centers from the very beginning ... we stormed the Mang Ca military base, which was the command post of the puppet First Corps and the First Division. Then we attacked the regional command headquarters of Thua Thien at the Thuan-ba hotel, paralyzing the command capacity of the enemy for the entire province. And we attacked the areas where the Americans were living such as the areas on Dong Da, Ly Thuong Kiet, Le Dinh Duong and Duy Tan streets.[100]

Elements from two infiltrated battalions and 15 special force units were involved in the initial assault. It was later estimated that, overall, as many as 20 battalions may have become involved in the battle (the communist account offered the lesser figure of some 3,000 fighters in the Hue environs). 6th PAVN Regiment supported by 12th VC Sapper Battalion led the assault from the southwest. 800 and 802 Battalions quickly invested the Palace and southern half of the Citadel but failed to take the airstrip and the 1st ARVN Division headquarters. 4th PAVN Regiment's 804 Battalion attacked the MACV compound but was also repulsed. The tough defense mounted by the ARVN and allied soldiers doomed the PAVN attempt to seize Hue. Had these compounds and the airstrip fallen, the psychological shock would have been huge and the problem of retaking Hue magnified several-fold. Even as these desperate actions were being fought, 806 and 810 Battalions deployed north and south of the city respectively to cut off Highway 1. By mid-morning, 6th PAVN Regiment was lodged in the Citadel and 4th PAVN Regiment had taken control of the modern city south of the river.

As the events unfolded, the question pressing American and Vietnamese commanders was: which units were close enough to react? The majority of 1st ARVN Division (which was at half strength because of the national holiday) was already committed and providing security north of the city on Highway 1. The nearest unit was 3rd ARVN Regiment based just five miles away. Arguably the single most important decision in the battle was taken by Truong on the first day. Appreciating the seriousness of the situation he ordered 3rd ARVN Regiment, reinforced by two airborne battalions, to rush to the defense of his headquarters before 806 Battalion could cut Highway 1. Truong's alacrity and reinforcement meant the PAVN would never be able to dislodge the ARVN and the battle effectively became a siege within a siege. This forceful response contrasted with marine Brigadier General Foster C. LaHue's complacency, later attributed to an intelligence failure. Further up the command chain, both Cushman and Lieutenant General Hoang Xuan Lam, commander of all South Vietnamese forces in I Corps, were even less clear over events in the old imperial capital.

The odd coincidence of LaHue's name in the battle for Hue, with hindsight, comes across as a jinx. He commanded Task Force X-Ray, based at Phu Bai, eight miles south of Hue. This formation included two regiments, 5th Marines whose Second Battalion was commanded by a Lieutenant Colonel Ernest C. Cheatham, a former professional footballer with the Pittsburg Steelers and Korea veteran, and the understrength 1/1 Marines, commanded by a Lieutenant Colonel Gravel. In the event, LaHue ordered just one company – A Company from 1/1 Marines – to trundle up the road to find out what was happening, supported by four M-48 light tanks. This piecemeal response, which continued for the next 48 hours, was a recipe for disaster.

The previous evening, Marine Scott Dawson had enjoyed a beer, the first in months, when "we got an alert that something much bigger was going down and to get ready."[101] In the morning his company deployed to Hue, a 45-minute ride away. The first thing they saw was a destroyed ARVN tank "and out of the driver's hatch was hanging the remains of the driver who had looked like he had been just cut in half." Then they reached a roundabout and petrol station and "dead in the center of the circle there was a dead NVA ... He had fresh web gear, a chest pack where he carried grenades and magazines, all his clothes looked new, and he was sort of crouched in the street with one arm pointing up." When they reached the causeway to enter the old city "all hell broke loose up at our front ... Captain Bacheller, had got caught in an ambush at the front of the column and he and, I guess about four, other people got killed."[102]

A Company was mauled. The tanks were caught by RPG fire and one crew panicked and crashed into a wall. "I remember the radioman," Marine Dawson later recounted, "He was every girl's high school sweetheart dream; tall, blonde, handsome, always a good word, and he lost both his legs, and that was that."

Gravel responded by commandeering G Company from 2/5 Marines, which had only arrived in Phu Bai that morning, and racing up Highway 1 to their rescue. Bolstered by more firepower, the combined force of A and G Companies made it to the MACV compound by mid-afternoon, but the relief cost the lives of ten marines, with 30 wounded.

LaHue then ordered Gravel to relieve the Citadel, a quite impossible task for the two exhausted companies. Gravel's protests fell on deaf ears: the obdurate LaHue was uninterested in excuses and ordered his subordinate to get on with it. The outcome was a predictable fiasco. Only G Company was in any shape to attempt a crossing of the 150-yard Nguyen Hoang Bridge, so it fell to this unlucky company to make the worthless sacrifice. Amazingly, a handful of marines did make it across the bullet-swept bridge, inspired by Lance Corporal Lester Tully who single-handedly charged a machine gun post. But they were never going to hold their lodgement. An account of what transpired is best left to Marine Dawson, who observed the disaster:

> It was just madness ... I would say they lost probably 80% if you think killed and wounded. That soured me because there was no need for that loss. The people who ordered the attack ... okay, we're Marines, that's what we do, we did it. But, we don't want to be wasted and that was a waste ... It wasn't a matter of having a fighting chance; it was just a matter of shooting fish in a barrel. That spirit, that ... the orders are go, you go.
> Nobody hesitated ... So, off they went and many of them didn't come back.

After two hours of fighting the marines retreated. In fact, a third of the company had been killed or wounded.

Cushman and Lam needed to come up with a plan quickly and the obvious option was to use the Perfume River as the boundary between Marine and ARVN forces committed to retaking Hue. Unwilling to cause damage to Vietnam's cultural jewel it was agreed that American forces would retake the modern city, south of the river, and the ARVN would expel the enemy lodged in the Citadel and Palace. There would be no artillery or air support. This restriction barely lasted 48 hours. By February 3 it became obvious the city would only be repossessed by bombing and shelling the North Vietnamese into submission. When Abrams pointed out to Vice President Ky and General Lam that there was concrete evidence the enemy was deliberately setting up positions in Buddhist temples and other historic buildings, Ky's riposte was unsentimental: "Those things were made by men. They can be rebuilt by men. Hit them."[103] The division of the task between the Marines and the ARVN, although it made perfect military sense, also contributed to a lack of coordination in the early phases of the battle. It, too, would be abandoned and the Citadel trashed.

By the third day, guerrilla Van recalled, "We became the complete master of the city." Now under communist control were the base camp of 7th Armored Regiment in the Ngu Binh area, most of the Tay Loc airstrip, the Thua Thien Province HQ, the provincial security forces HQ, the provincial pacification program HQ, the city police force HQ and numerous other command posts. Only the 1st Division HQ at Mang Ca military base held out.

However, the battle for Hue was not just being fought in the city. PAVN and Viet Cong units had dug defensive positions in the countryside surrounding the city perimeter and these had to be dislodged. Crucially, resupply routes and reinforcements had to be cut off. Lacking manpower, this vital task was at first neglected. Over the course of the 25-day battle, elements of PAVN 24th, 29th, and 99th Regiments all managed to infiltrate into the city from the north and west. The communists used the river to ferry supplies and casualties were successfully evacuated by the same route. Eventually the North Vietnamese and Viet Cong survivors escaped west along routes that were never properly interdicted. This glaring omission was probably the most important failure in the battle plan to retake Hue.

Although LaHue now had a better appreciation of the scale of the problem facing his marines, he still failed to muster sufficient forces to the task. Instead, he ordered the exhausted Gravel to take his depleted 1/1 Marines and expel the PAVN from the Thua Thien Province HQ building. The attack was launched at daybreak on February 2 in a cold rainstorm, and got nowhere.

The confusion was total:

You don't know what's going … People are shooting, people are firing back, there's noise, you hear a yell, the only thing that you understand is either, "Go there," or "Come here!" You just rattle through it and try and keep your wits and your ears open so that you don't get left behind … I was scared … those bastards were trying to kill me.[104]

Marine Dawson would in fact be wounded (twice) and eventually be medevaced. When he was returned to A Company, 1/1 Marines in April – now on Hill 861 at Khe Sanh – just six members of his platoon remained.[105] Faced with withering fire, the battalion failed to make one block. LaHue responded to this failure by peremptorily appointing Colonel Stanley Hughes, the newly arrived commander of 1st Marines, overall commander of all marine units committed to the retaking of Hue.

Unfortunately, Hughes proved as peremptory as his superior. Without properly appraising the situation, he ordered Gravel to undertake an attack to relieve a trapped detachment of communications specialists near the US Consulate. With only one company to spare (F Company from 2/5 Marines), the attack failed. The following morning 1/1 Marines made a second attempt and reached the beleaguered signalers. Frustrated by the apparent lack of progress, Hughes established a tactical HQ and devised a hasty plan to clear the western half of the city. The now depleted 1/1 Marines would secure the MACV compound and Highway 1 (both of which were under intermittent attack), while 2/5 Marines, now reunited with its commanding officer, Lieutenant Colonel Cheatham, would sweep west.

This plan had some merit, but sweeping a quarter comprising nine blocks by 11 blocks was not a straightforward proposition. The problem facing Cheatham was that G Company was at half strength, F Company had been exhausted in the misjudged attempt to relieve the communications detachment, and H Company had lost men battling its way up Highway 1. Cheatham himself was hardly in a position to make a sound appreciation of the tactical situation after only a matter of hours in the city (a problem exacerbated by the fact that nobody had city maps, rectified by stealing a pile of maps from a petrol station). The attack went ahead anyway, with F and H Companies leading.

For 24 hours, 2/5 Marines fought over the same blocks, making no progress. Five or six attempts were made to capture the post office and treasury building and each was repulsed. A single company could only realistically tackle one block – there were nearly 100 to clear. Despite the setback, on February 4, Hughes ordered a second attack. By now the marines were learning fast, or they were learning that the only way to make progress was to blast each enemy strong point with overwhelming firepower (the "creative way" of opening doors, as Dawson put it before his wounding). For this task, the six-barrelled 106mm ONTOS proved very handy. No building was spared, not even the Joan of Arc Church in which a French and Belgian priest luckily survived after it was demolished. Even with this change of tactics, the marines were still short of their objectives.

In fact, 2/5 Marines was doing much better than the situation suggested. 4th PAVN Regiment was running out of men, bullets, and options. It was a matter of one more push, and by the afternoon of February 5 the determined marines had retaken the Thua Thien Province HQ building. The event was celebrated by raising a US flag over the building, filmed by a CBS crew. Criticism of this gesture was dismissed by the marines, for whom tearing down the North Vietnamese flag after three days of continuous fighting had become an obsession.

Cheatham had not just taken down the offending flag. He had also taken out the 4th PAVN Regiment HQ. With the loss of the command element, the remainder of the regiment began to disintegrate. It took a further six days to clear all the way to the confluence of the canal and Perfume River, and two more days to link up with 1/7 Cavalry and 2/501 Infantry on the outskirts of the city. Intermittent sniping continued for another two weeks. Nonetheless, 2/5 Marines had fought doggedly. Thirty-eight marines were killed and 320 were injured – an entire battalion had effectively been wiped off the order of battle. Over 1,000 PAVN and Viet Cong corpses were later reportedly recovered, an exaggerated number that also included civilians.

It was then the turn of 1/5 Marines under Major Robert H. Thompson to sacrifice themselves on the altar of Hue. The ARVN in the Citadel had managed to hold off the communists but had insufficient forces to evict the enemy. 1/5 Marines was deployed into the Citadel and ordered to clear the eastern wall. The assault began on the morning of February 13, in another cold downpour. A Company led, and in a short but violent gunfight lost 15 marines with 40 wounded. A well-entrenched enemy position established around a prominent ornamental archway and tower had stopped the marines dead in their tracks. For the next 48 hours 1/5 Marines attempted to overwhelm this redoubt with no success. The position finally fell on February 15 when D Company was inserted by boat to outflank the tower. Captain Myron Harrington, commanding D Company, recalled a scene of "utter devastation."[106] Simultaneously, the position was battered by naval gunfire and artillery. This action cost another 50 marines. By February 17, after just five days of fighting, the unit had suffered 47 killed and 240 wounded.

It took a further week to clear the southeast corner of the Citadel. M-48 tank crewmen discovered to their amazement that 90mm shells bounced off the stone walls, although one marine avowed: "If it had not been for the tanks, we could not have pushed through that section of the city."[107] A critical role played by the tanks was ferrying the wounded. Unable to use medevac helicopters, the marines relied on the M-48 tanks, the only protected vehicle capable of negotiating the rubble-strewn streets, to act as field ambulances. Many wounded marines owed their lives to the tank crewmen who risked their lives and machines to pluck the injured to safety.

As the battle lengthened, the destruction mounted. As many as 10,000 houses were damaged or destroyed, or half the city was reduced to rubble. It was later reported that the PAVN and VC murdered as many as 3,000 South Vietnamese "collaborators" in Hue. Some of the victims were reportedly found to have been buried alive. Nobody was spared – women and children were among the dead. This number subsequently proved exaggerated, but a large number of civilians were undeniably murdered. Around 150 corpses were exhumed from a mass grave in the Citadel. Similar mass graves were found elsewhere in the environs, one containing the remains of three German doctors. A total of 809 bodies were eventually recovered from 24 sites southeast of the city. An American observer tasked with unearthing some 250 corpses in a shallow creek recalled the deep black eye sockets and water flowing through ribs. The mass murders proved a propaganda gift to Saigon, but the whole truth was suppressed. A proportion of the violence seems to have been the consequence of revenge-taking by families who had suffered Diemist repression during the Buddhist riots of 1962. In the testimony of one witness to this blood-letting, there was little "revolutionary commanders could do to control the population," or perhaps they did not try too hard.[108]

How many civilians were killed in crossfire would never be properly determined. Hue became a nightmarish place – the calm elegance of the pagodas and Buddhist gardens magnifying the madness of the rain-drenched killing spree that was taking place. Marines became hallucinogenic with tiredness. The rush to get reinforcements to the Citadel meant that some of the killed marines had literally stepped out of basic training in Camp Pendleton in California and were still wearing their US pattern boots and fatigues when they died.[109] Reporters flocked to the place to witness the surreal spectacle. The smell of the unburied dead and a plague of hungry rats added to the sense of horror in the macabre streets.

The battle turned when 1st Cavalry finally managed to block the western approaches to the city on February 21. Up to this point, the PAVN had been successfully infiltrating from a staging area 11 miles west of the city. With this lifeline closed it was only a matter of time before the enemy in the Citadel would begin to crumble. The denouement came on February 23–24. 3rd ARVN Regiment mounted a determined surprise attack that succeeded in dislodging the pockets of surviving North Vietnamese. Gas was used. A petty vindictiveness overtook the victors. When the bodies of two female guerrillas were found, they were stripped and paraded like trophies in the Cong marketplace.[110] Survivors fled west out of the city gates, eventually escaping to sanctuaries on the Laos border. Some estimates suggested that as many as 8,000 PAVN and Viet Cong had been killed or wounded in the battle, again an exaggeration. Twenty-five days after the communist forces launched their attack the South Vietnamese flag was once again flying on the Citadel flagpole. The battle was declared over on March 2. Three quarters of the 147 marine fatalities had been suffered in the Citadel, an indication of where the fighting had been heaviest.

The fallout from Hue was severe. This was Vietnam's Monte Cassino and Dresden in miniature. A cultural jewel had been destroyed, a consideration that barely bothered the communists but which agonized American opinion. Entire quarters of old Hue were turned to rubble, creating the incongruous juxtaposition of a canopy of ornamental trees floating over trapezoidal lumps of brick and stone, a puzzle of geometric shapes that had long lost proportion. As at Khe Sanh, a hostile media could only lament the battle, failing to acknowledge that the marines and ARVN had comprehensively beaten their enemy. The gallantry of 5th Marines – the regiment that gave the most – was conspicuous, but passed over in the hand-wringing that followed. The main outcome of the battle should have been a cause for some optimism. A communist attempt to provoke a general uprising in the north had completely failed. The chief military lesson – that the PAVN could not take and hold a city – did not raise the morale of a dispirited White House.

There is no agreed estimate for how many men Hanoi committed to the Tet Offensive. MACV claimed 85,000, of which only a fraction actually took part in serious fighting. CIA analyst George Carver later asserted that "as many as 400,000" main force, local forces, and militias troops may have taken part.[111] Tet, it seems, only served to disinter the corpse of the great order of battle debate of 1967. Nor is there an agreed number for how many were killed or wounded. By the time the offensive blew out, 2,100 American and more than 4,000 ARVN had been killed. As many as 50,000 Viet Cong and PAVN were assessed to have been killed, or a fifth of the enemy strength – most slain in the first month of the offensive. The people did not rise. The government did not collapse. Not a single American base was overrun.

Against any pure military measure, Tet was a total failure. Davidson and Weyand both thought so by the end of the first day. Indeed, there was a certain gloating that at last an elusive enemy had been unmasked and could be destroyed.[112] The enemy were only able to hold one of the over a hundred cities and towns they attacked, although as late as early March remnants of cadres continued to be active in Saigon, Da Nang, Kontum, Pleiku, Hoi An, Con Tho, and My Tho. By February 2, Westmoreland had already started preparing Operation *Recovery*, a plan to re-breathe life into the shocked South Vietnamese patient – such was the level of confidence in MACV.[113] The urban war created a lull in the rural war which MACV was quicker to exploit, re-invigorating pacification through an Accelerated Pacification Program, which enjoyed some success. By July, the MACV intelligence verdict was that the "B3 Front was a dead loss," that "things were comparatively good on the DMZ," and that as a result of the "high-cost failure at Tet," the "war is not going well for him [the enemy]."[114] Faced with this draining of the human pond, Hanoi reacted as only it could: by pumping even more recruits down the drain pipe of the Ho Chi Minh Trail to make up for the catastrophic losses. By the summer, another two divisions' worth made the journey south to reinforce depleted units.[115]

Internally, the Hanoi Politburo mixed high delusion with a cold-blooded and accurate assessment of the new situation. In an April 3 missive to the COSVN, the Northern leadership celebrated "our massive victories in all areas, military, political, and diplomatic, especially the victories we won in the general offensive and uprisings during the Tet Lunar New Year."[116] The NLF and Viet Cong leadership knew this was rubbish. Hanoi probably sensed the discontent because the directive concluded with the advice that the COSVN should develop a plan to stifle dissent, or in communist parlance, to maintain "the correct ideological position in order to strengthen solidarity, so that they [the NLF/VC] continue to fight and work well, and to guard against and overcome any erroneous trends or deviations," chief of which was telling the truth of what had happened. Yet the deduction drawn from this abject failure was unimpeachably true: "The situation on the battlefield in South Vietnam and the situation in the U.S. and throughout the world is developing in directions that are very favorable to us and very unfavorable for the enemy." It concluded, "This is a victory for us."

There were other surprising winners. The Tet Offensive proved a redemptive experience for the ARVN. The CIA thought "the ARVN's confidence had been shattered," and assessed that swathes of the countryside had been abandoned as soldiers fled to the safety of towns and cities, often to protect their families.[117] This had happened, and perhaps as many as 15 percent of pacified areas were temporarily lost, but the ARVN also demonstrated that it could not be rolled over by a communist assault. Ground lost was soon recaptured, and Tet provided the stimulus for the rearmament of the South Vietnamese armed forces under a RVNAF Improvement and Modernization Plan – the "Vietnamization" that would herald an American withdrawal.[118] Moreover, ARVN effectiveness, the "lousy divisions" as Weyand characterized the South Vietnamese, varied greatly between corps areas. 1st ARVN on the border had always been aggressive; in II Corps the ARVN seemed to change with the seasons; in the Saigon area, indolence and corruption were rife. Much depended on personalities and local circumstances. Yet many ARVN units did fight well.

The sequel in South Vietnam, however, was panicky. Tet destroyed the fragile unity of the South Vietnamese leadership. A sense of desperation, cynicism, and corruption comingled toxically. For some, only self-preservation now mattered. Government-leased Boeing 727s were prepared (sitting in safe berths in Thailand and Hong Kong) with passenger lists of the elite, ready for flight. In a heavy-handed backlash, politicians arguing for peace negotiations were imprisoned. Fearful of an American collapse of will, the Saigon government launched a charm offensive on the US Embassy. But the truth was that the South Vietnamese camp had been in danger of collapsing and became divided and chaotic.

In this respect, at least, the communists had always been right: the "puppets" were dancing to tired tunes. Ky and Thieu fell out almost immediately; the latter accused Ky of irresponsibility, treason, and disloyalty and the former lambasted Thieu's lack of leadership.[119] An alarmed Bunker was forced to dissuade Ky from leading an impromptu coup, which he eventually mounted anyway. Over the course of February, Thieu and Ky barely spoke or conferred, running separate operations from the Presidential Palace. The collapse in the relations between these two men ran so deep they appeared at the same meetings, unaware that the other had put himself forth as the legitimate South Vietnamese interlocutor. The legislature hopelessly splintered into three factions of the ruling Dai Viet party, two factions of the Socialist Party, five other factions, and around a dozen splinter groups of the nationalist-religious Cao Dai movement. It was a political disaster.

The economic damage caused by the communist offensive was also great. Some 20,000 homes were damaged or destroyed, and a further 600,000 temporary refugees were added to the over-strained economy. This human flotsam added to an already jittery and demoralized civilian population, and constituted a blow to the credibility of the Thieu-Ky junta. In CIA analyst George Allen's later estimation, "Most Vietnamese then and there came to the gut realization that a Communist takeover was just a matter of time."[120] But the worst effects were in Washington, where there were few fresh ideas and plenty of gloom, despite the fact that Westmoreland was actually winning. The chief military outcome of Tet was the "virtual decimation" of the VC, later acknowledged by the communists, but Washington failed to see it this way. DePuy was absolutely right when he later observed, "After TET it was a North Vietnamese war."[121] The Southerners were spent and never recovered. But also by the spring of 1968, American air power had disgorged over 2 million tons of high explosives over Vietnam, or as it was calculated, 31.8 tons for every square mile of the country.[122] Just how many more tons would need to be detonated to "win" in this wretched war? Again in DePuy's recollection, "the effort was too expensive, lasted too long, became too frustrating, was too complex, involved too much television, resulted in too much gore, and required too much patience. In short, the American people decided that Vietnam wasn't worth it."[123]

Tet also marked a great watershed because there was a significant change of dramatis personae, but most of this convulsion could not have been anticipated by Hanoi, and nor was it caused by the offensive. Who would have imagined that Martin Luther King would not sit down at the table of brotherhood, but collapse on a balcony of the Lorraine Hotel in Memphis, felled by an assassin's bullet that split his eloquent jaw? King may have feared no man, but many feared him. Who would have imagined Bobby Kennedy lying on the floor of a kitchen passageway of the Ambassador Hotel in Los Angeles, his brains splattered by a .22-caliber revolver? He had been, as his brother Ted eulogized, "A good and decent man, who saw wrong and tried to right it, saw suffering and tried to heal it, saw war and tried to stop it." All too late. At the requiem mass, Andy Williams sang "The Battle Hymn of the

Republic," but the Top Twenty song that week was Simon and Garkunkel's "Mrs. Robinson" – any way you look at it you lose.

The official transfers of power, a Washington merry-go-round as the press morbidly reported, took place unhurried by an assassin's bullet, but they were no less momentous. On March 1, McNamara handed over the office of defense secretary to Clark Clifford, a Kansas lawyer who had served in the war as a naval aide to President Truman. In his own way, Clifford was another "whiz kid" elevated to the beltway, where he served two more presidents. Johnson hoped the urbane Clifford would back him in the war, but privately the latter had other ideas, eschewing as he put it, the "ornithological division" of hawk or dove. Prior to Tet, Clifford had been relatively optimistic: "I still believed in our policy." Following a joint visit to Saigon with Maxwell Taylor in the winter of 1967, he returned imagining "some of our men might even be back by Christmas."[124] "When Tet came," he recalled, "it was a complete shock to me." Within his first two weeks in the Pentagon, he resolved that his mission was to "get this country and our President out of this mess."[125]

Two days before quitting his post, McNamara had a lunchtime meeting with Rusk. Over the course of the fare, he became "very emotional," "his voice broke and there were tears in his eyes" over the futility of the entire war.[126] Johnson's chief speechwriter Harry McPherson's open-mouthed observation of this episode was acute: Tet had left everyone in Washington with "that sense of the awfulness, the endlessness of the war."[127]

Three weeks after Clifford's appointment Westmoreland was appointed Army Chief of Staff. On April 11, Creighton Abrams was promoted to COMUSMACV, but full command was assumed awkwardly in stages, the first completed on May 29 and the second on June 10. The bespectacled Lieutenant General Andrew Goodpaster was appointed his deputy. Westmoreland departed from Tan Son Nhut with little fanfare. On his departure, US forces had suffered some 15,000 fatalities. A Vietnamese band discordantly played "Auld Lang Syne." Westmoreland curtly wished his successor "good luck," and was gone. The night before, in a press conference, he warned that the Allies could not win the war in a classic sense, but "only because of our national policy of not expanding the war." As if to prove him right, hours before he left, Viet Cong ambushes in Saigon left 19 dead and 67 wounded.

On March 26, facing a major speech to the nation, Johnson reunited the "wise men," now more an antiquary of shocked men. The Joint Chiefs had secretly requested 206,000 more troops be sent to Vietnam, prompting the President to set up a task force under Clifford, concerned with "what the social, political, economic impact might be on the United States."[128] The engine behind this appeal was a concerned General Earle Wheeler, who wanted to use the proposed troop uplift to build-up strategic reserve forces depleted by the Vietnam commitment. Johnson "wanted out, but he did not want to bug out."[129] In an unexpected volte-face, Clifford advised just that – quit the battlefield – counsel which Johnson found "exceedingly disturbing." Only Rostow held out as an unrepentant hawk, even proposing a madcap scheme to invade North Vietnam in a massive amphibious operation, a move which every expert advised would end up with Hanoi requesting assistance from Peking "and we would then be embroiled in a land war in Southeast Asia with Red China which had no limitation as to the millions of men that they could put in the field against us."[130]

The well had been poisoned, Johnson conspiratorially suspected, by a growing band of skeptics, and the chief "traitor" was the very man Johnson had appointed to succeed McNamara, Clark Clifford. He was right, as Clifford wasted no time in finding allies:

> I remember talking with Harry McPherson, I talked to people... in [the] State Department, like Nick Katzenbach. We began to develop a group and I know that after a while the question would be very secretly, "is he with us?" ... is he part of this group ... organized and dedicated to changing Lyndon Johnson's mind? ... [From this moment] The relationship between him [Johnson] and me became very strained at that time, and it remained quite strained thereafter. He felt that when he had assigned me to the Pentagon post that I would be a strong resolute supporter of the previous policy and here I was crumbling before his very eyes. [131]

Yet none of these men were actually in the room when the decision was taken, and they did not need to be. Instead it fell to Acheson, McGeorge Bundy, and Ball to stab Caesar. Taylor was "dismayed" and Abe Fortas loyally stood by his old friend Lyndon, decrying "drama for the sake of dramas," but both men were heavily out-voted by the doves.[132] Johnson wondered whether it was all "a diabolical plot."[133] As he reflected on these judgments, he privately scrawled on a White House notepad "can no longer do the job we set out to do," as if signing off his own presidency.[134] "Congress and I are like an old man and woman who've known each other too long, and have yelled at each other and begged from each other" – now it was time to go.[135]

The "abdication speech" was jointly drafted with speech writer Harry McPherson, who ironically set out to save his President, but the emotion was all Johnson's. Three days before the speech was delivered, a meeting was held in Rusk's office attended by Clifford, Rostow, William Bundy, and

McPherson. "What was started out as a speech ... became a deep seated divisive policy meeting," with heated arguments between the hawks and doves, leaving "the whole matter ... absolutely at sea again."[136] Clifford thought the speech was a "disaster," merely offering more of the same bankrupt policies. Neither Rusk nor Rostow contested the argument. McPherson proved the key:

> as the drafts proceeded, I think his influence was an important one and, by time we came to the final reading of the speech, the speech had changed very materially ... it was no longer the warlike hawkish speech that it had been.[137]

An all-day Saturday meeting followed. With time running out, McPherson fretted but Johnson mischievously told him, "You don't need to worry about time. I may have a little ending of my own."[138] At this point, McPherson knew the presidency was over. Supported in secret by Special Assistant Horace Busby, who only learned the day before of Johnson's intentions, the valediction was drafted.[139] The circumstances were hardly propitious: Busby arrived in the presidential bedroom in the morning to find a room full of family and friends, with Johnson standing in the middle making telephone calls at the end of a very long cord, while simultaneously dive bombing his chuckling grandson with his spare hand. Eventually, space and quiet was found in the Treaty Room for Busby to work, while Johnson lingered in the West Wing, teasing that "Buzz" was pushing him into retirement.

At 5pm on Sunday March 31, just four hours before the television address, Johnson and McPherson exchanged brief words over a telephone:

- "Do you know what's in it?"
- "I think so."
- "What do you think about it?"
- "I'm very sorry, Mr. President."
- "Okay. So long, partner."[140]

Fifty-two months and ten days after the presidency fell in his lap, Johnson spoke to the nation. Luci Johnson, the youngest daughter, led a rearguard action to stop her father, to no avail. With only an hour to airtime, Busby was still unsure whether Johnson would see the matter through.[141]

The speech lasted for over 40 compelling minutes. "Tonight I want to speak to you of peace in Vietnam and Southeast Asia." In the first draft, the word had been "war." It was, as Clifford recalled, "just a complete 180 degree turn." He spoke woodenly, like a schoolboy reading an end-of-term report, but soon got into his old stride, leaning into the camera as if addressing each individual citizen, cajoling and persuading.

The substance of the address was a bombing pause.

> I have ordered our aircraft and our naval vessels to make no attacks on North Vietnam, except in the area north of the demilitarized zone where the continuing enemy build up directly threatens allied forward positions and where the movements of their troops and supplies are clearly related to that threat.

The bait was the promise of "serious talks on the substance of peace," the same offer he had made in his Johns Hopkins University speech three years previously, and in the Manila proposals the preceding year. The plea was to the South Vietnamese to get their house in order and accept "the main burden" of defending their nation. And the giveaway was a darted glance at Lady Bird who was watching him deliver the speech, pausing as he lifted his hand to wipe away a bead of sweat. In Clifford's later estimation, "90% of the credit for that decision [to resign] [went] to Mrs. Lyndon Johnson."[142] Concluding, Johnson faced the camera to deliver his "little ending." "I do not believe I should devote an hour or a day of my time," he continued in his swinging Texan drawl,

> to any partisan causes or to any other duties other than the awesome duties of this office – the Presidency of this country. Accordingly, I shall not seek, and I will not accept, the nomination of my party for another term as your President.

The emotional release filled the room. Lady Bird, then George Christian hugged Johnson, released from the prison that the presidency had become.

Johnson's abdication speech confirmed the real significance of Tet: Hanoi had turned military defeat into a massive psychological victory. For hawks, this was the stab in the back moment. American soldiery won, only to discover the civilians were already running. The shock was almost immediate – within one week commentators were noticing the collapse of morale in Washington. The "brutal surprise" of Tet indisputably beat Johnson.[143] But the fact is that he had already been beaten before Tet. Johnson first informed his press secretary George Christian that he was contemplating resignation in August 1967.[144] In December, Horace Busby had urged him not to run again.[145] Johnson had privately intended to make his candidacy withdrawal speech on the occasion of his State of the Union message on January 19, 1968. To maintain secrecy, he asked three aides, Busby, Christian, and John Connally, to append the words to the State of Union message. At the last minute, Johnson requested the words not be added to the teleprompter and instead took a hard copy stuffed deep in a pocket. It was never pulled out of the pocket. Unbeknown to congressmen, the press, guests, and a national television audience, their President had been carrying a message of his resignation which he could not bring himself to deliver.

The stab in the back myth was greatly inflated by the media reaction. The *coup de grâce* was delivered on Sunday February 27 by Walter Kronkite, CBS News's most respected anchorman and the voice of Middle America. He delivered the dignified valediction framed by a map of the Pacific Ocean with Southeast Asia, almost symbolically off shot:

> To say that we are closer to victory today is to believe, in the face of the evidence, the optimists who have been wrong in the past. To suggest we are on the edge of defeat is to yield to unreasonable pessimism. To say that we are mired in stalemate seems the only realistic, yet unsatisfactory, conclusion. On the off-chance that military and political analysts are right, in the next few months we must test the enemy's intentions, in case this is indeed his last big gasp before negotiations. But it is increasingly clear to this reporter that the only rational way out then will be to negotiate, not as victors, but as an honorable people who lived up to their pledge to defend democracy, and did the best they could.[146]

Westmoreland felt betrayed and MACV fumed at the torrent of negative reporting, but reporters like Kronkite were only the messengers, not the protagonists.[147] Americans were making up their own minds. Johnson was not directly influenced by Kronkite's report, which he missed anyway on the night it was broadcast. At the time of the Tet Offensive, there were around 450 accredited correspondents in South Vietnam. The relationship between this ill-disciplined battalion and MACV was not as bad as commonly portrayed. The worst sanction applied by MACV was a 30-day suspension of accreditation, and this was only applied in three cases.[148] Most American reporters did get behind the war effort. "Paint it Black" was a pop song, not the universal tenor of war reporting. They followed the voluntary code of practice promulgated by MACV and more or less reported what they were witnessing objectively. There was no media conspiracy to get Westmoreland, although there was certainly a phalanx of reporters who gained notoriety for challenging the military reporting. On the other side of the argument were correspondents like Alsop who consistently promoted the government propaganda. The MACV Office of Information was extremely generous in the amount of information it afforded to reporters, in total contrast to the

South Vietnamese government that maintained rigid censorship, or Hanoi that controlled the media.

The heart of the problem was that over time the media stopped believing the perfectly truthful information offered, and MACV began to weary of a press pack that seemed obsessed with highlighting scandals and failures. In the official war historian William Hammond's verdict,

> In the process, they fell in a vicious circle. For when the promises failed to materialize, the credibility of official statements declined, and the press redoubled its criticism. That prompted more official optimism, leading to more failed promises and to further recriminations in the press.[149]

The media did not lose America a war. It went over the cliff, locked in a squabbling embrace with MACV.

Whatever the misgivings broadcast by Kronkite, MACV had to get on with the war. It is a golden rule that generals in trouble call for reinforcements, and the Joint Chiefs in the spring of 1968 proved no exception. Wheeler was a sick man recovering from a heart attack, a former mathematics graduate whose sums no longer added up. Since the beginning of the ground deployment in 1965, he had sought ways of persuading McNamara and Johnson on the necessity of mobilizing the US strategic reserve, under the guise of reinforcing MACV. Once again he tried this gambit; Wheeler's worst moment in the war, and a naked attempt to dupe the national, civilian leadership. In late February, he visited Saigon and, supported by a compliant Westmoreland, concocted a half-baked plan to bag an additional 206,700 troops over and above the 1967 Program Five agreement. Both men would later emphatically argue that the proposal amounted to a contingency plan, not a firm request. The only option by which such a large body of men could be mustered quickly was by activating the National Reserve – which was unconscionable to Johnson.

Over the first three weeks of his appointment as defense secretary, Clark Clifford was absorbed by the request for additional troops. His staffs were unchanged from McNamara's tenure, who now viewed the war through the dark eyeglass of the Tet Offensive. De-escalation, not escalation, was required. "What is the plan to win the war in Vietnam?" he demanded of the generals?[150] Every question raised more questions, not answers: "We had long talks. How long would it take? They didn't know. How many more troops would it take? They didn't know. Would 206,000 answer the demand? They didn't know."[151] "The only plan is that ultimately the attrition will wear down the North Vietnamese and they will have had enough," but this was hardly a plan, more a Calvary of mutual slaughter. It was at the conclusion of this inquiry that Clifford decided, "I had turned against the war." An immediate additional reinforcement of 10,500 troops was authorized – made up from 3rd Brigade from the 82nd Airborne and 27th Marines – but a decision on the larger reinforcement was deferred.

The desperation of these ploys bordered on recklessness. By the spring of 1968, the Vietnam War had seriously hollowed out the US Army and Marine Corps. The regular army could now only count on the 82nd Airborne and four skeleton divisions (1st Armored, 2nd Armored, 5th Infantry, and 6th Infantry). Aside from the airborne division, none were combat effective, nor could they be realistically deployed to Indochina. The Marines were in a similarly dire situation. This corps was now reduced to 2nd Marine Division and a newly activated but incomplete 5th Marine Division. Scraping soldiers and marines from these skeleton formations to feed the Vietnam War had already provoked open dissent. The decision to deploy 3rd Brigade, 82nd Airborne was taken so precipitously, the billets could only be filled by re-deploying paratroopers who had recently returned home from Vietnam. This flew in the face of the Army's own individual deployment criteria and caused widespread protest. Eventually, the Army was forced to relent and offered the paratroopers the option of returning to the United States. From 3,650 paratroopers hastily despatched from Fort Bragg, a total of 2,513 voted with their feet and flew home without firing a shot in Vietnam.[152] A greater snub to Wheeler's machinations could hardly have been delivered.

In Washington, the block was now Clark Clifford. The recommendations submitted to the President on March 4 reflected this change of view. Clifford proposed a modest 22,000-strong reinforcement from existing resources, to be reviewed on a weekly basis, and a mobilization sufficient to meet the requested reinforcement, if the decision were taken to support the Wheeler-Westmoreland request. More effectively, Clifford emphasized the requirement for more Vietnamese manpower, not American boys, on the front line. Johnson straightway approved the 22,000 reinforcement, and four days later raised the number to 30,000. These numbers, though modest, still represented an augmentation above the 11,500 already sent, and would exceed the Program Five ceiling (which at this stage had not yet been reached). In a further round of playing with the abacus, Johnson also agreed to the immediate reinforcement of 13,500 support troops to follow the airborne brigade and marine regiment. To achieve these numbers, around 100,000 reservists would have to be called up in March.

In fact, the early-February emergency deployment of 11,500 combat troops, and the additional 13,500 support troops, would be the only reinforcements announced in Johnson's March 31 address to the nation. This raised the total force to 549,000, or 24,500 more than the Program Five ceiling. In what was almost certainly a deliberate leak, the media was apprised of the Wheeler-Westmoreland 206,700 troop request. The *New York Times* ran the story and all hell broke loose. These revelations, coupled with the entry of Robert Kennedy into the presidential race and Senator Eugene McCarthy's shock near-win in the New Hampshire primary, pulled down the edifice. In a hasty political retreat, the White House disavowed the Wheeler-Westmoreland package, and formalized the 24,500 reinforcement in what was now dubbed Program Six, the last of the Johnson presidency and the high-water mark of escalation. The graph would now only trend in one direction, downwards.

For Westmoreland, the decision not to ramp up the reinforcements amounted to the missed opportunity in the war. In retrospect, the departing general judged that Tet should have been exploited more aggressively. He wrote,

> Yet even with the handicap of graduated response, the war still could have been brought to a favorable end following defeat of the enemy's Tet offensive in 1968. ... Had President Johnson changed our strategy and taken advantage of the enemy's weakness to enable me to carry out the operations we planned over the preceding two years in Laos and Cambodia and north of the DMZ, along with intensified bombing and the mining of Haiphong Harbor, the North Vietnamese doubtlessly would have broken.[153]

Hanoi, probably, would have agreed. But what might have been no longer counted, and MACV was busy enough commanding the troops it did have as it swung into its counteroffensive, while deliberately downplaying the significance of its offensive operations to a hyper-sensitive media.[154]

Between the end of February 1968 and Nixon's inauguration in January 1969, MACV conducted nearly one hundred major operations. The Tet Offensive was met with an emphatic riposte – an avalanche of counteroffensives. This was a portrait of a command taking the fight back to enemy. Far from provoking a popular uprising, Hanoi provoked counterattack. And, overwhelmingly, it was an American-led fight back. The ARVN participated in a small number of operations, and was especially strong in the capital district and surrounding areas, but mounted virtually no independent operations. Allies like the Australians raised their tempo, but the ROK division was supine. Even as the sands were running out on the hourglass of Johnson's presidency, he was, finally and indisputably, winning the war on the battlefield.

In mid-March, MACV launched a major clearance operation in the greater Saigon area involving 50,000 troops drawn from 1st, 9th, and 25th Infantry Divisions, supported by 11th Armored Cavalry Regiment. 7th and 25th ARVN Divisions, an airborne task force, and 5th Ranger Group also participated. It was a massive effort and only finally closed on April 9, by which time a kill count of 2,658 had been claimed. This was followed by Operation *Toan Thong* – the biggest concentration of allied troops in the entire war. This involved 42 US and 37 ARVN battalions. *Toan Thong* claimed an even bigger kill count of 7,600. Regardless of the certain exaggeration, these offensives preempted and blunted the Viet Cong's "mini-Tet," mounted in May. A high-ranking defector had given the game away anyway, and although 119 towns and cities were attacked, the offensive came as no surprise.

By now MACV had ringed Saigon with steel. From east to west, 1st Australian Task Force covered Long Thanh; 1st Division blocked the northern approaches; 199th Infantry Brigade remained in situ at Bien Hoa; 25th Infantry screened the west of the capital; and 3rd Brigade, 9th Infantry defended southern approach routes from Long An Province. Tan Son Nhut air base was assaulted again, but the attackers were easily repulsed. Elements of as many as 13 VC battalions managed to infiltrate Saigon, but these were beaten up, with the majority of the fighting effectively over by May 12. One of the toughest fights took place at "Y Bridge" over the Kinh Doi Canal that joined Saigon with Nha Be. Here, it took 2/47 Infantry and 5/60 Infantry six days to winkle out two determined Viet Cong battalions. Cholon and the Phu Tho racetrack once again became the scenes of heavy fighting, only finally subsiding at the end of the month.[155] The city was subjected to random 122mm rocket attacks, nicknamed "the whispering death." The attacks killed 75 civilians and wounded a further 200, provoking a run on the supply of sand bags. This amounted to harassment, not a serious threat to the city. To mark Ho's birthday (May 19) 20 such rockets were lobbed into Saigon. The futility of the offensive was evident, and the losses on the communist side were heavy. But the destruction, once again, was widespread.

In the north, MACV was determined to strike back against the infiltration corridor that had been used by the People's Army to funnel troops to Hue and adjoining provinces – the A Shau Valley. 1st Cavalry was chosen for the task, now commanded by Major General Tolson. On April 19, 1/7 and 6/7 Cavalry from 3rd Brigade kicked off Operation *Delaware/Lam Son 216*, air assaulting the northern end of the valley. North Vietnamese antiaircraft gunners shot down ten helicopters and crippled a further 13. Terrible weather then threatened to grind the operation to halt. Eventually the late monsoon clouds lifted and 1st Brigade was flown in, followed by 3rd ARVN Regiment. A massive sweep was conducted of the entire length of the valley which revisited the abandoned A Shau Special Force Camp, but the PAVN refused to fight. The operation was officially ended in mid-May having uncovered and destroyed significant quantities of war materiel. North Vietnamese troops reoccupied the valley as soon as the Americans departed. On August 4, Major General Melvin Zais's

101st Airborne launched a second operation in the A Shau code-named *Somerset Plain/Lam Son 246*. This mission barely lasted two weeks and experienced the same fate of the first: the cost in helicopters proved high and the communists simply evaded into the hills rather than confront the valley intruders.

On the DMZ, 3rd Marines could not counterattack without crossing the border, and by the end of the year all US offensive operations would be banned in this sector anyway. This meant the stoic marines continued holding the line of Route 9 using the tactic of mobile defense. Most of the action over the spring and summer took place in the vicinity of Dong Ha, where 320th PAVN Division made three serious incursions. At the height of the fighting, virtually every marine artillery gun was ranged on this front. The marines were also greatly assisted by the 16-inch guns of the USS *New Jersey* battleship, as well as by the arrival of 1st Brigade, 5th Infantry Division which included a useful tank battalion (1/77 Armored). Further south, the sister 1st Marines swept Thua Thien and Quang Nam Provinces, later supported by 101st Airborne (Operation *Nevada Eagle* in May). The Americal Division undertook numerous battalion-level operations in Quang Ngai, including the operation in My Lai, visited in a later chapter.

By this stage, the Batangan Peninsula had become notorious as a "heavily, heavily mined" area. "I mean we found mines every day," recalled Stephen Dant with 5/46 Infantry, "We had guys, it seemed like every few days we would have somebody wounded who had hit a mine ... So everybody was just very uptight, nervous, and getting angry."[156] Dant in fact patrolled the same area at My Lai as Lieutenant William Calley, who would later go on trial for his part in the massacre. Dant said, "So we were feeling the same frustration as his troopers were," adding, "[but] as frustrated as we all were out there, none of us could ever picture ourselves going in and massacring a village. There was something wrong with that unit."

Even as the Viet Cong mounted the hiccough of a mini-Tet offensive, the long-awaited announcement was made on May 3 that peace talks would begin in Paris. Ten days later, chief delegates Averell Harriman and Cyrus Vance arrived in the French capital. If Paris in spring could not provide inspiration, where could it be found? The American delegation was so "euphoric," hotel rooms were rented in the expectation that the talks would not last long.[157] Washington's offer was genuine and could not have been stated more plainly in Johnson's March 31 television address. In return for a bombing halt, Washington expected Hanoi to engage in substantive peace talks which would include the Saigon government and the National Liberation Front. America also expected Hanoi to refrain from violating the DMZ and attacking towns and cities, an expectation based on misjudged "assurances" from the Soviet Politburo. All this proved to be so many false hopes.

The peace talks were finally convened in the neo-classical Majestic Hotel, a Gestapo HQ in the Second World War, now reconverted into an international conference center. The North Vietnamese delegation was led by the bespectacled and immaculately dressed Xuan Thuy, assisted by his aide-de-camp, Colonel Ha Van Lau. Thuy (born in 1912) was a hard-liner, a guerrilla from the age of 14 who carried the struggle for Vietnamese independence like a calling card. Seemingly selected because he had participated in the 1954 Geneva talks, Thuy was not a man versed in the minuets and caracoles of diplomacy. If he had learned anything from dealing with Westerners it was that their promises were worthless. A secret CIA memorandum got it absolutely right when it observed, "the Communists see themselves more as revolutionaries opening a second front than as negotiators exploring the possibilities of compromise."[158] Later allegations that presidential candidate Nixon sabotaged the peace talks were mostly spurious.[159] The Republican camp did intrigue in what Johnson later labeled a "sordid story," but these machinations did not derail Johnson's peace efforts. The South Vietnamese government had already made up its mind and decided that "anything is better than those two guys [Johnson and Humphrey]."[160] Kissinger was not the great malefactor he was later portrayed to be, but only indulged in some self-promotion and jockeying for jobs. Nor was all the quibbling over places at the table, and who could speak to whom, which so entertained the press, really the sticking point. No matter what shape the table, and no matter who had authority to speak to whom, the peace talks were foredoomed to failure. "Fighting while negotiating" or *danh vua dam* had been implicit in Hanoi's Tet Offensive, but just more fighting followed, and a good deal of pointless, ritual talking. In mid-August, a third wave of the Tet Offensive was launched but by now the communists were so weakened, only 15 assaults were launched, and just two were of battalion size.[161] The intransigent North Vietnamese delegation did not arrive in Paris to negotiate peace, but rather to demand surrender terms, even in the face of battlefield defeat. Working with this obdurate rock, no amount of diplomatic chiseling was going to carve out a peace statue.

The crucial period fell over October 9–31, precipitated by an apparent softening in the North Vietnamese negotiating position after five fruitless months of talks. On October 14, Johnson met with his security advisors to take a decision to suspend the bombing of North Vietnam. There followed another 13 days of prevarication provoked by a North Vietnamese demand for an unconditional end to the bombing, and the granting of full status for the NLF at the peace talks. On October 23, Johnson consulted with Momyer, who gave his assent to a cessation of the bombing. On October 27, the North Vietnamese delegation appeared to drop their demands. Two days later, Abrams returned to Washington and also gave assent to a bombing halt. Painfully, agreement was reached with Thieu to attend talks with NLF participation, but Washington agreed not to recognize the Front as a separate negotiating party. At 8am Eastern Time, on Friday November 1, Johnson finally made the long-awaited announcement of a halt of the bombing campaign over North Vietnam.

In four years of conflict, Washington had attempted 36 significant peace initiatives, a number Dean Rusk liked to quote to skeptics doubtful of the administration's sincere efforts to end the war. Diplomacy, Rusk would argue

> must always act on an optimistic base, because you must always try in the hope that something positive can be accomplished. Whether you would predict that it could have a successful end or not, you've got to try. Otherwise, we'd turn everything over to the soldiers and we'd all burn up.[162]

The number of indirect, unofficial, and third-party peace feelers was believed to exceed 2,000. All had come to nought.

The history read like the bleakest catalog of dashed expectations. The first initiative emanated from the National Liberation Front, one week after the assassination of Diem, but was ignored. A succession of mainly Western and international institutions then attempted to blaze a peace trail. The first was F. Blair Seaborn, a Canadian working for the International Control Commission, who visited Hanoi twice in the summer of 1964 and again in the winter of 1965. The UN, the Russians, and the French also had a go over this period. Tito tried in mid-March 1965. Johnson gave his "carrot and stick" speech on April 7 at Johns Hopkins University in Baltimore. North Vietnamese Premier Pham Van Dong retaliated with his own four-point proposal the following day. A flurry of half-hearted peace attempts by the British, Indians, and Canadians followed these two speeches. In May, the bombing suspension was ordered and a covert communications channel was opened with the North Vietnamese Embassy in Moscow. Hanoi replied via French intermediaries but tarried too long and the bombing was resumed. In the summer Johnson made a second speech and prodded the UN, to no avail. In October, Pope Paul VI made an appeal for peace at the UN. In November the non-aligned Hungarian Foreign Secretary János Péter joined the club of forlorn hope peace negotiators. In December he was joined by the Italian Giorgio La Pira, a professor at the University of Florence who made an eccentric private citizen's bid to secure a peace deal. Also in December, the British Foreign Secretary Michael Stewart made a peace appeal on Russian state television (this was a period when the Wilson government was indulging in controversial chumminess with the Soviet Union).

In January 1966, Averell Harriman made a marathon tour of 34 capitals and passed Johnson's latest peace proposals to 115 governments. In February, Chester Ronning, another Canadian diplomat, made a secret four-day trip to Hanoi following the resumption of the bombing. In June he made a second trip but this also failed. Over the summer, U Thant talked of de-escalation even as the war was visibly escalating. Then another non-aligned nation boarded the peace ship in the form of the Polish representative of the International Control Commission, Janusz Lewandowski, who proposed a ten-point peace plan, or six more points than Hanoi was proposing, and all irrelevant and doomed. In December, once again in the middle of a bombing suspension, American diplomat John C. Guthrie exchanged messages with North Vietnamese diplomats in Moscow. At the same time, Prime Minister Wilson and Soviet Foreign Minister Kosygin again acted as best friends but failed to get "their friends" to talk.

On February 8, 1967 a frustrated Johnson sent a personal letter to Ho Chi Minh; Ho replied dismissively via the Pope on the day bombing resumed in North Vietnam. In the summer, U Thant made an umpteenth, but mercifully short, three-point peace proposal, backed by a Ceylonese government (mired in its own ethnic conflict). Also in the summer, the indefatigable Canadians re-joined the fray and proposed a "super-DMZ." This idea was roundly ignored. In August, a "mystery man" engaged in a secret exchange of messages between Washington and Hanoi (Johnson, apparently, placed great faith in this interlocutor). On September 29, Johnson made another peace speech in San Antonio, Texas. Hanoi replied through an interview with an Australian journalist named Wilfred Burchett on October 21 and the answer was "no." Finally, over the winter of 1967–68, Hanoi hinted that a definitive end to the bombing might do the trick, but this was a ruse as, on January 30, the Tet Offensive detonated.[163] It could not be argued that Hanoi had not been wooed by damsel peace. Nor could it be denied that the communists had been entirely indifferent to her blandishments.

Nothing had really changed in this dolorous litany of failures since the first Seaborn visit in the summer of 1964. Hanoi set out its demands – the unilateral and unconditional withdrawal of American forces, the primacy of the National Liberation Front in the south, and the reunification of Vietnam under a communist government – and it was as if nobody believed that Hanoi was serious. These were never negotiable diplomatic postures. These were from the beginning unyielding demands. The South Vietnamese position was equally severe and boiled down to two propositions: the Viet Cong would be offered amnesty or safe passage north; every other proposal, from Hanoi or Washington, was off the table. Henry Kissinger's later achievement in chipping away at this granite block of Vietnamese intransigence deserves far more credit than it ever received. He succeeded where battalions of peace negotiators marched up the hill, only to march down empty-handed. With the November presidential election now in purview, the stage entry of this colossus of American foreign policy was now just a matter of weeks away.

Chapter 5

EXPANDING A WAR,
JANUARY 1969–DECEMBER 1972

Richard Milhous Nixon won the 1968 presidential election because in his own words he appealed to "the great majority of Americans." These were the forgotten citizens, the non-shouters, far removed from "the tumult and the shouting" of a liberal-dominated media. Along the way he had reached out to save "Americans hating each other" in "cities enveloped in smoke and flame."[1] In the electoral reckoning, the solid American rooted in practical sense and hard work had won.

All this may have been true, but he also triumphed because the Democrats imploded under the Hubert Humphrey-Ed Muskie ticket, and because the Independent George Wallace carried the South. In the end, it was the tightest of affairs. Humphrey boasted he would repeat the feat of the underdog Truman and snatch victory at the eleventh hour, which he almost did. Just over half a million votes separated the two principal candidates. But still it was evident when Americans woke up on November 6, that the electoral map, from sea to shining sea, was now a deep Republican red. How unfortunate that the Nixon about to assume the presidency – who saw himself appealing to "the good people" – could only see enemies everywhere.

Both Johnson and Nixon were haunted by the thought of inheriting the title of the first American president to lose a war, but only Nixon had the iron to forge this anxiety, his hatred of the war, into decisive action. Vietnam did not win Nixon the presidency, but his clarity did. "Never has so much military, economic and diplomatic power been used so ineffectively," he flourished in his nomination acceptance speech at the Golden Gate Hotel on Miami Beach. "The first priority foreign policy objective of the next administration will be to bring an honorable end to the war in Vietnam. We shall not stop there – we need a policy to prevent more Vietnams."[2] He would later write a book entitled precisely *No More Vietnams*. As if signaling a symbolic rebirth, Nixon flanked himself in a semicircle of the candidates' wives and their four daughters, all dressed in white, like archangels in a Byzantine frieze.

There were other memorable moments as power seeped like a draining tank from a now bankrupt White House: a departing Johnson beaming from the steps of Air Force One, clutching his grandson Lyn Nugent, so devoted to his gigantic grandfather. He quit office a "caged eagle," as Kissinger memorably put it, dignified and proud but ultimately beaten.[3] Belying the popular view that it was Nixon who introduced the vial of poisonous paranoia into the White House, Johnson's one piece of advice to Kissinger was that he should sack any staff member praised by the columnists, on the grounds that he would almost certainly be "your leaker."[4] The executive high office had already become a thoroughly venomous nest before Nixon's foot crossed the threshold. The following morning, a liberated Johnson jumped into a pick-up and headed off into the prairie to shoot deer, a 19-year-old once again on his home ranch.

But Johnson had crumpled, and seemed to take the Democrat party with him into a wilderness of electoral isolation. At the investiture, Nixon garbed himself in Woodrow Wilson's peace "with healing in its wings," but lofty rhetoric, like small talk, was not something Nixon did well. His appeal to the anonymous "quiet voice" and the "backbone of America," however, was genuine. This had been his family experience, the landscape of his youth that had since darkened. The inaugural parade was assailed by protestors and hecklers, as many as ten thousand, representing the raucous minority he so detested. When one group began waving Viet Cong flags a predictable brawl erupted with fellow parade-watchers who judged waving the enemy's flag in the nose of the president-elect an insult too far. Few presidencies had started so awkwardly.

Richard Nixon was the second of four sons, born to Californian Quakers, of mixed Scots-Irish, English, and German heritage. The abstinence, seriousness, and self-improvement all came from the roots of a religious family, working a failing farm and later a grocery business. But the drive to succeed, relentless, and later ruthless, all came from the boy. Nixon's favorite phrase was "the bastards," a descriptor he machine-gunned at everyone who stood in his way: the Hanoi Politburo, political rivals, a hostile East Coast press, his staff, and even his own air force. Yet the former lawyer and naval officer had not started out in politics this way. The invective accreted to his nervous political body like a tumor growing with his political success. He entered the House of Representatives in 1956 then leaped to the Senate in just four years. Eight years as Eisenhower's Vice President was followed by a period of setbacks in the early and mid-1960s.

Finally, he arrived at the White House where he believed, with certain fervor, he belonged. On the journey, he made or found enemies. By the time he was handed the keys of power, he had convinced himself that the State Department "had no loyalty to him" and the CIA were a bunch of liberals determined to undo him.[5] Macbeth strode into the banqueting hall only to find hissing and booing courtiers, and the ghosts of many slain Banquos.

This was the self-victimizing Nixon, but there was another side to this complex man. Nixon can only be understood through the lens of his long service as vice president in a decade when the promise of the American dream finally seemed to be realized for millions of ordinary families, families like his own, before the horrible sixties unraveled the dream. In many ways, he was a fifties president catapulted into the seventies, and in no respect was this truer than in his visceral anti-communism. Nixon hated the Marxist creed with an obsessive passion, viewing it as an ideology of tyranny and oppression that had poisoned the hopes of a postwar world. This was a former vice president who had impressed on Khrushchev the virtues of the capitalist automatic spin wash in the great "Kitchen Debate." For Nixon, the great cause of the age was the defeat of communism, behind the shield of strong-armed forces, but achieved through a grand peace deal and not war. "Let historians not record," he would later voice, "that when America was the most powerful nation in the world we passed on the other side of the road and allowed the last hopes for peace and freedom of millions of people to be suffocated by the forces of totalitarianism."[6] This thought evolved into correcting the historic mistake of "losing China," seeking entente with the Soviet Politburo, and replacing the orthodoxies of containment and military interventions with diplomacy. To this end he was absolutely determined to run foreign policy from the White House. Nixon also hauled another trunk of popular policies and folkloric beliefs into the White House: a determination to restore fiscal discipline, a resolve to recharge a frontier and entrepreneurial spirit, and the will to curb an encroaching big government. It was not a surprise that, when given a second chance, he won a landslide victory in the subsequent 1972 election.

The Republican team that entered the White House understood that few if any military options were tolerable to a wearied American public. Nixon confessed that when he took office the only military strategy that merited serious consideration was ramping up the war: bombing the North, crippling the vital Haiphong Harbor, threatening invasion, and extending operations into Laos and Cambodia – or the very strategy advocated by the departed Westmoreland.[7]

All these options seemed foreclosed, first because Nixon would be unable to carry the country; second, because there was unanimity that the war needed a political and not military resolution; and lastly because Nixon sought rapprochement with the two communist giants, the Soviet Union and the People's Republic of China. It was a measure of just how quickly attitudes hardened that within months, three of the options, bombing, mining, and hot pursuit, were all back on the table.

"Courage, boldness, guts! Goddamn it! That is the thing." This, Nixon advised Kissinger, is how he wanted to be remembered over Vietnam.[8] His loyal factotum, however, sketched a more awkward and hesitating psyche. Nixon's decision-making was "tortuous." He threw out many and contradictory ideas, expecting to be challenged. When the moment came to take a decision, he could display great calm, and even coldness. He relied on small inner circles of loyalists, and held interminably long meetings. Yet he also displayed a great capacity to seize on the essence of a problem and was unafraid to take brave but unpopular decisions.[9] Johnson wrung his hands over "young men dying in the fullness of their promise."[10] Nixon also detested the slaughter. But what crippled the Texan galvanized Nixon.

State went to William Pierce Rogers, a leathery-faced East Coast attorney who like the rest of his generation had seen wartime service, in his case on the carrier USS *Intrepid* in the battle of Okinawa. A distinguished career in private practice and government service followed, over which period his path frequently intersected with an impressed Nixon. By 1957 he had stepped into the top job, US Attorney General, serving out the last years of the Eisenhower presidency. His appointment at State was a reward for loyalty, not a statement of confidence. Indeed, Nixon viewed Rogers' lack of knowledge of foreign affairs an important qualification for the job, or as Kissinger put it, not unkindly, few secretaries of state can have been selected precisely because of their ignorance of foreign policy.[11]

The affable Rogers provided light to the chiaroscuro inheritance from a lugubrious Rusk, but both men presided over a diminished office. Nixon had no intention of allowing the life blood of his foreign policy to pump through the bureaucratic, cholesterol-clogged arteries of the State Department – this would be passed to the only man he viewed as an equal, his National Security Advisor, Henry Kissinger. Thus, within one day of assuming office another feature of the Nixon presidency manifested itself – the back-channel communications – appropriately in this case, an instruction to Cabot Lodge in Paris, then negotiating with the maddening North Vietnamese, to bypass State and send his recommendations direct to the White House.[12] Nixon's tactical emasculation of this important office of state proved a mistake. Rogers was too proud and Kissinger too arrogant to make compromises and cooperate.[13] Rogers' chilliness later extended to Nixon, who mistook old acquaintance with enduring friendship. Over time, the secretary of state would become more the mouthpiece of East Coast opinion and Congress, and less the advocate of his boss.

The post of defense secretary fell to Melvin Robert Laird, a son of Nebraska and another naval man who had been awarded a Purple Heart serving on a destroyer in the war. The round-faced Laird, known by his childhood nickname "Bambino," incongruously shortened and pronounced "bomb" by his mother, seemed destined for political office. At the age of 23 he inherited a Wisconsin Senate seat following the death of his father. Six years later, he gained a seat in the House of Representatives, which he held for eight consecutive elections, eventually assuming the role of Chairman of the House Republican Congress. By the time Nixon offered him the poisoned chalice of the Department of Defense, he had built a reputation over a quarter of a century as a solid, grassroots Republican, tough on communism, skilled in the merry-go-round of Washington politics, but with his nose to the ground on public opinion outside the Beltway.

As Laird later recounted, two bundles of reports shocked him on his first day in office, and these set the course for the next four years of his tenure as defense secretary.[14] The first was "a multivolume set of binders in my closet safe that contained a top-secret history of the creeping U.S. entry into the war." These were the "McNamara papers," later leaked and popularly known as the Pentagon Papers. "Infinitely more troubling," however, was Westmoreland's secret request to raise American troop levels to 700,000 in Vietnam. Appalled by this "more-is-better philosophy," he made it his mission to pursue exactly the opposite path.

Melvin Laird proved an inspired choice, his championing of the policy of "Vietnamization" – a phrase he deployed in an NSC meeting on March 28, 1969 – run close by the longer-lasting legacy of a downsized but better-equipped armed forces.[15] He could not re-make a department molded by the McNamara years, but he was able to repair frayed relations with the services (stimulating the joke "Praise the Laird"). As an experienced politician he understood viscerally that a dented and bruised armed forces needed a deal, a way out, not more internecine confrontation. In this respect, he was the civilian counterpart to Creighton Abrams who, on leaving Vietnam, devoted the last two years of his life to reforming the divisive draft system, laying the foundations for the modern National Guard and Regular Reserves. In return for quitting America's only shooting war, stalemated, and accepting steep cuts in personnel (over one million in four years), the soldiers, sailors, and airmen got what most fluttered their hearts: shiny, new gizmos. It is notable that so many of the icons of America's wars in the succeeding 40 years all had their origins in the Laird years: from cruise missiles, to the F-16 fighter, to the Abrams tank. Laird would leave office just two days short of the signing of the Paris Peace Accords and outlive McNamara by four years, both men surviving into their nineties, or long enough to witness another cycle of discordant American wars in Iraq and Afghanistan.

However, the most important appointment in Nixon's cabinet was Assistant to the President for National Security Affairs, bestowed on Professor Henry Heinz Alfred Kissinger. With a voice that sounded like a rumble, Kissinger was the giant waiting to emerge from the caverns of academia to rescue America's war. Few countries have owed so much to an intellectual. And few have had to endure so much petty academic envy and semi-hysterical vilification from an offstage audience that, as Kissinger philosophically observed, mistook argument for shouting. The son of Bavarian Jews who fled Nazi persecution, Kissinger would always hold up his childhood experience as an example of what America meant, and what she should continue to be – a shining Statue of Liberty still summoning the huddled masses. Whereas many of his contemporaries could invoke distinguished wartime careers, Private Kissinger had been variously employed in intelligence and administrative roles, serving with 84th Infantry Division in France and Germany, and later in counter-intelligence. Postwar, he entered Harvard and quickly displayed interest in two masters of European diplomacy, Castlereagh and Metternich, historical mentors who laid the intellectual foundations for his time in office. Rockefeller gave him the necessary bunk-up, but it was his erudition that propelled the rocket of his career. Fittingly, he received the invitation to an interview with Nixon in the middle of a meeting with Rockefeller. The meeting had convened to discuss what job Rockefeller should accept when the inevitable call came – embarrassingly, the protégé vaulted the master.[16] Like many academic colleagues, Kissinger had been "sick at heart" over Nixon's victory, but now this politician who seemed to provoke so many paroxysms of liberal vilification and disdain was offering him a job. At least on one point both the President-Elect and his soon-to-be National Security Advisor were in complete concurrence: Vietnam was a "genuine tragedy" in which nobody had a monopoly on the anguish.[17] The task now was to withdraw as a matter of deliberate national policy, and not in reckless and irresponsible flight. Kissinger would later lament that one's intellectual capital drained the moment you entered public office, but he had made terribly good use of this fuel in his two decades as a Harvard professor.

When Nixon entered the White House there were over 440,000 soldiers and marines in South Vietnam serving in 110 combat battalions.[18] The total number of servicemen in-theater including airmen and sailors exceeded half a million. Soon after assuming command of MACV in the spring of 1968, Abrams joked that there was not a lot of sympathy out there, and he was right.[19] Whichever direction the embattled command turned, there were enemies. MACV was fighting not one but three wars: in Vietnam, at home, and with world opinion. This same sense of self-pity shrouded the incoming Republican team. It was a doubtful achievement of many critics, Kissinger later wrote, including many from previous administrations, that debate over the war became debate over decisions taken by the Nixon administration, as if Nixon had dragged the country into Vietnam. The Democrats had hauled America into the unholy mess, but somehow Nixon very quickly assumed the blame.

Notwithstanding the undiminished fight in America's soldiers and marines, Nixon inherited a war that had become infected with the psychology of futility. The media had created an air not of victory but of defeat, Westmoreland lamented. Reinforced by vocal anti-war elements, this profoundly influenced officials in Washington. The contest was like two boxers in a ring. One had the other on the ropes and was close to a knock-out, then the second had inexplicably thrown in the towel.[20] In this judgment, he was correct. MACV had been touchingly close to the elusive victory Westmoreland promised. 1969 proved disastrous for the communists – "hunger, pain, bullets and enemies" – as General Chu Huy Man later recollected.[21] Northern soldiers actually starved to death and no meaningful operations were mounted anywhere in South Vietnam. Hanoi became divided after the failure of Tet. One camp led by Foreign Minister Nguyen Duy Trinh favored negotiations; Giap seemed to favor insurgency in the South; and the most influential camp led by Truong Chinh argued for "protracted war on Maoist lines." Regardless of these doctrinal divisions, however, Hanoi was united in its determination to continue the war to ultimate victory. The same was not true in Washington. Post-Tet, Vietnam fell off the wires. Americans had tired of the bad news, buried it, and yearned for an end to the fiasco.

Johnson had elevated Westmoreland on a pedestal then pulled the pedestal away. Nixon inherited "Abe," a wartime hero who had taken part in the relief of Bastogne, the "world champion" tank commander in Patton's estimation, and a quite different personality.

Creighton Williams Abrams was 54 when he assumed command of MACV, a square-jawed man with an ambling gait, scented with the smoke of cigars, imported for him from Hong Kong. Where Westmoreland had been the epitome of the Southern gentleman, Abrams preferred to punctuate with the odd profanity. At press conferences the Westmoreland monotone was replaced with Abrams' melody; an upbeat music, like the jazz records he liked to listen to in the evenings in his villa. The former had won the respect but not necessarily the affection of his staffs; Abe's command meetings were broken by laughter, commonly his loud guffaws. Over the course of the war Abrams adopted a black Labrador, named Devil, and promoted it, remarking that it was hard to be negative in a headquarters that had such a lovable dog. Westmoreland, by contrast, had rationed his smiles. Beyond these differences of personality, so heavily in Abrams' favor, was a more fundamental difference between the two generals which makes any comparison unfair. Westmoreland led an army that intended to win a war; Abrams withdrew an army that no longer believed this was possible. Like his predecessor, he worked formidably long hours to achieve this inglorious goal. But like many of the generals of his generation he suffered from ailments; ulcers, a dodgy gall bladder, and weakening smoker's lungs. After quitting Vietnam in 1972 he would survive for just two more years, felled by cancer.

Every commander seeks to stamp his authority and style on a campaign, but there were far more similarities than differences between Westy's and Abe's wars than critics of the former are willing to concede. Promoting Abrams as the better general, a comforting view that scapegoats Westmoreland, ignores the fact that Abrams was the beneficiary of Westmoreland's four-and-a-half-year slog in South Vietnam, first as deputy and then as overall commander. Westmoreland had to scale the logistic mountain of escalation, while fighting a war. Abrams inherited that half-a-million-strong force, now superbly equipped and generously serviced by a war machine in full motion. The enemy was now on the run across South Vietnam. The country team relationships in the US Embassy were better than ever. Where Westmoreland was shackled to a tortured president, Abrams was liberated by a president who advised him candidly that he would back him up if he used "any dirty tricks."[22] Critically, the inadequacies of MACV's intelligence apparatus had largely been addressed, although relationships with the CIA remained prickly. In Abrams' estimation, the intelligence problem now was not its paucity or timeliness but rather that it had become "massive" and overwhelming for commanders to digest and analyse.[23] In one month alone (July 1969), 780,000 pages of captured documents landed on the desks of the staffs manning the Combined Intelligence Center at Bien Hoa.[24]

Like Westmoreland, Abrams avowed that progress was being made; that offensive action was paramount; that the bombing campaign should not be curtailed; and that more should be done in Laos and Cambodia, including ground incursions if necessary.[25] He believed in attrition warfare and was as addicted to body counts as every other American general in Vietnam. In his very first conference as commander he instructed his subordinates to kill the enemy, inflict attrition, and destroy him. This was the "payoff."[26] In another conference he ordered his divisional commanders to slaughter the communists "in droves."[27] Search and destroy may have been replaced by the more euphemistic "spoiling attacks" or "reconnaissance in force," but it was the same thing and Abrams enthusiastically promoted both. Attrition warfare did not die out with the departure of Westmoreland. When Abrams finally promulgated his first Combined Campaign Plan for 1969, there was little in the document that may not have been written by his predecessor.[28]

Nor did Abrams wind down the war, until he was forced to by his political masters. Between mid-1968 and mid-1971 he ramped up the category of "battalion days spent on large unit operations per month." It was only after this period, with withdrawal in progress, that MACV's tempo of operations began to decline below the highpoint of Westmoreland's tenure. In Westmoreland's last full year in command there had been 3,328 battalion days dedicated to large-unit operations.[29] Under Abrams, the numbers jumped to 4,557 (1968–69), 3,648 (1969–70), and only finally fell to 2,225 days by mid-1971. These numbers only reflected US operations. When operations conducted by allies and the South Vietnamese were added, it was evident that the war truly took off under Abrams. In 1968 there had been 4,407 total battalion days in the field. By 1972, the number had hiked to 34,263.[30]

The more enlightened policy of pacification, aligned with Abrams by critics of Westmoreland, was simply not reflected in the intensity of fighting between 1968 and 1972. In this he was fully supported by his subordinate generals. Even a pacification enthusiast like Weyand was a convert, in one discussion with Abrams agreeing that he could not believe more in the truth "about killing people." MACV's essential task was "find him and kill him" – or search and destroy.[31]

Overwhelmingly, both committed to offensive operations. This deep cultural instinct in America's armed forces, manifest from Pershing to Patton, could not be diluted by the civilian leadership in Washington. Pre-Tet, Westmorland had dedicated 80 percent of operations to "combat" (the other categories were security, training, reserve, and pacification).[32] Abrams ramped this up to 92 percent. American withdrawal did not mean the end of fighting: Hanoi was going to "screw us," so MACV had to respond in kind.[33] As late as 1971, nine out of ten US operations were classified as "Combat." It is just not the case that MACV ever fully embraced the tenets of pacification, regardless of who was in charge. Find, fix, and destroy was the unaltered mantra, from start to finish, with its concomitant casualty bill. Just over 16,500 American fatalities had been experienced before Tet; the majority of battlefield deaths were suffered under Abrams.

In one important respect, however, Westmoreland and Abrams did differ, but the difference was principally in semantics and perception, not substance. Where Westmoreland had become associated with search and destroy, attrition warfare, and statistical analysis, Abrams became indissolubly linked with the simplified concept of "one war." Fighting such a war, Abrams argued, required understanding, rather than more charts apparently proving progress:

It finally gets to the point where that's really the whole war – fucking charts, and where they are supposed to go up if you can make them rise and where they are supposed to go down if you can push them down … instead of really thinking about what the whole thing's about, and what really has to be done ... somehow the chart itself becomes the whole damn war, instead of the people and the real things.[34]

In fact, "one war" had also been a feature of the Westmoreland command, but was labeled as the "two-fisted" strategy.[35] This envisaged exerting simultaneous pressure on the entire communist war machine, from village cadres to the regular battalions in the People's Army. Abrams had coined the phrase "one war" while still deputy commander in the spring of 1968, and then made it his own.[36] MACV had to "get after the whole thing," a phrase he often repeated. By this he meant the main forces, the local forces, the guerrillas, and the infrastructure. But after a period in command, even he began to judge it a hackneyed phrase.[37] When Abrams told his staffs that all operations should proceed against the full spectrum of enemy forces, organizations, and activities, he was mirroring the same exhortatory demands being made north of the border.[38] Both sides were waging, or trying to wage, "one war." In a joking aside, Abrams mused whether Hanoi would be open to swapping divisional commanders. He would take two, in return for two ARVN commanders. An aide asked, but who would win? Abrams replied with a laugh that he knew "who wouldn't lose."[39]

In other respects, Abrams was a mix of views, pragmatic, political, and sometimes resigned. He cultivated the press but assumed their hostility, remarking in private that the bureau chiefs were like a baseball umpire, calling you out before the throw. He understood that the US Army was good at conventional warfare but still struggled with the type of war being waged in Vietnam.[40] He had little faith in the civilians at the Paris peace talks, whom he judged "a bunch of nightmares." He had even less faith in Congress: when Weyand once teased that he might address a joint session of Congress, Abrams retorted that this would be like parachuting into Hanoi "without a parachute."[41]

Above all, Abrams understood that he was in a race against time. The United States was betting on "Vietnamization" and Hanoi was betting on pouring troops down the Ho Chi Minh Trail. The war had become "a liar's dice game." One day, somebody would lift the cup and instead of four fives there would be "garbage."[42] At the beginning of 1969, nobody could be quite sure who had rolled garbage.

The swollen belly of the Cambodian panhandle had always been the great strategic irritant, placed tantalizingly out of reach by the 1954 Geneva Accords that guaranteed Phnom Penh's neutral status. Since the early 1960s, this neutrality had been methodically disregarded and violated by Hanoi. In turn, Washington had responded with a small-scale and covert special force campaign. This had been supported by a very modest air campaign: from 1965 to 1968, just 2,565 sorties were launched over Cambodia, and 214 tons of bombs dropped. The clear winner in this war, publicly denied by both sides, was Hanoi.

The bitter truth was that for five years MACV had presided over an undeclared, frustrating, and ultimately phony war in Cambodia, or exactly the sort of war Nixon was unprepared to contemplate. The Joint Chiefs were even more deeply dissatisfied with the status quo and wasted no time in making their arguments to the new president. Just ten days after the presidential inauguration, General Wheeler suggested to a receptive administration that Viet Cong sanctuaries in Cambodia be added to the target lists. This proposal was supported by Abrams, one week later, specifically identifying the "Fishhook" area as the choice target. Both these commanders were making their appeals to a very receptive listener. Even before assuming the presidency, Nixon had advised Kissinger on January 8 that changing the bombing policy towards "neutral" Cambodia would be one of the "first orders of business."[43]

The opportunity to unleash the bombers arose early, precipitated by communist bad faith during the February Tet Offensive. Nixon at the time was traveling to a NATO conference in Brussels when he was informed of indiscriminate rocket attacks in Saigon. This, in Nixon's eyes, was unforgivable. Washington had unilaterally held to its bombing pause since the previous November. Even during the bombing phases, Hanoi had always been spared. Such casual contempt infuriated the President, who instructed Kissinger to initiate the planning for retaliatory raids (an irate Nixon in fact demanded immediate bombing and had to be dissuaded by a panicked Kissinger – Rogers, in all this, was kept out of the loop, and Laird was only informed when Al Haig, Kissinger's aide, returned to Washington).

As the bombing suspension over the North was still in place, satisfying Nixon's call for retaliation meant planning raids on the Cambodian sanctuaries in secret. The sticking point was not world opinion, which could be deflected by denial, but Congress, which could not.

Three weeks later, on March 15, the Viet Cong again launched rocket attacks against Saigon. By now, Nixon's patience had evaporated. With an impetuosity that betrayed his dislike for argumentation, Nixon informed a nonplussed Kissinger, late in the afternoon, that he had just issued an "unappealable" order to the Air Force to bomb the Cambodian sanctuaries. A stunned Kissinger insisted that a meeting was necessary, if only to confirm the President's decision.[44] The following day, a Sunday, Nixon attended church service then chaired the necessary meeting in the Oval Office. As the previous secret meetings had been held during working breakfasts at the Pentagon, the operation was dubbed *Breakfast*, but it soon metamorphosed into a rolling Operation *Menu* (Kissinger could not help but later record that he found the Air Force's choice of code words both meaningless and tasteless).[45] In Guam, 60 unsuspecting B-52 crews from 3rd Air Division were issued their orders for a massive Arc Light raid on War Zone D. Unbeknown to the airmen, only 12 of the bombers would actually attack the pre-determined targets in South Vietnam. Using elaborate command and control procedures to conceal the real target grids, the remaining crews were diverted at the last safe moment and sent over the border. Some 4,200 tons of high explosives spilled out of the bellies of the Stratofortresses on "Base Area 353." The results were spectacular: the bombers reported 73 secondary explosions, indicating that a major enemy dump had been struck. Kissinger was described as "beaming" at the news, although subsequent analysis suggested the COSVN had not in fact been hit.

As gratifying was the lack of a reaction. Hanoi maintained a guilty silence; Phnom Penh pretended to look the other way; and both Moscow and Peking refrained from diplomatic demarches. As far as a global audience was concerned, nothing had happened. There had been no carpet bombing in Cambodia, or at least no bombing that could not be explained away as an unfortunate error, if challenged.

Encouraged by this success, Operation *Menu* expanded. Within a year, 3,100 B–52 sorties were launched under Operation *Menu*, dropping over 91,000 tons of bombs, the majority reporting successful results. By the end of the Cambodian bombing campaign in August 1973, 2,756,941 tons worth of bombs would be dropped in 230,516 sorties, striking 113,716 sites.[46]

Given this level of military effort, the secrecy could not be maintained indefinitely. In fact, it barely lasted two months. On May 9, the *New York Times* published an article by one of its Defense Department reporters, William Beecher, entitled "Raids in Cambodia by U.S. Unprotested," that is, not protested by the Cambodian government. This was true, but who had agreed to bomb in Cambodia in the first place? The article was short, mostly buried on page seven, but clearly well-informed. The administration's goals, Cambodian leader Sihanouk's complicity, the bomb tonnage, and the divisional identities of PAVN units – all appeared in the article. Beecher had practically written an apologia for the White House, except that the whole business was meant to be a secret.

The revelation of the B-52 raids in Cambodia incensed Nixon who, in characteristic fashion, demanded the source of the information be "destroyed." A shoddy witch hunt followed that eventually alighted on the bookish and innocent Morton Halperin, one of Kissinger's own aides. No guilt was ever proven, but the FBI wire-tapped as many as 17 individuals over this affair, such was Nixon's determination to unmask the impertinent leaker.

The revelations actually made no difference to any of the protagonists, and barely stirred the peace movements. The mass Vietnam Moratorium marches would come at the end of the year (provoking a weary Wheeler to lament America's "interminably vocal youngsters, strangers alike to soap and reason").[47] The White House persisted with its policy of denial, which passed unchallenged by the media or by Congress. Relations with Cambodia improved: Sihanouk restored formal diplomatic relations, which had been severed for the last four years, and a US embassy was opened in Phnom Penh. Hanoi continued to maintain a blank silence over the whole matter. In Washington the circle of the initiated widened to include Laird, who had been bypassed in the first instance, as well as five senior Congressmen.[48] None challenged the policy. In Guam, the bomber squadrons filed their post-mission paperwork in the normal way, maintaining an auditable trail of Arc Light raids that concealed the true target grids.

From Kissinger's perspective, exculpation was unnecessary. Why was it moral, he later asserted in defense of the policy, for the North Vietnamese to have 50,000 to 100,000 troops in Cambodia, from which sanctuary they were killing Americans, and why was there a moral issue when the host government advised that if Washington bombed the border areas "they would not notice." This was a stout defense, but the morality of carpet bombing the Viet Cong's border sanctuaries was not the fundamental issue. Operation *Menu* expanded beyond its original intent and raised much wider questions. Like the ground escalation in 1965, the B-52s became a drink whose effects, once worn off, demanded even more B-52s, and it was this expansion of the air war over Cambodia that would provoke unresolved controversies, accusations, and counter-accusations.

For the anti-war lobby, the bombing campaign over Cambodia became a cause célèbre, the most heinous war crime perpetrated by a heinous president and his executioner-in-chief, Henry Kissinger. This lobby would peddle enduring myths that the B-52s killed half a million Cambodians, that the raids hastened the fall of the government, that they emboldened the Khmer Rouge and that they drove the North Vietnamese even deeper into Cambodia. The subsequent Cambodian genocide would also be blamed on Washington by strident voices that were as dismissive of the facts as they were reasonableness. All these charges were exaggerations.

Notwithstanding tactical successes of individual sorties, 2.7 million tons of bombs failed to eliminate the Cambodian sanctuaries, or destroy the Viet Cong's logistic infrastructure, or even ultimately save Prime Minister Lon Nol's government. For the majority of the four-year-long campaign the bombing remained at a modest monthly total of around 2,000 tons. Air power alone could not reverse the tide of fortune against the communists, although it certainly complicated their operations. Crucially, it could not substitute boots on the ground. The end of America's war in Indochina effectively witnessed a resurrection of the same dilemmas that were presented at the beginning. Hanoi was undeterred by this weight of aerial power, but Washington was now withdrawing, not escalating its ground forces. Bombing became the only option, not because it was right, but because it was the only card left in the hand, and this contributed to the caricature of a malevolent Washington thrashing out against defenseless Cambodia even as it pulled out the last of its soldiers from Indochina. For Nixon, this was the one and last chance to win "this goddamn war" and his patience with "assholes" screwing it up was thin.[49]

The morality of Operation *Menu* remains an intractable question because the morality of state violence shifts with cultural values and importantly technological progress. The Vietnam-era generation may be proximate, but there is a gulf between the freefall bombing of the 1960s–70s and the precision bombing available to a modern generation. The choice in March 1969 was binary: do not bomb at all, and therefore concede the field to the enemy – or bomb and accept the cost of civilian deaths. Johnson had not faced this decision and it remains an open question whether he would have played the same card. As no US president would have countenanced being chased out of Indochina by a victorious Hanoi, it is not unreasonable to suppose that Johnson would have concluded the war much as he started it – by calling on the bombers. For the decision-makers at the time, at any rate, this was a straightforward choice because it was judged there would be minimal civilian casualties. Prince Sihanouk gave his agreement to bombing on the grounds that no Cambodians lived in the border areas anyway. But he fell to a coup and it is equally probable that Sihanouk had no real idea who lived in these remote areas of his kingdom, because he had never visited them. Had Operation *Menu* been constrained to targeting the Viet Cong border sanctuaries, there may well have been no great controversy. The assertion that few civilians were killed would have been defensible.

But with the departure of Sihanouk and ensuing civil war (agitated by Hanoi, not Washington), the bombing expanded dramatically. The B-52s, flying at high altitude, enjoyed no better odds than their predecessor B-17s. In fact, they faced far worse odds because the most lucrative target for carpet bombing remained densely populated urban areas – a Dresden or Tokyo – not sparsely populated jungle. Washington would never have countenanced flattening Cambodian towns, any more then North Vietnamese towns, so the bombers were restricted to evacuating thousands of tons of high explosives over the least promising target set, wilderness. The B-52 became the iconic, sinister image of a senseless war, but it was more a reflection of expensive frustration.

None of this was missed by the administration that was well aware of the *ineffectiveness* of Operation *Menu*. An irritated Nixon thought the pilots were just "farting around."[50] Late at night, on December 9, 1970, he vented his frustrations on Kissinger over the way in which the Air Force was "running these goddamn milk runs." Anti-war protestors saw mass murder, but a skeptical Nixon suspected "the whole goddamn Air Force ... get one or two trucks a day and fly 800 sorties." The exchange was memorable:

P. The thing that concerns me about this thing you sent over on Cambodia was Moorer's ... lame excuse that they did not have any intelligence because the weather is bad. I don't think they are trying to do a good enough job in trying to get the intelligence over there. You understand what I mean?

K. Yes I do.

P. There are other methods of getting intelligence than simply flying. They've got the methods of the Cambodians to talk to and hell of a lot of other people ... now I want you to get ahold of Moorer tonight and I want a plan where every goddamn thing that can fly goes into Cambodia and hits every target that is open.

K. Right ...

P. I want this done ... They are running these goddamn milk runs in order to get the air medal ... It's horrible what the Air Force is doing. They aren't doing anything at all worth a damn.

K. They are not imaginative.

P. Well, they're not only not imaginative but they are just running these things – bombing jungles ... They have got to go in there and I mean really go in ... I want everything that can fly to go in there and crack the hell out of them. There is no limitation on mileage and there is no limitation on budget. Is that clear?

K. Right, Mr. President ...

P. It's a disgraceful performance and they are going to get off their ass and start doing something on it ... I want it done!! Get them off their ass and get them to work now.

K. Well we will get it done immediately Mr. President.[51]

It took all of Kissinger's tact to deflect Nixon from sacking the Air Force commander and court-martialing a second.

However, the ineffectualness of carpet bombing, which both Nixon and Kissinger recognized, gives more reason to critics than to its excusers. Kissinger was too quick to dismiss the question of the morality of Operation *Menu*. A figure of half a million deaths may have been exaggerated but a stick of bombs, however widely dispersed, is no less lethal for that dispersion. Operation *Menu* did claim tens of thousands of civilian lives (a minimum of 40,000 and maximum of 150,000 is generally reckoned, although the true number will never be known). Once the decision was taken to expand the bombing beyond its original parameters, it was inevitable the casualty count would start climbing. Nixon's histrionics prompted Seventh Air Force to bomb in circumstances where the planners may have assessed there was no valid target, and where civilians would be killed. The intelligence was imperfect. Lon Nol, a confused and contradictory man, was not afflicted with the same inhibitions over the deaths of his countrymen as Sihanouk, or they were overtaken by the urgency of survival at any costs. Cambodian acquiescence did not excuse Operation *Menu*'s advocates from raising the ethical questions. Faced with presidential ire, they simply didn't, and large areas of southeast Cambodia were effectively treated as if they were the depopulated or uninhabited free fire zones of South Vietnam, which they were not. MACV had no reliable technical means of determining precise targets beyond the border areas reconnoitered by special force teams, and no forward air control teams were deployed into Cambodia. A self-imposed restraint of not designating aim points within a mile of a settlement was a token gesture. Mapping was not necessarily accurate and bomber crews could not always achieve this level of precision anyway.

Ultimately, Operation *Menu* was both disproportionate and indiscriminate. As a way of waging war, its principal value was that it bought time for the American withdrawal by exacting a cost to communist operations in Cambodia. This was a sufficient if not essential dividend for an administration extracting the nation from an unpopular and unwinnable war. Kissinger was right over Hanoi's double-values. But the cloak of secrecy also acted as a moral blindfold. The White House would never have stomached a comparable campaign in South Vietnam because it could not have been concealed and there would have been uproar. In the end, all sides hypocritically pretended that Operation *Menu* did not exist – Washington, Hanoi, and Phnom Penh – because all placed ruthless national calculations over civilian lives. The cost of this collective moral blindness, in the final balance, was steep.

The weakness of a strategy based entirely on bombing was exposed within a year of the commencement of Operation *Menu*, but in a manner entirely unanticipated by Washington. Both Washington and Hanoi had assumed Cambodian "neutrality." Appended to this premise was a second assumption that the backward kingdom was timeless and unchanging. The only matter of political consequence was a generational change of royal power. This had been settled after the Second World War. Militarily, Cambodia was insignificant, economically she was feeble, and culturally, a mystery, except to French archaeologists and ethnographers who had become entranced by her charm.

The postwar period witnessed conflict between nationalists, conservatives, reformers, and revolutionaries; a confusing and eddying rapid of patriotic aspirations and crude power grabs skilfully navigated by Norodom Sihanouk. What emerged from the period – by the beginning of the 1960s – was a reassertion of historic Vietnamese control of the eastern border regions; a CIA-backed Khmer Serei ("Free Khmer") insurgency, led by Son Ngoc Thanh; an outlawed Prachea Chon party (the communist People's Party that emerged from the ranks of the 1950s Khmer Issarak or "Free Cambodia" insurgency); and Royalist control over the capital and surrounding provinces.[52] But Sihanouk was weak, or as Abrams quipped, the king-god was only capable of taking on a wounded squad of Italian motorcyclists.[53] North Vietnamese infiltration of Cambodia had begun in 1962 and within a matter of years as many as 50,000 soldiers were encamped in Stung Trang, Ratanakiri, Kratie, Prey Veng, Svay Rieng, Takeo, and Kampot Provinces. Sihanouk feared the communist cuckoo would swallow his country and engender a second Laos, but he was even more distrustful of American intentions in Indochina. In 1964, both the American and British embassies in Phnom Penh were sacked by government-instigated mobs. In May of the following year Sihanouk took the decisive step of severing diplomatic relations with Washington, making a Faustian bargain with the communist forces now operating from eastern Cambodia and hoping to save his country.

When Cambodia suddenly unraveled, at the beginning of 1970, it took everyone by surprise. Lloyd Rives, the US chargé d'affaires, was completely wrong-footed. Senate opposition to the perennial fear of "expanding the war" meant the CIA had been blocked from posting a single official in-country.

There were two principal actors in the plot: Prince Sirik Matak, Sihanouk's cousin and Deputy Prime Minister, and Lon Nol, a former army general and now Prime Minister. It was Matak who acted as Cassius to Lon Nol's Brutus. Fearing Sihanouk's ever-deepening complicity with Hanoi, the former persuaded a reluctant Lon Nol to land the fatal stab wound. With Sihanouk absent on a foreign junket, mass anti-Vietnamese rallies were organized in the capital, and in several provincial capitals. On March 12, Lon Nol was pushed into demanding the withdrawal of all North Vietnamese troops from Cambodian soil within 72 hours, an ultimatum summarily rejected by Hanoi. One week later the National Assembly deposed Sihanouk and installed Lon Nol as Head of State. Lon Nol, who had never wanted to dethrone the king, reportedly wept. Prince Matak, the cousin and rival for the throne, was less lachrymose.

The deposition of Sihanouk – the intermediary between Heaven and Earth – inevitably provoked unrest amongst a superstitious peasantry. "How are we going to work the rice fields, this year, since the Prince is no longer here to make it rain," complained one panicked villager.[54] When two government representatives sought to calm the crowds, they were beheaded and their livers grilled in a market place.[55] The government responded with artillery fire to disperse the mobs. In the capital, a quite different mood erupted: "wild ... real enthusiasm" for the revolution.[56] The chief manifestation of this enthusiasm was a wave of atrocities against ethnic Vietnamese and the embarrassment (to Washington) of mutilated bodies floating down the Mekong River.

If the Politburo in Hanoi was surprised by these events, it nonetheless reacted with alacrity. By the spring of 1970, Hanoi had established substantial forces in eastern and southern Cambodia: the 1st PAVN Division based in the area south and southeast of Phnom Penh; 5th, 7th, and 9th PAVN Divisions, east of the Mekong in the border sanctuaries; and an independent C40 Division, northwest of the capital near Tonle Sap Lake.[57] These moved quickly to seize control of a swathe of land from the Laotian border to the coast. One by one, every major town in northeast Cambodia fell to a mostly unopposed advance.[58]

By the last two weeks of April every highway other than Route 5 to Battambang and Thailand had been cut, and within the month, eight of 17 provinces had fallen to an alliance of the People's Army, Viet Cong, and the Khmer Rouge. Squeezed from the northwest and southeast, the helpless and retitled National Army of Cambodia (FANK – Forces Armées Nationales Khmères) was left in control of a diagonal corridor of land running through the middle of the country.[59] The fighting came to an exhausted halt on the "Lon Nol" line north of Phnom Penh, at the height of the summer, but it was clear to every observer that Lon Nol, soon to be nominated the president of a Khmer Republic, was fighting for survival.

Concurrent with this eruption of country-wide violence was a rush to militarize the Cambodian population. General mobilization was announced on June 25, driving the FANK from 35,000 to over 100,000 strong. Kissinger became an enthusiast even as the special force officer entrusted with the mission of building up the FANK, Colonel Jonathan Fredric Ladd, became convinced that the situation had "gone to pieces and was totally out of hand."[60] Where before Washington had pulled back from supplying weapons to Cambodia, there was now a rush to arm Phnom Penh. On July 1, Nixon authorized the expenditure of $10 million from contingency funds to support the FANK.[61] By the following year a Military Equipment Delivery Team, Cambodia (MEDTC) had been set up in the US Embassy in Phnom Penh. Wild plans were concocted to raise a quarter-of-a-million-strong force comprising 32 brigades and 202 battalions. Alarmed, Congress moved to hobble Nixon. The January 1971 Cooper-Church amendment prohibited the assignment of US advisors to the FANK, and the February 1972 Symington-Case amendment restricted the number of official American personnel in Cambodia to 200.

Faced with this obstruction, the administration exploited the loophole of covert operations to keep the supply lines open. Vinnell Corporation, Air America, Bell Aircraft Company, AVCO Lycoming Aircraft, and Helio Aircraft Corporation were all co-opted into this secret war.[62] The Military Assistance Program (MAP) grew exponentially: from $180 million in 1971, to $414 million by 1974. Over 260,000 M-16s, 12,000 machine guns, and more than 500 howitzers were flown to Cambodia.[63]

Hanoi clearly won the first round in the spring of 1970, but also suffered an important strategic setback about which it could do nothing; the closure of Sihanoukville (renamed Kampong Son), which for many years had served as a secret and vital maritime Ho Chi Minh Trail. The first arms shipments arrived in Sihanoukville in October 1966. From the quaysides, convoys of trucks ferried the supplies to Kampong Speu where they were distributed to two depots, one operated by the Viet Cong and the second by the Cambodian army at Lovek, northwest of Phnom Penh. The entire operation was run by a well-connected impresario called Hak Ly who owned a fleet of 200 trucks. The supplies were then further broken down and transported to the border bases that also served as training camps and rest areas. From December 1966 to the spring of 1969, mainly Chinese ships had delivered 21,600 tons of military supplies to the port. This included as many as 222,000 rifles and 16,000 machine guns and mortars, or enough for 600 battalions. One hundred million bullets and half a million grenades and mines had been delivered.[64] All this had been happening with the full complicity of the Sihanouk government and largely undetected by American intelligence.

The loss of Sihanoukville aside, by far the most important consequence of Hanoi's undeclared war on Lon Nol's government was that it provided the White House with the pretext to break the taboo of violating Cambodian territorial sovereignty. Faced with a mortal threat, Phnom Penh had requested US assistance – why should it not be granted? Nixon now found himself in the same position as Johnson five years previously: all the indicators were flashing red over the imminent collapse of a second Indochinese country to communist forces, but for an American intervention. Unlike the spring of 1965 there was less agonizing, at least in the White House. One month into the coup, Kissinger recorded that the administration, hobbled by critics, "had barely lifted a finger." At this juncture, no military aid or intelligence support had been authorized, although the developments over the border threatened Washington's entire position in Vietnam.[65] This wonderland of inaction could not last.

On March 25, Nixon instructed the Joint Chiefs to prepare a plan for a limited invasion of Cambodia; or as he put it "the time has come for action." But its aims were modest. In its original conception, only the sanctuaries would be targeted and the South Vietnamese would be involved. Rogers fretted over derailing the peace talks, and Laird was later left in an embarrassing position having assured the House Appropriations Subcommittee on April 23 that the administration had no intention of escalating the war into Cambodia, but Nixon was dismissive of these concerns. In fact, he was furious that every instruction was being obstructed. Kissinger was similarly unimpressed with what he dimly judged as "bureaucratic foot dragging." Over this period, the administration was unhelpfully distracted by other concerns, not least the aborted Apollo 13 mission. In Cambodia, it appeared Phnom Penh might collapse anyway, and Nixon was still faced with navigating a hostile Senate and media.

The sequence of events that led to the decision to attack the sanctuaries took place in one dramatic week.[66] On April 18, McCain briefed Nixon on the military options. Two days later he repeated the brief to Nixon and Kissinger in San Clemente. The following day, Nixon and Kissinger flew to Washington and conferred with CIA Chief Helms. At this point, there was still no plan to attack the sanctuaries. On April 22, the National Security Council met. By now Nixon was despairing: every advisor was offering suggestions on "how to lose," and none on "how to win."[67] The President secured Council agreement on intervention, but it was evident that all the protagonists were extremely cagey. Vice President Spiro Agnew, who made the decisive intervention, challenged the conferees with the familiar dilemma that America should either get in or get out (which annoyed an upstaged Nixon). As nobody was prepared to sign their names to quitting and running, there really was only one choice, but in the by now practiced art of being "on the right side of history," all parties started covering themselves for the expected backlash. Still, there was no action.

Notwithstanding the prevarications, two credible military schemes had emerged: Operation *Shoemaker*, an American-led affair against the COSVN in the so-called Fishhook area; and Operation *Toan Thang 42*, a South Vietnamese mission that would be launched against the Parrot's Beak, some 40 miles to the south, where it was believed the Provisional Revolutionary Government (PRG) was decamped. Four days after the NSC meeting, on the evening of Sunday April 26, Nixon signed the executive order to mount the attacks following a "charade" National Security Council meeting in which the attendees (Rogers, Laird, Wheeler, Helms, and Kissinger) pretended they were attending a briefing, but knew that Nixon was simply issuing an order.

In the usual way, this was not the end of the matter, as all departments had become experts at "bureaucratic exegesis" – in Kissinger's phrase – which commonly amounted to disobedience. A further meeting was required on April 28 to confirm what Nixon had already decided two days previously.

Finally, and with a decisiveness that delighted the Joint Chiefs, Nixon instructed MACV to attack on May 1.

Intelligence had previously estimated that there were as many as 125 border camps running from base area "704" on the coast to base area "609" in the Central Highlands. In addition to these there were scores of other military installations including 57 storage areas.[68] Over four years, the Viet Cong and PAVN had been allowed to build up this military infrastructure with virtual impunity, effectively controlling large swathes of eastern Cambodia. Tempted by such a lucrative target set, the original proposed double operation was expanded into 12 separate operations running from April 29 to July 1.[69] US forces were limited to a 20-mile exploitation line, but ARVN forces had no such constraint and would eventually penetrate as far as Kampong Cheu, a distance of 60 miles.

ARVN forces under the competent if eccentric Lieutenant General Do Cao Tri mustered in an area north of Tay Ninh on Route Coloniale 22 (he originally objected to the timing of the mission on astrological grounds and stayed in bed to avoid the imagined ill effects of misaligned stars).[70] Nearly 9,000 troops comprising 12 battalions drawn from 5th and 25th ARVN Infantry Divisions provided the spearhead. These were supported by four cavalry squadrons mounted in light tanks. 2 Ranger Group bolstered this invasion force with a further four battalions. Their objective was the headquarters of the COSVN based in the border town of Krek. Co-located in the same general area were elements of the 5th, 7th, and 9th PLAF divisions. The total enemy strength was estimated at 7,000. On April 29, the ARVN units crossed the border and quickly put the Viet Cong to flight.

The following evening, a combative Nixon addressed the nation. "To protect our men who are in Vietnam, and to guarantee the continued success of our withdrawal and Vietnamization program, I have concluded that the time has come for action."[71] Then, following a methodical itemization of North Vietnamese perfidy, Nixon announced to an unsuspecting nation the Cambodian incursion. "It is not our power, but our will and character that is being tested tonight." The Republican President had no intention of being found wanting.

Within hours, Operation *Shoemaker*, renamed *Toan Thang 43*, was launched against Base Areas 352 and 353 in the Fishhook. Drawing from all-source analysis intelligence, 381 targets were identified. These were pounded by six Arc Light sorties and 148 tactical air sorties that announced the launch of the operation at 4.15am on May 1. As many as 13,400 American troops and 8,000 ARVN then raced across the border. *Toan Thang 43* ran from May 1 to June 10. The speed of the advance caught the enemy "apparently flat-footed."[72] The main thrust was led by 11th Armored Cavalry, supported by 3rd ARVN Airborne Brigade, dropped to the rear of the Viet Cong base areas. 2nd and 3rd Brigades, with 1st Cavalry, secured the left and right flanks respectively. It took 11th Armored just five days to reach the border town of Phum Khcheav and secure Highway 7. The regiment then pressed north as far as Snoul in pursuit of the retreating PAVN units. Resistance was patchy or non-existent.

Over the course of the next five weeks 204 significant caches were uncovered. The principal logistic hubs were discovered at "Shakey's Hill," "Rock Island" in Base Area 351, and "the City" in Base Area 352. The latter comprised 182 separate bunkers containing more than 175 tons of supplies. At "Rock Island" a further 330 tons was discovered. "Shakey's Hill," named after a fallen soldier and the best concealed of the three base areas, contained more than 170 tons.[73] The full extent of the incursion ranged from Snoul in the northeast to Kampot on the Gulf of Thailand. Kampong Spoe, Prey Veng, and Svay Rieng all fell. Vanguard ARVN units reached the outskirts of Phnom Penh. According to MACV estimates 11,562 enemy were killed and over 1,000 prisoners taken. US losses were 338 and the ARVN reported 809 killed. By any measure, the combined *Toan Thang* operations had been a resounding success.

An indisputable foundation for the success of the operation, hidden to the communists and only relatively recently declassified for historians, was the top-secret work of the Radio Research companies, or SIGINT community.[74] Using the technique of "radio finger printing" (RFP) – essentially following the transmissions and locations of individual radios from unique identifiers recorded on light sensitive paper – the NSA and MACV SIGINT units were able to maintain constant surveillance on virtually the entire array of enemy forces across the border. Crucially, this intelligence was forwarded to tactical commanders. In the words of the NSA cryptologic history on the Cambodian incursion: "RFP coverage was not restricted to COSVN and Hq, SVNLA [South Vietnam Liberation Army]. Information from RFP was gathered on almost every target believed to be of significant value to the military operations being conducted inside Cambodia." The coverage was so good, wrap-up reports on the activities of the COSVN and subordinate units were being churned out every half an hour. It is quite likely that American commanders knew more about the dispositions and locations of the retreating communist forces than their counterpart commanders.

The decision to launch a ground invasion had the important result of expanding the air war. Notwithstanding the opening salvo of B-52 strikes, tactical maneuver could only be supported by tactical air strikes. This implied extending the Laotian Steel Tiger interdiction missions south of the border. The code name given to this new front was Freedom Deal and the effects were deleterious across northeast Cambodia and the border regions.

From the outset, the rules of engagement were inadequate. Authorization to attack a target relied on two English-speaking FANK officers based at Seventh Air Force; three aerial observers based at Pleiku; or confirmation of the target via a VNAF liaison officer based in Phnom Penh.[75] These liaison officers only had the haziest intelligence on the location of communist forces, and none could truthfully distinguish non-combatants from combatants. The Cambodians had no experience of air support and were unwilling to lose face with their new-found American allies. As a consequence, they proved very permissive, agreeing to whatever targets were suggested to them (their US mentors found themselves in the unusual position of urging restraint). As the campaign proceeded, non-English-speaking Cambodians were rotated through these liaison posts, complicating the process.

Timothy Eby, hailing from a family of Ohio pacifists, was assigned to act as a Forward Air Controller (FAC) on the top-secret spotter missions over Cambodia (code-named *Rustic*). He recalled, "by the time I got there some of the ground commanders still didn't have anybody that could speak English and they spoke only French and Cambodian."[76] A call was put out for French speakers and unwitting volunteers presented themselves at Bien Hoa Air Base. We would "throw them in the backseat of an OV-10 and away we'd go." The volunteers had no training whatsoever. Eby recalled a sergeant who was given the simple instruction: "'I will never say "Bail out" unless I want you to reach down and pull up on that handle. Is that clear?' 'Yes, sir.' I said, 'Sergeant, congratulations. You are now combat qualified,' and away we went."

Despite proscriptions against attacking settlements (unless attacked), the combination of weak target authorization mechanisms, generous rules of engagement, and a lack of accurate US-sourced intelligence, were bound to result in high civilian casualties. Eby recalled "we had to confim and confirm and confirm," but the Cambodians on the ground simply didn't care about civilian casualties. "You bomb village" was the instruction he would invariably receive. The only civilian casualty avoidance measure was warning by loudspeakers and leaflet drops, two totally impractical measures that were as widely ignored in Cambodia as they had been in South Vietnam.

This unsatisfactory situation was further inflamed by a Nixon who already harbored suspicions over the Air Force's performance in Operation *Menu*, and who now transferred his qualms to the tactical air strikes, with good reason. Every strike had to be personally authorized by the four-star 7th Air Force commander in Saigon, a process that could take three hours, by which time the target was gone. If the commander was at lunch, or in a meeting, he could not be interrupted.

In mid-June, Nixon summoned Admiral Moorer, now Acting Chairman of the JCS, and bluntly told him that he wanted more "action."[77] A stung

Moorer responded on June 17 by firing off a message to Abrams informing him that Freedom Deal had now been elevated to Freedom Action. "You are authorized," he wrote, "to employ U.S. tactical air interdiction in any situation that involves a serious threat to Cambodian positions such as provincial capitals whose loss would constitute a serious military or psychological blow to the country." As the entire territory of Cambodia was in this parlous state, and would remain so until the fall of the government in 1975, this instruction gave Seventh Air Force free rein to bomb liberally. In 1970, at the height of the air surge, Seventh Air Force flew almost 2,000 weekly interdiction and tactical support missions. An estimated 6,269 "structures" and 5,720 bunkers were destroyed, as well as 50 bridges. As many as 653 Arc Light missions were despatched, striking border targets as well as targets beyond the 20-mile limit.[78] Swathes of Cambodia had, in effect, become free fire zones.

Predictably, the action Nixon craved in Cambodia provoked counter-action on the streets of Washington. Protests erupted in as many as a third of university campuses nationwide. On May 9, a balmy spring day, more than 100,000 protestors converged on the Mall, many stripping off and cooling themselves in the ornamental pond at the Lincoln Memorial. Five days earlier, at Kent State University, flighty Ohio National Guardsmen had opened fire on protesting students, killing four. Inflamed by this gross act, it appeared the White House itself might be threatened by an incursion of thousands of anti-war protestors, brandishing swastika placards at the President. Laird panicked, but Nixon held his nerve and firmly instructed Abrams to keep throttling the communists. In a bold if awkward gesture, Nixon even mingled with the protestors, the king disarming the rebellious peasants by showing his face.

In an unprecedented gesture, some 250 State Department officials, including diplomats, signed a statement objecting to their own government's policy.[79] If Nixon needed any excuse to believe the world was against him, this was it – the government's own employees were now in opposition to him. Congressional rebellion – which by now had become a routine, monthly ritual – gained new wind. In mid-May, Senators John Cooper and Frank Church proposed their amendment to the Foreign Military Sales Bill, which if passed would have resulted in no weapon transfers or indeed any US military activity in Cambodia after June 30. In effect, the two Senators preferred the collapse of Cambodia (followed by South Vietnam), with the chaos that would have ensued, to the White House's calibrated efforts to prevent just that eventuality. In the event, a promised deadline for the conclusion of operations on June 30 was comfortably met, after it became apparent by the end of May that the mission's objectives had been met.

Nixon dismissed the "fatuous nonsense" that the United States had invaded neutral Cambodia, and was jubilant over the results of the incursion. He later itemized the haul like Croesus counting his treasures: 22,892 individual weapons; 2,509 crew-served weapons; 15 million rounds of ammunition; 14 million pounds of rice; 143,000 rockets, mortars, and recoilless-rifle rounds; 199,552 antiaircraft rounds; 4,852 mines; 66,022 grenades; and 83,000 pounds of explosives.[80]

Nixon, with some justification, described this as "the most successful military operation of the entire Vietnam War."[81] The Viet Cong campaign in the Delta was crippled for two years, Lon Nol's government was temporarily saved, and Sihanoukville remained closed to Hanoi's weapon smuggling. The allegation that the White House expanded the war, which Nixon angrily refuted then and subsequently, was simply not founded in fact. North Vietnam had occupied the Cambodian border regions since the mid-sixties, with the compliance of Sihanouk. In the course of this occupation, Hanoi raised and trained the Khmer Rouge, from which ranks a bunch of semi-crazed henchmen would emerge to perpetrate the 1975–79 Cambodian genocide. Nixon did not widen the war; he attacked Hanoi where it was vulnerable and where it had enjoyed sanctuary for the last five years. Although MACV could not have anticipated such a decisive outcome, the fact is that communist operations in the Cambodian fronts buckled and would not recover until the collapse of the South Vietnamese government in the spring of 1975.

Following the release of the Cambodian genie from the bottle, it was inevitable Laos would follow. It was here that the Ho Chi Minh Trail started, and it was in this somnolent kingdom that Kennedy had first raised the prospect of a communist takeover of Southeast Asia. Laos's neutrality was guaranteed by the 1954 Geneva Accords, subsequently reaffirmed in the July 23, 1962 Declaration on the Neutrality of Laos. These agreements had been totally abused by Hanoi. A departing Eisenhower had described Laos as the "cork in the bottle," but the communists smashed the bottle. Over the following decade, Hanoi trained and armed the Pathet Lao insurgency, keeping Premier Souvanna Phouma in Vientiane on the back foot, and even threatening his overthrow. Washington's response to this dribbling civil war had been ineffective at best. A covert CIA program had been an irritant to Hanoi, but no more. Under Johnson, the Barrel Roll and Steel Tiger interdiction missions had never been sufficiently resourced. Moreover, an aversion to upsetting the fragile status quo in Laos had been reinforced by Ambassador William Sullivan (1965–69) who consistently foreclosed more forceful military options (Westmoreland's perfectly sensible proposal that the communist war effort could be asphyxiated by throttling the Ho Chi Minh Trail at its source in

Laos never stood a chance because of Sullivan's opposition). The problem with Laos, as Abrams put it, was that there was no intelligence "worth a shit" and the special force campaign had been run by a bunch of guys "playing soldier."[82]

Under Nixon, all this changed, but not before the usual departmental sparring. Even the President, sensitive to the political implications, was lukewarm at first. After Souvanna Phuoma made a personal appeal Nixon changed his mind, authorizing the first air strikes on 17 February 1970. In the now customary fashion, as Kissinger later noted, just one B-52 strike – authorized after a month of painful discussions and in the face of an unprovoked communist offensive that threatened to overthrow the Laotian government – "was enough to trigger the domestic outcry."[83] A queue of senators formed, impatient to lambaste the administration – Eugene McCarthy, Frank Church, Mike Mansfield, Mathias, Gore, Symington, Cooper, and Percy – and all motivated not by the plight of the poor, suffering Laotians, but by the opportunity to embarrass Nixon. This was the culmination of a campaign extending over many months, Kissinger sarcastically wrote, "to get at the 'truth' in Laos."[84] The "truth" was not at stake. The previous three administrations had kept the Senate informed of operations in Laos in secret hearings. The media knew what was going on and had done so for years through leaks. There was no secret to keep. What Nixon's political enemies wanted was public confession and humiliation, a gesture he was hardly likely to grant.

The Steel Tiger missions in southern Laos expanded. A combined air-ground effort code-named *Commando Hunt* was launched. Royalist forces, now bolstered by the offending B-52 strikes, checked and then pushed back the encroaching Pathet Lao. However, as in Cambodia, this military effort came with a cost to the civilians. In short order, there was an inflationary spiral. As many as a quarter of the kingdom's population of three million would be displaced over the next three years. The price tag to the communists was also significant – optimistic assessment suggested less than 20 percent of war materiel entering Laos now reached the South.

The iron logic of air operations engendering ground operations also played out in Laos. The Cambodian incursions had highlighted the lucrative rewards gained from striking directly at the cross-border sanctuaries. It was just a matter of time before the Laotian sanctuaries would be similarly targeted. However effective the bombing, neither Pathet Lao nor the Ho Chi Minh Trail could be neutralized from 20,000 feet. Truck bombing was a successful game but supporting the Laotian ground forces effectively was proving much harder in what was described as a "loose as a goose situation."[85] The snag was the same as that experienced in Cambodia: MACV sent a planning team to Vientiane to work out a plan of attack, but there was none to plan. The

Royalist forces did not know where their own units were, still less enemy positions. They didn't know "what the hell is going on," as Abrams recalled.[86]

The prospect for an incursion into Laos arose at the end of 1970. In a war that had thrown up the most arcane arithmetical calculations, it should perhaps have come as no surprise that Laos would eventually add to the strange calculus. Following a series of studies on the progress of Vietnamization, it was concluded the ARVN was suffering from an "eight-battalion deficit" (this in a country which had mobilized one million soldiers and militiamen). This pedantic conclusion would not have mattered greatly, except the same studies suggested that if Hanoi succeeded in dominating Laos and Cambodia, then Saigon would be facing a 35-battalion deficit – a more serious imbalance of forces.[87]

The consequence of this fretting over abstract battalion deficits was Operation *Lam Son 719*, an operation "conceived in doubt and assailed by skepticism," which then "proceeded in confusion."[88] *Lam Son 719* dangled two hopes before the planners' eyes, neither of which would be fulfilled. The first addressed the perennial strategic frustration of the cross-border sanctuaries. By mounting a dry-season offensive against the communist logistic supply lines – the Ho Chi Minh Trail – it was hoped Hanoi's offensive plans could be set back a year. The second offered an opportunity to shore up the foundations of the policy of Vietnamization, on which Washington's withdrawal strategy critically rested. Why could *Lam Son 719* not repeat the success of the Cambodian operations? Why not reduce the battalion deficit by taking the war across the border?[89]

However, not everyone was convinced. In Washington, the Kissinger camp championed the proposal through Al Haig. Abrams remained doubtful, at first, and the Joint Chiefs were similarly unconvinced. In fact, from Kissinger's account, his original concept envisaged another incursion into Cambodia, specifically against the Chup Plantation, not Laos. Following a fact-finding mission to Saigon, led by Haig, it appears Thieu, MACV, and the Embassy all rejected another major Cambodian operation but agreed to a Laotian incursion.[90] It is difficult to determine how much real enthusiasm there was for the idea, and to what extent various actors were responding to signals and political imperatives. Abrams, for example, always felt operations in Laos were a poor joke. Thieu, it subsequently transpired, had placed a 3,000 casualty limit on the operation, a threshold which, if reached, would trigger the withdrawal of ARVN units from Laos regardless of whether the aims of the operation had been met. After the operation, nobody wished to be publicly associated with its failure, which muddied the waters further. In Kissinger's retrospective analysis, Washington allowed itself to be carried away by the "daring conception," by unanimity in both Saigon and Washington, and by the memory of success in Cambodia. Energies were soon absorbed not in careful analysis but in interdepartmental maneuvering through which the Nixon administration made its decisions.[91] The latter point was unimpeachably true, but Kissinger may have been self-deceived over the unanimity of responsible military planners – in fact, there was little.

Despite the misgivings, tentative planning for the operation began on December 8, 1970, encouraged by reporting of a PAVN logistic build-up in the Tchepone area, an important juncture of the Ho Chi Minh Trail just 40 miles from the border. Over the Christmas period, Nixon swung behind the operation, but knew he would face opposition from within his own administration. An elaborate game of chess then developed between Nixon and his principal secretaries. Two meetings were crucial in this game: on December 23, when he coaxed Laird on board, and on January 18, when he lured Rogers – or so he thought. In fact, no sooner had Nixon presumed consensus than Rogers began to find flaws in the plan. This was always likely as XXIV Corps, commanded by Lieutenant General James Sutherland, was given just nine days to submit a plan, a hopelessly short schedule later exposed when weaknesses in the operational and logistic concepts became evident. Faced with cabinet rebellion, first Kissinger and then Nixon turned to Moorer (a sailor), who pronounced himself confident that the operation would be a success. Thus armed, another meeting of all the senior advisors was held on January 27.[92] Unfortunately, for a quietly despairing Nixon, Rogers proved a far cleverer general than Admiral Moorer. In a bravura performance he dismantled the Chief's plan, leaving Nixon little choice but to order the go-ahead without consensus.

The rushed plan became two operations: a US marine-led *Dewey Canyon II* that would establish a firm base for the incursion west of Khe Sanh (following the same route the PAVN had traced in reverse during the 1968 siege); and *Lam Son 719*, the incursion itself conducted solely by ARVN units. Following the January 27 meeting, Nixon authorized *Dewey Canyon II* but disingenuously held back from authorizing support for *Lam Son 719*, although all the protagonists knew the second step was inevitable once the first had been ordered. It was not until the early evening of February 3 that phase two was authorized, but this show of deliberation only served to compress military timings even more. The stated objectives of this second phase – *Lam Son 719* proper – were Base Area 604 in the Tchepone area, and, optimistically, Base Area 611 in the A Shau Valley. On paper the scheme may indeed have appeared realistic, but for several flaws, some already identified by Rogers.

The chief flaw was that the North Vietnamese were aware of the impending incursion but not the exact scope or timing. A reliable network of spies and the difficulties of concealing the movements of over a division's worth of soldiers and their vehicles had flagged allied intentions. Far from worrying, Hanoi welcomed the chance to entrap and destroy so much ARVN combat power on ground of its own choosing, and even made an announcement on Radio Hanoi revealing a secret agreement between the South Vietnamese and Laotian governments to allow two ARVN divisions to penetrate 20 miles into Laos.

Hanoi was not the only city buzzing with news of the impending operation. An agreement with the press corps in Saigon to observe an embargo on reporting the build-up of forces simply served to uncork a bottle of leaks and speculation in Washington. So much talk provoked the usual backlash from hostile legislatures. Within 24 hours of ARVN troops crossing the border, Representative Thomas P. O'Neill and 37 co-signatories raised legislation opposing any US military action in Laos whatsoever. This was just the beginning of a stampede of self-indulgent, pious congressional resolutions: five were raised over the course of *Lam Son 719*, and a total of 17 House or Senate votes were held between April and July.[93] Every one of these resolutions sought to severely limit or totally foreclose the administration's ability to end America's military commitment in Indochina in good order. Scoring political points in the Beltway mattered more than soldiers' lives. The front pages of national newspapers once again filled with critical headlines and war protestors found one more reason to reinforce their unswerving prejudice that Richard Nixon was a mad warmonger. "They [the South Vietnamese] have one of the world's biggest armies," editorialized the *Milwaukee Journal*. "If they can't stand on their own feet now it is too late."[94] Kissinger's recollection of this "brutal" line pointed to an important truth. Too many Americans simply did not care if South Vietnam collapsed. After so much discord, abstract arguments over American prestige and domino theories now rang hollow to a generation asked to make the sacrifice.

The tactical defect in the plan was the proposed axis of advance. The ARVN invading force would be squeezed down the single Route 9, following the narrow valley traced by the course of the Xe Pon River. With no flanking options, Lieutenant General Hoang Xuam Lam, Commander I Corps, had to trust in this poorly maintained road and several rickety bridges to maintain the momentum of his advance. Aware of this vulnerability, the plan envisaged leap-frogging infantry battalions ahead of the column to seize key hilltop features, but this depended on American helicopters and safe air corridors, which the North Vietnamese antiaircraft batteries were not likely to grant.

Lam was probably not the best choice of commander. He looked like a boy scout and bedecked the entire left side of his chest with rows of medals that dripped over his waist belt. None of his subordinates, who actually outranked him in seniority, placed great faith in his leadership. Both the marine and airborne commanders whose troops would be crucial to the success of the operation, Lieutenant Generals Le Nguyen Khang and Du Quoc Cong respectively, sulked and remained in Saigon throughout the operation. In an effort to maintain secrecy, participating units were not involved in the planning until a very late stage and there were no opportunities for rehearsals. Few had experience of cooperating with other formations, let alone within their own.

The ARVN launched on February 8 following a 48-hour weather delay, forfeiting all surprise. Announced by a B-52 strike and massive artillery bombardment, 4,000 men from 3rd ARVN Armored Brigade, supported by 1st and 8th Airborne Battalions, proceeded to trundle up the undefended road. Simultaneously, 1st ARVN Infantry secured four landing zones and three forward support bases south of Route 9. In a follow-up, 2nd and 3rd Airborne Battalions secured a further two landing zones, and 21st and 39th Ranger Battalions seized two hill features forward of the armored column. The spear point of 3rd Armored succeeded in reaching the halfway point of its advance – a settlement called Ban Dong (A Luoi) – within three days. One week into the operation, by February 16, the ARVN had squeezed over 10,000 soldiers into Laos. It was a commendable effort and a measure of just how far the ARVN had developed as a capable, conventional army. This, at least, is what a satisfied MACV at first saw in the performance of its protégés.

Then the column of M41 Bulldog tanks halted. Abrams and Sutherland urged Lam to maintain momentum, and Laird was forced to defend the general in a press conference, but it was evident that the Laotian incursion was unraveling. Lam was not entirely to blame. Both Thieu and General Vien, the Chief of Staff, were beginning to see an unfolding disaster sealed by a politically unacceptable casualty bill.

In accordance with the importance of the battle, Hanoi mustered the biggest combined arms concentration of forces of the war, and Colonel General Van Tien Dung, Chief of the General Staff, was despatched to oversee the operation.[95] This amounted to 13,000 men and 10,000 support troops.

The operation crucially depended on American helicopters, but the 101st Aviation Brigade pilots found themselves running a gauntlet of heavy antiaircraft fire from PAVN gunners, well-concealed by both the thick jungle canopy and low cloud. Matters worsened when it became plain that Route 9 was in such a dilapidated state that virtually all resupply would have to be by helicopter. This provoked a second crisis. The calculated aviation fuel requirement for the operation had significantly underestimated helicopter usage. Faced with a stalled advance, a supreme effort was made to reroute emergency supplies to the front, but by now expectations of success were being dashed by the sluggish Lam.

Lam's prevarication contrasted with the alacrity of his counterpart General Le Trong Tan. Counterattacks were launched with PT-76 and T-54 tanks. ARVN

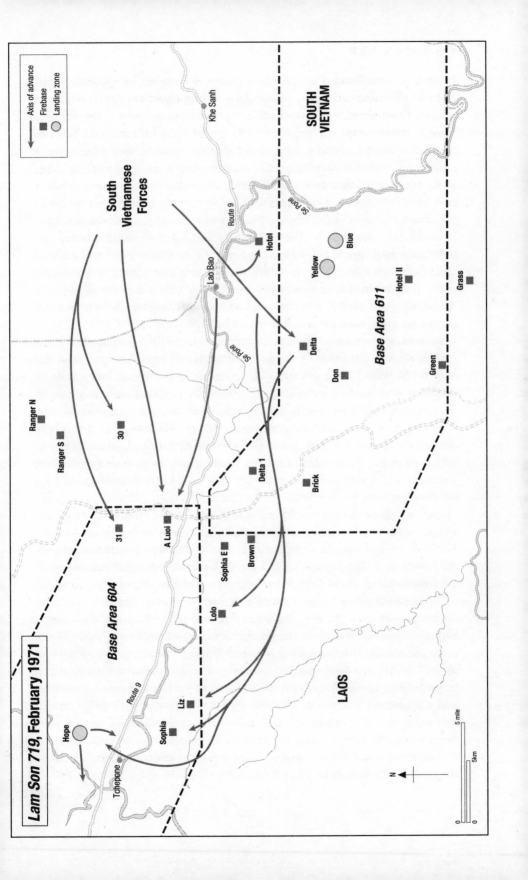

batteries in the forward support bases were out-ranged by Soviet-supplied 130mm guns and received a pummeling. The Ranger battalions were then subjected to concentrated assaults. By the time 39th Rangers fell back, three days later, it had suffered 75 percent losses. 21st Rangers lasted a further two days before also withdrawing with more heavy losses. A worried President Thieu ordered General Do Cao Tri to assume command of the faltering operation, but in an unfortunate twist he was killed when the helicopter ferrying him north crashed. Lam then fell out with the airborne commander Dong. Order was matched by counter-order. In the ensuing confusion, first one forward support base collapsed, then a second one week later. Both airborne battalions holding these bases were decimated. By the last week of February, there were numerous tank clashes on Route 9. 17th ARVN Cavalry stood its ground but, with the hills falling on its flanks, it was just a matter of time before the cavalrymen would be forced to withdraw. But for MACV organizing more B-52 strikes and tactical air missions, they probably would have.

Retreat now was politically unacceptable. Abrams was urging that a second ARVN division be fed into the fight. Three weeks into the operation, the only achievement was a pointless blood-letting on Route 9. From Saigon's perspective, a symbolic occupation of Tchepone was necessary before closing the operation. This would achieve little as Base Area 604 was actually west of the town, a point that did not escape Abrams. Nevertheless, MACV felt obliged to support the new plan, which involved lifting elements from 1st ARVN Division to three landing zones south of the town. Eleven helicopters were lost and 44 damaged. Three days later, on March 6, the bulk of 2nd ARVN Regiment was flown to Tchepone in the biggest helicopter operation of the war (involving 276 UH-1s). Careful route selection and a massive amount of preparatory fires ensured that just one helicopter was lost. The furthermost landing zone was named "Hope," but there was little to be found. All this effort was largely wasted. Within 48 hours of "taking" Tchepone, itself a worthless prize, Thieu ordered the withdrawal of the incursion force.

Withdrawal became retreat, which evolved into an extended rout. The operation did not officially end until April 7, by which time the ARVN had abandoned or lost 298 vehicles, including 54 tanks. One quarter of the original force was either killed or wounded, although some estimates suggested more than half the force was lost (the official count was 1,549 killed, 5,485 wounded). Over 215 Americans were killed (137 pilots and crew were killed and a staggering 818 wounded). The People's Army also suffered grievously defending Route 9 – how could it not when 53,000 tons of bombs were dropped on the PAVN divisions? PACAF reckoned it destroyed over 2,000 trucks, 100 tanks, and 300 antiaircraft guns. Some 13,000 communist soldiers were assessed to have been killed.[96]

But the cost to the allies was the more shocking. The aviation squadrons lost 103 helicopters, with another 631 damaged (the ARVN only flew around three percent of sorties – it was, as ever, an American effort). *Lam Son 719* had been the last sacrificial altar to US Army aviation. Over a six-week period, MACV lost ten percent of all the helicopters lost during the entire war. One company started with 32 machines and had eight left at the end of just two weeks. Every pilot was shot down at least once.[97] Base Area 604 was not dismantled and the traffic flow on the Ho Chi Minh Trail immediately increased following the operation. The following day, with considerable aplomb, Nixon announced on national television that "Vietnamization has succeeded."

A hostile American press only saw a fiasco: photographs of South Vietnamese soldiers clinging to the skids of American helicopters did not look like a victory. In Saigon, assessments were more positive. An initially skeptical Abrams thought it delivered a "death blow" to Hanoi. Admiral McCain was characteristically bullish, and blind: "In ten years' time," he asserted, "people would look back and acknowledge the allies were a 'goddamn' closer to success than the politicians and newspapers cared to admit."[98] Weyand later pointed out that the People's Army was unable to mount a single major operation for the remainder of 1971. This was true, because the ARVN maximum effort had required a corps-level defense by Hanoi using troops that otherwise would have been employed in South Vietnam. But it was only true for one year – by the spring of 1972, the communists were ready to resume the offensive. In the short term, secret French reporting suggested that *Lam Son 719* had a devastating effect upon the morale of communist soldiers and on the civilian population of North Vietnam.[99] At least two enemy divisions had been wiped out (tallying with MACV's estimate of 17 battalions). Nixon was unimpressed and later fumed at the manner in which a treasonous press dissected the corpse of the operation. Kissinger avowed the plan would not have been approved if it had been known the South Vietnamese were unwilling to complete the job.

With the controversies over Cambodia and Laos, it was easy to forget there was also a war in South Vietnam, the war MACV was supposed to be fighting and which had never gone away. Against a backdrop of imminent withdrawal, MACV continued to mount an aggressive ground war. General Frederick Weyand, the former commander of 25th Division and II Field Force, was promoted to Deputy COMUSMACV in late 1970. As a consequence of the Tet Offensive, a new Provisional Corps – eventually XXIV Corps – had been stood up on March 10, 1968 and placed under the command of General William Rosson, now a veteran of two Vietnam tours (as MACV Chief of

Staff, and I Field Force Commander). This new corps fell under General Cushman's I Corps command that already included 1st Marine and the Americal Divisions, with Rosson directly commanding 1st Cavalry, 101st, Airborne and 3rd Marines. Rosson, who had previously commanded the early incarnation of the Americal Division – Task Force Oregon – proved the judicious choice. Under the Cushman-Rosson double act, frayed army-marine relations mended.

An Accelerated Pacification Program was signed off by an enthusiastic Thieu on November 1, 1968. The original HES (Hamlet Evaluation System), based on 18 questions, grew to 137 questions. This was warfare by management tools and programs: the Accelerated Pacification Program would eventually give way to a Community Defense and Local Development (CDLD) plan, and the marine CAPs (Combined Action Platoons) became CUPPs (Combined Unified Patrol Programs). But re-branding programs and playing musical chairs with acronyms changed nothing on the ground. Under the hood of the MACV war engine, a covert campaign called the Phoenix Program had begun to attract unwanted attention. CIA Chief Colby felt obliged to defend the program, blaming "the good offices of our friends in the press" for the "assassination" label which the secret war quickly gained.[100] Few believed him.

In keeping with the philosophy of Vietnamization, US divisions were allocated pairing missions. The Americal paired with 2nd ARVN; 4th Infantry continued to screen the Central Highlands; and 173rd Airborne paired off with 22nd and 23rd ARVN Divisions. 1st Cavalry logically paired with the ARVN Airborne Division covering the western approaches to Saigon, while Major General Ellis Williamson's 25th Infantry covered Tay Ninh and Hua Nghia Provinces, alongside the sister 25th ARVN Division.

In mid-April 1969, Operation *Montana Raider* saw the paratroopers take on the 1st and 7th PAVN Divisions in War Zone C, while a third brigade tackled 5th PAVN Division in War Zone D. Now under the command of Major General Elvy Roberts, many of 1st Cavalry's operations were preceded by massive B-52 strikes, all restraints lifted as MACV sought to punish and degrade communist forces. 1st Infantry under Major General Orwin Talbott, now nicknamed "The Big Dead One," paired with 5th ARVN Division in the three provinces directly north of Saigon, supported by 11th Armored Cavalry Regiment.[101] Security of Route 13 continued to be a perennial headache. In late March, 11th Armored became engaged in a stiff fight with 320th PAVN Regiment in the Michelin Plantation. MACV had lost count of how many times this area had been fought over. To the east, 1st Australian Task Force paired with 18th ARVN Division. South of Saigon, 3rd Brigade, 9th Infantry was left as the only US Army formation guarding the approaches to Long An Province.

In the far north, Lieutenant General Richard Stilwell's newly formed XXIV Corps comprised 3rd Marine Division, 101st Airborne and the mechanized 1st Brigade from 5th Infantry. At the beginning of the year 4th Marines mounted *Scotland II* in the Khe Sanh area and 9th Marines re-entered the A Shau and Da Krong Valleys in Dewey Canyon. The latter involved a rare Laotian cross-border raid which netted 525 tons of weapons and ammunition.[102] 101st Airborne followed up this success with *Massachusetts Striker* that ran from March 1 until mid-May. 1st Brigade, 5th Infantry mounted *Montana Mauler* in the Con Thien area and became engaged in heavy fighting near a feature named Hill 208. Major General Charles Getty's American Division continued to launch small-unit operations in Quang Ngai Province. There was heavy fighting in Quang Nam Province, in the vicinity of the coastal provincial capital Tam Ky, and the foothills at Tien Phuoc.[103]

When Major General Lloyd Ramsey assumed command in the summer, the fighting shifted to the Hiep Duc Valley, 35 miles south of Da Nang (Operation *Frederick Hill*). At Da Nang, 1st Marines, now commanded by Major General Ormond Simpson, swept the Que Son and An Hoa basins much as they had done for the last four years. Many operations were defensive in nature and aimed at pushing back the Viet Cong "rocket belt" from the air base. When the marines were not fighting the Viet Cong, they were fighting the elements. In April 1969, a bush fire spread into the base, setting off 38,000 tons of ammunition and 20,000 drums of fuel.[104] A measure of the futility of marine efforts in this sector can be gauged by an operation conducted against the coastal hamlet on Go Noi Island, just 12 miles south of Da Nang. Countless operations had failed to eradicate the Viet Cong presence in this settlement. Finally, in the spring of 1969, the marines lost patience. A massive operation was mounted and the entire 6,750 acres of the island were flattened with dozers, completely altering the geography of the land.[105]

The beating meted out by MACV forced Hanoi to make a radical strategic volte-face. The delusion of winning a conventional war was replaced by the pragmatism of pursuing a sapping guerrilla war. In effect, the Politburo conceded that the Tet Offensive had been a disaster. This change of direction was signaled in COSVN Resolution 9, promulgated a year later on July 9, 1969, fortuitously captured by a unit of 199th Light Infantry Brigade.[106] This change of policy was subsequently reinforced by Resolution 14 in October 1969 which conceded, "the only way to cope with an enemy that has a large number of troops and war facilities is to wage guerrilla warfare."[107] Ground attacks were substituted with "ABFs" in the military acronym, or "Attacks By Fire." Logistic nodes, civilian infrastructure, and vulnerable routes – Highways 13 and 19 in particular – were all targeted. A campaign of terror in the countryside was stepped up. In a significant evolution, and for the first time since the Johnson intervention in 1965, Hanoi abandoned any plans for mounting large-unit operations in the South. The People's Army would not stand it and the Viet Cong had sunk in a mire of poor morale and internal dissension.

The possibility that Washington might now actually be winning its war was entirely discredited by a national mood as black as that afflicting the other side. Now out of power, there was no restraint in an anti-war Democrat faction, led prominently by Ted Kennedy. Senator Fulbright, the most acerbic and intelligent critic of Johnson's war, was no less propitiated by Nixon's war. Elder statesmen like Harriman, feeling snubbed by the administration, joined in the chorus of disapproving voices. The reality was that Nixon had no domestic war allies, even if he had sought them, which he did not.[108] This further uncoupled national politics from a MACV that sensed in the Viet Cong a "crouching beast cornered" and sought to plunge the mortal lance.[109]

Nowhere was this disjuncture more evident than in the events that took place between May 10–20, 1969 on Dong Ap Bia (Ap Bia Mountain), annotated Hill 937 on military maps, but which later became known with grim humor as "Hamburger Hill." To outsiders, the entire battle was a pointless bloodbath over a worthless lump of ground. To the protagonists, it was a sacrificial experience played out at the airy altitude of 3,000 feet in triple canopy jungle.

If battles were fought for the possession of features of imposing natural beauty, then 3rd Brigade, 101st Airborne had every reason to assault Ap Bia Mountain. But 3rd Brigade was not in the game of claiming the possession of hills, imposing or not – it was in the business of search and destroy. And a regiment from the People's Army was squatting on the feature because it overlooked the A Shau Valley, yielded after the fall of the special force camp in 1966. Over time, this had become the key infiltration route west of Hue. Successive attempts to close down this trail had failed and it had become a de facto sanctuary, just one and a half miles from the Laotian border. The mountain did not greatly matter, the valley did.

In the spring of 1969, the PAVN had redeployed its 6th, 9th, and 29th Regiments deeper into the A Shau after suffering heavy losses in February, following the US marine-led Operation *Dewey Canyon*. The successful *Dewey Canyon* was subsequently exploited by 2nd Brigade 101st Airborne in Operation *Massachusetts Striker*, in the mouth of the valley. Neither operation was costly in lives and both paid handsome dividends. It was against this background of success that a decision was then taken by Stilwell to root out any remaining enemy forces still lingering in the valley. To the protagonists it did not seem like the "madness" Kennedy would later charge. Rather, it seemed the obvious next move against a beaten enemy.

The operation was called *Apache Snow*, and it involved three paratrooper battalions drawn from Major General Melvin Zais's 101st Airborne. All three battalions were taken from the division's 3rd Brigade, commanded by Colonel Joseph Conmy. The lead unit was 3rd Battalion, 187th Infantry Regiment, the "Rakkasans" (meaning "falling down umbrella men," or paratroopers in Japanese). This battalion, led by a Lieutenant Colonel Weldon Honeycutt, was no stranger to tough battles, having fought at Dak To, Cu Chi, and Long Binh. The other two units were 2nd Battalion, 501st Parachute Infantry Regiment, the "Geronimo" boys who jumped in Normandy, commanded by Lieutenant Colonel Robert German; and 1st Battalion, 506th Parachute Infantry Regiment, a veteran unit from the Battle of the Bulge, under Lieutenant Colonel John Bowers.

Of the three battalion commanders, it was Honeycutt who would attract the most criticism. A former private soldier, Weldon Honeycutt used the propellant of the Korean War to jump the ranks to captain, ending the war as a company commander, and coincidentally serving under Westmoreland. He gained a nickname – "Tiger" – and a certain reputation from being "abrasive." Some judged him a martinet, others just a typical paratrooper. If Honeycutt's character predisposed him to aggressive actions, that of his commander, Joe Conmy, was equally combative. Known by his call sign "Iron Raven," Joseph Bartholomew Conmy was born into a service family and spent his entire life fighting wars. His career in conflicts started in Europe in 1944 and ended one week after the battle of Hamburger Hill, when he was wounded in a night attack. Along the way he was awarded three Silver Stars for gallantry in action, and three Purple Hearts. To liberal opinion in Washington, he was probably the worst example of that dying breed of wartime commanders careless of soldiers' lives. To his soldiers he was the opposite: a caring and greatly respected commander.

His immediate commander, Major General Zais, son of Russian immigrants, was a wartime paratrooper who had taken part in a similar battle to wrest the Col de Braus from the German 34th Infantry Division.[110] In his mind, this was a familiar tactical problem. Indeed, there were significant similarities between both battles which involved failed frontal assaults, followed by pounding artillery bombardments and irresistible but costly cumulative attacks.

Both Zais and Conmy belonged to a deep-rooted tradition of military service. Zais had two sons who also served as paratroopers in Vietnam, and three grandsons who would serve as future paratroopers in the Iraq War.[111] The clash in perspectives between Washington liberals and the generals, ultimately, was cultural and probably irreconcilable.

The scheme for *Apache Snow* was straightforward and had been replayed many times before in Highland battles. The valley floor would be sealed by 2/3rd ARVN Regiment. Then a composite force of 9th Marine Regiment supported by 3rd Squadron, 5th Cavalry Regiment would sweep towards the Laotian border, acting as beaters. The three paratrooper battalions would be lifted into the valley, search in their designated areas, and destroy any enemy units in their path. As Stilwell had amassed as many as nine artillery batteries to support this operation, there was some confidence that any enemy encountered would be destroyed. The great unknown was the exact dispositions of the People's Army units lingering in the valley. Four years of fighting Americans had taught the North Vietnamese the importance of maintaining the highest standards of camouflage and radio discipline. The reality was that Conmy entered the A Shau Valley without any clear idea – beyond unit designations – of where the enemy was or in what strength.

The battle for Hill 937 did not start in controversy. For the first four days, the main controversy was not the casualty rate, which was relatively moderate, but the number of friendly fire incidents (there would be a total of five). The operation kicked off at dawn on May 10 with a 74-minute fire preparation of 30 potential landing zones by artillery, Cobra gunships, and close air support. This was followed by a 65-helicopter lift of 1,800 paratroopers into the valley, accomplished without resistance.

The first good intelligence came from a document captured by 3/187th on the first day. This appeared to indicate that 29th PAVN Regiment was decamped on Ap Bia Mountain. At the time, 3/187th was located roughly half a mile northwest of Hill 937 on an adjoining hill feature separated by a shallow valley. Zais conferred with Conmy and ordered 3/187th to seize the hill. With the lie of the land predicating against a tiring march down the valley, Honeycutt led his battalion in a wide loop north, following the contours of the range and approached Hill 937 from the north. Unfortunately, and unbeknown to the Rakkasans, this led the paratroopers straight into three well-concealed, concentric trench lines.

The following morning – May 11 – Honeycutt ordered a two-company assault involving A and B Companies advancing from a roughly northwesterly axis. This ran into determined resistance. C Company attempted to scale the hill directly from the north but also failed to make headway. The attacks were called off after a Cobra gunship mistakenly attacked the battalion command post, killing two and wounding another 25. Stalled by this setback, the battalion spent the next two days regrouping, replenishing, and probing the hill. The North Vietnamese in the meantime used the pause to reinforce their positions and harass the encroaching paratroopers, provoking random gun battles that incurred more casualties. This period marked the end of the first round of fighting.

Both Honeycutt and Conmy had by now appreciated that 3/187th faced a substantial enemy on Hill 937. Without reinforcement, it was unlikely the Rakkasans would succeed in dislodging the defenders. In addition, the brigade had suffered another setback after 2/501st, located across the valley and to the north, was attacked on the night of May 12, suffering 26 fatalities and well over 50 wounded.

The additional necessary manpower was drawn from the sister 1/506th "Currahees," the nearest available and intact unit. This battalion was located just two and a half miles south of Hill 937. On May 14, Conmy ordered 1/506th to be in a position to mount a coordinated attack in support of 3/187th no later than May 15. However, he gravely underestimated the difficulties of the ground and the possibility of undetected enemy positions. Eventually, it would take the Currahees five days to cover the distance and involve assaults on two further defended features, Hills 916 and 900.

Conmy was not the only commander underestimating the scale of the task. Honeycutt, in a moment of impatience and imprudence, decided to assault anyway, without the support of 1/506th. On the morning of May 14, the Rakkasans launched their second bid for the hill. D Company was ordered to make a flanking attack from the north. B Company was tasked to advance up the main ridge, with C Company providing support from a finger ridgeline 150 yards to the south. None of the attacks succeeded. B Company was halted in its tracks by withering automatic fire and concealed Claymore mines; C Company's gains were quickly reversed and the company withdrew suffering 52 casualties; and D Company barely managed to advance past its start line. By late afternoon, it was obvious the assault had been repelled and withdrawal was ordered. Twelve paratroopers had been killed and 80 wounded for no gain. A second friendly fire incident involving a Cobra gunship had cost one life and a further three wounded. At dusk, as the paratroopers regrouped in the shadow of the hill, one soldier recalled seeing over one hundred cooking fires on the summit, confirmation if it was needed that the feature was strongly held by a confident enemy.

On May 15 – the day of the second aborted attack – Associated Press reporter Jay Sharbutt arrived on the scene, in time to witness the messy scenes at the base of Hill 937 as the battalion regrouped and gathered the wounded. These scenes made a deep impression on the reporter. 3/187th had unquestionably been worsted. One company's worth of soldiers was now *hors de combat*. The survivors were tired and some angry.

An irrational obsession then seemed to seize certain officers. The Rakkasans had twice attempted and twice failed to claim Hill 937. It was clear the objective was too big for one battalion. The ground was impossibly difficult, complicating command and fragmenting units. Conmy had already ordered 1/506th to advance north to enable a coordinated two-battalion assault, and this battalion had made some yards, although it was still short of the objective. It was now just a matter of waiting another few days, organizing the fire support, and launching a deliberate attack. 29th PAVN Regiment had given no indication that it was preparing to abandon the hill. There was no compelling reason to attack again, and yet this is exactly what happened.

On May 16, the Rakkasans mounted their third assault on Hill 937. B Company managed to get within 150 yards of the summit, but then fell back following another friendly fire incident involving a helicopter gunship. A Company made no better progress and also withdrew. The only outcome of this forlorn hope attack was another 38 paratroopers killed or wounded. 1/506th simultaneously launched its assault on the adjacent Hill 916, but capture of this feature still left it just over a mile short of Hill 937. And 1/506th still faced a second obstacle – Hill 900 – and an unknown enemy. Faced with this double reverse, the following day, May 17, was used to reorganize and prepare for a concerted assault on the stubborn North Vietnamese soldiers still holding out on Hill 937.

The battle's reputation as a "meat grinder," Sharbutt's phrase in the despatch he filed the following day, was earned from the two-battalion assault mounted on the morning of May 18. The most serious charge against Zais, Conmy, and Honeycutt was that all three commanders were still significantly underestimating the enemy resistance, despite the evidence of the previous week's fighting.

The assault was initiated at 8am with an aerial bombardment, followed by a 60-minute artillery barrage. 1/506th then launched from the south against Hill 900, while 3/187th pressed from the west and south. In the event, the scheme collapsed. The Currahees clawed their way forward but were not in a position to support their sister battalion. To the north, the Rakkasans' attack was led by D and C companies. The former managed to get within touching distance of the summit, then fell back after suffering 50 percent casualties. Every officer was either killed or wounded. Overall, including the attrition from the earlier battles, this company could now muster about a fifth of its strength. C Company was stopped by a freak rainstorm and had now suffered 80 percent casualties. Both A and B companies had been reduced to half strength. In a third fratricide incident, the latter company received a volley of rockets from a Cobra gunship, incensing Honeycutt, who canceled all further gunship support.

The shock of these high casualty rates, coupled with growing media attention, jolted Zais. The option of aborting the assault on Hill 937 was considered but discounted following consultation with Stilwell and Abrams. The relief of 3/187th was also mooted but Honeycutt protested against an order that would deny his battalion the glory of standing on the summit of Hill 937. A blood debt could now only be expiated by further spilling of blood. As the Rakkasans were now technically combat ineffective, Zais augmented the battalion with one company from Lieutenant Colonel Gene Sharron's 2/506th, a fresh unit that Zais had intended as a replacement for the depleted Rakkasans.

On May 19, three additional battalions were deployed to the southern base of the hill: 2/501st, 2/506th and the ARVN 2/3rd. The following morning, a massive barrage fell on the peak. One million pounds of high explosive bombs and 152,000 pounds of napalm were dumped within a half-mile radius of Hill 937. Some 20,000 shells were lobbed by the division's nine artillery batteries. The ancient triple canopy jungle stood little chance against this fearsome assault. Hill 937 was reduced to a moonscape of craters and blasted tree stumps. Remarkably, this barrage did not kill off all the defenders. The majority, it seems, had actually exfiltrated and evaded to Laos the previous day. A small number – possibly two platoons – found refuge underground and met the final attacks with patchy resistance. How many North Vietnamese were in fact killed by the bombardment is entirely unknown. Regardless, the firepower demonstration did break any remaining resistance.

The main assault was led by the survivors from 3/187th, the reinforcement company from 2/506th and the ARVN battalion. It proved an anticlimax after the thunder of the bombardment. South Vietnamese soldiers reached the top of the deserted peak by mid-morning, exploiting an undefended route. To satisfy honor, they were ordered to pull back and 3/187th claimed the hill. The first paratroopers reached the blasted summit at just before midday. Finally, after 11 assaults and over 440 casualties, Hill 937 was in the hands of the Rakkasans. The overwhelming majority of the casualties had been endured by this battalion that lost over 50 soldiers and suffered 290 wounded. Just three prisoners were taken. Over 600 North Vietnamese soldiers were believed to have perished – in effect, PAVN 29th Regiment had ceased to exist – or so it was claimed.[112] On the summit, an anonymous soldier scrawled "Hamburger Hill" on the cardboard lid of a C-Ration pack and posted it against a tree stump. A second jaundiced comrade added the obvious comment: "Was it worth it?" On the same day, Sharbutt's despatch hit the newsstands, missing the denouement but provoking a political storm.

Such a battle needed a scapegoat and Sharbutt certainly clattered his typewriter keys with some indignation. "The paratroopers came down the mountain, their green shirts darkened with sweat, their weapons gone, their bandages stained brown and red – with mud and blood," he wrote.[113] "Many cursed Lt. Col. Weldon Honeycutt, who sent three companies on Sunday to take this 3,000-foot mountain just a mile east of Laos and overlooking the shell-pocked A Shau Valley ... They failed and they suffered." Then, in an inflammatory addendum, Sharbutt quoted one of the paratroopers allegedly cursing, "That damn Blackjack (Lt. Col. Honeycutt's radio call sign) won't stop until he kills every one of us." Whether or not these words were accurately reported, on June 27, *Life* magazine featured a montage of 241 recently killed American soldiers which became conflated with the battle in A Shau, adding to the sense of outrage that so many were killed over the possession of an apparently worthless hill. The myth of the butcher Honeycutt then grew with rumors that the underground magazine *G.I. Says* had posted a $10,000 bounty on his head, but this subversion did not come from within the Rakkasans. Despite the trauma of the battle, or perhaps because of it, the unit remained close-knit. In postwar reunions, the paratroopers would stand behind their former commanding officer.

The mission had always been to destroy the enemy, which was accomplished. An unapologetic veteran dismissed the criticism. "We went after them and in the end we got 'em." But the butcher's bill was too high and the political fallout proved as costly as the attack. Zais and Westmoreland both felt obliged to defend the battle. Kennedy was joined by Senator McGovern in criticism over the "irresponsible ... madness." Senator Stephen Young made comparisons with the butchery of the Civil War. On June 5, as Washington fulminated, the hill was quietly abandoned. Three weeks later, the People's Army reoccupied the feature – the A Shau Valley was back in enemy hands. A withdrawing US Army would never again engage in another "meat grinder" battle.

Nixon's war had been driven by the imperative to keep Hanoi off-balance while MACV withdrew. In this aim, it succeeded. But there had to come a moment when the downward graph of US troop strengths would intersect with the upward graph of communist war aims. The two strategies were not so much mutually exclusive as mutually reinforcing. This moment arrived far sooner than the White House anticipated or wished.

The 1972 Easter Offensive (*Chien dịch Xuan he*) fell at the most awkward moment for Washington. Kissinger was pursuing secret peace talks. Nixon was about to make his historic visit to Peking. Later in the year, he hoped to woo Moscow. In South Vietnam, MACV's rapid withdrawal had raised questions over South Vietnamese readiness.

The other side was also traversing a difficult period. The Politburo feared both the possible loss of its Chinese ally and fallout from Soviet-Chinese rivalry. The Viet Cong had failed to recover momentum. Cambodia and Laos had proved great distractions, as MACV had intended. In the North, the strain of urging the masses to greater revolutionary sacrifice was provoking domestic tensions. Hanoi was well aware it faced the likelihood of a re-elected and stronger Nixon. Faced with these multiple and severe challenges, the Easter Offensive aimed to achieve a position of maximum negotiating advantage over a withdrawing Washington and weakening Saigon. This would be a conventional invasion of South Vietnam with clear tactical aims. The People's Army would physically and morally defeat the ARVN, grab territory, and establish political ascendancy. However, as in the 1968 Tet Offensive, Hanoi massively underestimated American firepower, and – to everyone's surprise – South Vietnamese resistance.

The surprise from Washington's perspective was that it happened at all. If the communists consistently underestimated American firepower, American intelligence consistently failed to appreciate the communist capacity to make good its losses. At the beginning of the year, Abrams still commanded 139,000 troops. As a result of an accelerated redeployment program, his successor would be left with just 15,000 by November.[114] MACV could still count on two infantry brigades in extremis (3rd Brigade, 101st, and 199th Brigade), but there was never any question that US troops would be used again to fight South Vietnam's battles. In fact, at the time of the offensive, just 65,000 American soldiers remained in South Vietnam, the majority support troops. Only one of the combat brigades remained, waiting impatiently for the final redeployment. The evidence of the previous year of fighting suggested the ARVN remained fragile and dependent on US advisors. Saigon remained a nest of vipers, disunited, corrupt, and self-serving. The question was not could Hanoi launch a major offensive in the dry season, but rather why would it not.

Hanoi named its spring 1972 campaign the Nguyen Hue Offensive, after an 18th-century emperor who defeated an occupying Chinese army. To ensure the best chances of success, the campaign was vested in Hanoi's three most trusted commanders. The DMZ battle would be fought by Van Tien Dung, overall commander of the Tri-Thien-Hue Region. B2 Front in the far south would be commanded by the bespectacled Tran Van Tra, and B3 Front in the Central Highlands by Hoang Minh Thao. Collectively, they boasted 82 years of warfighting experience. Across the border they faced in I Corps the hapless Hoang Xuan Lam (soon to be replaced by Ngo Quang Truong); Ngo Dzu in II Corps (who was also sacked and replaced by Nguyen Van Toan); and in the III Corps, Nguyen Van Minh, a Thieu loyalist and favorite who survived the purge of senior officers. All three North Vietnamese generals would play key roles in the final denouement two years later.

Unlike the 1968 Tet Offensive, the Nguyen Hue Offensive made a supreme effort in the north as well as mounting a significant offensive in the south. There was little choice as the Viet Cong in the south were a spent force. The burden fell therefore on the veteran 308th PAVN Division located on the DMZ; 304th PAVN Division perched on the elbow of the Laos border; and 324B Division funneled into the A Shau Valley. The I Corps commander, Lam, would have been challenged whatever the status of opposing forces, but in the spring of 1972 his hand was even weaker through the deployment of the untested and newly created 3rd ARVN Division to the border forts – the so-called "Alpha line" – just south of the DMZ.

3rd ARVN "Ben Hai Division" had only been created on October 20, 1971 as a hasty contingency measure. Just one of its regiments – the 2nd ARVN, stolen from 1st ARVN Division – was reliable. The other two – the 56th and 57th – were hastily cobbled from unwilling volunteers. As poor luck would have it, it was precisely these two regiments that would receive the communist avalanche. A former deputy commander of 1st ARVN Division, the competent Brigadier General Vu Van Giai, was entrusted with the defense of the border trip line, but he could not magic poor troops into stout troops overnight. Doubly unfortunately, Giai was absent, having decided to take a long weekend in Saigon.[115]

The offensive broke with the convention of dawn attacks and was launched at midday (or midnight in Washington). Across the length of the front it was obvious straightaway that a major assault was under way. Hundreds of guns opened up, picking their targets with accuracy. There was no coordinated response and little leadership at divisional and corps levels. It was a case of each firebase fighting its own war, or fleeing. Behind the cover of this massive bombardment, 308th PAVN Division dispensed with clever maneuvers and simply charged across the DMZ, a move which Lam had previously dismissed as impossible. Advisor Colonel Raymond Battreall later confessed that nobody had seriously countenanced the idea the communists might just drive across the demilitarized zone.[116] The border town of Cam Lo was quickly overrun and three US advisors disappeared. Helicopter pilots despatched to rescue trapped comrades recalled that every hill looked like a Christmas tree, such was the weight of antiaircraft fire.[117]

Nixon was enraged by what he perceived as Hanoi's perfidy and later raised the possibility of using a nuclear bomb to rattle the communists. Saigon was stunned and "bewildered" – "we couldn't even raise the general on the phone."[118] The media became alarmist. Only Abrams calmed nerves. The South might bend, he avowed, but it would not break.[119]

The Nguyen Hue Offensive was the closest the communists would come to "winning it" with US troops still deployed in Vietnam, but in Nixon they

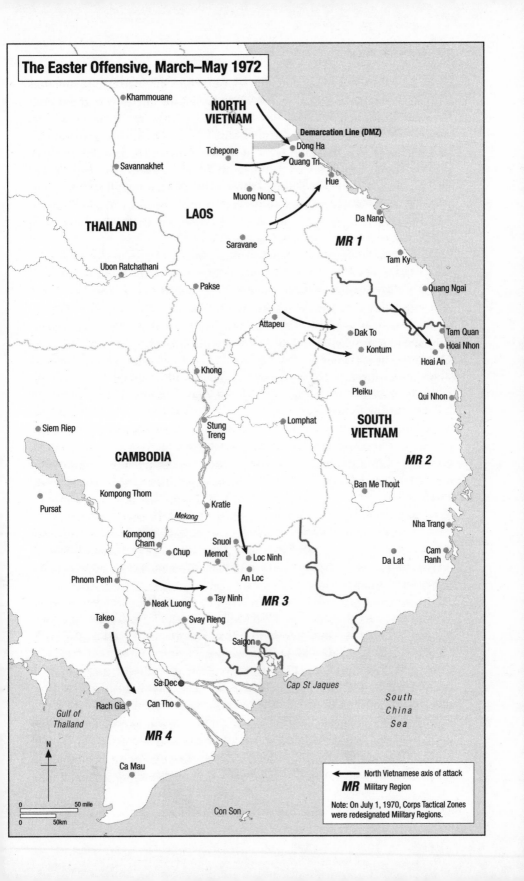

The Easter Offensive, March–May 1972

Khammouane

NORTH
VIETNAM

Demarcation Line (DMZ)

Tchepone
Dong Ha
Quang Tri

Savannakhet

Hue

Muong Nong

LAOS

Da Nang

MR 1

THAILAND

Saravane

Tam Ky

Ubon Ratchathani

Quang Ngai

Pakse

Attapeu
Dak To
Tam Quan
Hoai Nhon

Kontum
Hoai An

Khong

Pleiku
Qui Nhon

Lomphat

SOUTH
VIETNAM

Stung
Treng

MR 2

Siem Riep

CAMBODIA

Kompong Thom

Ban Me Thuot

Pursat

Kratie

Mekong

Nha Trang

Kompong
Cham

Snuol
Memot

Chup
Loc Ninh

Da Lat
Cam
Ranh

Phnom Penh
An Loc

Neak Luong
Tay Ninh
MR 3

Takeo
Svay Rieng

Saigon

Cap St Jaques

South
China
Sea

Sa Dec

Gulf of
Thailand
Rach Gia
Can Tho

MR 4

N

Ca Mau

0   50 mile

0   50km

Con Son

North Vietnamese axis of attack

MR   Military Region

Note: On July 1, 1970, Corps Tactical Zones
were redesignated Military Regions.

found a commander-in-chief dismissive of "bastards" critical of the war and more than willing to wield the hammer of American air power. In his later recollection, the 1972 spring offensive was "Hanoi's last chance."[120] As the communists had chosen war, so would he. Nixon would have agreed with a CIA judgment that in this war "the matter of will is crucial." I have will "in spades," Nixon told Kissinger, and he also had the means.[121] In the first half of the year, the navy doubled its carrier presence in the Gulf of Tonkin to six ships, and augmented its gunfire support from 16 to 54 ships. The B-52 fleet tripled to 148 aircraft. Tactical support aircraft doubled from 212 to 480.[122] Air strikes were ordered against the North, the first since the 1968 bombing suspension. It was time to give Hanoi a "severe jolt." In the second week in May 11,000 mines were dropped into Haiphong harbor, trapping 27 resupply ships for the next ten months.[123] As four fifths of Hanoi's imports were arriving by sea, this was a heavy blow.

This was Washington's angry riposte, but the war was being fought on land and at first this did not go well. On the DMZ, a communist armored spearhead trundled up the flat coastal plain, using Highway 1 as the axis of advance. A second aimed itself at Gio Linh, the district capital. Faced with a collapsing situation, I Corps ordered the total abandonment of the border firebases north of the Mieu Giang River. Every base US marines had doggedly defended over five years, at such high cost, fell to the enemy in a matter of 24 hours. Faced with an increasingly desperate situation, Giai ordered the remnants of his division, now mostly stragglers seeking safety further south, to form a new defensive line, using the natural barriers of the Mieu Giang and Cua Viet rivers. By now, the streams of retreating soldiers were swollen by a torrent of civilian refugees adding to the problems of command and control. In a matter of days, just one firebase remained in South Vietnamese hands north of Thach Han River. This was Pedro, where a combination of marine and ranger battalions finally halted the communist advance after some bitter fighting.

The action at Firebase Pedro marked a sort of turning point in the battle. Two weeks into the Nguyen Hue Offensive, 308th PAVN Division was blocked at Dong Ha on the coast. To the west, both 304th and 324B PAVN Divisions stalled. 320B and 325C Divisions, now fed into the battle, were making no better progress. Despite the collapse of the northern firebases, a shaky defensive line had been re-established. The communist penetration at this stage amounted to no more than ten miles – thin reward for so much expenditure of manpower and firepower. When tested, Dung, a world-class guerrilla leader, had proved a poor commander of a conventional corps. Giap liked to boast knowledge of military strategy but he too seemed bereft of ideas. The situation demanded boldness but there was no élan to be found.

The inevitable corollary of this absence of momentum was stalemate, which descended on the battlefield like a pall.

From I Corps' perspective, the crisis appeared over. The American estimate was that 3rd ARVN Division "can still be counted an effective force," despite its mauling.[124] The provincial capital Quang Tri had not been captured. The only town of any significance to fall was the district capital Gio Linh. The People's Army had mostly filled the vacuum of no-man's-land on the DMZ.

But this relief was tempered by the growing realization that the enemy had used Route 9 to infiltrate as many as three regiments down the Ba Long Valley. Ejecting these would be the first task to establish a more solid defensive line. The operation was called *Quang Tran 729*. It kicked off on April 14 and three days later the ARVN had managed to advance just one mile. Sensing the danger, Dung threw elements from 210th and 204th Tank Regiments into the fray. MACV responded with air strikes.

As the battle expanded, it became evident the command relationship between Lam and Giai was totally unsatisfactory. Simply put, the political appointee Lam was out of his depth and effectively abrogated his responsibilities to his divisional commander. In doing so he placed an impossible burden on Giai: all nine brigades in I Corps (33 battalions) were subordinated to Giai's divisional HQ. This crazy re-subordination was exacerbated by rifts that existed between the different branches of the armed forces. The two marine brigades answered first to their own Commandant (Lieutenant General Le Nguyen Khang, comfortably based in Saigon), and the Rangers also demonstrated an independent streak. In the meantime, Lam never once visited the front line. Indeed, he never stepped out of his headquarters. Many ARVN units were simply unwilling to leave the sanctuary of their positions without US saturation bombing.

On April 23, the People's Army swung back into the offensive, and by the following day it was clear *Quang Tran 729* had run its course. As many as 240 vehicles, including almost a battalion's worth of tanks, had been lost, and more than 60 artillery pieces. Unlike Hanoi, the South Vietnamese could not simply feed more troops to the front line. There were none. This had an inevitable implication: Quang Tri city was doomed.

On Thursday April 27, an overcast day, the front line erupted again. On the coastal plain 308th Division redoubled the pressure and threatened to turn the flank at Dong Ha. Within 24 hours the communists were within one mile of Quang Tri and raining shells on the disorganized defenders. ARVN units mingled with fleeing civilians and retreat turned to rout. The communists mercilessly bombarded the vulnerable columns, killing and wounding hundreds of civilians, which added to the chaos. There were instances of resistance but too few. The uneven battle was mostly waged by artillery.

The ARVN had precious few guns or ammunition, and the People's Army had plenty of both. Demonstrating supreme indifference to the destruction being wreaked, and lacking all tactical subtlety, Dung's brigades bombarded their way to Quang Tri, mile by bloody mile. One American advisor who observed the retreat along Highway 1 later recorded, "Any respect I had for the North Vietnamese military, I lost that day."[125] He had just witnessed a helpless column of civilians deliberately targeted by artillery fire. As many as 2,000 were killed or injured, including patients evacuated from Quang Tri Hospital for their safety.

What was left of Giai's command was now split between one combat base north of Thach Han River, and Quang Tri. A single bridge spanned the river. Fearing annihilation, Giai ordered the marines to hold the city then ordered every remaining unit north of the river to withdraw. This was an order more easily delivered than executed, as every point on the withdrawal route was now covered by North Vietnamese artillery.

The withdrawal became a scene of chaos and desperation. Lam then intervened, under pressure from Thieu who had publicly vowed not to surrender territory. The order to withdraw was duly countermanded dooming 3rd ARVN Division. By now, as many as four PAVN regiments and a battalion of T-54 tanks had tightened the noose around Quang Tri. A sobbing Giai broke down and was eventually rescued along with 80 US advisors from the city citadel. His command dissolved.

His woes did not end there – Saigon needed a scapegoat, so Giai was duly imprisoned for dereliction of duty. South Vietnamese soldiers fled south by whatever route they could find, or sought sanctuary on the coastal flats. All of Quang Tri Province was now effectively in communist hands, and the only formation in a position to stop the tide overflowing south into Thua Thien Province was the relatively untouched 369th VNMC Brigade which had taken defensive positions at My Chanh, halfway between two bridges over the O Khe and Tach Ma rivers. If this brigade collapsed then the road was open to the imperial city of Hue.

Led by a determined Colonel Pham Van Chung, 369th VNMC Brigade now held the key to the battlefield – his men had to hold the two bridges and bottle up the People's Army in Quang Tri. Chung tasked 9th Battalion to hold the northernmost O Khe bridge and held 5th Battalion in reserve near My Chanh. Then the marines waited for the inevitable onslaught. It came at dawn on May 3, with a massive artillery bombardment followed in now characteristic fashion by a reckless charge headed by 18 T-54 tanks. The marines stood their ground, and even used howitzers in direct fire mode to blast their assailants. Just one tank survived. A succeeding human wave assault by infantry was totally decimated, leaving hundreds of bodies on the battlefield.

This drama was overtaken by events in I Corps HQ. At the instigation of Abrams and Bunker, the woeful Lam was flown back to Saigon and kicked upstairs in the Defense Ministry. His departure was so sudden he did not even bother to inform his staff, who had no idea the corps now lacked a commander (and may not have noticed). It was not until the evening of May 3 that the announcement was made that the IV Corps commander – Lieutenant General Ngo Quang Truong – would assume command, effective from the following morning. Truong was a nervous, chain-smoking man with a frail physique, but his appearance belied a steely determination to reverse the debacle he had inherited from the hopeless Lam.

With insufficient troops to hold both bridges, the decision was taken to blow the My Chanh bridge, effectively trapping any stragglers who had not made it to safety, but ensuring that the enemy vanguard would now be delayed at the gates of Thua Thien Province. Quang Tri was definitively lost. The main effort for the battered I Corps now had to switch to saving the imperial city, Hue, and this seemed far from assured. Swollen by refugees from the north, panic began to grip the population. Hue was the only city in South Vietnam which had experienced a communist occupation during the 1968 Tet Offensive. The memory of this bitter experience served as tinder to an already inflammable situation. For one week, Hue became a scene of looting, drunkenness, and fighting between rival gangs of deserting soldiers.[126] As many as 150,000 civilians fled south to escape the mayhem, adding to the chaos on Highway 1. It was not until a shoot-on-sight order was promulgated that order was restored, but by now Hue was a ghost city, awaiting its death sentence.

Hanoi crowed its victories and prophesied the imminent fall of Hue, but the truth was that Giap's divisions were burned out. The supply lines were overextended and the ranks badly depleted. Although no protagonist could see it, the high-water mark of the invasion had been reached.

The key to Hue lay in the A Shau Valley. It was here the People's Army had built its redoubt over many years, and it was from this valley that Route 547 ran from the town of Ta Bet, 40 miles to Hue. The communist commander on this front was Lieutenant General Tran Van Quang and he held up his sleeve the veteran 324B Division. However, unlike the situation in Quang Tri, Quang faced a far more capable opponent in Major General Pham Van Phu, commander of 1st ARVN Division. In the opinion of many officers in MACV, 1st ARVN was the best division in South Vietnam. Much of this was due to Phu, an "excellent tactician."[127]

The defense of Hue rested on a ring of fire support bases: Bastogne, Veghel, Birmingham, Checkmate, Anzio, Barbara, Rakkasan, and Rifle. Where Lam had been static and sluggishly reactive, Phu was dynamic and preemptive.

As early as February it had become obvious the enemy was preparing a major offensive. Rather than wait for the deluge, Phu mounted a series of aggressive spoiling operations that pushed back the communist schedule and dissipated its force. Pulverizing B-52 strikes and curtains of artillery barrages did the rest. The result of this campaign was the decisive erosion of Quang's offensive. It took 324B Division a full month to finally force the evacuations of Bastogne and Checkmate, but by then the issue was over. Route 547 was an open road, but the communists no longer had the strength to exploit it.

All this would have been for nought had MACV not committed to a massive rearmament program of the debilitated I Corps. In a race to pump bullets, bombs, and shells to the front line, Hanoi was always going to come second-best. The decimated 3rd ARVN Division was reconstituted in one month – a remarkable logistic achievement. The marine brigades re-inflated and received the latest TOW anti-tank missiles mounted in jeeps and crewed by personnel from 101st Airborne Division. Hundreds of pallets of artillery shells were unloaded at Da Nang. Truong later observed that no unit ever ran out of ammunition despite the colossal expenditures.[128] But if this was the way to win battles, would it win the war? The acute dependence on American largesse begged a question none asked over the fraught spring and summer of 1972. How many more communist offensives would Congress thwart? The last US combat units had now quit the country. Were the USAF's bomber fleets now the permanent guarantor of South Vietnam's independence? For how long?

By mid-May, the pressing concern was now no longer the salvation of South Vietnam but rather the ejection of the communists from Quang Tri Province. With the Paris peace talks deliberately stalled by a jubilant Hanoi, returning the battlefield to the status quo ante had become the political as well as military imperative. Never mind that the ARVN would be recapturing a desolation of burned villages and rubble. What mattered now was demonstrating that not one field of South Vietnam was negotiable.

Truong barely paused to resume the counteroffensive. Starting on May 12, I Corps mounted a series of increasingly bold operations into Quang Tri, testing the communist defenses and opportunistically nibbling back lost territory. Operation *Song Than 5-72* provoked a retaliatory attack on the My Chanh line, but the People's Army was decisively beaten. In a matter of five days, further south, 1st ARVN managed to recapture Bastogne and Checkmate. In a first ever amphibious assault, 147th Marines seized a beachhead immediately south of Quang Tri. Again, the communists retaliated with a counterattack but this failed in the face of massive air and artillery strikes. Emboldened, Truong launched *Song Than 8-72* on May 8, committing three marine brigades across the Tach Ma River. Ten days later the marines again leaned on the communist defense line and advanced to a position three miles north of the My Chanh line.[129]

There was no question that American firepower was again turning the tide, but the use of that firepower was also turning heads, in the habitual way. Following *Lam Son 719*, a suspicious Nixon had begun to lose faith in Abrams. The communist irruption on the DMZ only served to further erode relations. In a manner reminiscent of Johnson, Nixon began to usurp his military commanders, designating targets and ordering bomber sorties. A disgusted Abrams threatened to resign and it took the combined efforts of the Chairman of the Joint Chiefs, Admiral Moorer, and McCain to mollify the aggrieved old soldier.[130] But the matter did not rest there. For Abrams, the absolute priority was saving South Vietnam. For Nixon, the point of wielding the cudgel was to make Hanoi pay a cost in destroyed factories, railways, and bridges.

For the North Vietnamese defenders, all this debate was irrelevant. "I never had to witness such a big loss," Pham Xuan later wrote.[131] Serving with 9 Battalion, 66th Regiment, he took shelter in cellars, but this offered little protection against B-52 carpet bombing. On May 2, a refuge where he and comrades were hiding received a direct hit. "I got knocked out of the tunnel into a puddle next to a stream," he remembered. Then the disorientated Xuan ran away shouting until he found the battalion headquarters. Here he fainted after reporting that the entire command team had been killed.

An opportunity presented itself to take over the air war – or at least to appoint a more pliant character – when General John Lavelle's tenure as commander Seventh Air Force ended abruptly in the spring with recall and demotion. The former P-47 Thunderbolt pilot had barely been in post six months when he fell foul of a murky backroom agreement between the White House and MACV to stretch the highly restrictive rules of engagement that governed bombing north of the DMZ. The joke went that the F-4 Phantom had a two-man crew because a second crewman was needed to carry all the volumes of rules.[132] For pilots, the joke had long worn thin. The fact was that everyone had been in a top-secret conspiracy to "liberalize" the rules of engagement: Moorer, McCain, Abrams, Kissinger, and of course Nixon, who was the most keen to bomb the hell out of the North. But only Lavelle would be found guilty by a hostile (and hypocritical) Congress.

Given how sneaky the air war had become by the beginning of 1972, the White House might have been forgiven for assuming that a few more below-the-belt punches would go entirely unnoticed. Unfortunately for all the protagonists, and especially Lavelle, a too-honest 23-year-old Sergeant Lonnie Franks decided to tell all to his senator, Harold Hughes (Ohio), who was also serving on the Senate Armed Services Committee.

What followed was the circus of the "Lavelle Affair"; more sound than fury, but with real costs to a number of victims of this institutional deceit. Lavelle was demoted two ranks and forced out of the air force. He maintained his dignity and silence and was only finally exonerated in 2010, 31 years after his death. In a spiteful gesture, Congress delayed the promotions of a further 160 air force and navy officers. The media had a field day over an exaggerated story. Lavelle was charged with mounting 28 unauthorized bombing raids out of 25,000 sorties. Just four reports were found to have been falsified. These were totally trivial charges. The real story was the manner in which his political and military masters had encouraged him to bend the rules, but none of these men were censured. Nixon thought the whole business was "crap" and deplored the manner in which Lavelle had been scapegoated. Kissinger compared the generals to rats, saving their own skins. The only honest voice was that of Representative William Dickinson (Alabama). "I am not sure why we are here today," he confessed to Lavelle. "If I had been in your position, I would have done the very same thing … good for you."[133] Within one week of Lavelle's recall, the Easter Offensive was launched and Nixon authorized the bombing raids anyway. Today, John Lavelle's headstone in Arlington Cemetery reads "General," reversing the injustice.

Lavelle's demise created an opening for General John Vogt, an officer who had previously impressed Nixon and crossed paths with Kissinger at Harvard. Vogt embarked for Saigon with the false impression that he was Nixon's man – specifically that that would assume the post of Deputy COMUSMACV and run the entire air war without hindrance. This would end what Kissinger dubbed the "institutionalized schizophrenia" that had characterized America's air war from the start.[134] This hope was dashed but Vogt still managed to play the Trojan Horse, bypassing both Abrams and McCain and communicating directly with Moorer through secret back channels, who in turn communicated with Kissinger. To the very end, America's factional generals could not resist intrigue and politicization.

The appointment of Vogt, however, did not solve the fundamental difference between the White House and MACV over where the air power should be applied. This came to a head at the beginning of May with Hue, Kontum, and An Loc in the south threatening to collapse. For Abrams, supported by Laird (now thoroughly distrusted by Kissinger and labeled "vicious"), it was obvious the weight of B-52 strikes had to be tasked in the south to save these cities. For Nixon, preparing the ground for the Moscow summit, and Kissinger in secret peace talks, the bombers had to go north.[135] The fundamental difference was between tactical and strategic outlooks. For Kissinger, it was a matter of demonstrating "implacable determination," and this meant bombing the North.[136]

On May 3, and assuming the role of commander-in-chief literally, Nixon demanded air strikes on Hanoi and Haiphong, which he intended to use as bargaining chips later that week. Bravely, Abrams refused to comply, arguing that the bombers were needed over the skies of Quang Tri. The White House backed down but rankled at the perceived disloyalty. The solution was to create yet another back channel from the White House direct to Abrams, via Ambassador Bunker, and bypassing Laird, Moorer, and McCain. Abrams was firmly told "in the bluntest terms" that the administration was not interested in "half-measures."[137] Furthermore there should be "no question" that any instructions received over this channel were a non-negotiable order. Simultaneously, the number of tactical air sorties was increased, effectively defusing the situation. By the following month, roughly half of all air raids were being mounted against the North, up from just over one tenth, but Abrams was allowed to deploy his B-52s where they were most needed to batter the People's Army in the South.

The mining of Haiphong harbor was both a surprise and heavy blow to the Politburo: some 2 million tons of supplies and all oil were at a stroke paralyzed. The rail network carried around one seventh of this total, making a quick switch to alternate transport means impossible without massive resource and time investments.[138] On May 8, Nixon justified the latest escalation in a television address preceded by fraught meetings and careful diplomacy with the Soviet Union (now only two weeks away from summit talks) and China. Kissinger had previously been despatched to Moscow (on April 20), and held a secret meeting with the North Vietnamese negotiator Le Duc Tho (on May 2). The only reward for these initiatives had been the usual "bombastic rhetoric" and Hanoi's habitual demands for surrender – a sure way to incense Nixon.[139] In fact, Nixon had made his most generous peace offer to the Politburo. Faced with "insolence and insult" what choice did he have? Abandon South Vietnam to "a long night of terror"? Jeopardize the lives of 60,000 US servicemen?

None of this placated a domestic audience that predictably exploded: Edmund Muskie, George McGovern, Mike Mansfield, and William Proxmire all denounced Nixon. The media went hysterical, bypassing the greater importance and prize of negotiations between the great powers. The *Times* argued the President should be saved from himself; the *Washington Post* that Nixon had lost touch with the real world; and the *New York Times* warned of threats to world peace from a US-Soviet crisis (relations had never been better and Ambassador Anatoly Dobrynin was amazed at this description, given that Nixon was about to become the first US president to visit Moscow). It was the media, not Nixon, that had totally lost touch with reality, or the only reality it recognized was that Vietnam was an unpopular war and America should get out, in any way. As Kissinger tirelessly argued, nobody had a monopoly on the anguish, and none had worked harder to withdraw from the war than the present administration.

The subsequent *Linebacker I* raids were classic Nixon. From June to October, when the bombing was finally wound down, a total of 155,548 tons of bombs were dropped on North Vietnam's energy and oil infrastructure, and on her lines of communication with China. Imports were savagely cut and industrial output collapsed. The attacks witnessed the first use of "smart" "tele-guided" bombs, with devastating effects. Whereas in the past, several hundred bombs might fail to drop a bridge, jets from USS *Midway* needed just two 1,100lb bombs to drop the Tho Tuong Bridge north of the port city of Vinh, using the new steerable wonder bombs guided to the target by the co-pilot using a television nose camera.[140] The age of precision bombing had arrived. A naval task force of three cruisers and two destroyers bombarded coastal targets almost as far north as Haiphong. Train yards were wrecked, rail lines cut, and dozens of road bridges destroyed. North Vietnam's two biggest power plants were damaged. Hanoi persisted with a desultory fight, but by this stage the Easter Offensive had run out of momentum, and war materiel was now being hidden in Laos and Cambodia or cached in South Vietnam.

The reversal of fortunes on the battlefield was marked by a change of command in Saigon. On June 30, Abrams handed over to Weyand – not a moment too soon as far as Nixon and Kissinger were concerned. No American general had served so continuously in Vietnam, first as Deputy COMUSMACV, then as overall Commander. He had witnessed US forces swell to over half a million men, then trickle away like sand in an hour glass. He had shared the drama of the Tet Offensive with his boss Westmoreland and beheld the subsequent, sad dissolution of Johnson. Search and Destroy had metamorphosed into One War and Vietnamization, but these were escape routes from Vietnam, not paths to victory. An oxymoronic Accelerated Pacification Program had acted as a spur to widening circles of violence. The idealism of the Kennedy generation had given way to the decay and corruption of an angry, disenchanted, and drug-taking soldiery. Through all these vertiginous changes, he kept his good humor. But a lifetime of soldiering and a chronic smoking habit had taken their toll. He left like his predecessor without fanfare.

What nobody expected, perhaps not even Abrams, was that he would go so quickly. On September 4 1974, Abrams passed away, almost unnoticed by an America that had moved on from the war news. His death merited one picture in the local *Tuscaloosa News*. Gerald Ford was pictured on the steps of the Fort Meyer Chapel. But the announcement of his death competed with front page news of the opening game of the Tuscaloosa Black Bears, increasing unemployment, and an uptick in university enrolments. Further down the page Tuscaloosans were being reminded that downtown in the Dale Cinema there was a screening of *The Teacher*, an "adult color movie" starring an Angel Tomkins whose strap line was "She corrupted the youthful morality of an entire school!" Who knows what the jovial tank man would have made of this company on his deathbed.

Frederick Weyand assumed the reins, carrying the baggage of all the hopes and bankruptcies of the last seven years. Like his predecessors, this was the 55-year-old's third major war. First sent to Vietnam as an intelligence officer in 1966, he had ascended the rungs and commanded 25th Infantry Division and II Field Force. Probably the most cerebral of his generation, Weyand's war had been waged with the rigor of a mind that eschewed the easy recourse to more and more high explosives. Still he struggled, like every other divisional commander, to make sense of the senseless. His political skills were recognized by an administration that appointed him military advisor to the peace talks, and he later returned as Deputy COMUSMACV. With Abram's departure, it naturally fell to this son of Arbuckle, California to finally close America's war in Indochina.

In I Corps, Truong had launched the ARVN's first corps-level operation. It was called *Lam Son 72* and kicked off on June 28, two days before Abrams' departure. The aim of the operation was to retake Quang Tri, an objective Truong hoped to achieve in just over one week (the city would not be captured until mid-September). The Cua Viet River served as a start line. Truong further divided the battlefield into three phase lines – Gold, Brown, and finally Blue – each advancing the front line by decisive bounds, or so he hoped. The marines were given the task of pushing the People's Army back up the coastline and the task of recapturing Quang Tri fell to Lieutenant General Du Quoc Dong's paratroopers. Unfortunately, the habitual lack of security within the ARVN higher command meant that Dung was well aware of the plan. He arrayed his forces in three defensive belts: the first based on a line of old forts on Route 1; the second on a ring of bunkers south of Quang Tri; and the last on the citadel itself. This Vauban bastion had been erected in the early 19th century. The perimeter walls were over six feet thick and quite impenetrable to anything short of a direct strike from a large bomb. Within the compound there were numerous underground refuges. Built on the banks of the Thach Han River, it would prove the toughest of objectives.

At first, *Lam Son 72* made good progress. Preceded by massive B-52 strikes and naval gunfire support from Seventh Fleet, the paratroopers of 2nd Brigade succeeded in advancing 18 miles from the My Chanh line to the outskirts of Quang Tri. For the next two weeks (July 8–22), 2nd Brigade found itself mired in a street battle of attrition where all the odds were in the defenders' favor. Over 2,000 B-52 strikes and almost 5,500 tactical air sorties failed to break the deadlock.[141]

However, for the communists, Quang Tri had now become an urban Dien Bien Phu without rationale. Possession was symbolic, but the symbolism came with a heavy cost in lives. In a cynical move typical of Hanoi, the best regular units were evacuated from the doomed citadel, which left the city in the hands of expendable irregulars and inexperienced units. Dung knew the defenders were doomed, but he also knew the Politburo would accept nothing less than a sacrificial fight to the death. By now, the Thach Han River had become the only open escape route. Relentless air attacks were interdicting supplies and neutralizing half-hearted counterattacks by elements of 325C and 312th Divisions to the west and south. Still the besieged Northerners held on, surviving in deep cellars and bunkers and protected by the massive citadel walls.

By the end of the month, the exhausted paratroopers ceded to Brigadier General Bui The Lan's marines. 147th VNMC Brigade, which had borne the brunt of the fighting on the coastal plain, was deployed north of the city as a block on Route 560. 369th VNMC Brigade was deployed in reserve nine miles southeast of the city. The task of assaulting the citadel thus fell to 258th VNMC Brigade. Like the paratroopers before them, the marines encountered a uniquely stubborn enemy. Determined to cling on to what had become a pile of historic rubble, Dung committed units from 326th, 308th, and 320B Divisions into the fray. Communist gunners lobbed more than 50,000 shells into Quang Tri and its environs. It was later estimated the city center received 10,000 shells per square yard.[142] The Southerners responded in kind. The ruined city had become a vortex of violence sucking in men and shells, and spinning out corpses and the maimed. By the end of the month, 1st Rangers had relieved 147th VNMC Brigade, allowing Truong to mount a two-brigade assault on the citadel from the north and south. Still, it took a further two weeks of bitter house-to-house fighting before victory could be declared. On September 16, the elated marines raised the yellow flag of South Vietnam over the western gate and broke open a bottle of champagne. The 81-day battle was over. One in four marines from the division had either been killed or wounded – some 5,000 men.[143] The cost to Hanoi had been even higher, probably five times this number. The civilian death toll was uncounted. Quang Tri Province had become a moonscape of deserted villages and its city a mound of shattered masonry. In the ornate chambers of the Paris peace talks, one counter had been removed from Hanoi's stack of chips.

The communist expenditure of blood in the north was surprising in many ways because here they really did not have to win. Hanoi merely had to fix its enemy in the five northern provinces, as it had done throughout the war. The 17th parallel carried a symbolic weight – the original sin of partition – but no more. For the Politburo, this was atoned with blood.

Further south in II Corps, a quite different campaign developed. This was not thanks to the ARVN commander, the inadequate Lieutenant General Ngo Dzu, a Catholic appointee whose family was involved in heroin trafficking and who inherited the command through a series of accidents, but rather to a controversial former US Army officer who had returned to Vietnam as Director Second Regional Assistance Group with the State Department. He was John Paul Vann and his post made him the most senior American in II Corps. Reporter Arthur Higbee described him as a short, slight man with thinning reddish-blond hair and freckles, but possessed with "a hawk-like face" and "eyes like Greenland glacier ice."[144] His helicopter call sign was "Rogues' Gallery." A man of driven physical and moral courage, it is no exaggeration to state the Central Highlands survived the communist assault in part thanks to his initiative and energetic leadership.

This was one side to Vann, and the hagiographies have been fulsome. But there was also another side. The press loved him because he had been one of the "honest" officers in the bad old days of General Harkins and MACV's upbeat press briefs. He talked and shot from the hip. This trait appealed to one audience but also aggravated many others. The eccentricity bordered on rudeness. His self-appointed mission to save South Vietnam was ultimately mad. Not all Americans shared his views or methods. Krulak considered him "a wicked, mischievous man ... a moral jackal."[145] The chronicler of the ARVN's war, Van Nguyen Duong, acknowledged his bravery but also thought him stupid and unforgivably condescending. He hardly ingratiated himself by loudly proclaiming that Vietnam's women made good lovers, but its menfolk were not heroic soldiers.[146]

Thanks to good intelligence, Hanoi's plan was in fact well known. In the opening phase, 3rd "Yellow Star" PAVN Division would mount distracting attacks on the coast in Binh Dinh Province. This would be the prelude to a concerted attempt to capture the towns of Tan Canh and Dak To. With this area secured, the People's Army would then neutralize the ARVN bases west of Kontum, and finally threaten Kontum and Pleiku. If these fell, the Central Highlands would be lost to Saigon. On the coast, Qui Nhon was the prize, though not realistically attainable. 320th and 2nd PAVN Divisions were committed to the campaign, supported by 202nd PAVN Regiment. In total, B3 Front, commanded by General Hoang Minh Thao since 1967, could count on as many as 50,000 troops.

The defense of II Corps was entrusted to ARVN 22nd and 23rd Divisions reinforced by 2nd Brigade from the Airborne Division (redeployed to Quang Tri), and a single company of tanks. The Airborne 3rd Brigade would later deploy to Kontum. A sprinkling of Ranger battalions and territorial forces added flesh, but the command was poorly led. Of 24 battalions in II Corps, ten were rated "ineffective" and another ten "marginal." In fact, the only formation which MACV rated at all was 44th ARVN Regiment, considered one of the best in the army. Both 40th and 42nd Regiments were judged worthless.[147]

And all protagonists were aware of the vulnerability of the two roads that knitted the Central Highlands – Route 14 and Route 19. If these were cut, or even interdicted, the II Corps command would likely fragment and collapse.

The decisive battles were all fought in the Highlands. Here, the contest opened on April 3 against six ARVN-held firebases on "Rocket Ridge."[148] The 20-mile feature was so named by 1/92nd Field Artillery, who had endured multiple rocket attacks from the area in previous scraps.[149] In 1969, a furious border battle had been fought northwest of the ridge at Ben Het (the area had also witnessed major battles in the fall of 1967 and spring of 1968). In the succeeding years there had been numerous small-unit actions. The Laotian and Cambodian borders were a mere six miles from the ridge, which pointed like a dagger at Kontum, and enjoyed dominating views to Dak To. For the communists, possession of Rocket Ridge opened the way to capturing the Central Highland towns. For the same reason, the ARVN could not afford to cede the feature.

The initial assault against the ridge was mounted by regiments from 320th PAVN Division. The response was swift and retributive. The lead regiments were shredded by a combination of air strikes and some stout defending. However, with the ARVN defenders fixed, the main axis of the communist advance then swung around the northern end of Rocket Ridge, threatening to outflank the hills to the west. The objectives of this axis were clearly signaled: the border town of Ben Cat, an airfield adjoining a settlement confusingly known as Dak To II, Dak To itself, and the 22nd ARVN Forward Division HQ at Tan Canh.

At Dak To, 42nd and 47th ARVN Regiments were engaged by units from 2nd PAVN Division, supported by 202nd Tank Regiment.[150] Flustered by these simultaneous assaults, Dzu became increasingly fatalistic. After some reshuffling of units, 22nd ARVN was reinforced, but the majority were deployed in a defensive arc immediately north of Kontum. By April 21, most of Rocket Ridge was in enemy hands, after Dzu ordered an evacuation. At Firebase Charlie, US advisor Major John Duffy led some 200 survivors into the sanctuary of the surrounding jungle. They left behind several hundred dead enemy from 64th PAVN Regiment stacked "like cordwood."[151] Two days later, Tan Canh was attacked. The poorly led 42nd ARVN panicked at the appearance of T-54 tanks and 24 hours later the town was captured (their commander, Colonel Dat, hid in a toilet). Vann led a daring helicopter rescue of the nine remaining US advisors, but his plan was upset when desperate South Vietnamese soldiers clung to the skids of his machine.[152] The defenses at Dak To also finally collapsed, but only after some resolute resistance from territorial forces led by an ethnic "Black Thai," Lieutenant Colonel Lo Van Bao, who refused evacuation and vowed to fight "to the death."[153] The loss of the towns left the People's Army in control of the minor Route 512, and free passage south down Route 14. Some survivors of these battles fought on but most fled down Route 14 to Kontum. Across the front there was near-total confusion, with roaming, leaderless South Vietnamese soldiers, some still accompanied by their US advisors, seeking escape routes. In a matter of three weeks, 22nd ARVN had been routed.

Then the ARVN got a lucky break. Rather than exploit to Kontum, just 25 miles to the southeast, Thao spent the next three weeks reorganizing his forces.

The city of Kontum sat within the meandering bow of the Dak Bla River and was surrounded on three sides by low-lying hills. The only viable approach was from the north, on Route 14, and this was eminently defensible, if the ARVN could be persuaded to stand and fight. This defense now lay in the hands of the 42-year-old 23rd ARVN Division commander, Colonel Ly Tong Ba, heavily guided by Vann, who had essentially assumed personal responsibility for the salvation of the Central Highlands. The relationship and trust between the two men stretched back over a decade, which would prove a decisive factor.[154]

Remarkably, at this stage, both the northern and southern anchors to Rocket Ridge – Ben Het and a Ranger camp at Polei Kleng respectively – still held. This was one reason why Thao delayed. The other was that the capture of the ridge and bead of towns on Route 512 had completely exhausted his supplies and significantly decimated his combat units. 22nd ARVN Division may have been rendered combat ineffective, but 320th PAVN Division had wasted itself in the effort. Following the necessary pause, Polei Kleng then came under attack on May 5. Four days later, following an increasingly desperate defense against impossible odds, the remaining survivors evacuated by foot. The besieged ARVN commander had requested helicopter evacuation but this was refused. "Fuck you," was his reply.[155] At Ben Cat, the situation was complicated by a Montagnard mutiny. This was quelled but the isolated camp remained in grave danger. Several attacks were rebuffed. In one incident, American advisor Mark Truhan helped repel an attack by ten PT-76 tanks. A single tank reached the main gate, but the "poor sucker ... got tagged seven ways to Sunday."[156] Despite the pressure, Ben Het held, raising the faltering morale of the ARVN leadership.

Notwithstanding, II Corps still faced significant problems. Only 53rd ARVN Regiment was immediately available to defend Kontum, supported by some 50 guns. The coastal-based ROK Division in Qui Nhon refused to keep open the vital supply route on Route 19, cut at An Khe by the communists. Highway 14 had been interdicted in seven places.[157] Two weeks of unsatisfactory bartering followed. Personal cajoling by an exasperated Vann and hundreds of tons of high explosives delivered by American aircraft finally served to embarrass the Koreans into action. Meanwhile in Kontum, panic had gripped the population. Stragglers from 22nd ARVN Division turned to looting and drinking. Mobs fought at the single airport north of the city in frantic bids to catch the few flights out of the city. Unscrupulous South Vietnamese pilots extorted bribes even as American pilots risked their necks saving South Vietnamese families. As many as 30,000 civilians fled, presaging the tragic flight of the spring of 1975. Vann, meanwhile, remained bullish: in ten years he had never predicted a battle wrongly. Kontum, he avowed, would hold.[158]

Despite these difficulties, and with remorseless determination, the Vann-Ba command team began to orchestrate a successful resistance. The key to the defense of Kontum lay with the B-52s. With the enthusiasm of a child coloring in a map, Vann drew an interlocking scheme of "kill boxes" across the northern approaches to the town, which the B-52s duly blasted. In six months, Vann appreciatively predicted, there would no more North Vietnamese army left.[159] This was exaggeration, but it was also undeniable that Thao's sluggishness and the concentration of lucrative targets had changed the balance on the battlefield. 23rd ARVN Division was being besieged on the ground, but 320th PAVN Division was now being besieged from the air. The longer the siege lasted, the more likely communist forces would be worn down to a point of ineffectiveness, as Vann confidently calculated. Even where the B-52s missed their target – and there is uncertainty over how much destruction they did wreak – their mere presence massively complicated North Vietnamese plans.

On May 10, the useless Dzu was replaced by Major General Nguyen Van Toan, further strengthening Vann's grip on the II Corps command (Vann had actually loyally defended Dzu). By this time, North Vietnamese gunners were indiscriminately shelling the town. Toan was an equally hopeless and corrupt bon viveur who owed his promotion to good connections. His ineptness as chief of staff to Lam in Quang Tri was being rewarded by promotion. But this suited Vann, who was able to manipulate the pliant general. Toan needed Vann to save his career, and Vann needed Toan to obey his every instruction – it was a perfect if dysfunctional match.[160]

By now, the defense of Kontum had been bolstered by three regiments: 44th ARVN held the center; 45th ARVN was deployed on the left flank just north of the Dak Bla River; and 53rd ARVN was left in place guarding the airport and right flank. Regional and Popular Forces were entrusted with the defense of the town itself.

The three-pronged communist assault fell on May 14. 1st PAVN attacked the airport; 28th PAVN supported by 64th PAVN assaulted 44th ARVN; and 48th PAVN supported by 203rd Tank Regiment used the axis of Route 14 to descend on 45th ARVN.[161] Probably from a lack of shells, the offensive was not preceded by a massive artillery bombardment. For the rest of the day, the two sides traded blows across the flatlands north of the town.

On the American side, TOW anti-tank missiles were used for the first time in the Central Highlands.[162] They proved devastating: 47 vehicles were destroyed, including 24 tanks.[163] Concentrations of artillery fire decimated the advancing communist ranks. Still the attackers pressed on and by nightfall succeeded in forcing a gap between 53rd and 44th ARVN Regiments. The crisis was resolved the following morning in dramatic fashion. Vann and Ba agreed a partial withdrawal, skilfully executed, to allow the B-52s to do their work. In one of the most successful single strikes of the campaign, the bombers devastated the unsuspecting units of 320th PAVN Division. When ARVN soldiers returned to reoccupy their positions they found hundreds of bodies and body parts. One company had been reduced to a single wounded survivor, who was taken prisoner. Perhaps 3,000 enemy had taken part in the previous day's assault. A large number now lay dead, wounded, or stunned.[164] The siege of Kontum was over, for now.

There were further reckless assaults over the next week, but each was checked. 53rd ARVN cracked at one point, and the Rangers proved less than effective in opening the Route 14 resupply route, yet 320th PAVN Division was no closer to capturing the town. Through sheer suicidal force, a salient was driven between 45th and 53rd ARVN Regiments on May 21, but a concerted pummeling wrecked the attacking force (a B-52 strike was mounted every hour for a period of 24 hours).[165]

Now it was time to counterattack. 44th and 53rd ARVN Regiment tentatively pushed north, discovering the grisly returns of the B-52 strikes as they advanced. A prisoner from 48th PAVN Regiment told his captors that every company in his battalion had been reduced to around ten men.[166] On May 24, Thao made another desperate bid to capture Kontum using a mix of infiltration tactics and more precise artillery fire. Footholds were gained in the south of the town and north of the airport. In doing so the communists managed to capture the city's cathedral, a nunnery, the hospital, and an orphanage – now crammed with Montagnards fleeing the violence. The hospital's single American doctor, Pat Smith, who had worked in Kontum for 13 years, managed to shift her patients and staff to Pleiku, eluding the communist advance.[167] Lurid reports that the North Vietnamese had crucified two French priests north of the city were probably just propaganda.[168] The assault put every South Vietnamese battery out of action, but American air power again saved the day.

Extraordinarily, Thao did not accept the failure of this sixth assault. A massive artillery bombardment fell on 45th and 53rd ARVN Regiments, some from captured guns, and the former regiment was almost cut off by

64th PAVN, which again exploited the gap between the two formations. Meanwhile, 44th ARVN holding the hospital area of the town found itself under a double assault from 52nd and 66th PAVN Regiments. In the midst of all this mayhem, an ammunition dump blew, spewing tons of CS gas from exploding shells across the battlefield. This mixed with thick black smoke from a burning petroleum storage area to create a toxic cloud.

By now, Kontum was a scene of house-to-house fighting, the communist soldiers unwilling to withdraw and the ARVN hesitant to eject them. The guarded battle ran for four days. On May 30, Thieu visited the front and promoted Ba to the rank of brigadier general. An attendant press pack was meant to record a moment of victory, but the fighting was not quite over. Nonetheless, by the following morning it was evident that the PAVN was retreating. The final death toll was gruesome: as many as 4,000 enemy soldiers may been killed in these forlorn hope attacks. The total butcher's bill for Thao's bludgeoning campaign was estimated at somewhere between 20,000 and 40,000 soldiers. A mountain of vehicles had been lost, including most of B3 Front's tanks, laboriously transported down the Ho Chi Minh Trail. In total, across all fronts, possibly 420 T-54 and PT-76 tanks were lost, a more grievous mauling than communist forces received in the Korean War.[169] But the 44th, 45th, and 53rd ARVN Regiments were also exhausted after a month of constant fighting, and 22nd ARVN Division had been scratched from the order of battle.

Over June and July, II Corps gradually clawed back lost ground. It had weathered the Easter Offensive and even redeemed itself. But as in the north, the ARVN really only held the major towns and cities, and importantly kept open Highway 1, as well as Routes 14 and 19. The perennial challenge remained the sheer size of the region – there was no realistic hope of controlling a 400-mile border. For the communists, manpower and resupply had proved the limiting factors. It was stalemate with a repeated history dating back to the 1950s.

There was an unexpected coda to this clear victory. Over the course of the campaign, 142 US helicopters were damaged and 21 destroyed;[170] one particular airman, Captain Jim Stein, was shot down three times (on his previous tour he had survived five shoot-downs).[171] But one incident was especially poignant. On June 9, John Paul Vann was killed, crashing into a hillside on the Chu Pao Pass in an OH-58 Kiowa, 15 minutes short of Pleiku. *Stars and Stripes* mordantly described it as "a meaningless crash on a low priority mission to a non-crisis spot."[172] His machine flew into the only tall grove of trees in the immediate area, which concealed an ancestral graveyard with carved statues.[173] Vann had literally careered into the final resting place of tribesmen he had spent the last month of his life defending. That evening he had attended a farewell dinner in Saigon. The night flying conditions were poor: low cloud and drizzly rain. Typically, he was not wearing a helmet when he died and the autopsy revealed that he was intoxicated, though not heavily.[174] He died as he lived, a maverick at the controls. It seemed fitting that a helicopter was his bier. The measure of the man was evident at his funeral in Arlington Cemetery. Who else could have brought together as contradictory an assembly of mourners as Westmoreland, Daniel Ellsberg, Melvin Laird, and Edward Kennedy, all peering into the black hole of his grave, the tomb of America's hopes in South Vietnam? Westmoreland delivered the necessary eulogy; he had been a man "who lived up to his convictions."[175]

The battles in the far north and Central Highlands had shaken the tree, but one battle of the Easter Offensive threatened to sever the trunk. This took place in An Loc, just 60 miles from Saigon, and for many it was the epic struggle of the entire communist campaign. Yet, for Hanoi, III Corps faced significant challenges. Too distant to be reinforced and facing a ring of formidable defenses, B2 Front had little hope of thrusting all the way to the capital. It was the proximity to Saigon and the ease with which journalists could commute to the front line that imbued the battle with importance. The larger-than-life presence of another American advisor – Major General James Hollingsworth – added color to the collision.

Hollingsworth was one of the last of the line: a world war veteran who had served under Patton and a tank man like Abrams. His disrespect for Washington politics was matched by a coarse tongue. The only arena that mattered was the battlefield, where Hollingsworth enjoyed "killin' hell out of the communists."[176] The general's final fling would be a direct counterpart to Vann's heroics in II Corps. Too easily overlooked in the drama was Colonel William Miller, whose 41-year career had started as a private on the battlefields of the Second World War, and ended in Vietnam, via the Korean War. "No guts, no glory," he exhorted his sons, one of whom ended up a major general in America's war in Iraq in the 21st century. Miller was 5th ARVN's advisor and as this division bore the brunt of the fighting, it was this mid-ranking officer who played the stellar part. For many, it was Miller who saved An Loc.[177]

With the withdrawal of American forces, III Corps was now defended by three strong divisions commanded by Lieutenant General Nguyen Van Minh. These included the veteran 25th ARVN in Tay Ninh, Hau Nghia, and Long An Provinces; 18th ARVN in the provinces of Bien Hoa, Long Khanh, Phuoc Tuy, and Binh Tay; and 5th ARVN in Binh Duong, Phuoc Long, and Binh Long Provinces. It was in the latter where the opposing forces collided; it seemed for no better reason than that Loc Ninh, an insignificant town ten miles from the Cambodian border, was easily overrun. With Loc Ninh in communist hands, the enemy columns continued to trundle down the road where they fell on Brigadier General Le Van Hung's 5th ARVN Division in An Loc. Thus was a classic battle engendered.

In fact, the People's Army was not irredeemably weak in the south. All the usual suspects lurked across the border: 7th PAVN and 9th VC Divisions north and west of Tay Ninh Province respectively, and 5th VC Division northwest of Loc Ninh, a small plantation settlement astride Route 13. By this time in the war the "VC" designation had lost some meaning as these were now formations manned by PAVN regulars from the north. Furthermore, the communists had hatched a realistic plan to upset the balance of forces in III Corps and add some useful counters for the negotiating team in the Paris peace talks.

Traditionally, Tay Ninh was the prize, and indeed this city was the assumed objective of the communist spring offensive. The communists reinforced this assumption by feinting with 24th and 271st Independent Regiments along the traditional axis of Highway 22, while throwing the weight of 7th PAVN and 5th/9th VC Divisions against the overlooked Binh Dinh Province. If the scheme played out as intended, 5th VC division would seize Loc Ninh, 7th PAVN Division would block Route 13 south of An Loc, and 9th VC Division would annihilate the surrounded 5th ARVN Division.[178]

An Loc was not, in fact, an accidental destination. In an ambitious plan, Hanoi fully intended to install a provisional government in this ignored town.[179] Under the French, An Loc had actually been a prosperous market town surrounded by hundreds of acres of rubber, coffee, and pepper plantations, as well as durian, rambutan, and mango orchards. The communists also had their eyes on these prizes. In the usual way, various intelligence strands had managed to piece together the enemy plan, but an unwillingness to believe the intelligence meant that III Corps was ill-prepared when the communist offensive opened on April 2.

To many Americans, Hung was probably not the best general for the moment. A Catholic, corrupt, in cahoots with the bigwig generals in Saigon to whom he owed the patronage of command, many would have predicted his demise. But the wayward Hung would prove durable, "the hero of An Loc" who resisted the longest communist siege of the war. Hung may have had flaws but he also belonged to a breed of Southerners that detested the communists and would not suffer living under Hanoi's rule. When Saigon fell, two years later, he was one of only five senior officers who chose suicide over captivity or flight.[180] He died, according to his family, with his "eyes wide open and filled with anger."[181]

The first formation to feel the brunt of the offensive was 9th ARVN Regiment at the border town of Loc Ninh, commanded by Colonel Nguyen Cong Vinh. Vinh's career stretched back to the days of the French colonial army and he should have long retired. The aging colonel confided to US advisors that he fully expected the communists to win the war, and openly confessed he would choose surrender over death. There was little surprise then when Loc Ninh fell, despite the angry specter of Hollingsworth in call sign Danger 79 hovering over the battlefield. A-7 Crusaders were despatched from USS *Constellation* and USS *Saratoga* – all to no avail.[182] By then Vinh had stripped to a pair of shorts and T-shirt and was ordering his officers to quit fighting before the base had even fallen. One US advisor considered shooting Vinh (three would be captured, along with the French photographer Yves Michel Dumont).[183] With all escape routes blocked, a wounded Lieutenant Colonel Schott took his own life rather than burden his comrades. Over 1,000 ARVN surrendered, in stark contrast to the handful of US advisors who fought to save Loc Ninh, all of whom were either killed or captured. 74th Rangers, who may have been expected to put up a fight, threw away their weapons and ran. Less than one hundred of Loc Ninh's defenders made it back to friendly lines.[184] In a foretaste of the fate that awaited South Vietnam's civilian population, the victorious People's Army set about looting and bullying the "liberated" locals. Vinh's capitulation had been disgraceful, but his sense of resignation carried a warning US advisors might have heeded. Far from being the exception, Vinh represented an exhausted segment of South Vietnamese society that had witnessed a lifetime of fighting and which could only foresee the inevitability of a communist victory. The colonel in his shorts may have cut a pathetic figure, but he was also pathetically right.

All that stood between the victorious 5th VC Division and An Loc, just 15 miles further to the south, was an ad hoc Task Force 52, a composite formation of 52nd and 48th ARVN Regiments commanded by Lieutenant Colonel Nguyen Ba Thinh. Over the next week Thinh retreated in the face of overwhelming odds. The demoralized Task Force 52 was ambushed at several points on Highway 13. One thousand soldiers were reduced to 600, and all heavy equipment was abandoned.[185]

As the Thieu government could not tolerate the seizure of a town that would leave the communists within striking distance of the capital, saving the small rubber plantation settlement of An Loc became a vital political imperative. Reinforcements from 8th ARVN Regiment were flown into the city by helicopter following the loss of the Quan Loi airstrip on April 7, the single available air bridge. 21st ARVN Division was ordered to redeploy from the Delta, joined by 1st Airborne Brigade, the strategic reserve. Both these formations would have to drive up Route 13 from Chon Thanh, the only route open for reinforcements. Thus, by April 12, as many as nine infantry battalions were marshaled to the defense of An Loc.[186] Unfortunately, these decisions were taken too late. By the second week in April, a regiment from 7th PAVN Division had cut Highway 13 between Chon Thanh and An Loc.

By now the communists had massed 35,000 troops in a tightening noose around the town. The defenders numbered less than 5,000 including militiamen. The sense of claustrophobia was intense. On a 1:50,000 scale map An Loc was a small dot surrounded by plantations and low-lying hills. The settlement had grown around the crossroads of Highway 13, and Routes 246/303 that led west and east respectively. Laid out in grid fashion, the town resembled a long rectangle comprising a dozen east-west streets intersected by a smaller number of north-south streets. The majority of the buildings were single story, and a good number of the town blocks were in fact empty lots of open land, which made perfect killing zones. In traditional fashion, the French had built a small square in the center. It was possible to drive the length of An Loc in a minute. Viewed from the air, one would have been forgiven for making the judgment that the town was basically indefensible. When it is considered that 78,000 communist shells were eventually lobbed into this small settlement (not counting the contribution of American bombers and tactical strike aircraft), it was a wonder anything survived at all.[187] For the besieged there was absolutely no direction to go, except underground.

Hanoi was obsessed with capturing a symbol, and Thieu's public appeal to save An Loc "at all costs" created a battle of wills. This proved the Northerners' undoing. The obvious move for the communists would have been to bypass An Loc, march south to the strategically vital Tau O Bridge just north of Chon Thanh, and isolate Binh Long Province. An Loc would probably have fallen without a fight.

But a fight was demanded, and the main assault was launched on April 13. This followed increasingly intense artillery bombardments that culminated in a barrage of 7,000 shells. At this stage, An Loc's defense was vested in two weakened battalions from 18th ARVN Division blocking Route 13 to the north, 3rd Ranger Group securing the east flank, and 7th ARVN Regiment holding the west flank.

9th VC Division's main effort fell to the north and west, spearheaded in typical fashion by a cavalcade of T-54 tanks. As in the Central Highlands, the South Vietnamese soldiers were intimidated and even panicked by the presence of tanks. The cry "*Thiet Giap!*" ("tanks") was enough to send them scurrying from their positions in an effort to escape the unfamiliar monsters.[188] But the ARVN soldier soon learned that the humble, shoulder-launched M72 LAW rocket launcher was perfectly capable of disabling the T-54s and quickly turned them into piles of smoking, communist junk. As the US Army's *Armor* magazine observed in an after-action analysis, "expensive mechanical marvels can be quickly reduced to ignominious rubble."[189] So it came to pass in An Loc. Like the ubiquitous AK-47, the Russian T-54 became the world's most sold tank. But it was also the worst: cheap, vulnerable, and a death trap to its crew.

The attacks failed because the tanks did not coordinate their assaults with the infantry, and because the isolated crew became easy prey for tank-hunting teams in An Loc's narrow streets. 8th ARVN Regiment formed 24 such teams and deployed them in the northwest corner of the town covering Highway 13. They did not have to wait long. A double file of 12 T-54s rumbled down the road with infantrymen riding the tanks. "One group of tanks approached the town lackadaisically with all hatches open ... they were told the town had been taken and no resistance was to be expected!"[190] This was far from true. Preplanned artillery barrages knocked the soldiers off, leaving the tanks vulnerable to ambush parties. Some of An Loc's surviving 105mm howitzers fired over open sights at ranges as close as 50 yards with high explosive shells. This defiance had not been anticipated.

The first tank only succeeded in reaching the outskirts of An Loc before it was taken out by a single shot. Unable to spot their assailants, the crews resorted to wildly swinging the turrets and firing co-axial machine guns. Very few tanks actually fired their main gun.[191] Cleverly, many tank-hunting teams had occupied the second or third storys of destroyed buildings, presenting an angle that was too steep for the tanks to engage at close range. Pounding B-52 strikes, tactical air strikes by F-4 Phantoms and A-7 Crusaders, and tank-hunting sorties by Cobra gunships from the Blue Max Squadron of the 1st Cavalry Division all contributed to stopping the assaults dead.[192] By the end of the day every tank had either been destroyed, fled, or become bogged down in the cratered ground.

The few tanks that did penetrate the town became disorientated and attacked random targets. One crew senselessly fired shells into An Loc's Catholic church, killing or wounding all the civilians who had sought refuge in the building. Irate South Vietnamese slaughtered the Northern soldiers.[193] Another tank drove the entire length of the main Ngo Quyen Street, reaching the southern end of An Loc, before turning around and retracing its route.[194] This crew was also killed. Seeing how easily the tank thrusts had been defeated raised the spirits of the beleaguered ARVN soldiers. The morale of the defenders was further buoyed when a lift managed to bring in 6th Airborne Battalion (1st Brigade) and 81st Ranger Group, both units committed to securing the high ground immediately south of the city. 5th and 8th Airborne Battalions followed and were deployed to the perimeter defense.

But the battle had not gone all in favor of the besieged. Through sheer numbers and human wave tactics, the communists had succeeded in creating an enclave in the northern half of the city. Here, the east-west Nguyen Trong Truc Street had become the de facto new front line. To the west, the communists used the axis of Route 246 to seize another two town blocks. Worse, Hung had become, in Miller's candid pen picture, "unstable – irrational – inadvisable – and unapproachable."[195] If An Loc was to be saved, it would be the Americans who would do the saving.

On April 19, the communists tried again. Three regiments from 9th VC Division rumbled down the axis of Highway 13, while 275th VC Regiment and 141st PAVN Regiment moved against the southern sector. Thanks to documents found in the possession of a killed COSVN political officer, the ARVN was aware of the plan. Indeed, the communists were so brazenly confident, a premature announcement was made that An Loc would become the seat of the provisional revolutionary government the following day. How wrong they were.

The two hilltop positions south of An Loc – Windy Hill and Hill 169 – were overrun. Just 60 or so paratroopers survived from the virtually annihilated 6th Airborne Battalion. But 9th VC Division's attempt to roll over the northern defense line failed under the weight of crushing B-52 strikes that stacked "the little bastards up like cordwood."[196] Faced with this face-losing defeat, the People's Army resorted to bludgeoning An Loc with artillery fire. As many as 1,000 shells were indiscriminately lobbed into the city every day, eventually damaging or destroying every public building, including the hospital where 300 medical staff were killed or wounded.[197] To the frustration of American pilots, targeting the enemy batteries proved extremely difficult, an experience that was repeated across all fronts. In a manifestation of supreme cynicism, any attempts by civilians to leave the city were met by communist artillery fire. In one incident, a group led by a Catholic priest and Buddhist monk was decimated, leaving the dead and injured strewn across Highway 13.[198] To avoid an epidemic, corpses were unceremoniously dumped in their hundreds in mass graves. Over the course of the next few weeks, repeated bombardments disinterred the corpses, adding to the general ghastliness.

In the end, survival rested on a football pitch south of the town. By now, some 15,000 soldiers and civilians were trapped in a square-mile bastion. These needed between 60 and 70 daily tons to survive.[199] Over April 7–14, VNAF helicopters ran the gauntlet of antiaircraft fire, making 42 resupply and medevac sorties.[200] Then a helicopter was shot down and a decision was taken to only undertake fixed-wing resupply. Five days later this stopped after a second South Vietnamese C-123 was shot down. Only 301 tons had been delivered. The temporary closure of the air bridge was disastrous for the wounded. Soldiers were left to die. Small wounds festered, which led to unnecessary amputations. One disenchanted US advisor observed that only the "Olympic" wounded could make it out, or perfectly fit soldiers with sufficient strength to leap up and grab the skids of a helicopter, abandoning the wounded in the dust.[201]

Then the C-130-equipped 374th Tactical Airlift Wing took over, experimenting with a variety of drop techniques: jettisoning loads, low parachute drops, high parachute drops, and employing improvised parachute drop technologies. At first, the returns were poor: by the third week of April, 845 tons had been delivered but only 45 fell inside the perimeter. Two aircraft were lost, one with all crew killed. But by the end, the drops became very accurate. From May 4 to June 25, there were 230 sorties delivering 2,984 tons. Only 249 tons fell to the enemy.[202] It was a triumph of American determination and ingenuity.

Tran Van Tra, the B2 Front commander, could not accept defeat. There would be one more attempt to overrun An Loc, advancing on the town on four axes: 9th VC would attack from the north and northeast, and 5th VC supported by 7th PAVN would stab with two prongs from the south. As before, the plan was known, thanks to a rallier. But the communists were bereft of ideas and it became a battle of firepower which they were always going to lose. On May 11, over 8,000 rounds landed within the perimeter, presaging the assault.[203] This bombardment stopped at 4.30am, then resumed half an hour later. Then for the next 12 hours, another 10,000 rounds pummeled the town. In response, MACV, in a plan that was the brainchild of Major General Hollingsworth, had pre-prepared a ring of B-52 strikes. Round the clock bombing thundered over An Loc. Tactical air flew a staggering 297 sorties. The ring of antiaircraft defenses was intense (four aircraft would be downed) but spraying the skies with cannon shells could not stop the weight of air attacks.

The effects proved devastating. Around 40 tanks were committed to the assault and not one survived. To the south, a half-company of six tanks that approached up Highway 13 was interdicted by an F-4 Phantom lobbing 500 pounds. Two curious ARVN paratroopers mounted an immobilized tank to inspect it. To their surprise, the engine restarted and the tank trundled off. "After some hand wrestling with the tankers the hatch was pulled open and a grenade was dropped in, killing the crewmen."[204] Even where T-54s evaded the predatory aircraft, they now had to contend with the ARVN, who had become expert tank-killers.

The experiences of Sergeant First Class Cao Tan Tai serving with 8th Regiment was typical. He destroyed one T-54 with a single shot fired from 30 feet that penetrated the turret front, igniting the ammunition bustle and converting the tank into a flaming torch. A second he immobilized by taking out a front road wheel. He then fired a further two M72s into the turret, setting the tank alight. The surviving crewmen were killed by small arms fire when they bailed. Neither tank had actually fired a single round.[205]

The sheer weight of the assault succeeded in creating two salients, but both were quickly snuffed out. VC battalions vanished, engulfed in the inferno. The battle continued for another day before communist will collapsed. The 66-day siege had ended. That night the heavens broke, washing the battlefield in cleansing rain.

On July 7, Thieu visited the destroyed town, promoting every soldier and officer and waffling about a victory for the Free World: South Vietnam now had its own Stalingrad. An equally jubilant Hollingsworth described it as "the greatest victory in the history of warfare."

In the aftermath, the protagonists interpreted the battle according to their prejudices and audiences. Nixon lauded the success of Vietnamization but a skeptical American press was unconvinced. Another South Vietnamese town had been utterly razed. Aerial photography revealed the remarkable image of a settlement entirely blasted flat. By July, just 1,000 hardy souls remained in An Loc; several thousand had been killed or wounded. Some 5,400 ARVN were killed, wounded, or missing – in effect the entire garrison was wiped out, but for the reinforcements that re-inflated the manpower pool.

Whatever their faults, and despite the failings of their leaders, it was unquestionable that the common South Vietnamese soldier had sacrificed on the altar of An Loc. But it was also the case that a small group of US advisors who never numbered more than 25, combined with devastating air power, had saved the day.[206] Tran Van Tra only succeeded in decimating three of his precious divisions, and losing most of the kit. As many as 25,000 dead and wounded was a steep price to pay for this folly. Prisoners from 141st and 165th PAVN Regiments confessed that entire battalions had been annihilated.[207] A communist enclave remained on the northern edge of the town and it was still there when the winter monsoons set in. An equally exhausted III Corps made no attempt to push back this new front line or recapture Loc Ninh.

Where had six months of fighting left all the protagonists? It had taken the communists four years to recover from the Tet Offensive – had the Easter Offensive been worth it? The minimal strategic aim had been to gain a favorable negotiating position in Paris. In the best case, Hanoi had hoped to sever South Vietnam in the north and Central Highlands and force the installation of a provisional government under the noses of withdrawing Americans. None of these aims was achieved. Operational competence had been poor, tactics unimaginative, and the behavior towards South Vietnamese civilians abominable. The only popular uprising was a general flight away from communist forces. Another one million South Vietnamese were displaced by the fighting. Fourteen divisions were committed and 14 were decimated. A mountain of equipment – tanks, trucks, artillery guns – was reduced to junk. Somewhere between 40,000 and 75,000 communist foot soldiers were killed and three times this number wounded, a tremendous sacrifice of fighting age males. By any measures, the Nguyen Hue Offensive had been a grand failure.

The rewards would come in the future. The offensive may have been a flop but it left Hanoi in control of enclaves in South Vietnam: in Quang Binh and Quang Tri Provinces in the north, at Khe Sanh, now turned into a communist redoubt, in the Central Highlands, and beyond to Binh Long Province. All these lodgements would become the launching pads for the decisive battles of 1975. Virtually every critical land route was either interdicted or hazardous for travel: Routes 1, 1A, 2, 4, 13, and 20 in III Corps; Routes 14 and 19 in II Corps; and every route in I Corps. South Vietnam had been filleted.

In the usual way, the fighting had resulted in many civilian deaths: perhaps 25,000 were killed compared to only 10,000 ARVN fatalities and 33,000 wounded.[208] However, the true numbers may have been three times this size. With so many units collapsing then re-constituting, accurate nominal rolls became hard to tally. Where the fighting was heaviest, in particular on the DMZ, there had been great economic damage.

The big debate had been over the competency and effectiveness of South Vietnam's army. This surprised many, but also left pessimists doubtful. Thieu had proved an uncertain war leader, complacent at first, obsessed with protecting Saigon, and slow in his decision-making. The ARVN command had been poor and lacking in coordination. Individual bravery could not compensate for collective failure. Too many units had been at half strength, and too many were simply war weary. Equipment serviceability was dire. Without American cajoling, there had been little appetite for incurring casualties and regaining lost ground. Too many abandoned bases, or fled, or changed into civilian clothes and discarded weapons. US military aid had built up the fourth largest air force in the world but half the aircraft never flew.[209] Strike aircraft failed to make an important contribution and helicopter pilots shirked the more dangerous missions. While recognizing the sacrifice on the ground, the reality was that a handful of courageous US advisors and air power had defeated the North Vietnamese. As the Year of the Rat ended, those advisors and bombers would be flying home. How would Saigon fare without the protective shield?

Chapter 6

LIQUIDATING A WAR, FEBRUARY 1969–MARCH 1973

Nixon's war was memorably described by a State Department official as "backing out of the saloon with both guns firing."[1] So it was. For the White House, "getting out" was a national and political imperative. This had three facets: ground withdrawal behind the shield of the bombers, "Vietnamization," and the Paris peace negotiations. It was also an ethical imperative, and this proved the most agonizing aspect of the war for Americans. For Hanoi, it was matter of plowing the same bloody furrow: *ta ta, t'an t'an* ("fight, fight, talk, talk").

In the first month in office, and in a blizzard of interrogation aimed at shaking up perceived bureaucratic inertia of the Democrat governments, the Nixon administration commissioned 26 National Security Study Memorandums (NSSMs).[2] Seven related to Vietnam or the Far East. Over the next two months the pace slowed (reaching 47 NSSMs), but another seven were devoted to the same subjects. A third of the intellectual capacity of the national security team was being thrown at one corner of Indochina. No fresh American administration since the end of the Second World War had started with such determination to review and change the bearing of the national compass.

Both Kennedy and Johnson had deferred or ducked the important questions in the beginning, the former inheriting an Eisenhower program tentatively expanded, and the latter following a gradualist approach that led to escalation and then a full-blown war.

Nixon was sharp to observe that his predecessor's biggest mistake had been to pretend the country was not at war. The deployment of ground troops was announced briefly in an afternoon press conference. Congress was not consulted. There was no reservist call-up, or even a supplemental appropriations bill. No plan was presented. The true scale of the proposed commitment was never revealed. The combat role was never properly justified. Johnson had gone to war without putting America on a war footing.[3] In deliberately downplaying the war, Johnson had never been able to carry the nation.

The new president had no choices left but to confront this legacy, and end it. This meant starting with a blank sheet of paper and reviewing the war from first principles. Directed by Kissinger, who lost no time in stamping his authority, NSSM 1 was fired to the US Embassy in Saigon, MACV, the Joint Chiefs, State, and Defense.[4] The omission of the CIA, whom Nixon suspected was against him, was later corrected.

NSSM 1 was despatched on Tuesday January 21, a fittingly cloudy and windy day after the presidential inauguration. The addressees were requested to respond to this stormy missive by February 10. The very title was epochal and told its recipients that an Old Testament had given way to a New: NSSM 1 "Situation in South Vietnam" – as if the conflict had only started the previous week.

But for all its thunder, NSSM 1 was a short document – just seven pages – confirming the newly appointed National Security Advisor had been caught unprepared by his appointment. It was typical of Kissinger that the question of negotiations was elevated to the top of the paper, and introduced by the vexed question: "Why is the DRV [Democratic Republic of Vietnam] in Paris?" Over the next four years every possibility would play out, like dissonant notes on the score of the peace negotiations, except the first: "Out of weakness, to accept a face-saving formula for defeat." Of all hypotheses offered, it was the third that proved prophetic – "To give the U.S. a face-saving way to withdraw" – but it was not followed by the inevitable corollary: and to subsequently defeat the South Vietnamese government, because this was not an outcome that could be admitted.

It was also expressive of Kissinger that follow-on questions focused on the Soviet Union and China, as the Nixon administration had entered government with the big play in mind – "linkage" as it came to be known – a grand strategy to replace a constricted, soiled war. NSSM 1 could not avoid the questions of attrition or the enemy order of battle that had dogged the Johnson years, but offering a significant clue to Nixon's predispositions, three out of the five questions on "U.S. Operations" related to bombing. In a shift that would surely have pleased Curtis LeMay, humiliated in the 1968 election as Wallace's running mate, the new president was asking the taboo question: should we "bomb them into the Stone Age," a statement LeMay denied he ever made, to force the war to an end?[5]

A total of 28 key questions were listed in NSSM 1, and all had been posed in one form or another in the last decade. The respondents all conformed to their roles in the drama: Abrams, CINCPAC Admiral John McCain, and Wheeler, offered a positive prospect; the CIA, State's Bureau of Intelligence and Research, and the disenchanted civilians in the Pentagon, all forecast gloom. In a sense, nothing new had been uncovered or determined. It was the urgency that imbued the script with the founding quality of a new administration.

Of the three levers in America's liquidation of her Vietnam War, troop withdrawal was the easiest to execute, if only because it was the single lever the White House could pull without controversy. Even so, the road was littered with the potholes and bumps of departmental in-fighting. Whatever war Abrams had hoped to fight, he had to answer to a new defense secretary who was a self-styled "disciple of the Eisenhower philosophy," and firmly convinced that America should not embroil herself in Southeast Asian land wars.[6] When Laird visited Saigon on March 5–12 – his first trip of the Nixon presidency – he bluntly informed the country team that the only acceptable outcome now was "the eventual disengagement of American men in combat."[7] He repeated the same message to Thieu. In his March 13 visit report he reinforced the message, recommending the withdrawal of as many as 70,000 troops by the end of the year. In taking this stance he knew he would face opposition from MACV, CINCPAC, and the Joint Chiefs, all of whom were arguing that the South Vietnamese were not ready to assume responsibility of the war, and that withdrawal should be conditions-based, a policy dubbed "cut and try."

He also faced hesitation from Kissinger, still finding his feet in the corridors of power, who proved chary of a precipitous withdrawal, although this opposition would soon evaporate. Laird's winning hand was the defense budget, swollen, unbalanced, and now running at close to $77 billion per annum, coupled with a pressing requirement to re-balance America's armed forces to meet other defense priorities.

The plan that eventually emerged from Laird's forceful maneuverings went by the uninspiring acronym CRIMP – Consolidated RVNAF Improvement and Modernization Plan – but it was the only realistic plan on offer. CRIMP was, in effect, the "Vietnamization" of the war. The program was actually submitted by MACV to CINCPAC in May 1968, so it represented an inherited scheme rather than a fresh start. But whether the RVNAF could be improved, after two decades of mentoring, first by French and now by American trainers and advisors, was an awkward question. And did medicating the RVNAF with modern equipment necessarily translate into modernized forces, or simply more hardware rusting in tank parks and aircraft aprons?

In the end, the single measure of success that suffused CRIMP with an obsessive quality was sheer numbers. If America was to withdraw her half-a-million-strong force, then the South Vietnamese would have to find another half a million men at arms, or more. At Laird's insistence, funding was secured for just over one million men in the RVNAF in fiscal year 1971, 1,090,000 in fiscal year 1972, and for 1,100,000 in fiscal year 1973.[8] What war this million-strong army might fight – conventional, guerrilla, or a mix – became muddied. What mattered was a *levée en masse*, a nation in arms. None had the foresight, in 1969, to suppose that an army of another million soldiers might just unstitch into another million deserting or surrendering soldiers, if Hanoi leaned hard enough on the door.

If there were any lingering doubts in the minds of the Joint Chiefs, or MACV, that Johnson's war was over, they were quickly dispelled. NSSM 36 "Vietnamizing the war" was pushed out on April 10. Just two pages long and dispensing with all the usual preambles and casuistry of previous Vietnam policy documents, NSSM 36 read like a peremptory order, which it was. From July 1, US forces would begin withdrawing from Vietnam, regardless of whether the North Vietnamese reciprocated, and regardless of communist force levels, although these would be taken into account to determine the pace of withdrawal. Nixon requested a plan by June 1 to cover the remainder of 1969, and full plan by September 1 to achieve complete withdrawal. In a timetable that stunned the JCS, NSSM 36 commanded full withdrawal from combat roles by December of the following year, 1970, or failing that, by the end of the December in the subsequent two years in increments.

The Joint Chiefs had every right to be taken by surprise. On March 28, a National Security Council meeting was held that skirted detailed discussion of withdrawal.[9] Based on the discussions from this meeting, four days later on April 1, National Security Decision Memorandum (NSDM) 9 "Vietnam" was promulgated. This document directly contradicted in spirit and principle NSSM 36, issued nine days later.[10] The former stated, "There will be no de-escalation except as an outgrowth of *mutual troop withdrawal* [author's emphasis]." Nixon reinforced this position. "I have decided that we should be prepared to withdraw all combat forces from South Vietnam *if* [author's emphasis] Hanoi meets specific conditions of a mutual withdrawal agreement."[11] As none of the conditions stipulated were likely to be met, a reader of NSDM 9 would have been forgiven for concluding that Nixon was digging in for an escalated military campaign, not withdrawal. What had happened in just nine days to bring about this abrupt volte-face?

Over several weeks, frustration had mounted over the state of the Paris peace talks, led by Ambassador Lodge, and now judged to be in a complete state of disarray. Seizing the opportunity of the presidential interregnum, some officials had taken to "saving the President from himself" by pushing for an end to the war without preconditions, and in direct contradiction to policies now being articulated by the administration. In a sure sign of institutional anarchy, members of the negotiating team, "devoid of loyalty or discipline," were indulging in freelance diplomacy – or committing every sin likely to antagonize Kissinger's tight, disciplined national security team.

This frustration was privately shared by Nixon, who viewed the negotiations as valueless "when the other side constantly accused us of insincerity, when every private meeting so far had been initiated by us, and when every proposition was put forward on a take-it-or-leave-it basis."[12] Unlike his national security advisor who was prepared to invest in the long haul of negotiations, Nixon was far too impulsive – too wedded to action and results – to accept such a deal in the first months of his presidency. Accordingly, Nixon had confidentially decided to make one more approach to Hanoi before taking the decision to end the war unilaterally. Negotiations should be concluded "within two months," or not at all, a remarkable stance in retrospect as these lasted, with interruptions, four years. NSSM 1 and NDSM 9 were launched by an administration still tacking between the crosswinds of conflicting and irreconcilable policy options. By April 10, the prevailing wind had settled, at least in Nixon's mind.

However, this private determination to "get out" was not presentable or presented to a domestic audience. Nixon waited four months before making his first public address on the war in a radio and television announcement on May 14 (by which time another 3,602 servicemen had been killed in Vietnam).[13] A statement that the United States would unilaterally quit the war would have delighted critics, but dismayed and shamed many more. The fetish of American "prestige" and Nixon's horror at being the first president to lose a war could not stand it. The Joint Chiefs might have resigned. Instead, Nixon concealed the covert policy of unilateral withdrawal and used the address to promote his statesmanship. "The old formulas and the tired rhetoric of the past," he loftily pronounced, would not be enough, although he repeated many.[14] His administration rejected "a one-sided withdrawal from Vietnam." But the corollary was a terribly lame request: "We ask only that North Vietnam withdraw its forces from South Vietnam, Cambodia, and Laos into North Vietnam, also in accordance with a timetable." This was a fantastic hope. Only then, or "as soon as agreement can be reached," would "all non-South Vietnamese forces ... begin withdrawals from South Vietnam." This was not so much fanciful as false – the administration had already decided to program withdrawals, regardless of "agreement," which Hanoi was not going to grant anyway.

Within two weeks of the address, on June 2, Laird consulted with his defense chiefs and the in-country team, and arrived at an agreement of a maximum withdrawal of 50,000 troops in 1969, with half the balance leaving from July, as NSSM 36 had mandated. The tenor of the May 14 announcement had been entirely bypassed. Abrams naturally struggled with this recommendation, offering just one regiment from 3rd Marine Division and two brigades from the Delta force, 9th Infantry Division.[15]

A showdown followed at Midway Island, six days later, in a Vietnam summit attended by Thieu, the first of Nixon's presidency. The uninhabited Midway was chosen to avoid the unpleasantness of protestors, and because Honolulu had become tainted by association with the previous administration. However, Nixon did make a stopover in Honolulu, where the triumvirate of Abrams, Bunker, and McCain, encouraged backstage by Wheeler, sought to influence the President with warnings over the risks posed by an early withdrawal. It was wasted effort. With obvious reluctance, so Kissinger recalled, the supplicants agreed to the 50,000 number, cognisant that this single decision effectively foreclosed the possibility that MACV could ever win its war.[16] The key meeting took place in the luxury resort of the Kahala Hilton. Thieu also accepted the decision and indeed was gracious – all the finessing had been unnecessary. Two days later, an unwavering Nixon made the public (and popular) announcement that 25,000 US troops would withdraw from Vietnam by August. The first unit home was 3/60 Infantry of 9th Infantry Division. On July 8 it was flown home to McChord Air Force Base in Seattle, fêted with a parade, and promptly disbanded.[17]

As expected, the Joint Chiefs balked at an accelerated withdrawal timetable, and in confirmation of the institutional waywardness, sidestepped Nixon's instruction to prepare a full withdrawal. NSSM 36 could not have been more explicit in what it commanded Defense to plan. Laird had confirmed the instruction at the beginning of June. Nixon had made a public announcement. And yet the Joint Chiefs could not have been more barefaced in their rejection when they presented their scheme to CINCPAC on July 22. In a counter-proposal, "Vietnamization" was interpreted as partial withdrawal: as many as 270,000 US troops would remain in Vietnam, including almost three combat divisions, with the balance leaving in six stages within 18, 24, 30, or 42 months. Had this plan been implemented, a quarter-of-a-million-strong force would have still been deployed in Indochina in 1973 (the actual date of the final American withdrawal). Wheeler, now supported by Westmoreland, must have known this proposal would be totally unacceptable to the administration, but the Chiefs elected to buttress an unhappy Abrams in Saigon, as well as the firebrand McCain, whose pilot son the future Senator John McCain was now a prisoner of war, and whose appetite for war on communists was undiminished.

McCain, in many ways, was the quintessential example of a politicized military hierarchy Nixon faced. He probably should never have been appointed CINCPAC, owing his four stars to the energetic lobbying of Senator Everett

Dirksen, who wanted him to collect the rank like "his father [who] was an admiral before him."[18] When Johnson posed the question to McNamara, "[But] Is he competent?" his secretary advised him that he was not. Al Haig, now working for Kissinger, cuttingly opined to Nixon, "I don't have much confidence in his brainpower." Nevertheless, McNamara had felt obliged to find him a four-star appointment. In a testament to the extraordinary power of insider influence on Pennsylvania Avenue, McCain got his four stars and the Pacific command. Dirksen died a year later, like many of his generation, from lung cancer. Nixon would quickly tire of the "crap" of "half-assed command," but it was the Joint Chiefs who shortened his fuse within months of assuming office by challenging presidential authority. Ironically, Nixon actually admired McCain, with or without brainpower, because he viewed him as a "hard-line little son of a bitch," or just the sort of person he liked to be surrounded by.

Three days after the Joint Chiefs made their pitch to CINCPAC, Nixon articulated the first hints of his grand strategy for Asia. This took place in the unlikely setting of Top O' The Mar Officers' Club in Guam, where the presidential party found itself en route to Indochina.[19] In Kissinger's estimation, the so-called "Nixon Doctrine" came about by accident. Nixon had no intention of making a major policy pronouncement but had simply been trying to "make some news" over the dead period produced by crossing the international dateline. The press pack was in a hungry mood and Nixon got "more news than he bargained for."[20]

> Asians will say in every country that we visit that they do not want to be dictated to from the outside, Asia for the Asians. And that is what we want, and that is the role we should play. We should assist, but we should not dictate. We will give assistance ... We, of course, will keep the treaty commitments that we have. But as far as our role is concerned, we must avoid that kind of policy that will make countries in Asia so dependent upon us that we are dragged into conflicts such as the one that we have in Vietnam.[21]

These remarks were made in an almost throwaway fashion, in the middle of a long and informal, discursive session. But a domestic press pack, reflecting a country tired of being "dragged into conflicts," pounced on the message. The simplicity was beguiling: this was restatement of the containment of the Eisenhower years, without the tensions of atomic confrontation that bedeviled the height of the Cold War, sprinkled with Kennedy's light footprint of military and civilian assistance missions.

At Guam, Nixon had been in an expansive mood. The press had similarly been animated. Five days earlier, Apollo 11 had landed on a silvery-gray plateau on the Moon. The previous day, a triumphant Nixon had been flown to the hangar deck of USS *Hornet* to greet the returning astronauts. The United States had planted the Stars and Stripes 8,000 miles away in Vietnam. They had now transplanted the same flag 240,000 miles away. There was no better metaphor for the changes overtaking America and the world. It was apt the astronauts landed in a Sea of Tranquility.

The Joint Chiefs' withdrawal plan was eventually presented one day short of the deadline, on August 29. This was loyally endorsed by Laird on September 4. Effectively based on MACV's campaign scheme for the renamed transitional support force, a compromise 24-month withdrawal timetable was recommended, which became the de facto planning guide incorporated into the defense budget. Nixon deferred a decision, husbanding his options carefully, but to mollify the Joint Chiefs, an incremental "cut-and-try" approach to withdrawal was accepted in principle. The problem with "cut-and-try" was not just that it was a phrase too easily subverted to "cut and run." The administration had no intention of reversing course – there was nothing to "try." No matter what happened in South Vietnam over the next two or three years, Nixon was determined to get out. "Cut-and-try" was a sop, a fig leaf for the generals that would be abandoned by the spring of the following year.

The White House was well aware of MACV's and the Joint Chiefs' positions, even if it had not yet mustered its artillery to foil their flanking attack. However, with his foot now wedged in the door of military obstructionism, Nixon then moved swiftly. In August, the bulk of 3rd Marine Division and two brigades of 9th Infantry Division were withdrawn, completing the Phase I withdrawals. On September 16, the Phase II withdrawals exceeded the previously agreed ceiling: 40,500 troops were pulled out, including the balance of 3rd Marines and 3rd Brigade from 82nd Airborne (rushed to Vietnam during the Tet Offensive). By April 15 of the following year, the due date for the completion of Phase III withdrawals, 1st Infantry Division and a brigade from 4th Infantry were out. Thus by the end of 1969, the administration had withdrawn or committed to withdraw 115,500 troops, a fifth of the overall force.[22]

But withdrawal was not a strategy, rather a clear retreat and intolerable policy hole that needed filling.

The big-unit war had once again degenerated into a war of terrorism for ordinary Vietnamese. Vietnamization was not an exchangeable currency with Pacification. More not less violence was being fomented, and for millions of peasants nothing had really changed since 1965. Civilian casualty figures were getting worse, not better. The war economy had become a ghastly burlesque of shocking inequalities, a sort of Indochinese version of Otto Dix's Great War

Metropolis triptych, but now painted by photographers like Larry Burroughs. Legless veterans, dogs, prostitutes, cigarette vendors, the stinking rich, all returned to the stage to play their sad parts.

If Guam had been an accidental articulation of national strategy, the President's next appeal to the nation was not. On November 3, Nixon delivered his first full public statement of an identifiable Nixon Doctrine.[23] The speech was significantly given after Ho Chi Minh's death (he died on September 2). Three days before his demise, Ho's response to Nixon's private peace overtures was received in the White House. It was a rude rejection, drafted not by the ailing president, but by the hard-liners who had moved swiftly to claim the imminent succession, notably Le Duan. The immediate backdrop to the television address was the looming Moratorium Day marches, during which period Washington would witness one of the biggest ever peace marches, attended by a quarter of a million protestors. From Capitol Hill, the war had opened not just a Pandora's Box of rowdy peaceniks, but a host of discontented, placard-waving minorities: blacks, ("Be Brown & Be Proud"), Hispanics ("Chicano Power"), and homosexuals ("Gay Is Good"). On the Mall, Pete Seeger orchestrated a cheery sing-along of "Give Peace A Chance," but his president had preempted him.

"Let us all understand," Nixon intoned, "the question before us is not whether some Americans are for peace and some Americans are against peace. The question at issue is not whether Johnson's war becomes Nixon's war. The great question is: How can we win America's peace?" The answer to this question was not to clutch at the temptation of abandoning Vietnam, which notwithstanding Nixon's absolute aversion to "losing" remained a political possibility for a new president who could have blamed predecessors, and cast himself as the man tasked with cleaning up the mess. This possibility was foreclosed because Nixon not only believed in the domino theory; he invested it with his own peculiarly strong anti-communism. "In my opinion," he argued, "for us to withdraw from that effort would mean a collapse not only of South Viet-Nam, but Southeast Asia." Such abandonment would "promote recklessness in the councils of those great powers who have not yet abandoned their goals of world conquest," sparking violence "in the Middle East, in Berlin, eventually even in the Western Hemisphere."

Unlike the Johnson administration that maintained a certain veil of secrecy over peace negotiations, Nixon was keen to reveal the depth of Hanoi's perfidy, and abject failure of the peace talks: "The effect of all the public, private, and secret negotiations ... can be summed in one sentence: No progress whatever has been made except agreement on the shape of the bargaining table."

This depressing admission encapsulated the intractable contradiction in his address. Nixon had arrived at the last great fork in the road of the war.

His administration sought "a plan which will bring the war to an end," but ultimately it would do so "regardless of what happens on the negotiating front." The contradiction was never resolved, if it ever could have been. As Nixon put it, there were now only three options left, but the reality was that these were Goldilocks options. Either he could take the "easy way" and quit the war, or the government could

> persist in our search for a just peace through a negotiated settlement if possible, or through continued implementation of our plan for Vietnamization if necessary – a plan in which we will withdraw all our forces from Vietnam on a schedule according with our program, as the South Vietnamese become strong enough to defend their freedom.

Nixon could and only intended to pursue the last option. In the same way that the previous administrations had believed they could control the war, turn the tap on or off, through incremental escalation and bombing, so Nixon chose the reverse path. He would control the war through incremental de-escalation, against his own timetable, regardless of the enemy. But he would not hold back on the single weapon that had so exercised passions for the last four years – bombing. Johnson had sought to "touch up" Hanoi's leaders. Nixon would knock them flat. "Vietnam cannot defeat or humiliate the United States. Only Americans can do that." This he could not allow.

Nixon viewed his "Silent Majority speech" as a signal triumph, the most effective of his presidency. The address provoked the biggest ever response to any presidential speech. A Gallup poll indicated a 77 percent approval rating. Three days before the Moratorium Marches, on November 12, 300 members of the House of Representatives (119 Democrats and 181 Republicans) co-sponsored a resolution of support for the government's Vietnam policy. Fifty-eight senators (21 Democrats and 37 Republicans) similarly expressed support. Over the next few days, more than 50,000 telegrams and 30,000 letters poured into the White House.[24] Nixon was so proud he piled up the telegrams in the Oval Office, making it impossible to conduct routine business for a matter of a few days. During the marches he professed to be uninterested and watched a football game on television instead.

Withdrawal, couched under the euphemism "redeployment," was the only option, but it proved as divisive as escalation, and the gradualist principle "cut-and-try" was soon abandoned. By April 1970, decisions were required on the Phase IV redeployments, but by now the strategic landscape in Indochina had been dramatically changed by the coup in Cambodia and communist offensive in Laos. Prime Minister Lon Nol's rebellion had taken Washington completely by surprise. As Nixon later recalled, the CIA did not have a single

General William Childs Westmoreland (COMUSMACV 1964–68). Americans hate a loser.
As a consequence, his hard slog in the first half of the war has never been properly acknowledged.
(Photo by PhotoQuest/Getty Images)

Lieutenant General Frederick Weyand – probably the most cerebral of the Vietnam generals, but with no better answers than anybody else. (US Army)

The jovial tank commander General Creighton Abrams. It fell to this Bastogne veteran to close America's war in Vietnam. Within two years he was dead, felled by lung cancer. (Photo by PhotoQuest/Getty Images)

The three wise men: Rusk, Johnson and McNamara. (NARA)

An impassive Prime Minister Ky and Lieutenant General Thieu face Johnson at the
February 1966 Honolulu Conference. This was Johnson's chance to stamp his authority on the war.
He was unable to take it. (NARA)

Secretary of Defence Clark Clifford: he took the job determined to save Johnson from himself.
(Photo by Keystone/Hulton Archive/Getty Images)

Premonitions of exile? Thieu contemplates his country from afar in 1968. (NARA)

The newly appointed National Security Advisor Henry Alfred Kissinger in 1969. America has never owed so much to an academic; nor has an academic been so vilified by off-stage critics. (Photo by Jack Robinson/Condé Nast via Getty Images)

We smashed them right here. Nixon was delighted by the results of the controversial April 1970 incursion against Viet Cong sanctuaries in Cambodia. (NARA)

The great political double act of the war: Nixon and Kissinger. (NARA)

Kissinger and Le Duc Tho at the peace negotiations in Gif-sur-Yvette in 1972. Peace is at hand, said Kissinger. Peace is at the stroke of a pen, quipped the North Vietnamese, if only the other side would sign. (Bettmann / Getty Images)

Pham Van Dong's revolutionary struggle began in 1925. He probably never imagined half a century would pass before he would witness the conclusion of that struggle. (Photo by Keystone/ Getty Images)

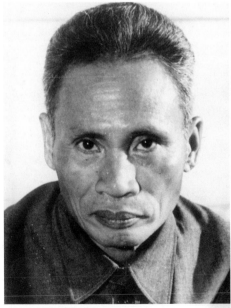

Nobody was more determined than Le Duan to unify the two Vietnams. (Photo by Sovfoto/ Universal Images Group via Getty Images)

Kissinger's nemesis: Le Duc Tho at the Paris peace talks. Here the two men shake hands after reaching final agreement on a peace deal on January 24, 1973.
(Photo by Daily Express/Archive Photos/Getty Images)

The eyes that witnessed a million deaths: Giap, Hanoi's most durable general. (Photo by Photo12/
Universal Images Group via Getty Images)

"Big Minh": the Japanese pulled his teeth out and in April 1975 he surrendered the Republic of South Vietnam to the communists. His last days were spent in exile in France. (Photo by Howard Sochurek/The LIFE Picture Collection via Getty Images)

Nguyen Van Toan was tasked with organising the last ditch defence of Saigon but fled the country after tricking his fellow officers over his whereabouts. (US Navy)

Ngo Quang Truong pins a medal on a soldier of 3/21 Infantry during the unit's deactivation ceremony at Da Nang. Americans rated him Saigon's finest general. (Bettmann / Getty Images)

Portrait of a war-losing army. (Bettmann / Getty Images)

He needed more help than that. (Bettmann / Getty Images)

Go home Yankee: North Vietnamese Lieutenant Colonel Bui Tin bids farewell to the last American servicemen to quit Vietnam in May 1973. The unidentified serviceman was only too happy to oblige. In 1990, Bui Tin would defect, disenchanted by the communist regime. (Bettmann / Getty Images)

The convoy of tears, March 1975: the disastrous retreat from the Central Highlands that led to the collapse of South Vietnam. (Bettmann / Getty Images)

Afros and peace symbols from a reluctant soldiery.
(Photo by David Hume Kennerly/Bettmann/Corbis via Getty Images)

The agony is almost over: the fight for Newport Bridge in downtown Saigon.
The following day, the city fell. (Bettmann / Getty Images)

Saigon, April 29, 1975: the CIA helicopter was meant to be rescuing the deputy prime minister. Pilot Robert Caron later joked, "I didn't realise he had such a large family." (Bettmann / Getty Images)

The face of defeat: an exhausted Ambassador Graham Martin on USS *Blue Ridge* following the emergency evacuation from the US Embassy in Saigon. (Bettmann / Getty Images)

The lucky ones: a South Vietnamese helicopter pilot and his family, safely aboard the USS *Hancock*, are escorted by a marine security guard to the refugee area during Operation *Frequent Wind*. (Photo by PhotoQuest/Getty Images)

agent in the country, an unfortunate omission which had origins in State's resistance to widening the war dating back to the Kennedy years (two years later, when Kissinger confessed to Chinese Prime Minister Chou En-lai that no CIA man had been based in Cambodia, he disbelieved him. Kissinger retorted, "Perhaps we can talk socially about it at dinner. I believe it might be to some advantage to us to maintain CIA's bad reputation," provoking laughter in the Chinese camp).[25] This strategic wrong-footing passed over peace demonstrators who once again swelled in the Mall, charging American culpability in the expansion of the war. Against this difficult backdrop and following a period of backroom haggling it was agreed that 150,000 troops would be withdrawn by April 30, 1971, with the majority pulled out towards the end of the period. American troop levels would then rest at about 284,000, or as many as in the year of escalation in 1966. This proposal satisfied both the NSSM 36 two-year timetable and reassured Abrams.

However, the fingerprint of Nixon's style of government was all over this compact. Neither Laird nor Rogers were kept abreast of what was being proposed, and indeed both were encouraged to continue preparing policy papers and options on redeployment. Kissinger instead used a CIA back channel with Saigon to cut the deal, later judging this calculating episode "one of the tours de force" which allowed the administration to stay on track with its plans for disengagement.[26] Abrams was resistant but understood that Washington was now adamant in its demands.[27] Only when the final agreements were in place, on April 20, did Kissinger inform the two secretaries. By then it was too late for debate: that evening Nixon addressed the nation on national television and announced "we have now reached a point where we can confidently move from a period of 'cut and try' to a longer-range program for the replacement of Americans by South Vietnamese troops."[28]

"Cut and try" did not make great sense to soldiers on the ground. For Marine Anthony Goodrich whose tour of Vietnam spanned 1969–70, the overwhelming feeling was one of the pointlessness of it all:

> We're here as fodder basically, so the politicians in Paris can do their flapping of their mouths in Paris at the peace talks while we sit here and get killed ... Nothing was being accomplished ... the war was over, it was coming to an end we just didn't understand why we all weren't pulled out at once.[29]

The announcement, rather than settle the matter, provoked another three months of bartering over what became known as Alternatives A and B, neither of which were palatable to Abrams or the Joint Chiefs. Of the two, Alternative A, which preserved a maximalist force posture for the longest possible period, was most favored, but in typical fashion, political and budgetary pressures squeezed out a third, Alternative C. It was this last alternative, proposed by Abrams, that was adopted. Under Alternative C, 50,000 men would be withdrawn by October 15, 1970, a further 40,000 by December 31, and the remaining 60,000 by April 30, 1971. Both Saigon and Thieu recognized the risks this posed to Cambodian operations, as well as to the balance of power in the Central Highlands and DMZ, but acquiesced. Nixon and Kissinger also belatedly acknowledged they were now running the risk of undermining the successful accomplishment of "Vietnamization," but had become passengers on an express locomotive they had set in motion.

Even before the Phase IV withdrawals had been completed, in February 1971, Laird instructed the Joint Chiefs to prepare plans to provisionally reduce troop strengths to 153,600 by mid-1972.[30] If Kissinger had first seized the initiative, it was now Laird who took firm control of the levers. In fact, the defense secretary intended to play another hand, which he was keeping close to his chest. Bypassing both the Joint Chiefs and the White House, Laird had visited Abrams a month previously, on a trip via Paris and Bangkok, and confidentially informed the in-country team that his intention was to remove *all* combat troops by the end of the year, leaving behind only a military assistance group – in effect, catapulting the American commitment back to the Kennedy years, albeit with a more substantial force (60,000 by September 1972).[31] In what Laird was now terming a "de facto withdrawal timetable," a suggestion the White House had assiduously downplayed to avoid giving succor to Hanoi, Abrams dutifully instructed his staffs to prepare an augmented Phase V withdrawal plan (re-labeled Contingency Plan 208).

In the same way that Washington had entered the war betting on its air power, so Contingency Plan 208 made the reverse calculation: the risks of redeployment would be borne by the threat of unleashing the B-52s. Unlike the earlier period, Abrams could now count on a president who was not crippled by indecisions on this point. MACV labored for two months on the new plan, which was presented to Laird on March 16–17, 1971. In a quite dramatic reversal of his original position – Abrams had always maintained that MACV would require a 200,000-strong force until the end of 1972 – Contingency Plan 208 proposed the removal of 224,000 between May 1, 1971 and August 31, 1972. For COMUSMACV, the calculation had become a simple question of military common sense: with almost all combat troops withdrawn anyway by the end of 1971, there was little profit debating the retention of individual brigades. There came a point where you could not have too few; you could not have any. MACV would no longer enjoy the mass required to make a decisive difference on the battlefield. In this respect, by March 1971, America's war was sentenced.

Ironically, Abrams' capitulation had the contrary effect of galvanizing Nixon and Kissinger into reasserting White House primacy over "the endless maneuvering over withdrawal rates" and slowing down the redeployment rate.[32] With presidential elections due to be held in South Vietnam in September 1971, the administration judged it imperative to maintain stability through the presence of at least 200,000 US troops. An announcement of troop withdrawals stained with the taint of defeatism might have the opposite result.

In fact, Kissinger's revised proposal only proved marginally different to the Abrams plan (the withdrawal of 100,000 troops between May and December 1971). To avoid departmental in-fighting, both Laird and Abrams were cut out and only Rogers and Ambassador Bunker were kept in the loop. The difference between the two plans was largely in the presentation, delivered by Nixon. On April 7, 1971, the President informed the nation that the end was in sight. The goal was now "total American withdrawal from Vietnam." That the announcement was made against the background of the abortive South Vietnamese operation in Laos – *Lam Son 719* – sat uncomfortably at odds with the purported success of the policy of "Vietnamization" portrayed by Nixon. Congress little cared: with the Democrats in disarray, "Vietnamization" was now a breezy tailwind that would see the Republicans return Nixon to the White House for a second term.

For the marines who had spearheaded America's entry into the Vietnam War the end was now in sight. At the beginning of 1971, the now redesignated 3rd MAB (Marine Amphibious Brigade), commanded by Major General Donn Robertson, comprised just over 24,000 marines, based on 1st and 5th Regiments, located in Da Nang. In the first week of May, F Company, 2/1 Marines undertook the last marine combat operation in South Vietnam. The clearance operation took place a few miles south of Hill 34 near Da Nang – a spot Philip Caputo would have recognized. On June 26, the 3rd MAB commander, ten staff, and 53 marines boarded a KC-130 loaded with 2,000 pounds of paper files and flew away to Okinawa.[33] An era was over.

At the beginning of 1972, MACV's strength stood at 139,000. Combat operations officially ended. The 1972 Easter Offensive upset the withdrawal program, but only temporarily. For the White House, any hesitation might be interpreted as a failure of "Vietnamization" and undermine the bombing campaign. Preempting the offensive and responding to domestic pressures, Nixon announced another tranche of withdrawals on January 13. Couched under Contingency Plan 208, this would see another 70,000 men withdrawn (reducing MACV's strength to 69,000 by May 1, against the original 84,000 target).[34] On the same date, MACV would transition to Interim Vietnam Assistance Command (Interim VAC).

Alarmed by this accelerated timetable on the eve of a communist offensive, the Joint Chiefs, now led by Admiral Moorer, backed Abrams' call to halt or at least slow the pace of the withdrawals. Laird, however, took a hard-line position, insisting on an end-of-year strength of 15,000. This allowed Nixon to act as the moderate voice. Following a fact-finding mission by Haig, Nixon announced on April 26 that Increment (Phase) Twelve would see MACV reduced to 49,000 by July 1, 1972 (this was actually 11,000 more than Abrams had argued would be the minimum acceptable number). By now, Increment Eleven had been completed and the US Army's last full division, the 101st Airborne, had been shipped home. This respite lasted one month. On June 28, Nixon made a second announcement: no more draftees would be sent to Vietnam and MACV's strength would be reduced to 39,000 by September 1 (Increment Thirteen). In the event, total strength would fall below this figure before the end of August, which also witnessed the withdrawal of the last combat units. With some haggling, the war closed on schedule.

Against this background of interdepartmental scheming, a conspiratorial use of back channels, and controversies over the criteria for withdrawing individuals and units, it should be recognized that MACV's withdrawal from South Vietnam was a significant accomplishment. Between the summer of 1969 and the end of 1972 – over 13 redeployments – MACV withdrew 410,500 troops.[35] This amounted to the equivalent of 168 combat and combat support battalions. The downward trajectory of withdrawal was inexorable. In August 1969, MACV commanded 524,500 troops. By December, the number had fallen to 484,000; then 384,000 (October 1970); 254,700 (June 1971); 139,000 (January 1972); 49,000 (June 1972); and finally a rump of 27,000 support troops by November 1972.[36]

The formations tumbled out of South Vietnam as quickly as they had arrived. In the winter of 1969, 1st and 2nd Brigades, 9th Infantry departed. In 1970 they were followed by 1st Infantry (April, redeployed to Fort Riley, Kansas); 25th Infantry Division (complete in Schofield Barracks, Honolulu by May); 199th Infantry Brigade (October, redeployed to Fort Benning, Georgia); and 4th Infantry Division (December, redeployed to Fort Carson, Colorado). 9th Infantry also completed its redeployment in 1970, disbanded, and was subsequently stood up again at Fort Lewis, Washington as a test-bed division for new warfighting concepts in 1981.

By the beginning of 1971, MACV's field strength was down to 54 combat battalions. In March, the US Army's only tank formation in Vietnam, 11 Armored Cavalry Regiment, returned home, was inactivated and then 14th Cavalry in West Germany was reflagged as 11th ACR, preserving the name.[37] Some 600 M48A3 Patton tanks and 270 M551 Sheridan light tanks had made the Pacific crossing; roughly a third stayed in Vietnam, destroyed. In the same month, 5th Special Forces Group returned to Fort Bragg, North Carolina (a small element remained behind). These formations were followed by 1st Cavalry, less 3rd Brigade (April, redeployed to Fort Hood, Texas); 1st Marines and 1st Brigade, 5th Infantry in the summer; and 173rd Airborne in August (subsequently inactivated, an inglorious end to a good formation). Thus, by the summer of 1971 only nine combat brigades remained in South Vietnam, seven of these deliberately deployed in I Corps. This stance both reflected the threat of an opportunistic PAVN invasion from the north – which would be attempted the following year – but also the weakness of the Viet Cong in the south. In November, the notorious 23rd Americal Division was brought home and inactivated.[38]

The last major US Army operation was blandly named *OPORD 13-70*. It ran from July to early October 1971 and involved three battalions of 101st Airborne on the coastal plains of Thua Thien Province.[39] By February of the following year, the last full American division, 101st Airborne, had come home. Only two veteran brigades remained in-country: 196th Infantry in Da Nang, and 3rd Brigade, 1st Cavalry in Bien Hoa. Their role was defensive, or exactly the same role first proposed by Westmoreland in the spring of 1965, when the possibility of an American ground intervention became reality. South Vietnam was far from pacified, and the Easter Offensive served as an untimely reminder that the country faced an existential threat from the North, but, against the odds, Thieu seemed to be repeating the 1950s "miracle of Diem." Yet like his Viet Cong adversary, he too had become a client entirely dependent on the largesse of a patron. The question was: which stockholder cared most about the investment?

This question, in the summer of 1972, was unanswered. On June 26, 3rd Brigade 1st Cavalry quit Vietnam. Three days later, 196th Infantry followed. The last two combat battalions departed in August: 3/21st Infantry and, appropriately, 1/7 Cavalry, the veterans of Ia Drang.

The casualty statistics told the story of America's ground war.[40] Just over 58,000 servicemen lost their lives, 17 percent from non-combat causes. Over 300,000 were wounded. The mortality high-water mark was reached in 1968: 16,511 were killed. The US Army had suffered the bulk of fatalities (38,190), and within the army, the infantry had borne the brunt of the sacrifice (20,460). The two Marine divisions bled 14,836 lives. Only 725 tank crewmen were killed, but this represented a third of all tank crewmen sent to Vietnam. By a surprising margin this proved the most dangerous combat role. In a war of air mobility, it was unsurprising that 3,007 helicopter crewmen also lost their lives.

The most dangerous provinces were in the north: Thua Thien (2,893 fatalities), Quang Ngai (2,342), and Quang Tin (2,068). The incessant fighting around Kontum claimed 1,641 lives. In III Corps, the most violent provinces were Binh Duong (2,742), Tay Ninh (2,648), and Hua Nghia (1,424). These were the old War Zones C and D, and even older insurgent bastions from the First Indochina War. The Viet Minh had never really gone away. On a more mundane level, the highest casualty levels had simply correlated with the highest presence of US military. The lowest casualties, and therefore safest place to serve, were recorded in IV Corps (the Delta). This was the region with the shortest US military presence, which partially accounts for the low numbers, but it was also where the US Army stained its reputation with a campaign that poorly respected civilian life.

The ground withdrawal was matched by a curtailment of the air war, but this proved more divisive, opening a breach between Laird, who was determined to reduce the cost of the war, and a White House that increasingly viewed air power as a necessary vice in the peace negotiations. In 1969, B-52 sorties were cut from 1,800 to 1,400, and tactical air sorties fell to an average of 20,000 per month, from 24,000.[41] These savings foreshadowed much steeper cuts the following year. B-52 sorties were reduced to 1,000, and tactical air sorties were halved to 10,000. Laird was only prevented from implementing further cuts by the direct intervention of Nixon, who insisted on maintaining the 1971 sortie levels through the next financial year, and then only modestly cutting at the final withdrawal. He was only partially successful on this score: by 1973 Laird had out-maneuvered his boss and reduced tactical air sorties to just 6,000 per month.

The long, melancholy withdrawing roar of one army was replaced by the exponential growth of another: the ARVN. The administration had predicated its Vietnam strategy on "Vietnamization." It was the only credible way to sell quitting and avoid casting it as losing. Under the "One War" concept, Vietnamization became conjoined with Pacification. After so many false starts dating back to the Diem presidency, these two programs finally reaped tangible results. A Land to the Tiller Act, passed in 1970, promoted the biggest revolution in land ownership in Vietnam's postcolonial history. Over three years, 2.5 million acres of cultivable lands were transferred from landlords to farmers, virtually eliminating the pernicious tenant class which the French period had created. A revised Hamlet Evaluation Scheme (HES), not without its controversies, suggested that 95 percent of South Vietnam's rural population was now living in a "secure" area. This was partly due to rural depopulation away from contested areas, but it was also the case that the Viet Cong's grip had been weakened. It was too easy to criticize Pacification and forget that Hanoi deeply feared this program. Governance was spread through elected councils at district and provincial level, although the reality was that Thieu maintained iron control through the patronage of military and civil service posts. The unsatisfactory 1971 presidential election which confirmed Thieu's one party rule deepened this trend.

The militarization of South Vietnamese society proceeded apace, generating prodigious numbers. A roughly 1.4-million-strong People's Self-Defense Force at the beginning of 1969 swelled to 3.9 million by 1972. The National Police grew from 74,000 to 121,000. The Regional and Popular Forces were expanded from 300,000 to over half a million.[42] The ARVN, also roughly half-a-million strong, had never been better equipped, benefiting not only from a generous military aid program but also from equipment and facilities gifted by the departing US military. Over the same period, the enemy had never been weaker. On the eve of the Tet Offensive, the Viet Cong had mustered some 80,000 regular fighters. Two years later, the impact of this disastrous campaign was still evident. Guerrilla strength stood at 40,000, with perhaps an additional 20,000 in the local forces. The PAVN was distracted in Cambodia and Laos, and at bay in the north where a bombing campaign continued to exact attrition. MACV could justifiably claim that the period from the end of 1968 to the end of 1971 was the best of the war. In an unfortunate double irony, American soldiers and marines had become terribly good counterinsurgents, despite the reduced strength and discipline problems. But nobody was claiming victory, and Westmoreland's hope in 1967 that the allies would now start "winning it" had come to pass four years too late.

By the end of 1972, American boots were no longer on the ground, but the boot prints could not be so easily erased. The war held a reflected mirror to Americans, which provoked horror and denial in equal measure. Kissinger was right to observe that nobody had a monopoly on the anguish. He also recorded in his memoirs the many sincere attempts he made (as did Nixon) to reach across to those anguished Americans. A profound humanity illumes *The White House Years*. Any less interpretation is baseless yelling of histrionic critics determined to condemn Kissinger to "war criminal" status. Yet on the matter of war crimes, Kissinger, like virtually all the protagonists, fell dumb. It was as if Americans did not wish to believe, and therefore could not bring themselves to discuss, the possibility that an army sent to fight for the cause of freedom could have acted in such morally abhorrent ways. Volume one of *The White House Years* (covering 1969 to 1973) is over 1,400 pages long. Not one page is devoted to this issue.

The powder was laid from the beginning. From 1965 to 1971, taking the example from one corps area, just 27 marines were convicted of the murder of Vietnamese civilians. There were 16 charges of rape and 15 of manslaughter. The majority of cases were recorded in rear echelon units. The prosecution of a marine for murdering on a battlefield was extremely rare, yet an unknown but very high number of innocent South Vietnamese had been killed, in questionable circumstances, in the five northern provinces. The sentencing in these cases was inadequate. In the most notorious incident – the massacre of five women and 11 children in a village called Son Thang, an act conducted by a five-man "killer team" – three defendants were acquitted on trial, one received a five-year sentence, and one received a life sentence. US Marine Major General Charles Widdecke intervened and reduced these to one-year sentences. Perhaps the most shocking aspect of the episode was that the oldest member of the team was a 21-year-old. Three were teenagers and one was on his first patrol in Vietnam. Their youngest victim was a three-year-old boy. Another was a blind girl.

There were other disturbing aspects to this case which suggested a cultural unwillingness to acknowledge that American boys could "do wrong." The patrol leader and alleged instigator of the murders had been Private Randall Herrod. Herrod hailed from Calvin, Oklahoma. There was no local repulsion, quite the opposite. A petition in defense of Herrod was signed by 160,000 locally patriotic Oklahomans. Experienced Oklahoma attorneys volunteered their services pro bono. Character witnesses testified to Herrod's sound character (he actually had a poor record). A well-known Oklahoma psychiatrist was hired to testify that Herrod had been suffering from battle fatigue. The government was accused of persecution. Herrod, not the 16 Vietnamese, was the victim. The panel of seven officers on the court-martial acquitted him.[43]

The powder of war crimes eventually detonated in a manner neither Nixon nor Kissinger could have imagined. It was parceled in ten pages in the December 5, 1969 edition of *Life* magazine, Volume 67, Number 23. The contents could not have been guessed from the magazine's cover photograph which incongruously featured an African antelope. The title of the piece was "The Massacre of Mylai."

The story was introduced with a photograph resembling a Boschian phantasmagoria. The picture showed around 15 adults, as many as three infants and children, and two babies lying prostrate on a track. All were barefoot, some were naked, and all had been shot by American soldiers. In the center of the photograph was the strangest image of all: a young girl, bare legs splayed, with both hands reaching across her vagina, and there between her legs, a baby whose head seemed to have disappeared back inside her womb. Another lay on its back, staring upwards. A third naked baby lay strewn across the track like a rag doll with part of its foot taken off and a bullet mark across its left knee. One woman in a red shirt seemed to be asleep. Another had covered her face. A pool of blood spilled from her brain darkening the earth. A third woman in a red blouse seemed to grin lopsidedly, her face slashed by a bullet. About half the bodies lay face down and the rest drew their last breaths looking up at a perfectly blue spring sky. Thus, the image accusingly seemed to say, did American boys deal with the enemies of liberty.

The My Lai massacre took place on March 16, 1968, a year and a half before the story broke. The perpetrators of the massacre – C Company, 1st Battalion, 20th Infantry, of Task Force Barker – might well have got away with it but for a photographer and a conscientious soldier. On the day of the operation C Company invited US Army photographer, Sergeant Ronald Haeberle, to accompany the troops. The company wanted a record of their action which everyone believed was going to be "hot." He took with him three cameras: a camera with black and white film to record official photographs for publication in an army magazine, and two personal cameras with color film. The former he handed over to his superiors. The latter he kept hidden until November 20, the following year, now a discharged civilian. These he offered to *The Plain Dealer*, a newspaper in his hometown of Cleveland, Ohio.

The collection of photographs was met with incredulity and disbelief. There was agonized debate over whether the photographs could or should be published at all. Haeberle's credentials were checked and an army prosecutor advised that the newspaper should refrain from publishing the images. But news of a massacre had already leaked in a story authored by an unknown reporter called Seymour Hersh and the photographs corroborated the story. The publisher of *The Plain Dealer*, Thomas Vail, resisted official pressure and published Haeberle's pictures, supported by a story written by one of Haeberle's college friends, a reporter called Joe Eszterhas. Haeberle briefly became a household name before slipping back into obscurity working as a factory supervisor (in 2000, Haeberle cycled from Ho Chi Minh City to Saigon and stopped at the My Lai Museum where his photographs now hang. "It's beautiful," was his comment, "for something that didn't have to happen, but did.")[44]

The second route to exposure was the conscience of a former GI and helicopter door gunner, Ronald Ridenhour, now discharged and a college student, who wrote a letter on March 29, 1969 to 30 congressmen and Pentagon officials exposing the massacre. The letter started innocently enough: "It was late in April, 1968 that I first heard of 'Pinkville' and what allegedly happened there."[45] The clue was in "Pinkville." The name was taken from the map sector coloring, which happened to be pink, but the word had connotations with "Commie" and death. Americans, it was said, seemed to go "psycho" and abandon reason whenever the word communist was invoked.

The letter then went on to describe the massacre:

2nd Lieutenant Kally (this spelling may be incorrect) had rounded up several groups of villagers (each group consisting of a minimum of 20 persons of both sexes and all ages). According to the story, Kally then machine-gunned each group ... [it was] estimated that the population of the village had been 300 to 400 people and that very few, if any, escaped.[46]

Ridenhour conceded that he had no way of knowing the truth of the events of that day, but of course, what he exposed was the truth.

Orders for the assault mission had been given the previous evening by Captain Ernest Medina to C, B, and E Companies of Task Force Barker (the Task Force Commander, Lieutenant Colonel Frank Barker, would be killed three months later). The target was known as "Mylai 4" (four hamlets known to the Vietnamese as Son My). Two companies would act as cordons and C Company would assault enemy believed to be hiding in the hamlet. The intelligence was very specific: 48th NVA Battalion of 98th NVA Regiment was holed up in the village. At least one attendee at the orders group stated that Medina, a tough company commander of Mexican origins, was unambiguous on the point that the soldiers would only find NVA, VC, or their families in "Mylai 4."[47] By a perverse logic that had long overtaken the war, the hamlet, and every living thing inside the hamlet, therefore had to be destroyed. Hundreds of communities had suffered this fate in the past three years. This was a mission of routine, not extraordinary destruction. Medina, known as "Mad Dog" by his soldiers, later denied he made such an explicit statement or that he ordered the subsequent killing of innocent peasants. Nonetheless, there is sufficient anecdotal evidence that the tone of his orders group was heavy with mindless, ra-ra aggression that would have left many of his soldiers with the impression that they were entering My Lai to torch and kill.

The intelligence was flatly wrong – the 48th NVA Battalion was 150 miles away. Not a single hostile shot was fired at the soldiers. What the "intelligence" actually revealed was the hollowness of the strategy of "Clear and Hold."[48] The presence of US bases stiffening ARVN or militia satellite bases was neither clearing nor holding the countryside. Brigade intelligence cells had a poor understanding of what was happening in the countryside because a mere patrolling distance from the nearest base was an unknown world whose dynamics they never understood. Probably not a single soldier in Task Force Barker knew that Quang Ngai was inhabited by a mix of Hre, Co, Xo Dang, and Vietnamese ethnic groups with long histories. They were ignorant of the events of the First Indochina War (and indeed many of the mines trodden by American soldiers in this area were in fact legacy French devices, not VC booby traps).[49] They didn't even know what the last unit had done in the area. Nothing had substantially changed since the first marines landed in Da Nang in 1965. There had been countless operations and pacification initiatives in the environs and they had all come to nought. The sediment of resistance had not greatly changed since the French colonial period (Quang Ngai had been the first province to raise a guerrilla force in 1945). Incursions into the area by C Company proved pointless contrivances for incurring casualties as the soldiers stepped on mines or were shot by unseen snipers. This was later cited as a reason for the vindictiveness displayed by C Company, but acting as dumb bait for guerrilla traps was hardly a novel experience for American soldiers in Vietnam.

The operation began after sunrise, with C Company enjoying a five-minute helicopter ride from LZ Dottie and landing in fields west of My Lai. Haeberle landed in the second wave. By the time he was on the ground, a 19-year-old platoon leader was describing how they had entered the village, burned down a few hooches, taken a number of prisoners, and shot "five or six" people. There was nothing unusual in this except that the "prisoners" were all plainly civilians. Haeberle pressed on and encountered a GI emptying his M-16 into an uncomprehending cow. Nearby was a burning body twitching (which he photographed). The body had been deliberately covered in thatch so that it would burn better. All that was visible was a white sleeve and the outstretched hand of a young woman. The soldiers joked the body had ghosts in it.

He continued following the soldiers who found a terrified young woman hiding in the brush. The soldiers opened fire on the woman, whose body slumped against a wooden fence, leaving her head unnaturally upright like a practice target. The soldiers continued firing at the head. Haeberle recalled seeing pieces of bone flying through the air "chip by chip." The magnetic pull of gunfire drew Haeberle further down a track. He found a shocked boy who had been shot in the arm and leg. It was clear the child had absolutely no idea what was happening. A soldier alongside Haeberle ended the bewilderment. He fired one shot that sent the child reeling back, a second that knocked him flat and a third that killed him.

The myriad tracks leading away from the hamlet were proving death traps. Haeberle came across two boys running away. The younger one was shot and the elder boy then covered the body of the sibling as if to protect him from further fire. He too was shot. This scene became one of the most disturbing photographs of the set.

A father appeared out of the elephant grass leading two infants and carrying a basket of possessions. All three were gunned down. An elderly man who could barely walk and seemed to have eyesight problems stared into Haeberle's camera. Moments later two shots rang out and he was killed. Private Varnado Simpson opened fire on a man with a weapon running away, or this was the claim he later made. He actually fired on a woman carrying a baby whose startled wide-eyed face Haeberle photographed. They were only 20 yards away when Simpson opened fire – there could not have been any confusion.

A bullet had ripped through the baby's mouth, creating a ball-shaped, bloody orifice. The only soldier to escape My Lai was one of the black soldiers, named Carter. Sickened by what he was witnessing, he drew a Colt.45 and put a bullet through his foot. He was the only American casualty of the day.

These murders were mere sideshows to what Lieutenant William Calley was up to. This insecure and unimpressive 25-year-old officer from Miami was rounding up the peasants in groups and when he had a big enough group he was ordering his soldiers to kill them. In his personal statement at the subsequent court-martial Calley stated:

> I was ordered to go in there and destroy the enemy. That was my job that day. That was the mission I was given. I did not sit down and think in terms of men, women and children. They were all classified as the same, and that's the classification that we dealt with over there, just as the enemy. I felt then and I still do that I acted as I was directed, and I carried out the order that I was given and I do not feel wrong in doing so.

He also acted as rewarded. After the action at My Lai, Westmoreland awarded 11th Brigade a special commendation. In a war where the kill count was king, Calley was incentivized to do just that.

Interestingly, defense lawyer Major James Endicott, an impartial figure, believed Calley.

> Rusty Cally [sic], I think, was a misfitted commissioned lieutenant, an OCS graduate, a shake and bake lieutenant who honestly I think then and to this day thinks that his mission was to go in and do what they did. I honestly think Lt. Cally [sic] thought he was following orders.[50]

This, however, does not explain how a lieutenant in the US Army could believe that his given mission was to massacre 400 villagers.

As his soldiers were at first hesitant, he led the way and opened fire first. This "business-like" killing spree produced the second great and searing photograph of the series. A squad of soldiers came across a group of women and children and turned their rapine attention on a teenage girl dressed in black who they began to strip. Her name was Do Thi Can.[51] A fight broke out as her presumed mother tried to stop the Americans from raping the girl. The soldiers stopped when they noticed Haeberle's presence but only momentarily. Haeberle then took the photograph. It showed the girl buttoning her blouse while cradling a five-year-old boy, Do Hat, with her spare arm. In front of her was an elderly woman grimacing with another woman's arms wrapped around her waist. This was Pham Thi So. Behind her, to her right, was "the balding lady" "Phu" (Nguyen Thi Cung), the wife of the village headman. She was cradling Do Thi Be, her daughter. To her left was a boy in striped pants holding the leg of the baby. Within seconds they were all dead, mown down by a volley of automatic fire. Haeberle did not turn round or take a second photograph.

The experience of Phom Dat, a 40-year-old farmer, was typical of the day. He was taken with his wife and four children to a ditch immediately east of the hamlet. His house was burned down and his four cows and three pigs were killed. About one hour after arriving at the ditch, two soldiers opened fire on the villagers. He was shot in both legs and a bullet shattered his chin. Playing dead, he waited until the soldiers had gone. His wife, Phung Thi Ly, and three-year-old daughter, Pham Di Thu, were killed outright. The infant died cradled in her mother's arms. His 12-year-old daughter, Pham The Lom, had been shot in the leg but survived. His other two children, Pham Tai Chi (eight) and Pham Dan Danh (five), were also wounded in the lower limbs. Twelve other family members were killed in that group, including his mother.

Some peasants had miraculous escapes. Truong Thi Tung, an elderly widow, was living with her son, Do Tham, his wife, Pham Thi Em, and a three-year-old son, Do Thi Loc, when a group of three soldiers appeared outside her hooch and ordered the family outside. Her two cows and three pigs were shot by the soldiers and her house was burned down. The family was then frog-marched to the eastern edge of the village where they were made to sit in a ditch. Around 40 to 50 villagers were corralled in the ditch guarded by eight soldiers, while their houses were systematically burned. During a moment when the soldiers were distracted, Tung slid backwards into the elephant grass and crawled away. None of the guards noticed the missing old woman. It proved her salvation. Sometime later the ditch erupted with gunfire. Tung only re-emerged from her hiding place later in the afternoon when she was certain all the soldiers had left. All the villagers had been shot where they sat, including her son, daughter-in-law, and grandson. She then wandered back into the burned-out village and found a dazed 13-year-old girl, Do Thi Tang, whom she took under her protection. With no family or means to start a new life elsewhere, Truong Thi Tung, the unlikely survivor, restarted her life in Son My surrounded by the ghosts of the dead.

A similar escape was enjoyed by another illiterate widow in her late seventies, Pham Thi Tuu. She was forced into a ditch of water along with a large group of villagers (now a tourist site). When the villagers tried to protest at the two uncomprehending soldiers guarding them, they opened fire. Tuu was shot in the wrist and fell back in the water. The bullet ricocheted into her side. Bodies of the dead and wounded piled on top of her. Despite the pain she remained still until the afternoon when she recognized the voices of fellow villagers and called out for help. Amazingly, as many as ten other villagers were also still alive within the group. Tuu the widow would later identify a body of an elderly man found in the village well. The man was called Thuong Tho. Too old to march with the rest of the villagers, she had witnessed a soldier, described as "the boss," lose patience with the elderly Tho and cast him down the well.

Rape was piled on murder. Staff Sergeant Kenneth Hodges was alleged to have raped a girl. The same girl was also witnessed being forced to have sex simultaneously with three other soldiers.[52] Sergeant Charles Hutto gave testimony to witnessing two comrades, Esequiel Torres then Jolly, raping a young woman. Other members of the platoon watched the rape through the windows of the hooch. After Jolly had ejaculated, the girl was killed.[53] In the later inquiry the soldiers turned on each other in self-preservation: Hutto was himself accused of being one of the rapists along with soldiers Wright, Hutson, Rucker, and Mower by Varnado Simpson. Others accused of rape included soldiers Gunnen, Goodson (raping an old woman), James Dursi, Dennis Conti (a soldier who allegedly decorated his helmet with braids of hair from girls he had raped), and West. The casualness that some displayed to raping Vietnamese women was breathtaking. In his trial, Conti was asked: "Didn't you carry a woman half-nude on your shoulders and throw her down and say that she was too dirty to rape? You did do that, didn't you?" "Oh yeah," he replied, "but it wasn't at My Lai."[54] A full account of the sexual depravity demonstrated by the soldiers of C Company was never satisfactorily established.

Elsewhere, the horror show multiplied in geometric progressions. Piles of slaughtered Vietnamese were appearing at every turn. A bare-chested old man was found with a "C" slashed across his chest. To save bullets a soldier was found madly stabbing a calf that was vainly trying to seek the protection of its mother. A fountain of blood was spouting from its nose. Other soldiers were amusing themselves by killing piglets. Another soldier seemed to have lost all reason and was running after an elusive duck with his bayonet. In an unfortunate juxtaposition that seemed to symbolize the unscrambled end to the tumultuous sixties, the *Life* report was immediately followed by a festive gift advertisement for Canadian Lord Calvert Scotch.

The many arguments framed to "explain" the My Lai massacre – that is, bound the events within boundaries that serve to disinfect guilt – amount to abject exercises in gross moral bankruptcy. There are no "explanations" for the wanton murder of some 400 villagers.[55] It is arresting that from top to bottom, and across the spectrum of American society, this is exactly what was sought, or denial and cover up.

It is a banality to observe that no human being with a modicum of moral sense massacres defenseless men, women, and children in cold blood. Massacres classically happen as a consequence of religious extremism, secular ideological extremism, ethnic hatreds, racism, or a mix. Their substrate is the poison of dehumanization. The other person is no longer a human but a "gook," a "dink," a "slant-eye," vermin to be shot.

There was nothing special about C Company, 1st Battalion, 20th Infantry to distinguish it from any other infantry company in Vietnam. The soldiers of C Company later protested their ordinariness. They were not "baby-killers." They were regular Americans, "just like you." In this assertion, at least, they were bleakly truthful. Medina had moronically encouraged his men to leave an ace of spades on the bodies of dead guerrillas, as a calling card, but fluttering over My Lai was the far more disturbing battle standard of an out-of-control, anti-communist, racist religiosity.

It was no surprise the soldiers thought My Lai was "no big deal," or that they were amazed by the furor it provoked. The point about My Lai was that a soldier sent to Vietnam could be a trigger-pull away from acting like a thug. Americans could not face or discuss this (and mostly remain unwilling to do so today). "How do you shoot babies?" one of the perpetrators, Meadlo, was asked. "I don't know," he replied vacantly, "It's just one of them things."[56] But it wasn't. The villagers at My Lai were the victims of a particular face of fifties America – the America that upheld a self-righteous and fundamentalist self-image. Calley pointedly saw the whole episode in Biblical terms. When he eventually came to trial, Reverend Michael Lord, leading a revivalist meeting in the Memorial Stadium in Columbus, Georgia, compared his court-martial to the crucifixion of Christ.[57]

Faced with the growing scandal, Nixon placed politics above ethics, perhaps not a challenging personal choice. Four months before the Calley trial, Nixon set up a "My Lai Task Force," employing a cabal of White House loyalists to minimize the public relations fallout. He shamefully suggested the use of "dirty tricks," such as discrediting Hugh Thompson, the helicopter pilot and single American soldier who acted with courage and honor to protect the villagers.[58] This was hardly necessary as Thompson had already become a public hate figure, a "traitor" living with death threats and enduring the macabre display of dead animals left on his porch. Two corrupt congressmen serving on the House Armed Services Committee, in cahoots with Nixon, set about exploiting arcane constitutional arrangements in an attempt to sabotage the forthcoming trial. Two days after the conclusion of the court-martial, in which Calley received a life sentence, Nixon instructed that Calley be placed under house arrest, pending appeal. Three and half years later Calley was paroled and discharged. Today he lives a quiet life in Columbus, Georgia.

Calley had been charged with the premeditated murder of "Oriental human beings," revealing even in the trial proceedings the suggestion of subconscious racism. As Calley's case was the first to be heard, the effect of this presidential intervention was the collapse of the cases against 29 other defendants. Nobody, in the end, was convicted. At the time, the White House was receiving 25,000 letters a day in defense of Calley. Voters mattered.

On the eve of the public revelation of the massacre a worried Laird held a telephone conference with Kissinger.[59] At no point did either individual express moral outrage or even the necessity to establish the truth. Laird suggested he would "like to sweep the whole thing under the carpet." Kissinger wisely advised not. Neither was Laird especially troubled by the fact that American soldiers committed atrocities, only that they had gone too far on this occasion: "You can understand a little bit of this, but you shouldn't kill that many." In a rehearsal of the many excuses that would be made, Laird suggested that "insanity" was to blame, or "that those boys had been suffering terribly" – they, not the villagers, were the victims. Both men agreed that the pressing imperative was "a game plan" and a "press policy," as morally insolvent a response to a massacre as may be imagined. This was an especially low point for two officials of generally honorable dispositions.

The participants predictably resorted to the Nuremberg defense. Hodges, charged with alleged murder and rape, defended himself, "As a professional soldier, I had been taught to carry out the orders and at no time did it ever cross my mind to disobey or to refuse to carry out an order that was issued by my superiors."[60] There is no such thing as a lawful military order to murder or rape civilians.

The Peers Commission subsequently revealed the depth and scale of the military cover up. Individuals charged included Major General Samuel W. Koster, the Americal Division's commanding officer, Brigadier General George H. Young, Jr. his assistant, the 11th Infantry Brigade commander, Colonel Oran K. Henderson, and the Task Force Barker commander, Lieutenant Colonel Frank Barker – or every level of command. A further ten mid-ranking officers were also charged. Not only did 11th Infantry Brigade cover up, it openly lied, filing an after-action report in which it claimed "the enemy suffered a hard blow" with over one hundred killed (hence Westmoreland's unit citation). This behavior may have been expected from a corrupt operational chain of command. But it extended in surprising directions. The outraged pilot Thompson not only reported the massacre to his operational chain of command, he also told the divisional chaplain. This man of God, it seems, was no less morally inadequate than the rest.

The truly shocking response, however, brilliantly examined in both Joanna Bourke's *An Intimate History of Killing* and Bernd Greiner's *War Without Fronts: The USA in Vietnam*, was manifested by majority American public opinion, the media, and the troops themselves. Americans were simply unwilling to accept that their soldiers could do wrong. "We're the good guys," as Captain Larry Burke serving with 1st Infantry put it, "We're the ones who are going to go save the world from Communism."[61] Their attitude echoed the unrepentant and self-exculpating outlook of some Germans after the war (and majority Japanese opinion). State capitals lowered their flags to half-mast in protest over the Calley trial.[62] One poll found that two thirds of respondents dismissed the massacre as one of those things that happens in wars. Another found that four fifths disagreed with the trial. From within this group, a stunning 20 percent judged the massacre not a crime. A third survey found that roughly half of respondents judged that Calley was merely doing his duty, by implication untroubled by the proposition that the duty of an American soldier was to massacre civilians. "Free Calley" rallies were witnessed across the country. The lyrics of "The Battle Hymn of the Republic" were rewritten in a paean to Calley. The record sold one million copies in one week. Pete Seeger's reply, "Last Train to Nuremberg," fared less well. When a book was eventually written on Calley, it was entitled "The Making of a Hero."

The endurance of this cultural self-righteousness and denial has been remarkable. It is evident in scores of veterans' websites, hundreds of Vietnam blogs, and in forums where a commitment to historical truth might be expected. Forty years after the My Lai massacre, the Laurens County Historical Society, on the opening page of its "Pieces of Our Past" webpage, included a missive on Sergeant Kenneth Hodges – accused of rape and murder – portraying him as a "sensitive and caring," God-fearing, wronged man, from a good local family.[63] In the stock inversion of this genre of writing, he was the victim, not the villagers he was alleged to have raped and murdered. The encomium concluded:

> And today … you may find him at home, doing what he loves to do, cooking a delicious meal and enjoying life with this wife, Margaret. Sometimes he closes his eyes and watches himself starring in a bad biographical movie which is now showing the good parts. And, it looks like there will be a wonderful and oh so happy ending.

It would be difficult to imagine tolerance of such a web post if the subject were a retired German soldier who had murdered Jews. Distinguished historian Stephen Ambrose has made exactly that comparison and begged the question: "I have spent a lot of time since trying to understand how this could happen – how American boys could do what SS boys did …"[64] He was unable to answer his own question.

This denial is balanced by the many veterans who have faced up to dark pasts. "It wasn't that we were fighting the bad guys," marine veteran Calixto Cabrera has expressed, "it was that we were the bad guys."[65] The same individual blamed the "rabid" anti-communism in American culture which could justify any excess "and call it freedom."

> In Vietnam it was just denials after denials after denials and then they would deny it some more. It took something like My Lai to come along that it was so big by comparison to what had been going on generally speaking throughout the whole war theater. It was just so big they couldn't cover it up and too many leaks they couldn't cover it up and they had to address it.

In this last judgment, he was only half-right.

Westmoreland lamely and wrongly asserted that My Lai was an "aberration." From January 1965 to August 1973 there were 36 US Army trials for crimes against civilians in Vietnam, excluding the My Lai massacre proceedings.[66] By comparison, US soldiers committed an estimated 3,500 acts of rape in France from June 1944 to the end of the war. From just over 900 convictions, 29 men were executed, all but five of whom were black soldiers.[67] The US Army was far more diligent in pursuing the rape of European women. Even the Soviet Army in the Second World War – notorious for its abuses, especially in Germany – convicted 4,148 officers and soldiers for atrocities.[68]

Across the 36 Vietnam trials, roughly a third were for murder, and one sixth for rape charges. This total is totally unrepresentative of the scale of either crime. The secret Vietnam War Crimes Working Group found 320 substantiated incidents, and a further 500 that could not be properly investigated. The 9,000-page study was declassified as a matter of bureaucratic routine in the mid-1990s. It was subsequently removed from public record in 2002 as its existence became more widely known and its contents investigated. Before reclassification, graduate student Nick Turse managed to obtain copies of some 3,000 pages. Combined with veteran interviews, this material served as the basis for his harrowing *Kill Anything That Moves: The Real American War in Vietnam*. Specific "rogue" units and operations had been identified by previous authors – Operation *Speedy Express*, Operation *Wheeler/Wallowa*, the Phoenix Program, the "Tiger Team" – but Turse's book highlighted that many formations in Vietnam manifested problems and these were more endemic than ever admitted.

It is at this juncture that the "explanations" for the war crimes committed in Vietnam are typically invoked. The average age of the soldiers; low educational standards; poor junior leadership, and peer pressure; the desire to be accepted; misplaced group loyalty; fears of sexual inadequacy; the unpopularity of the draft; inadequate training; a tactical philosophy that placed so much weight, literally, on firepower; the moral hazard of free fire zones; the perverse incentivizing of the body count; the intense competition in the officer promotion ladder (15,000 lieutenant colonels chasing 300-odd battalion commands in Vietnam) and the concomitant rewards that fell to those who could demonstrate aggressive spirit; the destructive effects of bombing, and especially weapons like napalm, that struck many as far worse than the acts of a simple infantryman; the difficulties of separating guerrilla from civilian; the intrinsically dirty nature of a guerrilla war; the difficulties of dealing with "the unseen enemy"; the casual attitudes to civilian death engendered by the mantra "if it's dead it's VC," the neutral personal pronoun dehumanizing Vietnamese, whether dead or alive; cultural clashes and incomprehension; the language barrier – all are invoked and all were undeniably contributing factors.

But none exculpate a US military culture that failed to face up to a moral degeneration, that colluded to cover up this reality, and that even fomented it through its doctrine and tactics. The true number of US military war crimes in Vietnam will never be determined. There is sufficient evidence to indicate it is a four-figure number. There were just 23 convictions of US Army personnel. The maximum sentence was given to a military intelligence interrogator who raped a 13-year-old girl. He received a 20-year term and served seven months.

The failure was institutional and the fish rotted from the head. As early as the fall of 1965, rules of engagement predisposed a war that would treat civilian life casually. In tandem with escalation, Westmoreland issued directives allowing both unobserved artillery fire and "free bomb zones" (MACV Directives 525-18 and 95-4). When the latter attracted media criticism the term was changed to "specified strike zones," but this changed nothing. The principle that an assessed VC village was "fair game" was also very quickly established. But this category also embraced any settlement from which soldiers or marines received fire. In practice, virtually any hamlet or village was a potential "target."

When marine gunnery officer Charles Allen (son of an Episcopalian minister) first deployed to Vietnam he was "very concerned" by the notion of "free fire zones" because of the obvious "fallacy" that families living in these areas were de facto enemy.[69] Following an incident in which six comrades were badly wounded, his attitude hardened. "From that point forward I figured I would shoot first and ask questions later." Asked later whether this was the common experience he replied, "Definitely, no question about it."

Marine Calixto Cabrera recalled the same desensitization of outlooks. After "some random fragging" of an area, the company he was with came across "an eight-year-old boy" with a leg wound.

> He had a chunk of his leg the size of a tennis ball ... it was a weird wound, gone from his leg. So he's standing there and we're all walking by and he's pointing to this chunk of his leg that is gone. Basically he was asking for

help and we just all walked by. We just all walked by. He was not offered aid. The corpsmen or nobody did a thing for this boy, nobody.[70]

Within a matter of months of entering the war, MACV was well aware that American firepower would result in large numbers of civilian fatalities and injuries unless more stringent rules and restraints were agreed and imposed. What forced consideration of the problem, however, was not unease of these civilian deaths but a "rash" of media reports landing on the desk of the Chairman of the Joint Chiefs in Washington suggesting that US forces were bombing and blasting their way into South Vietnam in an indiscriminate fashion. It was for this reason and under pressure from Wheeler that Westmoreland requested a study of the problem in September of 1965.[71] Actually, for Westmoreland, the real problem was the "wasteful" application of air power. When the study reported, a conclusion was drawn that "Incidents of errors were surprisingly few in number," but "changes were necessary only to cope with the US buildup in RVN."[72] The problem of civilian deaths was judged marginal and the focus fell instead on proposing measures to avoid the "wasteful" use of air power.

The notion that incidents of civilian deaths were "few" demonstrated myopia at best and untruthfulness at worst. In this judgment, the military was supported by more patriotic correspondents like Joseph Alsop who described critics of bombing as "twaddle merchants" engaged in a "loud, goose-like cackle."[73] Consequent recommended procedural changes were either unrealistic (such as issuing a warning before bombing or shelling a village); euphemistic (the "specified strike zones" which became the even more mealy-mouthed "jettison areas"); or just frankly inadequate (collating all rules of engagement in a single document, as if the tiresomeness of having to read multiple documents was contributing to civilian deaths). Helicopter pilot Fred Beck remembered that the so-called "Jepp manual" (named after the civilian company that printed the manuals – Jeppeson Company) was around 300 pages long and changed every month.[74] But the fundamental reason why MACV's rules of engagement were woefully and arguably criminally short was that the command hierarchy, from Wheeler downwards, abrogated moral responsibility over civilian deaths in the formulation of policy, and furthermore never revisited this policy in any meaningful way when it was evident that US firepower was plainly killing and injuring large numbers of innocent civilians.

The refusal to acknowledge the truth over the scale of civilian deaths was arresting. Concerned with the drift of the campaign, Senator Fulbright sought figures on civilian deaths as early as the beginning of 1966. The totally incredible response received from McNamara's office was six dead and 15 wounded civilians from all US military actions, across Vietnam, in the first two months of the year. As this period coincided with Operation *Masher/White*

Wing, to name one major operation, the reality was that many, many more than this number of civilians were being killed or injured every day.

Education was not lacking. Soldiers were issued with the "Nine Rules" card, emphasizing "strength, generosity and understanding" in conduct towards Vietnamese. By December 1965, US servicemen received a rules of engagement card and one-hour mandatory lecture on the avoidance of civilian casualties. The latter warned against "wild and indiscriminate firing against populated places, or vengeful burning of houses and hamlets as blind and wholesale reprisal for Viet Cong sniper fire."[75] Appeal was made to a mythologized sense of honor:

> Throughout our history, American fighting men have fought clean. American fighting men don't kill non-combatants, if they can possibly help it. American fighting men don't kill women and children, either in the heat of battle or in cold-blooded reprisal against enemy sniper fire. American fighting men don't molest or insult the women. American fighting men don't deliberately destroy the houses and private property of innocent civilians.

The lecture script advised that such behavior was "not only wrong in and of itself, but if there is anything that could cause us to lose this new kind of struggle we're in, this kind of thing is it." This common sense and basic morality were roundly ignored. In Vietnam, the mythologized "American fighting man" committed all these acts.

From 1965 to 1968, MACV and subordinate formations promulgated some 40 directives on the minimization of civilian casualties.[76] A revelatory aspect of the My Lai preliminary investigation by the Department of the Army was a bureaucratic obsession with such directives: an entire volume of the investigation report totaling almost 500 pages was devoted simply to *itemizing* these directives.[77] Review of this body of official documentation presents a culture of self-delusion and outright denial. Efficient process and paperwork acted as a moral blindfold. As long as the paperwork was all in order, everything was fine. The Americal Division published its own seven-page Rules of Engagement (Regulation 525-4), suspiciously on the same day of the My Lai massacre, and its policy on the Safeguarding of Non-combatants, eight days after the massacre.[78] But as a member of the division later testified, "I became absolutely convinced that as far as the United States Army was concerned there was no such thing as murder of a Vietnamese civilian."[79] Commanded by the autocratic and feared Kosner, any suggestion that the division was acting wrongly was suppressed, a collective mendacity described as "a game," as everyone knew what was going on.

The facts are that US divisions in South Vietnam did not just pay lip service to these regulations; they deliberately pursued tactics that contradicted in spirit and in specifics MACV's own avoidance of non-combatant casualty doctrine and regulations. Westmoreland's personal policy guidance to senior commanders unequivocally stated: "Minimize non-combatant battle casualties through discreet, controlled application of firepower."[80] As the American war in Vietnam may be characterized as the exact opposite of this guidance, it at least raises questions over the commitment to this policy. At soldier level, in individual and unit cases, there was flagrant disregard. This was tolerated and covered up when it led to civilian deaths.

Westmoreland knew that US operations were resulting in large numbers of civilian deaths, but his response was inadequate and deflecting. On August 28, 1966 he held a commander's conference in Nha Trang attended by over 40 officers of general rank. In that year there had been 103 recorded incidents, almost certainly an underestimation. While conscious that this was a "very sensitive subject," he nonetheless described the number as "miniscule" and attributed the problem to "mechanical failure" or "human error," not the tactics that he himself was promoting.[81] The following year there was a fivefold increase in reported incidents (567). At a December 3, 1967 commander's conference he cast this as a problem of "safety" and training, not ethics or tactics.[82] To concede that "the American way of war" was fundamentally incompatible with the conflict in Vietnam would have fatally undermined the entire basis of his campaign plan.

The Nuremberg defense invoked by the perpetrators of the My Lai massacre was a widespread self-exculpating sentiment, tacitly or openly stated. That soldiers were being ordered to burn villages or shoot fleeing Vietnamese as "suspect VC" undoubtedly served to confirm in their minds that what they were doing was not "wrong." The destruction of villages, the killing of domesticated animals, the spoiling of rice supplies, and the poisoning of wells were all officially sanctioned tactics. Excessive and indiscriminate use of firepower added to this destruction. Reward for high kill counts inflated it. Extraordinarily, this scorched earth policy was in direct contradiction to MACV's own policy on the control, disposition, and safeguarding of Vietnamese property, captured materiel, and food supplies, described in MACV Directive 525-9 (and numerous other directives).[83] In practice, American formations and units were deliberately flouting this policy. There is undeniably a strong case that at soldier level, confusion over what constituted ethical conduct in war may have been expected.

But this argument only offers so much "explanation." Westmoreland infamously allowed himself to be filmed opining that Asians held life in less regard than Westerners: "The oriental doesn't place the same high price on life as the Westerner."[84] By implication, the loss of Vietnamese lives was not an equal calculation. This subconscious racism was widespread. Veteran Scott Camil expressed a common sentiment:

> As time went on, I came to a point where I didn't consider them people at all … I called them gooks. I considered them gooks. I didn't know what a gook was but … they weren't like human beings. I didn't have the same feelings if I saw one of them laying there hurt that I would have towards an American or even a dog.[85]

MACV addressed racism with aide-memoires and a plethora of directives. In practice, this education and training was competing against incomprehension, hostility, condescension, a sense of superiority, and the temptation of sexual exploitation, far more powerful forces. A failure of leadership only deepened the problem. The number of bastard children fostered by US serviceman serves as one measure. In 1987, Congress passed the Amerasian Homecoming Act, permitting resettlement of these children. By 1994, some 25,000 had arrived in the United States.[86] The total number of Vietnamese Amerasians has been estimated at 77,000.[87]

In the summer of 1971, *Armed Forces Journal* published an article penned by USMC Colonel Robert D. Heinl, Jr.[88] Heinl was an Iwo Jima and Korea veteran who 15 years earlier had written a noted essay on the necessity for strong leadership in the armed forces.[89] His second piece was entitled "The Collapse of the Armed Forces." In it, Heinl charged: "The morale, discipline and battle-worthiness of the U.S. Armed Forces are, with a few salient exceptions, lower and worse than at any time in this century and possibly in the history of the United States." Over 18 painful pages, he itemized with candor the symptoms of this collapse, concluding "we have met the enemy and they are us." No revelation was especially new. What mattered was that a senior serving officer was openly discussing these in an official journal. Before ending his command at MACV, General Abrams begged the question, "Is this a god-damned army or a mental hospital?"[90] Heinl's article amounted to a description of that mental hospital.

This was an army riven by "pandemic drug addiction, race war, sedition, civilian scapegoatism, draftee recalcitrance and malevolence." Individuals and units refused orders and combat. Fragging officers had become commonplace, notably in formations like the American Division. Grenades were used as escalatory warnings: first a yellow smoke grenade, then red smoke, then CS gas, and finally a white phosphorus or high explosive grenade.[91] Soldiers were placing bounties on officers' heads. Unauthorized dress regulations had spread, evident in the body of war photography showing soldiers with long hair, sporting peace symbols, or other peace paraphernalia. Blacks segregated themselves in rear areas (race relations were rarely a problem on the front line) and substituted the army salute with the Black Power salute. Officers were too intimidated to stop this practice.

Fragging became more than an isolated problem. Ninety-six incidents were reported in 1969. In the subsequent two years the numbers grew to 209 and 215. In total, some 551 fragging incidents were reported, resulting in 86 deaths.[92] "You could run into a lot of officers in the military who were jerks," opined Jerry Benson who served as an infantryman with 1/18 Infantry, "That were trying to play the 'I'm in charge' scenario ... I'm in charge and you're the private."[93] Some 90 percent of the assailants were under the influence of drugs when they attacked (but only seven percent were draftees, scotching the notion that these reluctant soldiers were more susceptible to ill-discipline). "Combat refusals" also rose – nobody, as the saying went, wanted to be the last soldier to die in Vietnam. In 1968, there were 68 convictions for "combat refusals." In the subsequent two years there were 248 convictions.[94] The most notorious case involved a platoon from 7th Cavalry that refused to advance in the middle of a live CBS Evening News broadcast, describing the order as "nonsense."

Draftee Charles Sabatier vividly recalled a general discontent with young, inexperienced officers regarded as "buffoons":

> By this stage in your life ... you're not going to put your life on the line for somebody just because they gave you an order to do it ... we're not going to die for nothing. We're not gonna ... be court-martialed by some fool, either.[95]

Marine Chuck Sawyer felt the same way about his "idiot" officer:

> Our captain, who, to this day I still consider an idiot, took us back three nights in a row to this same hilltop. Common sense tells you, you don't do that ... Now, they didn't do a ground attack, thank goodness, but they did blow the dickens out of everything in sight, including me. It blew my foot, my right foot apart, put some shrapnel in my head and then my left forearm and made me pretty mad.[96]

In retirement he offered, "We were inept, totally inept. Supposedly the most technically advanced war machine you could put on the field and some of the best troops you could ever have, and yet we couldn't beat these guys." On his second tour, Marine Calixto Cabrera also became truculent: "To take a patrol out just because some fucking lieutenant was told by some fucking captain who was told by some fucking colonel to send a patrol out there, there's no way."[97] Others, by contrast, were more understanding. David Adcock, serving with 1/7 Cavalry, had sympathy for the lieutenants:

> The lieutenants had a rough time. They had a rough job because they were just young soldiers like we were and carrying an awesome responsibility but a lot of times they'd make mistakes in their judgment and it would cause the rest of us to be kind of wary of them.[98]

Reflecting trends in civilian society, drug use rose alarmingly, again overwhelmingly in the rear areas. By the first full year of Nixon's presidency, probably a majority of servicemen had used drugs in Vietnam, principally marijuana. This widespread use was evident in drug arrests, which only captured a relatively small proportion of users. In 1966 there had been 344 arrests. Three years later, the number was 8,466.[99] Two years later, heroin and high potency opiate use raised even greater concern. As many as one in ten soldiers was using heroin, which cost as little as a "pack of cigarettes." Overall, one fifth of servicemen may have experimented with these hard drugs. In rear areas, this rose to half.[100] Drug use and the speed with which it spread seemed to catch MACV by surprise. Westmoreland raised the issue with Sharp and Wheeler in January 1968, distracted by the imminent Tet Offensive.[101] A coherent anti-drug strategy – Directive 190-4 – was only finally promulgated in December 1970. Medical corpsman George Cantero recalled of his unit that as many as 20 soldiers were using heroin, and by the time he left "everybody I knew was gone."[102] Pot smoking had become fashionably rife and brazen. Again, in Cantero's recollection, for a box of Tide soap powder a soldier could buy a carton of marijuana cigarettes soaked in opium. A vial of pure heroin cost ten dollars.

Some 144 seditious underground newspapers proliferated, one openly urging soldiers to kill their officers. A plethora of civilian organization was dedicated to undermining the armed forces. University campuses became hotbeds of anti-war resistance. Subversion was abetted by sympathetic litigation. Racial tensions and violence were common. Desertions were on the rise. Heinl wrote from the perspective of a proud serviceman who could not bear the spectacle he was witnessing. His dismal survey of the state of affairs in the US armed forces was not inaccurate.

Of the three facets of Nixon's liquidation of the Vietnam War, securing a peace settlement proved the most intractable and ultimately the most controversial.

There were two forums for the peace talks. The public negotiations were held in the Paris *belle époque* Majestic Hotel on Avenue Kléber, a former headquarters of the German Army of occupation, later requisitioned by the US Army. These talks were a necessary charade. Over four years there were 174 meetings. In Kissinger's sarcastic verdict they achieved the great distinction in the history of diplomacy in that not "a single accomplishment however trivial" was achieved. Four senior American public figures dutifully took their penitential turn at the negotiating table, whose shape was the only point of agreement between the parties: Averell Harriman, Henry Cabot Lodge, David Bruce, and William Porter. The forum was only sustained because both parties needed to be seen to be seeking a peace deal, for international and domestic audiences. Crucially, for Hanoi, the public peace talks were linked with the 1968 bombing suspension. Nixon was quite right when he observed that the pretense in the Majestic Hotel amounted to little more than a weekly forum which Hanoi used to erode American domestic support for the war.[103]

If the war was to be concluded through a peace deal, however imperfect, then this process would have to take place in private, in secret talks. These clandestine discussions brought about the collision of two contrasting personalities: Henry Kissinger and Le Duc Tho. For Kissinger, diplomacy was the epitome of civilized behavior, a gracious and nuanced game which had inspired him as an academic. Now elevated to statesmanship himself, it was a stage where his battery of intellectual powers would be exercised in a measured *pas de deux* in which the natural conclusion should be compromise and mutual respect. The tall, angular Le Duc Tho took a quite different view. Diplomacy for Hanoi's chief negotiator was a matter of relentlessly wearing down your opponent with long monologues, conceding nothing, and casting your side as absolutely morally right. Hanoi had no intention to negotiate – at least as any American interlocutor would have understood it – the communists sought and demanded surrender.

Johnson had originally justified the war to himself on the grounds of American "prestige." This proved a treacherous concept. Saving South Vietnam had been dismissed as just "ten percent" of the reason why the United States should take a stand in Indochina, a point conveniently forgotten by Democrats who subsequently criticized Nixon for cynically sacrificing Saigon. Nixon would quit a war invoking the very same reason, but in radically different circumstances. Giving up on Vietnam would amount to "a renunciation of our morality, an abdication of our leadership among nations, and an invitation for the mighty to prey on the weak," or constitute the fatal blow to American prestige. "This," he had emphatically stated in his April 26 speech, "we shall never do."[104]

For Nixon, the peace negotiations were always about America's destiny and place in the world, not personal, electoral salvation. By 1968, this had distilled to ending the trauma of a deeply divisive war. But how this could be achieved with dignity and due recognition to the sacrifice was not obvious at his investiture, and policy evolved in tandem with the course of the war over the next four years. This took place against a background of increasingly constrained options and a hostile Congress. The Republican administration did not start out with the intention of selling an ally down the river. The contemptuous view that the White House sought a "healthy interval for South Vietnam's fate to unfold" – in Kissinger's phrase – does not acknowledge that Nixon consistently adopted unpopular policies, often relishing his solitary stand against critics, which no vote-grubbing politician would have countenanced.[105] Nixon boasted he did not care if he served as a one-term president, and it was no idle boast. Over Vietnam, he acted like one too. "We can lose an election," Nixon once confided privately to Kissinger, "but we're not going to lose this war, Henry."[106]

The other actors hardly played ethical or helpful parts. A coterie of congressmen sought to humiliate Nixon, even at the cost of losing the war and peace. This offstage audience found nothing good to say over Kissinger's contortions to secure a just peace settlement, and in some instances supported amendments that deliberately undermined his efforts. The East Coast press remained uniformly hostile. At first ignorant of the secret talks, no major broadsheet found a spirit of generosity in editorials when they were eventually revealed. The notion that the United States should withdraw from Vietnam as an expression of policy, and not government implosion, was dismissed. Many actively sought that implosion. Protestors and critics collapsed Vietnam into a single "Madman Theory" and berated the lunatic in the White House with a stridency matched only by their unrealistic demands. Academia turned its back on the government, snobbishly and sometimes with intellectual dishonesty. Thieu went along with the secret talks, feigning agreement then pulling the rug from under the negotiations at the eleventh hour. Ironically, Nixon's best support came from Moscow and Peking, both making the pragmatic decision that their support for Hanoi was outweighed by their separate desires for rapprochement with the United States. But they were no more able to influence the hard men in the Hanoi politburo than Washington could guarantee South Vietnam's survival. At the United Nations, Vietnam became background white noise, best ignored because nobody could offer a credible resolution to the war. Perhaps the only party that actually enjoyed the peace negotiations, if with a sense of *Schadenfreude*, were the French. It is inconceivable the Sûreté did not bug all the talks and intercept North Vietnamese diplomatic communications.

Despite starting out with all the zeal of a new administration, 1969 proved a wasted year. Nixon inherited both the form of Johnson's peace negotiations and the chief negotiator – Averell Harriman. The inheritance proved empty. The quite unrealistic position advanced by Harriman, supported by his deputy, Cy Vance, essentially boiled down to a total withdrawal of communist forces from South Vietnam, a supervisory period of six months during which the United States would test Hanoi's good faith, free elections, and an indefinite period over which a small, residual US force would remain in the South. This position had roots in Johnson's earlier and equally bankrupt "Manila formula," which had similarly been spurned by Hanoi. This should not have surprised. From the North's perspective the American negotiating posture was a treacherous twin to French proposals 20 years previously, which had proved empty and duplicitous. In the communist narrative – shared by Peking – 1954 was the critical year when America's relationship with East Asia took a wrong turn. Every subsequent ill had flowed from decisions taken by the arch villain of the period – in the communist view – Secretary of State Foster Dulles. Neither should it have come as a surprise that Hanoi's riposte to this stance was utterly disdainful: all US forces should unilaterally withdraw and the Saigon government be replaced by a communist-led Provisional Revolutionary Government.

Despite Kissinger's considerable intellectual firepower, he entered the vexed cockpit of peace negotiations a self-confessed novice (albeit a quick learner), and shackled, like the rest of the protagonists, by the intractable legacy. The exquisite torture that Kissinger would later record in *The White House Years*, describing his dealings with the implacable North Vietnamese delegation, would be matched by the equal torture of domestic enemies who sabotaged reasonable debate on a strategy for ending with war with moralizing lectures, as if the White House incumbents were wayward, arms-toting teenagers. Kissinger entered the game doubtful that "Vietnamization" would work, accepting that military victory was a distant prospect, and, as he later confessed, naive in his belief that the two parties might achieve equitable agreement. Where Kissinger entered the negotiations fortified by a belief in "the efficacy of goodwill and the importance of compromise" he faced an opponent armed with a "ferocious self-righteousness ... [compounded by] ... an infuriatingly doctrinaire technique of advocacy."[107] For Le Duc Tho, the talks were a monologue of demands stated in the imperative voice. As Kissinger later recalled, it felt like a great breakthrough when the haranguing imperative "must" subtly mellowed to a more reasonable conditional "should" – after two years of negotiations.

In fact, over the first months of the administration, Kissinger had little control over the peace talks which were still dominated by the Harriman agenda and an institutional momentum State was unwilling to surrender. The first peace talks of the Nixon presidency took place on March 22.

They produced the usual pointless restatement of positions but no more. Led by Xuan Thuy, a Foreign Minister functionary with no authority to negotiate settlement anyway, there was little hope the North Vietnamese would be more forthcoming to the new president. On May 8, at the 16th plenary meeting, the communists threw down the gauntlet of a ten-point plan, a prickly document bunged with the usual "musts" and lectures on what was "correct and logical." The chief "must," naturally, was that neo-imperialist America and her lackey allies should quit South Vietnam, and the puppet clique of Thieu-Ky-Huong should hand over power to the "liberation" forces. Nixon felt obliged to respond to this proposal on May 14 with an eight-point plan, announced on television. Significantly, the White House signaled an abandonment of the Harriman position with a more conciliatory stance offering recognition of the National Liberation Front (NLF), tacit understandings over withdrawal of communist forces, and a general ceasefire. Predictably, the compromise elicited rejection.

Kissinger made just three contributions to the peace talks in 1969, and all ended in frustration. In the spring, an abortive Vance mission attempted to create "linkage" between improved relations with Moscow and a Vietnam peace settlement. Hanoi ignored Moscow as determinedly as it ignored "signals" from Washington. On June 1, against Nixon's instincts, Kissinger attempted to resurrect secret channels through an old friend, Jean Sainteny, who had held the post of Delegate-General in colonial Hanoi. His "beautiful and intelligent" wife Claude had studied at Harvard and Kissinger had previously used the auspices of Sainteny to establish communication channels with the communist leadership.[108] Sainteny met Nixon and Kissinger on July 15 and agreed to pass a letter to Ho Chi Minh, but Hanoi demurred and the message was eventually passed via Paris representatives. It came to nothing. A reply was received on August 3 (the message received by the White House three days before Ho Chi Minh's death). The reply repeated the standard communist sermons and said nothing new. On the day of Ho's funeral US forces observed a unilateral ceasefire as a mark of respect. Hanoi, characteristically, did not.

Even as these tentative feelers were being pushed out, Kissinger was beginning to experience grave concerns over the entire Vietnam policy. On the domestic front, mollifying critics was undermining the strategy of an honorable withdrawal. On the front line, unreciprocated concessions were simply emboldening Hanoi.[109] The United States government needed a plan to end the war, not just to withdraw troops, or in other words, a real strategy and not just an exit plan.[110] In 1969, this did not exist. Few officials in the administration believed in the negotiations and Kissinger's own memoranda were self-confessedly becoming "quixotic."[111] State officials, clever policy advisors, columnists, senators – all were negotiating with themselves.

When they were not squabbling, they were ganging up on the White House. At the epicenter of this discordant choir of voices was a fulminating Nixon, who in turn was leaning on Kissinger to find the key to breaking a seemingly intransigent Hanoi.

It would have required great foresight to imagine that an option subsequently proposed, but then abandoned, would in fact prove the decisive act four years later. In collaboration with the Joint Chiefs, Sharp and Abrams, Kissinger's national security team sketched out a scheme code-named *Duck Hook* that would involve making a generous peace settlement, which, if rejected, would result in an all-out aerial offensive against the North, backed by the mining of Haiphong Harbor. *Duck Hook* evolved into *Pruning Knife*, an attack involving "all available U.S. air and naval bombardment forces committed to Southeast Asia and contiguous waters" to achieve "maximum military and political impact in minimum time."[112] Neither plan was immediately accepted, but the idea had been planted, waiting to seed at a more propitious time.

The lava was not just flowing in the White House. The long, hot summer of 1969 witnessed the Moratorium Day marches. The word "peace" had never been chanted in a more hostile way. In the comfortable surroundings of the Amsterdam Hilton Hotel, John Lennon and Yoko Ono began the first of their "bed-ins" against the war. A October 12 *Washington Post* editorial argued, "a loud shout to stop the war ... is not a strategy," but this passed over the protesting classes. Kissinger later wrote that the common feature of the protests was condescending ridicule over the notion that a United States government should seek an honorable peace, leavened with equally condescending lectures on the general "undesirability of war."[113] In a dairy farm in upstate New York, half a million revelers converged near the town of Bethel for the Woodstock Music Festival. The festival was opened by the yoga guru Sri Swami Satchidananda who urged the crowds to repeat the chant "Hari Om Hari Om, Hari Hari Hari Om." This was not an answer either. Even at the height of the "M Day" hysteria, Nixon enjoyed a 58 percent approval rating and the lowest recorded percentage for his conduct of the war was 44 percent.[114] The boisterous placard-wavers were not representing mainstream American opinion, which detested the war, but also disliked the notion of surrender.

The White House also faced serious challenges in the Senate. Between September 24 and October 15, 1969 as many as 11 anti-war resolutions were raised, each more shrill.[115] On September 25, Senator Charles Goodell raised a resolution requiring total withdrawal of all US troops by the end 1970; on October 2, Mike Mansfield demanded that Nixon impose a unilateral ceasefire; and on October 3 Senator Charles Percy called for the end of all offensive operations. None of these amendments was realistic or even practically achievable.

Away from the clamor, on August 4, Kissinger finally managed to meet Xuan Thuy and his deputy Mai Van Bo in Sainteny's apartment in the Rue de Rivoli. The meeting proved pointless and the timing awful. Within the week Hanoi launched a late summer offensive against scores of towns and cities, incensing the White House (and provoking the only occasion when Nixon threatened to stall troop withdrawals). This last gesture marked the end of Kissinger's attempts to revive the stalled talks. By the fall Harriman had resigned; Nixon had tired of "the clowns" in Paris; and a completely new strategy of unilateral withdrawal and "Vietnamization" was evolving.

1970 thus opened on a note of pessimism. Kissinger remained doubtful that Hanoi was anywhere near quitting, or that the ARVN was ready to assume the defense of South Vietnam without significant US assistance. Always skeptical of the culture of success statistics, he also disbelieved that pacification was working.[116] But Lodge was now gone and this created an opportunity. At the beginning of the year, the Paris Defense Attaché, General Vernon Walters, discreetly approached the North Vietnamese delegation in Paris with an offer of secret peace talks. After an initial rebuff, a meeting was agreed between Kissinger and Le Duc Tho. This represented a significant breakthrough. Tho ranked fifth in the Politburo hierarchy. The first meeting was held on February 21 and three more would follow over the next six weeks.

The secret talks took place at 11 Rue Darthé, Choisy-le-Roi, a lower-middle-class suburb on the outskirts of Paris. The meeting room was on the ground floor, furnished with red, upholstered easy chairs. The American party comprised Kissinger, Vietnam expert Richard Smyser, assistant Tony Lake, and the Paris Defense Attaché, General Walters. Tho led a team of six negotiators. The two groups sat a mere five feet apart, but were separated by "eons of perception."[117]

From the outset, the silver-haired Tho, who had spent ten years of his life in French prisons, set out to cajole, lecture, and taunt Kissinger – even drive him mad to distraction. If America and its allies had failed to win with a million troops, he sneered, how could America possibly win now?[118] Although Kissinger could not concede this point, privately, the same question tormented him. Multiple and intractable issues faced the negotiators: the status of the DMZ as international boundary or interim partition line; prisoner exchanges; the withdrawal of North Vietnamese forces from the South; ceasefire arrangements; the status of the cross-border sanctuaries; and most centrally, political settlement in South Vietnam. There was no agreement on any of these points. Despite imaginative efforts on the part of the American delegation to find some way of encouraging the North Vietnamese to negotiate rather than make surrender demands, the meetings ended in deadlock. On April 4, with the eruption of fighting in Laos and Cambodia, further talks were canceled.

The only tangible result from the first four meetings between Kissinger and Tho was agreement on the appointment of David K.E. Bruce – a gracious veteran diplomat – to head the public peace negotiations from June. In typical fashion, the North Vietnamese, who had protested Harriman's resignation the previous November, dismissed the 72-year-old Bruce as a lightweight.

These were small distractions. As ever, Kissinger had an eye on the long play and could see the growing contradiction in the administration's policy. A strategy of "Vietnamization," he warned Nixon on July 20, could not be indefinitely compatible with the current negotiation strategy.[119] Each unilateral withdrawal was weakening the American bargaining position. By the middle of 1971, the administration might be forced to choose between negotiations or "Vietnamization." Or ramp up the bombing, a choice that resurfaced but was dismissed as too controversial.

In a certain sign of the administration's desperation, the White House then became bewitched by a proposal for mutual ceasefires (which Cy Vance had previously championed and failed to sell). On September 7, Kissinger duly held another secret meeting with Xuan Thuy in Paris. The meeting was held on the premise that the proposed mutual ceasefires (and no mention of a communist withdrawal, a substantial concession) might melt Thuy's hard heart, or at least that of his masters. How wrong. Just over a week later, the Foreign Minister of the Provisional Revolutionary Government (PRG) in the South, Madame Nguyen Nhi Binh, published an eight-point "peace program" which brazenly restated the communist demands for total and unconditional US withdrawal and overthrow of the Saigon government. To Kissinger's dismay, critics seized on this offer – in effect surrender demands – as an example of Hanoi's goodwill and Nixon's bad faith. Kissinger returned to Paris on September 27, but the second meeting with Thuy proved fruitless. The only certainty was that talk of ceasefires was dead, yet Nixon was now hooked on the idea and could not be stopped. On October 7, he delivered a speech outlining the proposal to widespread praise. In Paris, the following day, Thuy rejected it out of hand. By November, all of Kissinger's initiatives had fizzled out, squeezed between the intransigence of the North Vietnamese and Nixon's growing disinterest.

On January 21, 1971, the 100th plenary session of the public peace talks was held. This meeting was only notable as a numerical milestone. After three years, the sole point of agreement remained the shape of the table. However, this gloomy start to the New Year was deceptive. The failure of the public peace talks was now about to be reversed by the promise of progress in the secret meetings. This evolution was partly due to Kissinger's sheer persistence, but also reflected a Politburo shaken by the *Lam Son 719* offensive and at odds over the direction of the war.

At the first secret meeting, held on May 31, a magnanimous Kissinger presented a fresh and frankly generous seven-point peace plan. This was, in his own words, the proposal which marked "a turning point in our diplomacy in Vietnam" and which ultimately Hanoi accepted, with revisions, 16 months later.[120]

The first point set a firm date for the total withdrawal of US forces – which Hanoi had demanded from the beginning – and dropped the proposal for mutual withdrawals. As MACV was on an irreversible course of total withdrawal anyway, the former was a moot concession. In counterpoint to Hanoi's insistence on the overthrow of the Saigon government, point two stated that Vietnamese and other Indochinese parties should be allowed to determine "the manner in which all other outside forces would withdraw from the countries of Indochina." This was an elliptical way of saying that the final political settlement was a Vietnamese affair in which the US government would play no part. Point three proposed a ceasefire, and point four an end to infiltration. The penultimate two points projected international supervision of the ceasefire, and respect for Laotian and Cambodian neutrality, as set out in the1954 and 1962 Geneva Accords. The last point dealt with the release of prisoners, the most emotive issue for Americans.

Xuan Thuy appeared to feign diffidence over the seven-point peace plan but Kissinger sensed a change of attitude. For the first time, Hanoi did seem keen to keep talking in secret and this raised hopes. On the home front, the administration was continuing to take a battering. Early June witnessed the leaking of the Pentagon Papers, and Congress voting 57 to 42 in favor of the Mansfield amendment. This called for a total US withdrawal in nine months following agreement on the release of prisoners. In effect, Congress had handed Hanoi a gold-plated bargaining chip – one more in an accumulating stack of chips.

When Kissinger returned to Paris on June 26, it was clear that something had changed. Tho was "cordial." The usual somewhat cramped living room was swapped for the dining room and a more formal, green baize conference table.[121] These nuances mattered in negotiations where the very shapes of tables had been the subject of interminable discussions. The two men took to perambulating in the garden like old friends. Kissinger jovially invited Tho to lecture on Marxism-Leninism at Harvard after the war, adding the not untruthful observation that he would probably be better received than Kissinger in his alma mater.

This apparent thaw belied unresolved tensions. Through the auspices of the public peace negotiations, Xuan Thuy now countered with a nine-point peace plan, joking that its additional two points proved Hanoi was more serious about peace. Notwithstanding, substantial if ambiguous concessions were offered. The removal of the Saigon government was no longer couched as a non-negotiable demand, and there was agreement on prisoner release in parallel with withdrawals. A penniless Hanoi also threw in a totally new demand: reparations. Kissinger was "elated" by the change in atmosphere. Every one of Hanoi's proposals was negotiable, except the lingering uncertainty over political settlement, and the unacceptable demand for reparations.[122] The June 26 meeting marked a turning point for another reason. For the first time in three years, Hanoi had presented its ideas as a negotiating document and not as a set of demands.[123]

Kissinger's elation, however, was premature. Less than one week later, on July 1, Foreign Minister Madame Binh publicly announced a seven-point peace plan (one less than her previous offer) that only partly reflected the secret concessions offered by Tho, and more reflected the intransigent demands made in earlier negotiating sessions. Kissinger despaired: with predictable eagerness, once again every major US newspaper seized on Binh's plan. And with predictable gullibility, every liberal editorial portrayed the bogus offer as a "reasonable chance" to end the war.[124]

Undeterred by this setback, Kissinger was willing to try again. Following a colorful telephone conversation with Nixon who offered him "graphic and bloodcurdling instructions" on how to deal with the North Vietnamese delegation, Kissinger secretly met with Tho on July 12.[125] Despite some ill-temper, the four-and-a-half-hour talks did "sharpen" the respective positions. The key stumbling block, as in previous meetings, was Hanoi's now tacit demand for the overthrow of the Thieu government. With a misjudged air of complicity Tho even started making outrageous proposals to his imagined co-conspirator, Kissinger. Why not rig the elections? Or stage a coup? Why not simply assassinate Thieu?

Despite the North Vietnamese delegation dragging the talks down to the level of mafia dons discussing a hit, Kissinger persevered. Another secret meeting was held on July 26. Again, this came unstuck on the question of Thieu's premiership. Tho's insistence on this point seemed to reflect a growing loss of nerve in Hanoi and a perception that Thieu might just repeat "the miracle of Diem" and create a strong and immovable regime. The prize of peace, Kissinger ruefully noted, was "as far away as ever."[126]

Unwilling to give up, there were two further meetings on August 16 and September 13 – neither attended by Tho. By now, Thieu was heading for electoral victory and Hanoi was brewing its forthcoming Easter Offensive. The sole purpose of the meetings, it appears, was to keep the American delegation engaged while war preparations got under way. Following the second fruitless meeting with Thuy, it was clear to both sides that an impasse had been reached. In an effort to break the deadlock, Kissinger made one final play. In private communication, Kissinger proposed to Nixon that a compromise eight-point plan be offered. This would make an offer of presidential elections within six months of signing a peace agreement, under international supervision, and would include communist candidates. One month before polling, Thieu would resign and an interim caretaker government would be established. Thieu was consulted and agreed to the proposed arrangements. Using the offices of Defense Attaché Walters, the re-worked plan was secretly transmitted to the North Vietnamese delegation on October 11. The initiative proved a triumph of hope over experience. Thuy stalled and eventually informed the US Embassy in late November that Tho was ill and would be unable to meet. The secret talks of 1971 thus ended on a flat and inconclusive note.

At the beginning of 1972 it was clear that a major North Vietnamese offensive was imminent. It was also abundantly clear that Hanoi's offensive might decide the outcome of the American war. MACV would either be quitting the field in ignominious withdrawal, its ARVN ally defeated, or Hanoi's divisions would be wrecked trying. As Nixon would not countenance defeat on the battlefield, the likelihood was always that the Easter Offensive would fail in its maximal objective of toppling the South Vietnamese regime. But Nixon was not just the street fighter; he was a consumed, implacable politician. The administration could not preempt the offensive (the official end to US combat operations had been declared). It would have to wait until it fell before ramping up the military response. However, Washington could preempt Hanoi in other ways, and undermine the chorus of domestic critics that would object to America again saving South Vietnam from collapse.

On January 25, in a theatrical coup, Nixon decided to disclose the entire trajectory of secret talks to an American public, completely wrong-footing a Hanoi that had become accustomed to playing off the public and secret talks to manipulate American congressmen, newspapers, and public opinion. The broadcast was one of Nixon's "most dramatic and impressive" television appearances from a president who was turning the television appeal to "the silent majority" into an art form.[127] Hanoi's surprise was matched by that of political opponents and a hostile media – for the first time in many months, these were caught off-balance and silenced.

There was one sour note – offering a foretaste of what was to come – but which was rolled over in the triumphalism. For the last two years Thieu had tacitly assented to the administration's proposals for securing peace. In an unexpected volte-face, he jarringly protested that not insisting on a communist withdrawal and allowing communist participation in the government would erode his authority. Hanoi similarly panicked. On January 31 it mirrored Nixon's television announcement by revealing its own secret proposals, making the excuse that it had refrained from being more open because the US government had insisted on secrecy.

With the Easter Offensive just weeks away, there was a certain irrelevance to these gestures, but both sides continued the diplomatic sparring. The day after Nixon's address, Washington made an offer to resume talks. On February 14, Hanoi replied with a counter-offer to meet on any day, at the American delegation's convenience, after March 15. This was straightaway interpreted as a signal of the imminent offensive, especially by Thieu, who was not fooled by the communist maneuverings.[128] The proposed delay nonetheless suited Washington, as by this date Nixon's historic China visit would be a fait accompli. A compromise date of March 20 was agreed. Hanoi's timing of its Easter Offensive then unraveled, throwing the timings again. On March 6, with no forewarning, Hanoi requested the meeting be postponed until April 15, by which time it secretly expected to have captured the city of An Loc, northwest of Saigon, and installed the Provisional Revolutionary Government. Playing along in this game of brinkmanship, Washington rejected the new date and offered April 24 as an alternative.

All this scheming came to nothing after Hanoi launched its offensive on March 30. Plainly, with nothing to talk about, the peace talks were suspended. After two months of bitter fighting, on May 2, the two delegations eventually convened in an encounter described by Kissinger as "brutal."[129] This was the first meeting in eight months. Tho calculated his side now held the upper hand and he was determined to let Kissinger know it. For too long, the American delegation had been deprived of the "epic poem" of American perfidy and Vietnamese valor, a deprivation Tho fully intended to redress. With infinite patience, Kissinger once more found himself having to sit through a litany of demands without "explanation, modification, or attempt at negotiation."[130] Unsurprisingly the meeting failed to make any progress. But Tho was far too confident, on all fronts. On the diplomatic front, Nixon's trip to China was about to be garnished by rapprochement with the Soviet Union, both valuing their relationship with the United States above the "miserable, little" country of Vietnam that was souring international relations. And on the battlefronts of South Vietnam, Hanoi's early victories were being inexorably reversed by a combination of American air power and South Vietnamese resistance.

In the event, Tho's bombastic mood barely lasted one month. By June, in a dramatic volte-face, Hanoi seemed to accept that decisive victory in the field was now an unattainable goal, and that settlement before a likely Nixon re-election would be advantageous. In past meetings Tho had irritatingly lectured Kissinger on American domestic politics. In reality, Hanoi was not as astute as it believed and did not fully comprehend the Beltway. The administration was in a far weaker position than Hanoi imagined, and a re-elected Nixon would be a more constrained, not stronger, president. Acutely, the escalator of congressional resolutions was eroding the administration's room for maneuver – from May to July alone there were another 19 votes in the Senate or House relating to amendments to end the war.[131]

At the beginning of July, faced with what it perceived to be a deteriorating military and negotiating position, Hanoi requested a resumption of the peace talks. Eager to reciprocate, Kissinger agreed to meet on July 19. In the interval, Haig was despatched to brief Thieu on the American negotiating positions. These meetings offered the first hints that the South Vietnamese president was far from sanguine over the proposed peace terms. Over the last two years Thieu had only been signaling his agreement to the secret talks because he knew perfectly well that Hanoi would reject the terms proposed by the American delegation. Now that settlement was possible, Thieu stalled. Unfortunately, the allusive, elliptical style that drove Kissinger mad in his dealings with the North Vietnamese was also evident in Saigon. When Haig returned to Washington, he did not appreciate (or did not wish to acknowledge) that Saigon had indicated rejection of the peace settlement being hatched in its name, only that it had "difficulties" over some points.

Against this confused backdrop of mixed expectations, the two sides convened again on July 19. Kissinger straightaway apprised the mood had changed. Tho promised "a turning point" and duly delivered a constructive six-and-a-half-hour meeting (the longest ever), which ended with an agreement to meet again on August 1.[132]

If all was going well with Hanoi, disaster now loomed with Saigon. With no forewarning, Thieu indicated that he would only accept a ceasefire linked to a full North Vietnamese withdrawal, to be completed in three months. This was a totally unrealistic demand. The sudden retrenchment of the South Vietnamese position felt like duplicity, if not betrayal. Thieu had known and concurred with every single previous ceasefire term. These included agreements over an in-place ceasefire (October 7, 1970); abandonment of the principle of mutual withdrawal (May 31, 1971); and agreement over a ceasefire decoupled from a requirement to withdraw (January 25, 1972, reaffirmed on May 8, 1972).[133] Now the South Vietnamese president was effectively threatening to tear up the last two years of painful negotiations with an impossible demand, long ceded by the American delegation.

Despondency over this setback was briefly overtaken by the excitement of a real breakthrough with Hanoi. On August 1, the two sides held a marathon eight-hour meeting that yielded three entirely unexpected concessions. On the issue of a ceasefire, Hanoi agreed to a general ceasefire, contingent and integrated with all other agreements (previously Tho had offered a limited ceasefire linked to the departure of US troops). On the question of the postwar political settlement, Hanoi repeated its demand for a tripartite government, but no longer insisted this body would represent a provisional government formed expressly to negotiate a final settlement with the Northern communists. Instead, the proposed body would now be established as the permanent government. In a second, complementary concession Hanoi dropped its long-standing demand to appoint and approve the composition of the non-communist two thirds of the tripartite government. In its place, it only requested that it have a say over the appointments of half of the "neutral" third, thus making it a 50/50 split government. Remarkably, Tho did not even insist that the "puppet" Thieu should go. If the American delegation was taken by surprise by these sweeping concessions, it was just as baffled by the proposed protocols for settling – arrangements described as necessitating "an advanced degree in metaphysics" to understand.[134] Hanoi had swung from being padlocked and unhelpful to more open and unctuous than a second-hand car salesman.

This unanticipated breakthrough had different effects on different actors. Nixon, now riding a crest of popular approval, was skeptical. In typically insensitive fashion he told Haig, "We have made no progress in 15 meetings!" so dismissing Kissinger's last two tortuous years of secret negotiations in one sentence. In Saigon, Thieu was privately panicking over the realization that the moment of reckoning was arriving fast. And Kissinger now began to fret that Hanoi would gain by stealth what it had failed to gain by confrontation.

The protagonists nonetheless reconvened on August 14 in what was largely a procedural meeting, and agreed to meet again on September 15. Following this meeting, on August 17 Kissinger flew from Paris to Saigon to brief Thieu on the status of the secret negotiations. At this stage the president's national security had only received weak warnings from Haig that the Saigon government might just attempt to scupper the deal. Indeed, nobody on the American side seems to have seriously questioned South Vietnamese compliance over this matter. The assumption was always that Saigon would accept the terms, with some cavils, but certainly not reject them.

It was at this critical juncture that two spoiling players entered the game: Thieu's nephew and press special advisor, Hoang Duc Nha, and special advisor Nguyen Phu Duc. On instructions from Thieu, Nha now embarked on a campaign of rumor-mongering and selective leaking. This could have only one purpose – to sabotage the talks in the eyes of the South Vietnamese. Duc, in tandem, acted like a fussy grammarian, picking apart every sentence and questioning the sense of every clause.

Even to the purblind, it was now clear that Thieu was digging in his heels, and he was doing so on the most maddening of technical points – the composition of the tripartite electoral commission. To neuter communist aspirations,

Kissinger had proposed renaming this body the Committee of National Reconciliation. In a significant concession, Hanoi had agreed this provisional committee would have no purpose other than supervising the elections fairly. Or, in other words, it would have no influence on the government that would emerge from the popular vote. This important concession left the field open for the election of a candidate approved by Saigon. Even as Kissinger and his team patiently responded to Saigon's pernickety lines of questioning, they began to observe that Thieu was basically raising objections to "whatever aspect appeared closest to a solution."[135] The only conclusion that could be drawn from this behavior was that Thieu simply did not want a peace settlement, a conclusion that at this late stage nobody in the American delegation wished to believe. Faced with this intransigence, Kissinger could only warn Thieu that if Hanoi accepted the original May 8 peace proposals and a general ceasefire, Washington would settle – but Thieu was not listening.

How could Americans have understood the unbridgeable "chasm" and "primeval hate that animated the two sides," Kissinger later reflected?[136] There was some truth to this exculpation. The chasm, however, reached deeper than that. From the perspective of Saigon's presidential palace, what was being proposed was fundamentally unacceptable: it would deliver both a "shock" to the South Vietnamese people, with Hanoi's army now permanently lodged in Southern territory, and it would tarnish Thieu as the man who surrendered South Vietnam to the communists. Unlike Washington, Thieu and his compatriots viscerally understood this was a fight to the death. Kissinger's sophisticated compromises and artful ways had yielded a set of peace terms that would merely offer a pause before a resumption of fighting. Saigon had never truly believed in the peace negotiations any more than Hanoi. The entire business, from Saigon's viewpoint, was a shoddy con trick, and the terms offered, far from disarming the North, would dismember the South. In this respect, Thieu was right. The proposed peace agreements were no such agreements.

However, critics who judge that Nixon and Kissinger engaged in a deliberate, calculated policy to wash America's hands of South Vietnam – after "a decent interval" – are bypassing evidence. What is striking from many hours of taped conversations is that both protagonists genuinely believed a "good deal" had been agreed. There was surprise and later anger over Thieu's rejection of the peace agreements. A stronger case can be made that both Nixon and Kissinger (and aides) had fallen into a self-congratulatory trap. The many hints and signals were being ignored because the White House could not countenance failure when success was just the stroke of a pen away.

The greater irony surrounding the entire "decent interval" controversy is that Hanoi saw exactly the opposite. Rather than selling off South Vietnam, the Politburo conspiratorially imagined that Kissinger had cooked up a "devilish plot" to recover American POWs; disengage from a politically costly war; and instead build up the Thieu regime with military and economic aid. The co-conspirators in this dastardly plot were none other than the communist leaders in Peking – or so Hanoi imagined – who had fallen for Kissinger's and Nixon's blandishments. From the perspective of the North, the proposed peace proposals carried risks as much as rewards. It would have amazed the tortured policymakers of the Kennedy and Johnson presidencies, who fretted over the dangers of a communist Chinese intervention in Vietnam, that Hanoi was equally vexed, not due to any such worry, but because it presumed Peking had been sending secret signals to Washington indicating "if you don't bother us, we won't bother you."[137]

If Kissinger felt dispirited after his difficult sojourn in Saigon, he was about to be surprised again by Hanoi. On September 15, the two delegations met again in Paris as previously agreed. Tho now proposed the two sides meet over two days, the following week, to resolve and conclude all remaining issues. A settlement was ready for the signing – if Washington was willing. On the same day Quang Tri was finally recaptured by the ARVN, and all polls indicated that Nixon was heading for a comfortable victory. Tho's sudden rush of urgency could only be interpreted as a signal that the Politburo sensed the imminent defeat of its Easter Offensive. Faced with this prospect, Hanoi was now seeking the most expeditious route to hasten the departure of the American neo-imperialists and their bombers, at whatever cost.

The September 26–27 meeting went ahead as scheduled. To avoid a press pack now scenting a news-breaking story, the meeting venue was relocated to a discreet address on the outskirts of Paris (in fact, the former home of painter Fernand Léger in Gif-sur-Yvette). Over the course of discussions Tho continued to offer expansive concessions. In addition to the previously agreed terms, Hanoi would withdraw from Laos and Cambodia, release prisoners unconditionally, and agree to a general ceasefire – all this goodwill garnished with caviar, shrimps, sherry, and wine.[138] The principal stumbling blocks now appeared to be terminological as well as securing agreement on the proposed powers of the provisional political body. In place of Kissinger's Committee of National Reconciliation Tho suggested a "Provisional Government of National Concord." This body would not supplant the existing government, but it would leave the communists in a stronger position. Notwithstanding this last-minute bartering, these were barely believable offers. Still driven by the same urgency of the previous fortnight Tho requested a final three-day meeting, within the next two weeks, to close the deal. After almost four years of sparring, a peace agreement seemed to be in touching distance.

It fell to Bunker and Haig to face the South Vietnamese president in a reunion held on October 4. This meeting, predictably, proved disastrous. In what had now become a ritual, the two Americans were confronted by a phalanx of government ministers including Vice President Huong, Prime Minister Khiem, Foreign Minister Lam, and the ever-present Duc and Nha. The excruciating collision of expectations lasted almost four hours, leaving the Americans baffled and angry, and Thieu hysterical and tearful. This extravagant display of Vietnamese emotionalism dispelled any lingering doubts that may have rested in the American camp. Saigon could not agree to terms that it viewed as the opening bars of its own funeral mass. If this turn of events caused Kissinger to despair, his master remained phlegmatic. With characteristic paranoia, Nixon was convinced that Hanoi's amenability was just one huge trick. If the bluff were called, Hanoi would surely pull back. More pertinently, Nixon had no intention of letting the tail wag the dog, as he put it. Should Hanoi settle, he advised Kissinger, he was under instructions to take the agreement to Saigon and "cram it down his [Thieu's] throat."[139] Not for Nixon the graceful art of diplomatic persuasion.

Four days later, on Sunday October 8, Kissinger sat down with Tho in the Gif-sur-Yvette hideaway for what was anticipated as a decisive meeting. After some opening jousts that lasted all morning, Tho requested a recess. When the two sides met again in the afternoon, Hanoi capitulated on virtually every remaining demand: the removal of Thieu, the requirement for a coalition government, and the unilateral withdrawal of American troops. To all intents, Hanoi had agreed to Kissinger's May 8 terms – a signal triumph of his patient and epic trial, but one that would not have been achieved without the equally persuasive force of the B-52s. Kissinger had waited four years for this moment, but when it came there was anticlimax. In place of rhetorical flourish there was "the droning voice of an elderly revolutionary" quibbling the last few points of legal ambiguity.[140] Anxious to complete the technicalities, the delegations worked through October 9–11, the last day extending into a 16-hour marathon session that ended at 2am on October 12. In what may have represented some sort of endurance record, Kissinger's heroic stenographer, Irene Derus, produced a 122-page transcript of the historic agreements.[141]

In broad terms, the two sides agreed on all the major issues except the securing of ceasefires in Laos and Cambodia (which Hanoi could not guarantee, even if it wished); the release of Viet Cong prisoners (which Washington could not guarantee without Saigon's agreement); and the replacement of military equipment in South Vietnam. This latter point was mired in technicalities that were eventually resolved by agreement on a piece-by-piece replacement policy.

Had the October 12 terms been accepted, the United States would have withdrawn all forces within two months of signing, the bombing would have stopped concurrently with a ceasefire in South Vietnam, and POWs would have been released in tandem with the final withdrawals. To ensure impartiality, all this process would have been supervised by an International Commission of Control and Supervision (ICCS). So close was Washington to its first Christmas without war dead in over a decade.

Buoyed by this prospect, all that remained to be agreed was a timetable to seal and sign the peace terms. Barring final hitches, Kissinger would return to Paris on October 17, meet with Xuan Thuy, and tidy up any loose ends in the draft documents. He would then travel to Saigon (October 18–22), stop over briefly in Hanoi (October 22), before returning to Washington no later than October 24. A public announcement would be made on October 26. The signatory ceremony would be held in Paris on October 31. Without hindsight, this timetable was wildly optimistic.

On October 18, Kissinger arrived in Saigon with high hopes. Despite the recent tensions with the South Vietnamese government, the mood in the Embassy was ebullient. Nobody, it appeared, wished to confront the truth – except Bunker's deputy, Charles Whitehouse, who made the honest assessment that Thieu would flatly reject the proposed peace agreement.

As Whitehouse predicted, Thieu, backed by his National Security Council and with the "obnoxious" Nha acting as interpreter, set about stalling the talks. Kissinger hand-delivered a letter from Nixon to impress on his hosts the criticality of the situation. In it Nixon argued:

> I believe we have no reasonable alternative but to accept this agreement. It represents major movement on the other side, and it is my firm conviction that its implementation will leave you and your people with the ability to defend yourselves and decide the political destiny of South Vietnam.[142]

This did not persuade. The South Vietnamese delegation was "completely incredulous." When Kissinger described how Le Duc Tho embraced him and wept (an anecdote that does not appear in *The White House Years*), Nha retorted, "Be careful of the crocodile tears."[143] Kissinger subsequently suggested, "Let's get this over with ... we have a peace treaty, you and I will go to Hollywood ... we'll have a grand time," but Nha was unimpressed.[144] The list of demands and questions lengthened. The failure to offer a Vietnamese text of the proposed agreements was perceived as a deep insult. It took 24 hours to find the requisite text, which proved to be a copy of the North Vietnamese draft, suffused with communist rhetoric and garnished with a few insults which the American delegation had failed to spot due to the peculiarities of the Vietnamese language.

The terms, as presented in English, were wholly unacceptable. The PAVN had to withdraw from South Vietnam, but this was both an impossible and unenforceable condition. What aid package and armaments would the United States offer to secure the South's survival? What was the exact composition and function of the now many times renamed "National Council of National Reconciliation and Concord"? How would the White House respond if the agreements were violated? Eventually, the South Vietnamese delegation offered 26 proposed amendments.

Even as the discussions unraveled, the South Vietnamese began to act in rude, "insolent," and frustrating ways from the American perspective. Thieu was not just objecting to specific terms – this amounted to delay and obfuscation – he was objecting to the very fact of a peace agreement. After eight years of American support, which had become dependency, Saigon was not ready to confront Hanoi. Thieu's "nightmare" was not any particular clause or term but the "fear of being left alone."[145] For years Washington had been laboring to achieve something her ally did not really want. Thieu knew, like his compatriots, that peace would only be a prelude to the end. Without firm American military commitment, there was no hope.

On October 21, Foreign Minister Lam presented 23 formal objections to the peace terms to the US Embassy. He then spent the remainder of the day blatantly refusing to talk. Finally, at 9pm, Bunker's telephone rang, but it was only a vituperative Thieu accusing Haig of plotting a coup against the government. Awkwardly, on the same evening, Hanoi again signaled its agreement to all last-minute, proposed amendments in the draft documents. Every party was now agreeing and compromising except Saigon, which had become semi-hysterical.

This dire situation was unexpectedly but only partly rescued by an injudicious interview given by Prime Minister Pham Van Dong to French reporter Arnaud de Borchgrave, in Hanoi, in which he made various factually incorrect and misleading statements over what had been agreed. This unexpected faux pas presented Kissinger with an excuse to complain and delay his flight to Hanoi, but it was clear the hourglass was running out of sand.

The following day Thieu appeared to calm down and agreement was secured to meet later in the evening. In the interim, the American delegation paid lightning visits to Souvanna Phouma, Lon Nol, and the Thai government. All supported the proposed peace agreements as a good deal, without knowledge of its full details (Lon Nol went so far as to break open a bottle of champagne). Finally, at 5pm, Bunker and Kissinger met with Thieu and Nha. By now, it was too late. That afternoon, Thieu had addressed the National Assembly and revealed the terms of the proposed peace agreement. The meeting lasted just two hours. Kissinger's subsequent telegram to Haig was terse and to the point:

"Thieu has just rejected the entire plan or any modification of it and refuses to discuss any further negotiations on the basis of it."[146] In a pantomime performance, Thieu refused to speak English (a usual tactic by now) and burst into tears. Nha, in synchronicity, reportedly howled alongside his uncle. After all the years of American sacrifice, Thieu's behavior was condemned as "outrageous," yet both sides knew that Washington could not simply ditch an ally, however "appalling" its behavior.

As Kissinger rightly feared, Thieu's disclosures to the National Assembly had now effectively canceled out Prime Minister Dong's public revelations. Hanoi's knowledge of Saigon's rejection would likely encourage the North Vietnamese to exploit the divisions between the allies. This point came just four days later. On October 26, Hanoi published details of the proposed peace terms, insinuating that it had been wronged. This divulgation needed a quick response. Kissinger and Nixon hastily conferred and agreed that the administration had to reply, in public, to reassure both parties that the talks were still on track, and that America was determined to settle. But Nixon was on the campaign trail and Kissinger had never appeared on national television, a deliberate policy enforced by the White House public relations staff who judged his voice unacceptable if not weird to Middle America.[147]

For an individual over-endowed with a surfeit of eloquence, presenting the administration's case was not a challenge to Kissinger. He had spoken to the press many times before, off camera. Nor did Kissinger intend to deliver a flight of Churchillian rhetoric. But four words in his televised statement – "peace is at hand" – rocketed to the front pages of newspapers and would provoke a perfect storm. Ironically, the White House's initial reaction to Kissinger's speech was enthusiastic.[148] Nixon's wife had been impressed. Aide Charles Colson thought the speech had wiped out Hubert Humphrey's chances in the polls. In an eight-minute telephone call at close to midnight later that day, both Nixon and Kissinger were jubilant. It is plain from their conversation that the two genuinely believed peace was at hand. Kissinger opined that Thieu was "too wily" not to know that America would protect him, so his whistleblowing could be discounted. Nixon felt insulted that Teddy Kennedy was suggesting America would sell out an ally. Both agreed there were differences still to be resolved but the peace deal was "90 percent there." We have them "where the hair is short," as Nixon colorfully put it.

But as the repercussions of the speech spread the following day, jubilation turned to apoplexia; opponents seized on the words as another example of the administration's duplicity; and the North Vietnamese spokesman in Paris, Nguyen Thanh Le, cheekily quipped that peace was at the end of a pen, if only the other side would sign. Both the Soviet and Chinese governments, which had been secretly kept informed on the progress of the negotiations, were totally confused, and began bombarding the White House with questions. Within 24 hours, a spiral of paranoid speculations had been engendered: the Democrats suspected an electoral trick; Hanoi suspected betrayal; the media suspected Nixon; and Saigon sank in a pool of self-pity and torment. The reality was that Kissinger knew perfectly well that peace was most certainly not at hand.

A second statement on national television was necessary, which Nixon duly delivered on November 2. "We are not going to allow an election deadline or any other kind of deadline to force us into an agreement which would only be a temporary truce and not a lasting peace," he warned. "We are going to sign the agreement when the agreement is right, not one day before. And when the agreement is right, we are going to sign, without one day's delay." This rescue act was, in some respects, wasted. By now the country was engrossed in the final days of electoral campaigning, and Vietnam seemed a distant and forgettable problem.

Five days later, Nixon won his stunning victory. But as Kissinger observed, this contradictory, tortured man seemed least happy in his most triumphant moments. It was as if his whole life had been propelled by a need to succeed, smashing anyone standing in his way, but in the very achievement of this goal, he found himself thrown into a deep and alienating sense of loneliness, almost baffled by his own self-fulfillment. On November 7, Nixon was as far from brimming with good cheer as he possibly could be. "Grim," "remote," and filled with "pent-up hostility," he seemed bent on revenge, not celebration. The day after his victory, in a grossly insensitive gesture, Nixon briefly addressed his cabinet and staff before handing over to Haldeman, who curtly told the assembled personnel they were required to submit their resignations. Although this was a ritual of office, no president had acted with such perfunctory callousness against the very people who had kept and supported him in office, the day after a thumping electoral win. Having despatched his own staff, he was now about to unleash the same foul mood against the North Vietnamese.

First, there was the matter of the Saigon government. On November 9, Haig flew to South Vietnam in an effort to persuade Thieu to at least prioritize his objections to the peace terms. After two days of fruitless meetings, Thieu obstructively announced that all objections were equally important, and his government would not yield on the requirement for a complete withdrawal of North Vietnamese troops from Southern soil.

Still smoldering from Kissinger's unhappy television debut, Nixon had by now begun to lose confidence in his national security advisor. In fact, relations between the two men had been strained for some period and Kissinger fully expected to be sacked following the presidential investiture in February. National leaders who lose confidence in advisors place greater stock in their own powers of persuasion. Nixon was no exception to this rule.

The over-academic "Henry" was failing, so the moment had arrived for robust personal intervention. The problem with Kissinger, Nixon sweepingly and ungratefully confided to Haldeman, was that he was "not a good negotiator … He does not know – shit."[149]

This fecal dismissal of his national security advisor left behind the spoor of a historical millstone. In a personal letter sent to Thieu on November 14, Nixon wrote:

> But far more important than what we say in the agreement on this issue is what we do in the event the enemy renews its aggression. You have my absolute assurance that if Hanoi fails to abide by the terms of this agreement it is my intention to take swift and severe retaliatory action.

The problem with this promise was that he could not realistically keep it. Congress was a few votes short of emasculating America's war. The likelihood was that it would carry out this painful surgical procedure in the near future. Nixon's absolute and genuinely offered assurance was worthless.

In telephone conversations over the next three days, Nixon and Kissinger discussed the possibility of proceeding on the basis of a bilateral peace agreement with Hanoi, but dismissed the idea as "a terrible thing" ("repugnant" in Kissinger's words).[150] Surely, Nixon reasoned, Thieu understood that if forced down this route, Congress would cut military assistance to South Vietnam (which it would do anyway). "If South Vietnam goes down," Nixon mused, "we don't want it [to], that's what bothers me." Kissinger concurred and argued that the agreement would "put them [Saigon] in a position where they can defend themselves."[151] According to a CIA map (Kissinger was probably referring to the Hamlet Evaluation Scheme), 95 percent of South Vietnamese territory was now in government hands – why was Thieu so concerned over the five percent? Both men were baffled.

Thieu's response indicated no confidence in the White House's promises. On November 19, Kissinger returned to Paris, even as Saigon fired back a raft of fresh objections to the peace terms (in total, 69, with almost no part in the draft terms agreed). Over the next five days, the American delegation struggled to regain the confidence of an understandably suspicious Tho. In what Kissinger later conceded was a "major tactical mistake," all of Saigon's objections were revealed to the North Vietnamese. This was meant as a gesture of transparency but was interpreted as a puzzlingly devious trick – with some justification, as even Kissinger was describing the objections as "preposterous."[152] For Hanoi, the new position was utterly confusing. At the beginning of October, the two parties had been two weeks away from settlement. If this was the deal on offer, Tho protested, both sides should prepare for another four-year cycle of war.

Surprisingly, after studying the objections overnight, the North Vietnamese delegation demonstrated some willingness to negotiate on a number of technical points. This glimmer of hope was somewhat spoiled by a trio of South Vietnamese ambassadors – in London, Paris, and Washington – now all decamped in Paris, who were demanding a nightly brief. This chore proved a pointless exercise – every American proposal was met with blank rejection.

The prospects could hardly have been bleaker, but through sheer persistence the two sides again inched closer to agreement. By the end of a five-day marathon, 12 amendments had been secured in Washington's favor, all small, and four more important changes were agreed in Hanoi's favor. These minor tactical victories won, the two parties agreed to meet again at the beginning of December, notwithstanding Saigon's obstructive stalling.

By now, a shift had occurred in Kissinger's mood and calculations. Faced with the prospect of failure, Kissinger recommended to Nixon consideration of "a drastic step-up in our bombing" to nudge along the North Vietnamese.[153] This was the first mention of the bombing option – as a means to break the deadlock – and it had Kissinger's name on it (the wider bombing option as a mechanism for ending the war, as earlier described, had been discussed since the Operation *Duck Hook* scheme in 1969). Nixon later unkindly professed that his national security advisor had an "inferiority complex" which he tried to compensate for through the use of force. With hindsight, it is easy to see the media would have linked failure in the talks to Kissinger's premature "peace at hand speech," which would almost certainly have ended his public career in some humiliation. But by Kissinger's own admission, he sensed his relationship with Nixon was coming to an end anyway, and he did not anticipate re-employment following the elections. At the beginning of December, Kissinger civilly indicated to Nixon that, in the event of failure, he would take responsibility for that failure.[154] He was prepared to resign. In the same three-page cable Kissinger was equally concerned with Thieu and indeed ended his analysis advising Nixon that the chances of Saigon compromising were "discouraging," regardless of agreement with the North.

Nixon's response to the recommendation was expressed in two cables to Kissinger, sent only six hours apart, on November 24. In the first, Nixon cautioned, "We have now reached the point where the resumption of heavy bombing of the North is no longer a viable option for us."[155] This cable was sent following a 4.37am meeting with Colonel Richard Kennedy (who acted as the liaison between Nixon in Washington and Kissinger in Paris). In the second, later that morning, he changed his mind: "For your information, I would be prepared to authorize a massive strike on the North."[156] In characteristic fashion, Nixon recognized this would constitute a public relations disaster but dismissed the popular challenge: "We must take our lumps and see it through." The abrupt volte-face has no certain explanation. A possibility is that Nixon, on reflection, realized his national security advisor needed some support and firepower.

On November 25, Kissinger met with Tho. The North Vietnamese delegation continued to bargain, quibbling the size and composition of the international monitoring force, the status of the DMZ, and the withdrawal of North Vietnamese troops from the South. Kissinger did not lose heart although it was plain the terms were worse than those proposed on October 12. Agreement was reached to meet again the following week, following consultations with Saigon. In the meantime, on November 29, Thieu's special advisor in Washington, Nguyen Phu Duc, met with Nixon and repeated Saigon's consistent message: the South Vietnamese government would not sign without a withdrawal of Northern troops. The following day, Nixon met with the Joint Chiefs, in a meeting attended by Kissinger and Laird, and instructed Admiral Moorer to prepare contingency retaliatory air raids that should be "massive" and "all out."[157] However, this instruction was not delivered in the context of forcing Hanoi to settle, but rather to punish potential communist violations, after settlement. At the end of November, no protagonist was preparing to bomb the North to force an end to the peace talks.

Interestingly, Hanoi was anticipating exactly the latter. On November 27 the Party Central Committee warned command elements that a resumption of US bombing was likely, including over Hanoi and Haiphong, a message reinforced by the Political Bureau the following week.[158] Whether through well-placed spies in Saigon who were picking up the signals, or astute assessment, Hanoi expected the worst.

The December 4 Paris reunion proved a disappointment. It was now obvious to Kissinger that Hanoi was "playing chicken" – and why shouldn't it? Again, Kissinger suggested bombing preceded by a television address.[159] Nixon demurred on the television address (too "melodramatic"), but concurred that in the event of a breakdown, "we will act immediately on the military side." Elaborating and demonstrating unconditional willingness, Nixon added:

> You can assume I will order a very substantial increase in the military action against the North, including the use of B-52s over the Hanoi-Haiphong complex. I would be willing to order that tomorrow prior to the next meeting. I would like your recommendation on this. In any event we should have the whole salvo ready to go when the talks break down, if they do.[160]

Between and November 24 and December 4, Nixon had decisively swung behind the bombing option.

On the flanks, Saigon was beginning to exploit the increasingly public Nixon-Kissinger split. Hanoi was acting like a jilted lover. When the two sides reconvened over December 6–7 there was deadlock, and again the status of the DMZ was re-opened, threatening to derail settlement. Kissinger advised Nixon that compromise with the North was possible, although this would constitute a "murderously difficult accomplishment," but that getting Saigon on board would be "nearly impossible."[161] In a sign of some desperation, Kissinger concluded that "massive bombing" until the following summer would now probably be necessary to secure the bare minimum US demands (the release of POWs). A more moderate Nixon rejected this somewhat apocalyptic "crossroads," instructing Kissinger to present minimum conditions, then advise the North Vietnamese delegation that further deliberations would be necessary in Washington.[162] Specifically, Nixon instructed that Hanoi should not be threatened with military action, a declaration that would obviously backfire in the forums of the public relations war. However, in private, Nixon was fully in accord with Kissinger's hard line:

> However your meeting comes out ... and of course I know and agree with you that there is a very remote possibility that you will make a breakthrough on the settlement side, we will embark on a very heavy bombing program in the North.[163]

Three days later the parties met again, with an increasingly irritated Nixon offering advice over fraught telephone links. Hanoi's stance at this meeting would later be described as "clumsy, blatant and essentially contemptuous of the United States" but the real fault lay with Saigon.[164] As well as questioning the status of the DMZ, Tho again raised problems over the composition of the International Commission of Control and Supervision, the body that would monitor the ceasefire, as well as technical questions over the meaning of the ceasefire. Faced with an impasse, the talks were recessed on December 13.

The following day, Nixon, Kissinger, and Haig met to discuss strategy. By the end of the one-and-a-half-hour meeting, a consensus to bomb emerged. With some perverseness, Hanoi was blamed for the fiasco, but it was Saigon that had created all the problems. Kissinger was certainly in an ill-tempered mood. For an individual whose voluminous memoirs would elevate the art of gracious and generous recollection of opponents, his description of the Vietnamese as a "tawdry, miserable; filthy people" was both uncharacteristic and below his usual magnanimous nature.[165] The three interlocutors were conscious that time was running out. The White House was now staring at a two-week window before a swelling regiment of hostile congressmen marched back to Washington. This annual migration would bring with it the likelihood of a terminal cut to supplemental appropriations for the war. For this reason, Nixon again rejected Kissinger's suggestion that a six-month bombing campaign would be necessary, instead proposing an intensive two-week campaign.[166]

Argument over ultimate responsibility for the bombing decision emerged after the events, from protagonists taken aback by the scale of the international and domestic response, and now wishing to gloss their place in history. At the time, there was matter-of-factness and some vagueness in the discussions (albeit Kissinger did suggest at one point that Washington should bomb "the bejesus out of them"). This wariness has been interpreted as Kissinger and Nixon attempting to place themselves on "the right side of history," but such conspiratorial interpretations ignore that nobody was taking a record of the meeting anyway, and only one person in the room knew that all conversations were being taped.[167] The possibility of bombing had been discussed for the last three weeks. The only real points of difference between Nixon and Kissinger had been when and for how long. In characteristic fashion, Nixon was more concerned with his domestic enemies, advising Kissinger never to forget "the press is the enemy, the press is the enemy, the press is the enemy, the establishment is the enemy, the professors are the enemy, the professors are the enemy" and suggesting his national security advisor write these words down 100 times on a blackboard.[168]

Nixon was always at his most decisive when cornered – indeed, he almost seemed to relish challenges that would crush ordinary mortals. This was never truer than in mid-December 1972 when he took the single most unpopular foreign policy decision of his presidency – to bomb Hanoi into submission.

There was no television address. On December 16, Kissinger delivered a sober 52-minute press conference expounding in great detail the course of the negotiations and current impasse. This necessary prelude gave no hint of what was to follow. We are "one decision away from a settlement" Kissinger advised a packed press room, but nobody guessed that the military decision had already been taken (Hanoi, ironically, did know because Nixon despatched a secret cable warning the Politburo that military action would follow if agreement were not reached).[169] On December 17, US aircraft began to seed Haiphong Harbor with mines, and the following day, at 7.43pm local time, the B-52s arrived over the skies of Hanoi, dumping their first loads on Hoa Lac Airfield west of the capital. Kissinger chuckled that the raids would "break every window in Hanoi" and pointed out to an approving Nixon that the bomb loads would be equivalent to a 4,000-strong raid in the Second World War. Hanoi would "think twice before they break the agreement" in the future, Nixon added, but of course, there would be no future, for Nixon or the bombers. This was the last hurrah.

Even by the standards of the last four years of anti-Nixon rhetoric, the eruption in the national and international media was unprecedented. "Outrage," "shame," "terror bombing," "madness," "slaughter," all were invoked in a Niagara Fall of protest. Nixon's sanity was questioned. NATO allies criticized the bombing. The Swedish government went so far as to liken the White House to Nazis, a barb which particularly irritated Kissinger whose family had escaped the genocide by fleeing to America.

The "Christmas Bombings" played out against the awkward distraction of *Time* magazine voting Nixon and Kissinger joint "Men of the Year." Knowing all too well that Nixon would be furious over celebrity status bestowed on one of his aides, Kissinger pleaded with the editor-in-chief, Hedley Donovan, to remove him from the billing. This only served to provoke a mischievous Donovan into threatening to promote Kissinger as sole "Man of the Year." Nixon was not amused and unsubtly signaled that Kissinger's time was up. But for the prolongation of the peace talks, and later the Watergate scandal, this is the course the career of America's most talented national security advisor of the modern era would likely have taken.

The irony was that Operation *Linebacker II* has some claim to be the most successful single operation of the entire American war in Vietnam.[170] Over 11 days (December 18–29), Nixon achieved what had eluded three predecessor presidents over two decades – Hanoi's submission. Robert Thompson later commented: "you won the war, they were at your mercy" – and he was right.[171] *Linebacker II* was the bludgeon that LeMay would have wielded in 1965, raising the question whether the old warhorse had been right all along. The heavier irony, however, is that Hanoi did not need to be pummeled into submission. The Politburo wanted to settle, notwithstanding its infuriating haggling. But for Saigon's obstructive attitude, there would have been no *Linebacker II*. America's unnecessary war would end, fittingly, in an unnecessary crescendo of violence.

The heaviest bombing runs since the Second World War involved both Seventh Air Force and Navy Task Force 77. At the time, it felt like a huge risk. This would not only be the longest ranged bombardments in the history of aerial warfare, but America would be risking irreplaceable aircraft and crew against one of the mostly densely defended cities in the world.[172] In total, some 200 B-52s and several hundred tactical aircraft were involved in various roles. The combined air forces dumped 20,237 tons of bombs in just over 1,500 sorties (or 14 times the bomb tonnage dropped on Monte Cassino). Hanoi's skies filled with "flying telegraph poles" and 15 B-52s were shot down (some crews described the SAMs as "deadly doughnuts" because of the corona light effects against the night cloud cover).[173] However, virtually all the losses were experienced in the first week. By the second week, the SAM batteries lost their sting, Hanoi's MiG-21s abandoned an unequal fight against superior F-4 Phantoms, and the skies belonged to the bombers.[174] The low point came on day three, when the loss of seven aircraft provoked a certain amount of panic within Strategic Air Command and a quick revision of tactics. The climax was witnessed on December 26 when 120 bombers supported by 113 tactical aircraft attacked from seven different directions, plastering ten targets in the Hanoi area. One aircraft was lost. Between 884 and 1,242 SAMs were launched over the 11 days, which suggests a less than three percent success rate.[175] American counter-measures, with the improved tactics, had whipped Soviet technology.

For some, this lashing was well overdue. Lieutenant Colonel Hendsley Connor, commander of 486th Bombardment Squadron, made no apologies:

> As we gathered for the meeting, speculation was running about fifty-fifty that we would be going home. Others of us had a premonition and were saying nothing. The General came in and the meeting got underway. The briefing officer opened the curtain over the briefing board, and there it was – we were not going home. Not yet, anyway. We were going north. Our targets were to be Hanoi and Haiphong, North Vietnam. At last the B-52 bomber force would be used in the role it had been designed for.[176]

A fellow squadron leader, Lieutenant Colonel George Allison, caught in the excitement of the moment, felt the same way:

> It is difficult to describe a feeling which develops gradually around intuition, hunches, rumors, logic, and so forth, but subsequently draws its substance from fact. Was it happiness, relief, a sense of "we're finally going to do it; it's long overdue"? ... Glad that we were finally going to show them a thing or two?[177]

General James McCarthy, their briefing officer and a veteran of over 1,000 sortie briefings, reported, "I can truthfully say that that group of combat crews was the most attentive I have ever seen."[178]

For pilot Michael Connors, the actual sorties were "quite hectic, quite exciting."[179] Connors was a veteran of 265 B-62 missions over South Vietnam, where the pilots faced no risk. Bombing the North was quite different. This was "really going to go to war" and "frightening." From his eyrie at an altitude of five miles, "you could see little firecrackers like going off and it was very distinct, very obvious that those were SAMs ... and as you got closer they just started going up around you." But Hanoi's ring of air defenses was insufficient to deal with the weight of attacks. Connors observed,

> They had shot their best SAMS on nights one and night two ... by the end ... toward night eight or nine or ten, they were shooting the worst SAMs ... They would go out of control. They would go up and spin ... we could just watch them blowing up, at wrong altitudes, blowing up on the pads, failing.

For crew unlucky to sustain a SAM strike, the overwhelming question was: could they nurse the aircraft back to Thailand, the nearest safe haven? One such crew (Peach 2), piloted by Major Cliff Ashley, recalled the awful moment when this prospect became a reality:

> The SAM had exploded right off our left wing. The fuel tank on that wing was missing along with part of the wing tip. We had lost #1 and #2 engines. Fire was streaming out of the wreckage they had left. Fuel was coming out of holes all throughout the left wing. Most of our flight instruments were not working. We had lost cabin pressurization. We were at 30,000 feet. Our oxygen supply must have been hit, because the fuel gauge was slowly decreasing.[180]

Determined not to be taken prisoner, the stricken Peach 2 was coaxed for the next desperate hour, accompanied by two F-4 Phantoms, until she was safely over Thai air space. By this time the entire left wing was on fire and one of the Phantom pilots was advising that the aircraft appeared to be on the point of breaking up. The red ABANDON light was switched on and all six crew members ejected safely (or in the case of Lieutenant Colonel Connor and the radar operator, jumped out of the hole left in the fuselage after the navigator ejected). The abandoned airframe banked left, torched spectacularly, and exploded when it hit the ground. As luck would have it, they had bailed out near a Marine base at Nam Phong. Twenty minutes later, a search and rescue helicopter was retrieving the uninjured survivors.

Others were not so lucky. Lieutenant Colonel Bill Conlee was shot down over Hanoi on December 21, on his third mission.[181] With a bleeding face and arm from shrapnel wounds, he landed in an open field under gunfire. No sooner had he dumped his parachute than he was "set upon by a mob of North Vietnamese, both military and civilian." He was stripped to his underwear and made to run a mile "through a gauntlet of people with farm implements, clubs, and bamboo poles." This ordeal left him with a broken rib and damaged knee. He was then loaded onto a truck and driven to the "Hanoi Hilton." Thrown off the back of the flatbed, he suffered a dislocated shoulder. Added to the compression he had suffered from the ejection, Conlee was now unable to sit up, let alone walk. He spent Christmas Day in solitary confinement drinking a pot of tea. The following day the walls of his cell shook from nearby B-52 strikes, which gave him "great encouragement." His visibly shaken captors were later unimpressed when he smiled at them. "This proved to be a mistake," he recalled, "as I was quickly subjected to a rough beating, the worst I received during captivity." Unbowed by this treatment, Conlee "responded with laughs" when subjected to clumsy, North Vietnamese propaganda. Although he could not have known it at the time, he only had to endure a few more weeks of this treatment before release. Some of his fellow inmates in "Heartbreak Annex" had endured years of abuse.

As much as anything, *Linebacker II* was a magnificent planning and logistic exercise. "Every 90 seconds after the first takeoff another fully loaded B-52 would roll down the runway. Anyone who has ever witnessed such an event can never forget it," so wrote one participant.[182]

The planners had been given just three days to prepare the scheme. This would have been an impossible task, but Andersen Air Base in Guam had evolved into an industrial bombing hub. Over 12,000 servicemen were crammed on the island, many living in 12-man tents. Aircraft were refueled and pre-flighted in four hours to meet the demanding schedules. Phase inspections were completed in eight hours, or five times faster than would normally be permissible in peacetime conditions.[183] Support and maintenance staff worked grueling 12-hour shifts with one day off per week (usually spent sleeping). The inflight kitchen found itself churning out 500 meals (the normal demand was 18 meals every 90 minutes).[184]

Once airborne, 43rd Strategic Wing's B-52s taking off from Guam made their night-time rendezvous over the northern coast of the Philippines with tankers which had flown from Okinawa. As they approached North Vietnam they were met by another stream of bombers flying in from 307th Strategic Wing, based at U-Tapao, Thailand. Obeying a tactical philosophy known as "press-on," pilots were forbidden from aborting a sortie regardless of the loss of two engines, all bombing computers, the radar systems, defensive gunnery, or ECM. Pilots who broke the "cell" formation (essentially a three-ship of B-52s), to evade SAMs, were threatened with court-martial. Unsurprisingly, given these draconian regulations, just two B-52s aborted in the entire operation.[185]

The longest mission involved an 8,200-mile round trip with the crew airborne for 18 hours.[186] Despite working in tropical climates, the crews had to carry thermal wear to mitigate the loss of cabin heat, an eventuality that befell more than one aircraft. It all worked like clockwork and despite the constant fear of "mid-airs" (collisions), there were none.

The range of struck targets was wide: airfields, rail depots, power plants, warehouses, and storage areas. The inviolable ten nautical mile no-bomb zone centered on Hanoi was penetrated. There was one significant incident of collateral damage – the bombing of Bach Main Hospital – a facility based within a military airfield. Overall, the damage done was huge but civilian casualties were light. Four fifths of the North's electrical power production was put out of action. Three million gallons of petroleum products went up in fire and smoke, or one quarter of Hanoi's reserves. The railways were devastated and Haiphong Harbor totally blocked. The import of war materials collapsed by several hundred percent. Some 1,624 civilians were killed, far fewer than anyone had anticipated given the severity of the bombing raids. The operation wound down, in part, because there were no more strategic targets of value to attack.

Despite the controversy over carpet bombing, the B-52s actually conducted radar-directed bombing, which proved so accurate one pilot later reflected, "It's amazing to me that even under those circumstances [enemy SAM launches] we managed to be as accurate as we were."[187] The North Vietnamese later privately conceded how impressed they had been with the accuracy of the targeting.

More significantly, *Linebacker II* had its intended effect on the peace negotiations. Using the diplomatic channels of the plenary sessions, the Politburo communicated that it wished to resume talks and settle. On a grim January 8, the two sides reconvened and within 48 hours Tho had agreed to virtually all the terms on the table. Ironically, the North Vietnamese party agreed to the draft form of words as they had existed on November 23 – following the first, post-election victory meeting – where Nixon would have happily settled for the October 8 form of words that were more favorable to Hanoi. Who won or lost which trade or concession was rapidly becoming an irrelevant question. Five days later, on January 13, the final form of words was agreed and the two delegations enjoyed their first ever joint meal.

Only Saigon remained to be brought into the fold. Nixon peremptorily informed Thieu in a letter that the United States would sign, and that if Saigon did not, he would announce publicly that the South Vietnamese government had obstructed peace. This would result in an "inevitable and immediate termination of U.S. economic and military assistance."[188] With near-suicidal defiance, Thieu held out until the eleventh hour, only finally capitulating on January 20, on the eve of Nixon's inauguration.

The final meeting between Kissinger and Tho took place on January 22 against the backdrop of Johnson's sudden death. The following day, after a cordial lunch, the two negotiating teams stepped out on a rainy Parisian street and shook hands for the press corps. They were never to meet again. Tersely, Kissinger recorded: "America's Vietnam War was over."[189] The public signing of the Paris Peace Agreements took place on January 27, garnished with the all necessary confection befitting a historic occasion. Kissinger did not attend.

The sense of anticlimax reached across the Atlantic to an indifferent and changing America. The *New York Times* was listing *Jonathan Livingstone Seagull* in its top ten bestseller list, the fable of a gull that rejected materialism and found spiritual enlightenment. Stevie Wonder was climbing the charts with "Superstition." O.J. Simpson was set to become the first player in the

NFL league's history to complete more than 2,000 yards in a single season. "Peace with honor" had been achieved, or so Nixon sought to portray it in his television address to the nation, yet history would dwell on the phrase "decent interval" to explain the events of the middle two weeks of January 1973. Both Kissinger and Tho received the Nobel Peace Prize, but the latter would turn down the award, observing with some honesty that peace had not been secured. Within a year Thieu would officially declare that the agreements were no longer in effect. The epic journey of negotiations between Washington and Hanoi had yielded a peace treaty that barely lasted a year, if that.

Notwithstanding the ultimate failure, it is clear from an abundance of taped and documentary records that both Nixon and Kissinger sought an honorable end to the war, compatible with America's dignity and status, and both worked for the survival, not collapse, of the South Vietnamese government. The later criticism by political opponents that Nixon chiefly sought settlement to boost his re-election prospects also fails. Nixon instructed Kissinger to ignore electoral implications and "do what is right to secure an honorable peace."[190] His consistent preference was to wait until after the election. And nor was Nixon prepared to settle at any price: in the absence of a settlement, he was resolved the United States would do "whatever is required" to thwart Hanoi's aggression, however difficult and regretful this course.[191]

The "decent interval" argument, nevertheless, raises difficult questions.[192] The sentences, "We want a decent interval. You have our assurance," were jotted on page 64 of a lengthy top-secret briefing folder, prepared for the historic China trip (in fact there had been 164 meetings between US and Chinese officials since 1955, all unfortunately fruitless).[193] The words were annotated against the bullet point: "We are ready to withdraw all our forces by a fixed date and allow objective realities shape the political future." This was reinforcement of the first sentence on the page and the salient point Kissinger wished to impress on his Chinese hosts, namely, that the United States had no desire to interfere in the final political resolution of the conflict in South Vietnam: "On behalf of President Nixon I want to assure the Prime Minister that the United States is prepared to make a settlement that will truly leave the political evolution of [S] Vietnam to the Vietnamese alone."

This was consistent with "the Nixon Doctrine" articulated in Guam, and Nixon's November 3 address to the nation. The document as a whole was informed with the re-posturing of the United States as detached, constructive partner in securing global peace, rather than interfering military hegemon.

Critics have interpreted the "decent interval" negatively. This interpretation depends on viewing the phrase "objective realities" as a euphemism for "eventual and probably violent North Vietnamese takeover of South Vietnam." However, the phrase was actually a reprise of Kissinger's broader point, made on page 16, that the world's geopolitical map was changing, and the United States wished to "deal with the [changing] objective realities of the post-war world." This new reality meant dealing with countries with opposing views not necessarily shared by the United States. Insofar as "objective realities" might then be a communist government in Saigon, critics are right. Kissinger was almost certainly indicating that an eventual North Vietnamese takeover was possible, and the United States would tolerate this evolution over the long term. But this was not an evolution Washington would tolerate if achieved by force in the immediate aftermath of a peace settlement. The administration sought "a ceasefire for all of Indochina" (the fourth annotated bullet point), which would allow the possibility of "a fair political solution." This was Nixon's and Kissinger's consistent desideratum.

The tenor of the whole page was reassurance to Peking that Washington had no long-term designs in Indochina and wished to pursue a broad policy of "Asia for Asians." At the same time, the United States would not be party to a dishonorable deal. Kissinger bluntly told Prime Minister Chou En-lai, when pressed on this matter, America "cannot be asked to engage in major acts of betrayal as a basis of its foreign policy."[194] The scrawled words in the margins of page 64 were not the jottings of a "squalid" or "sordid" deal, as later charged.

In the context of the entire document, a different picture emerges. Kissinger's very first bullet point under "My Objectives" (page nine) was: "– Indications firm enough to be taken as assurances that the Chinese will use their influence on the North Vietnamese to move them toward a peaceful and acceptable settlement of the Vietnam War."

This general objective was repeated on pages 12, 26, 27, 28, 31, and 60. The overall argument presented was that the United States wished for settlement now; that prolonged conflict was in nobody's interests; and that Washington considered the overthrow of the Saigon government as "flatly unacceptable." The flaw was not so much misjudgment of Hanoi (Kissinger was under no illusions over Hanoi's long-term strategic intentions) as misplaced hope in Peking's influence on its neighbor, which in reality was negligible. The same misjudgment was evident in Nixon. Both, to an extent, had become self-deceived by the historic rapprochements with China and the Soviet Union (Nixon was so proud of this achievement, he suggested a book should be written, simply entitled *1972*). Both, wrongly, believed that Moscow and Peking could rein in their client. In an end-of-November meeting with the Joint Chiefs, Nixon confidently but mistakenly argued, "Whether the war resumes depends on Chinese and Soviet intentions."[195] Both wholly underestimated Hanoi's willingness to fight on at any cost, regardless of what any outside party said.

Both also misread Hanoi's quite different perspectives on Peking and Moscow. From the mid-1950s, the former had pressed Hanoi to seek a political solution. In the mid-1960s Peking reversed this position, memorably captured by Taylor's quip, "the Chinese are determined to fight the USA right up to the last Vietnamese."[196] In the early 1970s, the Chinese position was reversed again. This was perceived by Hanoi as an unconscionable "betrayal." Enduring historic enmity further soured relations. By contrast, the Soviet Union was perceived as the reliable ally. In truth, this perception was quite misplaced. Brezhnev was little interested in the problem of Vietnam, and Russians viewed Vietnamese communism with a certain condescension.

If the "decent interval" argument is overstated, then, on the other side of the ledger, there are also too many avoided issues. The first is the title of the document that was signed in Paris: "Peace Agreement on Ending the War and Restoring Peace to Vietnam." It was just not true and the signatories knew it. The war was not going to end and peace was not going to be restored – both amounted to fraudulent promises. The purpose of the Paris Agreement was to extract America from an unpopular war, with dignity, and to recover her prisoners of war. This goal coincided with Hanoi's overall aim which was to remove US troops from Vietnam, once and for all, as a prelude to concluding the war of liberation. The threat of US air power remained, and would concern Hanoi right to the end, but it was clear that as long as American soldiers remained in the South, the North faced years of uncertain struggle and no guarantee of victory. The Peace Agreement was a ticket home and Hanoi acted as the obliging ticket seller. Saigon was left standing on the platform.

Kissinger privately appreciated this reality. In his December 6 cable to Nixon, he warned:

> Moreover, as I have consistently told you since mid-September, this is a very high risk operation. The eventual outcome of this settlement will essentially turn on the confidence and political performance of the two sides. Having seen the total hatred and pathological distrust between the Vietnamese parties, and knowing as well that Hanoi has no intention of giving up its strategic objectives, we must face the reality that this agreement may lack the foundation of minimum trust that may be needed. Thus it could break down. It will certainly require from us a posture of constant readiness and willingness to intervene.[197]

Over the course of the historic Peking trip he had candidly confided to his hosts: "We are realistic about the future. We recognize that after our forces leave we will be 10,000 miles away and the North Vietnamese will still be at hand in Indochina."[198] He added, "we are not children, and history will not stop on the day a peace agreement is signed … we are not proposing a treaty to end history."[199] He also explicitly recognized the war might restart and the United States would be unlikely to intervene:

> If the North Vietnamese … engage in serious negotiation with the South Vietnamese, and if after a longer period it [the war] starts again after we were all disengaged, my personal judgment is that it is much less likely that we will go back again, much less likely [underlining in the original].[200]

Kissinger thus both recognized the worst could happen and the importance of a "decent interval" for the sake of America's reputation. Nixon also recognized the fragility of the Southern political entity, on one occasion admitting to his national security advisor, "South Vietnam probably is never going to survive anyway."[201] But it was one thing to accept this reality and probable evolution of the Indochinese conflict, and another to engage in cynical machinations. The United States could not indefinitely engage in a war to prevent this evolution. This central point is too quickly bypassed by critics. The frenetic climax to the 1972 peace negotiations is better viewed through the prism of Walter Cronkite's 1968 Tet broadcast: these were the actions of a noble nation that did the best it could. A strident antechamber of hecklers has never afforded a stitch of nobility to the two principal protagonists in the last act of the war: Nixon and Kissinger.

Both men acted, almost quixotically, as if they could somehow defy the gravity of eventual defeat. From Kissinger's perspective, the North's unyielding claim over the South was reason to ensure terms in the agreement that Hanoi would "have an interest in maintaining," by force if necessary. This was a genuine sentiment, not a bargaining ploy. But the terms of the peace agreement ultimately pre-ordained that South Vietnam would not survive anyway. What Nixon could not abide was reunification by communist aggression. It was for this reason he had instructed Admiral Moorer to prepare contingency retaliatory air raids.[202] Nixon had every intention of bombing, if necessary, to save South Vietnam, while conscious of the opposition he would face in Congress and from the "American left." As he never seemed more fulfilled than when landing punches on these enemies, it may be reasonable to assume he meant it.

Technical details also raise questions. Kissinger consistently invoked the clauses prohibiting infiltration as a reason why the South could tolerate the presence of the PAVN on its soil (Hanoi, of course, publicly denied the presence of its soldiers in the South, a lie tolerated to secure the settlement). Over time, without further infiltration, the North Vietnamese forces would wither and cease to be a threat – so went the argument. This argument was crucial because of all objections raised by Saigon the presence of communist soldiers on Southern soil was viewed as the chief objection. Leaving the North Vietnamese in place was tantamount to defeat. Kissinger's counter-argument was just not credible and it is difficult to believe that Washington, dogged and obsessed by the intractable problem of infiltration, actually believed that the mere signing of a piece of paper was going to end infiltration. The only factor that had curtailed – but never stopped – infiltration was B-52 strikes. These were ending. In these circumstances, urging Thieu to grab as much land as possible before the signing ceremony was hardly a credible strategy.

Surprisingly, even on this matter, there was a certain measure of self-delusion, shared by all parties. Nixon thought Hanoi had painted itself into a corner by leaving troops in the South. Kissinger argued that the illegal presence of the North Vietnamese would allow the United States to retaliate strongly to violations. He also seemed to believe (or misunderstand) Hamlet Evaluation Scheme assessments that portrayed 95 percent of South Vietnam in government hands. In complete denial, at the time of signing, the issue of infiltration was not judged mortal.

The same ambiguities and wishful thinking were evident in other aspects of the peace terms. The DMZ provisions called for respect of the 17th parallel and an end to cross-border hostilities. There was no realistic prospect the North would respect this border – it never had. Article 20 called for ceasefires in Laos and Cambodia and the withdrawal of North Vietnamese forces. Hanoi had no intention of abiding by these clauses and relinquishing its handsome advantage in the cross-border sanctuaries. Neither could the signatories guarantee, still less enforce, a cessation of hostilities in these two countries now destabilized by civil wars. The likelihood – and surely every signatory knew it – was that Hanoi would now redouble its efforts in Laos and Cambodia, and renew its operations on the DMZ. The articles were empty promises.

In his defense, Kissinger would later argue that Saigon was offered an "understanding" that in extremis the United States would back its ally and prevent a communist takeover (notably in Nixon's November 14 letter to Thieu). But this discounted the spoiling role of Congress, which Kissinger and all the other actors in the White House were well aware of (Laird flatly told Nixon that congressional support would be "impossible," even before the signings). It was the very fact that Congress was likely to pull the rug from under the war that had driven Nixon's calculations in the closing months of 1972. Had the peace talks unscrambled again at the beginning of 1973, the likelihood is that this scenario would have played out, and the withdrawal from Vietnam would have ended in some disarray, if not ignominy. Why did Kissinger believe this same hostile Congress which had come close to sabotaging his own honorable efforts to secure a dignified peace would now act as South Vietnam's guardian and protector? In his memoirs Kissinger described as "inconceivable" the proposition that Congress would throw it all away, but it is also inconceivable he did not realize this was at least a possibility, if not the probability, given the administration's rough ride with the senators. In private conversation with Chou En-lai he had admitted so.

Even suspending these open questions and their corresponding mitigations, it is difficult to ignore that the signatories did not actually sign up to anything. The 1973 Paris Agreement in this respect repeated the 1954 Geneva Peace Accords (despite Kissinger's avowal that this pitfall was being avoided). The United States and South Vietnamese governments signed on one page; and the North Vietnamese and Provisional Revolutionary Government signed on a separate page. To appease Saigon, the latter was not even mentioned in the text of the Agreement. Misquoting Kennedy, the signatories may as well have been referring to different countries.

The background to the Peace Agreement was a frantic burst of aggressive operations, dubbed "Land-grab 73," in which Hanoi sought to maximize its territorial and bargaining position before the ceasefire. Blasted landscapes were revisited: Quang Tri, An Loc, Kontum, Pleiku, Route 21, Tay Ninh, a rash of hot spots that had never truly been cleared, held, or won over to the government side. Serious clashes with the PAVN were witnessed in over two thirds of South Vietnam's provinces – a true measure of the scale of infiltration, but not of communist success. Just one part of one South Vietnamese province – Quang Tri on the DMZ – was "liberated" and under North Vietnamese governance. All the parrying had achieved very little: the immovable weight of over a million men under arms could not be decisively shifted by a combined PAVN-VC force perhaps seven times smaller.

The reality was that the PAVN had become a demoralized and homesick army supporting a depleted and even more demoralized guerrilla force. Although frowned upon, cadres listened to BBC or Voice of America broadcasts. In February 1973, the average communist soldier saw little to cheer and plenty to complain about. If you were squatting in a jungle camp, it was difficult to see why a ceasefire implied victory, or even whether victory would ever be attainable. Many simply wanted to return to homes in the North. For this brief moment, Nixon and Kissinger had won their war of endurance with Hanoi.

At An Loc, on January 27, 1973, just 11 hours before the guns fell silent, Lieutenant Colonel William Benedict Nolde – who had taught ROTC at Central Michigan University and was later drafted into the army during the

Korean War – was killed. Nobody, it was said, wanted to be the last soldier to die in combat in Vietnam. It fell to Nolde to be that last American.[203] He was 43 years old. His funeral at Arlington Cemetery was attended by Nixon and Haig.

Despite the near-scuttling of the Peace Agreement, Nixon kept his equipment pledges with Thieu. Under the auspices of Project Enhance Plus, the RVNAF was furnished with 105,000 items of equipment, from aircraft to tanks, which augmented unit holdings well beyond normal levels.[204] The total cost of this transfer was in the order of $5 billion (or roughly $30 billion in today's prices). The immediate outcome of this prodigious dumping of war materiel was the creation of the fifth largest armed force in the world.[205]

The ARVN comprised 12 divisions, including the airborne division. This force was stiffened by three tank battalions, 11 cavalry squadrons, five heavy artillery battalions, 15 medium artillery battalions, and 41 light artillery battalions. A further seven Ranger groups and 33 border defense Ranger battalions (derived from the Montagnard CIDG) added a well-motivated corps of troops. This regular force of some half a million men was doubled by the Regional and Popular Forces, and self-defense militias. The VNAF (the fourth largest air force in the world) was now squatting on a fleet of over 2,000 aircraft of all types. The Navy fielded a marine division and around 1,500 craft and ships.

It was too easy to be dazzled by this bull market of war stocks and too inconvenient to question whether it mostly amounted to military boom and bust. No other small or even medium-sized nations in the world maintained such large armed forces, for the good reason that they were totally unsustainable. How would South Vietnam's agricultural economy sustain this force? It could not possibly do so, at least not without continued, generous US support. How would an industrially backward country maintain this equipment? South Vietnam neither had the infrastructure, organizations, nor trained personnel to keep in service, repair, or refurbish the pyramids of equipment now sitting in warehouses and depots. And what of the Pharaohs in the RVNAF – the corrupt cliques of generals who were personally benefiting from this sudden dumping of stocks? Why did anyone believe they had changed their ways after years of failed promises? Did the numbers really stack up anyway? Tires, batteries, and fuel all vanished into the civilian economy. Statisticians in MACV had spent a decade forlornly calculating desertion rates and actual rather than claimed unit strengths. Regardless of the true numbers, the vital question was how many would fight for South Vietnam's survival, which nobody could answer.

For MACV, under Weyand, these intractable questions were suspended. The absolute priorities were the return of American POWs and the total withdrawal of remaining US forces within a 60-day period. Over the course of Operation *Homecoming*, 587 POWs were returned (three had been released in August 1969, in a propaganda gesture). One hundred and fourteen had died in captivity. The fortunate returnees were treated to "cigarettes, candy, and Playboy magazines" on the flight to Clark Air Force Base in the Philippines.[206]

From a total of 802 POWs (661 military and 141 civilians or foreign nationals), 472 had been held in North Vietnam, 263 in South Vietnam, 31 in Laos, 31 in Cambodia, and five in China.[207] Just four percent had managed to escape.

From the beginning, their treatment was appalling. Hanoi roundly ignored the 1947 Geneva Conventions, refused to acknowledge prisoner of war status or reveal names, and did not permit inspections by the International Red Cross. Prisoners were wretchedly tortured and kept in solitary confinement. They were not allowed to communicate with each other or their families. They were not allowed to read, exercise, or attend religious services. This barbaric treatment was only finally relaxed in the fall of 1969, in a public relations offensive which backfired and only served to cause outrage at the manner in which POWs had been treated.[208]

The longest-serving aviator POW in the North was Navy pilot Everett Alvarez (3,113 days). Two prisoners were held in China for 19 years, on "spying" charges. One remarkable pilot, Vern Ligon, had previously escaped from Stalag Luft 1 during the Second World War. The infamy of the "Hanoi Hilton" was miserably deserved. There is no extenuation, but it is worth observing that many facilities had previously been French colonial prisons, which also witnessed abominable acts.

POW endurance was frankly astonishing. During the Korean War, exaggeration over American prisoners "collaborating" with communists provoked a rash of dubious psychological warfare programs (how else to explain why a patriotic American boy cooperated with "Commies"?), as well as the development of interrogation techniques such as water-boarding that would become notorious in the 21st century. In Vietnam, quite the reverse happened. The brutality of the North Vietnamese provoked dogged resistance. A grim humor and ridicule of naive communist attempts at indoctrination was one plank. Ingenuity (tap codes between cells) was another. Sheer willpower was another, although no prisoner was able to tolerate the excruciating pain and cruelty of "the ropes." The servicemen prisoners were fortified by a military ethos. Civilian prisoners were not but showed equal courage. Missionary nurse Betty Ann Olsen was captured during the Tet Offensive. She resisted barbarous mistreatment for months before succumbing to malnutrition and illness. The last three days of her life were spent lying in her own feces, too weak to move or eat.[209] A misjudged visit to North Vietnam by actress Jane

Fonda widened the controversies (and enduring opprobrium from veterans groups: "Politicians, wars and scandals come and go, but hating Jane Fonda is forever").[210] As a group, the Vietnam War POWs demonstrated remarkable collective solidarity. Perhaps it is not coincidental that so many former POWs went on to pursue distinguished military and civilian careers.

The final withdrawal of US troops proved quick and efficient. Weyand's staffs had pre-prepared a Countdown Plan which was activated the day after the signing of the Peace Agreements. At the time, there were just over 23,000 US servicemen in South Vietnam, and a further 35,000 from contributing allies.[211] In total, there were four phases to the withdrawal, each lasting two weeks. Notwithstanding a last-minute delay provoked by disputed arrangements over prisoner releases, all troops quit the country on March 29, or two days ahead of the cut-off date.[212]

Concurrently, on January 29, a civilian Defense Attaché Office (DAO) assumed responsibility for US affairs from MACV, led by Major General John E. Murray.[213] The loyal Ellsworth Bunker prepared to hand over his ambassadorial post to the highly strung Graham Martin. In Washington, Laird ceded to Elliott L. Richardson, a veteran of Utah Beach who would only serve briefly under Nixon before resigning on principle over the Watergate scandal. The DAO was established for 1,200 posts but the unpopularity of Vietnam left a third of the appointments unfilled.[214]

A mixed coda to the war was played out at the Rex Hotel in Saigon. The building had started life as a two-story car dealership, Bainier Auto Hall, which showcased Citroen and other European cars. In 1959 the building was turned into a Rex Complex hotel with three cinemas, a cafeteria, dance hall, and library. It became better known for its conference room which daily hosted the MACV press brief. On Monday February 12, the eight-year-old spectacle of the 5 O'Clock Follies had its final performance. Army Major Jere Forbus, the last Follies star, sighed, "Well, we may not have been perfect, but we outlasted Fiddler on the Roof." Associated Press Saigon bureau chief, Richard Pyle, was less jocular, describing it "the longest-playing tragicomedy in Southeast Asia's theater of the absurd." [215] In a calculated act, Hanoi overlaid its own sediment of history on the hotel, using the same conference room to announce the formal reunification of Vietnam two years later.

The final hour of the final day came quickly. There was perfunctory media coverage. That week *Time* magazine led with a cover on the new class of Arab leaders and followed with a topical story on rising beef prices. On Thursday March 29, the 500,000-strong force which had once made up Military Assistance Command Vietnam had been reduced to some 140 Saigon-based embassy guards and a 50-strong liaison contingent in the DAO.[216] Some 575 naval personnel also remained in-country, awaiting repatriation.[217] More than

7,000 civilians employed by the Defense Department made up a rearguard, contracted to remain in South Vietnam beyond March 31 to assist in the transfer of equipment and technical skills. The intention had been to hand over logistic responsibilities to the South Vietnamese armed forces. The reality was a "farce" in the estimation of the US general in command of the program.[218] Some 200 logistic bases collapsed to 37. The everyday running of the armed forces – maintenance, warehousing, construction, and stevedoring – all now depended on a small army of Americans, Singaporeans, Filipinos, Chinese, and Koreans, the "happy contractors" who "liked the money." At the time, MACV had 383 contracts on its books with a value of $255 million ($1.2 billion at current prices, a relative bargain compared to the Pentagon's recent "trillion dollar wars").

A gossamer layer of cloud tempered the spring sunshine. Bored servicemen with suitcases waited outside Camp Alpha, the out-processing center. A chartered TWA airliner and USAF C-141s waited for them on the tarmac. Curious North Vietnamese and Viet Cong representatives took the opportunity to snap photographs of the historic occasion. A four-strong ceremonial party representing each of the four services furled the American flag for the last time. Elsewhere, unrecorded disestablishment ceremonies took place in Da Nang, Qui Nhon, Cam Ranh Bay, Can Tho, and Vung Tau. Always one of the more thoughtful generals of the war, Frederick Weyand did not prolong the ceremonies. The former criminology graduate had no inclination to dwell at the scene of the crime. Later that afternoon, Weyand bade farewell to an honor party of Saigon's generals. In a generous gesture he made a short speech in Vietnamese: "Our mission has been accomplished. I depart with a strong feeling of pride in what we have achieved, and in what our achievement represents."[219] The sentiments were politic but feigned. Across the airport, another 30 coffins were being unloaded. Colonel Eimar Himma made the honest observation: "There's going to be a full-blown war starting up after we leave."[220] But it would not be an American conflict. Nixon said he would not be the first president to lose a war. He kept the promise.

Chapter 7

LOSING A WAR,
MARCH 1973–APRIL 1975

The ceasefires across South Vietnam proved a thin fiction. The dying days of January 1973 witnessed encroachment, flag-planting, and land-grabbing on both sides, even as the ink was drying on the Paris Peace Agreement. In the north, the true border ran 20 miles south of the 17th parallel where South Vietnamese marines held on to the ruins of Quang Tri City, but little else. Swathes of the Central Highlands adjacent to the Laotian and Cambodian borders lay in communist hands. And in the south, in the Delta, government control was measured by dyke lengths. A map of South Vietnam revealed a "leopard-spot" pattern of communist occupation, much of it unbroken since the 1950s. It was not accidental that the Viet Cong referred to communist-held settlements as "maquis" villages. When chronicler of the final battles on the B2 Front, Lieutenant General Tran Van Tra, was taken from An Loc by American helicopter to settle ceasefire arrangements in Saigon, the pilot turned to him and said, half jokingly, half seriously, "You have won the war." Tra was more impressed with the bomb-devastated landscape below him, a view he had never seen before.

A Four-Party Joint Military Commission, led by General Gilbert Woodward, proved ineffective. This gave way to a Two-Party Joint Military Commission, which collapsed immediately. The International Commission of Control and Supervision – whose task it was to prevent territorial violations – proved impotent or biased.[1] Within a matter of weeks the Canadian contingent quit, frustrated. The North Vietnamese delegation proved paranoid, convincing themselves that every meeting was a "trick" of the Saigon "lackeys and puppets."

Game American officers at Tan Son Nhut plied the dour communists with whiskey, grateful that they would soon be leaving.

The general ceasefire in South Vietnam was in fact broken the day after the signing ceremony in Paris (over 1,000 violations). Hanoi used the truce to implement a three-phase "opportunity plan of the High Command," seizing hundreds of outposts and hamlets as well as cutting strategic routes. There was a run on sewing machines and blue and red materials as the communists sought to mass-produce National Liberation Front flags.[2] Thanks to a document captured the previous October, Saigon was well aware of Hanoi's scheme and responded with its own preplanned "Ly Thuong Kiet 1973 Plan," reversing some communist incursions, especially in the Saigon environs and Delta.[3] Over 1.6 million South Vietnamese flags were hastily distributed in what had become a war of flag-planting gestures. The communists complained that Saigon mounted almost 20,000 "land-grabbing operations" in the space of two months, but both sides played this game.

Hanoi's response was even more violence, intimidation, and terrorism. In the 20 weeks following the ceasefire, 1,017 incidents were recorded in Military Region 1 (with the withdrawal of US forces, the former CTZs became Military Regions 1 to 4).[4] At the opposite end of the country, in Military Region 4, there were 800 in the first three weeks. Much of this violence was due to the "rice war" – as many as 600 tons were being smuggled north every month to feed the People's Army.[5] By the mid-year, some 3,000 incidents were being recorded every month.[6] Laotian and Cambodian neutrality was never respected. Exploiting the departure of American troops, more than 100,000 communist soldiers were rotated south, flagrantly disregarding the terms of the ceasefire. The North even mounted four brazen, divisional-sized attacks; on the DMZ, on the Cambodian border, in the Central Highlands, and in the old War Zone D. Kissinger's hopes that Northern infiltration would cease were always naive.

At the time of the signing of the Agreement, as many as 13 PAVN divisions and 75 regiments – 148,000 combat troops – were deployed in South Vietnam.[7] Combined with support units this number rose to 219,000. Thirteen regiments were based in Cambodia (30,000 men). Another 70,000 were based in Laos. Opposing this force was the 1.1-million-strong RVNAF, but this was a misleading figure because too many units were unreliable if not useless. Villages pacified by day were occupied at night by the Viet Cong. There was no more security than existed before, and in some districts security deteriorated. The South Vietnamese government held all the provincial capitals and major towns, but this was shallow governance when so many outposts could only be resupplied by helicopter or parachute drops. A nationwide matrix of 3,400 South Vietnamese bases and outposts was impotent to stop the infiltration routes. In response to the repeated incursions the ARVN resorted to prophylactic fire. Over the course of 1973, IV Corps artillery batteries fired off more than 190,000 shells in the Delta. A single artillery shell cost $225, or the monthly salary of a major general in the ARVN.[8] The profligacy soon ended.

An estimated 80,000 South Vietnamese lost their lives to the violence in 1973, a period when the country was purportedly at peace.[9] Both Vietnams seemed to enter a period of decay. In the South, galloping inflation and the loss of tens of thousands of jobs following the American withdrawal worsened the lot of an already exhausted population (160,000 directly employed and perhaps ten times this number in indirect employment). Military families were especially badly hit, fueling corruption. In some notorious cases, South Vietnamese officers traded weapons and ammunition to Northern counterparts. Shameless helicopter pilots would only fly if bribed. Thieu's "three-selfs" program (self-defense, self-management, self-sufficiency) proved another empty initiative in a country dizzied by a merry-go-round of failed programs.

For the communist leadership, the signing of the Paris Peace Agreement created the challenge of sustaining bellicosity and further self-sacrifice in an equally exhausted civilian population and weary soldiery. In a candid interview with Italian journalist Oriana Fallaci, Giap confessed the war had cost the North half a million casualties.[10] After three decades of warfare, Northerners as much as Southerners craved peace. American servicemen had served one-year tours. Northern soldiers could spend three or four years away from their families.

Hanoi viewed with dismay "the rather widespread phenomenon of pacifist thought and a lack of vigilance."[11] This "negative tendency" was reinforced by

> the rather widespread ideological tendency ... to believe that the Agreement could be implemented, to believe in the role of the International Commission of Control and Supervision and the Joint Military Commission, and to believe in the possibility of setting up the National Council of Reconciliation and Concord and the tripartite coalition government.[12]

For the Politburo, the peace negotiations had always been a deeply cynical game. It came as a surprise – even a shock – that Hanoi's foot soldiers did not share this attitude and genuinely believed, or wanted to believe, in the possibility of peace.

At the beginning of 1974, a traditional flurry of fighting over the Tet period gave way to the so-called Ceasefire II in the summer, but this only served as a temporary respite. In the north, 304B and 711th PAVN Divisions made a thrust into the Que Son Valley but were deflected by 3rd ARVN Division. Further south, 324B PAVN Division threatened to cut the coastal Highway 1 between Hue and Da Nang but was also repulsed. In the Central Highlands, 320th PAVN Division was parried south of Pleiku by 22nd ARVN Division. 3rd PAVN Division actually did succeed in interdicting Highway 1 at three points in Binh Dinh Province. Across all fronts Northern "strategic raids" were gradually eroding the South's capability to hold ground and resist. Over a six-month period, both sides suffered more than 15,000 casualties.[13] Unit strengths in the South declined as one quarter of draftees simply deserted. Nixon looked the other way, doubly hobbled by the growing Watergate scandal and an antagonistic Congress. By now, the clock was ticking against both the President and America's involvement in Indochina. In June, legislation was passed cutting funds for military operations in Cambodia and Laos. On August 15, further legislation came into effect terminating the authorization of funds for combat operations anywhere in Southeast Asia. Meaningful Indochinese policy effectively expired on this mid-holiday Wednesday; a day when Americans flocked to movie theaters to enjoy the vicarious horrors of *The Exorcist*, or tuned in to Maureen McGovern crooning *The Morning After*, a sugary song about rebirth and sunshine following the night. For Nixon – who had resigned the presidency six days previously to avoid the indignity of impeachment – there was only penumbral gloom.

In December, operational and maintenance funds for the South Vietnamese forces were cut precipitously. The manner in which this happened was shoddy. The Senate, led by Ted Kennedy, drastically cut the 1974 Defense Appropriations Bill. Fearing a loss of morale, Ambassador Martin refused to allow communication of the reduced funding to the ARVN. As a consequence, the South Vietnamese Central Logistics Command continued to expend and order war materiel at the usual rates, unaware that it was approaching a cliff-edge.[14]

Martin's iron control of reporting had already manifested itself in other ways. The reality was that the massive logistics support offered by Washington – Operation *Enhance Plus* – was sinking in a quagmire of corruption and insufficient funding. Martin was determined that this reality not be communicated to Washington. CIA chief analyst Frank Snepp was strictly ordered not to "look at the warts" and reporting on corruption was discouraged or downgraded (a lengthy study was undertaken, but CIA boss George Carver in Washington "caveatted it out of existence").[15] To the very end, America's war in Vietnam was crippled by false or misleading reporting.

Martin's fears of alarming Saigon were nevertheless justified: at current rates of expenditure, he wrote, "Tentative ammunition replacement through the balance of the fiscal year would leave a projected balance ... far below the ceasefire level that represents a minimum safety position against both enemy capabilities and also present estimates of intentions."[16] In plain language, the South Vietnamese would run out of bullets. By May 1975, it was estimated, Saigon's soldiers would be clean out of fuel. Infantrymen were being restricted to one or two magazines of ammunition. Bandages were being rewashed and re-used. Martin's military advisor, General John Murray, exploded at Washington's false promises, which left him as "point man in the duplicity."[17] Murray, a thoughtful world war veteran, already held dim views of the modern US Army which he judged had institutionalized mediocrity and hypocrisy. Vietnam convinced him that "the best way to handle idiocy is to laugh at it," but the effective termination of support to the ARVN left him unsmiling. The effects of the funding cuts were immediate: one fifth of the VNAF's aircraft were grounded; 400 pilots in training in the United States were recalled mid-course; half of all APCs were rendered non-operational; 35 percent of all tanks were immobilized; and lavish artillery support ended. In one year, the VNAF lost 281 aircraft – just eight replacements were received.[18] This was not a sustainable war. Few in the Senate cared. America was a country not only facing a constitutional crisis but also the aftershocks of a global oil crisis and recession.

In South Vietnam, the collapse of American military and economic support had the same effect as switching off a life support machine. The patient gasped for breath, struggled, and then went into terminal decline. It fell to the increasingly dictatorial Thieu to put up the struggle with yet another policy fantasy: the "Four No's" – no negotiations, no communism, no coalition government, and no surrender.[19] It was tough talk but he was beating a drum that his demoralized and war-drunk nation could not follow.

In a mirror opposite to the declining military strength of the South, the communist pugilist was now re-invigorated with the oxygen of an effective logistics and materiel build-up. A secret CIA report estimated that from 1970 to 1974, Hanoi received $5.6 billion in aid from the Soviet Union and China, of which just under half was military aid.[20] The assessment warned, "in 1974, delivery of ammunition to Hanoi markedly increased and reached a level as high as that of 1972" – or a certain indicator that the communists were planning another major offensive. It further cautioned that comparisons with Saigon were treacherous because the South was required "to maintain roughly twice the number of men under arms to defend all of South Vietnam –and thus must have commensurately larger logistic support." Washington needed to be doubling down on the communist support to the North but military aid to Saigon was being choked off.

However, the view that an enfeebled South fell to a strengthened North is somewhat simplistic. Saigon did need commensurately more support, but so did Hanoi. Three Northern corps were raised following the withdrawal of US forces. These devoured resources. The principal reason why Hanoi planned a two-year campaign over 1975–76 was because materiel and ammunition stockpiles were judged "still very deficient." The memory of the 1972

Easter Offensive hung like a pall. Following early successes, the campaign had become unsustainable. The Military Commission of the Party Central Committee did not wish to repeat the experience. A regional command such as the southernmost B2 Front was under orders *not* to use tanks or artillery at the start of the 1975 dry season, except with authority from Hanoi, such was the concern over resourcing the war effort.[21]

A critical shortage was artillery shells. At the end of 1974, the North held stocks of roughly 100,000 shells across all fronts, including reserves. An eight-gun battery firing at a deliberate rate of fire for just ten minutes consumed 480 shells. These were insufficient numbers to sustain a prolonged campaign. So desperate was the situation, shell casings were being recycled and refilled – a dangerous practice.

The key difference ultimately lay not in the numbers. Neither side, in fact, was receiving sufficient aid to prosecute and sustain a general war. Hanoi would win its war looting Southern stocks and stealing fuel to keeps its columns on the road. The difference between the two protagonists lay in the psychology of the struggle; one defeatist and the other determined.

———

The vertebral column of the communist enterprise remained, as it always had been, the Ho Chi Minh Trail. Since the mid-19th century, Vietnamese had known no national achievement, except as coolies to the French. Modernity and industrialization had been imposed but not shared. The *routes coloniales*, railways, and iron bridges had served as the commercial arteries of an exploitative colonial master. When the French quit, they left behind a rudimentary industrial base, geared to their export markets. The Soviet and Chinese engineers that later flooded into Hanoi and Haiphong were even more rudimentary and just as self-serving behind a veneer of communist fraternalism. The Ho Chi Minh Trail by comparison was indisputably a Vietnamese achievement, the "great accomplishment of our people" as Le Duan put it, and the first of the modern age. Few North Vietnamese memoirs fail to mention the Trail and all do so with veneration. When Kissinger invited Le Duc Tho to deliver a lecture at Harvard University, Tho responded by suggesting Kissinger visit the mighty "Truong Son."

Over the course of 1973, equipment lost in the Christmas bombings was made good, including, crucially, tanks and long-range artillery. The vital Route 9 in Quang Tri was linked with the supply routes east of the Annamite Range. An unbroken communications network was established from Hanoi to the Cambodian sanctuaries. According to Hoang Van Thai's memoirs – that likely inflated numbers – a 3,000-mile network of fuel pipelines stretched from

Quang Tri, through the Central Highlands, and south to Loc Ninh. In total, 12,500 miles of jungle roads were built, resembling "lengths of sturdy hemp rope being daily and hourly slipped around the neck and limbs of the monster who would be strangled with one sharp yank when the order was given."[22]

Over 1974, the construction effort redoubled, untroubled by air raids. The vital oil pipeline infrastructure was extended further south. Some 4,000 miles of north-south roads, 2,500 miles of east-west roads, and nearly 3,000 miles of detour roads were either expanded or consolidated – a prodigious effort. Over the first six months of the year, again according to Thai, 25 fresh tank, armored, and artillery battalions infiltrated south. CIA reporting, likely more accurate, suggests more modest numbers: over 1974, the People's Army received just 15 T-59 tanks and some 40 artillery pieces from communist China. The Soviet Union added another 15 T-54 tanks and 45 artillery pieces.[23] A series of caches and supply depots was established extending from the A Shau Valley, in a network across the Central Highlands and west to the coast. In the second half of the year, Hanoi planned to fill these stores with more than 500,000 tons of war supplies.[24] By the end of the year, the North had mobilized some 400,000 troops across the fronts, organized as three corps – the three "strong fists" that would smash the South. Even compensating for Thai's inflationary numbers it was undeniable the North was preparing for a major push.

This Sisyphean project swallowed up 75,000 soldiers in the Binh Trams (logistic companies), 30,000 "shock youths," and a small army of women workers.[25] Tens of thousands of Chinese soldiers also served in the "rear base," an unprecedented and secret effort that allowed Hanoi to release troops for front-line duties. This included 150,000–170,000 Chinese troops that rotated through the 16–17 antiaircraft divisions which were credited with downing 1,707 American aircraft (as early as July 1965 the CIA detected and was reporting "the introduction of some [Chinese] rear service elements into North Vietnam"; it was never a secret, or at any rate, it was a poor secret).[26] North Vietnam's logistic feats rivaled anything the Allies achieved in the liberation of Europe in 1944–45.

Surprisingly, at least to observers circling the victim like vultures, South Vietnam clung on despite Hanoi's steady encroachments of government-held areas. It even struck back. In Military Region 3, an armored sweep was conducted into Cambodia in an area known as the "Angel's Wings" in Svay Rieng Province.[27] The objective was to disrupt 5th PAVN Division. Led by Lieutenant General Pham Quoc Tham, the 3 Corps Commander, the operation proved a success. But much like the archetypal Battle of the Bulge, it was the last throw of the dice. Debilitated by fuel and ammunition shortages, the ARVN pulled back, leaving in its tracks the melancholy of what might have been.

This last sweep could not mask that across South Vietnam, the din of war was getting louder as the People's Army nibbled away at the ARVN's matrix of bases in a series of "strategic raids." From north to south, an unmistakable process of strangulation was all too obvious. Notwithstanding its growing numbers, Hanoi was not yet strong enough to make a final push. But as Saigon softened, so Hanoi hardened.

It seemed fitting – as the players reached the final act – that fresh and untainted American leadership was left with the difficult task of delivering the requiem lines. The bluff Gerald Ford, who assumed the presidency in August 1974, had no military options and could not have exercised them anyway in the face of an antagonistic Congress. His policy towards South Vietnam rested in naive hopes and unrealistic expectations. When later pressed on what grounds he had based these hopes, his lame answer was that as President he felt "I ought to be optimistic."[28] For the first time in many years, the poisonous word "Vietnam" was not even mentioned in the State of the Union address. One week later, Ford openly stated in a press conference that America's armed forces would not re-enter the war.[29] His predecessor was in disgrace and Johnson dead. Kennedy had become an embroidered myth. Both Truman and Eisenhower had also passed away. Every American president embroiled in Vietnam was now either dead, or in Nixon's case, as good as.

The same passing of the old guard could be witnessed elsewhere. Bunker had surrendered his post to Ambassador Graham Martin. Lodge had taken up an occasional post as envoy to the Holy See, an appointment that offered plenty of opportunities for penance. Nolting joined academia and Taylor was retired. Rusk was teaching law and Rogers practicing it. Abrams was dead, Westmoreland was retired, and Wheeler had a few months to live. Harkins had long retired and drifted back to happier memories of wartime service with his beloved Third Army in Europe. Curtis LeMay, who would have bombed North Vietnam, whether or not "back into the Stone Age," was in political limbo. McNamara continued to slave away at the World Bank with his customary energy. Even Laird had thrown in the towel, eventually succeeded by a young Donald Rumsfeld. The entire, odd conjunction of generals – formed by the experience of a world war, hitched to tortured civilian masters in the White House and Congress, commanding rebellious sixties kids in a war they little understood and had less chance of winning – had quit the stage.

———

The issue was now going to be settled by the conflicting strategic calculations made by the two remaining players.

In the South, Thieu fell into a sort of depressed necromancy. The divinations that emerged from this communion with the dead were expressed with arithmetical fatalism. One year before the final communist avalanche Thieu made bleak calculations on how much territory the South Vietnamese armed forces could hold based on the scale of US aid. According to his sums, Saigon required an annual $1.4 billion to secure the entire country. If the aid fell to $750 million, Thieu assessed he would "lose all of Military Region 1 and Military Region 2," or effectively cede half the country.[30] His pessimism ran deeper. If military aid levels fell below a critical $600 million, only the Saigon enclave and parts of the Delta would remain in government hands. This, precisely, is what came to pass. When the general offensive erupted in February 1975, Thieu's decision to abandon the north and Central Highlands should not have surprised – he had already made up his mind to retreat.

This fatalism – or realism – was compounded by two other factors. Thanks to a well-placed spy, Hanoi was aware that Thieu was contemplating strategic retreat into defensive enclaves. The second and more important factor was that these gloomy prognostications were not being forged into a national plan for survival – and anything less now guaranteed extinction. In fact, the notion of withdrawing to more defensible lines had been a subject debated by South Vietnam's generals since the Paris Peace Agreement. Amongst the civilian population, particularly in the north, rumors had swirled that Saigon might exchange territory for security with Hanoi. But paralyzed by a private and correct conviction that retreat would be a prelude to defeat, Thieu did not act. There was no plan. The strategy amounted to a bottled-up, festering thought in the president's mind, shared with only a handful of confidantes, and couched as vague lines of resistance. Thieu routed himself.

In the North, the algebra was more pleasing. South Vietnam's *coup de grâce* was planned in a nondescript house at Number 33, Pham Ngu Lao Street, Hanoi.[31] It was here that a collection of generals and party officials met in March 1974 to discuss the deliberations of the party Central Committee's 21st Plenum, held the previous year, from April to June.[32] "The summer weather had just begun," Thai later reminisced, and "the flamboyant trees along the streets of Hanoi had produced their first bright red blossoms."[33]

The directives that emerged from this plenum were the final great statement of the communist liberation struggle. As such they were the logical conclusion to a narrative that began with Resolution 15 (1959) which committed Hanoi to supporting the National Liberation Front; the resolutions that emerged from the 11th Plenum Special Session (1965) that aimed to defeat the "special war" initiated by Kennedy; and the resolutions that fell out of the 12th Plenum (1968) which sought to defeat Johnson's "limited war" with a general offensive.[34] In party leader Le Duan's later hagiography, it was the 21st Plenum

that "affirmed the continuation of the path of revolutionary violence …
[opening] the way for the final victory of … liberating the south."[35]

The delegates of the Central Military Party Committee met in an ebullient
mood.[36] Their excitement increased when the bald and bespectacled President
Ton Duc Thang took the platform to address the cadres.[37] Thang was born in
the same year that Wilhelm II was crowned emperor of Germany and when the
feudal world of Tsar Alexander III was in decline. In Britain, Queen Victoria
ruled an empire as wide as the oceans. His birth predated cars, aeroplanes,
the radio, and mass electrification. He could not have recognized, let alone
named, the appliances in an average American suburban home. Now, this
octogenarian with six years of breath left in his body was on the threshold of a
famous victory. The frail boy whose first languages were classical Chinese and
French was about to become the first President of a unified Socialist Republic
of Vietnam. His message to the generals was uncompromising: the decisive
moment had arrived. Saigon's "puppet army" faced defeat; now was the time
for the war to "surge forward."

This war was being driven by the twin pistons of the Political Bureau, led by
the hard-line Secretary Le Duan, and the Central Military Party Committee,
steered by Giap. Le Duan, or "Brother Ba" to fellow party members, played
the revolutionary fabulist to Vietnam's revolutionary war. Only communist
"objectivity" and "correctness" counted; two portals through which all his
utterances passed, each new event, each twist and turn on the battlefield,
fitted into a Homeric, unfolding and irreversible narrative. But the machinery
of war needed a good mechanic, not just poets. Giap, "Brother Van," was
the pragmatic, even cautious, foil to Le Duan's romanticism. For all the past
miscalculations, there was no one more experienced than Vo Nguyen Giap in
the technical science of running Hanoi's military machine. North Vietnamese
memoirs have promoted one or other individual, depending upon in which
camp the author sits. Perhaps the balanced verdict is that the major strategic
decisions taken in the final months of the war were shared between these two
personalities. The other members of "Uncle Huong" – the secret code word
for the Politburo – completed an impressive cast of remarkable survivors, but
largely played supporting roles.[38] On the battlefield, General Van Tien Dung,
commander of the southern B2 Front, would steal the glory.

In contrast to Washington, in Hanoi there was continuity, both in
personalities and schemes. The overall strategy had not greatly evolved since
1965. What had changed was that Hanoi would no longer face American
soldiers, and more pertinently, American bombers.[39] The possibility of an
American intervention was not wholly dismissed – indeed it remained a fear –
but Prime Minister Pham Van Dong's view prevailed: Washington was pleased
to be out of South Vietnam and would not return.[40] It was confidence over

American non-intervention that encouraged Giap in the spring of 1974 to sketch out a "two phase basic plan" for the defeat of South Vietnam. The first phase would be mounted as a spring offensive in 1975. In this phase "we would win a victory of decisive significance," or the victory that had been denied in the 1968 Tet and 1972 Easter Offensives. This would involve the capture of one or more major cities: Hue, Da Nang, and possibly Can Tho in the south. The second phase would be mounted in 1976. With the balance of forces altered in Hanoi's favor, this phase would witness a victorious general offensive, blown along by the hurricane of a general uprising.[41]

The anticipated uprising would always remain a wild fantasy. Coyly, the Political Bureau seemed to understand that the theory of communist revolution was not matching the reality, admitting to itself that "control of the people was something with which we were always concerned."[42] No amount of proselytizing was encouraging industrial workers to take over factories, merchants to confiscate shops, or civil servants to seize public offices. Faced with this damp squib of revolutionary fervor in the South, all rested on the North's guns.

The other great paranoia was China. By 1974, febrile imaginations in the Politburo were seeing plots everywhere, especially in Peking, where conspiracy theories were rumoring a Kissinger-Chou-En-Lai scheme which would see Chinese troops advance south across the unguarded Sino-Vietnamese border.[43] Seemingly convinced of this "nefarious plot," reinforced by the Chinese seizure of the Paracel Islands in 1974, it was imperative the People's Army act quickly and decisively – to then switch and meet the historic enemy from the north – following Saigon's capitulation.

Giap's basic plan went through seven revisions by the General Staff before being presented on August 26 to the Political Bureau and Central Party Military Committee.[44] Over October, the strategic picture was hotly debated by these two parties. Overall, the military balance seemed pretty clear. In the north, the People's Army faced five entrenched ARVN divisions. Saigon was protected by another three divisions. The weak point was Military Region 2, the plateau of the Central Highlands. Here, the People's Army faced just two ARVN divisions and the terrain favored the communist vision of a decisive mobile war.

At the end of the summer dry season, even as these deliberations were taking place, two developments significantly bolstered communist morale. The first was Nixon's resignation on August 8. The second was the unexpected sequence of victories on the B3 Front that threatened to cut South Vietnam in half. In western Quang Nam Province, Que Son, Nong Son, and Trung Phuoc all fell. The towns of Gia Vut and Minh Long were also captured in western Quang Ngai. Two further settlements, Phu My and Deo Ngang, were ceded in northern Binh Dinh Province. Then on the day before Nixon's resignation, a decisive victory was won at Thuong Duc, a former Green Beret base 25 miles southwest of Da Nang.[45] With the exception of the latter – Thuong Duc was the first district capital to fall to the communists, provoking protests in Saigon – none of these settlements were particularly important. It was the manner in which ARVN units had collapsed that seemed to hint at a more widespread malaise. The rangers at Thuong Duc had barely resisted an hour before quitting.

The significance of these actions was not missed by the CIA. In a cautious but nonetheless prescient assessment issued on August 9, 1974, analysts judged,

> if the North Vietnamese perceive that the battlefield situation is turning in their favor and/or that the US is no longer willing to come to Saigon's defense, they might be tempted to undertake even heavier action and take greater risks to make major gains in South Vietnam.[46]

"The Communists," it added, "have moved supplies into South Vietnam at an unprecedented rate." Some 40,000 tons of ammunition were detected moving into South Vietnam through the southern Panhandle, a similar amount to the 1972 Spring Offensive.[47] Two new corps headquarters had been formed. In the key Central Highlands, the B3 Front Headquarters had moved over the border and was now deployed midway between Pleiku and Kontum. Two major logistics headquarters had followed – a sure sign that something big was brewing.

In a passage of arresting foresight, the 1974 end-of-year National Intelligence Estimate on the short-term prospects for South Vietnam further assessed:

> The South Vietnamese would be able to withstand the initial impact of an all-out Communist offensive only by trading space for time. They would probably lose all of MR-1 north of Danang, Pleiku and Kontum provinces in MR-2, and some territory in MR-3 and MR-4 ... The adverse psychological impact of Communist successes in the initial stages of the offensive might be more significant than the actual effect on the military balance ... The RVNAF would be unable to contain a sustained Communist offensive unless the US provided early and large-scale logistic assistance.[48]

This is exactly what transpired, and of course, the necessary support was never going to be provided. On the same day that Thuong Duc fell, a hostile Congress voted by 233 to 157 for a Vietnam amendment to the 1975 defense appropriation, reducing aid by $300 million to just $700 million.

The manpower ceiling of the US advisory mission was also reduced by ten percent to 2,850 posts (of which 438 were allocated to the Embassy).

With more refinement, Giap's scheme for the 1975 general offensive was broken into three inter-related phases. In the first phase (December 1974–February 1975), limited attacks would be conducted across all fronts. Phase 2 (March–June 1975) would witness "a large-scale campaign ... carried out in the western Central Highlands theater, along with coordinating campaigns in eastern Nam Bo [also known as Military Region 7, or the eight provinces describing an arc north of Saigon]; northern Military Region 5 [the coastal provinces of Quang Nam, Quang Tin, and Quang Ngai]; and Tri Thien."[49] In the pedantically technical language of the General Staff, eastern Nam Bo would be the "main force theater"; the Central Highlands the "primary theater"; and the Mekong Delta and Saigon hinterlands the "primary battlefields." Giap's orders were:

> In the Military Region 5 and Central Highlands theaters, use three main-force divisions to attack the Central Highlands, open up a corridor connecting the southern Central Highlands with eastern Nam Bo, and create conditions for the main force troops to move quickly into eastern Nam Bo and coordinate with the regional main-force troops in attacking Saigon. The opening battles will be fought to take Buon Ma Thuot, break through to Tuy Hoa and Phu Yen, cut the Military Region 5 lowlands in half, and create yet another direction from which to rapidly advance south and put pressure on Saigon.[50]

In the last phase, coinciding with the onset of the winter monsoons, (August–October 1975), Hanoi anticipated securing and consolidating its gains. There was no realistic expectation the People's Army would be capable of winning and ending the war by the end of the year. Rather, it was expected that the 1975 dry-season campaign would act as a foundation for a decisive push the following year. When the collapse happened, it was a complete surprise to everyone.

Cautious due to previous setbacks, the Central Party Military Committee sought firsthand intelligence from the National Liberation Front leadership represented by Pham Hung, Tran Van Tra, and Hai Van in meetings held on December 3–5.[51] The Northern leadership was especially interested in the state of the "Fifth Region" (the general term for the Saigon fronts). There were further deliberations over three weeks from December 18, 1974 to January 8, 1975.[52] Great encouragement was taken from the fall of Phuoc Long, just

75 miles from Saigon, in the first week of January, the first province to be "liberated" in South Vietnam despite spirited local defense. Less than 850 Southern soldiers survived from the original 5,400-strong force.[53] It was a disaster. Saigon declared three days of mourning and prayers. What especially caught Hanoi's attention was the lack of any significant American reaction to this reverse.[54]

Prime Minister Pham Van Dong was less surprised. In 1973 Dong had crossed paths with Kissinger. In the usual manner, the Northerner had assaulted Kissinger with the epic story of Vietnamese heroism. Three times the Yuannese had dared to invade Tonkin and three times they had been repulsed and sent home. How many times did the United States intend to send an army to Vietnam, he demanded of the American? Kissinger held up one finger.

The action at Phuoc Long mattered because Thieu refused to reinforce, electing to save Tay Ninh and Binh Tuy Provinces, and Washington refused to help. Thieu's decision was based on the impracticality of reinforcing the isolated city but had a certain racist tinge. Phuoc Long had a population of 50,000 mainly Ma and Mnong tribesmen. Who cared for these half-savages? In contrast, the People's Army demonstrated that concentration of force had no answer. Two infantry divisions supported by an armored regiment fell on Phuoc Long. The psychological shock from these realizations further eroded Southern morale. ARVN Lieutenant General Du Quoc Dong was duly sacked and replaced by the more capable Nguyen Van Toan, but this only saved the former general from being the man in charge when the collapse occurred two months later.

There were other unexpected consequences from the loss of Phuoc Long province to the communists. The Cao Dai abruptly declared themselves neutral, a clear signal that the leadership anticipated a communist victory. The Hoa Hao, implacable enemies to the communist creed, set about raising a self-defense militia, no longer trusting in the government forces. When Saigon decreed the militia illegal, fighting broke out. A whiff of the factional scuffles of the late 1950s hung in the air.

Notwithstanding divisions in the South, doubts remained in the Central Party Military Committee. When the conference closed on January 8, with the usual revolutionary exhortations, Hanoi was neither planning for, nor expecting, a South Vietnamese collapse in the spring. Rather, the General Staff envisaged a continuous campaign through to the rainy season, with the intention of securing the Central Highlands from Hue to Da Nang, and Binh Dinh Province.[55] If the campaign progressed favorably, a general offensive and uprising would be launched in 1976. The possibility that South Vietnamese resistance might disintegrate was expressed as an "if," and nowhere in the plan was the capture of Saigon articulated.

In fact, with the exception of Phouc Long, what was striking about the ebb and flow of fighting at the beginning of the 1975 was that everywhere else the communists had surprisingly lost ground. In Military Region 1, 1st ARVN Division had won back the hill features overlooking Phu Bai and forced a battered 324th PAVN Division to withdraw. Further south, the ARVN and not the PAVN seized the initiative in a series of clearance operations involving 2nd and 3rd ARVN Divisions. In Military Region 2, 22nd ARVN Division maintained pressure on the An Lao Valley. On the Pleiku and Kontum fronts, PAVN spoiling attacks were met aggressively by seven Ranger Groups arrayed in defense of the Highlands. In Military Region 3, 18th and 25th ARVN Divisions had shoved back against PAVN incursions and inflicted heavy casualties on the enemy. And in the Delta, a supreme effort by the COSVN was successfully contained, again with heavy losses to the communists.

Giap's operational plan for the campaign in the Western Highlands was passed to the B2 Front in conditions of absolute secrecy by a handful of officers, code-named "Group A.75." This group traveled incognito down the Ho Chi Minh Trail one month after the fall of Phouc Long and included Van Tien Dung, representing the Central Party Military Committee; Dinh Duc Thien, head of the Rear Services General Department; and Le Ngoc Hien, the PAVN deputy chief of staff.[56] Dung lyrically observed, "The road to the front at that time of year was very beautiful."[57] A small cryptography team accompanied the generals in anticipation of the burst of reporting that would be generated between the B2 Front headquarters and Hanoi. The plan was code-named "Campaign 275," and it followed the same gambit unsuccessfully played in the Tet Offensive. Large-scale diversionary attacks would be launched in Military Region 1 to fix attention in the north. Four divisions – the 320th, 10th, 968th, and veteran 316th – would subsequently be launched against Ban Me Thuot, the provincial capital of Darlac Province, then weakly held by elements from 23rd ARVN Division. So unlikely was this scenario, CIA chief analyst Frank Snepp recalled, "We were caught by surprise." In a pre-battle estimate he assessed, "The Communists wouldn't go after Ban Me Thuot." Instead he suggested they would attempt to interdict the road systems between the Northern Highlands and the Southern Highlands and probably attack Pleiku.[58]

Ironically, and with the hindsight of subsequent events, the selection of Ban Me Thuot as the primary objective was almost an afterthought. For two decades, the Northern obsession in the Central Highlands had been the control of Pleiku and Kontum. This was still the case at the beginning of the second week of January 1975 when the Politburo concluded its 20-day planning conference. The day after the conference adjourned, on January 9, the Central Party Military Committee met to turn the Politburo's resolutions into concrete military plans. The conference had already started when Le Duc Tho arrived, unannounced. Noting that the PAVN now boasted some five divisions in the Western Highlands, it would be "absurd," he argued, if the easy prize of Ban Me Thuot were not seized. After some deliberations, Tho's suggestion was accepted.[59]

However, when Dung, Thien, and Hien arrived at the COSVN in Cambodia they discovered that Hanoi's intelligence of the battle fronts presented an over-optimistic view of the situation – a perennial problem that had bedeviled the communists as much as Washington. Phuoc Long had been a handsome victory, but B2 Front was still locked in battles for the control of Route 14 – an unwelcome distraction – with the bulk of its combat units spread out between Duc Lap and Dac Soong. The significance of this was that it placed the assault regiments southwest of the town of Ban Me Thuot, the settlement selected as the main objective for the forthcoming push. Duc Lap and Dac Soong were old Hoa Hao bastions and consequently resistant to communist blandishments. "After discussions it was realized that because our force deployment was askew and would be difficult to readjust … [we] decided to attack Duc Lap first, then the next day attack Ban Me Thuot."[60] The attack on Duc Lap was scheduled for March 9, followed by Ban Me Thuot the following day. By this stage, PAVN units had infiltrated across the Western Highlands and were "firmly entrenched along routes 19, 14, and 21" preventing quick reinforcement of the threatened areas. The scene was now set.

———

Ban Me Thuot sat at an elevation of 1,700 feet, cool in summer, and wet in winter. It was a mixed city of 50,000 Buddhists, Catholics, Protestants, and Montagnards.[61] The surrounding areas were dominated by the Rhade tribe, but many North Vietnamese had also settled in the area, fleeing the communist regime. None of these groups would likely welcome "liberation" by the People's Army. From the air the city presented a pleasant aspect of one- and two-story buildings, tree-lined avenues, and rolling wooded hills. The town boasted an Emperor Bao Dai summer palace, USAID hospital, and Benedictine convent. In the 1880s the French introduced coffee plantations, dropped the indigenous name Lac Giao, and promoted Ban Me Thuot as capital of Bak Lak Province. Fertilized by civet dung (hence Vietnamese *ca phe chon*, or civet-cat coffee), small fortunes were made from the bean.[62] Later the French established a Bible Institute and the Collège Sabbatier, which they deliberately used to foster Montagnard nationalism at the expense of the Vietnamese.[63] In December 1945, soldiers from 5th RIC ousted local militias and reclaimed the town for the French.[64] In 1954, the survivors from the disastrous ambush of Groupement Mobile No. 100 fell back on the town.[65] In 1961 a detachment from 5th Special Forces Group arrived here, a vanguard in Kennedy's counter-revolutionary war, and henceforward there was an almost continuous US military presence until 1970.

US servicemen based at Ban Me Thuot remembered it as a sleepy hollow of colorful markets, afternoon tennis games, and barbeques. The MACV advisory team based itself in traditional Montagnard bungalows with steep-sided gable roofs, surrounded by lawns and ornamental plants. As in all South Vietnamese towns with a military presence, it had its fair share of "Cat Houses," known as "Hooky Laus," after a drunken airman mispronounced Ho Thi Lau, the name of a pharmacy specializing in venereal diseases set up by an enterprising South Vietnamese nurse.[66]

Ban Me Thuot had mostly escaped the war. In 1964 there had been a short-lived Montagnard rebellion against encroachment by Viet outsiders. During the Tet Offensive, as many as 2,000 troops from 233rd PAVN Regiment had assaulted the town. The attack plan was captured two weeks before the assault fell. Even so the ferocity of the assault took everyone by surprise. Over three days the city was pummeled with air strikes and artillery, damaging the summer palace. Supported by American firepower, Ban Me Thuot's defenders held firm. Those advisors had long departed, along with the firepower. Ban Me Thuot relapsed to somnolence. Nobody imagined that if South Vietnam were to fall, the collapse would start here.

Ban Me Thuot was well chosen to unpick the lock of South Vietnam, but for reasons that probably eluded Hanoi. Since the 1930s, the town and environs had been incorporated into a deliberate French policy of divide and rule.[67] Fearful of rising Vietnamese nationalism, the French had sought to foster an ally in the independently minded Montagnards. Under the influential administrator Léopold Sabbatier, after whom the school was named, Montagnard ethnicity was elaborated and embroidered. The Central Highlands were designated a "Special Administrative Circumscription" (Populations montagnardes du Sud-Indochinois – PMSI), and later an autonomous "Crown Domain" (Domaine de la couronne du pays montagnards du Sud – PMS). This awakened Montagnard identity was reinforced by Green Berets who, like the French, straightaway recognized the fighting qualities of the tribesmen.

However, by the early 1970s, Ban Me Thuot was a divided town. The Americans had gone and the single ethnic group that could be counted on to fight had been marginalized by racist Vietnamese officials (indeed, the Vietnamese word for "Montagnards" was "Moi," meaning "savages"). The town was now held by soldiers whose commitment to the defense of the land – Montagnard ancestral lands – was weak. This same pattern would be repeated across the Highlands as ethnic Viets sought to save their skins at the expense of the Montagnards.

Aware of Montagnard dissatisfaction, Hanoi had cultivated old members of the FULRO (Front Unifié pour la Libération des Races Opprimées) with promises of autonomy following a communist victory. These former partisans helped guide the communist forces into Ban Me Thuot. Their treachery done, the duped Montagnards were subsequently detained and despatched to "re-education" camps in the North as potential subversives.

Vietnamese racism, more broadly, was written across the general disposition of ARVN divisions in South Vietnam. Despite the historic importance of the Central Highlands and Saigon's consistent and correct deduction that Hanoi would seek a decisive outcome in this region – for the obvious reason that it would sever the country in two and likely precipitate collapse – it was the most-weakly defended. Just one division (23rd Division) was allocated to the area. Had Thieu and the Joint General Staff followed the logic of their own appreciations, at least three divisions would have been arrayed across this front. But who cared to save these mountain people? Or cared for a posting in the cold, damp hills away from the attractions of Saigon, or distractions of the coastal towns?

The assault on Ban Me Thuot was commanded by B3 Front Commander Lieutenant General Hoang Minh Thao, Dung's immediate subordinate. The intent was to seize the town then block and ambush any reinforcements. Once secured, it was planned that Ban Me Thuot would act as a funnel through which battalions would be poured to exploit across Military Region 2. There was perhaps no better illustration of the difference between the two sides than that Dung set up his headquarters in a forest of khopj trees (shared with a herd of elephants that unwittingly kept snapping communications cables), while his counterpart, the 2 Corps Commander General Pham Van Phu (only appointed the previous December), slumbered in a villa in Pleiku.

In the first week of March, in a "war of wits," B3 Front first set about isolating the Central Highlands from the coastal towns. This was achieved with almost casual ease. It took the communists just one day of coordinated actions to cut Route 14 (Pleiku to Ban Me Thuot), Route 19 (Pleiku to Qui Nhon), and Route 21 (Ban Me Thuot to Nha Trang), blowing five bridges in the process. In the course of these diversionary attacks, several small outposts were overrun. Route 19 was especially targeted with rocket attacks on Pleiku, supported by attacks on the Mang Yang and An Khe Passes (where Groupement Mobile

No. 100 had met its fate), at Binh Khe, and all the way down the coastal plain as far as Phu Cat Air Base.

At the 2 Corps HQ, the communist offensive was not a cause for immediate panic. The main routes linking the Highlands had been cut before in the last ten years. Those with longer memories of the First Indochina War had witnessed the loss and recapture of these strategic lines of communications many times before. The question facing General Phu was: where would the next blow fall? It was obvious that the routes had been cut as a prelude to an assault on one of the Highland towns, but which one? With so much sporadic action reported on Route 19, it seemed likely that seizing Pleiku would indeed be the main effort.

On March 9, an emergency meeting was held, attended by the 23rd ARVN Division commander, Brigadier General Le Trung Tuong, his second-in-command Vu The Quang, the Ranger commander in 2 Corps, Colonel Pham Duy Tat (soon to be promoted to brigadier general by a desperate President Thieu), and the commanding officers of units deployed between Pleiku and Ban Me Thuot.[68] The ARVN commanders knew of the existence of the three enemy divisions in the Central Highlands, including one deployed west of Pleiku. A fourth – the 10th PAVN Division – was likely to join the front. Viewing the dispositions, Phu argued that Pleiku remained the likely main objective.

There is some suggestion that Phu may not have been the best general for the moment. The CIA knew him as "the Barney Fife" of the ARVN (a comic actor deputy sheriff from a sleepy North Carolina town, in a series that ran for five years). But Phu had been fighting since the 1950s and indeed had parachuted into Dien Bien Phu. Weariness and wariness had set in. His family in Nha Trang weighed on his mind. When the situation later unraveled this is where he escaped to. The communist avalanche that Military Region 2 was about to experience would have tested any commander.

With some prescience General Phu's intelligence officer, Colonel Trinh Tieu, disagreed. He was seconded by Tuong, as well as by Phu's assistant, Brigadier General Tram Vam Cam. The immediate attacks had fallen in the Pleiku area, but recent reporting suggested there had been major PAVN redeployments west and south of Ban Me Thuot. Would it not be wise to at least despatch one regiment – the reliable 45th from 23rd ARVN Division – to stiffen the defenses at Ban Me Thuot?

Later criticism that this advice was ignored bypasses a hard reality. Even if Phu had accepted his intelligence officer's assessment there was still the question – was the redeployment of his best regiment a realistic option? Phu only had two trusted regiments: one was defending Pleiku and the second Kontum. There was no reserve. Ban Me Thuot was over 100 miles south of Pleiku. On March 8, the city had been cut off from Pleiku anyway, after

9th Regiment, 320th PAVN Division cut Route 14. If the assault fell on Ban Me Thuot, reinforcements could always be flown in (in fact, a forlorn hope). After some discussion, Cam remembered, "we rallied to Phu's view that Pleiku remained objective number one."[69] Faced with no good options, Phu waited for the blow to fall.

He did not have long to wait. Two days later, on March 10, three PAVN combined arms divisions fell on Ban Me Thuot like a "lightning flash." These faced just one ARVN regiment (the 53rd), and three civil guard units. A fourth division was held in reserve to deal with counterattacks. It was the classic application of strength against weakness. The battle was expected to last up to ten days, but effectively lasted one. Sapper units launched surprise attacks against the two airfields. Long-range artillery fire pounded the city. Tank units successfully concealed in nearby forests broke cover, some ferried across water obstacles in improvised rafts. By early morning, much of the northern sector of Ban Me Thuot had been overrun in a series of aggressive probing attacks.

By the evening, the list of objectives that fell with little resistance grew longer: the Hai Hac De ammunition depot, the city's rice depot, the broadcasting center, 23rd ARVN Division's command post, Hoa Binh District, and the Anh Dao Hotel, a prominent landmark on the strategically important six-point intersection in the city center (today, the location of a victory monument). By nightfall, the city was virtually in communist hands.

However, the communists did not have it all their own way: over a dozen tanks were knocked out, and as many as 400 PAVN were estimated to have been killed in the assault. 53rd ARVN Regiment resisted with some zeal, the stiffest defense mounted at Phung Duc airfield where the 3rd Battalion continued to hold out against the odds. Elsewhere, scattered pockets of Regional Force companies fought on but with dwindling resources. A company from 225th Regional Force Battalion continued to occupy the tactically important Hill 559. Despite the loss of Hai Hac De depot, the main ammunition depot in Ban Me Thuot still remained in South Vietnamese hands, held by 242nd Regional Force Battalion.

Notwithstanding this resistance, by the following morning, it was plain the defenders were in an increasingly dire position. The nearby 21st Ranger Group transmitted a last pleading message: "At present, munitions are nearly exhausted ... if not resupplied, we will be plunged into a most dangerous situation."[70] Neither resupply still less reinforcements were immediately forthcoming. The defenders would have to fend for themselves. As unit cohesion disintegrated many did, escaping and evading in the coffee plantations. The message had come too late anyway. A French reporter who conveyed news of the fiasco was shot dead by South Vietnamese police, but by now knowledge of Ban Me Thuot's collapse had spread across the Central Highlands.

Phu had in fact made a request for strategic reinforcements, but this was rejected by Saigon, faced with its own imminent threats. Left to control the situation as best he could, the 2 Corps Commander redeployed the 72nd and 96th Ranger Battalions by helicopter to the town of Buon Ho, 20 miles northeast of Ban Me Thuot, on Route 14. In an over-ambitious scheme, Phu planned to truck these two battalions the remaining distance south to block any further communist advances.

What followed, in Dung's words, was "a race with the enemy and the weather."[71] But only one side was racing, and the heavens favored the bold. This should never have happened. In the Central Highlands, the two sides enjoyed parity in foot soldiers, but the South enjoyed an 8.5:1 advantage in tanks, a 4.2:1 advantage in artillery, and owned all the aircraft and helicopters. The difference between the two sides was not equipment, but heart.

Even so, at this stage, all was not lost. The environs of Ban Me Thuot continued to be held by the surviving rump of 53rd ARVN Regiment and 21st Rangers. The command group of 23rd ARVN Division, protected by 45th Battalion, had been airlifted from Pleiku to Buon Ho. If this small town were held, the threat to Pleiku would be blocked. Unfortunately for the Southerners, this was exactly where Dung's troops intended to march next.

Leading elements from 320th PAVN Division charged down Route 14, swatting away weak opposition, and were soon in possession of a 50-mile stretch of this road. 316th PAVN Division, supported by 95B Regiment, similarly overcame the town of Phouc An. The domination of Route 14 essentially scythed the Central Highlands, the bottom of which had fallen away. Uncoordinated counterattacks by 44th and 45th ARVN Regiments, the only functioning formations in the crumbling 23rd ARVN Division, only served to hasten the complete annihilation of this division. By now, 53rd ARVN Regiment and 21st Rangers had also run out of steam.

Ironically, even as it began to enjoy success the PAVN was discovering the difficulties of coordinating a corps-level operation (success can be as tricky as failure), hampered by "old-fashioned practices" and by commanders unwilling to demonstrate initiative. Having seized Ban Me Thuot, the communists did not break out. Indeed, for the first seven days there was little movement, other than the interdiction operations on Routes 14, 19, and 21. It was a measure of the failure of the Southern leadership that this gifted operational pause was never exploited to recover the situation.

Unwilling to act without approval from Hanoi, this period was spent exchanging messages with the General Staff and debating what to do next. Fully expecting a reaction, much of the debate was about how to defeat the anticipated counterattack. The decision to exploit the success was only finally taken in the late evening of March 16 when messages began to arrive reporting the flight of the ARVN from Pleiku. The communist surprise was considerable: "Why such a retreat? And who had given the order for it?"[72]

The assault on Ban Me Thuot had fixed all eyes on events in the Central Highlands, but communist success in this region was not going to deliver the Republic of South Vietnam. This prize lay in Military Region 3 and the capital district. Here, the immediate Northern objectives were the captures of Tay Ninh, Binh Duong, and Long Binh Provinces. Standing in the way was 3 ARVN Corps, commanded by General Toan. The province of Tay Ninh was held by elements of 25th ARVN Division, supported by two ranger battalions and ad hoc units from four armored brigades. Binh Duong was held by 5th ARVN Division and a single armored brigade. Long Binh was only weakly held and lacked good defenses.

The assault on Toan's 3 Corps began on March 11, the day after the investment of Ban Me Thuot. It fell from the east and was led by the veteran 9th PAVN Division.[73] The initial objective was the seizure of the town of Tri Tam. Located on the intersection of Tay Ninh, Binh Duong, and Long Binh Provinces, Tri Tam offered valuable crossings over the Saigon River. Once captured, the greater prize of Tay Ninh city would be vulnerable to encirclement. This is in effect what happened. Tri Tam was defended by the best part of four Regional Force battalions. These resisted for just one day before being overwhelmed by superior numbers. A relief column from 3rd ARVN Brigade was beaten back and unable to advance beyond the town of Ben Cui. Advancing from the north and west, elements from 5th PAVN Division then broke out of Cambodian safe bases, bypassed Tay Ninh city, and cut three vital routes: Highway 22, Route 26, and the minor Route 239. The plantation areas in the hinterlands of Ben Cau and Ben Cui were also seized. All the PAVN columns were now pointing at Go Dau Ha, an important road and river crossing that dominated Tay Ninh Province. Responding to this threat, Toan despatched units from 18th ARVN Division, his sole remaining armored brigade, and 64th and 92nd Ranger Battalions to defend the vital node. Even as 3 Corps struggled to cope with this assault from the west, a greater crisis then developed in the center and east. Here, 6th, 7th, and 341st PAVN Divisions began converging on the main body of 18th ARVN Division from the directions of An Loc, Chon Thanh, Long Khanh, and Binh Tuy.

These events on the battlefield mattered. But more important was what unfolded in Thieu's mind. Just one day after the communist assault on Ban Me Thuot, on March 11, Thieu invited Prime Minister Tran Thien Khiem, General Cao Van Vien, the Chairman of the Joint General Staff, and Lieutenant General Dang Van Quang, the presidential assistant for security affairs, to a working breakfast in the presidential palace.

At the meeting, Thieu produced a briefing map depicting his visualization for the defense of South Vietnam. It should not have surprised, as he had long privately argued that the defense of the entire territory of South Vietnam was an impossible task. Nevertheless, it shocked. "Given our present strength and capabilities," he informed the meeting, "we certainly cannot hold and defend all the territory we want."[74] With a pen stroke, Thieu proposed to redraw the map of Indochina, redefining South Vietnam as the former Cochin China, with a new border some 300 miles south of the 17th parallel, or effectively Military Regions 3 and 4. North of the proposed new border, in Military Regions 1 and 2, Thieu drew four phase lines – cutting through Thua Thien, Quang Nam, Quang Ngai, and Binh Dinh Provinces. Vaguely, he suggested that only a number of prosperous coastal enclaves would be held. The Central Highlands, for which the South Vietnamese held no great emotional attachment, could go to the devil, or the communists. If the defense of the coastal enclaves proved too difficult, the ARVN would conduct a fighting withdrawal on the four phase lines to the new border.

The plan, if it could be graced with this title, suffered from a raft of obvious fatal flaws. Aside from the three conferees at the breakfast meeting, nobody knew what was in the President's mind. In other words, it was not a plan at all. It was just an idea, or hallucination. Not a single piece of paper – the planning – existed, beyond Thieu's private map. Not only were South Vietnam's generals and provincial governors clueless of what Thieu was preparing, but neither did he inform Ambassador Martin, the single interlocutor he should have told. The French learned of Thieu's intentions and in a chance encounter Ambassador Jean-Marie Merillon tipped off Martin. "It's not possible," the American Ambassador uttered, turning pale. The color should not have drained from his face. The previous summer, General Murray had honestly warned:

> In the final analysis, you can roughly equate cuts in [US] support to loss of real estate. As the cutting edge of the RVNAF is blunted and the enemy continues to improve his combat position and logistical base what will occur is a retreat to the Saigon-Delta area as a redoubt.[75]

This was now coming to pass.

Even if the concept of a strategic withdrawal had been staffed and prepared over the previous year, actually implementing it would have proved fearsomely difficult. The communist offensive had erupted. Withdrawal under fire is the most difficult of military operations. And even if this had been conducted successfully, what of the civilian population? No thought or planning had been devoted to coping with the certain exodus of several million civilians. It was all too late.

The second key event happened 12,000 miles away. Hanoi could not have guessed that its offensive in the south would coincide with a crucial vote in the House of Representatives. On March 12, even as Thieu was preparing to order the retreat from Military Regions 1 and 2, the House voted by 189 to 49 against sending further military aid to South Vietnam. A later and hasty fact-finding mission by Weyand, from March 26 to 31, amounted to gesture without substance. The B-52s would not be unleashed. Unrealistically, he suggested the ARVN should attempt its own offensive in Military Region 3 to score a symbolic victory and steady nerves. Military historian Colonel William Le Gro, intimately involved in the denouement, has argued persuasively that aid alone could not have saved Saigon.[76] It is indisputable that the House's decision ripped South Vietnamese morale beyond repair. But the scale of the emergency – many predicted collapse within a month – meant that any aid would have probably arrived too late anyway. American air power alone could save South Vietnam, as it had done in the past. In Le Gro's words, drafted for the visiting Weyand: "Only the application of U.S. strategic airpower in South Vietnam can give any degree of probability [of securing South Vietnam's survival]."[77] The words were wasted. American strategy in South Vietnam had become an empty chest.

In the meantime, an insouciant Phu, displaying more coolness than Saigon or Washington, had already devised a rescue plan. The situation was not so dire that it required the de facto surrender of the Central Highlands. He had already begun assembling a task force at Phuoc An, 12 miles east of Ban Me Thuot, under Brigadier General Le Trung Tuong, the commanding officer of 23rd ARVN Division. This composite force comprised 45th Infantry Regiment, elements from 44th Infantry Regiment, and one battalion from 21st Ranger Group. He planned to fight west and link up with the survivors from 53rd Infantry as well as the 72nd and 96th Ranger Battalions that had earlier been airlifted to Buon Ho.

This was entirely feasible. The city may have fallen, but Phung Duc airfield west of Ban Me Thuot was still holding out five days after the surprise attack. In fact, the ARVN defenders would only finally withdraw on March 18, after it became apparent that the proposed rescue attempt from the direction of Phuoc An to the southwest had been foiled by 10th PAVN Division, now in the line and blocking all movement on Route 21.

Nor was the situation so bad across the rest of 2 Corps. Phu still commanded a 50,000-strong force, the majority of which had not yet been committed to battle. The 6th, 22nd, and 23rd Ranger Groups were intact in the Kontum area and bullish over repelling PAVN attacks. Pleiku was being shelled and rocketed but not otherwise threatened. The capture of Ban Me Thuot had been a symbolic blow, but could the PAVN exploit this victory? It was now a mechanized army, as constrained by the few trafficable tarmac routes as its ARVN opponents. Ambushing these routes, as the communists well knew, was all too easy.

The decision that sealed South Vietnam's fate was taken on March 13, even as 10th PAVN Division began trundling down Route 21. In a secret meeting held in Saigon and attended by the 1 and 3 Corps commanders – Ngo Quang Truong and Nguyen Van Toan respectively – Thieu explained his concept of withdrawing to hold defensible enclaves. A bitter Thieu would later complain that Washington had asked the South Vietnamese to do impossible things, "like filling up the ocean with stones," but the person who should have kept a stone in his mouth was precisely the president.[78]

In a precipitous move that provoked a wider and unstoppable debacle, Thieu decided to implement his plan for the division of South Vietnam. In the immediate situation, an attempt would be made to save Ban Me Thuot, but at the cost of sacrificing Pleiku and Kontum. This implied that 2 Corps would have to undertake a total strategic retreat from the Central Highlands, leaving behind the Regional and Popular Forces. It also meant that Truong in 1 Corps would have to withdraw to an enclave based around the anchor of Da Nang. However, Thieu bypassed Phu, absent from the meeting, knowing that he would face resistance from this general. Instead, the instruction was transmitted over a fraught telephone conversation with Pham Duy Tat, commander of the 2 Corps Rangers. Tat was also resistant and offered to fight and die in Pleiku, but Thieu would have none of it.

In fact, despite Tat's bullishness, the situation in Pleiku was beginning to deteriorate. With the fall of Ban Me Thuot, where a majority of soldiers from 23rd ARVN Division had family, morale plummeted. There was a "flood" of demands for leave in particular from 44th Regiment, and "innumerable AWOLs." The Regional and Popular Forces began to disintegrate and unscrupulous staff officers pulled rank and absconded. The cost of air tickets to Saigon rocketed to 40,000 piasters as a frantic civilian population sought to escape the inevitable encirclement. Tat's stand was fast being overtaken by growing defeatism.

Thieu then asked to meet Phu at Pleiku. This was deemed too dangerous, so the two men met at Cam Ranh on March 14 in a building which had been erected for the visiting Johnson in 1966. The only other attendees were the triumvirate of Prime Minister Khiem and Generals Quang and Vien. Even at this late stage, no South Vietnamese institution of state – neither the government nor the Assembly – was being informed of Thieu's plan. Dismissing Phu's counterattack plan, Thieu explained his scheme for a strategic withdrawal. What then emerged from the day-long meeting was a completely hare-brained scheme that would involve withdrawing all ARVN units from Kontum and Pleiku using the minor Interprovincial Route 7B (LTL-7B). In an impossible maneuver, it was proposed that a counterattack force would then assemble at the coastal town of Tuy Hoa. This force would travel over 100 miles south on Highway 1 to Ninh Hoa, then double back up Route 21 to assault Ban Me Thuot from the southwest. While all this was happening, the Regional and Popular Forces would be expected to hold on in Kontum and Pleiku.

Phu has been saddled with the historical millstone of this dreadful scheme, but what choices did he have? Thieu ordered the withdrawal from the Central Highlands, but all the main routes – 14, 19, and 20 – were now interdicted by communist forces. The chosen axis of retreat – indeed the only viable option – was perforce the undefended and dilapidated Route 7B that ran from Pleiku 160 miles southeast to Tuy Hoa on the coast. This route was crossed by numerous fords and at one point was spanned by a partially collapsed bridge. It could not hope to bear the weight of traffic that was now about to be squeezed down its two lanes. Warning Phu that he might experience difficulties was hardly helpful.

Even as this alternative plan was being proposed, an emboldened 10th PAVN Division continued to push east down Route 21 (the same route that Thieu had proposed for his counterattack), facing increasingly weakening resistance from the surviving units of 23rd ARVN Division. The communist spearhead was only finally halted 50 miles down the route at Khanh Doung on 21st March by a combination 40th Regiment, 22nd ARVN Division and by 3rd Airborne Brigade, rushed south from Quang Nam Province.

Thieu's directive was not just rash and foolish – it was totally unrealistic. Every soldier would insist on bringing along his family members, which is exactly what happened. The civilian population in turn would panic and seek to flee. In *August 1914* Solzhenitsyn observed, "Retreat ... is instantly and unquestionably grasped from top to bottom, and the private soldier is infected by it with no less immediacy than the corps commander." So it came to pass in the Central Highlands.

The retreat did not start out as a rout. With some alacrity, 2 Corps HQ stitched together a reasonable plan which involved a phased withdrawal over four days (March 16–20). Three columns were organized each comprising of up to 250 trucks, escorted by M-48 tanks from 21st Tank Battalion. The first column would include three Ranger groups and 20th Engineer Group, tasked to open the way and clear obstacles. This would secure the midpoint at Phu Bon and prove the route from Phu Tuc to Tuy Hoa. The second column would comprise the corps command, the infantry, three artillery battalions, and the bulk of 21st Armor Regiment. The third column and rear guard would be made up from three Ranger groups.[79] In total, the withdrawing force would include elements from 19 infantry battalions, one tank battalion, three artillery battalions, and supporting units. To avoid provoking panic, the withdrawal was kept secret and no written orders were issued. This secrecy proved a recipe of chaos. Over the next four days as many as 400,000 civilians and soldiers attempted to negotiate Route 7B, setting the scene for one of the last tragedies of the war.

Dung first realized that something was afoot on March 16, but it was not until March 18 that an attempt was made to interdict the retreating columns between the settlements of Phu Bon and Cheo Reo (roughly halfway between Pleiku and the safety of the coast at Tuy Hoa). The nearest formation was 320th PAVN Division. This formation caught up with the defenseless flood of refugees at Cheo Reo, a small town of around 10,000 inhabitants, set on a river plain and surrounded by open fields. By the end of the day, hundreds of vehicles were either burned out or abandoned on its streets.

Now scenting a kill, 320th PAVN Division was ordered to cut the route east of Phu Bon and effectively trap the retreating columns. At the same time Viet Cong units were ordered to seal the bridges in Phu Yen, blocking any potential reinforcements from the west. Exploiting the collapse, 968th PAVN Division crashed into the now abandoned Pleiku, the first Central Highland city to fall.

On Route 7B, a disorganized column of hundreds of military and civilian vehicles now stretched from Cheo Reo east to the town of Cung Son, a distance of some 25 miles, and still 20 miles short of the coast. Midway between these two towns the column was forced to ford the Ca Lui River. The operation inevitably led to bogged down vehicles, blocking this escape route and adding to the confusion. Soldiers drowned. An airstrike called to relieve the beleaguered column accidentally targeted a Ranger battalion, killing and wounding many. The situation may have been salvaged, but a dispirited Tat discovered that the remaining sections of Route 7B had been so heavily mined by the departing South Korean division, he had no choice but to reroute the entire column south along the even more unsuitable local Route 436. This would entail bridging the Song Ba River. Dung anticipated this move and set up five road blocks on this minor road, forcing Tat to fight for every foot of road. To Tat's frustration, the Song Ba proved no more fordable than the Ca Lui, causing a log jam of vehicles waiting to make the perilous crossing.

Witnessing these developments, the Political Bureau and Central Military Party Committee met again in high excitement. Cryptographers in the Operations Department rushed to make copies of urgent messages now being received across the fronts. Over the 55 days of the final offensive, Hanoi's cryptographers would encrypt and decrypt a staggering 1,192,525 telegrams, a veritable Babel Tower of exhilaration mixed with disbelief.[80] To the communists' surprise, it appeared "the enemy were forming strategic enclaves earlier than we had expected."[81] Hanoi had always anticipated that Thieu might take the decision to withdraw to more defensible lines, ceding entire provinces if necessary, but the unfolding events were taking everyone by surprise. Either the South Vietnamese armed forces were collapsing, or a deliberate plan was being implemented to establish enclaves "at Saigon, Cam Ranh and perhaps Da Nang." But which was it? Whatever the state of the enemy camp, it was clear Hanoi was being presented with "a major opportunity" and had to act fast. "Secretary Van" (Giap) had no doubts. History was being compressed with a revolutionary intensity. The war, he told the Political Bureau, should be won now.[82]

Two contingency plans were proposed to exploit the situation. In the first, the offensive would be expanded from the Central Highlands along two axes. The main thrust, involving "most of the B3 forces," would "develop down into eastern Nam Bo [the provinces north of Saigon]." A secondary axis would "develop down into the lowlands of Military Region 5 [the DMZ] with the existing forces, possibly reinforced by the 968th Division and technical equipment."[83] In the second contingency, all available forces would be hurled at Military Region 5, effectively sweeping south from the DMZ, demolishing 1 Corps, and advancing as far as Binh Dinh, Phu Yen, and Nha Trang Provinces. Once these provinces were secured, the corps would thunder south towards Saigon.

By March 20, ARVN units and stragglers in the Central Highlands were fleeing south in three principal directions: on the fateful Route 7B to Tuy Hoa, on Route 21 to Khanh Duong, and on Route 19 east to the old 1st Cavalry base at An Khe. Dung, in the meantime, had begun to seize the initiative from the Central Military Party Committee which could no longer keep up with events on the ground. On the same day, Dung despatched "Message No 57" in which he advised his intention to pursue the routed enemy down these three routes until he reached the coast: on Route 7B to Phu Yen, Route 21 to Nha Trang and Cam Ranh, and Route 19 to Binh Dinh.[84] Brimming with confidence, he recommended only 316th PAVN Division be considered as a possible reinforcement on this front. All remaining, uncommitted divisions should be ordered to advance on Saigon by whatever practical route. In effect, Dung was implementing Giap's first choice contingency plan, and not waiting for further instructions. Indeed, he went further, advising Hanoi how they should now direct the campaign. "Because the situation is changing by the hour," he wrote, "we should not hold a general meeting … but should send brief directives from the Political Bureau and the Military Commission of the Party Central Committee, and immediately send people to disseminate their directives to each battlefield."[85]

In the meantime, and by the following morning, the retreating force on Route 7B had become split. The 4th, 23rd, and 25th Ranger Groups were now trapped between Cheo Reo and the blocking 320th PAVN Division. Beyond this block, the 6th, 7th, and 22nd Ranger Groups were caught between the Ca Lui and Song Ba fords. The tank regiment had virtually ceased to exist, with the majority of vehicles now abandoned, along with other heavy equipment. A hasty bridge over the Song Ba was finally completed on March 22, but a section collapsed in the headlong rush to escape. 34th Ranger Battalion (7th Ranger Group) – later dubbed "the block destruction heroes" – pressed on and cleared enemy blocks on Route 436. Three days later, the exhausted Rangers finally reached Tuy Hoa. Half their number had been killed or wounded. Behind them, around 60,000 civilian and military stragglers followed, but an estimated 100,000 were left behind.[86] Some 300 vehicles eventually made it to safety, but hundreds more were abandoned, including irreplaceable armor and artillery. At a stroke over 20 ARVN battalions effectively ceased to exist. In General Vien's later account: "At least 75 percent of II Corps combat strength, to include the 23d Infantry Division as well as Ranger, armor, artillery, engineer, and signal units, had been tragically expended within ten days."[87]

Five days later, 320th PAVN Division was shelling Tuy Hoa, the town from which Thieu had intended to assemble his counterattack force. It fell one day later. North of this drama, on the now largely undefended Route 19 from Pleiku, 3rd PAVN Division and 95B Regiment pushed back the demoralized 22nd ARVN Division, reaching Qui Nhon on the coast on April 1. Phu Cat Air Base also fell.[88] The remnants of this division were picked up from a beach south of the town by three navy ships. The commander of 42nd Regiment which had fought so solidly refused to leave and committed suicide instead, the first of several such acts. Further south, 316th and 10th PAVN divisions motored down Route 21 and reached the coast at Nha Trang one day later. A last-ditch defense by decimated airborne battalions proved hopeless. Just 300 paratroopers survived from 3rd Airborne Brigade.

In three weeks, the ARVN Military Region 2 had ceased to exist. Phu ended up in a Saigon hospital having suffered a mental breakdown. Two weeks later this Dien Bien Phu veteran shot himself. The entire territory he once commanded was fully occupied by the communist enemy by April 16, following a succession of disjointed and desperate actions by disparate surviving units. Military Region 1 had predeceased it by about two weeks.

As Vien later observed, "The operation to reoccupy Ban Me Thuot failed to materialize simply because 2 Corps no longer had combat troops." Dung later explained the Route 7B disaster:

> Once an error in strategy was committed, defeat in the war was certain; it would come sooner or later. The only thing is that it was we who led the enemy to commit this error, stepped up that process by the enemy,

and created that turning point in the war. By becoming faster, bolder, more decisive, and more active, and by rushing forward on the impetus of victories, we were certain to win the war.[89]

This representation was self-flattering. The error was Thieu's, but Dung was unarguably right that the turning point fell between March 9 and 13. The surrender of the Central Highlands was a gross strategic blunder from which Saigon could never have recovered.

———

The first and immediate consequence of the collapse in Military Region 2 was the isolation of the divisions holding the five northern provinces of South Vietnam, now effectively cut off from the rest of the country. This region was held by a mix of marines, paratroopers, rangers, elements of 1st, 2nd, and 3rd ARVN Divisions, and Regional Forces, all under the command of Lieutenant General Ngo Quang Truong based in Da Nang.

The two most northern provinces – Quang Tri and Thua Thien – were allocated to the Airborne Division and 1st ARVN Division, supported by 1st Armored Brigade, 14 and 15 Ranger Groups, and 369th VNMC Brigade. The central Quang Nam Province, encompassing Da Nang, was the responsibility of 3rd ARVN Division, reinforced by the balance of the Marine Division. The bottom two provinces – Quang Tin and Quang Ngai – fell to 2nd ARVN Division and 10 and 11 Ranger Groups. Facing them were five fresh PAVN divisions supported by numerous independent regiments.

Surprisingly, given their predicament, units fought hard to repulse communist attacks across the territory, ceding little ground and inflicting heavy casualties on the Northerners. The situation began to deteriorate after Thieu controversially ordered the withdrawal of the Airborne Division to Saigon on March 12, forcing the redeployment south of 369th VNMC Brigade to cover the now exposed districts of Da Nang and Phu Loc.

Even as General Truong struggled to implement this order, on March 13, as we have seen, he was secretly flown to Saigon and informed that both Military Regions 1 and 2 would be sacrificed to save the rump of South Vietnam (receiving these orders the day before Phu would be informed of the same fateful decision). Only Da Nang would be held, as an enclave. Instead of planning a defense, he now had to plan an evacuation. Like Phu in Military Region 2, Truong was asked to execute the most difficult of military operations, a fighting withdrawal, in the most unpropitious of circumstances.

In less than 24 hours, Truong concocted a plan which amounted to a last-ditch defense of Da Nang with his remaining forces. Unlike Phu, Truong correctly deduced that a military withdrawal would provoke a flight of the civilian population, but he was equally helpless to deal with the exodus. Sensing victory, PAVN units began to cut the coastal Highway 1, complicating the retreat. Counter-order then followed order. Following a lightning visit by Prime Minster Khiem on March 18 (the day the debacle was beginning to unfold on Route 7B), Truong was ordered to hold Hue, Chu Lai, and Da Nang, a quite impossible undertaking given the unraveling situation.

Again, Saigon was preempted. Following a hasty conference of PAVN and Viet Cong regional commanders held on March 16, a decision was taken to capture Quang Ngai and Binh Dinh Provinces.

Even as Truong was attempting to organize the withdrawal in Military Region 1, he was summoned back to Saigon on March 19. In a brief meeting attended by Vice President Tran Van Huang, Truong sketched two options. The first would involve all remaining units retreating on Highway 1 to Da Nang. This was not realistic. The vital coastal route was already being interdicted at several points. The second option involved withdrawing separately to Hue, Chu Lai, and Da Nang by whatever available routes, then organizing a sealift to the latter. In this also unrealistic plan, the city of Da Nang would harbor four divisions and four Ranger Groups, surely a sufficient force to create a defensible enclave. Unfortunately, this was a fantasy because the proposed formations were rapidly disintegrating and there was no real plan for the defense of Da Nang. In attempting to satisfy his president's scheme for a strategic withdrawal, Truong was necessarily making it up as he went along.

Thieu was not satisfied. In a volte-face, he passed over Truong's two options and instead informed the surprised general to suspend the withdrawals and hold all ground. He could even keep the Marine Division, which Thieu had intended to steal for the defense of Saigon. That evening, Thieu would address the nation and calm nerves.

But the pressure on the now porous defensive lines had become unbearable. After a week of fighting, communist forces reported that the "puppet 2nd Division" had been "annihilated." Quang Ngai Province fell quickly, including the coastal base at Chu Lai. Truong ordered the complete evacuation of the province and instructed all combat effective units to rally to the same city. But soldiers began to desert in droves, aware of the mass flight of the civilian population and desperate to find their families. The city of Tam Ky was captured on March 24 without great resistance and along with it the ARVN base at Tuan Duong. The PAVN then swept into the coastal lowlands and expanded operations across Quang Nam Province. In Quang Tri Province the PAVN rolled up the DMZ defenses and reached the My Chanh Line on the boundary with Thua Thien Province. Phu Loc crumbled under the combined assault of the 324B and 325th PAVN Divisions, although the marines held on to the important Bo Corridor. Hue was rapidly emptying of its civilian population, provoking massive traffic jams on the Hai Van Pass. Remarkably, some ARVN units continued to put up spirited resistance. Faced with the prospect of losing 1st ARVN division, the order was given to abandon Hue. The majority of civilians had already anticipated the military withdrawal and were streaming towards the coast, the same escape route earmarked for the military withdrawal.

On March 20, an increasingly erratic Thieu changed his mind again. Truong had barely settled back in his corps headquarters when he received a secret flash message from Saigon. Disregarding the pledge Thieu had made on national television the previous evening, Military Region 1 was not going to be defended at all costs. Facing the impossibility of holding Hue, Chu Lai, and Da Nang, the former two should be abandoned. Adding to Truong's difficulties, Thieu ordered the last airborne brigade to embark for Saigon. By midnight, it was gone.

Hue was now doomed. Over March 21 to 23, units from the Tri Thien Military Region and 2 PAVN Corps drove virtually unimpeded into the coastal lowlands, severing Highway 1 and encircling Hue. Overnight, ARVN units fled from Hue in the direction of the coastal towns of Cua Thuan and Cu Tu Hien – all too late. The communist forces had anticipated this move and bombarded the retreating troops mercilessly. In the resultant action, the disorganized mob of South Vietnamese troops was "annihilated, captured, or routed."

The now defenseless Hue fell on the subsequent day. In the communist hagiography, "the inner-city infrastructure and commando forces encouraged the masses to arise, eliminate the enemy administration, and guide the main-force troops in capturing … the city."[90] This hardly described the reality of Hue's second sacking by the predatory People's Army. There was no uprising. "Elimination" translated as the summary executions of scores of Hue's "puppet" officials and their families – nobody knows how many perished. As in other South Vietnamese cities, the fall to communist troops degenerated into an opportunity to loot and bully. The average communist soldier had only known privation and the grimness of the North. The jetsam of consumer goods that had washed into South Vietnam with the tide of American forces now proved irresistible. After months subsisting on rice, fish paste, and bananas, what could be more alluring than Winston cigarettes, a 7UP, humming white trunks that kept food cool (refrigerators), Panasonic color televisions, and improbably, badminton rackets, which were believed to be some form of portable radar.[91]

Effectively, all the former ARVN Military Region 1 was now in Northern hands and Da Nang was surrounded from the north and south.[92] A region that had cost the lives of 13,000 US marines and 88,000 wounded – a third of America's war casualties – was no more.

As many as 121,000 refugees poured into Da Nang (the American estimate was closer to 400,000).[93] In the communist narrative:

> The enemy were forced to abandon their plan to withdraw their marine division from Da Nang, and had to use the remaining forces to defend Da Nang, their last important base in Military Region I, in hopes of holding up our main force units in the north, so that they could have time to redeploy their strategic defences in the South. The enemy troops there still numbered about 100,000, but they were isolated, [and] their morale had collapsed.[94]

Da Nang's defense would be in the hands of the survivors from 1st and 2nd ARVN Divisions, two formations at breaking point and exhausted by long marches. The other available formation – 3rd ARVN Division – was crumbling through mass desertions. Surveying these apocalyptic scenes, Truong resignedly reported that the only units showing any semblance of order were the marines, the very units Saigon was stealing in a panicked move to save the capital.

In the end, there was no defense of Da Nang. 324B and 325C Divisions, reinforced by an armor regiment and two artillery regiments, surrounded the city from the north and west. 71st Division and 304th Division blocked the south. The encircled city became gripped with mass panic. Again in the communist narrative, this terrified population was recast as extras in a joyous mass uprising. "Thousands of people in Da Nang," an official account celebrated, "in private automobiles, buses, three-wheeled Lambrettas, and even Hondas came out to await our troops ... Tens of thousands of people in the outskirts gave rice, water, and gifts to the troops."[95] Many did line the streets, but from apprehension. Many took advantage of the chaotic situation and fled in the opposite direction. Yet it should be acknowledged that there were also winners. Some who had suffered under the Diemist and subsequent regimes were ecstatic. "It was impossible to describe the joy," recounted Nguyen Thi Nguyet Anh, who had worked covertly for the National Liberation Front.[96] Non Nuoc prison emptied. For those with the means, self-preservation became the order of the day. At Da Nang Air Base, South Vietnamese air force pilots commandeered ten surviving UH-1 helicopters in a bid to outrun the communist advance. Hopelessly overloaded and dangerously low on fuel, just four found safety. Two made forced landings and four were shot down.

No contingency plan had been put in place for a large-scale air evacuation and any such attempt would have probably failed anyway. In a last-minute forlorn hope gesture, the Saigon Embassy chartered 20 flights from World

Airways to make the perilous journey to Da Nang. Just three were completed before the contract was canceled because the trip had become too hazardous. The Embassy, however, had not counted on the idealism and determination of the company's founder – Edward Daly – a former army sergeant and semi-professional boxer. Unwilling to give up on the city, Daly personally commandeered a Boeing 727 and ordered the pilot, Ken Healey, to fly to Da Nang.[97] At the last minute, five newsmen jumped aboard, sensing a good story. The flight itself was uneventful but as the crew approached Da Nang they were met by a scene of "clouds of black smoke boiled up from where military vehicles, automobiles and buildings were burning."[98] Unbeknown to the crew, they were being observed by an Air America helicopter pilot, Tony Coalson, who had been despatched to the city to search for refugees. What he witnessed he later admiringly described as "the most idiotic and stupid display ... I have ever seen."

To Coalson's astonishment, Healey landed the jet. As the aircraft taxied it was confronted by a 19-year-old Tran Dinh Truc, a military policeman abandoned by his officers, who promptly began shooting at the cockpit. His attempt to stop the aircraft failed. The aircraft taxied to a halt, chased by a desperate crowd, then lowered the back stairs.[99] Daly's attempts to impose order were overwhelmed by an armed mob of soldiers and family members – several hundred wailing, screaming, and punching Vietnamese – all attempting to barge their way on board. His clothes were torn, his trousers pulled down by the panic-struck clinging to his legs, and he resorted to pistol-whipping the mob.

Pity was short in this hysterical scrum. Attendant Wollett reached out to help a family of five climb aboard. To her horror, "I stretched my arm out to grab the mother's hand but before I could get it a man running behind them shot all five of them and they fell and were trampled by the crowd ... And the man who shot them stepped on them to get closer to the air stair." Truc, with some companions, sneaked into the open body of the aircraft. There he found dozens more people, including some women and children, desperately feeling their way in the dark. In the confusion, station manager Hrezo was pushed off the stairwell and almost left behind. Others parked cars or lay across the runway trying to prevent the aircraft from taking off. Eventually the aircraft did take off from a taxiway, pursued by "thousands – and I mean literally thousands of people" on bicycles, motorbikes, and cars. An armored personnel carrier even joined this "tidal wave of desperate humanity." Angry Vietnamese soldiers opened fire. One motorcyclist rode headlong into the landing gear and was smashed to pieces.

Despite suffering wing damage from a grenade strike, and now unable to retract the landing gear (the body of an unfortunate soldier became trapped in the hydraulic mechanism preventing its operation), Healey succeeded in nursing the aircraft to Tan Son Nhut airport. Some 268 shaken escapees stepped off the jet, and the cargo hold disgorged perhaps another 60.[100] This remains a world record for passenger carriage on a Boeing 727. Seven died trying to cling to the damaged rear stair well. The first to fall was a young woman who strangely smiled and waved as she fell to her death. As many as 17 people lost their lives falling out of the wheel wells (but seven held on and survived). They fell, as one witness remembered, "like bombs."

The bestiality of the evacuation was measured by the genders of the evacuees: just five were women, with two or three children. For all his idealism, Daly had managed to save a crowd of panicky cowards with guns. Dan Rather on CBS news described the rescue as a Dunkirk. Attendant Valerie Witherspoon, many years later, remembered the life-saving aircraft as "our very precious angel."[101] Such was the last American flight from Da Nang.

PAVN main-force units and irregular cadres quickly seized the Da Nang city hall and overran the 1 Corps headquarters and air base.[102] In the chaotic free-for-all, every available boat was used to evacuate soldiers, marines, and civilians from the lawless city. Observers off the coast reported seeing "wall to wall people along the shore," desperate to escape.[103] Truong joined them, swimming from the beach before being rescued by a passing boat. Military Sealift Command hastily tasked two ships to the area: the SS *Pioneer Contender*, and her sister ship *Pioneer Commander*. As many as 9,000 evacuees were rescued, some lifted in nets like cargo. The majority were dumped further down the coast at Cam Ranh Bay, a facility that was about to fall within the next two days anyway.

The US consulate staff and six marines led by a redoubtable Staff Sergeant Walter Sparks escaped in a commandeered garbage truck. It seemed a fitting metaphor. They too eventually made it to the awaiting SS *Pioneer Contender*. The diligent Consul General stayed behind to oversee the evacuation of any remaining Americans. He swam to safety from a beach near Marble Mountain and was picked up by a South Vietnamese patrol boat. The last batch of Americans was rescued by a New Zealand skipper on the barge *Oseola*.

On March 30, less than two weeks after Thieu ordered the sacrifice of Military Region 1, this wish had come to pass. By the evening, all radio contact was lost with Da Nang. Just 6,000 marines and 4,000 ARVN were saved. The red flag and gold star of North Vietnam now flew over the airbase where Johnson's misadventure in Indochina had begun.

The chaotic fall of Da Nang created a situation that Giap was naturally keen to exploit. The advancing corps were ordered to "rapidly develop their attack southward," an order followed with some zest. In the ensuing days of rapid advances, communist forces "annihilated and disintegrated the remaining elements of the puppet II Corps," capturing the last districts of Binh Dinh Province by March 31. Nha Trang and Cam Ranh Bay both fell on April 1.[104]

Hanoi's gains, just one month after the assault on Ban Me Thuot, were stunning:

> we had annihilated or disintegrated more than 35 percent of the enemy forces. For the first time we had annihilated and knocked out of action two puppet military regions and two corps, totaling about 40 percent of their modern technical forces, took over or destroyed more than 40 percent of their material and rear services bases, liberated 12 provinces, and increased the total number of people in the liberated areas to 8 million.[105]

Exhilarated by this success, Giap became a possessed man. Thirty-one years had elapsed since his great victory at Dien Bien Phu. He was now on the verge of an even greater victory and the culmination of a lifetime struggle. General Hoang Van Thai, a witness to these last days, wrote:

> During that period, in which we received a flood of good news, it had almost become customary that every afternoon Van [Giap] would cross Hoang Dieu Street in the direction of the western gate, go to the operations duty office, and remain there until late at night. Sometimes he would sleep in the conference room of the Military Commission. At night he would take in the latest news from the battlefields, exchange opinions with us and the duty officers, and visit the communications and cryptanalysis personnel on duty there. Sometimes he would stand silent for long periods of time before a battle map hung on the wall of the operations room, or walk in the courtyard of the "Dragon House" [Zone A of the Citadel, where the offices of the Military Commission were located within the Ministry of National Defense]. At such times he was thinking, assessing and evaluating the situation, and preparing opinions to report to and exchange opinions with the members of the Political Bureau and Military Commission on the following morning.[106]

The reality was that, however hard Giap sought to stay in control of the situation, both the Political Bureau and Military Commission were now issuing daily directives that were out of date by the time they reached the front commanders. The order of the day was now a campaign of "miraculous speed and even greater miraculous speed."

On April 7, Giap issued a general order to the front-line commanders. It was a model of brevity:

1 Like lightning, and even more so; recklessly, and even more so; taking advantage of every hour, every minute, rush to the front and liberate the South. Be resolved to fight and totally win.
2 Transmit at once to the party members and soldiers.[107]

The formation at the head of this sprint was 2 Corps, northwest of Saigon, and now commanded by Major General Nguyen Huu An – Hal Moore's old adversary in the battle of Ia Drang. Ten years after that first bloody encounter with American soldiers, it was his soldiers that were now on the verge of complete victory.

To add more punch to 2 Corps' advance, Giap ordered the re-subordination of three divisions – the 325th and 304th, both now in Da Nang, and 3rd PAVN Division, sweeping through Binh Dinh – under the single command of Le Trong Tan.

Tan was yet another example in North Vietnam's long production line of survivors. Born at the outbreak of the First World War, he had witnessed all the great events of the 20th century and like many compatriots sniffed the winds of independence. An early career as a footballer was cut short by the Second World War when he elected to join the ranks of the Viet Minh. By 1954 he was a brigade commander in the Vietnam People's Army and fought at Dien Bien Phu. It was one of Tan's units that was first to enter the French headquarters and capture General Christian de Castries. As fate would play out, it would also be Tan's troops that would crash through the gates of Independence Palace and arrest South Vietnam's last president. In the interim years he had served on the Laotian fronts and led 1 Corps' battle for Quang Tri in the 1972 Easter Offensive. With his frail appearance and large, square-rimmed glasses he hardly looked the part of a dynamic field commander, but appearances were deceptive. Now, the sexagenarian "Vietnamese Zhukov," as he was later dubbed, was ordered to advance at best speed with this eastern column "to annihilate enemy troops ... and develop the attack in the direction of Saigon."[108]

After the frenetic events of March, the first week of April offered a window for reorganization and respite for Saigon. This would be the only pause during *Thang Tu Den* ("Black April"). Military Region 1 was lost. A border which had cost so many US marine lives was erased from the map as if it had never existed. The fight in the Central Highlands and Military Region 2 was also over, the last coastal enclaves swamped. The last coherent fighting formation in this region was 3rd Airborne Brigade, but it had lost three quarters of its soldiers. Military Region 4 in the far south was a landscape of numerous petty battles, none decisive, although 7th ARVN Division did get into a serious fight with 5th PAVN Division in Long An Province.

Military Region 3 still held, but the situation had obviously become desperate. Stout defending in Long Khanh, Binh Long, Binh Duong, and Tay Ninh had temporarily checked the communist avalanche. For the government in Saigon, re-establishing a line of resistance had become the absolute and urgent priority, but with so many shattered, dispersed, and disorganized units, this was an overwhelming task. The remnants of the Marine Division, still under Major General Bui The Lan, disembarked at Vung Tau, but now needed to be re-fitted. Just 4,000 had managed to escape, or one third of the force, abandoning all heavy equipment. 22nd ARVN Division had also managed to withdraw with over 4,000 men, but other divisions were not in such good shape. 23rd ARVN Division was reduced to a nominal strength of 1,000 but just 20 rifles.[109] 2nd ARVN Division swelled to around 3,600 with reinforcements but promptly lost an entire regiment in a final defense of the town of Phan Rang. 3rd ARVN Division somehow managed to raise over 1,000 men in Ba Ria and Phuoc Tuy and was joined by 1st ARVN Division, now comprising just two officers and 40 men.[110]

The disintegration of the ARVN was matched by a disintegration of the Saigon administration, now bypassed by an increasingly dictatorial and paranoid Thieu. Prime Minister Khiem resigned, along with most of the government, now contemplating flight not fight. In a pointless fit of pique, Thieu blamed his own colossal blunder in the Central Highlands on his military commanders and ordered the arrests of generals Du Quoc Long, Pham Van Phu, and Pham Quoc Tham. The gesture was meaningless because Saigon's generals no longer commanded troops, or cared to. Phu would commit suicide, but others, including Khiem, managed to slip the country before the fall. The majority simply went to ground, awaiting their fate. On the same day that Thieu ordered the arrests, a pilot called Nguyen Thanh Trung manifested his feelings towards the national President by bombing the Independence Palace. He then flew to the now communist-held Phuoc Binh airfield and handed over his F-5E to the Viet Cong.

For the communists, the beginning of April was a period to capitalize on the battlefield successes. On April 7, Le Duc Tho traveled to Loc Ninh to meet with the regional commanders. The message he brought from the political bureau was uncompromising: "At present, time is strength. We must act quickly, boldly and unexpectedly, and win certain victory."[111]

For Washington, the events of March were a profound shock. The Ford administration was caught totally unprepared by the speed of the collapse.

Da Nang's supine surrender had been an especially powerful psychological blow. For many months, skepticism over South Vietnam's ultimate survival was a tacit but unstated feeling within Congress and the government. But when the unraveling began, it fell like a blow.

It was apt that Washington's disengagement from Indochina was tinctured by the same venom that poisoned the entry – over-optimistic and false reporting. The printing press of this misleading reporting was being personally manhandled by Ambassador Graham Martin, an increasingly erratic and unreliable interlocutor. Son of a Baptist Minister, the upright Martin had first intersected with Indochina in the late 1940s and early 1950s when he served in Paris in the US Embassy. The "French lobby" in the State Department had been instrumental in prodding Washington into supporting the French war. A subsequent firsthand witness to the tragic unraveling of this ruinous conflict did not deter Martin from Indochinese entanglements. Rather, it fortified a belief that America could do better. This belief still held when he was appointed to the Saigon ambassadorship in June 1973. And much like the French before him, the war had become a personal cause. In November 1965 his only foster son, Marine 1st Lieutenant Glenn Dill Mann, was killed in fighting near Chu Lai.

Martin, like many other Americans in the Saigon mission, felt a deep and growing sense of betrayal over Washington's imperial cold-shouldering of its ally. Many officials shared US Information Agency Director Alan Carter's later verdict that the fall of Saigon was the most painful moment of their public careers.[112] Many found Washington's behavior "obscene."[113] Nobody had a monopoly over the anger, to misquote Kissinger, but only Martin refused to accept the reality of collapse. As an individual "he was tough, he was brave, he was indefatigable."[114] His sense of honor was unimpeachable. Yet this was not enough. The moment needed cold calculation. Congressman Pete McCloskey, spokesman to the final congressional visit to Saigon, over the last week of February, was not so much cold as icy. His hosts warned him that Hanoi now had 700 tanks and 400 heavy artillery pieces in South Vietnam. The DAO warned him that the enemy was preparing "a return to major offensive activity as the primary means of advancing the Communist revolution to a successful conclusion," but he played deaf.[115] The Embassy was in the grip of a "siege mentality," he decided, and living in an "unreal world." "I didn't see any indication that he [Martin] was insane," McCloskey dispassionately observed, "but ... he was obsessed with the virtue of his mission, beyond the point which he could make competent decisions."[116] Yet competent decisions were now urgently required.

In Deputy Ambassador Wolfgang Lehman's view, the congressmen had already made up their minds. On return to Washington, America's legislators voted against further provision of aid to the Saigon government. Ford attempted to veto the measure as "impractical and unconstitutional" but was hobbled because so many senators were in recess, on weekend leave, or abroad. This was the final reliquary note.

Abandoned by the congressmen, the Embassy became "magnetized" and "cowed." Only positive reporting, or a "rosy picture," was permitted by Martin. The ARVN was described as tenacious and determined. A growing body of signals intelligence (SIGINT) revealing the full scale of the debacle was suppressed. NSA Chief Tom Glenn was refused permission to evacuate his 43-man staff and their 22 dependents. When evacuation was finally authorized, the haste was such that the entire SIGINT apparatus fell into the hands of the North Vietnamese.[117]

Regardless of the Embassy's stance, by the end of March nervous Americans began filling outward-bound Saigon flights. The trickle quickly turned to a flood, inflated by demands for the evacuation of Vietnamese dependants, co-workers, and friends. As it was illegal for the latter to travel directly to continental America, Clark Air Base in the Philippines became the unprepared reception point for this increasingly desperate relay.

By now, various lobby groups were pressing Washington to act to save lives. The most vociferous was a confederation of charities that took up the cause of Vietnamese orphans.[118] At the time, these organizations were caring for several thousand orphans across South Vietnam.

Thus was born Operation *Babylift*, on April 3, a gesture intended to insert some good news in the uninterrupted ticker tape of bad news, but which backfired tragically on the very first lift. Twelve minutes after the first C5A Galaxy took off from Tan Son Nhut Airport, with its cargo of orphans, it suffered a catastrophic mechanical failure. Captain Dennis Traynor nursed the stricken aircraft back to land but it broke into four parts after hitting a dyke. One hundred and thirty-eight people were killed in the crash, including 78 children and 35 DAO staff. Over half, including the crew, survived, thanks to Traynor's cool airmanship. The setback provoked an immediate response from Friends For All Children who posted an advertisement in the *New York Times* announcing the charter of a Boeing 747 and urging Americans to contribute tax-deductible dollars that "can literally buy these kids their ticket to a new life."

The following day, April 5, a second attempt was made using a chartered Pan Am flight from Hong Kong. Nurse Joyce Harrington who accompanied the flight was overwhelmed by emotion as she watched

> the endless flow of little ones pouring into the plane filling every available space. Some were even being handed over by their mothers. Many were obviously not full Asian. I guessed they probably had American GI fathers.

I could only wonder how many families on both sides of the Pacific were being impacted by this one planeload of children.[119]

After an exhausting 30-hour flight via Guam and Honolulu, some 408 orphans were eventually disembarked at Seattle. A single four-month old baby did not survive the journey and was buried in Guam. Shocked by this "ultimate disaster in a country of endless disasters,"[120] Ford personally greeted the inbound flight, Clipper 1724, at San Francisco International Airport. Eventually, 30 evacuation flights were completed, processing a total of 2,547 orphans. But Operation *Babylift* was just the first chord in the frenetic fugue that would be the even more desperate Operation *Frequent Wind*.

The scene was now set for the last major battle for the survival of South Vietnam, and one of the hardest fought. The confrontation took place at Xuan Loc, a small town of some 30,000 people, 38 miles northeast of Saigon in Long Khanh Province. Much like Ban Me Thuot, the war had mostly bypassed Xuan Loc. During the Tet Offensive, D440th VC Battalion had launched an attack on the town. It had taken just one day for 52nd Ranger Battalion supported by 3rd Squadron, 5th Cavalry to see off the assailants. Since then, there had been very little enemy activity in the surrounding countryside. The town itself little mattered. Xuan Loc's significance lay in its position: it sat astride Highway 1 and near the intersection with Highway 20. It was the hinge around which Thieu was planning a last stand, and the central point of a defensive line that ran from Tay Ninh in the west to Phan Rang in the east. If it fell, the communist spearheads would enjoy a free run to Bien Hoa Air Base, just one hour's drive down the road, and beyond into the heart of Saigon.

The defense of the town was entrusted to 18th ARVN Division. Built on a flat plain and surrounded by rubber plantations, Xuan Loc was not naturally defensible.[121] In typical colonial style, the town center had been laid out in an open grid pattern. An east-west French railway line ran through the middle of the town. To the southeast, the suburbs gave way to a number of rubber processing plants, workers' accommodation, and a military air strip. Like every other small town on the outskirts of Saigon, the dusty streets abounded with children, recently resettled refugees, and the odd pig rooting for rubbish. The entire area was overlooked to the east by the Nui Chua Can, a volcanic massif, but this was too far from the town to be effectively defended. More handily, to the northwest, there were three pimple hills that offered better defensive options and complicated any assault from the north. Further afield, the ground gave way to jungle and banana tree plantations. From the air, evidence of past B-52 strikes could be seen in the beads of water-filled bomb craters. 11th Armored Cavalry Regiment had departed in 1968, leaving behind an infrastructure that had since become dilapidated. The only building of note was a Catholic steeple church, which featured in Bob Simon's reports for *CBS Evening News* and remarkably survived.[122] Simon reported, "People in Saigon feel that if Xuan Loc falls, the war is over," and he was of course right.

The 4 PAVN Corps' plan for the capture of Xuan Loc involved attacking on three axes. 7th PAVN Division would attack directly from the north. 6th PAVN Division would assault west from the direction of the Nui Chua Chan massif, hand-railing Highway 1. The trap would be closed by 341st PAVN Division, rolling down from the northwest and roughly following the axis of Highway 20 (in Tran Van Tra's account this is puzzlingly designated "1st Division" and is described as seriously understrength due to losses incurred in earlier fighting). Overall command was vested in the 55-year-old General Hoang Cam, a dour Northerner from the Hanoi hinterlands.

To block the imminent communist assaults, 18th ARVN Division had hastily established a lozenge-shaped defensive perimeter, roughly six miles wide, stretching from the Nui Cha Chan massif west to the intersection with Highway 20. The division itself was not in bad shape. As well as its organic regiments (43rd, 48th, and 52nd), the formation could count on two artillery battalions and four Regional Force battalions. As battle joined, further reinforcements arrived from 1st Airborne Brigade, 8th Task Force, 5th Infantry Division, and 33rd Ranger Battalion. Crucially, the division could also count on elements from 315th, 318th, and 322nd Armored Brigades to counter communist armored thrusts. In total, 18th ARVN Division was roughly 12,000 strong. 4 Corps perhaps mustered 20,000 soldiers in the three divisions now converging on Xuan Loc. The question was – could Cam make his numerical superiority count?

On paper, Xuan Loc should have fallen quickly. But for the stubbornness of its defenders it would have. The diminutive 18th ARVN Division Commander General Le Minh Dao was better known as an accomplished guitar player with an impressive repertoire of French ballads, not for his tactical skills. Always dressed in a neatly pressed uniform, wearing dark sunglasses, and bearing a swagger stick in his delicate fingers, he barely looked the part of an operational commander. But Dao was a patriot to his polished boots and a determined, wily opponent. He almost certainly knew the cause was doomed – he later confessed that the loss of the north had filled him with despair – but this fatalism filled him with steely anger.[123] If Saigon was to fall, the communists would have to do it the hard way, fighting for every last yard.

Dao arrayed his forces with 43rd Regiment blocking the eastern approaches on Highway 1, 48th Regiment securing the town itself, and 52nd Regiment screening the north. It was from this latter direction that the first attacks fell. On April 9, communist gunners dumped a barrage of 4,000 shells into the town center which signaled the beginning of an assault by 341st PAVN Division. One shell landed directly on Dao's two-story accommodation, crashing into the bedroom. The attack at first made good headway but then stalled when it was met by a counterattack from 52nd Regiment. To the east, an over-confident vanguard from 7th PAVN Division steamed down Highway 1 but was easily repulsed by 43rd Regiment. In the south, lead units of 6th PAVN Division became embroiled in running battles with 322nd ARVN Armored Brigade, holding a defensive line astride Highway 1 between the hamlets of Bong Con and Hung Nghia. Undeterred by this stiff resistance, Cam pressed on with the assaults. By the afternoon, several important objectives had been captured, including the 18th ARVN Division headquarters, the communications center, the governor's residence, and the police station. This should have been the prelude to a collapse of the town's defense, but the communists had underestimated their enemy.

For the next three days Dao beat back the three-pronged PAVN assaults. Then, on April 12, General Toan began to squeeze reinforcements to the front: 1st Airborne Brigade from the west, supported by Task Force 322; and a second, Task Force 315, from Cu Chi. By the fifth day of the battle, the US Embassy was cabling Washington with the news that "enemy losses have been staggering."[124] An entire enemy tank battalion had been annihilated. This was true, as was the concluding remark that the ARVN had confounded critics and demonstrated a will to fight, but these were eulogies to a dying army. Reporters flocked to the town to witness the unexpected reversal of fortunes, burnishing the heroic aura of the defenders.

On April 13, 4 Corps tried again, this time mounting a seven-regiment-strong attack. This too failed to make headway against a determined 43rd ARVN Regiment. Sensing a decisive confrontation, both sides now began shoveling troops into the battle: 320B and 325th Divisions on the communist side, and a further two ad hoc task forces on the Southern side. After two weeks of fighting, 18th ARVN Division was now faced with overwhelming odds and furthermore was completely surrounded. More urgently, Saigon was being threatened from the west and south. Holding Xuan Loc at any cost no longer made sense, if it was even possible.

The melancholy withdrawal was finally ordered on April 19. Just 200 vehicles successfully escaped, two days later, in a heavy rainstorm. The last unit to evacuate the ghost town was 3rd Battalion, 1st Airborne, which paid the price, suffering near annihilation. Over 2,000 South Vietnamese soldiers fell in the defense of Xuan Loc and more than twice this number was captured. Communist casualties doubled the casualty bill. Dao had scored a final moral victory for the South, but the monument that today stands in the center of Xuan Loc shows a peasant gesturing in the direction of Saigon, alongside a communist soldier bearing aloft an AK-47 in triumph. Dao's elevation proved brief and his subsequent imprisonment some 17 years long.

Notwithstanding the resistance at Xuan Loc, by the second week of April, and from the perspective of the communist eyeglass, a great victory was imminent:

> A vast liberated [area] extended from the southernmost part of Trung Bo and through Military Region 5 and the Central highlands, and to Tri Thien, where it connected with the great rear area in the North. Thus the entire nation had advanced as far as the land of the Bronze Bastion, had moved close to Saigon-Gia Dinh, and was orienting all actions toward the final strategic battle on the key battlefield: Saigon.[125]

A great victory deserved a grandiose title. So, on April 14, the Military Commission took the decision that the Saigon campaign be renamed the Ho Chi Minh Campaign – a symbolic gesture that reflected Hanoi's now total conviction that it was on the verge of triumph.

Even as the *coup de grâce* approached, Hanoi felt it necessary to fit the quickly unfolding events into an orthodox communist narrative. It was insufficient to smash your enemy – you had to smash your enemy according to the theory of revolutionary warfare. This demanded "a great uprising," which had so far eluded Hanoi. In preparation for this anticipated historic event, on April 12 the Saigon municipal party committee issued an urgent resolution urging its cadres to prepare for battle. This was all well, except that in a frank admission the National Liberation Front could only muster around 700 fighters in this city of several millions and possibly another 1,000 on the outskirts. A combination of the suicidal Tet Offensive and relentless security operations since had utterly decimated the Viet Cong in the capital district, reducing the guerrillas to near impotence.[126]

This same pattern was repeated elsewhere, although communist myth-makers would later present a picture of a mass mobilization. In Military Region 9, in the Mekong Delta, the claims were prodigious. It was reported that thousands of new recruits had rushed to join the ranks of the local force battalions, raising the number from 15 to 24 and creating 60 new companies. Overall strength had supposedly jumped in one month from 32,900 to 54,900. In Military Region 8, seven local battalions, 36 local companies, and 150 local platoons were reportedly established. Ben Tre Province raised two fresh battalions and another three were raised in My Tho Province. It was claimed that "each village had one or two guerrilla platoons," that 40,000 peasants had mobilized to transport weapons and ammunition, and that 4,000 commandos were poised to strike Highway 4, south of Saigon. None of this was remotely true. The reality was that the National Liberation Front and Viet Cong had become increasingly irrelevant to Hanoi's war and were heading towards a precipice of dissolution, along with the enemy government they had fought for the last two decades.

The Northerners faced other unanticipated problems. The "miraculous" speed of the communist advance had inevitably provoked logistic difficulties. Too few trucks were chasing too many demands for ammunition, especially artillery and tank shells. On April 19, the Hanoi General Staff sent an urgent message to the B2 Front advising that a convoy of 430 vehicles had been organized, loaded with 13,000 130mm shells and 8,300 tank shells, to support the final battles. An additional 20,000 shells were being sent by sea to the newly captured ports at Qui Nhon and Nha Trang. In fact, none of these supplies, despatched on April 17, actually reached the front-line units before the collapse of the Saigon government.[127]

By the beginning of the second week of April, Saigon had become an encircled city. The sound of communist guns could be clearly heard on the outskirts, drumming a menacing beat. Starting in the south and traveling in a clockwise direction, the divisions available to the Joint General Staff were as follows. The approaches from the Delta were held by the largely still intact 7th and 9th ARVN Divisions. But these were vulnerable to the Viet Cong blocking Route 4 and putting them out of the fight. The southwestern corridor in Long An was held by a single brigade – 12th ARVN Infantry – reinforced by survivors from 22nd ARVN Division. The northwestern approach was blocked by 25th ARVN Division, still holding on grimly to Tay Ninh City and Route 1. 5th Division defended Highway 13 to the north. The critical northeastern approach on Highway 1 was about to become the withdrawal route of the heroic 18th ARVN Division, forced to surrender Xuan Loc. Far to the north and east, along the coast, the remnants of 2nd ARVN Division maintained a weak claim on Binh Thuan and Ninh Thuan Provinces. And finally, to the south and east, the remnants of two airborne brigades guarded Highway 15. These formations belied their titles. All were understrength. Many had become paper divisions, with perhaps only one or two effective battalions.

The city of Saigon should have presented a ring of steel, but steel and men were now in short supply. The defense of the Capital Military Special Zone (CMSZ) was vested in General Nguyen Van Toan, the 3 Corps former tank commander. But he had become little more than a janitor in a crumbling apartment block. The puffy-faced Toan had survived the onslaught of the 1972 Easter Offensive thanks to American intervention and political favoritism. Neither card was now in the pack. He despatched his command for less than a week, treacherously deceiving his fellow generals and fleeing the country before the fall. No preparations had been made to turn the city into a bastion, and it was far too late now. In this most defendable city, no bridges had been prepared for demolition, no mines laid, and no barricades erected. In tardy and futile gestures, 6th, 7th, and 8th Ranger Groups were deployed to the southern and western suburbs. A still fresh marine brigade was redeployed to the south and east, but there was no significant threat from this direction. A disintegrating collection of various ad hoc regular units, territorial forces, and police milled in the city center, but the likelihood that any of these would contribute to the defense of Saigon was fast vanishing. For most Southerners, personal safety and the whereabouts of displaced family had become the paramount concerns.

Ranged against these forces were a formidable and growing number of People's Army divisions, many fresh and imbued with the zeal of a winning side. By far the biggest concentration had crossed over from Cambodia to the west of Saigon. This corps-level force included the 3rd, 5th, 8th, and 9th PAVN Divisions supported by 27th Sapper Division. From the opposite axis, following the line of the coast, 3rd PAVN Division was sweeping all before it. And 6th, 7th, and 341st PAVN Divisions were in pursuit on Highway 1. In total, as many as 16 People's Army divisions were now drawing the noose around Saigon.[128] Towns fell like collapsing dominoes: Phan Rang, Ninh Thuan (April 16); Phan Thiet, Bin Thuan (April 18), and finally Xuan Loc (April 20). At Phan Rang, President Thieu's ancestral home, retreating ARVN soldiers vandalized the family graves. Immediately to the north, 1 Corps had breached the Be river line and poured its units over this last major water obstacle. To the northwest, 3 Corps was poised menacingly on the western banks of the Saigon River. 4 Corps was astride Highway 1, having completed the capture of Xuan Loc, and 2 Corps was leaning against the eastern approaches of the city.

In synchronicity with his collapsing country, President Thieu resigned on April 21. He quit office cursing America's betrayal of South Vietnam, which he likened to "haggling for fish in the market." He blamed his generals, he blamed Kissinger, and he blamed the media. "[If] the country remains, everything remains; [if] the country is lost, everything is lost." He did not remain. Like the majority of the Saigon government he escaped – courtesy it appears of the CIA and carrying suitcases rumored to be filled with gold. Seemingly unwilling to live in the country which he felt had betrayed him, he went into a traumatized, reclusive exile in London.[129]

His successor, the 70-year-old nearly blind and arthritic Tran Van Huong, lasted a week before being succeeded by "Big Minh." The old general whose teeth had been pulled out by the Japanese was handed the keys, but only to surrender them to the enemy. By the time he acceded to the office at 5pm on April 28, Tan Son Nhut air base was under bombardment and the 25th ARVN

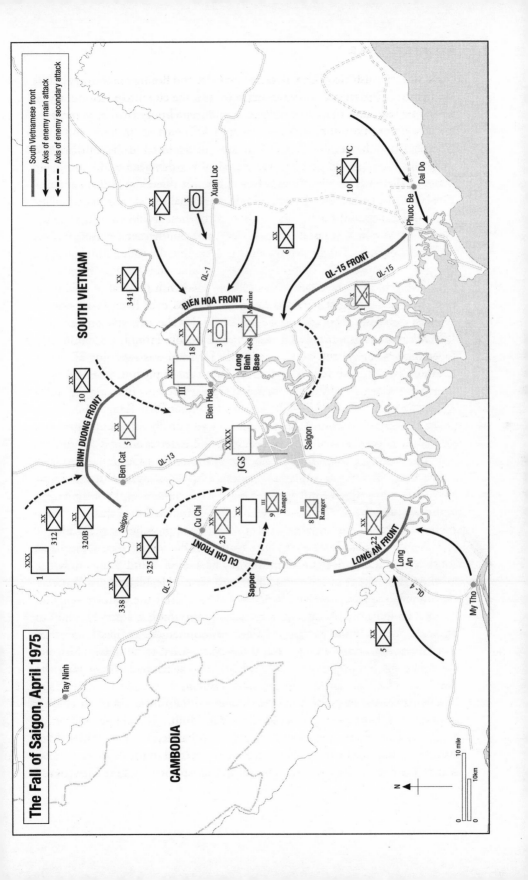

The Fall of Saigon, April 1975

Legend:
— South Vietnamese front
→ Axis of enemy main attack
⇢ Axis of enemy secondary attack

SOUTH VIETNAM

CAMBODIA

BIEN HOA FRONT
BINH DUONG FRONT
QL-15 FRONT
CU CHI FRONT
LONG AN FRONT

Xuan Loc
Dai Do
Phuoc Be
Bien Hoa
Long Binh Base
Saigon
JGS
Ben Cat
Cu Chi
Long An
My Tho
Tay Ninh

QL-1
QL-13
QL-15
QL-4
Saigon

Marine
Sapper

Units: 7, 10 VC, 6, 341, 18, 3, 468, III, 10, 5, 312, 320B, 1, 325, 338, 25, 9 Ranger, 8 Ranger, 22, 5

N

0 10 mile
0 10km

Division at Cu Chi had been pushed back. That same morning the ARVN command in Bien Hoa effectively dissolved, leaving the capital's surviving units without leadership.[130] The last intelligence report was submitted to the JGS Chief of Staff, Lieutenant General Dong Van Khuyen, on April 29. Whether or not he bothered reading it, later that morning he secretly hitched a ride on an Air America evacuation flight and by the afternoon he was a guest of the US Seventh Fleet.[131] Shortly before noon the entire JGS had vanished on board the evacuation flights, watched by embittered and disbelieving junior officers and soldiers.

Saigon was now a city in denial of its fate, surreally playing out the routines of urban life:

> Believing in the protection of the ARVN, which had been able twice to push back the communist attacks in 1968, people in the capital went about their daily activities. The face of Saigon appeared peaceful and quiet. Markets, stores and restaurants were open as usual and traffic was normal. Streets filled with pedestrians, bicycles, and cars. Schools around the city were not yet closed; kids were still playing in schoolyards or studying in classes. Everything appeared in its habitual state.[132]

In the skies above Saigon, CH-53s and UH-1s clattered above the rooftops even as the crump of shells signaled the encroachment of the People's Army.

In a pointless gesture, Minh despatched a delegation comprising a Buddhist monk, Chau Tam Luan, a Catholic priest, Chan Tin, and the lawyer, Tran Ngoc Lieng, to parley with Brigadier General Vo Dong Giang, now squatting in the newly captured Tan Son Nhut air base.[133] But what was there to parley about? The idea of negotiating had gestated from a single truthful insight resting on a profound delusion. "The Communists know that the people of South Vietnam do not like Communism," he argued, "Since it is impossible for the Communists to kill them all, it is to their advantage to negotiate."[134] Or conquer and subjugate.

The capture of Tan Son Nhut brought to an end what had become an increasingly unruly and fraught mass evacuation exercise. The final American evacuation from South Vietnam was always likely to have been caught between two contradictory impulses as well as legal entanglements. Setting aside the not inconsiderable logistic and transport challenges, the newly passed War Powers Act raised challenges over the use of military transports in a civilian evacuation. Even bigger legal question marks hung over the evacuation of Vietnamese to continental America. Hasty flight, it was feared, might provoke a backlash and hasten the collapse of South Vietnam; yet a tardy evacuation could endanger American lives. Regional countries had shamefully turned their backs on the impending humanitarian crisis and were refusing to offer assistance or sanctuary to fleeing Vietnamese. These problems required urgent resolution against the backdrop of a rapidly deteriorating situation. Both Ford and Kissinger were adamant that the absolute priority was the safety of US citizens. In this stance they were at odds with their senior official in-country, Ambassador Martin, who maintained that America should honorably offer evacuation to as many imperiled Vietnamese as practicable, and maintain a minimal but effective presence in Saigon, at least until the eleventh hour. Following interdepartmental haggling, and a further delay imposed by an unrealistic plan to furnish the South Vietnamese government with $722 million's worth of armaments, agreement was reached on an irreducible 1,250-strong rear guard, or as many staff as could be rescued by helicopter, in an emergency, in a single day. This proved a significant underestimate. Fortunately, a reconnaissance of potential landing zones in Saigon had yielded 13 sites, each of which was cleared of obstacles.

The timings were incredibly tight. State officials met with Senate committees on April 8 to seek the Attorney General's "parole" authority for evacuees from Indochina. Four days later the US Embassy in Phnom Penh closed in Operation *Eagle Pull*. On the same day, State officials met with UNHCR counterparts in Geneva. On April 14, "parole" was finally secured for Vietnamese dependants of US citizens (full parole for additional categories of relatives, third-country nationals, and up to 50,000 "high-risk" Vietnamese was only granted four days before the surrender of Saigon). An Interagency Task Force (IATF), led by Ambassador L. Dean Brown from the State Department, was not actually stood up until April 18 (the day that the defense of Xuan Loc was finally abandoned). Its mandate was daunting: "To coordinate ... all U.S. Government activities concerning evacuation of U.S. citizens, Vietnamese citizens, and third-country nationals from Vietnam and refugee and resettlement problems relating to the Vietnam conflict." At Tulane University, just one week short of the final collapse, President Ford consciously closed the war to an audience that represented the nation's future and not her divided past: "Today, America can regain the sense of pride that existed before Vietnam. But it cannot be achieved by refighting a war that is finished as far as America is concerned."[135]

There were not one, but two separate and linked operations: the military evacuation, Operation *Frequent Wind*, and the evacuation of Vietnamese civilians, Operation *New Life*. Thirteenth Air Force under Brigadier General Richard T. Drury activated ten military airlift wings.[136] Some 20,000 soldiers were mobilized, mostly drawn from 25th Infantry Division in Hawaii. Rear Admiral George Stephen Morrison, commander of US Naval forces on Guam (and father of the singer Jim Morrison), was tasked with pulling together the naval contribution. The logical evacuation point was always Tan Son Nhut airport (there were also US consulates in Da Nang, Nha Trang, Bien Hoa, and Van Tho, which closed precipitately in the face of advancing communist forces). The most efficient means of evacuation was commercial aircraft. Over 50,000 evacuees had already been processed through Tan Son Nhut over the course of March and beginning of April. This was the emergency plan the Embassy and DAO expected to implement, should it be necessary. Neither anticipated that the runways on Saigon's only civilian airport might be interdicted before the evacuation plan could be fully implemented.

Operation *New Life* was only formally initiated on April 23 – just one week before the loss of Tan Son Nhut. "If history judges the resettlement effort to have been a success," the subsequent Congressional inquiry reported, "credit will have to be given to many agencies of Government."[137] This was true – 14 different government departments and agencies scrambled to action and displayed uncommon alacrity and cooperation. A gauge of the massive effort undertaken to maintain the lifeline open until the very end can be taken from the numbers. Flying Tiger Airlines had actually started the airlift of the first 99 evacuees two days earlier on April 21. This turned into a deluge.[138] More than 130,000 Vietnamese were eventually evacuated in the last days of April. The military airlift alone included 201 C-141 flights and 174 C-130 sorties.[139] Twenty-three thousand arrived by sea in a mix of South Vietnamese Navy vessels and pressed ships, including a fleet ballistic nuclear submarine tender, the USS *Proteus*. CV-41 USS *Midway* abandoned her complement of F-5 Tigers in a parking lot at Orote Point, Guam. The surplus aircraft were eventually loaded on barges and dumped in the Marianas Trench. "Millions and millions of dollars" of military kit from Vietnam followed the same path to the bottom of the Pacific Ocean. Conditions were so fetid on the evacuation ships, refugees defecated where they stood. "One quickly learned to stay upwind of these ships as they arrived," a sailor related, "at least until they could be washed down."[140] As the operation settled, refugees were met by a reception party of doctors, aid workers, and priests, as well as long lines of sailors with commandeered supermarket trolleys used to carry worldly possessions to the island bus ferry.

The overwhelming majority of refugees were transhipped to Guam, with smaller numbers distributed to alternative locations like Wake Island. The island from which America had bombed Vietnam had now become a receptacle for the bombed. In total, some 111,919 evacuees were processed on Guam, more than doubling the population of the island, with a bewildered cargo now living in a vast tent city.

The intent was to save Vietnamese whose lives might be endangered by the communist takeover, but the stampede to escape overtook altruism. "Half the Vietnamese we intended to get out did not get out," the same Congressional inquiry reported, "and half who did get out should not have."[141] Many had fled in herd-like panic not knowing their final destination, or even intending to immigrate to the United States. Many had no idea where they were. Some two thirds spoke no English and one fifth spoke only rudimentary English. Families were separated. The oddest batch was the inhabitants of an entire fishing village. Some 16 percent were children under the age of five. In both genders, roughly half were under the age of 17 – the primal impulse to save children had been overwhelming. Around 1,500 were over 60.

A cross-section of the origins and status of the evacuees, however, revealed that Saigon's elites had mostly exploited the evacuation, almost certainly hastening the end. Over 40 percent were Catholics, the Diemists who had risen to power in a predominantly Buddhist country. One fifth held higher education qualifications and 1,955 PhDs fled. At a stroke Saigon lost its professional classes.[142] Indeed, a quarter of the evacuees classified themselves as "Professional, Technical and Managerial." Almost one in ten belonged to the medical professions.

Once resettled in the United States, the refugees faced navigating a plethora of questionnaires, guidelines, and regulations in an unfamiliar environment. The Internal Revenue Service's notoriously convoluted tax regulations were an especial difficulty. "When I left Vietnam, I was able to salvage some gold and jewelry that I converted into currency after reaching the United States. Will I be taxed on this conversion?" ran one question. The bureaucratic and somewhat confusing answer was: "The conversion will be a taxable exchange if the amount you received when you converted the gold and jewelry into United States currency exceeded your cost or other basis in the gold or jewelry actually converted." United States currency brought from Vietnam was not tax deductible, an inconvenient regulation for those who had done precisely that, filling suitcases with dollars.

Notwithstanding the trauma of evacuation, the refugees could only count themselves as deeply fortunate. In preparation for the conquest of South Vietnam the Political Bureau in Hanoi hastily cobbled together a mass "re-education" program for the "liberated" peoples. But this was not so much re-education as rather bizarre notions of Taoist purification frog-marched down the glum doctrinal corridors of communism, or *trai hoc tap cai tao* in the Vietnamese. Southerners needed enlightenment at the point of a gun. Hanoi had some practice in this. In 1961, a nervous Politburo formally established "re-education camps," worried over the continued existence of "obstinate counter-revolutionary elements" and "professional scoundrels" in Northern society.[143] These provided the model for the scheme imposed on the South.

Had the original plan been implemented, South Vietnam's purgatory would have been short-lived. But Hanoi's understanding of the Southerners was woeful. The abstract masses of communist fantasy were real, even alien. A plan to impose three-day, ten-day, and one-month re-education courses, according to rank soon broke down. The suggestion that this relatively benign program was always intended as a lure to net as many former government workers and soldiers as possible may be over-conspiratorial. It is equally likely that Hanoi simply failed to grasp that it would find itself master of 20 million people unmoved by the rapture of communist "liberation." Panic turned to punishment, the favored cold dish in authoritarian regimes. The willing volunteers for "re-education" – a failure to register risked worse sanctions – found themselves trapped in an increasingly pernicious system.

According to the North Vietnamese government, over one million Southerners eventually attended "re-education camps." Given that roughly half the population was under-age, and subtracting women, this implies that as many as one in five Vietnamese males of working age found themselves captured by the re-education program. French journalist Jean Lacouture who visited the country in 1976 estimated that one in three South Vietnamese families had a relative in the system.[144] This fell especially hard on the urban population, as the new regime could barely afford to depopulate the countryside. On a routine basis, between 20,000 and as many as ten times this number were incarcerated.[145]

But even Hanoi could not incarcerate an entire society (and collapse the economy). Five levels of "re-education" were therefore dictated. The majority of Southerners, possibly half a million, attended day courses in socialism. These lucky workers escaped lightly. Roughly 200,000 attended level two camps, some 300 facilities, which lasted as long as six months. These were minimally guarded but evasion was rare. Level three camps, or "socialist reform camps," were prisons and incarceration could last a couple of years. Level four and five camps were reserved for the most dangerous enemies of the new order.[146] The unfortunate prisoners of these camps – some 15,000 – were interned from anything between three and ten years, without charge. The longest sentence was 17 years. Eighty camps were built to cope with the numbers, all squalid and mismanaged. Saigon's already dire Hoa Prison, with 8,000 inmates, swelled to 40,000.[147] In the bleak tradition of communism, the category of "enemy of revolution" expanded rapidly. By the summer of 1976, 12 such categories had been designated, from "lackeys" to "criminals." Over the same period all foreign journalists were expelled from Vietnam. The National Liberation Front and Viet Cong, no longer allies but now potential subversives, were scooped up, alongside former ARVN soldiers they had once fought. The usual "dangerous" classes – poets, intellectuals, writers, artists – stood no chance. Over 500 Catholic priests ended up in the bag.

Prisoners were forced to chant their "gratitude" for the blessing of now enjoying "freedom" from their previous state as "oppressed and exploited Vietnamese citizens."[148] All the miserable staples of communist prison camps were evident: "confessions," an obsession with purifying minds from impure thoughts, such as the "enslavement" of capitalism, and a raft of petty, degrading rules. In an echo of Nazi concentration camps, prisoners were extolled with the slogan "Labor is Glory." Hard labor and starvation rations made for a mortal combination. Torture added to the misery. Making a "mistake" could be fatal, leading to a beating, gangrene, and death. Prisoners learned to catch rats, birds, lizards, grasshoppers, crickets, and snakes. In short order, fauna was exterminated in the environs of the camps, and then the internees resorted to eating leaves and plant shoots. But this was mere survival, not sustenance, and a morsel of food felt like "one breath of air blown into a vast empty house."[149] Prison authority indifference and incompetence contributed to the estimated deaths of 165,000 inmates, mostly from disease and malnutrition. Around 65,000 may have been executed. The worst concentration camps were in the North, where the mix of ignorance, deprivation, and the universal psychology of camp bullying led to many deaths. The insanity of "re-education" provoked flight and the later phenomenon of Vietnam's "boat people" – around 800,000 by the time the human jetsam ended. In total, some 2 million South Vietnamese found ways of escaping "liberation," or one tenth of the population.

The last five divisions of the Army of the Republic of Vietnam, totaling perhaps some 60,000 men, would exist for one more day. In a forlorn gesture, Toan organized five redoubts. The Cu Chi front, to the northwest, was allocated to 25th Division; the Binh Duong front, to the north, was given to 5th Division; the Bien Hoa front, to the northeast, to the depleted 18th Division; the Vung Tau and 15 Route front, to the southeast, to 1st Airborne Brigade and remnants of 3rd Division; and the Long An front to 22nd Division. This reorganization completed, Toan tricked his fellow officers and fled the country, the first of many to run.

America's 30-year misadventure in Indochina also now only had 24 hours to run, yet there was still blood to be exacted. In the early hours of the morning of April 29 a stray rocket struck a guard post at the DAO Compound at Tan Son Nhut. Two marine corporals were on duty at the time; 19-year-old Darwin Judge from Iowa, and 22-year-old Charles McMahon from Massachusetts. Both were killed instantly, the last two US servicemen to die on South Vietnamese soil. In the haste of the evacuation, their bodies were abandoned in a nearby Seventh Day Adventist Hospital (denying their families a burial until the following year when their bodies were released following intercession by Senator Kennedy).

By dawn, artillery fire had begun to land on the runways. With some aplomb, American pilots negotiated the random fire until one salvo succeeded in disabling a taxiing C-130. The crew bailed from their burning aircraft and were rescued by a second, but the incident called into question the possibility of evacuation by fixed-wing aircraft. For reasons that have never been ascertained, the three intrepid C-130s that landed that morning were each carrying a 15,000lb "daisy cutter" bomb, even though they were supposed to be picking up an assortment of journalists, contractors, and other sundry nationals. As the rescue attempt was abandoned, it can only be guessed what the passengers would have made of the cargo.

Tripped by this unexpected turn of events, the DAO quickly reassessed the situation and advised the embassy that evacuation from the airport was no longer feasible. A shocked Martin raced to the scene, as if by sheer willpower he might re-open the runways, but it was clear the situation had become dire. The carefully staffed evacuation plan that relied on Tan Son Nhut remaining open to air traffic had been shredded by communist shrapnel now skidding across deserted pans.

As Saigon awoke to another tense day, the imminent capture of Tan Son Nhut was not widely known. At just before 11am, Americans tuning into Armed Forces Radio Saigon heard the presenter announce, "The temperature in Saigon is 112 degrees and rising." They were then treated to the voice of Bing Crosby and the Ken Darby Singers crooning "White Christmas." This was the code signal for the initiation of the evacuation plan, Operation *Frequent Wind*.

Officially, "Operation *Frequent Wind Option IV*" began at 10.51am Saigon time, but participating units were only issued the execute order, for unexplained reasons, at 12.15pm. The operation got rolling at about 3pm. Across central Saigon, buses collected anxious evacuees at 28 pre-arranged rendezvous points. In a meticulously planned scheme, selected Americans had been trained to drive South Vietnamese buses and fake national police cars had been acquired to act as escorts.

At the DAO Compound, a ferry of 9th Marine Amphibious Brigade (MAB) CH-53 and CH-46 helicopters whisked the disorientated civilians away from the intermittent shelling now punctuating the Saigon skyline, and deposited their human cargos on Seventh Fleet ships offshore Vung Tau. The first lifts arrived in the early afternoon. By late evening some 4,000 Vietnamese and 395 Americans had been airlifted to safety in an operation that owed much to the skill, flexibility, and ingenuity of the air crew and controllers directing the airborne armada. Throughout, North Vietnamese gunners continued to shell

Tan Son Nhut, now a crazy scene of light aircraft crewed by South Vietnamese pilots attempting to escape to Thailand. Beyond, Saigon presented an eerie backdrop. One pilot recalled, "The sky was completely overcast … with the lights of the city and the burning buildings reflecting off it, giving one the sensation that you were seeing a strange movie about the Apocalypse."[150]

By midnight, a handful of marines had damaged, destroyed, or set fire to the DAO buildings before withdrawing back to the embassy. Thirteen million dollars were burned (that had only been despatched earlier in the month), but some classified documents survived the incineration. Thus did the former MACV HQ meet its lugubrious end: the site which Prime Minister Ky had hoped to turn into a hotel and golf complex; the block of land which Westmoreland commandeered to erect his magnificent headquarters, with its little America of chapels, bowling alleys, and swimming pools – all ended as a pile of smoldering buildings and scattered papers, washed in a Saigon rainstorm.

The iconic image of the last American evacuations in daylight hours, however, was not framed at the DAO compound, but at the Pittman Building, a CIA station at 22 Gia Long Street. It was here that a Jacob's ladder of desperate Vietnamese ascended to the rooftop water tower, waiting to be lifted away by pilot Robert Caron's Air America UH-1 helicopter. He had been briefed to rescue the deputy prime minister and his family, but as he remarked to his co-pilot Jack "Pogo" Hunter, "This prime minister has a pretty damned big family." Some 50 or more people had shown up, claiming to be "family."[151]

The drama now shifted to the US Embassy even as darkness was falling. Unbelievably, and shortly after the evacuation at the DAO Compound had got under way, Carey was informed that a second evacuation of roughly 2,000 persons would be needed at the US Embassy. This came as a complete shock. There was no plan for an evacuation from the embassy. The rooftop landing pad could only hold a single CH-46. The grounds could accomodate a single CH-53 (after felling a tree). The shock turned to anger when pilots subsequently realized the embassy was lying over how many were being pepared for evacuation.

Moreover, the embassy had now become a scene of chaos:

Between the intersection of Hai Ba Trung Street and Thong Nhut Avenue and the embassy building were thousands of people. The embassy was surrounded by a huge crowd of Vietnamese, American and third-country nationals who were trying to get in. The main gate was closed and numerous U.S. Marines had secured it. However, people were trying to climb over the walls. Some were taken in but many were pushed out. It was a complete mob scene, crazy and piteous.[152]

Van Nguyen Duong, who witnessed the scenes, recorded that "hundreds of thousands of Vietnamese wanted to go with them," yet there was a surprising lack of violence or bitterness directed against the departing Americans.[153] He later drove to Bach Dan Quay on the Saigon River, where the navy moored four capital ships. Many more thousands were pressing against the fence of the naval base seeking an alternative escape route. Giving up, Duong returned home, passing through the center of Saigon where he was amazed to see some city residents queuing to watch a film.

The more persistent, or desperate, were rewarded. In total, some 27 Vietnamese navy ships managed to sail to safety in the final hours of South Vietnam's existence, all overcrowded, and intent on reaching the US naval Task Force 76, led by USS *Blue Ridge*. They carried as many as 30,000 refugees but were joined by an estimated armada of 65,000 civilians who chanced their luck in sampans, barges, and fishing boats. Ten Military Sealift Command ships and 45 Navy ships continued to pluck this human jetsam from the sea. Nearly 40,000 South Vietnamese were rescued. However, before the end of the week, the task force commander Rear Admiral Donald B. Whitmire was ordered to sail away, abandoning what at night appeared to be a floating city of lights bobbing in the ocean. Most drifted or dispersed to Thailand, or further afield to the Philippines, where they were met with indifference.

As the evening sky darkened to stormy night the evacuation gathered pace. The first of multiple, hasty helicopter lifts landed at the US Embassy at around 5pm. In a final supreme effort, just over 1,000 Vietnamese and 978 Americans were plucked from the building and grounds. The giant tamarind tree in the Embassy's rear parking lot was felled to create a landing zone.[154] The operation did not go smoothly. Unbeknown to Carey, Whitmire suspended all flights to the embassy on safety grounds. Carey only learned of this decision in a telephone conversation with Ambassador Martin from the DAO Compound where he had alighted to supervise the last evacuations as darkness fell. "I was damned angry at his stopping my helos," Carey later recalled, "and I made this point in no uncertain terms." His immediate superior, Lieutenant General Louis H. Wilson, Jr., the FMF Pacific commander was even more exercised: "If General Carey was damn angry, I was out of my mind. I told Admiral Gayler and Admiral Weisner on the phone [CINCPAC and Commander Pacific Fleet respectively] that there was no such thing as Marines not evacuating Marines. We do not understand that."[155] The lifts resumed.

In total, the Operation *Frequent Wind* airlift succeeded in evacuating as many as 7,000 people from Saigon in the last day of the war in 662 sorties.[156] It was a phenomenal effort. Four fifths were Vietnamese. Just one helicopter crashed – a US Marine CH-46 Sea Knight, call sign YT-14 – taking the lives of Captain William Nystul and Lieutenant Michael Shea. They have some claim to be the very last two US servicemen killed in the war. In the later verdict of commanding general of 1st Marine Aircraft Wing, Major General Norman Gourley, an individual whose 36-year career spanned flying Corsairs in the Second World War to F-4 Phantoms in Vietnam, he had never seen "a group of pilots [who] performed so magnificently as the helicopter pilots who extracted those folks out of Saigon in late April, 1975."[157]

The deserving and undeserving escaped together. Lieutenant General Nguyen Van Manh landed with two suitcases filled with gold bars.[158] An intrepid South Vietnamese Chinook pilot disgorged his human cargo then ditched his aircraft, leaping from the cockpit as it plunged into the sea. The corrupt General Dan Van Quang talked his way to safety, dressed in a suit and towing Samsonite suitcases. A Lieutenant Trung Ma Quoi flew his family and possessions to safety, including Honda motorcycles. All the generals, colonels, majors, and captains had fled, he remarked, why not the lieutenants? In a celebrated event, a pilot in Cessna O-1 Bird Dog landed on USS *Midway* without the benefit of an arrestor hook or barricade. His wife and five children stepped out of the fragile aircraft unhurt. Ky fled in his own personal helicopter, having denounced his countrymen as cowards. A British ITN television crew "clawed and fought" to escape. Uncomprehending infants tottered off the ramps. Eventually, more than 30 Hueys ended up being ditched in the sea to create deck space as a cavalcade of ill-disciplined South Vietnamese pilots appeared out of nowhere trying to land their machines on any available deck space.

By the early hours of the morning, Martin had transformed into a Lear-like figure – a king without a kingdom raging in a storm. A helicopter was landing at the embassy every ten minutes but the list of evacuees appeared to be "a bottomless pit." It was suspected that Martin was deliberately refusing to evacuate to see if he could maintain the lifts indefinitely. Pilots had long passed their "12-hour rule" and in the case of air force pilots were forbidden from flying. Only the marines were still going, breaking every flight regulation to get people out.

At 3.45am, a concerned White House ordered an end to the evacuation and the rescue of any remaining Americans. One hour later, marines with orders to arrest the ambassador should he refuse to comply, escorted the drained Martin on board Lady Ace 09. Graham Martin departed Saigon at 4.45am on April 30 – almost the last to leave, according to his wish, but not his heart. He was accompanied by his loyal chef and by his black poodle, Nitnoy. By dawn, the abandoned embassy compound was invaded by a small army of looters who "mobbed in and carried out everything they could find."[159]

This was not quite the end. Eleven marines, led by Major James Kean, were inadvertently left on the roof of the Embassy. Just two days previously Kean had been told his wife in Hong Kong was pregnant. Now he and his colleagues found themselves temporarily abandoned due to confusion over the code words "Tiger is out," which pilots assumed meant the end of the mission (it only meant the ambassador had been retrieved, on the last scheduled lift).

The marines barricaded themselves and used CS gas to fend off Vietnamese imploring to be evacuated. As dawn broke, the men began to doze off, exhausted. A bottle of whiskey was passed round. The city became strangely quiet. After two hours, the unmistakable sound of a CH-46 Sea Knight, Swift 22, was heard. A red smoke grenade was tossed to attract the helicopter's attention. As Swift 22 approached the embassy roof it seemed that thousands of Vietnamese were milling about, still hoping for evacuation "like ants on a watermelon." They were disappointed, along with some 420 Vietnamese who had been promised evacuation, waiting by the area of the embassy swimming pool, abandoned to their fate. Master Sergeant Juan Valdez had the dubious honor of being the last American to leave his boot print in South Vietnam. He carried a neatly folded Stars and Stripes, wrapped in a paper bag.[160] "I felt like it was the end of the world," his fellow sergeant, Douglas Potratz, thought.[161] The last helicopter lifted at 7.35am.

Martin left behind a regime living out the last six hours of its existence, yet paradoxically four of the five communist axes of advance remained stalled outside the capital. Immediately north of the capital, on the Binh Duong front straddling Highway 13, 5th ARVN Division was holding the line in an arc that stretched from Ben Cat in the west to Ben San in the east. 1 PAVN Corps was struggling to make any headway. 10th PAVN Division was still short of the important Bay Hien intersection. The other divisions – 320th and 320B – were locked in messy fights at Lai Khe, Phu Loi, and Lai Thieu, still some 20 miles northwest of Saigon. A second column was embroiled in an indecisive fight on the Binh Phuoc and Bin Trieu bridges. Further to the southwest, on the Cu Chi front, 25th ARVN Division was holding off 325th and 338th PAVN Divisions on Highway 1, advancing from Tay Ninh. Here, the communists were also a good 12 miles short of the outskirts of Saigon. The southern approach on Route 4, the Long An front – always the least critical and most defensible – was being stubbornly defended by 7th and 22nd ARVN Divisions. The former, at My Tho, was fending off 3rd and 9th PAVN Divisions. 22nd ARVN Division had re-established positions on the Vam Co Tay river line at Tan An, roughly 30 miles southeast of the capital. The encroaching 5th PAVN Division and ad hoc Group 232, assembled from various Viet Cong main force and guerrilla units, stood little chance of breaching this obstacle, but in the end would not need to.

To the northwest, on the more promising Bien Hoa front, the lead units of 4 PAVN Corps had encountered unexpectedly stiff resistance at the ARVN General Staff HQ. On this front, 341st, 7th, and 6th PAVN Divisions, which had been bled in the fight for Xuan Loc, continued to slug it out with their old nemesis, 18th ARVN Division, supported by elements from 3rd Armored Brigade and 468th Marine Brigade. These divisions were also still well short of the capital. In fact, aside from Tan Son Nhut, none of the five objectives set by Dung for the 16 divisions encircling Saigon had been captured. Most units were now piled back in traffic jams.

Only An's divisions from 2 Corps on the far southeastern "QL-15 front" had actually made a decisive breakthrough, by hand-railing the mostly unguarded Route 25 approach. In the final week, the JGS had become so obsessed with the approaching PAVN corps from the north that this sector of Saigon's defensive ring had been neglected. A token redeployment of 1st Airborne Division to cover the southeastern approach was insufficient as this formation now largely existed in name only. Wheeling left at Long Thanh, and after overrunning ad hoc ARVN units at Thu Due and Nhoa Trach on the outskirts of the city, lead PAVN companies from 324th Division crossed the Rach Chiec Bridge spanning the Dong Nai River (this division had remarkably advanced all the way from Hue).[162] The bridge itself was actually seized by commando units Z22 and Z23 from 81 VC Battalion, 316th Brigade. Over 50 were killed. Because the Viet Cong were subsequently discarded by Hanoi, this action was written out of the history books. Their sacrifice was only finally recognized with a memorial park in 2015.[163]

The seizure of Rach Chiec Bridge placed the advancing companies within six miles of the city center and with only one more water obstacle to cross, the Newport Bridge on the Song Sai (Saigon) River. Camera crews that rushed to cover the action found themselves scrambling for cover, along with ARVN soldiers. On reaching the second bridge, the communists were now only a matter of two miles away from Independence Palace.

The surprise and relief was that there was no final battle for Saigon. The battles that mattered had already taken place elsewhere: at Ban Me Thuot, on Route 7B, and at Xuan Loc. A storm was approaching Saigon, but it was only meteorological. In the late evening of April 29, the city skyline was dramatized by lightning and thunder. Toan had fled Bien Hoa and informed Minh that the airport was lost. Ky made a final appearance on the still-functioning Armed Forces Radio and flamboyantly announced he would fight to the last drop of blood. He didn't, instead choosing flight on board the USS *Blue Ridge* and eventually settling in California, where he ran a liquor store.

The Republic of South Vietnam's army was always going to collapse – how could an army fight on when virtually its entire officer corps had deserted? But the ARVN was not a beaten army at dawn on April 30. The ARVN surrendered because at half past nine in the morning Minh announced on Saigon Broadcasting Radio that all Republic of South Vietnam soldiers should stop fighting to avoid any further bloodshed. The statement was agreed after a final meeting with Prime Minister Vu Van Mau and Vice President Nguyen Van Huyen.[164] In a final bizarre twist, retired French General Vannessen gatecrashed the meeting and implored Minh to continue the fight and declare an alliance with China. He was sent away. One hour later, Minh made a second and final announcement: "As President of the Republic of Vietnam, I, General Duong Van Minh, request all the armed forces give up their arms and unconditionally surrender to the Liberation Army." With this pronouncement he surrendered the 21-year-old state of the Republic of South Vietnam to Hanoi. Military Region 4 was the last to surrender, its commander Major General Nguyen Khao Nam committing suicide.[165] At the moment of surrender the ARVN still counted on its five infantry divisions, 18 Ranger battalions, pockets of paratroopers and marines, and some 500 tanks and 400 artillery pieces.

The Hanoi Politburo learned of the news after its Intelligence Department reported that Western radio stations were broadcasting that communist troops had entered Independence Palace, at just before noon. They had not so much entered as careered in, smashing the ornate French gates (because the gate guard could not be found to unlock them). Companies from two formations were involved in the drama: the 203rd Tank Brigade and sappers from 116th Sapper-Commando Regiment, commanded by a Colonel Tong Viet Duong. 66th Regiment soldiers also joined in the assault. Overall command lay with the tank brigade commander "Comrade Tai."

The honor of carrying out the symbolic demolition of the palace gate went to Tank 390 crewed by Le Dinh Phuong, Nguyen Van Tap, and Ngo Sy Nguyen. Gunner Do Cao Truong missed his chance of historical celebrity because he was injured and had been left behind. Tank 843, commanded by Captain Bui Quang Than, should have stolen the moment, but this tank rammed the side gate and got stuck.

On a first-floor balcony, a government official Nguyen Van Diep was given the dubious honor of waving a white cloth. In anticipation, camera crews had already pre-positioned themselves to capture the event. In the ensuing confusion, Western reporters and communist soldiers milled about together as if on holiday. An officer raced off to collect a Northern flag, then waved the winning team's standard from a balcony. This was reportedly Sapper Pham Duy Do. Another account suggests that a local sympathizer named Dao Ngoc Van, who had guided the lost soldiers to the government building, "carried the Liberation flag up to the balcony of the 2nd floor of Independence Palace."[166] Yet another accords the honor to the tank commander Captain Bui Quang Than who had earlier crashed into the side gate.

It was all strangely amicable. Outside the palace the city now presented the spectacle of curious crowds, looters helping themselves to the last valuable goods from government offices, and columns of North Vietnamese soldiers taking in the scenes, almost like tourists, bemused by the buzz of journalists in their pursuit.

Minh was dignified but impotent. A meal of beef tendon stewed with ginseng, and fish cooked in sugar cane juice had been prepared, but nobody was eating.[167] Lieutenant Colonel Pham Xuan, who accompanied the first group of soldiers to enter Independence Palace, remembered being greeted at the foot of a stairway by President Minh's assistant, Brigadier General Nguyen Huu Hanh. The raiding party was then led to "a large, beautifully decorated room with green carpeting, velvet seats, white curtained windows and a large number of people standing."[168] Minh invited "a ceremony of orderly transfer of power so as to avoid any unnecessary bloodshed in the population," but the People's Army was neither prepared nor in a mood for ceremonies. The tank company that had so rudely burst through the palace portals was accompanied by a senior lieutenant colonel, Bui Tin, a Dien Bien Phu veteran, then serving as an army reporter and political commissar. His superior, Tai, and the sapper commander, Duong, had spent their entire adult lives fighting. Xuan had been wounded three times, once severely. "You cannot give up what you do not have," Minh was brusquely told.[169] The delegation of 30-odd South Vietnamese officers and officials who had awaited their arrival was summarily detained. Later, contemptuous photographs were taken with the communist soldiers lounging and smoking on what had once been the seat of power of South Vietnam.

The last South Vietnamese government was probably saved from a roughing up by the large number of journalists jostling with the communist soldiers inside the palace. A brief press conference was arranged. It seemed apt that Duong Van Minh spoke in French. It was probably the handover of power that should have happened in 1945. He was then led away in a jeep adorned with a portrait of Ho Chi Minh. At gun point, Minh read out a final surrender statement from the Saigon Radio premises, now under the control of soldiers from 8 Battalion, 66th Regiment. He objected to being described as "President" but complied when his captors insisted he use this title. His words were recorded by a "Mr Morit," a journalist from the Federal Republic of Germany. In the chaos of the moment a People's Army mortar team, not realizing the fighting had ended, began lobbing bombs into the courtyard of Independence Palace. The only casualty, it appears, was a deputy head of corps operations, Nguyen Van Duyen, who received shards of shrapnel to his face.[170]

This was not the end of the journey for two of the protagonists that morning. Lieutenant Colonel Tin and President Minh later became conjoined in ways that neither could have imagined. In 1990, Tin went into voluntary exile in Paris, disgusted by the abuses of the communist regime. Minh had already made the same passage seven years earlier. They may have been on opposing sides but both men had roots in Vietnam's independence struggles from the 1930s. Their values and vision for French Indochina had long been overtaken by a new generation of communist leaders, removed from the history and roots of that struggle. Both ended up strangers in the very country they had fought for, exiled to the country from which they had sought liberation.

The final exchange of messages between Washington, Hanoi, and Moscow had already taken place in anticipation of the surrender. On April 28, the affable Ambassador Dobrynin in Washington passed a verbal assurance from Moscow that Hanoi favored "the establishment of good relations with the United States."[171] The message, artfully presented, read: "There is no animosity towards the United States in Vietnam and we seek the same from the American side." Brent Scowcroft replied for the Ford administration: "Washington also favored good relations ... there was no hostility in principle toward Vietnam, and ... the United States proposed to proceed on this basis in all relations between the two nations." With that the quarreling parties separated and the door closed.

The final word may be honorably given to Jack Smith, a survivor of the biggest single loss of American lives in South Vietnam at LZ Albany in November 1965.[172] At the time he was a teenage rifleman. He later became a correspondent, like his father before him, and revisited the battlefield of his youth. The experience proved cathartic. On his return he commented:

> What I discovered with time may seem obvious, but it had really escaped me all those years on my journey home from Vietnam: the war is over. It certainly is for Vietnam and the Vietnamese. As I said on a Nightline broadcast when I came back, "This land is at peace, and so should we be."

NOTES

CHAPTER 1: BATTLE OF THE BEACHHEADS

1 Talking Proud website: http://www.talkingproud.us/Military/Military/Walking Dead.html
2 Vietnam Veterans: Letter Home: http://www.vietvet.org/pocindex.htm
3 The "Expeditionary" would be changed to "Amphibious" (III MAF) to avoid connotations of the French Expeditionary Corps
4 Cosmas, Graham A., *MACV: The Joint Command in the The Years of Escalation, 1962–1967*, Center of Military History, United States Army, citing State cable dated January 6, 1965 [hereafter Cosmas, *1962–1967*]
5 CINCPAC, Eyes Only to Wheeler, March 5, 1965
6 *MACV Command History 1965*, Library of the US Army Military History Institute, Carlisle Barracks, Pennsylvania, 3
7 The loss of life was not trivial either; 155 servicemen would be killed and 1,702 wounded
8 Pentagon Papers, Part IV-C-4, xiii
9 JCSM 100-65, February 11, 1965
10 Pentagon Papers, Part IV-C-5, 89. The number would eventually grow to 11,141 civilians encompassed in a 12 square mile TAOR (Tactical Area of Responsibility)
11 Ibid, i
12 Pentagon Papers, Part IV-C-4, 22
13 EMBTEL 465, August 19, 1964
14 JCSM 982-42, November 23, 1964
15 3D Bn 9th Marines – Command Chronology, Covering Mar-65 dated 3/1/1965 Document No. 1201056111
16 Ibid
17 Pushing On blog spot: http://lde421.blogspot.co.uk/2012/12/george-mcarthurs-vietnam.html
18 *MACV Command History 1965*, 30
19 Pentagon Papers, Part IV-C-4, 8
20 http://www.recordsofwar.com/vietnam/usmc/3rdBn9thMarines.htm

21 Ibid

22 Pentagon Papers, Part IV-C-5, 90

23 Named after 1st Lt Frank Reasoner, killed in action on July 12, 1965

24 3/9 Marines, Command Diary for Period June 1–16, 1965

25 Ibid

26 Shelby, Stanton, A., *The Rise and Fall of an American Army: U.S. Ground Forces in Vietnam, 1963-1973*, Presidio Press, first published in 1985, 307 [hereafter Shelby]

27 Carland, John M., *Combat Operations, Stemming the Tide, May 1965 to October 1966*, Center of Military History, US Army, Washington DC, 2000, 16, citing Memo, Gen Johnson for Sec Dcf et al., March 14, 1965 [hereafter Carland]; interv, Col Glenn A. Smith and Lt Col August M. Cianciolo with Maj Gen Delk M. Oden, former Commanding General (CG), US Army Support Command, Vietnam, May 27, 1977, 20 (Johnson quotations), Senior Officer Oral History Program, MHI

28 Wood, David (August 30, 2016), "Would The Military Obey Commander In Chief Trump? Probably," *Huffington Post*: "Gen. Harold Johnson, the Army's chief of staff from 1964 to 1968, deeply regretted having never opposed the decisions of President Lyndon B. Johnson and Defense Secretary Robert McNamara that deepened U.S. involvement in the Vietnam War. 'I am now going to my grave with that lapse in moral courage on my back,' Johnson later lamented"

29 Cosmas, *1962–1967*, 203

30 COMUSMACV Estimate March 6, 1965

31 The suggestion of creating enclaves would become one of several strategic options bandied about for the rest of the war. The idea was originally mooted by Taylor, as a way of limiting the war, but was never pursued or argued with great enthusiasm until Johnson took it up

32 This would eventually become the largest combat command in the world

33 MACV 170747Z

34 JCSM 204-65

35 Westmoreland's March 1965 "Commander's Estimate of the Situation"

36 Wilson Center, Digital Archives: http://digitalarchive.wilsoncenter.org/document/ 113969

37 Halberstam, David, *The Best and the Brightest*, Random House Publishing Group, 1992, 362–379 [hereafter Halberstam]

38 Memo, Ball to Johnson, July 1, 1965

39 WGBH Open Vault, Interview with George W. Ball, 05/18/1981

40 Halberstam, 377–378

41 McNaughton notes, April 4, 1966, cited in: http://jtmcnaughtonfindawayout. blogspot.co.uk/2011_01_01_archive.html

42 McNaughton informal notes March 24, 1965, Pentagon Papers, Part IV-C-5(1), 60

43 JCSM 238-65, April 2, 1965

44 CINCPAC for Taylor 042058Z

45 MACV 110825Z

46 Carland, 34

47 EMBTEL 3373

48 Pentagon Papers, Part IV-C-I, 11

49 WGBH Open Vault, Interview with Nguyen Khanh, 1981

50 Ibid
51 Pentagon Papers, Part IV-C-I, 11, 89
52 Pentagon Papers, Part IV-C-5, 88
53 Ibid
54 Pentagon Papers, Part IV-C-5, 5
55 Carland, 51, Remarks of DePuy in *Operation Cedar Falls: I Corps Battle Analysis Conference/ 13–14 September* 1988, History Office, 1988, 36, copy in Historians files, CMH. In Lt-Gen William B. Rosson to author, February 28, 1993, Historians files, CMH, the former MACV chief of staff stated that "DePuy ... was the father of search and destroy, with General Westmoreland serving as senior proponent"
56 *Life* magazine, April 16, 1965
57 *Life* magazine, June 11, 1965
58 JCSM 321-65
59 Carland, 20–21
60 It was also the first significant combined operation with the ARVN, involving two battalions from the South Vietnamese Airborne Brigade
61 *MACV Command History 1965* estimate of enemy strength
62 The others were 305th, 324th, 330th, and 338th: Pentagon Papers, Part IV-A-5, 215
63 LIMDIS 19118, 070335Z Jun 65
64 Pentagon Papers, Part IV-C-5, 49
65 JCS, Report of Ad Hoc Study Group, July 14, 1965
66 McNaughton memo to General Goodpaster, JCS, July 14, 1965
67 MACV 19118, 070335Z. This was in fact a request for 35 battalions and a possible additional 9 battalions if required at a later date
68 Bill Moyers' Journal, *Bill Moyers on LBJ's Path to War Pt2*/PBS, excerpts from White House telephone recordings, https://www.youtube.com/watch?v=IQtMWtohrZE
69 A phrase coined by McGeorge Bundy and Moyers for a Los Angeles presidential speech in 1964
70 Later inherited by the Soviet Union in 1979
71 Lyndon Johnson and Robert McNamara on June 10, 1965, Conversation WH6506-02-8116-8117, *PRDE* (Presidential Recordings Digital Edition, Miller Center, University of Virginia)
72 Ibid
73 JCSM 457-65
74 JCSM 482-65
75 Deptel 3057, June 26, 1965
76 WGBH Open Vault, Interview with George W. Ball, 05/18/1981
77 Ball to President, "A Compromise Solution for South Vietnam," July 1, 1965
78 JCSM 515-65
79 WGBH Open Vault, Interview with Bill D. Moyers, 05/05/1981
80 Lyndon Johnson and Robert McNamara on July 2, 1965, Conversation WH6507-01-8302, *PRDE*
81 WGBH Open Vault, Interview with Bui Diem, 06/03/1981
82 Carland, 34
83 WGBH Open Vault, Interview with Jack Valenti, 04/23/1981

84 Cited in VanDeMark, Brian, *Into the Quagmire: Lyndon Johnson and the Escalation of the Vietnam War*, Oxford University Press, 1991, 195

85 VanDeMark, 178

86 WGBH Open Vault, Vietnam, Interview with Jack Valenti, 04/23/1981, for all quotes.

87 Ibid

88 WGBH Open Vault, Interview with McGeorge Bundy, undated

89 WGBH Open Vault, Interview with McGeorge Bundy, undated

90 WGBH Open Vault, Interview with Bill D. Moyers, 05/05/1981

91 *MACV Command History 1965*, 49

92 Hackworth H. David, *About Face: The Odyssey of an American Warrior*, A Touchstone Book, Simon & Schuster, 1989, 465

93 Cited in http://jtmcnaughtonfindawayout.blogspot.co.uk/2011_01_01_archive.html

94 Cosmas, *1962–1967*, 244

95 WGBH Open Vault, Vietnam, Interview with Jack Valenti, 04/23/1981

96 Herring, George, *America's Longest War: The United States and Vietnam, 1950–1975*, University of Kentucky, McGraw Hill Education, 1996 (3rd Edition), 168

97 WGBH Open Vault, Vietnam, Interview with Nguyen Cao Ky, 05/07/1981

98 Ball, July 1, 1965 Memo to President

99 WGBH Open Vault, Interview with George W. Ball, 05/18/1981

100 *MACV Command History 1965*, 35

101 The "E" of "Expeditionary" was replaced by the "A" of "Amphibious" on May 7

102 *MACV Command History 1965*, 12

103 The first major III MAF operation under command of a USMC officer was Op Lien Ket on July 28 involving 2/4 Marines and elements from the ARVN and VNMC

104 Walt was instrumental in promoting the enlightened CAPs (Combined Action Patrols) and wrote a thoughtful book *Strange War, Strange Strategy: A General's Report on Vietnam*, Funk & Wagnalls Co, 1970, on retirement.

105 A full account of the operation is in Andrew, Jr., Rod, Colonel, US Marine Corps Reserve, *The First Fight, U.S. Marines in Operation Starlite, August 1965*, Marines in the Vietnam War Commemorative Series, History Division, Marine Corps University, Quantico, Virginia, 2015

106 Believed to be 60th VC Bn, 80th VC Bn, 52nd VC Coy, and 45th VC Weapons Bn

107 *Life* magazine, September 3, 1965, "The Battle of Chu Lai – the Instant a Marine is Shot"

108 Shulimson, Jack, and Johnson Charles M., Major, USMC, *U.S. Marines in Vietnam, The Landing and the Buildup, 1965*, History and Museums Division, Headquarters, US Marine Corps, Washington, DC, 1978, 76

109 Operation Starlite 50th Anniversary Documentary, DC, US, 11/09/2015, Video by Cpl August Light, Communications Directorate, DVIDS

110 Op *Starlite* AAR, TCR: 21/2113H/AUG65/CCN-255/RB, 210634Z AUG 65

111 *MACV Command History 1965*, 163

112 The Vietnam Archive at Texas Tech University, The Vietnam Archive Oral History Project, Interview with Chuck Sawyer, Conducted by Natalie Swindle and Kelly Crager, Transcribed by Emilie Meadors, Date: April 3, June 12, 2009

113 The Vietnam Archive at Texas Tech University, The Vietnam Archive Oral History Project, Interview with Calixto Cabrera, op cit

114 *MACV Command History 1965*, 165

115 "Step Lightly" Tim O'Brien, *Playboy*, June 1970

116 "'They Been Fighting Around Here for a Long Time' – the legacy of the area near Hill 43", 1/6 Bn, 6th Infantry, The Americal Division website

117 "Why We Are in Vietnam" address, July 28, 1965

118 WGBH Open Vault, Interview with Charles Sabatier, 10/08/1982

119 The Vietnam Archive at Texas Tech University, The Vietnam Archive Oral History Project. Interview with David Adcock, Conducted by Natalie Swindle February 3, 2009; February 12, 2009, Transcribed by Cecily Darwin

120 The Vietnam Archive at Texas Tech University, The Vietnam Archive Oral History Project, Interview with Charles Allen, Jr., Conducted by Kelly Crager May 28, 2008, Transcribed by Cecily Darwin

121 The Vietnam Archive at Texas Tech University, The Vietnam Archive Oral History Project, Interview with David Crawley, Conducted by Stephen Maxner February 27, 2001, Transcribed by Tammi Mikel Lyon

122 The Vietnam Archive at Texas Tech University, The Vietnam Archive Oral History Project, Interview with Anthony Goodrich, Conducted by Steve Maxner April 11, 2002, Transcribed by Jennifer McIntyre

123 Clodfelter, Michael, *Mad Minutes and Vietnam Months: A Soldier's Memoir*, McFarland, 2015

124 This battle, as expected, has generated an extensive bibliography. Major works include: Moore, Harold G. and Galloway, Joseph L., *We Were Soldiers Once ... And Young*, Random House, 1992; and Summers, Jr., Harry G., *The Bitter Triumph of the Ia Drang*, American Heritage, February 1984. Others include: Coleman, J.D., *Pleiku, the Dawn of Helicopter Warfare in Vietnam*, St. Martin's Press, 1988; Pleiku Campaign, 1st Air Cavalry Division Headquarters, General Harry Kinnard, March 4, 1966; Pleime Battle Viewed From G3/I Field Force Vietnam, G3 Journal, I Field Force Vietnam, October 1965; Than Phong 7 Viewed From G3/I Field Force Vietnam, G3 Journal, I Field Force Vietnam, November 1965; Tribute to a brilliant commander, General Norman Schwarzkopf, *It Doesn't Take A Hero*, Bantam, 1992; General Vinh Loc, *Why Pleime*, Information Printing Office, September 1966

125 "Vietnam: A Television History; Brigadier General Richard T. Knowles, assistant commander of the First Air Cavalry," *Vietnam: A Television History*, November 10, 1965

126 See *Ia Drang: An Investigative Report by William Triplett*, VVA Veteran, The Vietnam Center and Archive, Douglas Pike Collection: Unit 02 – Military Operations, 1965

127 See the National Archive film *The Battle of Ia Drang Valley 1965*, a *CBS News* special report

128 Kinnard, 1st Cavalry Division (Airmobile), Combat Operations After Action Report, Pleiku Campaign, Pleiku Province, Republic of Vietnam, Oct 23–Nov 26, 1965, http://www.generalhieu.com/pleiku-2.htm 5 [hereafter 1st Cavalry AAR]

129 *CBS News* special report

130 USMC Presentation on Ia Drang, *Vietnam: The Big War and the Vietnam Syndrome*, Lesson 23, undated

131 Carland, 56, Ltr, Gen Paul L. Freeman, CG, USCONARC, to Gen Harold K. Johnson, June 26, 1965, Harold K. Johnson Papers, MHI; Headquarters, USCONARC, "The Role of USCONARC in the Army Buildup, FY 1966," 112, copy in CMH; Walter G. Hennes, "Department of the Army: The Buildup, 1965–1967," ch. 5, CMH.

132 Seven separate operations were eventually mounted over this period, from October 19 through to November 26: *Don Thang 21, Ingram, Long Reach, All the Way, Silver Bayonet I, Than Phong 7,* and *Silver Bayonet II.* See 7th Triennial Vietnam Center and Archive Symposium, March 10–12, 2011. The full sequence of battles from http://www.generalhieu.com/pleime_military_genius-2.htm was: Plie Me campaign (B3 Field Front, 10/19–27), Pleime campaign (II Corps, 10/19–11/25), Pleiku campaign (1st Air Cavalry Division, 10/23–11/25), Operation *Dan Thang 21* (3rd Armored Task Force, 10/20–27), Operation *Long Reach* (1st Air Cavalry Division, 10/27–11/25), Operation *All the Way* (1st Air Cavalry Brigade, 10/27–11/9), Operation *Silver Bayonet I* (3rd Air Cavalry Brigade, 11/9–18), Operation *Silver Bayonet II* (2nd Air Cavalry Brigade, 11/18–25), Operation *Than Phong 7* (Airborne Brigade, 11/18–25), Ia Drang Valley battle (1/7th, 2/7th, and 2/5th Air Cavalry Battalions, 11/14–17), LZ X-Ray battle (1/7th Air Cavalry Battalion, 11/14–16), LZ Albany battle (2/7th Air Cavalry Battalion 11/17).

133 Kinnard, Pleiku Campaign, from Intelligence Logbook, November 11, 1965

134 See http://www.lzxray.com/tactmap.htm

135 Lieutenant General Pham Xuan, *Memories of the Battle of the Ages*, The Military Publishing House, 2011, Ha Nam Library, https://www.quansuvn.net/index.php?topic=31363.0 [hereafter Xuan, *Memories*]

136 Lieutenant General Dao Van Loi, *Battle and Lecture Hall*, People's Army publisher, 2010, https://www.quansuvn.net/index.php?topic=31435.0

137 Ibid

138 Moore, After Action Report, December 9, 1965, IA DRANG Valley operations, 1st Battalion 7th Cavalry, November 14–16, 1965 [hereafter Moore AAR]

139 Carland, 114

140 Moore's AAR is substantially the basis for the account of the battle at LZ X-Ray given in this book

141 Moore AAR

142 Exact PAVN unit designations are problematic. There are inevitable inconsistencies in multiple sources. Given the confused nature of the fighting, it is possible that PAVN units became mixed up in the same way that 1/7 Cavalry sub-units were re-subordinated as the battle developed

143 An's testimony

144 The Vietnam Archive at Texas Tech University, The Vietnam Archive Oral History Project, Interview with Charles Gentry, Conducted by Dr. Richard Verrone, September 25, 2006; October 12, 31, 2006; November 2, 9, 2006. Transcribed by Jessica Fontenot

145 1st Cavalry AAR

146 Carland, 129

147 After Action Report, IA DRANG Valley Operation 1st Battalion, 7th Cavalry November 14–16, 1965

148 Ibid

149 Moore AAR

150 Ibid

151 The Vietnam Archive at Texas Tech University, The Vietnam Archive Oral History Project, Interview with George Thatcher, Conducted by Jonathan Bernstein, November 15, 2001, Transcribed by Shannon Geach

152 CBS Special Report on Ia Drang battle

153 1st Cavalry AAR

154 Originally published in *The Saturday Evening Post*, January 28, 1967: http://www.mishalov.com/death_ia_drang_valley.html

155 Ibid

156 Triplett, The Vietnam Center and Archive, Douglas Pike Collection

157 Kissinger, Henry, *The White House Years*, Weidenfeld and Nicolson and Michael Joseph, 1979, 232 [hereafter Kissinger]

158 Carland, 75

159 The Vietnam Archive at Texas Tech University, The Vietnam Archive Oral History Project, Interview with Larry Burke, Conducted by Steve Maxner April 21, 2001, Transcribed by Shannon Geach

160 Carland, 84

161 Carland, 87

162 Carland, 92

163 Carland, 78–80

164 JCSM 811-65, November 10, 1965

165 LBJ, McNamara telephone conversation, June 10 1965, https://prde.upress.virginia.edu/conversations/4002500/notes_open. Also see: https://millercenter.org/the-presidency/educational-resources/americanization

166 Ford, Ronnie E., Captain, *Tet 1968: Understanding the Surprise*, Cass Series – Studies in Intelligence, F. Cass, 1995, 37 [hereafter Ford]. The quote is from "General Nguyen Chi Thanh on the South's Ideological Task," *Hoc Tap*, Hanoi, No. 7, July 1966

167 McNamara's deliberations were summarized in a December 7 memo for the President

168 *MACV Command History 1965*, 14

169 *MACV Command History 1965*, Table I-I Viet Cong Incidents 1965

170 *MACV Command History 1965*, 78

171 WGBH Open Vault, Interview with Bill D. Moyers, 05/05/1981

172 Telephone conversation # 9305, sound recording, LBJ and ROBERT MCNAMARA, 12/2/1965, 12:15PM, Recordings and Transcripts of Telephone Conversations and Meetings, LBJ Presidential Library, accessed January 27, 2019, https://www.discoverlbj.org/item/tel-09305

173 A December 16, 1965 Opinion Research Corporation of Princeton, NJ poll showed 65 percent support in favour of continuing the war, and only nine percent in favour of withdrawal

174 http://digitalarchive.wilsoncenter.org/document/113971

175 *MACV Command History 1965*, 180 and 186

CHAPTER 2: A GALLOPING YEAR

1   This was the impression but not the reality. Johnson's decision against mobilising reserves in fact provoked a re-working of Phase II and a delay in the scheduling of the deployments. The main effect was to push back divisional deployments into the second half of 1966

2   WBGH Open Vault, Interview with David Christian, 07/07/1983

3   The Vietnam Archive at Texas Tech University, The Vietnam Archive Oral History Project, Interview with Calixto Cabrera, op cit

4   The Vietnam Archive at Texas Tech University, The Vietnam Archive Oral History Project, Interview with Chuck Sawyer, op cit

5   The Vietnam Archive at Texas Tech University, The Vietnam Archive Oral History Project, Interview with Charles Allen, Jr., op cit

6   The Vietnam Archive at Texas Tech University, The Vietnam Archive Oral History Project, Interview with General John Arick, Conducted by Richard Burks Verrone, PhD, January 22; February 19; March 19; April 16, 2003, Transcribed by Reccia Jobe

7   *Life* magazine, February 25, 1966

8   JCSM 811-65, November 10, 1965

9   13th Plenum of the Central Committee of the Vietnamese Communist Party, January 23, 1966

10 *MACV Command History 1965*, 265

11 Pentagon Papers, Part IV-C-6a, 64. This was fruit of the January 17–February 9 Honolulu Conference in which three "cases" were debated. "Case I," favoured by the JCS, was adopted but Johnson's continued reluctance to mobilize reserves led to further negotiations and an amended "Case I" plan that began to resemble more the "Case II" option

12 Cosmas, *1962–1967*, 268

13 *MACV Command History 1965*, Table II-6

14 *MACV Command History 1965*, Table V-I

15 *MACV Command History 1965*, 24

16 Cosmas, *1962–1967*, 272

17 CIA, Captured Viet Cong Documents: Collection, Translation, Dissemination and Analysis, May 24, 1967

18 Cosmas, *1962–1967*, 292

19 Cosmas, *1962–1967*, 488

20 *MACV Command History 1965*, 119

21 *MACV Command History 1965*, 124

22 F031700070124, Vietnam Archive Collection, The Vietnam Center and Archive, Texas Tech University

23 Cantigny Military History Series, *Blue Spaders, The 26th Infantry Regiment, 1917–1967*, 1996, 136 [hereafter Cantigny, *Blue Spaders*]

24 *MACV Command History 1965*, 139

25 Pentagon Papers, Part IV-C-6a, 56

26 Shelby, 217

27 WGBH Open Vault, Interview with Bui Diem, 06/03/1981

28 Berman, Larry, *Lyndon Johnson's War*, W.W. Norton & Company, 1989, 9–10 [hereafter Berman]

29 *Washington Evening Star*, February 7, 1966

30 *New York Herald Tribune*, February 8, 1966

31 Richard Critchfield in the *Washington Evening Star*, February 9, 1966

32 *Washington Evening Star* columnist, Marquis Childs, February 9, 1966, *New York Times*, 9 and 13 February 1966

33 *Baltimore Sun*, February 10, 1966

34 And popularizing the concepts of the "Strategic Corporal" and "Three-Block War" which became common currency in Iraq following the 2003 invasion by US and UK forces

35 The Vietnam Archive at Texas Tech University, The Vietnam Archive Oral History Project, Interview with Calixto Cabrera, op cit

36 The Vietnam Archive at Texas Tech University, The Vietnam Archive Oral History Project, Interview with Don Cuneo, Conducted by Dr. Richard Burks Verrone, November 18, 27, and December 13, 2002, Transcribed by Reccia Jobe

37 WGBH Open Vault, Interview with Edward J. Banks, 01/25/1982

38 The Vietnam Archive at Texas Tech University, The Vietnam Archive Oral History Project, Interview with David Adcock, op cit

39 A full account of the battle is at: http://www.ephemeraltreasures.net/operation-utah.html courtesy of Bob Ingraham

40 Ibid

41 Shulimson, Jack, Marine Corps Vietnam Operational Histories Series, Department of the Navy, *US Marines in Vietnam: An Expanding War 1966*, 1982, Ch 7, 114 [hereafter Shulimson]

42 http://www.ccfreedomfighters.com/scoggins.htm

43 The Vietnam Archive at Texas Tech University, The Vietnam Archive Oral History Project, Interview with Charles Allen, Jr., op cit

44 See Bob Ingraham: http://www.ephemeraltreasures.net/operation-utah.html. The Operation Utah AAR is also available at: http://www.recordsofwar.com/vietnam/usmc/OpsRpts.htm

45 http://www.popasmoke.com/kia/incidents.php?incident_id=44

46 Shulimson, Ch 7, 127

47 Shulimson, Ch 7, 109 http://forums.military.com/eve/forums/a/tpc/f/1450051361001/m/2450057661001

48 Shulimson, Ch 1, 48

49 West, Jr., Captain Francis J., History and Museums Division, HQ USMC, USMCR, *Small Unit Action in Vietnam Summer 1966*, 3 [hereafter West, Jr.]

50 The Vietnam Archive at Texas Tech University, The Vietnam Archive Oral History Project, Interview with David Crawley, op cit

51 Shulimson, Ch 7, 131

52 http://1stbn4thmarines.net/operations-history-folder/kansas.htm

53 Msg 1B1214Z Jun 66, III MAF SITREP OPERATION KANSAS

54 Statement by Staff Sergeant Jimmie Earl Howard, 1130610/0369/8651 USMC

55 Shulimson, Ch 4, 16

56 West, Jr., 119

57 Shulimson, Ch 7, 143
58 Shulimson, Ch 7, 139
59 Shulimson, Ch 4, 62
60 2/1, 1/3, 2/4 and 3/4 Marines
61 Shulimson, Ch 7, 171
62 Shulimson, Ch 10, 173
63 http://www.combatwife.net/chetdiestelhastings.htm
64 Shulimson, Ch 10, 166
65 Operation *Hastings* After Action Report, 1201064001, US Marine Corps History Division Vietnam War Documents Collection, The Vietnam Center and Archive, Texas Tech University
66. Shulimson, Ch 10, 176
67 Shulimson, Ch 4, 17
68 Shulimson, Ch 4, 191
69 Shulimson, Ch 4, 189
70 The Vietnam Archive at Texas Tech University, The Vietnam Archive Oral History Project, Interview with Calixto Cabrera, op cit
71 The Vietnam Archive at Texas Tech University, The Vietnam Archive Oral History Project, Interview with Chuck Sawyer, op cit
72 Shulimson, Ch 4, 222 (March–August 1966)
73 Shulimson, Ch 4, 192
74 The Vietnam Archive at Texas Tech University, The Vietnam Archive Oral History Project, Interview with Larry Burke, op cit
75 Shulimson, Ch 18, 284
76 Ibid
77 1st Infantry Division Operational Report –Lessons Learned, May 1–July 31, 1966, (RCS CZFOR-65) August 15, 1966
78 West, Jr., 59
79 The Vietnam Archive at Texas Tech University, The Vietnam Archive Oral History Project, Interview with Calixto Cabrera, op cit
80 History of the 1st Battalion 9th Marines 3rd Marine Division – "The Walking Dead", Sergeant Thomas J. Holmes USMC and Sergeant Major Larry E. Gugle USMC Retired, no date
81 History of the 1st Battalion 9th Marines 3rd Marine Division, slide 31
82 The Vietnam Archive at Texas Tech University, The Vietnam Archive Oral History Project, Interview with Calixto Cabrera, op cit
83 Marine J.C. Barrera would subsequently be involved in a rape, with two other marines, according to Cabrera's testimony. This incident was also covered up
84 Shulimson, Ch 4, 196
85 Shulimson, Ch 14, 281
86 The Vietnam Archive at Texas Tech University, The Vietnam Archive Oral History Project, Interview with Calixto Cabrera, op cit
87 WGBH Open Vault, Interview with Jane Barton, 05/12/1981
88 Walt letter to Westmoreland, November 17, 1966
89 Shulimson, Ch 14, 241
90 Shulimson, Ch 14, 234

91 West, Jr., 79

92 Shulimson, Ch 14, 249

93 Confusingly, General Chu Huy Man states that 1st PAVN Division was made up from 33rd, 66th, and 320th Regiments. However, he does subsequently record the appearance on the battlefield of the 24th, 88th, and 95th Regiments. General Chu Huy Man, *Vibrant Times*, People's Army publishers, 2004

94 Ibid

95 Ibid

96 Carland, 185

97 Carland, 193, citing Westmoreland Journal, March 22, 1966, Westmoreland History files, CMH

98 Carland, 193, citing Operation *Harrison* AAR and 1st Brigade reports

99 Carland, 197

100 Carland, 200

101 Carland, 256

102 Carland, 201

103 Also known as Song Lai Giang

104 Prados, John, "Operation Masher, the Boundaries of Force," *VVA Veteran*, Feb–Mar 2002

105 Operations Lessons Learned, Report 2-66, AD 502772, March 31, 1966

106 Carland, 207

107 Prados, "Operation Masher," 3

108 Combat Operations After Action Report (RCS MACV J3/32), April 28, 1966

109 Ibid

110 Ibid

111 Carland, 211

112 Carland, 213

113 Ibid

114 AAR 1st Cav Div (Airmobile) Bong Song Campaign, March 11, 1966

115 Ibid

116 The exact numbers remain disputed

117 http://legacy.h21.hani.co.kr/h21/vietnam/eng-jujoo.html

118 The Vietnam Archive at Texas Tech University, The Vietnam Archive Oral History Project, Interview with Anthony Goodrich, op cit

119 Combat Operations After Action Report (RCS MACV J3/32), April 28, 1966

120 Ibid

121 WBGH Open Vault, Interview with Douglas Kinnard, 04/01/1982

122 Carland, 256–262

123 Carland, 271

124 See YouTube: http://www.youtube.com/watch?v=jgCgyrUM8ag

125 The Vietnam Archive at Texas Tech University, The Vietnam Archive Oral History Project, Interview with Brian Glaspell, Conducted by Kelly Crager April 1, 2009, Transcribed by Rachel Haney

126 Carland, 287–288

127 Carland, 165–166

128 CMH Pub 70-23, 153

129 Cantigny, *Blue Spaders*, 143, citing CMH Pub 70-23

130 DePuy, CMH Pub 70-23, *Changing an Army: An Oral History of General William E. DePuy*, USA Retired, United States Military History Institute and United States Army Center of Military History, 1988, 150

131 As of December 1966, DePuy had sacked 11 commanders: one special force officer, four infantry battalion commanders, three artillery battalion commanders, and four divisional staff officers. CMH Pub 70-23, 153

132 CMH Pub 70-23, 144

133 The Vietnam Archive at Texas Tech University, The Vietnam Archive Oral History Project, Interview with Jerry Benson, Conducted by Stephen Maxner September 15, 2000, Transcribed by Christina Witt

134 1st Infantry Division Operational Report, Lessons Learned, May 1 to July 31, 1966, (RCS CSFOR-65), Part 1, August 15, 1966

135 WGBH Open Vault, Interview with Duong Long Sang, 03/10/1981

136 Carland, 173

137 See http://shelf3d.com/iX3kmgdDAGw for a short film on the operation

138 Carland, 80

139 Carland, see http://shelf3d.com/iX3kmgdDAGw for a short film on the operation

140 Carland, 324

141 Fromson, Murray (December 11, 2006), "Name That Source," *New York Times*

142 Carland, 339

143 Carland, 340–353

144 Carland, 350

145 Carland, 351

146 Cantigny, *Blue Spaders*, 148

147 1st Infantry Division Operational Report, Lessons Learned, May 1 to July 31, 1966, (RCS CSFOR-65), Part 1, August 15, 1966

148 *Stag* Magazine (Operation Attleboro – 1966), June Issue, "Report from HQ, 25th Infantry Division ... This is what happened next, according to Lieutenant P.J. McKeand," http://25thaviation.org/history/id731.htm

149 Lieutenant General Bernard William Rogers, Vietnam Studies, Department of the Army, *Cedar Falls–Junction City: A Turning Point*, 1989, Rogers, Part 5 [hereafter Rogers]

150 Ibid

151 1st Infantry Division Operational Report, Lessons Learned, May 1 to July 31, 1966, (RCS CSFOR-65), Part 3, August 15, 1966

152 RAND, Project CHECO Southeast Asia Report, Operation Paul Revere/Sam Houston, July 27, 1967, 24

153 4th Inf Div, Combat Operations After Action Report (RCS:MACV J3-32) January 28, 1967

154 1st Infantry Division Operational Report, Lessons Learned, May 1 to July 31, 1966, (RCS CSFOR-65), Part 3, August 15, 1966

155 RAND, Project CHECO Southeast Asia Report, Operation Paul Revere/Sam Houston, July 27, 1967, 53

156 327 Infantry Regiment: http://oldsite.327infantry.org/first/1_327th_history_page.htm

157 http://www.tigerforcerecon.com/

158 Sallah published his findings in a co-authored book (Weiss – Associated Press): *Tiger Force: A True Story of Men and War*, Little Brown and Company

159 http://www.pulitzer.org/archives/6822

160 Cited in Greiner, Bernd, *War Without Fronts, the USA in Vietnam*, Vintage, 2010, 178 [hereafter Greiner]

161 The Army did substantiate 20 war crimes against 18 Tiger Force members but none were prosecuted

162 WGBH Open Vault, Interview with Charles Sabatier, 10/08/1982

163 President to Def Sec, June 28, 1966. The so-called "Plan 3" may have been a ploy by Johnson to demonstrate that he was obliging the JCS as best he could

164 Lodge to President, August 10, 1966

165 Cosmas, *1962–1967*, 401

166 Sharp to Westmoreland and Wheeler, Operational concept for Vietnam, January 3, 1967

167 Pentagon Papers, Part IV-C-6-a, 111

168 The American Presidency Project: http://www.presidency.ucsb.edu/ws/?pid=27958

169 Berman, 19

170 JCSM 702-66, Deployment of Forces to Meet CY Requirements, November 4, 1966

171 "The Secret Diary of McNamara's Dove: The Long-Lost Story of John T. McNaughton's Opposition to the Vietnam War," April 2011, *Diplomatic History* 35(3): 505–534, DOI: 10.1111/j.1467-7709.2011.00961.x

172 *Life* magazine, January 14, 1966

173 Pentagon Papers, Part IV-C-6a, 97

174 Lodge to State, October 1, 1966

175 This became known as the Southeast Asia Deployment Program #4

176 CIA/DIA Report "An Appraisal of the Bombing of North Vietnam through 12 September 1966"

177 *MACV Command History 1965*, 13

178 SecDef memo for President, Actions recommended for Vietnam, October 14, 1966

179 Estimates were: 94 VC battalions and 86 NVA battalions with a total strength of 277,000

180 McNaughton diary, April 8, 1966 cited in http://jtmcnaughtonfindawayout. blogspot.co.uk/2011_01_01_archive.html

181 McNaughton diary, December 11, 1966 cited in http://jtmcnaughtonfindawayout. blogspot.co.uk/2011_01_01_archive.html

CHAPTER 3: THE BIG-UNIT WAR

1 Helms, Richard, *A Look Over My Shoulder: A Life in the Central Intelligence Agency*, Presidio Press, 2004, 150

2 DePuy letter to Alsop, January 24, 1967

3 Pentagon Papers, Part IV-C-6-b, 33

4 Pentagon Papers, Part IV-C-6-b, 3

5 Major General PGS-TS Ho Thanj Minh, Silent Victory (Episode 2), People's Army, 2005, https://www.quansuvn.net/index.php?topic=31443.0

6 Berman, 16

7 CIA, Memo 1/9/67, The War in Vietnam

8 *Life* magazine, January 28, 1967

9 Pentagon Papers, Part IV-C-6-b, 1

10 Pentagon Papers, Part IV-C-6-b, 4

11 Later published as Harrison Evans Salisbury, *Behind the Lines: Hanoi, December 23, 1966–January 7, 1967*, Harper & Row, 1967

12 http://www.history.com/this-day-in-history/johnson-administration-responds-to-harrison-salisburys-charges

13 D'Amato, Anthony A. et al, "War Crimes and Vietnam: The 'Nuremberg Defence' and the Military Service Register," 57 *California Law Review* 1055 (1969) Code A69d

14 MACV 29797 to CINCPAC, Subj: Concept of Military Operations in SVN, August 24, 1966, and Berman, 27

15 MACV 29797 to CINCPAC, Subj: Concept of Military Operations in SVN, August 24, 1966

16 Westmoreland, William C., *A Soldier Reports*, Doubleday, 1976, 133

17 Pentagon Papers, Part IV-C-6-a, 127

18 See http://www.capmarine.com/ for an overview of the CAPs. Also see: http://www.capmarine.com/cap/capunits.htm#CAP1-1-4

19 Shulimson, Ch 15, 258

20 Johnson final statement at Honolulu Conference, Plenary Documents, February 9, 1966

21 CORDS study, Project TAKEOFF, June 1967

22 Ibid

23 Maj-Gen JCF Tillen (J-3 MACV) Briefing to Mission Council, August 8, 1966

24 MAC-J311, Supplemental Data Sheet A, October 22, 1967

25 McNaughton diary, February 11, 1966

26 Rogers. The accounts of both battles in this book are greatly indebted to Rogers' monograph. See also Jonathan Schell's "The Village of Ben Suc," *The New Yorker*, July 15, 1967 [hereafter Schell]

27 1st MIBARS in Vietnam: http://military-intelligence.wikispaces.com/1st+MIBARS+-+7+August+1964+to+1+December+1966

28 Bluespaders: 26th Infantry Regiment Association: http://www.bluespader.org/uploads/haig.pdf

29 Frank Castro writing for the 1st Div newspaper, "The American Traveler" on January 28, 1967, cited in Rogers, 50

30 Rogers, 36

31 Rogers, 37

32 Rogers, 38. The after-action report stated that 149 were detained

33 1st Battalion, 26th Infantry, *Cedar Falls* operation report, January 23, 1967

34 WGBH Open Vault, Interview with Le Ban Va, 03/10/1981

35 The Vietnam Archive at Texas Tech University, The Vietnam Archive Oral History Project, Interview with Calixto Cabrera, op cit

36 Schell, 60–61

37 The Vietnam Archive at Texas Tech University, The Vietnam Archive Oral History Project, Interview with Calixto Cabrera, op cit

38 The Vietnam Archive at Texas Tech University, The Vietnam Archive Oral History Project, Interview with Alfred Alvarez, Conducted by Kelly Crager June 3, 5, 2008, Transcribed by Cecily Darwin

39 Schell, 62. Haig's counter-claim is in Haig, *Inner Circles*, cited in Cantigny, *Blue Spaders*, 206

40 Schell, 131

41 Rogers, 39

42 Schell, 76–82

43 Schell, 95

44 Rogers, 44

45 The Vietnam Archive at Texas Tech University, The Vietnam Archive Oral History Project, Interview with Stephen W. Dant, Conducted by Richard Burks Verrone, PhD, March 4, 9; April 20, May 5, 11, 18, 25, 2005, Transcribed by Brooke Tomlin

46 The Vietnam Archive at Texas Tech University, The Vietnam Archive Oral History Project, Interview with Jerry Benson, op cit

47 The Vietnam Archive at Texas Tech University, The Vietnam Archive Oral History Project, Interview with Larry Burke, op cit

48 The Vietnam Archive at Texas Tech University, The Vietnam Archive Oral History Project, Interview with Calixto Cabrera, op cit

49 Rogers, 18

50 WBGH Open Vault, Interview with Dang Xuan Teo, 1981

51 Rogers, 74

52 Tractors fitted with a dozer blade were made by Rome Caterpillar Company, Georgia

53 Rogers, 74

54 DePuy Cedar Falls AAR quoted in Rogers, 78

55 Rogers, 158

56 WBGH Open Vault, Interview with Dang Xuan Teo, 03/10/1981

57 Rogers, 83

58 A good example is Lieutenant General Dao Van Loi, *Battle and Lecture Hall*, People's Army publisher, 2010, https://www.quansuvn.net/index.php?topic=31435.0

59 Operation *Junction City 1* and *2*, Combat Comments 2-67, prepared by G-3, 1st Inf Div, 1967

60 *Life* magazine, March 10, 1967

61 Rogers, 135

62 Puckett, David H., *The Blue Spaders at the Battle of Ap Gu, Cantigny First Division Foundation* (1997), 5

63 Rogers, 148

64 Puckett, op cit, 14

65 The Vietnam Archive at Texas Tech University, The Vietnam Archive Oral History Project, Interview with Larry Burke, op cit

66 Rogers, 150

67 Pentagon Papers, Part IV-C-6-b, 108

68 Komer, R. W., Vietnam Prognosis for 1967–68, quoted in Pentagon Papers, Part IV-C-6-b, 4

69 WGBH Open Vault, Interview with Mark Smith [1] 1982

70 Powers, Robert, K., *1966 The Year of the Horse*, Dog Ear Publishing, 2009, 62

71 The Vietnam Archive at Texas Tech University, The Vietnam Archive Oral History Project, Interview with Brian Glaspell, op cit

72 Locke would barely remain in post for six months before returning to Texas to run for governor. His replacement Samuel Berger arrived after the 1968 Tet Offensive

73 Pentagon Papers, Part IV-C-6-b, 99

74 Komer, R. W., Vietnam Prognosis for 1967–68, quoted in Pentagon Papers, op cit

75 *New York Times* abstract, March 15, 1967

76 Transcript, Ellsworth Bunker Oral History Interview I, 12/0/80 by Michael L. Gillette, Internet Copy, LBJ Library

77 Pentagon Papers, Part IV-C-6-b, 59

78 Pentagon Papers, Part IV-C-6-b, 60

79 Pentagon Papers, Part IV-C-6-b, 61–63

80 The debate over force levels would only finally be resolved in the summer. On July 5, McNamara flew to Saigon to agree the so-called Program 5 uplift. Westmoreland was authorized to increase the MACV ceiling to 525,000 by the summer of 1968. This meant that an additional five tactical air squadrons and 19 battalions would be deployed to South Vietnam. See Cosmas, *1962–1967*, 420

81 Pentagon Papers, Part IV-C-6-b, 83

82 Pentagon Papers, Part IV-C-6-b, 105

83 Pentagon Papers, Part IV-C-6-b, 106

84 Pentagon Papers, Part IV-C-6-b, 146

85 McNaughton Diary, December 6, 1966

86 Ibid

87 Cosmas, *MACV: The Joint Command in the Years of Withdrawal 1968–1973*, 23, [hereafter Cosmas, *1968–1973*] quoting Special National Intelligence Estimate (SNIE) 14.3-67

88 Cosmas recommends Thomas K. Latimer, "Hanoi's Leaders and Their South Vietnam Policies, 1954–1968" (PhD diss., Georgetown University, 1972) for this topic.

89 Cosmas, *1968–1973*, 29, citing Col. Gen. Tran Van Tra, *Vietnam: History of the Bulwark B2 Theater*, vol. 5. Concluding the 30-Years War (Ho Chi Minh City: Van Nghe Publishing House, 1982), trans. Foreign Broadcast Information Service, Joint Publications Research Service, Southeast Asia Report no. 1247, Feb 2, 1983, 35

90 Brush, Peter, "The Story Behind the McNamara Line," first published in *Vietnam* magazine, February, 1996, 18-24: http://msuweb.montclair.edu/~furrg/pbmcnamara.html

91 Details of the "McNamara Line" are in the *MACV Command History 1967*, appendix to Vol III

92 Telfer, Major Gary L., USMC, Rogers, Lieutenant Colonel Lane, USMC, and Fleming, Jr., V. Keith, *US Marines in Vietnam Fighting the North Vietnamese 1967*, History and Museums Division Headquarters, US Marine Corps, Washington DC, 1984, 94 [hereafter Telfer et al]

93 See Eschwege, Henry, *The Use of Agent Orange in Vietnam*, Community and Economic Development Division, Report to Republican Ralph H. Metcalfe, August 15, 1978. The other important source is Major William A. Buckingham, Jr. who was an historian at the Office of Air Force History and who authored *Operation Ranch*

Hand: The Air Force and Herbicides in Southeast Asia, 1961–1971. This account is heavily indebted to his research and insights

94 Agent Orange consisted of a 50:50 mix of the n-butyl esters of 2,4-dichlorophenoxy acetic acid and 2,4,5-trichlorophenoxy acetic acid

95 TCDD: 2,3,7,8 - tetrachlorodibenzodioxin

96 From 1958 to 1971 the urban population of South Vietnam is assessed to have increased from 2.8 million to 8 million

97 Buckingham, Jr., William, *The Air Force and Herbicides in Southeast Asia, Office of Air Force History*, United States Air Force, Washington DC, 1982, 11

98 Eschwege, Enclosure II, op cit

99 Telfer et al, 12

100 Telfer et al, 45

101 The Vietnam Archive at Texas Tech University, The Vietnam Archive Oral History Project, Interview with David Crawley, op cit

102 Telfer et al, 38

103 Coan, James P., "The Battle for Con Thien," July 8, 1999 11370101002, James Coan Collection, The Vietnam Center and Archive, Texas Tech University

104 Telfer et al, 99

105 History of the 1st Battalion 9th Marines 3rd Marine Division, "The Walking Dead," Sgt Thoams J. Holmes USMC and Retd Sgt Mjr Larry E. Guggle USMC, slide 31, undated

106 http://mcvthf.blogspot.co.uk/2008/09/siege-of-con-thien.html

107 The Vietnam Archive at Texas Tech University, The Vietnam Archive Oral History Project, Interview with James Coan, Conducted by Kelly Crager, July 24, 2008; July 25, 2008, Transcribed by Cecily Darwin

108 Ibid

109 *MACV History of the War 1967*, 16

110 Hartzel, Jack, *Reflections of my Past*, BookSurge Publishing, 2001 [hereafter Hartzel]

111 The Vietnam Archive at Texas Tech University, The Vietnam Archive Oral History Project, Interview with James Coan, op cit

112 Operation *Malheur*, After Action Report, 1st Bde, 101st AB Div, October 3, 1967

113 Ibid

114 Ibid

115 Ibid

116 Ibid

117 The Vietnam Archive at Texas Tech University, The Vietnam Archive Oral History Project, Interview with Larry Casselman, Conducted by Jason Stewart January 31, 2009, Transcribed by Valerie Sopena

118 Telfer et al, 118

119 The Vietnam Archive at Texas Tech University, The Vietnam Archive Oral History Project, Interview with Calixto Cabrera, op cit

120 Operation *Swift*, AAR, October 5, 1967

121 http://www.lzcenter.com/Operations.html#Wheeler

122 Telfer et al, 256

123 Hartzel, 31

124 Hartzel, 32

125 Cited in Shelby, 164

126 Shelby, 167

127 Quote is from Tim Dyhouse, "33 Days of Violent, Sustained Combat," 2/503 Vietnam Newsletter No. 47, November 2012, 100

128 http://www.173rd.com/history.htm. Also see Murphy, Edward F., *Dak To: the 173d Airborne Brigade in South Vietnam's Central Highlands, June–November 1967*, Presidio, 1993

129 2/503 Vietnam Newsletter No. 29, November 2012, 13

130 Peers presentation to MACV commanders, December 3, 1967

131 Prados, John, "One Hell of a Fight," 2/503 Vietnam Newsletter No. 47, November 2012

132 In 2004 he published his memoirs: *Fighting in the Central Highlands*, by Senior Lieutenant General Professor Hoang Minh Thao, People's Army publishers, https://www.quansuvn.net/index.php?topic=30238.0. In 1966 he was appointed Deputy Commander to the overall Front Commander Chu Huy Man. His predecessors in this post were Huynh Dac Huong, Nguyen Chanh, Doan Khue, and Cao Van Khanh

133 See Prados, "One Hell of a Fight," op cit: 12,700 tons of supplies were delivered in November, including 5,100 tons by air

134 Scott, LTC B., USAWC Military Studies Program Paper, The Battle for Hill 875, Dak To, Vietnam 1967, 2/503 Vietnam Newsletter No. 47, November 2012, 86, General Chu Huy Man, *Vibrant Times*, People's Army publishers, 2004

135 2/503 Vietnam Newsletter No. 29, November 2012, 29

136 173 AB Bde AAR December 1967

137 Peers presentation to MACV commanders, December 3, 1967

138 Ibid

139 Hoang Minh Thao, *Fighting in the Central Highlands*, op cit

140 Editorial, *The Washington Post*, November 26, 1967

141 An excellent 71-page CIA report offering a summary of the state of play at the end of 1967 is in the CIA Library: Top Secret, Questions and Answers Relating to Vietnam, 25XI, Dec 8, 1967, https://www.cia.gov/library/readingroom/docs/CIA-RDP79T00826A003000320001-7.pdf

142 Cosmas, *1962–1967*, 448

143 Sorley, Lewis, *Westmoreland: The General who lost Vietnam*, Houghton Mifflin Court Publishing Company, 2011, 147–150

144 *Life* magazine, November 27, 1964

145 Cosmas, *1962–1967*, 450

146 Cosmas, *1962–1967*, 455

147 Cosmas, *1962–1967*, 456

148 Cosmas, *1962–1967*, citing Col Elmer Martin Affidavit, paras. 1 and 15, US District Court, Westmoreland v. CBS, CBS Memorandum, 33n and 130

149 http://indochine54.free.fr/cefeo/dinassau.html

150 Department of the Army Vietnam Studies, Command and Control 1950–1968, Major General George S. Eckhardt, 1991

151 A brief history of 9th Infantry Division in Vietnam can be found at http://www.mtholyoke.edu/~cormi22k/classweb/subpage2.html

152 http://www.mrfa.org/9kiabyunit.htm

153 http://www.warboats.org/vietnamboats.htm

154 http://www.rivervet.com/monitor.htm

155 See Keaveny, Captain Kevin, *Armor* magazine, "The 39th Cavalry Platoon on the Mekong Delta," July–August 1993. The British first used hovercraft experimentally in Borneo in 1965. The USN also trialled hovercraft in Vietnam from 1966 in PACV Division 107.

156 Longaker, Jr., Ray F., BMCM (SW) (CMC) USN/Ret, cited in http://www.warboats.org/vietnamboats.htm

157 http://www.warboats.org/vietnamboats.htm

158 MRF Summary Report July 1967, cited in http://www.warboats.org/vietnamboats.htm

159 Arrival Photos section, cited in in http://www.warboats.org/vietnamboats.htm

160 See Hain, Tom, "9th Division-Riverine," for a pen picture of life as a soldier on the Mekong Delta, http://www.vietvet.org/tjhain.htm

161 Ibid

162 http://www.9thinfantrydivision.com/html/619newspapersrticles2.htm

163 Vietnam Studies, Riverine Operations 1966–1969, Major General William B. Fulton, 1973-CMH Pub 90-18, 66

164 *The Old Reliable* (9th Infantry Division newspaper), Vol 1, No. 21, May 27, 1967

165 *The Old Reliable* (9th Infantry Division newspaper), Vol 1, No. 27, July 12, 1967

166 House, Jonathan M., *Into Indian Country*, undated, cited in http://www.9thinfantrydivision.com/html/619newspapersrticles2.htm

167 Ibid, and Hanson, Shannon, *Riverine Warfare on the Rach Nui*, www.vfw.org, November/December 2005, cited in http://www.9thinfantrydivision.com/html/619newspaperarticles.htm

168 Ibid

169 *The Old Reliable* (9th Infantry Division newspaper), Vol. 1, No. 27, July 12, 1967

170 9th Division recollections cited in http://www.9thinfantrydivision.com/html/619recollections.htm

171 Rosner, Joe, Vol. 1, Number 5, Summer 1994, Rach Gia River, June 19, 1967 – A Day Remembered, cited in http://www.9thinfantrydivision.com/html/619newspaperarticles.htm

172 Kayser, Evans, *Operation Concordia I – Mekong Delta, Memories of a Huey Gunship Pilot*, cited in http://www.9thinfantrydivision.com/html/619recollections2.htm

173 *The Old Reliable* (9th Infantry Division newspaper), Vol. 1, No. 27, July 12, 1967

174 *The Old Reliable* (9th Infantry Division newspaper), Vol. 1, No. 25, June 24, 1967

175 Ibid

176 John Bradfield, December 8, 2002, cited in http://www.9thinfantrydivision.com/html/619recollections2.htm

177 See http://www.thenation.com/article/my-lai-month#

178 Buckley, Kevin P., "Pacification's Deadly Price," *Newsweek*, June 19, 1972, 42–43, cited in http://msuweb.montclair.edu/~furrg/Vietnam/buckley.html

179 *The Cu Chi Tunnels*, 1990, produced, directed, and photographed by Mickey Grant

180 Ibid

181 Ibid

182 Ibid

183 http://www.diggerhistory.info/pages-conflicts-periods/vietnam/tunnel-rats.htm

184 Allen, George W., *None So Blind*, Ivan R. Dee, 2001, 233 [hereafter Allen]

185 Pentagon Papers, Part IV-B-3, Appendix III

186 *Life* magazine, January 28, 1967

187 One can only wonder what that generation would have made of today's equally fruitless trillion dollar wars

188 The BDM Corporation, *A Study of Strategic Lessons Learned in Vietnam*, Volume VI Conduct of the War, Book 1, Operational Analyses, Ch 3, 36, citing Congressional Record, Vol. 118, No. 76 (May 10, 1972), E4978, quoted in Thompson, Scott W., and Frizzell, Donaldson D., *The Lessons of Vietnam*, Crane, Russak, 1977, 92

189 Jenkins, Brian M., "The Unchangeable War," RM-6278-1-ARPA (Advanced Research Projects Agency), September 1972

190 Cited by Cosmas, *MACV Headquarters: The Years of Expansion, 1965–1967*, 295 [hereafter Cosmas, *1965–1967*]

191 Cosmas, *1965–1967*, 296

192 Pentagon Papers, Part IV-C-6a, 110

193 Pentagon Papers, Part IV-C-6a, 111

194 The CIA "Situation in Vietnam" reports which today are declassified and available online in the CIA Library

195 Pentagon Papers, Part IV-C-6a, 115

196 Pentagon Papers, Part IV-C-6a, 116

197 Berman, 96

198 Berman, 101, citing Isaacson, Walter and Thomas, Evan, *The Wise Men: Six Friends and the World They Made*, Simon & Schuster, 1986, 683, 646, and Ball, George, *The Past Has Another Pattern*, W.W. Norton, 1982

199 Cosmas, *1968–1973*, 20, citing Humphrey, Hubert H., US Congress, Senate, Committee on Foreign Relations, *The U.S. Government and the Vietnam War: Executive and Legislative Roles and Relationships*, Part IV: July 1965–January 1968, Washington, DC, Government Printing Office, 2002, 895

200 The Pacifica Radio/UC Berkeley Social Activism Sound Recording Project, Norman Mailer: Teach-In on the War in Vietnam, UC Berkeley, May 21–23, 1965, cited in http://www.lib.berkeley.edu/MRC/pacificaviet/mailertranscript.html

201 WGBH Open Vault, Interview with Bill D. Moyers, 05/05/1981

202 Cosmas, *1968–1973*, 3–4, citing Westmoreland, William C., *A Soldier Reports*, Doubleday, 1976, 361–362. Msg, Gen Earle G. Wheeler, Joint Chiefs of Staff (JCS) 11 081–62 to Westmoreland, Dec 22, 1967, Westmoreland Message files, Dec 1967; Ltr, Wheeler to Westmoreland, Dec 22, 1967, tab A–13, Westmoreland History file 27 (Dec 19–26, 1967); William C. Westmoreland Papers, US Army Center of Military History (CMH), Washington, DC

203 Cosmas, *1968–1973*, 16

204 Cosmas, *1968–1973*, 466

CHAPTER 4: TET

1 Cosmas, *1968–1973*, 10: "The command's actual strength stood at a little over 497,000, of which about 331,000 were Army troops. Rounding out MACV's force

were 78,000 marines, 31,600 Navy personnel, and 56,000 Air Force personnel plus a small Coast Guard contingent"

2   Cosmas, *1968–1973*, 11

3   Cosmas, *1968–1973*, 10: "The Republic of Vietnam Armed Forces (RVNAF) numbered about 650,000 officers and men in January 1968. About half of these troops were in the regular Army, Navy, Air Force, and Marine Corps; the other half were in two territorial security components, the Regional Forces and the Popular Forces"

4   Shelby, 216–217

5   Cosmas, *1968–1973*, 12, citing MACV and Joint General Staff (JGS) Combined Campaign Plan, 1968, AB 143, Nov 11, 1967, an. A (Intelligence), 1, Historians files, CMH

6   Cosmas, *1968-73*, 29

7   Ford, 17

8   Cosmas, *1968–1973*. The plan was captured by US forces on May 22, 1968: *Vietnam Documents and Research Notes*, No. 45; and Department of Defense (DoD) Intelligence Information Report No. 6–026–1418–68, Apr 18, 1968, sub: VC Plans. Both are in in CMH

9   Secret North Vietnamese cable from Politburo to Pham Hung COSVN Party Secretary, Jan 21, 1967, Wilson Center, Digital Archive

10 Newspaper Article: "Assessment of General Offensive Discussed" from Hanoi, Hoc Tap, January 30, 1968, Folder 11, Box 10, Douglas Pike Collection: Unit 01 – Assessment and Strategy, The Vietnam Center and Archive, Texas Tech University

11 Ford, 50

12 CIA   Library: https://www.cia.gov/library/readingroom/docs/VIET%20 CONGNORTH%20VIETNAMESE%5B15617869%5D.pdf

13 *Washington Post*, November 1, 2013, Bass, Thomas A., "Vietnam's Vo Nguyen Giap: More than a War Hero"

14 Ford, 95

15 Pribbenow II, Merle L., "General Vo Nguyen Giap and the Mysterious Evolution of the Plan for the 1968 Tet Offensive," University of California Press, *Journal of Vietnamese Studies*, Volume 3, Summer 2008, available at: https://text.123doc.org/ document/2099503-journal-of-vietnamese-studies-docx.htm

16 Ibid

17 The origins of the Tet Offensive are extensively covered in: Wirtz, James J., *The Tet Offensive: Intelligence Failure in War*, Cornell University Press, 1991; Nguyen, Lien-Hang T., "The War Politburo: North Vietnam's Diplomatic and Political Road to the Tet Offensive," *Journal of Vietnamese Studies* 1 (2006) (1–2); Ang Cheng Guan (July 1998), "Decision-making Leading to the Tet Offensive (1968) – The Vietnamese Communist Perspective," *Journal of Contemporary History* 33 (3); Doyle, Edward, Lipsman, Samuel, Maitland, Terrance, et al, *The North*, Boston Publishing Company, 1986

18 Ford, 12, 29, 87. This split in the Politburo later consolidated with Giap, Chin, Dong, Pham Hung, Le Thanh Nghi, and Hoang Van Hoan in the moderate group, and Duan, Tho, Thanh, Truong Chinh, and Nguyen Chi Tren in the militant group. Giap was not alone within the cadre of generals; in the South he was able to count on

the loyalty of Generals Tran Van Tra and Tran Do, as well as the North Vietnamese general appointed to command PAVN operations, General Hoang Van Thai

19 Nguyen, 22

20 Nguyen, 24–40

21 Ford, 81

22 According to Lieutenant Colonel Bui Tin, member of the PAVN general staff, the plan for the Tet Offensive was proposed by Thanh in January 1967, "History and the Headlines," ABC-Clio

23 Ford, 20–21

24 Ford, 23

25 Truong Son, *Five Lessons of a Great Victory – Winter 1966–Spring 1967*, Foreign Languages Publishing House, Hanoi – Two Copies, January 1, 1967, Folder 03, Box 08, Douglas Pike Collection: Unit 02 – Military Operations, The Vietnam Center and Archive, Texas Tech University

26 Nguyen, 34

27 Cosmas, *1968–1973*, 29

28 Ford, 25

29 Ford, 80

30 CIA, The White House, Memorandum for the President, December 16, 1967, "Are the Next Four Months Decisive?"

31 Ford, 66

32 WGBH Open Vault, Interview with Bui Tin, 02/20/1981

33 Ford, 97–100

34 Ford, 52

35 Ford, 126–130

36 WGBH Open Vault, Interview with Dang Xuan Teo, 03/10/1981

37 The Vietnam Archive at Texas Tech University, Vietnam Archive Oral History Project, Interview with Norm Gardner, Conducted by Stephen Maxner March 14, 2001, Transcribed by Reccia Jobe

38 Berman, 158

39 Berman, 149

40 Berman, 179

41 CIA, The White House, Memorandum for the President, December 16, 1967, "Are the Next Four Months Decisive?"

42 Ibid.

43 Allen, 257

44 Cosmas, *1962–1967*, 36 citing Msg, Sharp to Wheeler, Dec 26, 1967, Westmoreland Message files, Dec 1967, CMH

45 Berman, 114–116

46 Ibid

47 Ford, 184

48 The Vietnam Archive at Texas Tech University, Vietnam Archive Oral History Project, Interview with Norm Gardner, op cit

49 Cosmas, *1968–1973*, citing Davidson Interview, Mar 30 and Jun 30, 1982, session 1, 53–54

50 Cosmas, *1968–1973*, 56

51 Cosmas, *1968–1973*, bid, 55, citing Msg, Westmoreland MAC 01438 to Sharp and Wheeler, Jan 30, 1968, tab 53, Westmoreland History file no. 28 (Dec 27, 1967–Jan 31, 1968), CMH

52 CIA Directorate of Intelligence, Intelligence Memorandum, Communist Units Participating in Attacks During the Tet Offensive, January 30 through February 13, 1968, February 21, 1968

53 Shelby, 232

54 A comprehensive summary of the action in II CTZ can be found in "Press Briefing: 1968 Tet Offensive in II CTZ, 17 April 1968," 168300010697, Bud Harton Collection, The Vietnam Center and Archive, Texas Tech University

55 Shelby, 241

56 II Field Force After Action Report, attacks in III CTZ, Tet Offensive

57 Shelby, 243

58 Arthur Schlesinger letter to *Washington Post*, March 22, 1968

59 Prados, John and Stubbe, E., Ray, *Valley of Decision, The Siege of Khe Sanh*, Houghton Mifflin, 1991, 276 [hereafter Prados and Stubbe]

60 In a parallel move, in June, a separate Capital Military Assistance Command would be created under Major General John Hay, the deputy commander of II Field Force

61 Cosmas, *1968–1973*, 48

62 Cosmas, *1968–1973*, 45, quoting Westmoreland MAC 01011 to Wheeler, Jan 22, 1968

63 Major General George Keegan USAF in Thompson and Frizzell, *The Lessons of Vietnam*, op cit, 137, cited in BDM Corporation Analysis Book I, Operational Analyses, 1981, Department of the Army, US Army War College, 3-101; available online via "The Black Vault," "the largest online Freedom of Information Act/government record clearing house in the world"

64 A figure of 5,500 PAVN killed has been estimated. North Vietnamese sources claim 2,469. The contemporary boast of 10,000–15,000 PAVN killed was exaggerated

65 Oral history transcript of Major General R Tompkins, USMC History and Museums Division, *The Marines in Vietnam: 1954–1973*, 104, cited by BDM Corporation, op cit

66 The Vietnam Archive at Texas Tech University, The Vietnam Archive Oral History Project, Interview with Tony Gleaton, Conducted by Richard Verrone, PhD, August 19, 24, 2004; September 15, 2005, Transcribed by Eunice Lee

67 Oriana Fallaci, *Interviews with History*, Liveright New York, 1976, 85f, cited by BDM Corporation, op cit

68 Vietnam Maps: http://alphareconassociation.org/maps.htm

69 Prados and Stubbe, 199, 171

70 Prados and Stubbe, 172

71 Prados and Stubbe, 269

72 *Vietnam Chronicles, The Abrams Tapes 1968–1972*, Transcribed and edited by Lewis Sorley, Texas Tech University Press, 2004, 33 [hereafter *Vietnam Chronicles*]

73 *Vietnam Chronicles*, 33

74 Prados and Stubbe, 40

75 Prados and Stubbe, 70

76 Nalty, C. Bernard, *Operation Niagara, Air Power and the Siege of Khe Sanh*, Office of Air Force History, 1991, 40

77 Prados and Stubbe, 264

78 Prados and Stubbe, 251–252

79 Ibid

80 Cosmas, *1968–1973*, 52

81 "The Battle for Khe Sanh," Captain Moyers S. Shore II, USMC, History and Museums Division Headquarters, US Marine Corps, Washington DC, 1969, 64

82 Ten were killed

83 Moyers, "The Battle for Khe Sanh," 107, op cit

84 On February 21, 1968

85 Prados and Stubbe, 373

86 Ibid

87 Prados and Stubbe, 379

88 Cited in Nalty, 41, op cit

89 Prados and Stubbe, 166–167

90 Xuan, *Memories*

91 Prados and Stubbe

92 The Vietnam Archive at Texas Tech University, The Vietnam Archive Oral History Project, Interview with Scott Dawson, Conducted by Stephen Maxner September 14, 2001, Transcribed by Tammi Mikel Lyon

93 Prados and Stubbe, 46

94 Pearson, Lieutenant General Willard, *The War in the Northern Provinces 1966–68*, Department of the Army, Vietnam Studies, 1991, 92

95 Of which 700,000 were ethnic Chinese

96 YouTube: Tướng Nguyễn Ngọc Loan: Xử bắn Việt cộng (1968) https://www.youtube.com/watch?v=LD4zRszg5cQ

97 The Execution of Nguyen Van Lem: Poetry Against War, *Waiting*, unknown author

98 The Vietnam Archive at Texas Tech University, Vietnam Archive Oral History Project, Interview with Norm Gardner, op cit

99 The account of the battle in this book is greatly indebted to Willbanks, James H., PhD, *The Battle for Hue, 1968*, 3400102005, James Willbanks Collection, The Vietnam Center and Archive, Texas Tech University [hereafter Willbanks, *Hue*]

100 WGBH Open Vault, Interview with Nguyen Van, 03/01/1981

101 The Vietnam Archive at Texas Tech University, The Vietnam Archive Oral History Project, Interview with Scott Dawson, op cit

102 Captain Gordon D. Batcheller was in fact seriously wounded, not killed

103 *Vietnam Chronicles*, 516

104 The Vietnam Archive at Texas Tech University, The Vietnam Archive Oral History Project, Interview with Scott Dawson, op cit

105 Dawson was then deployed to the Rockpile and subsequently to Con Thien, where he was wounded for a third time and evacuated from Vietnam for good. His tour with 1/1 Marines visited every hot spot

106 WGBH Open Vault, Vietnam, Interview with Myron Harrington, 12/08/1981

107 1 Marines AAR March 20, 1968, cited in Shulimson, 202

108 WGBH Open Vault, Interview with Hoang Phu Ngoc Tuoung, 02/28/1982

109 Willbanks, *Hue*, 32
110 WGBH Open Vault, Vietnam, Interview with Nguyen Thi Hoa, 03/01/1981
111 Allen, 258
112 Cosmas, *1968–1973*, 64
113 Cosmas, *1968–1973*, 68 and Westmoreland, *Soldier Reports*, 332–333
114 *Vietnam Chronicles*, 11
115 Cosmas, *1968–1973*, 14: DMZ/MR-TTH 10,000–11,500, MR-5 12,000–13,700, B-3 Front 2,200–2,500, COSVN 10,900–12,400
116 Wilson Center, Digital Archive, 113977, April 3, 1968, Secret North Vietnamese Politburo Cable
117 Allen, 264
118 Cosmas, *1968–1973*, 121
119 Allen, 265
120 Allen, 266
121 DePuy, CMH Pub 70-23, 125
122 The quote is from *Life* magazine, March 22, 1968
123 DePuy, CMH Pub 70-23, ibid
124 WGBH Open Vault, Interview with Clark Clifford, 05/18/1981
125 Ibid
126 WGBH Open Vault, Interview with Harry McPherson, 04/23/1981
127 Ibid
128 WGBH Open Vault, Interview with Clark Clifford, 05/18/1981
129 WGBH Open Vault, Interview with George Christian, 04/30/1981
130 WGBH Open Vault, Interview with Clark Clifford, 05/18/1981
131 Ibid
132 Berman, 198–199
133 WGBH Open Vault, Interview with Clark Clifford, 05/18/1981
134 Berman, 199
135 WGBH Open Vault, Interview with Harry McPherson, 04/23/1981
136 WGBH Open Vault, Interview with Clark Clifford, 05/18/1981
137 Ibid
138 WGBH Open Vault, Interview with Harry McPherson, 04/23/1981
139 WGBH Open Vault, Interview with Horace Busby, 04/24/1981
140 WGBH Open Vault, Interview with Harry McPherson, 04/23/1981
141 WGBH Open Vault, Interview with Horace Busby, 04/24/1981
142 WGBH Open Vault, Interview with Clark Clifford, 05/18/1981
143 WGBH Open Vault, Interview with George Christian, 04/30/1981
144 Ibid
145 WGBH Open Vault, Interview with Horace Busby, 04/24/1981
146 *CBS News*, February 27, 1968
147 Hammond, M. William, *Public Affairs, The Military and the Media, 1968-1973*, The United States Army in Vietnam series, US Army Center of Military History, Government Printing Office, 1988
148 Hammond, Prologue
149 Ibid
150 WGBH Open Vault, Interview with Clark Clifford, 05/18/1981

151 Ibid

152 Shelby, 214

153 An argument made in *A Soldier Reports*

154 Cosmas, *1968–1973*, 110

155 Shelby, 273–275

156 The Vietnam Archive at Texas Tech University, The Vietnam Archive Oral History Project, Interview with Stephen W. Dant, op cit

157 WGBH Open Vault, Vietnam, Interview with John D. Negroponte, 04/24/1981

158 CIA Library/Reading Room, Hanoi's Negotiating Position and Concept of Negotiations, May 6, 1968, DOC_0001166486.pdf

159 By using Anna Chennault, wife of the wartime general, to encourage President Ky to take a hard line.

160 WGBH Open Vault, Interview with Hoang Duc Nha, 05/09/1981

161 Shelby, 276

162 WGBH Open Vault, Interview with Dean Rusk, 06/08/1982

163 This paragraph is indebted to Frank McCulloch's review of peace initiatives in *Life* magazine March 22, 1968

CHAPTER 5: EXPANDING A WAR

1 Nixon's Republican National Congress acceptance speech, August 8, 1968

2 Ibid

3 Kissinger, 3

4 Kissinger, 19

5 Kissinger, 11

6 Nixon's RNC acceptance speech, August 8, 1968

7 Nixon, Richard, *No More Vietnams*, W.H. Allen, 1986, 102 [hereafter Nixon]

8 Brinkley, Douglas and Nichter, Luke A., *The Nixon Tapes*, Houghton Mifflin Harcourt, 2014, 70 [hereafter Brinkley and Luke, *The Nixon Tapes*]

9 Kissinger, 1175

10 Johnson's Third State of the Union Address, January 12, 1966

11 Kissinger, 26

12 Kissinger, 29

13 Kissinger, 31

14 *Foreign Affairs Journal*: http://www.foreignaffairs.com/articles/61195/melvin-r-laird/iraq-learning-the-lessons-of-vietnam

15 The phrase "Vietnamization" was reportedly coined by Laird; see Kissinger, 272, and Cosmas, *1968–1973*, 144

16 Kissinger, 8

17 Kissinger, 229

18 Shelby, 284. Major formations were: 1st and 3rd Marines, 1st Cavalry, 101st Airborne, 1st, 4th, 9th, 23rd, and 25th Infantry, 1st Brigade of 5th Infantry, 3rd Brigade of 82nd Airborne, 173rd Airborne, 199th Infantry Brigade, 11th Armoured Cavalry Regiment, and 5th Special Forces Group. Major ARVN formations were: the Airborne and Marine Divisions, 1st, 2nd, 5th, 7th, 9th, 18th, 21st–23rd and 25th Divisions, 20 Ranger battalions, and 42nd and 51st Independent Regiments.

19   *Vietnam Chronicles*, 8

20   An analogy used in *A Soldier Reports*

21   General Chu Huy Man, *Vibrant Times*, People's Army publishers, 2004

22   *Vietnam Chronicles*, 132

23   *Vietnam Chronicles*, 70

24   *Vietnam Chronicles*, 239

25   Cosmas, *1968–1973*, citing Msg, MAC 14710 to All General Officers, November 1, 1968, Abrams Papers, CMH, 130

26   Ibid

27   *Vietnam Chronicles*, 12

28   Published on September 30, 1968

29   Birtle, J. Andrew, "PROVN, Westmoreland, and the Historians: A Reappraisal," *The Journal of Military History* 72 (October 2008): 1213–1247, 2008 by The Society for Military History, Table 1, from Bendix Aerospace Systems Division, Jul 73, Analysis of Vietnamization: Data Abstract, Final Report, III-14 to III-17, Historians files, CMH

30   Ibid

31   *Vietnam Chronicles*, 12

32   Table 3, from *MACV Command History, 1970*, 1: VII-105, Historians files, CMH; Memo, ODASD, (SA), Sep 2, 1969, sub: US Operations by Type of Mission in Vietnam, Thayer Papers

33   *Vietnam Chronicles*, 611

34   *Vietnam Chronicles*, 407

35   Cosmas, *1968–1973*, 136

36   Ibid

37   *Vietnam Chronicles*, 392

38   Cosmas, *1968–1973*, citing Msg, COMUSMACV MAC 30430 to Cdr 7AF et al, Oct 13, 1968, MACV History, 1969, Vol. 1, Ch 2, 16–17; and Msg, Abrams MAC 2127 to CAS Paris for Weyand, Feb 17, 1969, Abrams Papers, CMH

39   Cosmas, *1968–1973*, 239

40   Cosmas, *1968–1973*, 17

41   Cosmas, *1968–1973*, 628

42   Cosmas, *1968–1973*, 568

43   Kissinger, 241

44   Kissinger, 245

45   Kissinger, 247

46   The Walrus, Bombs over Cambodia: http://www.yale.edu/cgp/Walrus_CambodiaBombing_OCT06.pdf

47   BBC, "On This Day," October 15, 1969: http://news.bbc.co.uk/onthisday/low/dates/stories/october/15/newsid_2533000/2533131.stm

48   Senators John C. Stennis (MS) and Richard B. Russell, Jr. (GA) and Representatives Lucius Mendel Rivers (SC), Gerald R. Ford (MI), and Leslie C. Arends (IL)

49   https://nsarchive2.gwu.edu//NSAEBB/NSAEBB123/DNSA%20KA04472%20December%209%201970%208%2045%20PM%20Kissinger%20Telcons.pdf

50   Ibid

51   Ibid

52   The Khmer Rouge would emerge in 1967 from an alliance of anti-government, communist groups

53   *Vietnam Chronicles*, 68
54   WGBH Open Vault, Interview with Francois Ponchaud, 01/01/1982
55   Ibid
56   WGBH Open Vault, Interview with Lloyd M. (Mike) Rives, 03/25/1982
57   Sak Sutsakhan, *The Khmer Republic at War and the Final Collapse*, Monograph Program, Department of the Army, Washington DC, 1978, 28 [hereafter Sutsakhan]
58   Sutsakhan, xiv: Kratie on May 6, Stung Treng on May 18, Siem Pang on May 19, and Lomphat on May 31
59   Originally the FARK, or Forces Armées Royales Khmères
60   WGBH Open Vault, Interview with Jonathan F. (Jonathan Fredric) Ladd, 01/25/1982
61   Sutsakhan, 50
62   Sutsakhan, 53
63   Sutsakhan, 182
64   Cosmas, *1968–1973*, 304
65   Kissinger, 474
66   Kissinger, 487
67   Kissinger, 490
68   HQ PACAF, Directorate Tactical Evaluation, CHECO Division, The Cambodian Campaign April 1– June 30, 1970, Fig 4 [hereafter CHECO]
69   *Toan Thangs 42–46, Binh Tays I–III* in the Central Highlands; and *Cuu Lons I–III* in the Delta (*Shoemaker* was renamed *Toan Thang 43* to add a South Vietnamese veneer)
70   WGBH Open Vault, Interview with Douglas Kinnard, 04/01/1982
71   UVA/Miller Center, Presidential Speeches, April 30, 1970: Address to the Nation on the Situation in Southeast Asia
72   CHECO, 9
73   CHECO, 31–32
74   National Security Agency: Focus on Cambodia, Parts 1 and 2, Cryptologic History Series, Southeast Asia, NSA FOIA Requester Service Center: National Security Agency, Previously Released in 2004 by NSA in Freedom of Information Act Case #: 3058, January 1974
75   CHECO, 42
76   The Vietnam Archive at Texas Tech University, The Vietnam Archive Oral History Project, Interview with Timothy Eby, Conducted by Kelly Crager, August 28, 2008; September 3, 2008, Transcribed by Cecily Darwin
77   CHECO, 52
78   CHECO, xii
79   Kissinger, 513
80   Nixon, 121
81   Ibid
82   *Vietnam Chronicles*, 393
83   Kissinger, 453
84   Ibid
85   *Vietnam Chronicles*, 629
86   Ibid

87 Kissinger, 987

88 Kissinger, 1002

89 Kissinger, 989

90 Kissinger, 990–991

91 Kissinger, 994

92 Kissinger, 999

93 Kissinger, 1012

94 Ibid

95 By now, six regiments had been committed against the ARVN incursion: 24B, 102nd (of 308th Division), 1st PLAF (2nd Division), 64th (320th), 88th (308th), and 141st (2nd PAVN Division). These were reinforced in the north by 48th (320th), 36th, and 66th PAVN Regiments. In the south, 812th (324B), 29th and 803rd (both 324B), were closing on the battlefield. In total, 5B Front compressed over ten regiments in the Tchepone area, supported by the upgraded 70B Front controlling 320th, 304th, and 308th PAVN Divisions.

96 Secret PACAF Summary Report Feb 3– Mar 24, 1971 – Operation *Dewey Canyon II*

97 http://www.company-c--2nd-bn--506th-inf.com/LamSon_719_Battlefield_Diaries.pdf

98 *Vietnam Chronicles*, 537

99 *Vietnam Chronicles*, 659

100 *Vietnam Chronicles*, 381, Feb 25, 1971 briefing to Admiral McCain

101 In August he would be replaced by Major General Albert Milloy

102 Shelby, 297

103 See http://hill29.com/apr.html for a pen picture of operations in this area

104 Shelby, 306

105 Shelby, 307

106 Cosmas, *1968–1973*, 243

107 Cited in Davidson, B. Phillip, *Vietnam at War: The History 1946–1975*, Oxford University Press, 1988, 600

108 Cosmas, *1968–1973*, 246

109 The phrase is from the title of an article in *Vietnam Magazine* on the battle of Hamburger Hill. It is taken from Ap Bia, the name of the mountain, which means crouching beast.

110 Boian, Major Kelly Owen Carl, *Major General Melvin Zais and Hamburger Hill*, School of Advanced Military Studies United States Army Command and General Staff College Fort Leavenworth, Kansas, 2012, 2

111 http://earlcapps.blogspot.co.uk/2010/11/lieutenant-general-melvin-zais.html

112 Battle of Dong Ap Bia – Hill 937 May 10–21, 1969, Summary of Action and Results, Headquarters 101st Airborne Division, Office of the Commanding General, APO San Francisco 96383, May 24, 1969

113 Jay Sharbutt, AP despatch, May 19, 1969

114 OPLAN J208A intended to reduce MACV to 60,000 men by July 1, 1972. On January 13, Nixon announced an additional 70,000 redeployments by May 1, reducing MACV's strength to 69,000 (as opposed to 84,000 under OPLAN J208A). In April the numbers were revised downwards again to 30,000 men by July 1 and 15,000 by November 1

115 Andradé, Dale, *Trial by Fire: The 1972 Easter Offensive, America's Last Vietnam Battle*, Hippocrene Books, 1994, 47–51 [hereafter Andradé]

116 Andradé, 68

117 *Stars and Stripes*, "30,000 'Invaders' Hurl Back S.Viets," April 3, 1972

118 WGBH Open Vault, Interview with Hoang Duc Nha, 1981

119 *Stars and Stripes*, "Battles Seen as Big Test," April 3, 1972

120 Nixon, 145

121 Kissinger, 517

122 Cosmas, *1968–1973*, 360

123 Cosmas, *1968–1973*, 519

124 Andradé, 121

125 Andradé, 147

126 Andradé, 187–188

127 Andradé, 177–182

128 Andradé, 191

129 Andradé, 198–203

130 Cosmas, *1968–1973*, 366

131 Xuan, *Memories*

132 Correll, John T. (November 2006), *Air Force Magazine*, Air Force Association

133 Patrick, Joe (December 1997), "Air Force Colonel Jacksel 'Jack' Broughton & Air Force General John D. 'Jack' Lavelle: Testing the Rules of Engagement During the Vietnam War," *Vietnam Magazine*, HistoryNet.com

134 Cosmas, *1968–1973*, 371

135 Cosmas, *1968–1973*, 368

136 Kissinger, 1116

137 Kissinger, 1181

138 Ibid

139 Transcript: Address to the Nation on the Situation in Southeast Asia (May 8, 1972), Richard Nixon, Miller Centre, University of Virginia

140 *Stars and Stripes*, "Viets Win Part of Kontum," June 2, 1969

141 Cosmas, *1968–1973*, 212

142 WGBH Open Vault, Interview with Do Cuong, 07/27/1981

143 Cosmas, *1968–1973*, 226

144 *Stars and Stripes*, "Vann Was a Legend With 9 Lives," June 11, 1969

145 "General Krulak – big in Vietnam, big at the Copley Press: Brute knows war," Judith Moore, February 15, 1990: https://www.sandiegoreader.com/news/1990/feb/15/cover-brute-knows-war/#

146 Duong, Van Nguyen, *The Tragedy of the Vietnam War: A South Vietnamese Officer's Analysis*, McFarland & Company, Inc. Publishers, 2008, 147 [hereafter Duong]

147 Andradé, 289

148 Known as FSBs, 5, 6, V, C, D, and H

149 http://www.bravecannons.org/stories/B_DM_fsb6_1.html

150 1st and 141st PAVN Regiments were also attached to the division

151 *Stars and Stripes*, "Reds Paid High Price For Base, Adviser Says," April 17, 1972

152 *Stars and Stripes*, "Helo's Angels Save 9 Advisors," April 26, 1972

153 *Stars and Stripes*, "N.Viets March Towards Showdown," April 27, 1972

154 Andradé, 22

155 Ibid

156 http://www.thebattleofkontum.com/memories/15.html

157 *Stars and Stripes*, "Viets Pull Back Under Red Push," April 26, 1972

158 *Stars and Stripes*, "Red Tanks, Troops Near Kontum," April 30, 1972

159 Andradé, 301

160 Andradé, 313

161 All but the first regiment were drawn from 320th Division

162 The 1st Aerial TOW Team (UH-1D helicopters armed with TOW missiles), from Fort Lewis, Washington, had been rushed to South Vietnam at the request of John Paul Vann when the offensive started

163 Andradé, 318

164 Andradé, 322

165 Ibid

166 Andradé, 336

167 *Stars and Stripes*, "Red Tank Losses Heavy," June 20, 1972

168 *Stars and Stripes*, "2 French Priests Reported Crucified by Communists," May 12, 1972

169 *Stars and Stripes*, "Hospital Spared By Reds," May 31, 1972

170 http://thebattleofkontum.com/losses/index.html

171 *Stars and Stripes*, "Ups and Down of Flying," May 26, 1969

172 *Stars and Stripes*, "Epitaph for Vann: He Saw the Truth and Spoke It," June 12, 1969

173 http://globetrotter.berkeley.edu/conversations/Sheehan/sheehan-con4.html

174 Andradé, 363–365

175 *Stars and Stripes*, "Westy Mourns John Vann," June 12, 1969

176 Andradé, 380

177 Andradé, 381

178 5th VC Division (275th, 174th, and E6 Regiments), 7th PAVN Division (141st, 165th, and 209th Regiments), and 9th VC Division (271st, 272nd, and 95th Regiments)

179 Andradé, 384–385

180 The other suicides can be found at: http://www.vlink.com/history/?subaction=show full&id=1193767806&archive=

181 http://www.bcdlldb.com/Tuong_Le_van_Hung.htm

182 Willbanks, James H., Lieutenant Colonel, *The Battle of An Loc*, Twentieth-Century Battles, 1993, 31 [hereafter Willbanks, *An Loc*]

183 Andradé, 406–409

184 Willbanks, *An Loc*, 33

185 Willbanks, *An Loc*, 36

186 Howard, Major John D., *The War We Came to Fight: A Study of the Battle of An Loc – June 1972*, a student research paper written for the Student Research Report, June 1974, 10

187 Willbanks, *An Loc*, 75

188 Willbanks, *An Loc*, 1

189 *Armour*, Jan–Feb 1973

190 Ibid

191 Ibid

192 Blue Max was not a full squadron; F Troop, 79th Aerial Rocket Artillery was a company-size unit attached to 229th Aviation, part of TF Garry Owen

193 Andradé, 429

194 Howard, 11

195 Andradé, 439

196 Andradé, 445

197 Willbanks, *An Loc*, 57

198 Willbanks, *An Loc*, 42

199 Andradé, 458

200 Andradé, 452

201 Howard, 14

202 Andradé, 462

203 Andradé, 472

204 Ibid

205 *Armour*, Jan–Feb 1973

206 Willbanks, *An Loc*, 26

207 Willbanks, *An Loc*, 75

208 Andradé, 531

209 *Stars and Stripes*, "The Strength and Weakness of the ARVN," June 18, 1969

CHAPTER 6: LIQUIDATING A WAR

1 James Reston, *New York Times*, February 21, 1971, quoting an anonymous official. The article was titled "Backing Out of the Saloon"

2 Federation of American Scientists (FAS): National Security Study Memorandums (NSSM) [Nixon Administration, 1969-74]; also found in the Richard Nixon Presidential Library and Museum, https://www.nixonlibrary.gov/national-security-study-memoranda-nssm

3 Nixon, 78

4 See FAS/Richard Nixon Presidential Library and Musuem for the full list of Nixon NSSMs

5 LeMay, Curtis, *Mission With LeMay: My Story*, Doubleday, 1965, 565. In an interview two years after the publication of his book, General LeMay stated, "I never said we should bomb them back to the Stone Age. I said we had the capability to do it. I wanted to save lives on both sides"; *Washington Post*, October 4, 1968, A8

6 WGBH Open Vault, Interview with Melvin R. Laird, 06/03/1981

7 US State Department; Office of the Historian; *FRUS* 1969–1976, VI, 108-20

8 http://riciok.com/Cease_Fire/organization_for_the_cease_fire.htm

9 *FRUS* 1969–1976, VI, 164-76

10 National Security Decision Memorandum (NSDM) 9, sub: Vietnam, April 1, 1969, box 1008, NSC files

11 Ibid

12 National Archives, Nixon Presidential Materials, NSC Files, Box 489, President's Trip Files, Dobrynin/HAK, 1969 [part 2]. Secret; Nodis. A handwritten note on the memorandum reads: "Back from President, 4/16/69"

13 *Life* magazine, May 23, 1969

14 The American Presidency Project: http://www.presidency.ucsb.edu/ws/?pid=2047

15 Cosmas, *1968–1973*, 144–155

16 Ibid

17 Shelby, 284

18 The White House Tapes: http://whitehousetapes.net/exhibit/lbj-nixon-and-johns-mccain-sr-jr-and-iii; see also UVA, Miller Centre, Conversation with Everett Dirksen, April 25, 1966: https://millercenter.org/the-presidency/secret-white-house-tapes/conversation-everett-dirksen-april-25-1966; and Brune, Tom, "How Dirksen lobbied on behalf of Jack McCain; A series of documents show the influential Illinois senator pushing LBJ hard for a promotion for John McCain's father, Adm. John 'Jack' McCain, Jr.," https://www.salon.com/2008/10/29/admiral_mccain_2/

19 The American Presidency Project: http://www.presidency.ucsb.edu/ws/?pid=2140

20 Kissinger, 224

21 The American Presidency Project: http://www.presidency.ucsb.edu/ws/index.php?pid=2140

22 Cosmas, *1968-73*, 144–155

23 Kissinger, 311 and 1480–1482

24 Nixon, 115

25 http://www.scribd.com/doc/59087456/Transcript-of-July-9-1971-Secret-Visit-by-National-Security-Adviser-Henry-A-Kissinger-with-Chinese-Premier-Zhou-Enlai

26 Kissinger, 481

27 Cited by Cosmas, *1968–1973*, Abrams Papers, CMH, Abrams MAC 4527 to McCain, April 6, 1970, MACV, Force Planning Synopsis, 271–273, 279–280, 296–297

28 Cosmas, *1968–1973*, 163

29 The Vietnam Archive at Texas Tech University, The Vietnam Archive Oral History Project, Interview with Anthony Goodrich, op cit

30 Cosmas, *1968–1973*, 166, citing Historical Division, "Joint Chiefs of Staff and the War in Vietnam, 1969–1970," 401–402; Historical Division, Joint Secretariat, Joint Chiefs of Staff, "The Joint Chiefs of Staff and the War in Vietnam, 1971–1973," September 1979, CMH, 114–122, 136–139; MACV, Force Planning Synopsis, 363, 368, 373–374, 377–378. Memo, Westmoreland for CJCS, January 4, 1971, RVN Force Levels, End FY 71 and FY 72, box 1001; Memo, Admiral Robinson for Kissinger, January 8, 1971, Size of Residual MAAG Force in South Vietnam, box 152, NSC files, Nixon Papers, NARA

31 Cosmas, *1968–1973*, citing Laird for the President, January 16, 1971, Trip to Paris, Bangkok, South Vietnam, and CINCPAC, January 5–15, 1971, box 083, NSC files, Nixon Papers. Historical Division, "Joint Chiefs of Staff and the War in Vietnam, 1971–1973," 141–142

32 Cosmas, *1968–1973*, 167, citing Memo, Kissinger for the President (Mar 71), Troop Withdrawals, box 1013, NSC files, Nixon Papers, NARA

33 Cosmas, Graham A., and Murray, Lieutenant Colonel Terence P., USMC, *USMC, U.S. Marines in Vietnam, Vietnamization and Redeployment 1970–71*, CreateSpace Independent Publishing Platform, 2013, 246

34 Cosmas, *1968–1973*, 354

35 Cosmas, *1968–1973*, 175–176

36 Figures from Cosmas, *1968–1973*

37 The US Army also deployed 1/69th (1st Infantry), 2/34th (4th Infantry), and 1/77th Armor battalions (1st Brigade, 5th Infantry). The USMC deployed 1st, 3rd, and 5th Tank Battalions.

38 198th and 11th Infantry redeployed. 196th reconstituted as a separate brigade and was the last formation to leave Vietnam in June 1972. One of its battalions, 3/21st, was the last infantry battalion to serve in-country.

39 Shelby, 356

40 Courtesy of VVA, chapter 12: http://www.rjsmith.com/kia_tbl.html

41 Cosmas, *1968–1973*, 169

42 Cosmas, *1968–1973*, 49

43 *The New Yorker*, "Cover Up –1," Seymour M. Hersh, January 22, 1972

44 *The Plain Dealer*, "My Lai photographer Ron Haeberle exposed a Vietnam massacre 40 years ago today in The Plain Dealer," Evelyn Theiss, November 20, 2009

45 University of Missouri-Kansas City, Famous American Trials, The My Lai Courts-Martial 1970: http://law2.umkc.edu/faculty/projects/ftrials/mylai/ridenhour_ltr.html

46 Ibid

47 Sergeant Charles West quoted in *Life* magazine, December 5, 1969

48 A strategy, of course, repeated in Iraq and Afghanistan

49 The Vietnam Archive at Texas Tech University, The Vietnam Archive Oral History Project, Interview with Gary Franklin, Conducted by Jonathan Bernstein November 1, 2001, Transcribed by Tammi Mikel Lyon

50 The Vietnam Archive at Texas Tech University, Vietnam Archive Oral History Project, Interview with James Endicott, Conducted by Steve Maxner, September 17, 1999, Transcribed by Tammi Mikel

51 Also known as "Cong"

52 Dennis Bunning testimony, December 7, 1969

53 Charles Hutto testimony, November 18, 1969

54 My Lai Massacre Explained: http://instruct.westvalley.edu/kelly/Distance_Learning/History_17B/Readings/My_Lai.htm.

55 According to the US Army investigation, 347 villagers were killed (not including My Khe killings); other estimates suggest more than 400 killed, and the Vietnamese government lists 504 killed in total from both My Lai and My Khe.

56 Greiner, 76 (Kindle version)

57 Bourke, Joanna, *An Intimate History of Killing*, Granta Books, 1999, 194; also see Greiner

58 *New York Post*, "Nixon and the My Lai massacre coverup," Trent Angers, March 15, 2014

59 http://www.lib.berkeley.edu/MRC/pacificaviet/kissinger1.pdf.

60 Laurens County Historical Society, https://dublinlaurenscountygeorgia.blogspot.com/2011/11/kenneth-hodges-veterans-veteran.html

61 The Vietnam Archive at Texas Tech University, The Vietnam Archive Oral History Project, Interview with Larry Burke, op cit

62 Bourke, op cit, 191–193

63 Laurens County Historical Society, https://dublinlaurenscountygeorgia.blogspot.com/2011/11/kenneth-hodges-veterans-veteran.html

64 Cited in Greiner, 344

65 The Vietnam Archive at Texas Tech University, The Vietnam Archive Oral History Project, Interview with Calixto Cabrera, op cit

66 Offenses were generally not charged as war crimes and therefore did not depend on Congressional power under Article I, section 8, clause 10. Instead, the charges were addressed under routine articles of the Uniform Code of Military Justice (Article 118, 10 U.S.C. § 918 (murder), or Article 120, 10 U.S.C. § 920 (rape), dependant on congressional power to make "Rules for the Government and Regulation of the land and naval Forces"

67 Wikipedia: https://en.wikipedia.org/wiki/Rape_during_the_liberation_of_France

68 According to Oleg Rzheshevsky, President of the Russian Association of World War II Historians, *Gareev, Makhmut; Tretiak, Ivan; Rzheshevsky, Oleg (21 July 2005). Насилие над фактами [Abuse of Facts]. Trad (in Russian). Interview with Sergey Turchenko*

69 The Vietnam Archive at Texas Tech University, The Vietnam Archive Oral History Project, Interview with Charles Allen, Jr., op cit

70 The Vietnam Archive at Texas Tech University, The Vietnam Archive Oral History Project, Interview with Calixto Cabrera, op cit

71 Joint Board to Study Tactical Air Firepower – Briefing by Westmoreland, both in Historians files, CMH

72 *MACV Command History 1965*, 188

73 Cited in *MACV Command History 1965*, 192

74 The Vietnam Archive at Texas Tech University, The Vietnam Archive Oral History Project, Interview with Fred Beck, Conducted by Jason Stewart, April 20, 2009, Transcribed by Maci Gregg

75 Birtle, Andrew J., "PROVN, Westmoreland, and the Historians: A Reappraisal," *The Journal of Military History* 72 (October 2008), 1,237

76 Birtle, citing Memo, I Field Force Vietnam for Distribution, May 13, 1966, sub: Fact Sheet--The Nine Rules; Rpt, ODCSOPS, Dec 1970, sub: An Analysis of the Evolution of MACV Rules of Engagement Pertaining to Ground Operations, 1965–69; MACV, "Guidance for Commanders in Vietnam"

77 Report of the Department of the Army Review of the Preliminary Investigations into the My Lai Incident (U), Volume III, Exhibits Book I – Directives

78 Report of the Department of the Army Review of the Preliminary Investigations into the My Lai Incident (U), Volume III, Exhibits Book 2 – Directives, 141

79 Seymour M. Hersh, "The Massacre at My Lai: A mass killing and its coverup," *The New Yorker*, January 14, 1972

80 MACV Guidance to Commanders in Vietnam 1965

81 Summary of remarks by COMUSMACV relating to noncombatant casualties, August 28, 1966

82 Ibid, December 3, 1967

83 MACV Directive 525-9, April 10, 1967

84 YouTube: "Hearts and Minds" documentary, https://www.youtube.com/watch?v=n7PdCUSyZQg

85 Interview with Scott Camil, 1981, produced by Richard Ellison, fl. 1985, in *Vietnam: A Television History*, WGBH Boston, 1983

86 "American Experience: Daughter from Da Nang", PBS, April 7, 2003, https://www.pbs.org/wgbh/americanexperience/films/daughter/

87 Ohio State University survey, http://www.asian-nation.org/amerasians.shtml#sthash.IwbKH5GV.dpbs

88 Heinl, Jr., Colonel Robert D., *Armed Forces Journal*, "The Collapse of the Armed Forces," June 7, 1971

89 Proceedings magazine, Vol. No. 82, No. 5, May 1956, Whole No. 639, *Special Trust and Confidence*

90 Appy, Christian G., *Patriots: The Vietnam War Remembered from All Sides*, Penguin Books, 2004

91 WGBH Open Vault, Interview with George Cantero, 05/12/1981

92 History Net: http://www.historynet.com/the-hard-truth-about-fragging.htm/2. Different sources cite different totals. A higher total of 1,103 fraggings is cited in http://home.mweb.co.za/re/redcap/vietcrim.htm. Official DoD statistics are hard to determine

93 The Vietnam Archive at Texas Tech University, The Vietnam Archive Oral History Project, Interview with Jerry Benson, op cit

94 "Fragging" and "Combat Refusals" in Vietnam: http://home.mweb.co.za/re/redcap/vietcrim.htm

95 WGBH Open Vault, Interview with Charles Sabatier, 10/08/1982

96 The Vietnam Archive at Texas Tech University, The Vietnam Archive Oral History Project, Interview with Chuck Sawyer, op cit

97 The Vietnam Archive at Texas Tech University, The Vietnam Archive Oral History Project, Interview with Calixto Cabrera, op cit

98 The Vietnam Archive at Texas Tech University, The Vietnam Archive Oral History Project, Interview with David Adcock, op cit

99 Cosmas, *1968–1973*, 237, citing statistics from *MACV Command History 1970*, Vol. 2, Ch 12, 4

100 Ibid. Additional sources recommended by Cosmas, *1968–1973*, include: Spector, Ronald H., "The Vietnam War and the Army's Self-Image," Schlight, John, ed., *Second Indochina War Symposium: Papers and Commentary*, US Army Center of Military History, 1986, 169–185; and BDM Corp., *A Study of Strategic Lessons Learned in Vietnam*, vol. 7, *The Soldier*, BDM Corp., 1980

101 Westmoreland MAC 01227 to Sharp info Wheeler, Jan 26, 1968

102 Ibid

103 Kissinger, 1107

104 Nixon Address to the Nation on Vietnam, April 26, 1972: https://www.nixonfoundation.org/2017/09/address-nation-vietnam-april-26-1972/

105 See Kimball, Jeffrey, *The Vietnam War Files: Uncovering the Secret History of Nixon-Era Strategy*, University Press of Kansas, 2004, for a critique of Nixon's war strategy

106 Brinkley and Luke, *The Nixon Tapes*, 11

107 Kissinger, 259

108 Kissinger, 277

109 Kissinger, 265

110 Kissinger, 284

111 Kissinger, 286

112 Cosmas, *1968–1973*, 291, citing Abrams Papers, CMH

113 Cosmas, *1968–1973*, 291, citing Abrams Papers, CMH, 291

114 Cosmas, *1968–1973*, 291, citing Abrams Papers, CMH, 293

115 Kissinger, 290

116 Kissinger, 435

117 Kissinger, 440

118 Kissinger, 444

119 Kissinger, 971

120 Kissinger, 1018

121 Kissinger, 1021

122 Kissinger, 1024

123 Kissinger, 1023

124 Kissinger, 1025, quote is from *New York Times*, July 15, 1971

125 Kissinger, 1026

126 Kissinger, 1031

127 Kissinger, 1044

128 Kissinger, 1105

129 Kissinger, 1169

130 Kissinger, 1171

131 Kissinger, 1306

132 Kissinger, 1312–1313

133 Kissinger, 1314

134 Kissinger, 1316

135 Kissinger, 1323

136 Kissinger, 1325

137 Tran Van Tra, *Vietnam: History of the Bulwark B2 Theatre*, Volume 5: Concluding the 30-Years War, CSI, February 2, 1983, 89

138 Kissinger, 1337

139 Kissinger, 1340

140 Kissinger, 1345

141 Kissinger, 1352

142 Nixon Library, National Archives, NSC Files, Box 862, Camp David Memos, September–December 1972

143 WGBH Open Vault, Interview with Hoang Duc Nha, 05/09/1981

144 Ibid

145 Kissinger, 1375

146 National Archives, Nixon Presidential Materials, NSC Files, Kissinger Office Files, Box 25, HAK Trip Files, HAK Paris/Saigon Trip Hakto, October 16–23, 1972. Top Secret; Sensitive; Exclusively Eyes Only

147 Kissinger, 1399

148 Nixon Library, National Archives, audio tape WHT 32-63, President Nixon congratulates Kissinger for his performance in the "peace is at hand" press conference

149 Brinkley and Luke, *The Nixon Tapes*, 17

150 The Nixon Tapes, 153-028, 11/15/1972, 9:08–9:14am and 033-089 11/18/1972, 12:02–12:08 pm

151 Ibid

152 Kissinger, 1417

153 Nixon Library, National Archives, HAK Office Files, Box 26, HAK Paris Trip TOHAK November 18–25, 1972

154 Nixon Library, National Archives, HAK Office Files, Box 27, HAK Paris Trip HAKTO & Memos to Pres, etc., December 3–13, 1972

155 Nixon Library, National Archives, Nixon to HAK, 240507Z November 1972

156 Nixon Library, National Archives, Nixon to HAK, 241150Z November 1972

157 Nixon Library, National Archives, Memcon: Nixon to JCS, November 30, 1972

158 Memoirs of Vietnamese Senior General Hoang Van Thai, JPRS Report, Southeast Asia: The Decisive Years, 19980610 109, US Department of Commerce, National Information Technical Service, 4 [hereafter Thai]

159 Nixon Library, National Archives, HAK Office Files, Box 27, HAK Paris Trip HAKTO & Memos to Pres, etc., December 3–13, 1972

160 Ibid

161 Ibid

162 Ibid

163 Ibid

164 Kissinger, 1443

165 Nixon Library, Exhibits, The December Bombing, Ch IV

166 Nixon Library, National Archives, Oval 823-1 Log, Kissinger gives President Nixon his recommendation for breaking the impasse in the negotiations

167 Nixon Library, Exhibits, The December Bombing, tape excerpts, Ch IV

168 Nixon Library, National Archives, Oval 823-1, Kissinger tells President Nixon he would be "impotent" if he does not bomb North Vietnam

169 Vien, Cao Van, General, *The Final Collapse*, Indochina Monographs, Center of Military History United States Army, Washington DC, 1985, 37

170 See Stephen Ambrose, *The Christmas Bombings*, Random House, 2005 for a comprehensive account of *Linebacker II*. McCarthy, James R., Brigadier General and Allison, George B., Lieutenant Colonel, *Linebacker II: A View from the Rock*, Air Force Global Strike Command Office of History & Museums, Barksdale AFB, Louisiana, originally published 1976 by the Air University, is another good source [hereafter McCarthy and Allison]

171 Thompson and Frizzell, *The Lessons of Vietnam*, op cit

172 McCarthy and Allison, 1

173 McCarthy and Allison, 74

174 The late USAF pilot and later Vietnam historian Herman Gilster argues that the expenditure of SAMs was exaggerated and that a better explanation for the lower attrition rate was improved tactics. Gilster authored a number of publications including: *Vietnam Diary: From Inside Air Force Headquarters and The Air War in Southeast Asia Case Studies of Selected Campaigns*, Rosedog Pr, 2005

175 McCarthy and Allison, 171

176 McCarthy and Allison, 40

177 McCarthy and Allison, 76

178 McCarthy and Allison, 50

179 WGBH Open Vault, Interview with Michael J. Connors, 04/21/1981

180 McCarthy and Allison, 62

181 McCarthy and Allison, 94

182 McCarthy and Allison. 61

183 McCarthy and Allison, 14–20

184 McCarthy and Allison, 46

185 McCarthy and Allison, 32

186 McCarthy and Allison, 6

187 WGBH Open Vault, Interview with Michael J. Connors, 04/21/1981

188 Kissinger, 1469

189 Kissinger, 1473

190 Kissinger, 1364

191 Scribd: http://www.scribd.com/doc/58767074/Polo-I-Briefing-Book-Kissinger-s-Secret-Trip-to-China-July-1971, 58

192 History News Network; Ken Hughes, Presidential Recordings Program, University of Virginia Miller Center: http://historynewsnetwork.org/article/140712#sthash. bdsizfLV.dpufhttp://hnn.us/article/140712 for a summary of the charges against Nixon and Kissinger

193 Scribd: http://www.scribd.com/doc/59087456/Transcript-of-July-9-1971-Secret-Visit-by-National-Security-Adviser-Henry-A-Kissinger-with-Chinese-Premier-Zhou-Enlai

194 National Security Archives, George Washington University: http://nsarchive.gwu. edu/NSAEBB/NSAEBB193/HAK%206-20-72.pdf, 29

195 Nixon Library, National Archives, Memcon: Nixon to JCS, 30 November 30, 1972

196 WGBH Open Vault, Interview with Nguyen Co Thach, 02/24/1981

197 Nixon Library, National Archives, Oval 823-1 Log, Kissinger gives President Nixon his recommendation for breaking the impasse in the negotiations

198 Scribd: http://www.scribd.com/doc/58767074/Polo-I-Briefing-Book-Kissinger-s-Secret-Trip-to-China-July-1971, 59

199 Scribd: http://www.scribd.com/doc/59087456/Transcript-of-July-9-1971-Secret-Visit-by-National-Security-Adviser-Henry-A-Kissinger-with-Chinese-Premier-Zhou-Enlai

200 National Security Archives, George Washington University: http://nsarchive.gwu. edu/NSAEBB/NSAEBB193/HAK%206-20-72.pdf, 31 and 37

201 History.com, 7 Revealing Nixon Quotes From His Tapes, updated September 27, 2018, https://www.history.com/news/nixon-secret-tapes-quotes-scandal-watergate

202 Nixon Library, National Archives, Memcon: Nixon to JCS, November 30, 1972

203 Willbanks, James H., Lieutenant Colonel, *Thiet Giap! The Battle of An Loc April 1972*, Combat Studies Institute, US Army Command and General Staff College, Fort Leavenworth, Kansas, September 1993

204 Cosmas, *1968–1973*, 392, citing Dillard, Walter S., *Sixty Days to Peace*, University Press of the Pacific, 2002, 60–61; Clarke, Jeffrey J., *Advice and Support: The Final Years, 1965–1973*, 452–453; *MACV History, 1972–73*, Normanby Press, 2014, Vol. 1, 104 and an. C, 20–21, 74, 77. Memo, Laird for the Assistant to the President for National Security Affairs, October 13, 1972, sub: RVNAF Supply Status, box 162; Memo, Sec Def Elliot L. Richardson for the Assistant to the President for National Security Affairs, March 17, 1973, sub: Replacement of RVNAF Combat Losses, box 163, NSC files, Nixon Papers, NARA

205 Ibid
206 YouTube, "POWs: Stories of Survival": https://www.youtube.com/watch?v=c-7ktaSAjGA
207 The Vietnam POWs Home Page: http://www.nampows.org/
208 Wilson Center, Merle Pribbenow: https://www.wilsoncenter.org/publication/treatment-american-pows-north-vietnam
209 YouTube, "POWs: Stories of Survival": https://www.youtube.com/watch?v=c-7ktaSAjGA
210 POW Network: http://www.pownetwork.org/fonda/fonda_index.htm
211 Cosmas, *1968–1973*, 398
212 Ibid
213 Ibid
214 Ibid. The same problem would beset the missions in Iraq and Afghanistan in the 21st century
215 *Time*, "The Press: Farewell to the Follies," February 12, 1973
216 Around 800 servicemen were still assigned to Four-Party Joint Military Commission, monitoring the ceasefire; these departed over the subsequent week
217 http://www.history.navy.mil/content/dam/nhhc/research/archives/commander-naval-forces-vietnam/quarterly-summaries-1973/Jan-Mar1973.pdf.
218 http://www.transportation.army.mil/history/GO_bios/murray.pdf
219 *New York Times*, March 29, 1972
220 Ibid

CHAPTER 7: LOSING A WAR

1   The observers were drawn from Canada, Indonesia, Poland, and Hungary
2   Vien, Cao Van, General, *The Final Collapse*, Indochina Monographs, Center of Military History United States Army, Washington DC, 1985, 29 [hereafter Vien]
3   Named after a famous Ly Dynasty general
4   Le Gro, William E., *Vietnam from Cease-Fire to Capitulation*, University Press of the Pacific, 2006, 42 [hereafter Le Gro]
5   Le Gro, 66
6   Vien, 31
7   Le Gro, 10 and Vien, 34, who states 17 divisions and 62 regiments totalling 167,000 regular forces, and a combined force, with irregulars, 293,120 strong
8   Resume of Career Service, Major General John Einar Murray, http://www.transportation.army.mil/history/GO_bios/murray.pdf
9   Cosmas, *1968-1973*, 401
10 Vien, 36
11 Thai, 8
12 Ibid
13 Vien, 41
14 Le Gro, 88
15 WGBH Open Vault, Interview with Frank Snepp, 10/14/1981
16 Martin to White House, December 26, 1973, Log 930-73, quoted in Le Gro, 89

17 Murray résumé

18 Le Gro, 94

19 Cosmas, *1968–1973*,403.

20 CIA Library/Reading Room, Communist Military and Economic Aid to North Vietnam, DOC_0001166499.pdf

21 At the end of 1974, B2 Front had just 4,800 120mm mortar shells; 1,190 160mm mortar shells; 6,500 122mm rockets; 300 105mm rockets; and 7,500 130mm artillery shells (Thai, 79)

22 General Van Tien Dung, Great Spring Victory, Asia & Pacific Supplement, FBIS-APA-76-110, Vol. IV, No. 110, Supp 38, June 7, 1976, 6

23 CIA Library, Reading Room, Imports of Military Equipment and Materiel by North Vietnam 1974, DOC_0001166498.pdf

24 Thai, 49

25 All subordinated to what was known as Military Region 559

26 MilitaryHistoryOnline.com, Seals, Bob, *Chinese Support for North Vietnam during the Vietnam War: The Decisive Edge*, 2008, citing Xiaobing Li, *A History of the Modern Chinese Army*, The University Press of Kentucky, 2007, 217–219

27 April 27 to May 2, 1974 – the "Svay Rieng Operations"

28 WGBH Open Vault, Interview with Gerald R. Ford, 04/29/1982

29 Le Gro, 147

30 Thai, 64–65

31 Dung, 1

32 General Tran Van Tra, the senior commander of forces in the south, asserts that the 21st Plenum met in April 1973 and concluded its deliberations in June 1973. Directives from this plenum were then issued in September 1973. Dung states that the 21st Plenum was held in October 1973. Available documentation shows the resolutions of the 21st Plenum were released at the later date. Extracts of key passages are translated and available in the Wilson Center, Cold War International History Project, Digital Archive: https://digitalarchive.wilsoncenter.org/document/175857

33 Thai, 39

34 See Wilson Center, Cold War International History Project, Digital Archive. A great debt is owed to the translation skills and endeavour of former CIA officer Merle Pribbenow who has undertaken much translation and interpretation of North Vietnamese primary source documents. Useful sources include: North Vietnam's "Talk-Fight" Strategy and the 1968 Peace Negotiations with the United States April 16, 2012, Speech Given by Party First Secretary Le Duan to the 12th Plenum of the Party Central Committee; and North Vietnamese Decision-Making, 1973–1975: An Update, December 20, 2017

35 Thai, 29

36 The nomenclature of the communist state organisations is not straightforward. Thai refers to a "Party Military Commission of the Party Central Committee." The author has chosen the shorter title used by Vien

37 See Christoph Giebel, "Imagined Ancestries of Vietnamese Communism: Ton Duc Thang and the Politics of History and Memory," *Critical Dialogues in Southeast Asian Studies*, 2004, for a critical biography of the Socialist Republic of Vietnam's first president

38 In Thai's account of the final months of the war

39 Thai, 38

40 A view expressed in General Chu Huy Man, *Vibrant Times*, People's Army publishers, 2004. This and hundreds of other North Vietnamese primary source documents and memoirs relating to the war are now available on the Dung nuoc-Giu nuoc website: https://www.quansuvn.net/index.php?PHPSESSID=ipg9ei23j4afu9mvjookodr4s2&board=21.0

41 Thai, 44–45

42 Thai, 61

43 Thai, 56–57

44 Thai, 64

45 Thai, 62

46 https://www.cia.gov/library/readingroom/docs/DOC_0001166497.pdf. Throughout 1974, the CIA issued a number of prescient analyses and reports warning of Saigon's fragility and the possibility of decisive Northern operations. Another example is https://www.cia.gov/library/readingroom/docs/CIA-RDP78T02095R000700080098-1.pdf

47 CIA Library/Reading Room, Imports of Military Equipment and Materiel by North Vietnam 1974, DOC_0001166498.pdf

48 NIE, Short Term Prospects for South Vietnam, December 23, 1974

49 Thai, 68–69

50 Thai, 81

51 Tran Van Tra was the commander of B-2 Front. Dung was the overall commander for Campaign 275 and the Ho Chi Minh Campaign

52 According to Chu Huy Man, these last key meetings ran from December 18 to January 8 and were attended by First Secretary of the Party Central Committee Le Duan who acted as Chairman; Politburo members Truong Chinh, Pham Van Dong, Le Duc Tho, Vo Nguyen Giap, Pham Hung, Le Thanh Nghi, Van Tien Dung, Nguyen Duy Trinh, and Tran Quoc Hoan; front-line commanders Tran Van Tra (Southern front) and Vo Chi Cong and Chu Huy Man (Zone 5); Song Hao, Chairman of the General Department of Politics, and Dinh Duc Thien, Chairman of the General Department of Logistics, and several other secretaries. General Chu Huy Man, *Vibrant Times*, People's Army publishers, 2004

53 Le Gro, 145

54 Other than a lame protest from the State Department

55 Dung, 7

56 Dung, 87

57 Dung, 19

58 WGBH Open Vault, Interview with Frank Snepp, 10/14/1981

59 Dung, 6–10

60 Thai, 43

61 HistoryNet: http://www.historynet.com/dr-lawrence-h-climo-recalls-his-vietnam-war-service.htm

62 *The Economist*: http://www.economist.com/blogs/prospero/2012/01/coffee-vietnam

63 Université du Québec à Montréal (UQAM), Faculty of Social Science and Humanities, The Indochinese War (1945–56) Pays Montagnards du Sud (PMS)

64 "French Indochina" Gia Vuc Tribute website: http://www.gia-vuc.com/frenchindochina.htm
65 Wikipedia: https://en.wikipedia.org/wiki/Battle_of_Mang_Yang_Pass
66 Ban Me Thuot AB, Home of Pyramid! Hooky Lau, by SSgt Channler Drawdry, 2005
67 UQAM, op cit
68 Nguyen Van Hien, Viet Cong media *Tin Nguyen*, "The Retreat from the Central Highlands," *Vietnam Courier* #39 (August 1975), courtesy of Adam Sadowski
69 Ibid
70 Dung, 30
71 Dung, 39
72 Dung, 44
73 See Le Gro, Ch 17, "The Last Act in the South"
74 Vien, 77
75 Le Gro, 95, citing Murray message June 1, 1974
76 Le Gro, 170
77 Ibid
78 Thieu resignation speech April 21, 1973
79 Ibid
80 Center for Cryptologic History, National Security Agency, United States Cryptologic History, Special Series No. 5, *Essential Matters: A History of the Cryptographic Branch of the People's Army of Viet-Nam, 1945–1975*, Translated and Edited by David W. Gaddy, 1994, 191
81 Thai, 97
82 Thai,100
83 Thai, 97
84 Thai, 103
85 Dung, 46
86 Le Gro, 162
87 Vien, 95
88 Le Gro, 163
89 Dung, 48
90 Thai, 12
91 Untold Stories – vnafmamn.com, The Battle of Xuan Loc: http://vnafmamn.com/xuanloc_battle.html
92 Le Gro, 104
93 Le Gro, 159
94 Ibid
95 Ibid
96 WGBH Open Vault, Interview with Nguyen Thi Nguyet Anh, 03/02/1981
97 The other members of the flight crew included co-pilot Charlie Stewart, the World Airways station manager Joe Hrezo, chief flight attendant Jan Wollett, and flight attendants Valerie Withersooon and Atsako Okuba, both in their early twenties
98 Englemann, Larry, "Mission Improbable!," *South China Morning Post* Sunday Magazine, July 22, 2012: http://mofak.com/mission_improbable.htm
99 Ibid

100 Another estimate suggests 250 and 80 respectively, with seven survivors in the wheel wells

101 Valerie Witherspoon, quoted in Englemann, Larry, "Mission Improbable!"

102 The city fell on March 29

103 *New York Times*, March 30, 1975

104 Le Gro, 110

105 Le Gro, 111

106 Thai, 103

107 Center for Cryptologic History, National Security Agency, United States Cryptologic History, Special Series No. 5, *Essential Matters: A History of the Cryptographic Branch of the People's Army of Viet-Nam, 1945-1975*, Translated and Edited by David W. Gaddy, 1994, 176

108 Thai, 118

109 Le Gro, 173

110 Ibid

111 Tran Van Tra, Vietnam: History of the Bulwark B2 Theatre, Vol. 5: Concluding the 30-Years War, CSI, 2 February 1983, 160

112 YouTube, "55 Days – The Fall of Saigon": https://www.youtube.com/watch?v=EeD6cb7klx4

113 Ibid. Speaker here is Wolfgang Lehman, Deputy to Ambassador Martin

114 Ibid

115 Le Gro, 154, citing DAO presentation January 1975

116 YouTube, "55 Days – The Fall of Saigon": https://www.youtube.com/watch?v=EeD6cb7klx4

117 Aid, Matthew M. *The Secret Sentry*, Bloomsbury Press, 2009, 125–127

118 These included Catholic Relief Services, Friends of Children of Viet Nam (FCVN), Friends For All Children (FFAC), International Orphans, Holt International Children's Services, the Pearl S. Buck Foundation, and International Social Services

119 Adopt Vietnam, Operation *Babylift* (Vietnam Adoptions 1975), Remembering the 1975 Vietnam Babylift – Pam Am Airlift, Joyce Wertz Harrington, RN: http://www.adoptvietnam.org/adoption/babylift-joyce.html

120 Gerald R. Ford Library and Museum, Operation Babylift: http://www.fordlibrarymuseum.gov/library/exhibits/babylift/memoirs.asp

121 See YouTube: https://www.youtube.com/watch?v=7yM5GSX5G7Q for views of Xuan Loc in 1968–1969

122 YouTube: https://www.youtube.com/watch?v=NE1skoTOUNs

123 Untold Stories – vnafmamn.com, The Battle of Xuan Loc

124 Smith Cable to the CJCS, April 13, 1975, cited by Le Gro, 174

125 Thai, 120

126 Thai, 121–122

127 Thai, 126

128 Le Gro, 177

129 Safer, Morley, *Flashbacks: On Returning to Vietnam*, St Martin's Press/Random House, 1991

130 Duong, 210

131 Duong, 213

132 Ibid

133 Ibid

134 Thai, 145

135 The History Place, Great Speeches Collection: http://www.historyplace.com/speeches/ford-tulane.htm

136 Air Mobility Command Museum: 60th, 62d, 63d, 436th, 437th, 438th, and 446th Military Airlift Wings; 514th Military Airlift Wing (Associate); 314th and 374th Tactical Airlift Wings; 56th Special Operations Wing; 21st Special Operations Squadron; 9th Aeromedical Evacuation Group; and 40th Aerospace Rescue and Recovery Squadron.

137 United States Congress, *Indochina Evacuation and Refugee Problems, Part IV*, 1975, 5

138 Operation *New Life* April 23–October 16, 1975: http://tendertale.com/ttonl/newlife.html

139 Air Mobility Command Museum

140 Ibid

141 United States Congress, *Indochina Evacuation and Refugee Problems, Part IV*, 1975, 5

142 Kelly, Gail P., "Coping with America: Refugees from Vietnam, Cambodia, and Laos in the 1970s and 1980s," *Annals of the American Academy of Political and Social Science*, Vol. 487 (September 1986), 138–149

143 *The Indochina Newsletter*, October–November 1982, "Re-education in Unliberated Vietnam: Loneliness, Suffering and Death," Ginetta Sagan and Stephen Denney

144 *National Review*, Le Thi Anh, "The New Vietnam," April 29, 1977, 487

145 *The Indochina Newsletter*, op cit

146 Vietnam Re-education Camps: http://www.country-data.com/cgi-bin/query/r-14750.html

147 The Distributed Republic, *The Vietnamese Gulag*, submitted by Jonathan Wilde, May 2006

148 Ibid

149 "A Form of Torture: Food Deprivation," Cao Ngoc Phuong, *The Indochina Newsletter*, Burlingame, CA. February–March 1982, Issue No. 24, cited in The Distributed Republic, op cit

150 Dunham, George R., Major, US Marine Corps and Quinlan, David A., Colonel, US Marine Corps, *US Marines in Vietnam, The Bitter End, 1973–1975*, History and Museums Division HQ: citing Capt Edward J. Ritchie interview, June 16, 1986, Tape 116A (Oral I-list-Coil). MCHC, 188 [hereafter Dunham and Quinlan, *US Marines in Vietnam*]

151 *CNN*, Thom Patterson, 2015: http://edition.cnn.com/2015/04/29/us/vietnam-saigon-evacuation-anniversary/

152 Duong, 215

153 Ibid

154 Some accounts describe this as a Baobab tree

155 Dunham and Quinlan, *US Marines in Vietnam*, 198–199

156 A total of 81 helicopters evacuated 1,373 Americans and 5,595 Vietnamese

157 Dunham and Quinlan, *US Marines in Vietnam*, 202

158 *Newsweek*, The Last Helicopter: Evacuating Saigon, Newsweek Staff, 4/26/15: http://www.newsweek.com/last-helicopter-evacuating-saigon-321254

159 Duong, 216

160 *Newsweek*, op cit

161 *Military Times*: http://www.militarytimes.com/story/military/2015/04/30/last-us-marines-to-leave-saigon-describe-chaos-of-wars-end/26653001/

162 Also known as 324B Division

163 Vietnam: http://en.vietnamplus.vn/memorial-park-for-war-martyrs-inaugurated-in-hcm-city/87015.vnp

164 WGBH Open Vault, Interview with Nguyen Huu Hanh, 03/16/1981

165 WGBH Open Vault, Interview with Dang Van Son, 07/26/1981

166 Xuan, *Memories*

167 https://www.bbc.co.uk/news/world-asia-45195395

168 Xuan, *Memories*

169 Butterfield, Fox, "Duong Van Minh, 85, Saigon Plotter, Dies," *New York Times*, August 8, 2001

170 Xuan, *Memories*

171 Dobrynin, Anatoly, *In Confidence, Moscow's Ambassador to America's Six Cold War Presidents*, Times Books, Random House, 1995, 349

172 Jack P. Smith, website by Neil Mishalov: http://www.mishalov.com/death_ia_drang_valley.html

BIBLIOGRAPHY

BOOKS

Aid, Matthew M. *The Secret Sentry*, Bloomsbury Press, 2009.

Allen, George W., *None So Blind*, Ivan R. Dee, 2001.

Andradé, Dale, *Trial by Fire: The 1972 Easter Offensive, America's Last Vietnam Battle*, Hippocrene Books, 1994.

Berman, Larry, *Lyndon Johnson's War*, W.W. Norton & Company, 1989.

Blight, James G., Lang, Janet M., Welch, David A., *Virtual JFK: Vietnam If Kennedy Had Lived*, Rowman & Littlefield Publishers, 2010.

Bourke, Joanna, *An Intimate History of Killing*, Granta Books, 1999.

Bouscaran, Anthony Trawick, *The Last of the Mandarins: Diem of Vietnam*, 1965.

Brinkley, Douglas, Nichter A. Luke, *The Nixon Tapes*, Houghton Mifflin Harcourt, 2014.

Cantigny Military History Series, *Blue Spaders, The 26th Infantry Regiment, 1917–1967*, 1996.

Carland, John M., *Stemming the Tide May 1965 to October 1966*, United States Army in Vietnam, Center of Military History, United States Army, Washington DC, 2000.

Cosmas, Graham A., *MACV: The Joint Command in the Years of Escalation, 1962–1967*, Center of Military History, United States Army.

Cosmas, Graham A., *MACV: The Joint Command in the Years of Withdrawal 1968–73*, The United States Army in Vietnam, Center of Military History United States Army, 2007.

Currey, Cecil R., *Victory at Any Cost*, Potomac Books, Inc (formerly Brassey's, Inc), 1999.

Davidson, Phillip B., *Vietnam at War: The History 1946–1975*, Oxford University Press, 1988.

Dommen, Arthur J., *The Indochinese Experience of the French and the Americans: Nationalism and Communism in Cambodia, Laos and Vietnam*, Indiana University Press, 2001.

Dunn M. Peter, *The First Vietnam War*, Hurst, 1985.

Duong, Van Nguyen, *The Tragedy of the Vietnam War: A South Vietnamese Officer's Analysis*, McFarland & Company, Inc., Publishers, 2008.

Farrar-Hockley, Anthony, Official History, The British Part in the Korean War, Volume 1, *A Distant Obligation*, HMSO, 1990.

Hackworth H. David, *About Face: The Odyssey of an American Warrior*, A Touchstone Book, Simon & Schuster, 1989.

Halbertsam, David, *The Best and the Brightest*, Random House Publishing Group, 1992.

Ham, Paul, *Vietnam: the Australian War*, Harper Collins, 2007.

Hammer, Ellen J., *A Death in November, America in Vietnam 1963*, E.P. Dutton, 1963.

Helms, Richard, *A Look Over My Shoulder: A Life in the Central Intelligence Agency*, Presidio Press, 2004.

Herring, George, *America's Longest War*, 1996 (4th Edition).

Hilsman, Roger, *To Move a Nation*, Doubleday, 1967.

Jones, Howard, *Death of a Generation: How the Assassinations of Diem and JFK Prolonged the Vietnam War*. New York City, New York, 2003.

Kimball, Jeffrey, *The Vietnam War Files: Uncovering the Secret History of Nixon-Era Strategy*, University Press of Kansas, 2004.

Kissinger, Henry, *The White House Years*, Weidenfeld and Nicolson and Michael Joseph, 1979.

Langguth, A.J., *Our Vietnam: The War, 1954–1975*, Simon & Schuster, 2000.

Le Gro, William E., *Vietnam from Cease-Fire to Capitulation*, University Press of the Pacific, 2006.

Marr, David G., *Vietnam 1945: The Quest for Power*, University of California Press, 1995.

Miller, Edward, *Misalliance: Ngo Dinh Diem, the United States, and the Fate of South Vietnam*, Harvard University Press, 2013.

Milne, David, *America's Rasputin: Walt Rostow and the Vietnam War*, Hill and Wang, 2008.

Moyar, Mark, *Triumph Forsaken: The Vietnam War 1954–1965*. New York: Cambridge University Press, 2006.

Neville, Peter, *Britain in Vietnam: Prelude to Disaster, 1945–1946*, Routledge, 2007.

Nixon, Richard, *No More Vietnams*, W.H. Allen, 1986.

Pike, Douglas, *Viet Cong*, Cambridge MIT, 1966.

Plaster L. John, *The Secret Wars of America's Commandos in Vietnam*, Mass Market Paperback, 1998.

Powers, Robert, K., *1966 The Year of the Horse*, Dog Ear Publishing, 2009.

Prados, John, *The White House Tapes: Eavesdropping on the President*, The New Press, 2003.

Prados, John and Stubbe, E., Ray, *Valley of Decision, The Siege of Khe Sanh*, Houghton Mifflin, 1991.

Safer, Morley, *Flashbacks: On Returning to Vietnam*, St Martin's Press/Random House, 1991.

Schlesinger, Arthur, M., *A Thousand Days: John F. Kennedy in the White House*, Boston, 1965.

Selverstone, Marc J, *Constructing the Monolith, The United States, Great Britain, and International Communism, 1945–1950*, Harvard University Press, 2009

Shelby, Stanton, A., *The Rise and Fall of an American Army: U.S. Ground Forces in Vietnam, 1963–1973*, Presidio Press, first published in 1985

Shulishmon, Jack, Marine Corps Vietnam Operational Histories Series, Department of the Navy, *US Marines in Vietnam: An Expanding War 1966*, 1982.

Sorley, Lewis, *Westmoreland: The General who lost Vietnam*, Houghton Mifflin Court Publishing Company, 2011.

Spector, Ronald H., *Advice and Support, The Early Years, The U.S. Army in Vietnam*, Centre of Military History, United States Army, Washington DC, 1983.

Staaveran, Jacob Van, *Gradual Failure: The Air War over North Vietnam: 1965–1966*, Air Force History and Museums program, 2002.

Thies, Wallace J., *When Governments Collide: Coercion and Diplomacy in the Vietnam War 1964–1968*, University of California Press Berkeley and Los Angeles, 1980.

Thompson, Sir Robert, *Defeating Communist Insurgency: The Lessons of Malaya and Vietnam*, New York, 1966.

Vien, Cao Van, General, *The Final Collapse*, Indochina Monographs, Center of Military History United States Army, Washington DC, 1985.

Vietnam Chronicles, The Abrams Tapes 1968–1972, Transcribed and Edited by Lewis Sorley, Texas Tech University Press, 2004.

Westmoreland, William C., *A Soldier Reports*, Doubleday, 1st Edition, 1976.

Willbanks, Lt Col James H. *Thiet Giap! The Battle of An Loc April 1972*, Combat Studies Institute, US Army Command and General Staff College, Fort Leavenworth, Kansas, September 1993.

Wyatt, Clarence, *Paper Soldiers: The American Press and the Vietnam War*, University of Chicago Press, 1995.

ARTICLES, STUDIES AND REPORTS

2/503 Vietnam Newsletter No. 29, November 2012.

Anh, Le Thi, "The New Vietnam," *National Review*, April 29, 1977.

Berube, Claude G., *Ho, Giap and OSS Agent Henry Prunier*, originally published on HistoryNet.com.

BDM Corporation analysis Book I, Operational Analyses, Department of the Army, US Army War College

Birtle, J. Andrew, "PROVN, Westmoreland, and the Historians: A Reappraisal," *The Journal of Military History* 72 (October 2008).

Boian, Major Kelly Owen Carl, *Major General Melvin Zais and Hamburger Hill*, School of Advanced Military Studies United States Army Command and General Staff College, Fort Leavenworth, Kansas, 2014.

Brian M. Jenkins, The Unchangeable War, RM-6278-1-ARPA, September 1972.

Brush, Peter, "The Story Behind the McNamara Line," first published in *Vietnam* magazine, February, 1996.

Buckingham, Jr., Major William A., Office of Air Force History, *Operation Ranch Hand: The Air Force and Herbicides in Southeast Asia, 1961–1971*.

Center for Cryptologic History, National Security Agency, United States Cryptologic History, Special Series No. 5, *Essential Matters: A History of the Cryptographic Branch of the People's Army of Viet-Nam, 1945–1975*, Translated and Edited by David W. Gaddy, 1994.

Coan, James P., "The Battle for Con Thien," May 8, 1999.

Correll, John T., "Lavelle," *Air Force Magazine*, Air Force Association, November 2006.

D'amato, Anthony A. et al, "War Crimes and Vietnam: The 'Nuremberg Defence' and the Military Service Register," *California Law Review* 1055 (1969) Code A69d.

Deer Mission, summary report, September 1945.

Deer Report No. 1, July 17 1945.

Department of the Army Vietnam Studies, *Command and Control 1950–1968*, Major General George S. Eckhardt, 1991.

Department of the Army, Vietnam Studies, *The War in the Northern Provinces 1966–68*, Lieutenant General Willard Pearson, 1991.

Drea, Edward J., "Gulf of Tonkin Incident: Reappraisal 40 years Later," *MHQ*, Summer 2004 edition.

Dyhouse, Tim, "33 Days of Violent, Sustained Combat," 2/503 Vietnam Newsletter No. 47, November 2012.

Eschwege, Henry, "The Use of Agent Orange in Vietnam," Community and Economic Development Division, Report to Republican Ralph H. Metcalfe, August 15 1978

Ford, Ronnie E., *Tet 1968: Understanding the Surprise*, In Cass Series – studies in Intelligence, F. Cass, 1995.

Franklin, John K., *The Hollow Pact: Pacific Security and the Southeast Asia Treaty Organization*, ProQuest, 2006.

Giebel, Christoph, "Imagined Ancestries of Vietnamese Communism: Ton Duc Thang and the Politics of History and Memory," *Critical Dialogues in Southeast Asian Studies*, 2004.

Hammond, M. William, *Public Affairs, The Military and the Media, 1968–1973*, The United States Army in Vietnam series, US Army Center of Military History, Government Printing Office, 1988.

Hanyok, Robert J. "Skunks, Bogies, Silent Hounds and the Flying Fish: The Gulf of Tonkin Mystery 2–4 August," *Cryptologic Quarterly*, approved for release by the NSA on November 3, 2005.

Harrison, Benjamin T., Mosher, Christopher L., "John T. McNaughton and Vietnam: The Early Years as Assistant Secretary of Defense, 1964–1965," University of Louisville and Arlington, Virginia, 2007.

Harrison, Simon, "Skull Trophies of the Pacific War: Transgressive Objects of Remembrance," Journal of the Royal Anthropological Institute, 2006.

Heinl, Jr., Colonel Robert D., "The Collapse of the Armed Forces," *Armed Forces Journal*, June 7, 1971.

Hickey, Gerald, "Village in Vietnam," Yale University Press, 1964.

History and Museums Division, HQ USMC, Captain Francis J. West Jr. USMCR, *Small Unit Action in Vietnam Summer 1966*.

Howard, Major John D., "The War We Came to Fight: A Study of the Battle of An Loc – June 1972," a student research paper written for the Student Research Report, June 1974.

HQ PACAF, Directorate Tactical Evaluation, CHECO Division, The Cambodian Campaign April 1–June 30 1970.

Jakobsen, Mark, Dr., "Washington's Management of the Rolling Thunder Campaign, Naval Historical Centre, Command and Control of Air Operations in the Viet Nam War," Colloquium on Contemporary History January 23 1991, No. 4

Janes, Thomas W., "Rational Man – Irrational Policy (A Political Biography of John McNaughton's Involvement in the Vietnam War)," essay, March 31, 1977.

Jenkins, Brian M., "The Unchangeable War," RM-6278-1-ARPA, September 1972.

Johnson, Leland L., "U.S. Business Interests in Cuba and the Rise of Castro," RAND, P-2923, 1964.

JPRS Report – "East Asia, Southeast Asia, The Decisive Years: Memoirs of Vietnamese Senior General Hoang Van Thai, 19980610 109," Reproduced by U.S. Department of Commerce National Technical Information Service.

Kelly, Gail P., "Coping with America. Refugees from Vietnam, Cambodia, and Laos in the 1970s and 1980s," *Annals of the American Academy of Political and Social Science* Vol. 487 September 1986.

MACV Command History 1965–73

Nalty, C. Bernard, *Operation Niagara, Air Power and the Siege of Khe Sanh*, Office of Air Force History, 1991.

Naval Historical Center, *Command and Control of Air Operations in the Vietnam War*, Colloquium on Contemporary History, January 23, 1991, No. 4.

Nguyen, Lien-Hang T. (2006). "The War Politburo: North Vietnam's Diplomatic and Political Road to the Tet Offensive," *Journal of Vietnamese Studies* 1 (1–2), 34.

Nguyen, Van Hien, Viet Cong media *Tin Nguyen*, The Retreat from the Central Highlands.

Pollard, A. Robert, *Economic Security and the Origins of the Cold War, 1945*, Columbia University Press.

Prados, John, "Operation Masher, the Boundaries of Force," *VVA Veteran*, Feb–Mar 2002.

Prados, John, "One Hell of a Fight," 2/503 Vietnam Newsletter No. 47, November 2012.

Pribbenow II, Merle L., "General Vo Nguyen Giap and the Mysterious Evolution of the Plan for the 1968 Tet Offensive," University of California Press, *Journal of Vietnamese Studies*, Volume 3, Summer 2008.

Publications du service historique de l'armée de terre consacrées a la guerre d'Indochine, *1945–1946 Le retour de la France en Indochine*, textes et documents.

Report of the Department of the Army Review of the Preliminary Investigations into the My Lai Incident.

Rogers, Lieutenant General Bernard William, *Cedar Falls-Junction City: A Turning Point*, Vietnam Studies, Department of the Army, 1989.

Sagan, Ginetta and Denny, Stephen, "Re-education in Unliberated Vietnam: Loneliness, Suffering and Death," *The Indochina Newsletter*, October–November 1982.

Schell, Jonathan, "The Village of Ben Suc," *The New Yorker*, July 15, 1967.

Scott, Lieutenant Colonel B., "The Battle for Hill 875, Dak To, Vietnam 1967," USAWC Military Studies Program Paper, 2/503 Vietnam Newsletter No. 47, November 2012.

Seals, Bob, MilitaryHistoryOnline.com, *Chinese Support for North Vietnam during the Vietnam War: The Decisive Edge*, 2008.

Sutsakhan, Sak, *The Khmer Republic at War and the Final Collapse*, Monograph Program, Department of the Army, Washington DC, 1978.

Willbanks, James H., PhD, *The Battle for Hue, 1968*.

Wedemeyer Report, 1950.

AFTER ACTION REPORTS (AAR)

A comprehensive collection of AAR can be found at The US Army in Vietnam, The Bud Harton Collection at the Texas Tech Virtual Vietnam Archive, http://www. recordsofwar.com/vietnam/army/

1st Cavalry 1965 (Battle of Ia Drang)

1st Infantry Division – Lessons Learned (May 1 to July 31) Part 1
1st Infantry Division – Lessons Learned (May 1 to July 31) Part 3
1 Marines After Action Report, March 20, 1968
1/3 Marines After Action Report, Operation Utah, March 11, 1966
173 AB Bde AAR Dec 1967
1st Battalion, 26th Infantry, CEDAR FALLS operation report, January 23, 1967
II Field Force Tet Offensive, Parts 1–3
4th Inf Div, Combat Operations After Action Report (RCS:MACV J3-32) January 28, 1967
Combat Operations After Action Report (RCS MACV J3/32), April 28, 1966
Moore After Action Report, December 9, 1965 (Battle of Ia Drang)
Operation Junction City 1 and 2, Combat Comments 2-67, prepared by G-3, 1st Inf Div
Operations Lessons Learned, Report 2-66, AD 502772, March 31, 1966
Op Malheur, After Action Report, 1st Bde, 101st AB Div, October 3, 1967
Op Swift After Action Report, October 5, 1967

TELEVISION, NEWSPAPERS AND JOURNALS

Armed Forces Journal
Armour
Army Times
Baltimore Sun
Bill Moyers' Journal, Bill Moyers on LBJ's Path to War /PBS
CBS Evening News
CBS News, Special Reports
Foreign Affairs
Life
Newsweek
New Republic
New York Herald Tribune
New York Post
New York Times
Stars and Stripes
The Economist
The Nation
The New Yorker
The Old Reliable (9th Infantry Division newspaper)
The Plain Dealer
Time
Vietnam magazine
Washington Evening Star

INTERNET

1st MIBARS in Vietnam
Blue Spaders: 26th Infantry Regiment Association
British Pathé archives
Gerald R. Ford Library and Museum
National Security Archives, George Washington University, Vietnam Project
Nixon Library, National Archives
Pushing On blog spot (Vietnam recollections)
The Fog of War: Eleven Lessons from the Life of Robert S. McNamara
Talking Proud (US) military website
The American Presidency Project
The Black Vault (online US Government declassified documents archive)
The Vietnam Center and Archive, Texas Tech University
This Day in History
University of Texas Archives, LBJ Library, Oral History Interviews
Vietnam magazine online
WGBH Open Vault, Vietnam Files
Wilson Center, Digital Archives

INDEX

Page numbers in **bold** refer to maps.

Beckwith, Maj. Charlie 52
Beecher, William 266
Ben Suc 137–138, 140–141
Benson, Pte Jerry 110, 141, 360
Binh Dinh Province 26, 96, 97–99, 105–106
bombing raids 65, 67, 68, 104, 108, 125,
    130–131, 226, 315, 323
  on Cambodia 265–270, 276–277
  free bomb zones 49, 355, 356
  halt of 252–253, 265
  on North Vietnam 306–308
  and peace negotiations 383–391
  reduction of 342
  tele-guided bombs 308
booby traps 86–87, 166, 183
Bourke, Joanna 352
Bowers, Capt. Gene W. 167
Braun, Maj. Richard 95
Brown, Col. Thomas 53, 62, 63, 65
Bruce, David 362, 368
Buckley, Kevin 185
Bundy, McGeorge 39, 81, 194
Bundy, William 24, 28
Bunker, Ellsworth 133–134, 151, 159, 194, 410
Burke, Capt. Larry 70, 91, 141–142, 352–353
Burrows, Larry 17, 31–32
Busby, Horace 244, 245

Cabrera, Calixto 45, 75, 84, 90–91, 94, 140,
    167, 353–354, 355–356, 360–361
Calley, Lt William 348, 351–352, 353
Cam Rabh Bay 36
Cambodia 264–271, 336–337
  bombing of 265–270, 276–278
  Operation *Toan Thang 43*: 275–276, 278–279
  plan for US invasion 273–275
  political upheaval 271–272
Camil, Scott 358
Cantero, George 361
Caputo, 2nd Lt. Philip 18–19
Carey, Gen. 457, 458
Carey, Joe 86
Carrington, Col. 86
Carver, George 178, 239
Casselman, Larry 167
Castro, Frank 137–138
casualties 18–19, 31, 32, 168, 316, 445–446
  American 44, 49, 50, 54, 59–60, 61, 64,
    66–68, 71, 73, 85, 86–87, 92, 97, 100,
    102, 116–117, 142, 147, 148, 151, 160,
    162–163, 165, 173, 184, 239, 250, 276,
    286, 341–342
  ARVN (Army of Vietnam) 38, 276, 286, 325

body counts, obsession with 109–110, 262
civilians 43, 44–45, 49, 85, 138, 140, 161,
    270, 277, 302, 325
  exaggerations of 106, 117, 121, 166–167,
    168, 173, 185
  generals 168
  last American soldiers killed 397–398,
    455–456
  notification telegrams 50
  PAVN (People's Army of Vietnam) 50, 54,
    62, 64, 85, 108, 238, 239, 286
  retrieving bodies 161, 167
  Viet Cong (VC) 44, 50, 70, 71, 147, 148,
    160, 214, 226, 238, 239, 276
ceasefires 368, 373, 385, 396, 403, 404, 405
Central Office of South Vietnam
    (COSVN) 72, 110, 135, 144, 149
Central Party Military Committee 412, 413,
    415, 416, 418, 429, 430
Champa 13
chaplains 167, 183
Chau, La Ngoc 54, 59, 61
chemical warfare 156–159
China 392–395, 409, 413
Chinh, Truong 201, 261
Christian, 2nd Lt David 75
Chu Lai 33, 43–45, 79–80
CIA 78, 130, 178, 203, 208–209, 214, 240,
    252, 336–337, 414
  "Alternative Interpretations of Hanoi's
    Intentions" 209–210
  "The Vietnamese Communists Will to
    Persist" 121
Civil Operations and Revolutionary
    Development Support (CORDS) 133–134
civilians 16, 42, 46, 86, 140–141, 428, 434
  casualties 43, 44–45, 49, 85, 138, 140, 161,
    270, 277, 302, 325
  children 95, 119, 347, 348, 349, 355–356,
    442–443
  compensation 141
  destruction of villages 92–93, 137–138,
    140–141, 150, 358
  directives on minimization of
    casualties 357–358
  elderly people 348–350
  evacuations to US 450–453, 456–460
  executions and atrocities 93, 94–95,
    119–120, 150, 237–238, 343–344, 347
  forced evacuations 102–103, 138, 141
  inequalities 334–335
  mass graves 237, 322
  massacres 85, 103, 185, 344–354